Civics for Americans

Second Edition

John J. Patrick
Richard C. Remy

Civics for Americans

Second Edition

John J. Patrick
Indiana University

Richard C. Remy
Ohio State University

Scott, Foresman and Company

Editorial Offices: Glenview, Illinois

Regional Offices: Sunnyvale, California •
Atlanta, Georgia • Glenview, Illinois •
Oakland, New Jersey • Dallas, Texas

Authors

John J. Patrick is Professor of Education at Indiana University in Bloomington and directs projects at the Social Studies Development Center there. He was a high-school social studies teacher for eight years. Dr. Patrick has authored books for teachers about social studies curriculum and instruction. He has also authored high-school social studies textbooks. His articles on curriculum and instruction have appeared in numerous professional journals. He has also served as a consultant to many school systems, development centers, and to national ministries of education in Europe and Asia.

Richard C. Remy is Director of the Citizenship Development Program, Mershon Center, at Ohio State University, where he also holds appointments in political science and the College of Education. He began his career as a classroom teacher in the Chicago Public Schools. His articles about topics in political science, curriculum, and instruction have appeared in many professional journals. He has written extensively for young students on citizenship and decision making. He has also served as a consultant to numerous school systems, state departments of education, and federal government agencies.

Contributing Author

L. JoAnne Buggey provided the in-book tests and the chapter-by-chapter lesson plans, annotations, and bibliography for the teacher's annotated edition of *Civics for Americans*. She is also the author of the *Duplicating Masters: Tests*. Dr. Buggey teaches social studies methods courses in the Department of Education at the University of Minnesota. She began her career as an elementary school teacher and subsequently co-directed the Social Studies Service Center for the Twin Cities area in Minnesota. She has assisted schools and communities to develop their curriculum resources.

Consultants

Teacher-Consultants

Diane Cadei, Chairwoman, Social Studies Department, Greenfield Union School District, Greenfield, California

Claire Kitchin Dahl, Elementary social studies teacher—Wisconsin, Illinois, and Michigan

Dolly Juarez, Valley High School, Albuquerque, New Mexico

Richard F. Kraft, Los Altos High School, Hacienda Heights, California

Robert J. McCloskey, Social Studies Department Chairman, C.D. East Junior High School, Harrisburg, Pennsylvania

Peter Sgroi, Social Studies Chairman, Rye Neck High School, Mamaroneck, New York

F. Kevin Simon, Sayre School, Lexington, Kentucky

Joyce L. Stevos, Social Studies Area Supervisor, Providence School Department, Providence, Rhode Island

Warren F. Tracy, Supervisor, Social Studies, Duval County Public Schools, Jacksonville, Florida

Steven Trubow, Miller Junior High School, Durango, Colorado

Academic Consultants

David Currie, Professor of Law, University of Chicago, Chicago, Illinois

Anne Freedman, Professor of Political Science, Roosevelt University, Chicago, Illinois

Brian Haggerty, Citizens' Research Foundation, University of Southern California, Los Angeles, California

Dr. Larry Wolken, Department of Finance, Texas A & M University, College Station, Texas

Acknowledgments: Cover photographs: © **1983 Peter B. Kaplan.** The Decision-Tree device used on page 33 was developed by Roger LaRaus and Richard C. Remy. The device is used in this text with their permission. Further acknowledgments for quoted matter and illustrations appear on page 562. The acknowledgments section there is an extension of the copyright page.

ISBN: 0-673-35155-6

Copyright © 1991

Scott, Foresman and Company, Glenview, Illinois.
All Rights Reserved.
Printed in the United States of America.

12345678910-RRC-99989796959493929190

Table of Contents

Charts and Maps

Unit 1

Government and Citizenship

People from many ethnic groups, races, and backgrounds have joined together as one nation in the United States of America. Their experiences have given vital meaning to these words on the Great Seal of the United States: *"e pluribus unum,"* which means "out of many, one."

The uniqueness of its people is one reason why the United States is a very special nation. Its government, which has been a model to many nations around the world, is another reason why the United States is special.

The United States government, built upon the sturdy framework of the United States Constitution, provides its diverse citizenry with many rights and freedoms. Every citizen has the right to equal and fair treatment under the laws of the country. With these freedoms come many responsibilities. All citizens have the responsibility to respect the laws and to contribute to the success of their country. No citizen is more or less an American than any other citizen of the United States.

We should all be proud of the many rights and responsibilities we have as United States citizens. And we should always work to uphold these privileges. Civics is the study of this citizenship.

During the course of this book you will learn what it means to be a citizen of the United States and how important the Constitution is to every citizen today. You will also find out that, as a citizen of the United States, you can help decide what actions the government will take in the future. And you will discover that, to a degree, your nation's future is up to you to decide.

(opposite) Viewing the Statue of Liberty from the statue's pedestal.

Chapter 1

Citizenship in Your Life

Introduction. The Pilgrim ship *Mayflower* left Southampton, England, for the Virginia colony in the late summer of 1620. The 102 passengers aboard, many of whom had established a less-than-successful colony in Holland, were determined to reach Virginia. Their goal was to start a colony in which they could freely practice their religion and keep their English customs and traditions.

Rough winds plagued the tiny ship from the outset and drove it north of its intended course. Finally, more than two weary months after they had left England, the Pilgrims spotted land. Men, women, and children shouted, laughed, and wept.

The rejoicing did not last long, however. Some of the men said that, since they were outside of the Virginia colony, no one had the power to command them. These men planned to go off on their own and do as they pleased.

The others pleaded for order and cooperation. "We will need everyone's help just to stay alive," they argued. Those who agreed

pointed out that in this new land there would be no towns like those they had known in England. They would be outnumbered by Indians who might not welcome them.

After a long discussion, all realized that they had to cooperate. The leaders wrote a statement, now known as the **Mayflower Compact,** in which they agreed to form a government. The Compact was signed by adult, male passengers. Every household was represented. The men elected a governor, and then they landed.

The citizens of the new colony cooperated to build houses, gather food, and gain friendly relations with the Indians. They settled their arguments according to law, as they had pledged to do in the Mayflower Compact. The Plymouth Colony survived.

The Mayflower Compact was a very important agreement made by early colonists. It grew out of an experience in civics that remains important today—the need for government, law, and cooperation.

Membership in a family involves benefits as well as responsibilities. What are some of these benefits and responsibilities?

Section 1
Citizenship in Groups

Civics is the study of the duties, rights, and responsibilties of citizenship. Civics comes from the Latin word *civis*, which means "citizen." In ancient Rome, citizens were a small, privileged class of people. They were men who owned land and property. They had the right to go anywhere in the city, and they sat in the councils of government and voted for leaders and laws. With these rights came the responsibility to provide the city with fair laws and good government. Roman citizens took their duty to the city very seriously.

Today, nearly all of the people living in our nation are United States citizens. These people, like the Romans, have rights, duties, and responsibilities as citizens.

Rights and Responsibilities of Group Membership

Civics plays an important role in every group. As a citizen of many groups, you have the right to enjoy the benefits of group membership. In return, you assume certain responsibilities for the welfare of the groups to which you belong.

Tony Martin, age fourteen, takes part in many groups. He lives in a family that includes his parents, two sisters, and grandmother. He belongs to St. Francis Church and is a member of the Catholic Youth Organization. He is a ninth-grader at

Hamilton High School, where he is on the junior varsity basketball team. He has friends in the neighborhood with whom he spends his spare time. As a member of these different groups, Tony has certain rights and responsibilities. As a family member, he has the right to affection, food, a place to live, and guidance in growing up. In return, he owes his family consideration and support for the things it tries to accomplish. He has certain chores that help keep the home a good place to live in.

At school, Tony has the right to learn. He has the right to take part in school activities such as the basketball program. He has the right to take any courses he is capable of taking. Through education, he may prepare himself for any career he wants. In return, Tony has certain responsibilities. He should follow school rules. He should also cooperate with other students in helping make the school a good place to get an education.

Tony Martin also has certain rights and responsibilities as a citizen of his city, state, and nation. Tony has the right to enjoy the services of government. For instance, he expects protection by the local police force. He has the right to play baseball or to jog in the public park near his home.

In return for these benefits, Tony has a responsibility for seeing that the laws in his city, state, and nation are obeyed. First, he should obey them. After that, he should do all he can to encourage others to obey the laws.

Tony also has the responsibility to work to change laws that he thinks are wrong. In a democratic society, it is a citizen's duty to work for changes in laws that do not meet the needs of the people.

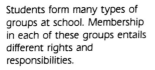

Students form many types of groups at school. Membership in each of these groups entails different rights and responsibilities.

A person who actively accepts these responsibilities is demonstrating **loyalty** to his or her government. Tony Martin is loyal to the United States because he believes that the people and groups he cares about can get along well here. He also feels free to express beliefs and ideas that are important to him.

Loyalty to a country or nation is called **patriotism.** Singing the national anthem and other patriotic songs, saying the Pledge of Allegiance, and participating in politics by voting, campaigning, and joining organizations that promote our interests, are some ways that we can show national loyalty. Cooperating with others for the benefit of the nation is another important way to demonstrate loyalty. President John F. Kennedy expressed this idea when he said, "Ask not what your country can do for you—ask what you can do for your country."

Decision Making in Groups

As members of groups, citizens take part in decision making. They decide about rules for the group. They decide what the group will do.

Deciding is choosing among **alternatives.** For example, your family might decide to vacation in Florida instead of Colorado or Utah. Taking a vacation in Colorado or Utah are alternatives to your **decision** to take a vacation in Florida. Sometimes you have many alternatives to choose from. Other times you do not have many choices. If you have no alternatives, you obviously cannot make a decision.

Group Decisions in a Democracy

In the United States, people make decisions as group members every day. In some small groups, all of the members directly take part in making decisions. Choices are made by **majority rule.** Majority means

Loyalty and patriotism can be expressed in many ways. These basketball players, and the students who support them, are showing loyalty to their school. Mary Lou Retton, the star gymnast of the 1984 Summer Olympics, stirred patriotic feelings in millions of Americans who watched the games.

(top) Student council voting on a proposal. In most schools, students elect representatives to serve on a student council. (above) The 1984 Republican Convention, which was held in Dallas, Texas. Delegates to a national convention represent people from their party and state.

most, or one more than half. All members are equal and have the same responsibilities to determine the policies and goals of the group. Government by such means is called a **direct democracy.**

In larger groups, members do not take part directly in day-to-day decision making. Instead, they elect representatives to make decisions that are consistent with the goals of the group. This type of government is often referred to as a **representative democracy.** Our national government is considered a representative democracy.

We are all members of both types of groups. As members of families and school groups, we make decisions every day that affect the direction of the group. As citizens of our city, state, and nation, we decide what the goals and directions of our governments will be. We then elect leaders who we believe will best carry out these goals.

Thomas Jefferson, our third President, strongly believed in government by majority rule. But he also believed that the majority should not violate the rights of individuals or minority groups. Jefferson's definition of democracy was "majority rule with minority rights."

In his first inaugural address, Jefferson said: "All . . . will bear in mind this sacred principle, that though the will of the majority is in all cases to prevail, that will, to be rightful, must be reasonable; that the minority possess their equal rights, which equal laws must protect, and to violate would be oppression."

As citizens of the United States, we all have many opportunities to make decisions concerning the way we want to live.

Section Review

Vocabulary:
alternatives, civics, decision, direct democracy, loyalty, majority rule, Mayflower Compact, patriotism, representative democracy.

Reviewing the Main Ideas
1. Why did the Pilgrims make the Mayflower Compact?
2. What does group membership have to do with civics?

3. How is decision making in groups part of daily life?

Skill Building

1. Organize the ideas in the section you have just read as they relate to your life. List three groups you belong to. Under each, give three rights you have as a member of the group. Then list three responsibilities you have for the group's welfare.

2. Which of these statements is the main idea of this section of the chapter?

a. Most people are group members.

b. In some groups, decisions are made by a few members.

c. Being a group member gives people rights and responsibilities.

Section 2
How Citizenship Is Gained and Lost

Every country has rules about how to gain the rights of citizenship. In the United States, there are two ways to become a citizen: (1) by birth, and (2) by **naturalization.**

Citizenship by Birth

Most people in the United States gain their citizenship by being born in this country. Anyone born in any of the fifty states, the District of Columbia, the Commonwealth of Puerto Rico, or the territories of Guam or the Virgin Islands, is a United States citizen at birth.

Some people gain United States citizenship at birth even though they are born outside of the nation. The law says that persons can claim to be citizens at birth, no matter where they are born, if both parents are United States citizens or if one parent is a citizen who has lived in the United States at least ten years.

Citizenship by Naturalization

Several million **aliens** live in the United States. Aliens are citizens of other countries.

Many aliens in the United States are **immigrants.** They enter the country and plan to stay here. They want to become **naturalized citizens,** and intend to take certain steps, required by law, to gain citizenship in the United States. More than 100,000 people become naturalized United States citizens each year.

Steps to Becoming a Naturalized Citizen

1 File a Declaration of Intention with the Immigration and Naturalization Service. (This step is optional.)

2 After 5 years residence in the United States (3 years if married to an American citizen), file a Petition for Citizenship.

3 Have two citizens testify that you have met the residence requirement, have a good moral character, and believe in the Constitution.

4 Take an examination to prove you can read and write English and know American history and government.

5 Pledge an oath of allegiance to the Constitution and laws of the United States and sign a certificate of naturalization.

(chart) What are the steps to becoming a naturalized citizen?

Some aliens are not immigrants. They come with the permission of our government to study in our colleges and universities, or to work for awhile. Others are permitted to visit relatives or friends. These aliens intend to remain citizens of their own countries.

Aliens who want to become United States citizens must first sign a statement that says they want citizenship. This statement is then filed with the Immigration and Naturalization Service.

For most aliens, the next step comes after living in the United States at least five years. (An alien who is married to a citizen waits only three years.) At this time, they file a petition asking for citizenship. Applicants must be at least eighteen years old and must have lived in the state where they seek naturalization for at least six months. In the third step, the alien goes before a judge. Two citizens must testify that the alien has lived in the country for the required period of time and that he or she would be a good citizen.

The fourth step is a citizenship exam that determines whether the alien can read, write, and speak English and knows basic facts about the history and government of the United States.

After a person passes the citizenship exam, he or she must wait thirty days. During this time, officials of the Immigration and Naturalization Service take a final look into the alien's background. They want to be sure that everyone applying for citizenship deserves this privilege.

Citizenship Oath

I hereby declare, on oath, that I absolutely and entirely renounce and abjure all allegiance and fidelity to any foreign prince, potentate, state or sovereignty, of whom or which I have heretofore been a subject or citizen; that I will support and defend the Constitution and laws of the United States of America. . . .

The final step in naturalization is to pledge an oath of allegiance. The alien swears to obey and defend the Constitution and other laws of the United States and to be loyal to this country above all others. Then the alien signs a certificate of naturalization and becomes a citizen of the United States of America.

Naturalized citizens have the same rights and duties as those who gained citizenship by birth except that they are not eligible to become President or Vice-President of the United States.

How Citizenship Is Lost

United States citizenship may be lost in three ways: (1) **treason,** (2) **expatriation,** or (3) **denaturalization.**

Citizenship may be taken from a person as punishment for treason. Treason is defined in Article 3, Section 3, of the Constitution. Anyone found guilty of trying to overthrow the government by force commits the crime of treason.

People who withdraw allegiance from their country are **expatriates.** Thus, people who take oaths of loyalty to other countries lose their rights of citizenship in the United States through expatriation. Children may be expatriated if their parents become citizens of another country.

Denaturalization happens when it is proved that a naturalized citizen received citizenship by fraud or that the oath of allegiance was not taken in good faith.

2. All aliens in the United States are immigrants.

3. Most immigrants must wait at least five years after entering the United States before they can become naturalized citizens.

4. Immigrants must show they can read, speak, and write English and know basic facts about United States history and government before they can become naturalized citizens.

5. Naturalized citizens have every right under the law that natural-born citizens have.

Section Review

Vocabulary:
alien, denaturalization, expatriate, expatriation, immigrant, naturalized citizen, treason.

Reviewing the Main Ideas
1. What are the two main ways to become a citizen of the United States?
2. What are the steps a person must take to become a naturalized citizen? Why do you think the government makes it so difficult and time consuming to gain United States citizenship?
3. How might a person lose United States citizenship?

Skill Building
Tell whether the following statements are true or false. For every false statement, rewrite it to make it true. Give the page number in this book that backs up your answer.
1. It is possible for a person born outside the United States to have citizenship in this country by birth.

(above) Italian immigrants on a ship heading for the United States in the early 1900s. (left) Haitian refugees on a boat en route to the Florida coast in 1980. Both groups hoped to make a new life for themselves in the United States.

Section 3

Government Decisions in the Lives of Citizens

United States citizens live under the **laws,** or rules, of national, state, and local governments. Any group that has the power to make and enforce laws acts as a **government.**

The United States has a national government that makes and enforces laws for the entire country. It is located in Washington, D.C. The state government of Alabama makes and enforces laws for people living in that state. The city of Birmingham, Alabama, has a government that makes and enforces rules for that city.

Decision making is the main activity of government. People in government make three kinds of decisions. One, they decide what laws a group should have. Two, they decide what goals a group should have. Three, they decide how certain benefits and burdens may be distributed within a group.

These three kinds of decisions have to do with how groups are governed. They involve rights, responsibilities, and benefits of citizenship. Thus, they are decisions about civics.

Governments Make Decisions About Rules or Laws

Laws are needed to keep order in a group. Governments decide what laws are needed to settle conflicts, defend the group, and provide services. For example, governments make traffic laws to regulate the use of motor vehicles. Drivers are required to obey speed limits, stop signs, and traffic lights.

Should the speed limit on Main Street be twenty-five or thirty miles per hour? Should Park Avenue be made into a one-way street? Should stop signs be placed at the corner of Market and Third streets? Your local government makes decisions to answer these kinds of questions about laws. Your government's decisions about laws affect what you and others may or may not do.

Governments decide about how to carry out laws. Drivers who are caught speeding must pay a fine. Government officials decide how much first offenders should pay. They may also decide that offenders have to attend classes in how to drive safely.

Governments Make Decisions About Goals

Your school's football team might have the **goal** of winning the league championship. A goal is something a person or group tries to attain.

Governments make decisions that set goals for a nation. For example, President Reagan decided in the early 1980s to strengthen the nation's defense. The state government in Alabama decided to develop more of its coal resources. And the city of Chicago, Illinois, focused on attracting more people to its hotels.

Governments Make Decisions About the Distribution of Benefits and Burdens

A **benefit** is anything that is for the good of a person or group. Examples of benefits are money, good health, safety, education, property, skills, and respect. Conversely, a **burden** is a duty or responsibility that a person or group accepts for the benefit of another person or group. Taxes are an example of a burden.

Your government's decisions about benefits and burdens have important effects on you and others. For example, suppose the government decides to build a recreation center in your neighborhood. This decision would provide benefits of jobs and money to the people hired to build the center. Jobs and money would be given to people hired to manage the center. People in your neighborhood would have the benefit of the programs and facilities of the recreation center.

Sometimes government decisions help some people while hurting others. For example, suppose the government of a community decided to stop the sale of fireworks to the general public. Only persons with special permits would be allowed to have a fireworks display.

This decision would take away benefits from the producers and sellers of fireworks. Their sales and profits would drop and jobs and money might be lost.

However, others might gain benefits from the decision. Doctors' groups and parent-teacher groups have argued that the open sale and use of fireworks is a threat to health and safety. They say that fireworks are the cause of many serious burns and accidents. So, passing a law to limit the sale and use of fireworks might bring benefits of greater health and safety to everyone.

Section Review

Vocabulary:
benefit, burden, goal, government, laws.

Reviewing the Main Ideas
1. What three kinds of decisions do governments make?
2. What do government decisions have to do with civics?
3. How do government decisions affect your life?

Skill Building
1. For each government decision below, tell whether it is about <u>rules</u>, <u>goals</u>, or <u>the distribution of benefits</u>.
a. The President announced that the United States will try to sell more goods to foreign nations than it buys from them.
b. The federal government passed a law that increases the amount of social security taxes.
c. The President of the United States announced today that the federal government will give disaster funds to farmers who had crops killed by the early freeze.
2. What specific local decisions affect the way you and your friends act in your community?

City governments make decisions that provide their citizens with benefits such as public swimiming pools.

13

Section 4
Why Citizens Create Governments

Whenever a large group of people live together, a government is usually formed to make and enforce laws. Governments help people in many ways. Governments in the United States have the power and duty to (1) provide many **public services,** (2) settle conflicts and keep order, and (3) provide security and a common defense against threats from other nations.

Providing Public Services
Governments make laws that provide many services we need. Government workers collect garbage, repair streets, and build parks.

Governments build libraries, schools, hospitals, and recreation centers. Governments keep records of births and deaths and issue licenses to hunters, door-to-door salespeople, and drivers.

Governments give help to poor and needy people. For example, each of the fifty state governments provides aid to poor families and to people who are out of work. These governments help handicapped people train for jobs.

Governments make and enforce many laws to keep you and others healthy and safe. For example, members of the fire department inspect your school to detect hazards that could cause damaging fires. Government workers enforce laws to protect the public from spoiled food or dangerous drugs. Government inspectors make restaurant owners and workers obey laws that protect the health of diners. Government officials enforce laws that keep

Services such as school lunch programs and special education classes for the handicapped are provided by governments.

14

factories safe for workers.

Providing for the public health and safety is a major goal of government. Yet at times governments do not always pass and enforce laws that meet these goals. Sometimes laws benefit some people and cause a disadvantage to others. It is the duty of citizens to closely watch their governments to make sure that laws are fair and that officials do not abuse the powers the people have given them.

Settling Conflict and Keeping Order

Most people want to live together in groups because people who cooperate to get things done can usually accomplish more than those who work alone. However, people who live and work together have **conflicts** from time to time. A conflict is a disagreement between people. Governments have the power and duty to keep order by settling conflicts according to law.

Conflicts may happen when people have different beliefs about their rights. For example, two people may disagree about who is the rightful owner of a piece of property. Two groups may have a conflict over which should have the right to use water from a spring or river.

Governments make laws about property rights and about who may use resources such as land and water. Government officials make decisions about how to settle conflicts and also have the power to enforce their decisions. Thus, conflicts between citizens living under the rules of government are settled in an orderly way.

Conflicts may occur whenever people disagree about what is best for their group. For example, some

United States citizens exercising their right to vote on election day.

Citizens create governments to maintain order, so they can live peaceful and productive lives. A government with too much power, however, can take away people's freedom. A government with too little power can't maintain law and order. The government of Shah Riza Pahlevi of Iran took away many of its citizens' political freedoms. Dissatisfaction with this and other aspect's of the Shah's rule led to a revolt against him in 1979. The photo shows Iranian revolutionaries rallying in support of the leader of the revolt, the Ayatollah Khomeini. The government under the Ayatollah failed to bring about the changes Iranians had sought from the Shah. Economic and political chaos plagued the nation in the early and mid-1980s.

people might want to use the group's money to build new and better roads. Others might think that it is more important to spend the money to buy new equipment for schools. Laws concerning public resources help reduce conflicts.

Conflicts may occur when members of a group try to decide who their leaders should be. Governments make and enforce laws that help people to select leaders. Thus, harmony can be kept in the group so that people can continue to work together for the good of all.

Providing Security and a Common Defense

Whenever a group of people occupies a given territory, one of its major concerns is **security**—how to protect its members and their land from hostile nations and groups. Arrangements must be made to fight off possible enemies. This is one of the reasons why governments have armed forces. Our national government has several branches of armed forces: the army, navy, air force, and marine corps are the main ones.

Even if neighboring nations have been historically friendly, it is useful to have agreed-upon ways of dealing with them. For example, the United States government oversees the trading of goods and services with the people of other countries. The need for ways to deal with foreign peoples and their governments is a chief reason for government.

What Would Your Life Be Like Without Government?

What would you do without government? Could you really get along without it?

Families, private businesses, and voluntary groups could take

care of some of the needs for goods and services. Private groups could provide schools, libraries, and hospitals. Neighbors could pitch in to build and keep up a street or road, and to collect and dispose of garbage. Churches and other private groups could take care of the needy.

For large groups, however, most of these things could be done more efficiently or more fairly through government. Without government, you might not have many services that you now take for granted. Rich people would be able to buy whatever services they needed. Less wealthy people would be unable to afford many services.

Without an orderly way to settle conflicts, there would be much fighting. The best fighters would triumph. People would be hurt and property might be damaged.

When fighting is the only way to settle conflicts, most people cannot feel safe or secure. They fear that some person or group may

Governments provide security for their citizens. Part of our nation's defense system is the North American Defense Command (NORAD). NORAD headquarters in Colorado Springs, Colorado control all American and Canadian defense forces.

seize what they have worked to create and save.

There is chaos and confusion when there is no government. Think about how confusing it would be to play basketball without rules. Players would not know what they could or could not do. If players did whatever they wanted, there could be no game.

People need rules to play a game of basketball or any other kind of game. They also need government to make and enforce rules if they want to live productively and peacefully together. However, government does not work naturally to provide security and order. Too much government can result in a **police state** —a state strictly controlled by government and where there is little

freedom. A corrupt government can abuse power to make its own members rich and powerful. History provides many examples of the dangers of government. Your newspaper and news magazines include modern examples of nations that have corrupt governments. In a free society, such as the one that we have, we decide what we do and what we do not want from government.

Section Review

Vocabulary:
conflict, police state, public services, security.

Reviewing the Main Ideas
1. Give examples of three public services governments provide.
2. How and why does government settle conflicts?
3. How and why does government provide security and a common defense against enemies?
4. Why do people need government?
5. Why must citizens closely watch the activities of their government?

Skill Building
1. Find evidence or examples in your text to support this statement: Without government you would not have many services.
2. Find evidence or examples in your text to support, or to contradict, this statement: People would live more freely and more peacefully without government.

Governments protect their citizens by providing services such as fire departments.

Law and Freedom

What Is Constitutional Government?

Most countries in the world have a **constitution.** The Constitution of the United States, written in 1787, is the world's oldest written constitution.

Each country's constitution is a plan for government that usually has three main features. First, it sets up a framework for government. Second, it grants and limits the powers and duties of government officials. Third, it is the highest law of a country. Let us examine each of these main features of a constitution.

A Constitution Is a Framework for Government

Most constitutions are brief, general plans for organizing and operating a government. A constitution provides a framework for the making of laws, the enforcing of laws, and the settling of disputes about the meaning of laws.

A constitution usually does not have many details to guide the daily management of a government. The Constitution of the United States, for example, is only about 7,500 words long. It is a general plan, not a blueprint, for the organization and operation of the government of the United States. Details that fit the framework are supplied by people who run the government, such as lawmakers, law enforcers, and judges.

Woodrow Wilson, the 28th President of the United States, said that the Constitution "is a cornerstone and not a complete building, or rather . . . it is a root, not a perfect vine." President Wilson meant that the Constitution establishes only a foundation for government. The structure must be completed and changed, if necessary, by citizens.

A Constitution Grants and Limits the Powers of a Government

A constitution both grants and limits the powers of government officials. It is a guide to actions that may or may not be taken.

Several parts of the United States Constitution grant powers and assign duties to different officials, such as the President, members of Congress, and justices of the Supreme Court. For example, Article 1 of the Constitution says that Congress has the power to make laws. It then lists, in general terms, the kinds of laws Congress can make.

The United States Constitution.

The Constitution also includes limitations on the powers of government officials. There are certain powers that the government does not have. Examples are depriving citizens of freedom of speech and the press, or interfering with a person's right to religious choice. Limits on the powers of government protect the rights and liberties of the people.

In the United States, powers are granted to the government in the name of the people. The government gets its right to rule from those who are ruled. The **Preamble,** or introduction, to the Constitution says: "We the People of the United States . . . do ordain and establish this Constitution for the United States of America."

A Constitution Is the Supreme Law of a Country

A constitution is the supreme, or highest, law of the land. For example, there is no law within the United States that is higher than the Constitution of the United States. Article VI of the Constitution says: "The Constitution, and the laws of the United States which shall be made in Pursuance thereof . . . shall be the supreme law of the land." This means that Congress should not pass laws that overrule the Constitution. If Congress does pass such laws, the Supreme Court has the power to declare them unconstitutional.

Statutes are the laws passed by Congress and the **legislatures** (law-making bodies) of the fifty state governments of the United States. Statutes are not supposed to conflict with the words of the Constitution. All laws, made either by the Congress or by the lawmakers of the fifty states, are supposed to conform to the supreme law, the Constitution, as its meaning is interpreted by the Supreme Court.

The Rule of Law

In a constitutional government, officials are not supposed to break the law. This means that there is government according to the rule of law.

Many countries have a written constitution, but some of them do not have a constitutional government. The Soviet Union is an example. In

The signing of the Magna Carta in 1215. The historic document marked an important step forward in the development of constitutional government in England. Some of the ideals of the Magna Carta were adapted by the framers of our Constitution.

the Soviet Union, the power of government officials is not limited in practice by its constitution. Article 50 of the Soviet constitution says that the people have freedom of speech. However, Soviet citizens who criticize the government in public are usually punished. Furthermore, newspapers, books, and television programs are carefully controlled by Soviet government officials. This is one of many examples that can be used to show that the actions of Soviet government officials are not limited by the Soviet constitution.

In contrast to the Soviet Union, Britain has a constitutional government even though it has no written constitution. Leaders of the British government follow traditions and laws that restrict their powers. In Britain, government officials, from the highest to the lowest, are expected to follow statutes and widely accepted traditions in carrying out their duties.

The United States has a constitutional government because government officials generally try to abide by the Constitution. The President, for example, is supposed to obey the Constitution and the statutes made under it. At times, Congress or the Supreme Court have disagreed with the President's interpretation of the Constitution. Our government, however, provides ways for dealing with such differences.

A Constitutional Government Protects the Freedom of Citizens

Citizens create constitutional governments to guard their freedoms. A government and laws are needed to have freedom with security and order. But what if the government is too strong? A government with unlimited power could take away rights and freedoms that citizens should have.

In contrast, what if a government is too weak? A government with too little power could not protect some citizens from others who might abuse or take away their rights and freedoms.

An effective constitutional government is neither too powerful nor too weak. It has all the powers necessary to perform tasks the people expect of it. At the same time, limits are placed on how the government's powers may be used in order to protect liberties of the people.

James Madison, one of the creators of the Constitution, said that "you must first enable the government to control the governed; and in the next place oblige it to control itself."

Madison believed that a government should be strong enough to enforce laws and keep order. At the same time it should be limited sufficiently to protect the rights of citizens. Madison believed the power of rulers should be limited by laws. Rulers in a constitutional government are supposed to perform their duties according to laws accepted by those whom they rule.

Review

1. What are the three main features of most constitutions?
2. Explain why the United States Constitution is a general plan, and not a blueprint, for the organization and operation of the government.
3. Why does the Soviet Union have a constitution and yet not have a constitutional form of government?
4. Why is it dangerous to have a government with too much power?
5. Why is it dangerous to have a government with too little power?

Case Study

The Coast Guard

All nations that border the ocean have rules about how far into the water their boundaries extend. They claim the right to enforce their laws within their territorial waters.

When George Washington was President, the United States government claimed control over three miles of ocean extending from the Atlantic shore. Today, the government claims that its territory extends two hundred miles into the waters surrounding its coastline. This claim includes all the natural resources within and below the water such as fish, oil, and minerals.

Government leaders and scientists hope that the land under our territorial waters might someday be a main source of natural resources. The United States Coast Guard patrols these waters day and night. One of its duties is to protect American resources from other governments.

A good example is the day a Coast Guard patrol spotted several Soviet ships fishing within American territorial waters. The patrol arrested the Soviet fishermen, and the United States government notified the government of the Soviet Union. The Soviets had to pay a fine to get their ships back and to have their sailors released.

The Coast Guard also stops United States citizens from breaking laws that apply to its waters. For example, it is against the law to catch salmon off the coasts of

Coast Guard patrol coming to the aid of some novice sailors.

Oregon and Washington from June 12 to July 1. The purpose of this law is to protect the supply of salmon. If fishermen could catch as many salmon as they wanted, whenever they wanted, there might be none left for future generations.

Coast Guard patrols also stop smuggling of illegal cargoes into the United States. For example, the Coast Guard is responsible for enforcing laws against the shipment of marijuana and other illegal drugs into the country.

Coast Guard patrols also go on many lifesaving missions every year. They rescue people from sinking ships, locate stranded vessels, and help sailors in stormy waters to reach port safely.

The motto of the United States Coast Guard is *"semper paratus."* These Latin words mean "always ready." The men and women of the Coast Guard patrol the territorial waters of the United States to enforce laws and help people.

Review

1. Find an example of a decision in this case study about rules.
2. Find an example of a decision that has to do with giving or withholding benefits.
3. Find an example of a decision that involves setting a goal.
4. What kinds of duties is the government carrying out in this case?
5. Use library resources to locate articles or books that deal with the various jobs performed by the Coast Guard. Prepare a report on your findings.

Coast Guard patrol seizing illegal drugs from a boat that had tried to enter the country.

Basic Social Studies Skills
Using Your Textbook

Your textbook is an important source of basic information about civics. It is an organized, easy-to-use resource that, if used properly, will provide you with a wealth of information about your governments and your role in their operation.

Table of Contents
The *Table of Contents* is a useful guide to information about the major topics that are covered in the text. It is found at the beginning of the text.

Units, Chapters, and Sections
The table of contents shows that this book has nine *Units* and twenty-seven *Chapters*. Each unit covers a major theme about citizenship and government in the United States. Each chapter within a unit is connected to the major theme.

Each chapter is divided into two, three, or four *Sections*. Each section is related to the main theme of the chapter.

Special Features
There are three types of special features that appear regularly throughout the text. The one you are reading now, *Basic Social Studies Skills*, is one of these features. It will appear in every chapter and will always appear opposite the *Chapter Review*. Another feature, *Case Study*, will also appear in every chapter. It will always follow the last section of each chapter. The other feature, *Law and Freedom*, appears once every unit.

Students' Resource Section
The *Students' Resource Section* in the back of your text is an integral part of your book. It includes informative charts, a helpful guide to flag etiquette, an acknowledgments page, and the following:
Writing and Research Skills. This part of the Resource Section contains information that will help you complete writing and research assignments that are given in various parts of the text.
Glossary. The Resource Section also includes a *Glossary* that defines words that are relevant to your study of civics.
Index. The Resource Section also has an *Index*. The index is an alphabetical listing of people, events, places, and topics that are covered in the text.
Atlas. The *Atlas* is another integral part of the Resource Section of your text. It contains maps that will help you locate places that are referred to throughout the book.
Documents of Freedom. This part of the Resource Section contains some of our nation's most historically important documents.

Skill Practice
1. Which section of the text would you use to find specific information about political parties?
2. Who took the photograph on page 22? Which section of the text gave you this information?

Chapter 1 Review

Summary

Section 1: Citizenship in Groups

Membership in any group involves both rights and responsibilities. Citizens of the United States have the right to receive certain services and opportunities from their local, state, and national governments. They also have the responsibility to demonstrate loyalty to their governments and to actively participate in their operation. Participation includes helping determine government goals and policies that are fair and that meet the needs of the people.

Section 2: How Citizenship Is Gained and Lost

People become citizens of the United States either by birth or by naturalization. Naturalized citizens have the same rights and duties as those who gained citizenship by birth except that they cannot become President or Vice-President. United States citizenship may be lost as a result of treason, expatriation, or denaturalization.

Section 3: Government Decisions in the Lives of Citizens

Citizens of the United States live under the laws of national, state, and local governments. These governments make decisions about laws, goals, and the distribution of certain benefits and burdens.

Section 4: Why Citizens Create Governments

People who live together in a community need government. Governments in the United States have the power and the duty to provide many public services, settle conflicts, keep order, and provide security and a common defense against threats from hostile nations. Although government is necessary, too much government can result in a police state. In a free society, citizens decide what they want and what they do not want from their governments.

Vocabulary

Define the following terms.

1. legislature
2. security
3. civics
4. patriotism

Reviewing Main Ideas

1. A citizen has responsibilities to:
a. obey laws
b. be loyal to the United States
c. both
d. neither
2. True or false: People form governments to make and enforce laws.
3. True or false: Loyalty is another word for faithfulness.
4. True or false: Patriotism means loyalty to your country.

Thinking Critically

Comprehending Information

Tell in your own words why people have governments.

Organizing Information

For each government activity listed below, tell if it is (a) a public service, or (b) a way of settling conflicts and keeping order, or (c) to provide security and defense against outsiders.

1. a trial in traffic court
2. job training for handicapped people
3. military training for sailors in the navy
4. garbage collection
5. a curfew law

Communicating Ideas

Write a paragraph explaining why civics is an important part of a person's life. Use at least five of the words from the Vocabulary. Underline each vocabulary word that you use.

Chapter 2

Citizens Make Decisions

Introduction. Dolores Johnson rubbed her eyes as she shut off the piercing buzz of the alarm. She was starting her day one hour earlier than usual. It was election day, and she wanted to have time to visit the polls before going to school.

Dolores had turned eighteen one month ago. This was her first chance to vote. She had decided to vote for Curtis for mayor and Rossi to represent her district in the city council.

After voting, Dolores caught the bus to school. As she walked into school, George Sawa stopped her.

"Hey, Dolores, you'll sign my petition, won't you?" he asked.

"What's it for?" asked Dolores.

"Well, some of us who drive to school want a bigger parking lot," said George. "Maybe the principal and school board will listen if we show that a lot of students agree with us."

"I don't know, George, I'll have to think about it."

During the day, Dolores decided to sign George's petition. She also decided to join the local chapter of the Sierra Club. The club was starting an antipollution campaign and she wanted to take part in it.

The choices Dolores made were civic decisions. By voting, she was taking part in the selection of people to represent her in government. She was using one of her rights as a citizen when she signed George's petition. She was using another civil right when she joined the Sierra Club.

To be free, you must have the right to make decisions. But this right is worth much more when you know how to make sensible choices. The main purpose of this chapter is to help you become a better citizen by teaching you a basic citizenship skill—how to make decisions.

Voting is one of the most important duties we have as citizens.

Section 1
Making Decisions

Citizens in San Francisco, California, faced an important decision recently. The **issue,** or occasion for decision, was "Proposition P," a law designed to restrict smoking in places of work. Proposition P would have required employers to limit smoking to certain areas. Workers who wanted to smoke would have to go to "smoking areas."

How did the voters in San Francisco make their decisions about Proposition P? If you were asked to vote on Proposition P, how would you decide?

When faced with a decision, you should ask yourself three questions: (1) What are my choices, or alternatives? (2) What are the likely **consequences,** or outcomes, of

each alternative? (3) Which consequence do I prefer?

What Are the Alternatives?
The voters of San Francisco had three alternatives regarding Proposition P. They could have decided for it, against it, or they could have **abstained,** which means to not vote.

Sometimes there is not much time to decide. For example, a quarterback has to decide quickly which play to call during a football game. The rules permit only twenty-five seconds to select one among numerous alternative plays. There is a five-yard penalty for taking too much time to choose a play in a football game.

Often, however, there is plenty of time to think of alternatives. When there is time, there often is

We are all called upon to make many types of decisions every day. Some of these decisions, such as deciding what play to call during a football game, must be made quickly. Others, such as deciding how to vote in an important election, must be thought about very carefully.

the chance to ask others for advice. You have a better chance of making a good decision when you are aware of all your choices.

Citizens of San Francisco had plenty of time to think about their alternatives in voting for or against Proposition P. Groups were formed to campaign for or against the proposed law.

One group, San Franciscans Against Government Intrusion, was *against* Proposition P. Another group, Californians for Smoking and Nonsmoking Sections, was *for* Proposition P. Both of these groups tried to influence the voters in the election about Proposition P. Both groups urged voters to think through the consequences of each alternative.

What Are the Consequences?

Decisions lead to consequences. When you choose one alternative over another, you choose one outcome rather than another. Therefore, an important step in decision making is to predict the good and bad results of each alternative. Your choice of a course of action will be influenced by what you think the outcomes of each alternative will be.

Think about the many consequences faced by voters in San Francisco in the decision about Proposition P.

A *positive outcome* of voting *for* Proposition P might be an improvement in the health of nonsmokers. A *negative outcome* of voting *for* Proposition P would be loss of freedom

to decide whether or not to smoke in certain places.

A *positive outcome* of voting *against* Proposition P would be the freedom of choice about when and where to smoke. A *negative outcome* of voting *against* Proposition P would be the increased health hazards for nonsmokers.

Which Consequence Do You Prefer?

Careful decision making is choosing the alternative most likely to lead to the outcome you want. You need to think about your goals in order to make good decisions.

You are thinking about goals when you ask the question, "What do I want?" A goal is something you think is important for you to have. People work to reach their goals.

When you answer the question about what you want, you show your **values.** Values are those things that people think are important or good and which they are usually willing to fight for.

When people have the same values, it is easy to make some kinds of decisions. For example, most people agree that cheating is wrong and that not punishing cheaters creates problems for the class. We expect teachers to make decisions that prevent cheating in the classroom.

Many decisions are difficult to make because they involve conflicts among different goals and values. Careful thought is needed to choose the alternative that will most likely lead to the best outcome.

Joe Reid, a voter in San Francisco, was a nonsmoker who valued public health. You might have expected him to decide easily in favor of Proposition P. However, Joe also believed that citizens should have the freedom to decide for themselves when and where to smoke. Joe had a difficult choice to make. He had to decide between two conflicting values. Did he prefer freedom of choice for smokers more than the elimination of risks to the health of both nonsmokers and smokers?

The voters of San Francisco decided in favor of Proposition P. The vote was very close. There were 80,740 votes for Proposition P and 79,481 votes against it. If you had had the choice, how might you have voted? In Section 2, you will find out about a method Joe used to determine how to vote.

Section Review

Vocabulary:
abstain, consequences, issue, values.

Reviewing the Main Ideas
1. What three questions should you ask yourself when faced with a decision?
2. Suppose you are trying to decide what the minimum legal driving age should be in your state. Name two possible alternatives and give two likely consequences for each.

Skill Building
Write several paragraphs explaining why values are important in the decision-making process.

Section 2
Judging Decisions

The headline of the morning newspaper said: Scenic City Council Bans Swimming in Lake.

Marcia Gordon showed the headline to her brother, Gregg.

"That's a dumb decision!" Gregg moaned. "I had planned to do a lot of swimming this summer."

"I did, too," said Marcia. "But the paper says the lake is polluted. I think the city council did the right thing."

"I don't agree," replied Gregg. "People should be free to make up their own minds about swimming in polluted water."

Marcia continued to read the newspaper. "Hey, Gregg! Listen to this," she shouted. "A group of people are going to demonstrate at city hall against the swimming ban. I don't think they should do that. Do you?"

"Of course they should, Marcia. They have the right to demonstrate as long as they do it peacefully and obey the law," replied Gregg.

Gregg and Marcia were judging the city government's decision to ban swimming. They were also judging the decisions of certain citizens about how to respond to the no-swimming rule.

What Are Judgments?
Everyone makes **judgments.** You make a judgment when you think a school rule is fair or not. You judge a friend's decision when you say, "that is a good idea," or "that's a silly thing to do."

Demonstrating against the use of nuclear power. Deciding to support or reject the use of nuclear power is a very difficult decision that many people all over the world have had to make.

Judging is deciding whether something is good or bad, better or worse, right or wrong. In Marcia's judgment, the city government made a good decision when it banned swimming. Marcia made a negative judgment of certain citizens who decided to demonstrate against the no-swimming rule.

When you judge objects to be good or bad, you are placing a value on them. You are determining their worth to you. Your judgments depend to a great extent upon your beliefs about right and wrong.

Marcia's judgment concerning the no-swimming decision and the protesters is based on her concern for public health and respect for the authority of the city government. In contrast, Gregg places the freedom of citizens to decide for themselves above public health and safety. He values free speech and the right to peacefully attempt to change laws.

Scenic City is a vacation resort. Many tourists come to swim and boat in the lake. The ban on swimming seemed to threaten the tourist business. Therefore, many owners of businesses and their employees were against the ban. Many workers feared they might lose their jobs if the number of people spending their vacations in Scenic City dropped. Like most people, they placed a high value on keeping their jobs. Thus, in their judgment, the city government's decision to ban swimming was a mistake.

As a citizen, you make judgments about candidates for government offices such as mayor, governor, or President. You judge the ideas, abilities, and decisions of the various candidates.

As a citizen, you make judgments about the decisions of government officials. These judgments are tied to your beliefs about what is right or wrong.

You also judge the decisions of other citizens—friends, teachers, and parents. You may like or dislike how these people decide to use their civil rights or carry out their responsibilities as citizens.

Finally, you judge your own decisions. After choosing an alternative, you may continue to think about the outcome. You may ask yourself, "Did I make the best choice? If I could do it again, would I make the same decision?"

Guidelines for Judging Decisions

Decisions may have positive and negative outcomes. Good decisions lead to outcomes that satisfy you and others. These four questions will help you judge choices and their probable outcomes:
1. Is the choice practical?
2. How will the choice affect me?
3. How will the choice affect others?
4. Is the choice fair?

Is the Choice Practical? Alternatives are not **practical** if they are tied to outcomes that cannot be reached. Some people can move from the city to the country to get away from air pollution. But flying to the moon to escape pollution is not a choice open to anyone. If you cannot really undertake a course of action, it is not a real choice. In a practical decision, there is a strong possibility that the choice will really lead to the result that you want.

How Will the Choice Affect Me?

Government decisions may affect your life in many ways. A government's decision to require all new cars to have air bags could affect your health and safety. A decision to end the sports program at your school could affect the skills you can develop. Laws that prevent unfair treatment because of your race, religion, or sex could affect your ability to earn money. Government decisions about how much income tax you have to pay will affect your budget. To judge these kinds of decisions, you must think about whether the outcomes will give or take away things that you believe are important.

How Will the Choice Affect Others?

Responsible citizens not only think of themselves, they also consider the welfare of others. When judging a decision, you should examine the consequences for all of the groups of people affected.

Suppose the government in your area decided to build a superhighway through your neighborhood. At first, you might like this decision because you and your family could drive more quickly to a nearby town to visit relatives and friends. However, you should also think about how the new highway might affect others.

Will the government have to tear down homes and stores to make room·for the new highway? Would the new road cause people to move their homes and businesses?

Would people who have to move be paid a fair price for their property and the troubles caused by moving? How many people would be helped by the new highway?

As you think about the worth of a decision, realize that different people might be helped or hurt by it. They might make very different judgments of the same decision. The owners of stores and homes being destroyed by a new highway might feel differently about the decision to build the highway than a truck driver who wants to use the new road. Do not rush to judge a decision as good or bad until you think carefully about how it might affect various people.

Is the Choice Fair? Good decisions are fair. The fairest decisions help both individuals and their communities. Fair decisions strike a balance between the needs of the individual and the needs of others.

Decision makers in government consider the needs of both the majority and minority of citizens in a situation. We often believe that the best decisions are those that serve the needs of the greatest number of people. However, this belief is an acceptable guide to judging decisions only if we remember the rights of minority groups and individuals.

Each person must at times give up some rights and freedoms in order to live in harmony with others. A community cannot exist when each person does exactly as he or she pleases. However, we should always remember that the basic reason for forming communities and

(above) Disappointed students learning that their school would be closed because of falling enrollment. (top) A final farewell to their school.

All the homes in this neighborhood, except the one shown, were sold and then razed by a developer to make room for a hotel complex. Although the owner was offered a fair price for her home, she decided that her personal attachment was far too great and could not be compensated for in money alone. After many attempts to convince the owner to sell, the developer finally decided to build his complex around the home.

governments is to serve individual citizens. A fair decision does not put undue hardship on individuals.

Using a Decision Tree

A good tool to use when making and judging difficult decisions is a decision tree. A decision tree can help you think carefully as you make or judge a decision.

The decision tree on the next page shows the choices that faced Joe Reid, who had to decide to vote for or against Proposition P. Notice that there are places on the tree to show the issue, or occasion for decision, the alternatives, the positive and negative outcomes of each alternative, and the conflicting goals that the voter has.

The trunk of the decision tree shows the issue, or occasion for decision. When you look at the branches, you find the three alternatives. One alternative was to vote against Proposition P. The second alternative was to vote for it. The third alternative was to abstain, or not vote, and let the majority of voters decide the issue.

Look higher in the tree and you will find the probable outcomes of each alternative. Choosing among alternatives means choosing among their probable outcomes, or consequences.

At the top of the tree are four goals Joe Reid had. The goals of decision makers help them to identify consequences they prefer. Joe Reid's goal of participating in government as a voter meant that he would reject abstaining.

Sometimes goals appear to be in conflict. Joe Reid valued both the freedom and health of citizens. Proposition P required limitations on the freedom of smokers to protect the health and comfort of nonsmokers. Furthermore, Proposition P restricted smokers in order to increase the freedom and rights of nonsmokers.

Decision makers usually rank their goals to help them choose the consequences they prefer. If Joe Reid had valued the health and comfort of nonsmokers more than freedom of choice, he certainly would have decided to vote for Proposition P. If Joe had valued freedom more than his other goals, he might have decided to vote against Proposition P in order to protect the rights of smokers.

After studying his decision tree, Joe Reid decided to vote for Proposition P because he valued *both* freedom and health. He wanted to support the health of nonsmokers and their freedom to avoid the discomfort from smoke at the workplace.

Although you certainly will not use a decision tree every time you have to make a decision, it is nonetheless helpful for analyzing the thought processes you should be going through when making choices. In some cases, when a really difficult decision is at hand, sketching out and filling in a decision tree can be very useful.

Section Review

Vocabulary:
judgment, practical.

Decision Tree

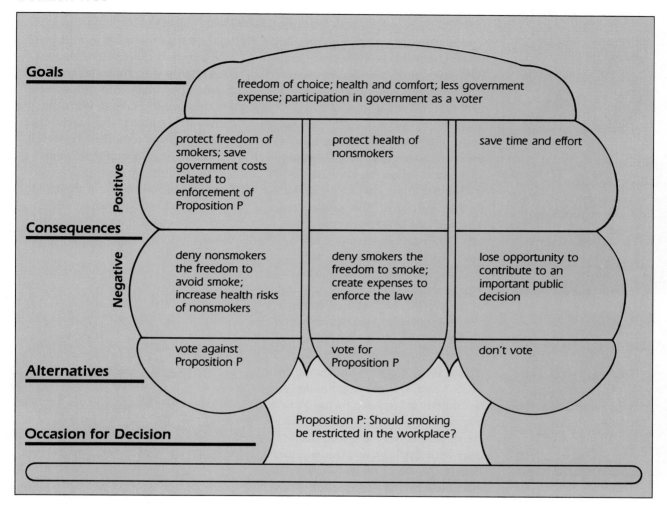

Goals

freedom of choice; health and comfort; less government expense; participation in government as a voter

Consequences

Positive

| protect freedom of smokers; save government costs related to enforcement of Proposition P | protect health of nonsmokers | save time and effort |

Negative

| deny nonsmokers the freedom to avoid smoke; increase health risks of nonsmokers | deny smokers the freedom to smoke; create expenses to enforce the law | lose opportunity to contribute to an important public decision |

Alternatives

| vote against Proposition P | vote for Proposition P | don't vote |

Occasion for Decision

Proposition P: Should smoking be restricted in the workplace?

Reviewing the Main Ideas:

1. What are four questions you should ask yourself when judging a decision?

2. How can you determine if a choice or decision is fair?

Skill Building

1. Look at Joe's decision tree above.

a. Which alternative might Joe pick if his main goal were to avoid participating in government?

b. Which alternative might Joe pick if his main goal were to give all citizens the freedom of choice?

2. Draw a decision tree for the Scenic City Council. Write in the alternatives and the good and bad consequences of each.

3. How would you judge the Scenic City Council's decision? Use the guidelines for judging decisions (page 30) to explain your answer.

Case Study

The Black Mesa Mine Decision

(top two) Black Mesa before and after. (above) Peterson Zah. (right) Peter MacDonald.

The Navajo [nav' ə hō] live in a large reservation in the Southwest. In recent years they have faced a severe conflict about how to use their natural resources.

Until a few years ago, the people of Black Mesa, Arizona, lived as their ancestors had lived—raising sheep and following ancient Navajo traditions. Then coal was discovered in the flat-topped hills of the area. Nothing has been the same since.

Geologists determined that Black Mesa covered a very rich, shallow vein of low-sulfur coal. They thought it could become one of the world's largest coal mines.

Peter MacDonald, Navajo tribal chairman, urged his people to sign a contract with a mining company. In return for the right to take coal from Black Mesa, the mining company would pay a large fee to the Navajo. The mining company would also share profits from the sale of the coal with the Navajo. Finally, more than three hundred Navajo would get jobs working at the mine. They would be paid more than $10,000 each year. Most of these people were then making less than $3,000 per year.

MacDonald said: "We must use our natural resources to create jobs for our people and put them on the road to economic self-sufficiency."

Many Navajo agreed with MacDonald. They believed that the growing population of more than 160,000 could not be supported by farming and herding. Too many people were poor and hungry. They believed that the mine would provide jobs and money. The money could be used to build better schools, hospitals, and other facilities the Navajo needed. With the money gained from the Black Mesa mine, everyone would be better off.

Some Navajo disagreed with MacDonald and his supporters. They wanted to preserve their old traditions. To these people, the Black Mesa was a sacred place that should not be ravaged in return for money.

They said taking coal from Black Mesa was a sin against nature. A traditional Navajo belief is that all things are sacred—people, animals, plants, earth, stones, and water. All natural resources should be used with care and passed on to the next generation unspoiled.

In addition, seventy-eight families living at Black Mesa would have to move if the mining contract were signed. Many Navajo thought this was unfair.

The decision was very difficult and the discussions were bitter. In the end, the tribal leaders agreed to sign a contract that gave the coal company the right to strip-mine coal from Black Mesa for thirty-five years. Strip mining involves removing thin layers of soil from the earth and then removing the valuable materials.

Judgments on the decision have been mixed. One outcome of the Black Mesa coal mine has been more money and a better standard of living for most Navajo.

As one young man said: "I have a steady job at the mine. I've never made so much money in my life."

A young woman said: "We already have been paid millions of dollars for leasing land to the coal company. We'll get lots more from our share of the profits. We can use this money to build the things our people need. We've never had it so good."

However, many Navajo are very unhappy with the situation. Smokestacks, machinery, and power lines now mark the land that previously had supported only trees, shrubs, and grass. Huge machines gouge the earth to remove coal that giant trucks carry away.

In May, 1976, more than six hundred Navajo gathered at Window Rock, Arizona, to protest the decision of their tribal leaders. Their viewpoint was expressed by an old woman: "The Earth is our mother. How much would you ask for if your mother had been harmed? There is no way that we can be repaid for the damages to our mother. No amount of money can repay; money cannot give birth to anything."

In the early 1980s, the Navajo were still plagued by poverty and high unemployment. Many people thought that the Navajo should be realizing more of a profit from the mining of their precious natural resources. Some Navajo criticized Peter MacDonald's ability to deal with the mining companies.

In November, 1982, the Navajo expressed their displeasure with MacDonald by not reelecting him to office. Instead, they elected Peterson Zah as their new tribal chairman. After taking office, Zah started to form plans that he hoped would increase the Navajo's share of the wealth being removed from their lands. But, as of today, there are still many Navajo who would rather return to the days of old.

Review

1. What was the first major occasion for decision in this case?
2. What were the alternatives?
3. What were the likely consequences of each alternative?
4. What consequence did Peter MacDonald and his supporters prefer?

Basic Social Studies Skills
Using the *Readers' Guide to Periodical Literature*

In this chapter you read about San Francisco voters who had to decide for or against a law to restrict smoking in places of work.

San Francisco is one of numerous places in the United States where voters have recently had to decide about restrictions on smoking in public. Suppose you wanted to find more information about this issue. You might begin by reading current magazine articles about this subject. But how would you, aside from skimming the contents pages of hundeds of magazines, find current articles dealing with this issue?

The best place to look would be the *Readers' Guide to Periodical Literature*, a reference source to which most libraries subscribe. The *Readers' Guide* alphabetically lists articles that have appeared in almost two hundred magazines. In addition, articles that appear in *USA Today*, a national newspaper, appear in this guide. *Readers' Guide* is published ten times a year. All issues for a particular year are combined into hardcover books and are usually found in your library's reference section. Most libraries carry issues of the *Guide* that go back many years.

Readers' Guide is well organized and easy to use. A list of all the periodicals covered in the *Guide* appears in the front of each volume. There is also a key explaining the abbreviations used in the listings.

Articles are listed under the general subject of the articles and by the author's name. For example, the following entry appears under the general topic of "smoking" in the March, 1981–February, 1982 volume.

Smoking
Antismoking campaigners. I. Steele. il
> *World Press R* 28: 57 My '81

The above entry tells you that an article titled "Antismoking Campaigners" appeared in Volume 28 of the *World Press Review*, which was published in May, 1981. The article is on page 57 and was written by I. Steele, and is illustrated.

Skill Practice
At your library, locate p. 1481 of Volume 43 (March, 1983, to February, 1984) of *Readers' Guide*. Then answer the following questions:

1. Find an article that is about San Francisco's Proposition P. In what periodical does the article appear? When was the periodical published? On what page does the article begin?

2. Find an article about the effects of smoking on health. Who wrote the article? In what periodical did it appear? When was it published? On what page does the article begin?

Chapter 2 Review

Summary
Section 1: Making Decisions
Citizens in the United States have the right and responsibility to make decisions concerning their governments. A decision involves alternatives, consequences, and goals. A decision maker should try to answer three key questions: (1) What are my alternatives? (2) What are the likely consequences of each alternative? (3) Which consequence do I prefer?

Section 2: Judging Decisions
Citizens judge decisions of government officials and others when they conclude that the decisions are good or bad, right or wrong. Citizens also judge their own decisions. There are four questions citizens should use to guide their judgments of decisions: (1) Is the choice practical? (2) How will the choice affect me? (3) How will the choice affect others? (4) Is the choice fair?

Vocabulary
Match the phrases with the terms.
a. useful; leading toward the desired result
b. results or outcomes
c. things believed to be good or important
d. an opinion about the worth of something
e. choose not to vote

1. values
2. consequences
3. judgment
4. practical
5. abstain

Reviewing Main Ideas
1. You are trying to make a decision. You have considered the alternatives. Next you should:
a. choose the alternative you like best.
b. consider the consequences.
c. judge the decision.
d. none of the above.
2. True or false: When making a decision, it is always necessary to have plenty of time to consider the alternatives and the consequences of each.
3. True or false: Once you have considered the alternatives and consequences you face, it is always easy to make a decision.

Thinking Critically
Finding Information
1. Use the headings in this chapter to find the guidelines for judging decisions. What page are they on?
2. If you wanted to review the parts of the decision tree, where would you look?
Comprehending Information
Write a paragraph of at least four sentences explaining what makes a decision *fair*.
Organizing Information
Copy the following story. Draw a line under the occasion for decision. Put circles around the alternatives. Put a star next to each consequence.

Wilona and Jim have asked Rose to go to the beach with them. She has a toothache. If she goes to the beach she might have so much fun that she'll forget about her tooth. On the other hand, the toothache might spoil her fun and everyone else's. If she goes to the dentist, she'll get her tooth fixed, but she'll miss out on the fun.

Unit One Test

Vocabulary

Write *true* if the underlined word or phrase is used correctly. Write *false* if it is used incorrectly. Rephrase each false statement so that the underlined word or phrase is used correctly.

1. <u>Civics</u> is the study of the rights and responsibilities of citizens.

2. Delegates from the different states voted to approve the <u>Mayflower Compact</u>.

3. A government passes <u>goals</u> for all the people to follow.

4. A <u>practical</u> decision is one that is possible and would lead toward desired outcomes.

5. When someone says, "That's a rotten idea!" that person is making a <u>judgment</u>.

6. One choice available to voters is to <u>abstain</u>.

7. <u>Government</u> is the authority that makes and enforces laws in a country or state.

8. <u>Values</u> are things that are believed to be good or important.

9. Government record keeping of births and deaths is not considered a <u>public service</u>.

10. <u>Patriotism</u> and <u>loyalty</u> to one's country mean the same thing.

11. The process of decision making does not include choosing from <u>alternatives</u>.

12. It is impossible to make a decision without having a <u>consequence</u>.

13. Governments have the power and duty to keep order by settling <u>conflicts</u> according to law.

14. People who withdraw allegiance from their country are <u>expatriates</u>.

15. Examples of <u>benefits</u> are good health and education.

16. A <u>constitution</u> is a plan for government.

17. The first ten amendments to the Constitution are called the <u>Preamble</u>.

Recalling Information

1. True or false: Being a group member gives a person both rights and responsibilities.

2. Governments usually help:
a. pick up garbage
b. provide security
c. fight fires
d. all of the above
e. none of the above

3. True or false: Decision makers should consider the consequences of the different alternatives they face.

4. Peter MacDonald, Navajo tribal chairman, urged his people to:
a. keep their old traditions
b. sign a contract with a mining company
c. continue farming and herding

5. True or false: Laws that promote unfair treatment because of race, religion, or sex could affect a person's ability to earn money.

6. True or false: Loyalty usually develops when a person supports, believes in, or identifies with the people and goals of a group.

7. Which of the following are public services?
a. a city worker repairing a damaged street
b. a police officer ticketing a driver for speeding
c. a firefighter building an addition to his home
d. a clerk issuing a couple a marriage license

8. True or false: You must make a decision whenever you face two or more alternatives.

9. True or false: The words "We the People" in the Preamble to the Constitution are important because they show that the government's authority comes from the people.

10. The United States Constitution
a. is the oldest written plan for government in the world.
b. grants great freedom and responsibility to individual citizens.
c. was replaced by the Articles of Confederation in 1787.
d. all of the above

11. True or false: Naturalized citizens have exactly the same rights and duties as those who gained citizenship by birth.

12. The Soviet Union has
a. a written constitution.
b. a constitutional government.
c. a democratic government.
d. none of the above

13. True or false: *"e pluribus unum"* means "out of many, one."

14. The Black Mesa Mine Decision
a. almost eliminated unemployment on the Navajo reservation.
b. had little or no effect on the environment.
c. has brought positive as well as negative results.
d. prohibited mining on Navajo lands.

Building Skills

1. If you wanted to find information about Martin Luther King, Jr., in your text, which of the following would you use?
a. glossary
b. index
c. table of contents
d. atlas

2. Which section of the text would you turn to if you wanted to find out how to correctly pronounce a vocabulary word?
a. glossary
b. index
c. table of contents
d. atlas

3. The *Readers' Guide* would be a good reference to use if you wanted to:
a. find a list of books dealing with Abraham Lincoln's years in the White House.
b. find newspaper articles dealing with nuclear power plants.
c. find lists of magazine articles dealing with nuclear power plants.
d. all of the above

4. Copy the following story. Draw a line under the occasion for decision. Put circles around the alternatives. Put a star next to each consequence.

"Amy asked Jenny to watch an important football game on television. Jenny thinks football is boring, and besides, she has a twenty-dollar nonrefundable ticket to the ballet that evening. Amy will be moving out of town in two days. If Jenny goes to the ballet she'll have a good time, but then she might not have the chance to see Amy before she leaves. If she goes to Amy's house, she'll get to say goodbye to her good friend, but she'll miss the ballet and lose $20."

5. James Madison said that "you must first enable the government to control the governed; and in the next place oblige it to control itself." Use one paragraph to explain what Madison meant.

6. Situation: You are tired and need to get some sleep but you have a big term paper due tomorrow that will require at least two hours to complete.
a. What are your alternatives?
b. What would be the probable consequence of each of your alternatives?

Unit 2

The Constitution and Your Rights

The United States has a plan for government that enables its citizens to actively participate in its operation. This plan, the United States Constitution, says that the citizens of the nation shall govern themselves. The Constitution has rules that discourage any person or group of persons from taking that power away from the people. The Constitution also states that the citizens of the nation have certain other rights and freedoms that shall not be taken away.

Theodore Roosevelt, the twenty-sixth President of the United States, said that people "can never escape being governed. Either they must govern themselves or submit to being governed by others." The Constitution of the United States is a contract made by citizens to establish the terms under which they will govern themselves. Citizens agree to obey laws made by their elected representatives in government. In return, they gain protection of rights and freedoms set forth in the Constitution.

Our Constitution, written in 1787, is the oldest written plan for government in the world. And yet the Constitution is new in some ways, too. It is an ever-changing document. Through the years the Constitution has been amended, or changed, twenty-six times. Most of these changes have increased the rights and freedoms of United States citizens.

Many of the freedoms and rights of citizenship are earned by exercising responsibilities and duties. Citizens of a free country must be ready and willing to participate in their government. They must also take the time and effort needed to make certain that officials in government follow the Constitution. Capable and responsible citizens have made the Constitution a practical and respected means of self-government.

(opposite)
Fourth of July parade in Philadelphia, Pennsylvania.

Chapter 3

Citizens Make a Constitution

Introduction. Early in 1787, George Washington had to decide whether to go to an important meeting in Philadelphia, Pennsylvania. Several of his friends favored having a convention of representatives from each state to decide how to strengthen and improve the young government. Many had written to Washington urging him to be at the convention. They said its success depended on his being there.

Washington was well aware of the nation's troubles. For several years he had been warning that the young nation might fall apart. The thirteen states had cooperated to win the war against the British. But after the war, the states quarreled. Washington often said that to save the nation each state would have to give up some independence to a more powerful, central government. There were riots around the country. Many citizens tried to settle their problems by mob rule.

Washington agreed with the goals of the convention in Philadelphia, but he was not certain that he should attend. He was fifty-five years old. Rheumatism racked his body with pain. His brother had just died, and his mother and sister were sick.

In addition to family problems, Washington worried about what the convention could accomplish. Some people viewed it as a meeting of traitors seeking to overthrow the national government. Would people think he was disloyal to the nation?

When Congress approved the convention, some of Washington's worries were eased. Now no one could think that those who attended were against their national government. He decided to attend and participate in what is known as the Constitutional Convention.

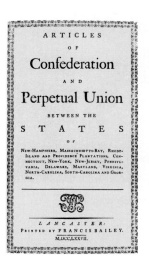

(left) George Washington presiding over the Constitutional Convention. (below) The Articles of Confederation.

Section 1
The Background of the Constitutional Convention

In 1786, a concerned George Washington wrote, "Wisdom and good examples are necessary at this time to rescue the political machine from the impending storm." Why did Washington compare the future of the United States to a "storm"?

In 1781, near the end of the Revolutionary War, the thirteen states had accepted a constitution called the Articles of Confederation. The weaknesses of the Articles led to the national problems that worried George Washington.

Government Under the Articles of Confederation

Under the Articles of Confederation, the main powers of government were held by the states. Each state was represented in a national Congress. The main job of the Congress was to make laws for the United States. Each state had one vote in the Congress. The Congress could not pass laws on certain important matters unless nine states agreed to do so. The thirteen states were a **confederation,** a group of independent states united only as a "league of friendship." The national government was very weak.

Leaders of the thirteen states were unwilling to grant very much power to a central government. Memories of the recent rebellion against the British government were too strong. They feared the creation of a powerful new central government that might infringe upon their liberties and rights.

Under the Articles, Congress had no power to tax the states. It could not regulate trade between the states. More importantly, Con-

43

gress had no power to make the thirteen states or their citizens obey its laws or the Articles.

The central government had only those powers listed exactly in the Articles. All other powers of government belonged to the states.

The states argued constantly among themselves over boundaries and taxes. The New York legislature, for example, started taxing New Jersey farmers who crossed the Hudson River to sell goods in New York. The states also created their own state armies and navies. Virginia and Pennsylvania fought briefly over conflicting claims to the area around Pittsburgh. An argument between Pennsylvania and Connecticut almost ended in war. The national government lacked power to settle these conflicts.

Another serious problem was money. Without the power to tax, Congress had to beg the states for money. They gave very little. As a result, Congress had little money to pay for government services. The government could not afford to keep a navy to protect its trading ships from pirates. It was also unable to pay its debts. (Large sums of money had been borrowed to pay for the Revolutionary War.)

There was no national currency such as we have today. Most states printed their own paper money. Often one state's money was not accepted in another state. Many people did not trust their own state's money. In North Carolina, people started to use whiskey to pay their bills. In Virginia, many people used tobacco instead of paper money.

George Washington.

All during the 1780s, leaders such as George Washington, Alexander Hamilton, John Hancock, Thomas Jefferson, and James Madison argued for a stronger national government. Hancock said that "our very existence as a free nation" depends on strengthening the national government.

George Washington warned: "I do not conceive we can exist long as a nation without having lodged somewhere a power, which will pervade the whole Union . . . ."

A Convention Is Called

In response to the warnings of Washington and other leaders, a **convention** (meeting of representatives) was held at Annapolis, Maryland, in September, 1786. The purpose was to discuss ways to solve the problems of the new nation's government. Each state had been invited to send **delegates,** or representatives, but only five states did so. Since less than half of the thirteen states were represented, those at the Annapolis Convention decided not to discuss revision of the Articles of Confederation. Instead, they issued a report which concluded that "there are important defects in the system of the federal government." The report included an invitation to the thirteen states to send delegates to a convention at Philadelphia in May, 1787, to change the Articles.

Shays' Rebellion. At first, Congress seemed reluctant to agree with the report of the Annapolis Convention. However, during the fall of 1786 and the winter of 1787, there were

(left) Shays' Rebellion. (below) Benjamin Franklin, the oldest and one of the most prominent members of the Convention.

disorders and riots in several states. The nation's economy was so weak that many farmers lost their farms because they could not pay their debts. In Massachusetts, Daniel Shays, a soldier in the Revolutionary War, led nearly one thousand farmers in an attempt to keep the state supreme court from meeting. If the court could not meet, it could not sentence poor farmers to jail nor make them give up their farms, the farmers believed.

Shays' Rebellion was over quickly, but it frightened citizens all over the new nation. By early 1787, it was clear that the national government had to be strengthened. Congress agreed there were problems with the Articles of Confederation. Each state was asked to send delegates to a convention in Philadelphia in May.

Who Came to the Convention?

Twelve of the thirteen states sent delegates to the convention. Rhode Island's leaders were strongly opposed to strengthening the national government and decided not to participate in the convention.

George Washington was one of the first to arrive. He came in a carriage escorted by local soldiers. Bells rang for the general. He was given a hero's welcome.

The fifty-five delegates to the convention in Philadelphia were practical men of knowledge and political experience. Many had served their country in the American Revolution. Eight of the delegates had signed the Declaration of Independence. Seven of them had been governors of their states. Thirty-one of the delegates had college educations. At that time, fewer people went to college than do today.

At eighty-one, Benjamin Franklin of Pennsylvania was the oldest delegate. He was also world famous as a diplomat, writer, inventor, and scientist.

(below) Alexander Hamilton. (middle) James Madison. (bottom) The mode of travel used by many Convention delegates.

Alexander Hamilton came from New York. At age thirty-two, he was one of the youngest delegates. However, he was one of the top lawyers in the country.

James Madison, a great scholar, came from Virginia. He was thirty-six years old. He knew a great deal about history, government, and public affairs. He contributed some of the most important ideas at the convention.

The delegates were a young group. Their average age was only forty-three. Half the delegates were in their mid-thirties. Most of these men had great careers ahead of them. Two men, Washington and Madison, later became Presidents of the United States. Another delegate, Elbridge Gerry, became Vice-President. Seventeen of the delegates went on to become United States senators. Eleven of the men went on to serve in the House of Representatives. Six delegates became Supreme Court justices. Clearly, the delegates were not a group of average citizens.

Two great leaders, Thomas Jefferson and John Adams, were not at the convention. Jefferson was in Paris, where he was serving as United States minister to France. Adams was working in London as the minister to Great Britain. Patrick Henry, another leader of the Revolution, was elected as a delegate from Virginia. But he was against the convention and did not attend.

It rained heavily the opening week of the convention. Roads from Maine to Georgia were deep in mud, and travel was very difficult. Many delegates were late in arriving. Once all were assembled, however, they were ready to make some of the most important decisions in American history.

Section Review

Vocabulary:
confederation, convention, delegate.

Reviewing the Main Ideas
1. What were the Articles of Confederation?
2. What were the main weaknesses of government under the Articles of Confederation?
3. Give the qualifications of the delegates to the convention in Philadelphia.

Skill Building
1. Make two lists. In one list, put the reasons George Washington thought he should go to the convention in Philadelphia. In the other list, put the reasons he did not want to go.
2. What event convinced Washington to attend the convention?

Section 2
Decision Making at the Constitutional Convention

The delegates met in Independence Hall in Philadelphia on May 25, 1787. They worked for more than sixteen weeks. Usually their sessions started at ten in the morning and ended about three in the afternoon. There was plenty of time to discuss the decisions they were making. During the evenings, they often met at the Indian Queen, a hotel where many of the delegates stayed. They also talked informally at dances and parties held for them by leading citizens in Philadelphia.

Decisions About Rules and Goals

The Convention started on a positive note. The delegates agreed **unanimously** that George Washington should **preside** over the meetings. A unanimous decision is one that is supported by *all* members of a group. As presider, he would recognize speakers and make sure that the meetings would be conducted in an orderly, efficient manner.

Before the meetings began, Washington reminded the delegates of the critical importance of their task, and challenged them to do their very best work. He said: "It is too probable that no plan we propose will be adopted. Perhaps another dreadful conflict is to be sustained. If to please the people, we offer what we ourselves disapprove, how can we afterwards defend our work? Let us raise a standard to which the wise and honest can repair."

One of Washington's first actions was to appoint a committee to write rules for conducting the business of the convention. The committee proposed several rules, and after much discussion, the delegates approved them.

One rule was to keep their discussions secret. The public was not allowed to attend meetings. Each delegate promised not to tell outsiders what was going on in the convention. To keep others away, sentries guarded the doors.

There were several important reasons for the "secrecy rule." It enabled the delegates to speak freely. They did not worry about pleasing the public with anything they said. It also made it easier for them to change their minds on the many issues debated.

Other rules dealt with keeping order during the meetings. No one was allowed to talk unless recognized by the presiding officer. While one person spoke, others were expected to listen. Meetings could not be held unless delegates from at

Independence Hall, Philadelphia, Pennsylvania.

least seven states were present. Decisions were to be made by majority vote of the states present. Each state had only one vote. The entire delegation from each state would decide by majority vote how to cast its one ballot.

After deciding what rules they should follow, the delegates discussed goals. The Congress had given them the job of revising the Articles of Confederation. The delegates agreed, however, that changing the Articles was not enough. They decided on a new goal. They would discard the Articles and write a new constitution. At this point, the meeting became known as the Constitutional Convention.

The delegates were determined to set up a government that all states would accept. Everyone knew that failure to write a new constitution would mean disaster. Elbridge Gerry of Massachusetts spoke for most when he said, "I would bury my bones in this city rather than [leave] . . . the Convention without anything being done."

Settling a Basic Disagreement

After agreeing on rules and general goals, the delegates began their discussions. From the start, it became clear that there would be conflict between the goals of some of the heavily populated states such as Virginia and Pennsylvania, and the goals of some of the less populated states such as New Jersey and Delaware. The states with large populations believed that they should have more power than states with small populations. The states with small populations, on the other hand, felt that population should not be a factor in determining power. These states wanted power equal to that of the large states. Thus, a basic question was: How should power be distributed among the states?

This cartoon was created in the 1980s. What do you think was the cartoonist's reason for drawing this cartoon nearly 200 years after the creation of the Constitution?

"Remember, gentlemen, we aren't here just to draft a constitution. We're here to draft the best darned constitution in the world."

The Virginia Plan. The Virginia delegates were among the first to arrive in Philadelphia. While waiting for the convention to start, they created a plan for a new constitution. On May 29, Edmund Randolph presented their plan to the others.

The Virginia Plan called for a government with three branches. A legislative branch would make laws. An executive branch would enforce laws. A judicial branch would decide whether laws were in agreement with the Constitution.

The legislative branch would be divided into two parts—a Senate and a House of Representatives. The states were to be represented in both houses of the national legislature on the basis of their population, or the amount of money they gave to the national government.

Delegates from Massachusetts, Pennsylvania, and Virginia promoted this plan. It gave the states with large populations more influence in the national government than they had before. Under the Articles, each state had been given one vote, no matter how big or small it was.

The New Jersey Plan. Delegates from the states with small populations did not like the Virginia Plan. William Paterson of New Jersey proposed an alternative. It was called the New Jersey Plan. This plan also called for three branches of government. However, the legislative branch would have only one house as in the Articles of Confederation, and each state would get one vote.

Delegates from Delaware, New Jersey, and Maryland approved of this plan. It made their states equal in power to the big states.

A decision had to be made. For six long weeks the delegates debated the issues. Each side thought it was right. Neither side wanted to give in. Some delegates even threatened to leave the Convention.

Fortunately, all the delegates shared the goal of creating a new constitution. They continued to work. They knew a **compromise** was needed.

A compromise involves giving and taking. In a compromise, each side gives up something it wants. Each side also gets something. Compromises are an important part of political life. They are a way to settle disputes when no one can agree. The delegates understood this. They looked for a third alternative.

The Great Compromise. A committee headed by Roger Sherman of Connecticut came up with the answer. It proposed that Congress have two houses—a Senate and a House of Representatives. The states would be represented equally in the Senate; each state would have two senators. This would please the small states. In the House, representation would be based on population. The big states would have more votes than the small states. This pleased the big states.

Sherman's alternative is often called the Great Compromise. After much discussion, the delegates

(top) Salem Harbor, Massachusetts, filled with ships carrying imported goods from China and the Indies. (middle) The north wing of the Capitol in Washington, D.C., in 1800. (right) Roger Sherman.

decided to accept this alternative. No group was completely happy, but the compromise was a solution all could accept.

Other Compromises

The Great Compromise saved the Convention. After agreeing to it, the delegates moved on to other important issues and decisions. When the delegates could not agree on an alternative, they compromised. As Ben Franklin said, the delegates spent a lot of time "sawing boards to make them fit."

The delegates at the Constitutional Convention have provided citizens of today with an important lesson in cooperation. Through compromise, the delegates settled various disagreements about the creation of their new government. Some delegates, for example, wanted members of the House of Representatives to be elected every year. Others argued for a three-year term of office. They compromised on two.

Delegates also argued about the powers and duties of the President and Congress. One issue was about whether or not Congress should have the power to tax trade with foreign nations. A compromise was reached that gave the federal government power to tax **imports,** goods coming into the country, but not **exports,** goods sent out of the country.

Sometimes, when the delegates could not agree on a particular issue, they simply did not solve the issue. They left a great deal for future generations to work out.

The Delegates Finish Their Work

The examples of arguments and compromises should not suggest that there was continuous bickering at the Constitutional Convention. A majority of delegates agreed on the most basic questions about the organization, powers, and duties of the new government.

During the ten weeks after the Great Compromise, the delegates created the basic parts of our Constitution. They decided upon the powers and duties of Congress and also provided for a President and a Supreme Court. The Constitution would be the supreme law of the country. In the interest of national unity, each state would give up some of its powers. The national government would be able to enforce its laws throughout the nation.

On September 17, 1787, the delegates met for the last time. The finished Constitution was placed on a table to be signed. Benjamin Franklin gave a speech urging the delegates to sign. He said that there were parts of the document that he did not approve, but, on the whole, he liked it.

Forty-two of the delegates were present at the final meeting of the Convention. Thirty-nine followed Franklin's advice and signed the Constitution.

Section Review

Vocabulary:
compromise, exports, imports, preside, unanimous.

Reviewing the Main Ideas
1. What decisions about rules did the delegates make at the start of the Constitutional Convention?
2. Why were these decisions important to the success of the Convention?
3. How did the Virginia Plan differ from the New Jersey Plan?
4. What was the Great Compromise?
5. What do you think was the most important difference between the Articles and the Constitution?

Skill Building
Use a decision tree to chart one decision (the Great Compromise) that the delegates made. Fill in the tree by answering these questions:
1. What was the occasion for decision?
2. What alternatives did the delegates have?
3. What was one likely consequence of each alternative?
4. What goals did the delegates have? Which goal did they share?

Section 3
How the Constitution Was Approved

Important decisions had been made at the Constitutional Convention, but additional decisions were needed. Voting citizens of the thirteen states had to judge the new Constitution. Nine states had to **ratify,** or approve, the Constitution before it could become the law of the land. The delegates' work would mean nothing if the Constitution was not ratified.

Taking Sides
Within days following the Convention, newspapers all over the country printed the Constitution. Many people were shocked. They had not expected a totally new constitution. Others were pleased. Citizens' judgments of the Constitution had begun.

Each state set up a convention to vote "yes" or "no" on the Constitution. Those for and against the Constitution worked hard to influence the state conventions.

The Federalists. Citizens who supported the Constitution were called **Federalists.** They were led by James Madison and Alexander Hamilton, who had been delegates at the Constitutional Convention.

The Federalists talked about the weaknesses of the Articles of Confederation. They warned that the country would face confusion and disorder unless the states united under a strong central government.

They were well organized and worked hard to promote the ratification of the Constitution.

The Anti-Federalists. Citizens against the Constitution were called **Anti-Federalists.** Such men as Patrick Henry, Samuel Adams, and Richard Henry Lee led this group.

The Anti-Federalists were against a strong national government because they feared that citizens would lose their civil rights and liberties. They believed that the new government might not treat all groups of citizens fairly. They were also afraid that the state governments might lose all their powers. Patrick Henry spoke for many of them when he said: "I look upon that paper [Constitution] as the most fatal plan . . . to enslave a free people."

Reaching Agreement
Many citizens agreed with the Anti-Federalists. They thought they might lose their rights under the strong central government set up by the Constitution. At the time, most state constitutions included a list of citizens' rights. People wanted the national Constitution to have the same thing. It was therefore suggested that a **bill of rights** be added to the Constitution. Thomas Jefferson argued in favor of a bill of rights. He said that "a bill of rights is what the people are entitled to against every government."

A bill of rights would list rights the national government could *not* take away from citizens—the rights of free speech and press, of religious

States Approve the Constitution

State	Date of ratification	Vote
Delaware	Dec. 7, 1787	30-0*
Pennsylvania	Dec. 12, 1787	46-23
New Jersey	Dec. 18, 1787	38-0*
Georgia	Jan. 2, 1788	26-0*
Connecticut	Jan. 9, 1788	128-40
Massachusetts	Feb. 6, 1788	187-168
Maryland	Apr. 28, 1788	63-11
South Carolina	May 23, 1788	149-73
New Hampshire	June 21, 1788	57-47
Virginia	June 25, 1788	89-79
New York	July 26, 1788	30-27
North Carolina	Nov. 21, 1789	194-77
Rhode Island	May 29, 1790	34-32

*These votes were unanimous

choice, of assembly and association, and certain other liberties. A bill of rights would also protect certain rights and powers of the state governments. (The Bill of Rights is discussed in detail in Chapter 5.)

The Federalists saw that ratifying the Constitution would not be easy. In at least six states, it seemed that the voters might reject it. To help influence the voting, the Federalists promised to add a bill of rights if the new Constitution was approved.

Some state conventions approved the Constitution quickly. In other states the struggle went on for eight or nine months. The table on this page shows the date each state approved the Constitution and the vote in each state. Notice how close the vote was in New Hampshire, Virginia, New York, and Rhode Island. The last two states ratified the Constitution after the new government was established.

In September, 1788, New York City was chosen as the temporary capital for the government. Members of the new Senate and House of Representatives for each state were elected.

As a member of the first Congress, James Madison proposed twelve **amendments** to the new Constitution. (Changes made in laws are called amendments.) Ten of these amendments became the Bill of Rights in 1791. The Federalists had kept their promise. The new government was well underway.

Section Review

Vocabulary:
amendment, Anti-Federalist, Federalist, ratify.

Reviewing the Main Ideas
1. What did the Federalists do to make sure that the Constitution would be ratified?
2. Why did the Federalists support the Constitution?
3. Why were the Anti-Federalists against the Constitution?

Skill Building
In judging the Constitution, people asked themselves: (a) How would it affect me? (b) How would it affect others? (c) Would it be fair?
1. How might a Federalist have answered each question?
2. How might an Anti-Federalist have answered each question?

(chart) Which state first ratified the Constitution? Which states passed the Constitution by unanimous vote?

Case Study

The Whiskey Rebellion

George Washington was sworn in as the first President of the United States at Federal Hall in New York City on the morning of April 30, 1789. A large crowd was there. Bells rang, and the people shouted: "Long live George Washington, President of the United States."

The President looked calm. But he was worried. Washington had earlier said to a friend that he faced "an ocean of difficulties."

Washington had to make decisions unlike those of any other President who would follow him. Washington did not inherit an operating government. Rather, he had to "create" the office of the presidency. He had to guide others as they put the Constitution into practice.

From the start, the President faced challenges to the government's authority. Many citizens were for the new Constitution only as long as it didn't inconvenience them. They defied the new government whenever it asked them to make sacrifices.

A serious challenge came from farmers west of the Appalachian Mountains. They refused to obey the new Excise Law of 1791, which taxed the sale of whiskey.

Western farmers turned much of their corn and rye into whiskey. For many farmers, whiskey was the only cash crop. Whiskey was easier to transport for sale than grain. A pack horse could carry only four bushels of grain. It could, however, carry twenty-four bushels once the grain was turned into two kegs of whiskey. The tax on whiskey would have cut deeply into the farmers' main source of money.

Farmers in western Pennsylvania were furious over the whiskey tax. For many months most refused to pay it. When tax collectors tried to force the farmers to pay, many of them rebelled. They beat up tax collectors and threatened law officers. One official who had the job of telling a farmer he had to appear in court was robbed, beaten, tarred and feathered, and left tied to a tree.

Federal Hall, the first capitol of the new government, served as the site of Washington's first inauguration on April 30, 1789.

(right) Western Pennsylvanians rebelling against a tax on whiskey in 1794. (far right) Washington putting down the rebellion.

The governor of Pennsylvania, Thomas Mifflin, did nothing to enforce the whiskey tax law. He was popular with the farmers and did not want to do anything that might cause them to turn against him.

In the summer of 1794, the conflict over the whiskey tax came to a head. There were meetings of angry farmers in western Pennsylvania. They signed agreements pledging never to pay the hated tax. There was even talk of separating from the United States. Local leaders urged resistance to the national government. Finally, on July 17, 1794, several hundred men burned the home of General John Nevelle, the tax collector in the area.

President Washington had to decide what to do. What were his alternatives? He could send messages to the rebelling farmers that they would be forgiven if they would stop their violence and pay the tax. He did this, but it did not work. He could ignore the situation, but that would make the government weak as it had been under the Articles.

Washington's goal was clear. He wanted to show that the new government was strong. He knew that a government that passes laws but does not enforce them cannot remain in power. Citizens lose respect for such a government. He had to act forcefully to end the Whiskey Rebellion.

President Washington asked the states for a large body of soldiers. Thirteen thousand men responded —a good show of support for the new government. Washington personally led the army into Pennsylvania.

Washington's show of force quickly ended the Whiskey Rebellion. Most rebel leaders fled to Ohio, and their followers paid the tax. Two leaders were captured and convicted of treason, but President Washington pardoned them. It was possible to show mercy; the authority of the national government had been established.

Review

1. What was the occasion for decision in this case?
2. What were President Washington's alternatives?
3. What was Washington's decision?
4. What were the consequences of his decision?
5. Was it a good decision? Why?

Basic Social Studies Skills
Reading a Table

Important information about government can be presented clearly in a table.

There are four rows that appear at the left side of this table. Each shows information about the powers of four aspects of government.

By reading across the first row of the table, you can compare powers of the legislature in the two plans for government. Likewise, by reading across Row 2, you can compare the powers of the executive branch.

Continue reading across the other rows of this table. Compare the information in each row.

Skill Practice

1. Under which plan does the legislature have greater power?

2. What weaknesses in government under the Articles were corrected by the Constitution?

Two Plans for Government

Powers of Government	Articles of Confederation	Constitution
Powers of the Legislature	Examples of Major Powers: • declare war • make treaties • coin and regulate values of money • establish post offices • borrow money and request funds from the states • regulate affairs with the Indians	Examples of Major Powers: • declare war • regulate trade between the states and with foreign countries • provide post offices and roads • coin and regulate the value of money • borrow money and levy taxes • establish courts of law • raise and support armed forces • regulate affairs with the Indians
Powers of the Executive	• no power to enforce laws was granted	• The President, as Chief Executive, has power to enforce laws. • The President makes treaties and otherwise manages relations with foreign countries. Treaties must be approved by ⅔ of Senate.
Powers of the Judiciary	• no specific grant of judicial powers	• Supreme Court and lower courts make judgments in cases involving the Constitution and laws of the Federal government.
Powers of the States	• states have all powers not granted specifically to Congress • Each state retains its sovereignty, or right to act independently.	• The Constitution, and laws of Congress made according to it, are supreme. • The Tenth Amendment says: all powers not delegated to the Federal government by the Constitution, nor forbidden by it to the states, are reserved to the states. • States give up their sovereignty. State government officials must pledge to support the Constitution of the United States.

Chapter 3 Review

Summary

Section 1: The Background of the Constitutional Convention

The first constitution of the United States was the Articles of Confederation. It provided a weak central government with no power to tax or enforce laws. In 1786, important leaders called for a convention to meet in Philadelphia to correct the flaws of the Articles. Some of the most capable men in the young nation were selected as delegates to the Constitutional Convention.

Section 2: Decision Making at the Constitutional Convention

During the summer of 1787, the Constitution was created in Philadelphia. Compromises were necessary to settle disagreements among the delegates. The Great Compromise between the small and large states saved the Convention. It provided for a Congress of two houses—a Senate and a House of Representatives. After the Compromise, the delegates decided how to organize the government and the kinds of powers and duties the different parts of the government should have. They signed the Constitution on September 17, 1787.

Section 3: How the Constitution Was Approved

Before the Constitution could be put into practice, nine states had to ratify it. Each state organized a convention to consider approval of the Constitution. Supporters of the Constitution were called Federalists. Opponents were known as Anti-Federalists. After promising to add a bill of rights to the Constitution, the Federalists were able to convince the state conventions to ratify the Constitution in 1788.

Vocabulary

Define the following terms.

1. imports
2. confederation
3. convention
4. delegate
5. compromise
6. preside
7. ratify
8. Federalist

Reviewing Main Ideas

1. True or false: Before the Constitutional Convention each state had its own military.
2. True or false: The Constitution was ratified by all the states at the Constitutional Convention.
3. True or false: The first state to ratify the Constitution was Delaware.

Thinking Critically

Finding Information

1. Use the index in this book to find all the pages that refer to the Bill of Rights. What are they?
2. Look at those pages until you find the complete Bill of Rights. On what page does it begin?

Comprehending Information

1. Name one way the Virginia Plan and the New Jersey Plan were the same.
2. Name two ways the Virginia Plan and the New Jersey Plan were not the same.
3. Name two ways the Great Compromise differed from the other two plans.

Organizing Information

Make a time line for 1785-1795. Include at least four events mentioned in this chapter.

Evaluating Information

The news of Shays' Rebellion persuaded many citizens they needed a stronger national government. Why? If people did the same thing today, would you feel your government was too weak? Explain.

Chapter 4

The Constitution— Our Plan for Government

Introduction. Our Constitution is almost two hundred years old. Other nations have had to write new constitutions many times. Germany, for example, has had four in just over one hundred years.

Life in the United States is very different now from when the Constitution was written. Yet it continues to serve us. Why has it stood up so well? Here are the opinions of three Presidents of the United States.

Theodore Roosevelt, our twenty-sixth President, saw the Constitution as a flexible plan for government. He said it is "an instrument designed for the life and healthy growth of the nation."

Woodrow Wilson was our twenty-eighth President. He had taught government and history at Princeton University. Wilson said the Constitution was not overly detailed, and could therefore be adapted to new circumstances. "Our Constitution has proved lasting because of its simplicity," he said.

Harry S. Truman, our thirty-third President, was a careful student of history. He read about the constitutions and governments of other nations. He studied what other Presidents had said about the United States Constitution. Truman said: "The longer I live, the more I am impressed with our American Constitution. Read it and think about it. It's a plan, but not a straitjacket, flexible and short. Read it one hundred times and you'll always find something new."

Every citizen should follow President Truman's advice and read the Constitution. (The Constitution appears on pages 76–99.) It is not necessary to become an expert on the Constitution. That is the job of lawyers, judges, Presidents, and other government leaders. However, all citizens should know the main ideas about government stated in the Constitution.

Viewing the Constitution at the National Archives in Washington, D.C.

Section 1
The Purpose of the Constitution

The Constitution is the plan for government in the United States. It tells how the government is organized. It says what the government can and cannot do.

The Constitution has three parts: (1) the Preamble, which states goals for our government, (2) the seven articles, which describe our plan for government, and (3) the twenty-six amendments, which have been added to the Constitution.

Citizens and Their Constitution

The Constitution is the highest law in the United States. No citizen is above the law, not even the President. Everyone is expected to obey the law.

In the United States, the government is supposed to act according to laws that are in accord with the Constitution. Conflicts between citizens and between citizens and government may be settled according to law. In this way, the Constitution is the foundation of a peaceful, orderly society.

The Constitution tells citizens what they can expect from government. It says what the government may do for citizens. It also lists some of the things that the government may *not* do to them.

Citizens who know the Constitution have an advantage over others. They have some idea of their legal rights. They know how to use the rules to gain services from the government. They know some of the ways they can protect themselves from any abuse of government power. Citizens who do not know what is in the Constitution cannot begin to use the rules to help themselves or others. Citizens who do not know their legal rights may lose benefits they deserve. Thus, it is important for citizens, young and old, to know their Constitution.

The Preamble: A Statement of Goals

The Preamble is the first part of the Constitution. It is a preface, or introduction, to the other parts of the Constitution. The Preamble tells why the Constitution was written. It is not law. Rather, the Preamble states purposes and goals.

The Preamble names six general goals that the writers wanted the United States to reach. These goals reflect the beliefs that the makers of the Constitution had about how government should serve citizens. Read the Preamble on page 76.

The first goal stated in the Preamble is "to form a more perfect union." The writers of the Constitution wanted a better union of the states than they had under the Articles of Confederation. They

believed that a strong central government would unite the state governments as one strong nation.

The second goal is "to establish justice." The founders wanted the United States to have a system of fair laws that would be used to settle conflicts between citizens and their government in a court of law.

The third goal is "to insure **domestic tranquility.**" This means that peace should be maintained in all the states. The government wanted to prevent behavior that could threaten health, safety, or property.

The fourth goal is "to provide for common defense." This means that citizens should be able to protect themselves and their country from enemies. The government wanted to have an adequate military force to defend citizens against attack by outsiders.

The fifth goal is "to promote the **general welfare.**" This means the health, prosperity, and happiness of all citizens. The founders wanted

Civil rights leaders joining in a tribute to Martin Luther King, Jr., the civil rights leader who was assassinated in 1968. Many of the ideals he held so closely are stated in the Preamble to the Constitution.

a government that would help citizens to work productively and enjoy the rewards of their work.

The sixth goal is "to secure the blessings of liberty." This means that citizens now and in the future should be free. The founders wanted a government that would protect the liberties of all citizens.

As shown by these goals, the makers of the Constitution valued the rights of citizens. They wanted the government to protect citizens' liberties. They valued security. They expected the government to preserve law and order. The creators of the Constitution also believed that government should be the *servant* of citizens, not their *master*.

Section Review

Vocabulary:
domestic tranquility, general welfare.

Reviewing the Main Ideas
1. Why should citizens of the United States be familiar with their Constitution?
2. What is the Preamble?
3. What six goals for government are stated in the Preamble?
4. In your opinion, which goal is the most important? Why?

Skill Building
1. Rewrite the Preamble in your own words. Include all the goals that are in the original version.
2. What additional goals, if any, would you include in the Preamble if you were writing it today?

Section 2
Three Branches of Government

The main body of the Constitution follows the Preamble. (See pages 76–91.) It is divided into seven parts called **articles.** Each article contains one or more rules or procedures for organizing the government and carrying out its business.

The Constitution separates the powers and duties of government among three branches. The purpose of this separation is to prevent any person or group from having all the power of government. If one person or group had all the power, the rights of citizens might be taken away. The chart on page 64 shows how the branches check and balance each other.

The three branches are (1) legislative, (2) executive, and (3) judicial. The first three articles of the Constitution explain these three branches of government.

President Ronald Reagan delivering his State of the Union speech to Congress and the Supreme Court.

Article 1: Legislative Branch

One main job of government is to make laws. Article 1 says that Congress is the **legislative** (law-making) **branch** of government. Congress is made up of the Senate and the House of Representatives. Article 1 gives the qualifications for members of the Senate and the House of Representatives and tells how these members are chosen. See the chart on page 63.

Article 1 gives the rules Congress must follow in making laws. One rule is that a majority of the members of both the Senate and the House of Representatives must vote in favor of any bill in order for it to become a law.

Article 1 lists the specific kinds of laws that Congress may make. For example, it says that Congress has the power to pass laws concerning taxes, regulating trade and business, coining money, and declaring war.

Article 1 also describes some of the powers Congress does *not* have.

For instance, Congress cannot pass a law granting **titles of nobility** such as "duke" or "duchess" to any citizen. (You will find out more about Congress in Chapter 6.)

Article 2: Executive Branch

The Articles of Confederation did not include an **executive branch.** It did call for a president, but he was just the person who presided over meetings of Congress. His job was to make sure the meetings ran smoothly. He had no special powers. The writers of the Constitution, however, believed the nation needed an executive branch. It would be the job of this branch to see to the day-to-day work of the government. In Article 2, the writers described the executive branch.

The executive branch is the law-enforcing part of government. The President is the **chief executive.** Thus, the President has the power to carry out laws passed by Congress. The executive branch also includes a Vice-President, who would become the chief executive on the death, incapacity, removal, or resignation of the President.

Article 2 explains how the President is elected and gives the qualifications for the presidency. It also tells how to remove a President from office, and gives rules about the President's salary.

Article 2 describes some of the President's powers and duties. It gives the President the power to command the armed forces, to deal with the leaders of other countries, and to appoint officials to help

(below) These copper sheets will be stamped into blanks that will then be made into pennies. Article 1 gives Congress the power to coin money. (chart) Which of these branches carries out laws passed by Congress?

Three Branches of Government

Legislative Branch makes laws

Executive Branch enforces laws

Judicial Branch settles conflicts by law

Rules about National Legislators (See Article 1 and the Seventeenth Amendment)

	Representatives	Senators
Term	2 years	6 years
Requirements	• at least 25 years old • a citizen at least 7 years • lives in state represented	• at least 30 years old • a citizen at least 9 years • lives in state represented
How many	at least 1 per state; the total number is based on the population in the state	2 per state
How chosen	by district election	by statewide election
Vacancies filled	by special district election	by special statewide election

manage the executive branch. (Article 1 gives the President power to **veto,** or reject, bills passed by Congress. The President vetoes bills that he thinks are unwise. Congress, however, can overturn a veto with a two-thirds vote.)

The President's oath of office is found in Article 2. Before becoming President, a person must take this oath: "I do solemnly swear (or affirm) that I will faithfully execute the office of President of the United States, and will to the best of my ability, preserve, protect, and defend the Constitution of the United States." A President may be removed from office for failing to live up to this oath. For example, a President who breaks the law is not carrying out the oath to "preserve, protect, and defend the Constitution." (You will read more about the executive branch in Chapters 8 and 9.)

Article 3: Judicial Branch

There are two sets of courts in the United States: federal courts and state courts. The Constitution describes the federal court systems in Article 3. (The states already had their own state court systems at the time the Constitution was written.) Federal courts are the **judicial branch** of our national government.

The Constitution makes the United States Supreme Court the head of the judicial branch. It gives Congress the power to create lower courts to help in the work of the judicial branch. The Constitution says that federal judges may keep their jobs until they die, as long as they work according to the law.

Article 3 lists what powers the federal courts have and describes the kinds of cases that will be heard in federal courts. For instance, federal courts hear cases concerning the

(chart) How do the qualifications for senators and representatives differ?

Checks and Balances in the Federal Government

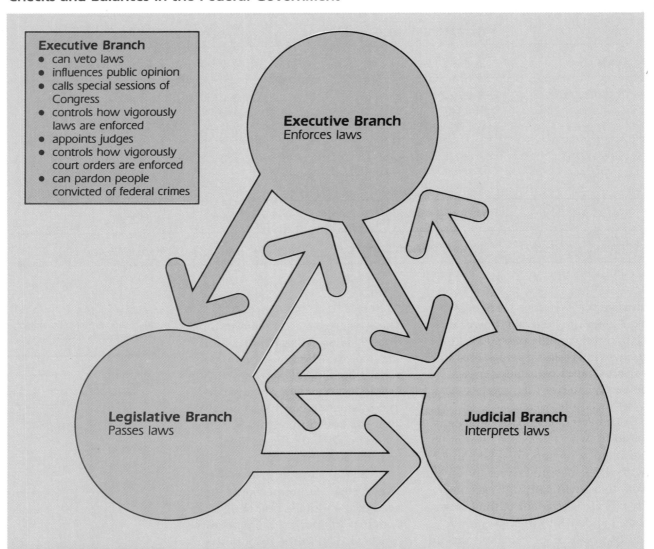

Executive Branch
- can veto laws
- influences public opinion
- calls special sessions of Congress
- controls how vigorously laws are enforced
- appoints judges
- controls how vigorously court orders are enforced
- can pardon people convicted of federal crimes

Executive Branch
Enforces laws

Legislative Branch
Passes laws

Judicial Branch
Interprets laws

Legislative Branch
- House can impeach President and other high officials
- Senate approves presidential appointments
- Senate approves treaties
- Congress can overturn President's vetoes
- Congress controls President's programs through "power of the purse"
- House can impeach judges
- Senate approves appointment of judges
- Congress establishes number of Justices on Supreme Court
- Congress can propose amendments to overturn Supreme Court decisions

Judicial Branch
- once appointed, judges are free from President's control
- can declare President's actions unconstitutional
- decides on the meaning of laws
- can rule that laws are unconstitutional

Constitution. This article also says that people who have been accused of committing crimes against the federal government have the right to a trial by jury.

The most serious crime a person can commit against a government is treason. Governments have often disposed of their critics by declaring that they were guilty of treason. The writers of the Constitution wanted to protect United States citizens from this misuse of government power. In Article 3, they defined treason: carrying on war against the United States or helping enemies of the United States. Article 3 provides only two ways to convict a person of treason. The accused person must confess in open court or at least two witnesses must testify that they saw the person commit the treasonous act. (There is more information about the federal courts in Chapter 10.)

Section Review

Vocabulary:
articles, chief executive, executive branch, judicial branch, legislative branch, title of nobility, veto.

Reviewing the Main Ideas
1. What are the three branches of government described in the Constitution?
2. Which branch makes the laws?
3. Which branch enforces laws?
4. Which branch decides whether laws have been broken?
5. Which branch is headed by the President?

6. Why were powers and duties of government separated into three branches?

Skill Building
1. Read the President's oath of office on page 63. What is the main idea of this oath?
2. Look at Article 1, Section 7, Clause 1, of the Constitution. What does this passage say about how Congress can raise money?
3. The Revolutionary War was fought over the issue of "taxation without representation." Considering this, why would the writers of the Constitution make the House of Representatives, and not the Senate, the place for tax laws to begin?
4. Look at Article 2, Section 3, of the Constitution. What does this passage say about the duties of the President?
5. Look at Article 3, Section 2, Clause 3, of the Constitution. What does this passage say about the trials of people accused of crimes?
6. Read your local newspaper. Find and bring to class articles about the legislative, executive, and judicial branches of the federal government.

Section 3
How State and National Governments Are Linked

How are the state governments linked to one another? How are they connected to the national government? What is the role of the state and national governments in

(chart, opposite) Which branch can veto laws? Which branch can declare a President's actions unconstitutional?

65

The United States flag and the Hawaiian flag. What do the sizes and positions of these flags suggest about the relationship of the federal government and the state governments?

amending the Constitution? Answers to *some* of these questions can be found in Articles 4 through 7. *All* of the questions are yet unanswerable. The relationships between the states and the federal government and among the states have been evolving over the years.

Articles 4 and 6: The States and National Supremacy

Article 4 describes how the state governments are linked to each other and to the national government. It says that only Congress has the power to admit new states to the Union. The national government must make sure that the laws, records, and court decisions of each state are respected in other states.

Article 4 declares that citizens of each state shall enjoy the rights of citizenship in any other state of the union. A citizen of any state may enjoy the rights of citizenship throughout the United States. Also, a citizen accused of a crime cannot escape justice by fleeing to another state. If an accused person does leave, he or she must be returned if the governor of the state where the crime was committed requests it. This process is called **extradition** [ek′strə dish′ən]. In some cases, where crimes have been committed in several states, the courts must decide which state has the right to try the accused person first.

The national government is supposed to protect the states from invasion and keep law and order in the states. Thus, the national government may send armed forces into a state to control riots or other acts that threaten the health, safety, and property of citizens. (Chapters 14 through 16 discuss in detail the

National Guard troops cleaning up after a damaging mud slide in California in 1980.

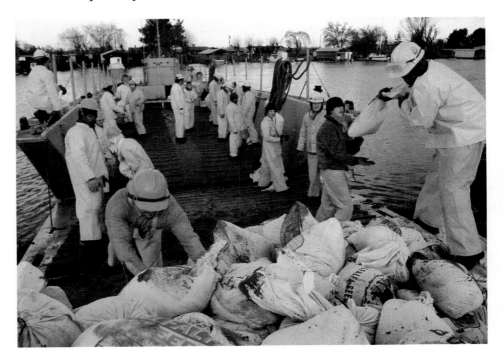

organization and duties of state governments. They also tell about the rights of citizens in the fifty states.)

Article 6 declares that the Constitution, laws passed by Congress, and treaties made by the national government shall be the highest law in the land. This basic constitutional principle is referred to as **national supremacy.** The state governments are supposed to accept that the national government is above them. No state government is supposed to act in any way that goes against the Constitution.

Since the Constitution is the highest law, the national government may *not* make a law which goes against the Constitution. Likewise, no state government is supposed to make a law that goes against either the Constitution or a law or **treaty** made by the national government.

A treaty is an agreement between the governments of two or more countries. Two-thirds of the members of the Senate must approve a treaty before it becomes an official agreement.

A Federal System of Government

The United States has a federal system of government. Power is divided between the national, or federal, government in Washington, D.C., and the fifty state governments.

The main idea of American **federalism** is that there are two levels of government—national and state—each with independent powers to act on people at the same time. Thus, under federalism, the

Construction of this bridge was halted when federal funds were cut off. Decisions made in Washington often call for budget adjustments at the state level.

state of Illinois has formal authority over its residents, but so does the national government in Washington, D.C. Illinois residents must obey the laws of their state government and their national government. They must pay state as well as federal taxes.

Unitary government is the opposite of federalism. In a unitary government, the national government has all the power. Regional, or local, governments may be created to help the national government carry out laws. However, these lower levels of government do not share power with the national government. They are only *parts* of the national government and may be created or abolished by it.

In the American federal system, the national government has certain exclusive powers that are granted to it by the Constitution. For example, Article 1 gives only the national government the power to coin money or make treaties with other nations. None of the fifty state governments may do these things.

The fifty state governments have certain powers that the national government may not exercise. For example, the Tenth Amendment to the Constitution says that the national government has only those powers granted by the Constitution. Other powers of government, which are not denied to the states by the Constitution, may be exercised by the state governments. Because of the Tenth Amendment, state governments have the power to make and enforce laws about fire and police protection, local and state elections, marriages and divorces, schools, and many other matters.

Articles 5 and 7: Ratifying and Amending the Constitution

Article 7 provided a way for the states to agree to the basic outline of the government. It required nine states to ratify the Constitution in order for it to go into effect.

The writers of the Constitution realized that if their work was to last, there needed to be ways to change the Constitution as society changed. They believed that both the national and state governments must take part in amending the Constitution. Article 5 describes how to amend the Constitution.

The most common procedure is for two-thirds of the members of Congress to vote for an amendment. Then three-fourths of the state legislatures have to approve the proposal in order for it to be added to the Constitution. All but one of the amendments have been approved in this way. The Twenty-First Amendment was approved by special conventions in three-fourths of the states rather than by votes in state legislatures.

Since 1789, there have been twenty-six amendments to the Constitution. The first ten amendments, known as the Bill of Rights, were added in 1791. The Bill of Rights is discussed in Chapter 5, along with other amendments having to do

Which method of amending the Constitution has been used only once?

Methods of Amending the Constitution

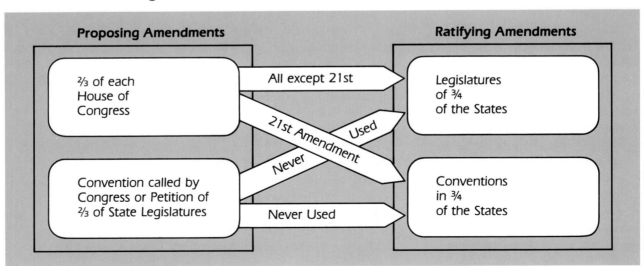

Proposing Amendments

⅔ of each House of Congress

Convention called by Congress or Petition of ⅔ of State Legislatures

All except 21st

21st Amendment

Never

Used

Never Used

Ratifying Amendments

Legislatures of ¾ of the States

Conventions in ¾ of the States

with human rights and liberties.

A number of amendments to the Constitution have been made to improve the way the government works. Three examples are the Sixteenth, Twenty-Second, and Twenty-Fifth amendments.

The Sixteenth Amendment. This amendment was passed in 1913 to allow the government to collect taxes on incomes earned by citizens. Before this, most taxes were on goods offered for sale. That is, they were sales taxes and tariffs. The income tax increased the money available to the government.

The Twenty-Second Amendment. This amendment was passed in 1951 to keep a President from serving more than two four-year terms of office. It was passed after President Franklin D. Roosevelt was elected four times. Many people feared that a President might gain too much power if allowed to hold office for too long. To avoid this risk, the Constitution was amended.

The Twenty-Fifth Amendment. This amendment became law in 1967. It clearly spells out how vacancies are to be filled in the office of Vice-President. The President nominates a Vice-President to fill a vacancy in that office. The President's choice must be approved by a majority vote of both houses of Congress. The Twenty-Fifth Amendment also tells how the Vice-President can take over the duties of the President if he or she is too ill to carry on. When the President recovers, he or she can take over again. If recovery does not seem likely, the Vice-President can be approved as the new President by a two-thirds vote of the Congress.

The Twenty-Fifth Amendment allows a President to resign from office. Whenever the office of President becomes vacant, the Vice-President either becomes Acting President or is sworn in as President.

The amendments to the Constitution have improved our plan for government. Chapter 5 includes a discussion of amendments that were made to protect citizens' rights and a discussion of responsibilities of citizens to preserve and protect the Constitution.

Vice-President Lyndon B. Johnson being sworn in as President after the assassination of President John F. Kennedy on November 22, 1963. The 25th Amendment outlines the procedure for the transfer of power when such a crisis occurs.

Section Review

Vocabulary:
extradition, federalism, national supremacy, treaty, unitary government.

Reviewing the Main Ideas
1. Why was the Sixteenth Amendment written?
2. Why was the Twenty-Second Amendment written?
3. Why was the Twenty-Fifth Amendment written?

Skill Building
1. In which article of the Constitution would you look to find out what rights citizens of one state have in the other states? What does this article say about the rights of citizens?
2. What is the main idea of Article 6?

Case Study

The Watergate Affair

During the summer of 1974, the government of the United States faced a crisis. President Richard Nixon was accused of misusing the powers of his office. Some government officials backed the President. Other officials wanted to remove Nixon from office.

The conflicts about President Nixon stemmed from the "Watergate Affair." On June 17, 1972, Washington city police arrested five men on charges of burglary. These men had broken into the national headquarters of the Democratic party located in an office building called Watergate. It seemed that the men were trying to get information that could help Nixon and other Republican candidates beat the Democrats in the 1972 presidential election.

Two reporters for the *Washington Post*, Carl Bernstein and Bob Woodward, turned the "Watergate Affair" into big news. They gathered information and wrote newspaper stories about the break-in. They found evidence that seemed to link the burglars to top government officials, including the President.

From the beginning, the President and his advisors denied any connection with the Watergate burglars. Yet as time passed, more and more evidence linked the President to the Watergate Affair. In addition, Bernstein, Woodward, and others learned of more illegal acts that involved the White House staff. Unlawful gifts of money were made to the Committee to Reelect the President. Illegal wiretaps were found on the phones of Nixon's opponents. Government officials were spying on American citizens that the White

The Senate Watergate Committee listening to testimony that linked President Nixon with illegal activities.

AUTH

During Watergate testimony, a White House aide revealed that President Nixon had had tape recorders installed in the White House. What does this cartoon suggest about the public's reaction to this practice?

House staff labeled "enemies." There was a long "Enemies List" that included many respected citizens—religious leaders, newspaper reporters, entertainers, and educators. The Internal Revenue Service had been told to harass people about their income tax because they had not cooperated with the White House.

The President and his advisors tried to cover up their involvement in illegal actions. They continued to deny any wrongdoing.

The United States Senate formed a special committee to investigate the case. The Senate committee found the same evidence. Top White House officials were apparently guilty of breaking federal laws. Even the President seemed to be involved.

Senator Sam Ervin, Chairman of the Senate Watergate Committee,

wrote in his official report: "Watergate was a conglomerate of various illegal and unethical activities in which various officers and employees of the Nixon Reelection Committee and various White House aides of President Nixon participated in varying ways and degrees. . . ." Ervin's report concluded that several high-ranking officials of the executive branch had misused their constitutional powers.

In early August, 1974, the Judiciary Committee of the House of Representatives faced a difficult decision. Should they vote to recommend impeaching the President?

Article 1 gives the House of Representatives power to impeach a President. This means that the House publicly considers evidence that the President has committed crimes or has otherwise misused

A security officer demonstrating some of the electronic equipment used to wiretap the Democratic national committee headquarters.

Vice-President and Mrs. Ford, and Mrs. Nixon and President Nixon shortly before Ford was sworn in as the new President.

his power. The House then decides, by majority vote, whether the accused person should stand trial in the Senate.

The Judiciary Committee realized that there was evidence that seemed to indicate President Nixon's involvement in questionable activities. Many members felt that, at least, he was guilty of foolish and unethical behavior unbecoming to a President. At most, he may have given approval for others to take part in illegal activities.

Some members of the Judiciary Committee decided that they would not vote to recommend impeachment. They believed it could cause the public to lose faith in the government. They also felt it might

weaken the government so that it could not deal with pressing problems. Finally, they believed that President Nixon had not done anything bad enough to risk impeachment. The consequences of leaving the President alone would be better for the country than the consequences of impeaching him.

The majority of the committee voted to recommend "the impeachment and trial and removal from office" of the President. The majority believed that President Nixon possibly took part in activities that no President should. Thus, he should be impeached and tried publicly for acts of wrongdoing. A consequence of not impeaching him, they believed, might be to cause the public to lose faith in the government. Citizens might believe that government leaders could get away with illegal behavior. They felt it would be bad for the nation if citizens believed any government official, even the President, is above the law.

It seemed likely that the full House of Representatives would follow the recommendation of the Judiciary Committee and vote to impeach President Nixon. If this happened, the next step would be a trial in the Senate. According to the Constitution, the Senate decides whether or not to remove a President from office. It takes a two-thirds majority vote to remove a President.

However, before the full House of Representatives voted on impeachment, President Nixon decided to resign because evidence had been uncovered that clearly showed that he had broken the law by trying to conceal a crime. He spoke on television to the nation on August 8, 1974: "I have concluded that because of the Watergate matter I might not have the support of Congress that I would consider necessary to back the very difficult decisions and carry out the duties of this office in the way the interests of the nation will require. . . . Therefore, I shall resign the presidency effective at noon tomorrow."

Thus, Vice-President Gerald Ford became President. A short time after taking office, President Ford named Nelson Rockefeller to be the new Vice-President. The Senate and the House of Representatives decided, by majority vote, to approve this appointment. These actions followed the rules written in Section 2 of the Twenty-Fifth Amendment: "Whenever there is a vacancy in the office of Vice-President, the President shall nominate a Vice-President who shall take office upon confirmation by a majority vote of both houses of Congress."

President Nixon's dramatic departure from office showed how well the Constitution works. The President had been forced from office according to the rules of the Constitution. Vice-President Gerald Ford replaced President Nixon according to constitutional law.

No riots or other serious disorders marked this change of government power. No soldiers or police were used to put a new leader in the country's highest office. A peaceful, orderly transfer of leadership took place. After taking office, President Ford remarked: "Our Constitution works; our great Republic is a government of laws and not of men. . . ."

Review

1. What were the alternatives facing the House Judiciary Committee in this case?
2. How did the majority of the Committee view the likely consequences of the alternatives?
3. Why did President Nixon decide to resign?
4. Explain what President Ford meant when he said that "our Constitution works."

73

Basic Social Studies Skills
Classifying Information

Classify means to organize, or arrange, things into different categories or groups. High-school students, for example, are classified by their status in school—freshmen, sophomores, juniors, and seniors. Members of a basketball team are grouped, or classified, by position on the squad—guards, forwards, and centers. Officials of the national government are also classified. They are members of one of three major branches—executive, legislative, or judicial.

Classifying involves three basic steps: (1) Identifying the common traits of items in a group, (2) putting similar items into groups, and (3) labeling each group or category.

Clear definitions of terms are essential when classifying. The definition of the executive branch, for example, is the part of government that enforces laws. According to this definition, agents of the Federal Bureau of Investigation (FBI), who are responsible for law enforcement, belong to the executive branch. The legislative branch is the part of government that makes laws. According to that definition, then, senators are classified as legislative officials. Federal judges are classified as members of the judicial branch. Judges perform duties that fit our definition of the judicial branch— the part of government that interprets laws.

Although classifying is not a difficult skill to master, it is nonetheless an essential one that has applications not only in the classroom but outside as well. Throughout this text you will have many opportunities to practice and sharpen your ability to classify items.

Skill Practice

Classify the items in the list below. Decide whether each item is a main power or duty of the executive branch, the legislative branch, or the judicial branch. The United States Constitution, which defines the powers and duties of these three branches, may be referred to if you need help. The Constitution starts on page 76.

Which Branch?

1. approves treaties
2. vetoes laws
3. creates lower courts in the federal judicial system
4. declares acts of government officials to be unconstitutional
5. appoints judges of the Supreme Court
6. pardons people convicted of federal crimes
7. overturns vetoes
8. settles disputes between two or more states
9. makes treaties
10. heads the nation's armed forces
11. borrows money
12. declares war
13. establishes post offices
14. prevents illegal entry of products into the country

Chapter 4 Review

Summary

Section 1: The Purpose of the Constitution

The Constitution is a plan for government by the people. The Preamble is a statement of purpose. It says that the makers of the Constitution wanted the government to provide law and order and, at the same time, to protect the rights and liberties of citizens.

Section 2: Three Branches of Government

The Constitution divides the powers and duties of government among three branches of government. The legislative branch makes laws, the executive branch enforces laws, and the judicial branch settles conflicts in courts of law. The Constitution provides means for each branch of government to check the powers of the other two branches. Thus, no person or branch of government is able to have too much power. This is known as a system of checks and balances.

Section 3: How State and National Governments Are Linked

The Constitution and laws made under it are supreme in the United States. The national government has the duty of protecting the states from invasion and of helping state governments maintain law and order. Under the federal system established by the Constitution, certain powers are given to the national government. Other powers are given to the state governments. Finally, some powers are shared by the national and state governments.

Vocabulary

Define the following terms.
1. federalism
2. domestic tranquility
3. treaty
4. executive branch
5. legislative branch
6. judicial branch

Reviewing Main Ideas

1. Which of the following can Congress make laws about?
a. taxes
b. regulating trade and business
c. coining money
d. all of the above
2. True or false: Congress is made up of the Senate and House of Representatives.
3. True or false: The main purpose of the Constitution is to help people live according to law.
4. True or false: The main part of the Constitution is divided into ten articles.
5. True or false: The first three articles explain the three branches of government.

Thinking Critically

Finding Information

The Preamble to the Constitution states six purposes for the Constitution. Find them and name them.

Communicating Ideas

Write a paragraph explaining why we have a Constitution. Use at least five of the words from the Vocabulary. Underline each vocabulary word that you use.

Comprehending Information

Rewrite the six purposes of the Constitution in your own words.

Organizing Information

1. Name the three branches of government.
2. List three purposes of each of the branches of government.

The Constitution of the United States

The Constitution is printed in black. The parts that are no longer in force have been crossed out. The spelling and punctuation have been modernized. An explanation of the Constitution is printed in color. The explanation and the headings are not a part of the Constitution.

The annotations to the Constitution were written by David P. Currie, Professor of Law, University of Chicago.

Preamble

We the people of the United States, in order to form a more perfect Union, establish justice, insure domestic tranquillity, provide for the common defense, promote the general welfare, and secure the blessings of liberty to ourselves and our posterity, do ordain and establish this Constitution for the United States of America.

The writers of the Constitution had six goals: (1) to set up a stronger central government than they had under the Articles of Confederation; (2) to improve the court system; (3) to have peace in all states; (4) to protect the country from enemies; (5) to have good living conditions; (6) to have freedom for themselves and for future Americans. Most important, the Preamble says that "We the people" are the authority for the Constitution.

Article 1/Legislative Branch
Section 1/Congress

All legislative powers herein granted shall be vested in a Congress of the United States, which shall consist of a Senate and House of Representatives.

Legislative power is the power to make laws. All of the federal government's power to make laws is given to the branch of government called Congress. Congress is divided into two parts, called houses. One house is the Senate; the other, the House of Representatives. The Senate is known as the upper house and the House of Representatives is known as the lower house.

Section 2/House of Representatives

Clause 1 The House of Representatives shall be composed of members chosen every second year by the people of the several states, and the electors in each state shall have the qualifications requisite for electors of the most numerous branch of the state legislature.

Representatives are chosen every two years by the voters of each state. People who are allowed to vote for representatives in the state legislature can also vote for members of the House of Representatives.

This clause gave each state the power to decide who could vote for members of Congress. All states once used this power to limit voting rights to white men who paid taxes or owned property. Several amendments have changed this practice by allowing first black men, then women, and then finally eighteen-year-olds, the right to vote.

Clause 2 No person shall be a representative who shall not have attained to the age of twenty-five years, and been seven years a citizen of the United States, and who shall not, when elected, be an inhabitant of that state in which he shall be chosen.

A representative must be at least twenty-five years old, must have been a United States citizen for at least seven years, and must live in the state from which he or she is chosen.

Clause 3 Representatives and direct taxes shall be apportioned among the several states which may be included within this Union, according to their respective numbers, ~~which shall be determined by adding to the whole number of free persons, including those bound to service for a term of years, and excluding Indians not taxed, three-fifths of all other persons~~.

The actual enumeration shall be made within three years after the first meeting of the Congress of the United States, and within every subsequent term of ten years, in such manner as they shall by law direct.

The number of representatives shall not exceed one for every thirty thousand, but each state shall have at least one representative; ~~and until such enumeration shall be made, the state of New Hampshire shall be entitled to choose three, Massachusetts eight, Rhode Island and Providence Plantations one, Connecticut five, New York six, New Jersey four, Pennsylvania eight, Delaware one, Maryland six, Virginia ten, North Carolina five, South Carolina five, and Georgia three.~~

The number of representatives a state has is based on the number of people in the state. So are some taxes called "direct" taxes.

When there were slaves, only three-fifths of them

were counted. This was changed by the Thirteenth Amendment.

Only "direct" taxes have to be based on population, and not all taxes are "direct." The Supreme Court said that income taxes and taxes on land were direct, but income taxes no longer have to be based on population because of the Sixteenth Amendment.

A **census,** or a count of the people, must be taken every ten years. Congress decides how the count will be made. It uses the census results to decide how many representatives each state shall have.

As the nation grew, the number of representatives also grew. Since 1910, Congress has limited the number of representatives to 435. This was done to keep Congress from getting too large. Too many members would keep Congress from getting its work done. By 1980, each member of the House represented about 521,000 persons.

Clause 4   When vacancies happen in the representation from any state, the executive authority thereof shall issue writs of election to fill such vacancies.

If a representative dies or leaves office, the governor—the executive authority—of the state calls an election to fill the vacancy.

Clause 5   The House of Representatives shall choose their speaker and other officers; and shall have the sole power of impeachment.

The House of Representatives selects its presiding officer and other officers every two years. The **speaker of the House** is usually a member of the political party that has the largest number of members—the **majority party.** You will find no mention of political parties in the Constitution. At the time it was written, political parties did not exist.

Only the House of Representatives has the power to **impeach,** or accuse, an official of the executive or judicial branches of some wrongdoing or misuse of power. The House of Representatives does not decide whether the official is guilty or not. If the House votes to accuse the official, the case goes to the Senate for trial.

Section 3/Senate

Clause 1   The Senate of the United States shall be composed of two senators from each state, chosen ~~by the legislature thereof,~~ for six years; and each senator shall have one vote.

The Senate is made up of two senators from each state. Each senator is elected for a six-year term and has one vote in the Senate.

Until 1913, senators were chosen by state legislators. The Seventeenth Amendment changed this. Now the people from each state directly elect their senators.

Clause 2   ~~Immediately after they shall be assembled in consequence of the first election, they shall be divided as equally as may be into three classes. The seats of the senators of the first class shall be vacated at the expiration of the second year, of the second class at the expiration of the fourth year, and of the third class at the expiration of the sixth year, so that one-third may be chosen every second year; and if vacancies happen by resignation, or otherwise, during the recess of the legislature of any state, the executive thereof may make temporary appointments until the next meeting of the legislature, which shall then fill such vacancies.~~

The senators in the first Congress were divided into three equal groups. One group held office for only two years. The second group held office for four years. The third group held office for six years. After each group finished its first term, the length of term for all senators became six years.

Today the terms of senators are arranged so that no more than one-third of the Senate is up for election at any one time. This allows the Senate to change in a gradual way, unlike the House of Representatives.

The Seventeenth Amendment changed the rules about replacing senators who resigned or died.

Clause 3   No person shall be a senator who shall not have attained to the age of thirty years, and been nine years a citizen of the United States, and who shall not, when elected, be an inhabitant of that state for which he shall be chosen.

A senator must be at least thirty years old and a United States citizen for at least nine years. At the time of the election, a senator must live in the state he or she represents.

Clause 4   The Vice-President of the United States shall be president of the Senate, but shall have no vote, unless they be equally divided.

The Vice-President **presides,** or is in charge, at Senate meetings. He or she can vote at these meetings only if there is a tie.

Clause 5   The Senate shall choose their other officers, and also a president pro tempore, in the absence of the Vice-President, or when he shall exercise the office of President of the United States.

The Senate chooses its other officers, including a presiding officer called the **president pro tempore.** This person presides at Senate meetings when the Vice-President is absent or when the Vice-President is serving as President.

Clause 6 The Senate shall have the sole power to try all impeachments. When sitting for that purpose, they shall be on oath or affirmation. When the President of the United States is tried, the Chief Justice shall preside; and no person shall be convicted without the concurrence of two-thirds of the members present.

Only the Senate has the power to try officials who are impeached by the House of Representatives. This means that the Senate sits as a jury. The senators must take an oath to try the case fairly. If the President is on trial, the **Chief Justice** of the United States presides over the trial. In other cases, the Vice-President presides. The senators vote on whether the accused is guilty or not guilty. To convict an official, two-thirds of the senators must vote guilty.

Impeachment gives Congress a check on the power of both the President and the judicial branch. However, it is a check that is not used very often. The House has impeached only twelve people. One was a President, Andrew Johnson. He was found not guilty by the Senate by one vote. Eleven judges have been impeached by the House. Only four were found guilty by the Senate.

Clause 7 Judgment in cases of impeachment shall not extend further than to removal from office and disqualification to hold and enjoy any office of honor, trust, or profit under the United States; but the party convicted shall nevertheless be liable and subject to indictment, trial, judgment, and punishment, according to law.

The Senate's power to punish a convicted official is limited. All it can do is remove the official from office and keep him or her from ever holding another office in the United States government. However, the official may also be punished by the regular courts.

Section 4/Congressional Elections and Meetings

Clause 1 The times, places, and manner of holding elections for senators and representatives shall be prescribed in each state by the legislature thereof; but the Congress may at any time by law make or alter such regulations, ~~except as to the places of choosing senators.~~

Each state may decide when, where, and how elections for its senators and representatives are held, unless Congress disagrees. As a result of the Seventeenth Amendment, senators are now elected at the same voting places as other officials.

Congress has set the first Monday in November of even-numbered years as the date for the election of representatives and senators. They must be elected by secret ballot.

Clause 2 The Congress shall assemble at least once in every year, ~~and such meeting shall be on the first Monday in December, unless they shall by law appoint a different day.~~

Congress must meet at least once a year. The Twentieth Amendment set January 3 as the regular meeting day for Congress.

Section 5/Congressional Rules

Clause 1 Each house shall be the judge of the elections, returns, and qualifications of its own members, and a majority of each shall constitute a quorum to do business; but a smaller number may adjourn from day to day, and may be authorized to compel the attendance of absent members, in such manner, and under such penalties as each house may provide.

The House of Representatives decides if its members are entitled to be in the House. The Senate decides if senators are entitled to be in the Senate. This clause gives each house the power to decide if the people elected to that house meet the age, residence, and citizenship requirements set out in Article 1, Sections 2 and 3.

Neither the House nor the Senate can hold meetings for business unless it has a **quorum.** That is, more than half the members must be present to conduct its business.

Many times the House and the Senate do conduct their business without a quorum. However, any member of the house can force others to attend a session by asking for a quorum call. In this case, business cannot be conducted if a quorum is not present. Each house also has the power to make members pay a penalty for not attending meetings.

Clause 2 Each house may determine the rules of its proceedings, punish its members for disorderly behavior, and, with the concurrence of two-thirds, expel a member.

The House and the Senate may each make rules for conducting business. They may punish their members for not following these rules. In either the House or the Senate, two-thirds of the members must agree if they wish to expel a member.

Clause 3   Each house shall keep a journal of its proceedings, and from time to time publish the same, excepting such parts as may in their judgment require secrecy; and the yeas and nays of the members of either house on any question shall, at the desire of one-fifth of those present, be entered on the journal.

The House of Representatives and the Senate must keep a **journal,** or daily record, of what is done at their meetings. When the members decide to keep some matters secret, these things are not printed in the record. If one-fifth of the members present favor it, the record must show how each member voted on any question. Much of what is said is printed in the *Congressional Record.*

Clause 4   Neither house, during the session of Congress, shall, without the consent of the other, adjourn for more than three days, nor to any other place than that in which the two houses shall be sitting.

While Congress is in session, neither the House nor the Senate can adjourn, or stop meeting, for more than three days unless both houses agree. Both houses must also meet in the same city.

Section 6/Congressional Privileges and Restrictions

Clause 1   The senators and representatives shall receive a compensation for their services, to be ascertained by law, and paid out of the treasury of the United States.

They shall in all cases, except treason, felony, and breach of the peace, be privileged from arrest during their attendance at the session of their respective houses, and in going to and returning from the same; and for any speech or debate in either house, they shall not be questioned in any other place.

Senators and representatives are paid out of the treasury of the United States according to the law that sets their salaries.

Members of Congress attending meetings of Congress, or going to and from meetings, cannot be arrested except for treason, serious crime, or breaking the peace. They cannot be punished for anything they say in their meetings, even if it is criminal, except by the house to which they belong. This allows members of Congress to say what they believe is best for the country without fear.

Clause 2   No senator or representative shall, during the time for which he was elected, be appointed to any civil office under the authority of the United States which shall have been created, or the emoluments whereof shall have been increased during such time; and no person holding any office under the United States shall be a member of either house during his continuance in office.

Senators and representatives cannot hold other United States government offices while they are members of Congress. During the term for which they have been elected, they cannot resign and take a government position that has been created during that term. They also cannot take any position for which the salary has been increased during that term.

The last part of this clause helps to keep the legislative and executive powers separate. The other provisions were included so that no member of Congress would be able to profit personally from laws he or she helped pass. **Emoluments** is another word for salary.

Section 7/How Bills Become Laws

Clause 1   All bills for raising revenue shall originate in the House of Representatives; but the Senate may propose or concur with amendments as on other bills.

All **bills** for raising money must begin in the House of Representatives. A bill is a proposal for a law that has not yet been adopted. The Senate may amend these money bills.

The House of Representatives originally was the only body in the government that was directly elected by the people. The framers of the Constitution remembered how Parliament had passed laws to tax the colonies without representation. By allowing only the House of Representatives, which was elected by the people, to initiate money bills, the delegates hoped Americans would never have to charge that there was unfair taxation without representation.

Clause 2   Every bill which shall have passed the House of Representatives and the Senate, shall, before it becomes a law, be presented to the President of the United States. If he approves, he shall sign it, but if not he shall return it, with his objections, to that house in which it shall have originated, who shall enter the objections at large on their journal, and proceed to reconsider it. If after such reconsideration two-thirds of that house shall agree to pass the bill, it shall be sent, together with the objections, to the other house, by which it shall likewise be reconsidered, and if approved by two-thirds of that house, it shall become a law. But in all such cases the votes of both houses shall be determined by yeas and nays, and the names of the persons voting for and against the bill shall be entered on the journal of each house respectively.

If any bill shall not be returned by the President within ten days (Sundays excepted) after it shall have been presented to him, the same shall be a law, in like manner as if he had signed it, unless the Congress by their adjournment prevents its return, in which case it shall not be a law.

For a bill to become a law, it must first pass both houses of Congress. Then, if the President signs the bill, it becomes law. If the President does not agree with the **provisions,** or parts of a bill, he or she can refuse to approve it. In that case the bill does not become a law unless it is passed again. This time two-thirds of the members of each house must vote for it. The bill then becomes a law without the President's approval.

This clause is an example of checks and balances at work. Congress must pass a bill before the President can sign or **veto** it. A veto is a refusal to approve a law. The President's veto is a check on the power of Congress. However, Congress has a power which serves to balance the President's veto. Congress has the power to **override,** or overturn, the veto by repassing the bill by a two-thirds vote.

The President may not approve one part of a bill and veto other parts of the same bill. He or she must approve or disapprove the entire bill.

After receiving a bill, the President has ten days (not counting Sundays) to consider it. If the President keeps it longer, the bill becomes a law without his or her approval. If Congress has adjourned, the unsigned bill does not become a law.

The President does not have to consider every bill. Bills can become law by not being signed or vetoed ten days after they were passed by Congress. However, any bill that is passed by Congress in the last ten days that Congress is in session must be signed by the President to become law. If the bill is not signed within these ten days, it has, in effect, been vetoed. This is called a **pocket veto.** The President puts it in his or her pocket and forgets about it, so to speak.

Clause 3 Every order, resolution, or vote to which the concurrence of the Senate and House of Representatives may be necessary (except on a question of adjournment) shall be presented to the President of the United States; and before the same shall take effect, shall be approved by him, or being disapproved by him, shall be repassed by two-thirds of the Senate and House of Representatives, according to the rules and limitations prescribed in the case of a bill.

The President's approval is needed for other matters in addition to laws. Any order, resolution, or vote that must be approved by both houses of Congress must also be approved by the President or passed over his or her veto by a two-thirds vote of both houses. However, Congress does not need the President's approval to end its meetings for the year.

Section 8/Powers of Congress
Clause 1 The Congress shall have power to lay and collect taxes, duties, imposts, and excises, to pay the debts and provide for the common defense and general welfare of the United States; but all duties, imposts, and excises shall be uniform throughout the United States;

Congress has the power to raise money by taxing. This money can be used (1) to pay the debts of the central government, (2) to defend the country, and (3) to provide services for the good of all people. Most kinds of federal taxes must be the same in all parts of the country.

There are many kinds of taxes. An **impost** is a tax on imports, that is, goods brought into the country. Imposts and some other taxes are called **duties.** An **excise tax** is a tax on the manufacture, sale, or use of goods. Only duties, imposts, and excises are required to be the same throughout the country.

Clause 2 To borrow money on the credit of the United States;

Congress has the power to borrow money for the government to use. The Constitution sets no limit on the amount of money the government may borrow. In times of great emergency, such as wars, the government has borrowed large sums of money. During World War II, the amount owed by the government—the **national debt**—skyrocketed. Since that war, the government has gone further and further into debt. In 1985, the national debt was more than $1.6 trillion.

Clause 3 To regulate commerce with foreign

nations, and among the several states, and with the Indian tribes;

Congress can pass laws to control commerce, or trade, with other countries, among the states, and with Indian nations.

This is one of Congress' most important powers. Under the Articles of Confederation, the states controlled commerce and the nation's economy suffered. Now Congress controls trade. It can regulate nearly everything that moves from one state to another or from our country to another country.

When you go to the movies, you will probably see a movie that was made in another state. When you eat in a restaurant, you will probably eat food that was grown or raised in another state. Congress has the power to regulate the movement of all these things from one state to another.

Congress can regulate other activities if they have a substantial effect on interstate or foreign commerce. For example, Congress has regulated the price of railroad tickets, the safety of airplanes, and the business of radio and television broadcasting. It has also required that restaurants and hotels serve people of every race. Congress has also required many employers to bargain with labor unions chosen by their workers.

Clause 4 To establish a uniform rule of naturalization, and uniform laws on the subject of bankruptcies throughout the United States;

Congress can pass laws that say how people born in other countries can be **naturalized,** or become United States citizens. At present, laws passed by Congress require that a person from another country must live in the United States for five years, pass a test about the Constitution, and meet several other requirements in order to become a citizen.

Congress also has the power to pass bankruptcy laws, but they must be the same throughout the United States. **Bankruptcy** is the legal term for not being able to pay debts. Bankruptcy laws set up rules for paying debts when a person does not have the money to pay them all. The Court will divide most of the debtor's property among those to whom he or she owes money. The Court may then cancel the rest of the debts so that the debtor can make a new start in life.

Clause 5 To coin money, regulate the value thereof, and of foreign coin, and fix the standard of weights and measures;

Congress has the power to coin money and to say how much it is worth. It also has the power to say how much foreign money is worth in American money. Congress has the power to define weights and measures so that they will be the same throughout the country.

Clause 6 To provide for the punishment of counterfeiting the securities and current coin of the United States;

Congress has the power to punish persons who make fake bonds, stamps, or money.

Clause 7 To establish post offices and post roads;

Congress can provide for a postal service and the roads to be used in delivering the mail.

Clause 8 To promote the progress of science and useful arts, by securing for limited times to authors and inventors the exclusive rights to their respective writings and discoveries;

Congress can encourage science, industry, and the arts by passing patent and copyright laws. Such laws prevent others from profiting from the work of inventors and artists for a certain period of time.

A **patent** is issued to a person who makes scientific or industrial discoveries. Most of the inventions you use every day are patented. A television set or car, for example, may have hundreds of patents—one for each important part.

A **copyright** is granted to a person who writes books, composes music, or creates artwork of some kind. The book you are reading, for example, is copyrighted. That means that no one may copy its pages without the permission of the copyright holder, Scott, Foresman and Company.

If you wish to make a copy of a book or use part of an invention, you must pay a fee to the copyright or patent holder for each copy you make.

Copyrights and patents do not last forever. After a number of years, anyone may copy a book or an invention without paying a fee.

Clause 9 To constitute tribunals inferior to the Supreme Court;

Congress has the power to set up courts that are lower in authority than the Supreme Court. It is Congress that determines how many federal courts we will have and what kind of cases these courts will hear.

Clause 10 To define and punish piracies and

felonies committed on the high seas, and offenses against the law of nations;

Congress has the power to make laws about crimes committed on international waters. Congress also has the power to make laws to punish those who break treaties or those who do not follow international customs, which we call international law.

Clause 11 To declare war, grant letters of marque and reprisal, and make rules concerning captures on land and water;

Congress has the power to declare war. Congress can also make rules about seizing enemy property on land or sea.

In 1856 Congress gave up the practice of granting letters of "marque and reprisal." That is, letters which gave people the right to capture and destroy ships and goods of enemy nations without being guilty of piracy. Congress now follows the rule of international law.

Clause 12 To raise and support armies, but no appropriation of money to that use shall be for a longer term than two years;

Clause 13 To provide and maintain a navy;

Clause 14 To make rules for the government and regulation of the land and naval forces;

Congress has the power to raise an army and a navy and to give them supplies. But Congress may not **appropriate,** or provide, money for the army for more than two years at a time. No limit was put on the appropriations for the navy.

Congress also has the power to make rules for the organization and conduct of the armed services.

Clause 15 To provide for calling forth the militia to execute the laws of the Union, suppress insurrections and repel invasions;

The volunteer armed forces of the different states used to be called the **militia.** Since the National Defense Act of 1916, the "militia" has been called the National Guard. This clause gives Congress the power to see that the Guard is called out (1) to enforce the national laws, (2) to put down rebellion, and (3) to drive out invading enemies.

Clause 16 To provide for organizing, arming, and disciplining the militia, and for governing such part of them as may be employed in the service of the United States, reserving to the states respectively the appointment of the officers and the authority of training the militia according to the discipline prescribed by Congress;

Congress can decide how the National Guard is to be set up and trained. It can also make rules for the conduct of these soldiers when they are called out by the central government. However, the states have the right to select the officers of the Guard and to see that the Guard is trained according to the rules made by Congress.

Clause 17 To exercise exclusive legislation in all cases whatsoever, over such district (not exceeding ten miles square) as may, by cession of particular states, and the acceptance of Congress, become the seat of the government of the United States, and to exercise like authority over all places purchased by the consent of the legislature of the state in which the same shall be, for the erection of forts, magazines, arsenals, dockyards, and other needful buildings;

Congress was given the power to establish a national capital on land given up by the states and to make laws for the national capital. Congress also governs all places bought from the states for use as forts, arsenals, navy yards, and public buildings.

The District of Columbia was set up as the site of the capital. Both Maryland and Virginia **ceded,** or gave up, land to form the district, but Virginia received its part back because the government didn't need it. The city of Washington was built in the District of Columbia. In 1974 Congress gave the District a charter that allowed a mayor and a thirteen-member city council to be elected. Still, Congress can overrule city council actions.

Clause 18 And to make all laws which shall be necessary and proper for carrying into execution the foregoing powers, and all other powers vested by this Constitution in the government of the United States, or in any department or officer thereof.

Congress has the power to make all laws needed to carry out the powers granted in clauses 1 through 17. Congress also has the power to make all laws needed to carry out powers that other parts of the Constitution give to Congress or other federal officials.

Clause 18 is sometimes called the **elastic clause** because it stretches Congress' powers. It does not give Congress power to do whatever it wants. However, this clause has been interpreted generously, so that the federal government has a good deal more power than you might think from reading the first seventeen sections.

This clause has allowed the government to adapt to needs of the times. For example, Congress used this power to create a national bank. Congress also used this power to create a new branch of the armed forces—the Air Force.

Section 9/Powers Forbidden to Congress

Clause 1 ~~The migration or importation of such persons as any of the states now existing shall think proper to admit, shall not be prohibited by the Congress prior to the year one thousand eight hundred and eight, but a tax or duty may be imposed on such importation, not exceeding ten dollars for each person.~~

Congress could make no law before 1808 to forbid the international sale of slaves. It could place a tax as high as $10 on each slave brought into the country.

This clause was part of the compromise over commerce. By agreeing that the foreign slave trade might be ended 20 years later, the Southerners gained a more favorable wording of other clauses. The writers did not use the word "slave" anywhere in the original Constitution. Even the expression "such persons" was part of a compromise.

Clause 2 The privilege of the writ of habeas corpus shall not be suspended, unless when in cases of rebellion or invasion the public safety may require it.

Only when the United States is in serious danger from rebellion or invasion can the courts be forbidden to issue papers called **writs of *habeas corpus.*** A writ of habeas corpus forces a jailer or other person to bring a prisoner into court so that a judge can decide whether he or she is being held lawfully.

The writ of habeas corpus was an important guarantee of personal liberty in England, and it is protected by the Constitution even against action by Congress. So long as the writ is allowed, the courts will set free anyone who is locked up by the government against the law.

Clause 3 No bill of attainder or ex post facto law shall be passed.

A **bill of attainder** is a law passed by a legislature to convict a person of a crime. It also sets a punishment. The person does not receive a trial in a court of law. An ***ex post facto* law** is retroactive. It punishes people for doing something that was not a crime when they did it. Congress cannot pass these kinds of laws.

Clause 4 No capitation, or other direct, tax shall be laid, unless in proportion to the census or enumeration herein before directed to be taken.

If Congress levies "direct" taxes, they must be based upon population. The wealth or physical size of states cannot be considered.

This clause repeats part of the other provision for direct taxes in Article 1, Section 2, clause 3. An income tax is a direct tax, but because of the Sixteenth Amendment, it no longer has to be based on population.

Clause 5 No tax or duty shall be laid on articles exported from any state.

Congress cannot tax goods or products being sent from any state to a foreign country.

Clause 6 No preference shall be given by any regulation of commerce or revenue to the ports of one state over those of another; nor shall vessels bound to, or from, one state, be obliged to enter, clear, or pay duties in another.

Congress cannot make laws that favor one state's harbors over another's. Ships from one state may enter the ports of other states without paying duties.

Clause 7 No money shall be drawn from the treasury, but in consequence of appropriations made by law; and a regular statement and account of the receipts and expenditures of all public money shall be published from time to time.

Government money can be spent only if Congress passes a law for that purpose. An account of how much money is collected and how it is spent must be kept and made public.

Clause 8 No title of nobility shall be granted by the United States; and no person holding any office of profit or trust under them, shall, without the consent of the Congress, accept of any present, emolument, office, or title, of any kind whatever, from any king, prince, or foreign state.

The United States government cannot give a title of nobility (such as count, duchess, earl) to anyone. No one in the service of the United States can accept a title, present, or a position from another country without permission of Congress.

The second clause was intended to prevent foreign governments from corrupting United States officials.

Section 10/Powers Forbidden to the States

Clause 1 No state shall enter into any treaty, alliance, or confederation; grant letters of marque and reprisal; coin money; emit bills of credit; make any thing but gold and silver coin a tender in payment of debts; pass any bill of attainder, ex post facto law, or law impairing the obligation of contracts, or grant any title of nobility.

This clause lists eight things that states may never do.

(1) States cannot make treaties with other countries or become part of another country. (2) They cannot give private citizens permission to fight other countries. (3) They cannot coin their own money or issue paper money. (4) They cannot pass laws that allow anything other than gold or silver to be used as money. (5) They cannot pass laws declaring a particular person guilty of an offense and describing the punishment. (6) They cannot pass laws that would punish a person for doing something that was not a crime when it was done. (7) They cannot pass laws that excuse people from carrying out lawful agreements. (8) They cannot give titles of nobility.

Clause 2 No state shall, without the consent of the Congress, lay any imposts or duties on imports or exports, except what may be absolutely necessary for executing its inspection laws; and the net produce of all duties and imposts, laid by any state on imports or exports, shall be for the use of the treasury of the United States; and all such laws shall be subject to the revision and control of the Congress.

Clause 3 No state shall, without the consent of Congress, lay any duty of tonnage, keep troops or ships of war in time of peace, enter into any agreement or compact with another state, or with a foreign power, or engage in war, unless actually invaded, or in such imminent danger as will not admit of delay.

These two clauses list the things that states may do only with the approval of Congress. States cannot tax goods coming from or going to other countries unless Congress agrees. However, states may charge an inspection fee if necessary. Any profit from state import or export taxes must go into the United States treasury. These state tax laws may be changed by Congress. Unless Congress provides otherwise, states may not tax ships for using their ports, or keep troops (except the National Guard) or warships in time of peace. States cannot make agreements with other states or with foreign countries unless Congress agrees. For example,

if three states want to form a compact to deal with a river that flows through their land, they must get the permission of Congress. States cannot go to war unless they have been invaded or are in such great danger that delay would be disastrous.

Article 2/Executive Branch
Section 1/President and Vice-President

✓ **Clause 1** The executive power shall be vested in a President of the United States of America. He shall hold his office during the term of four years, and, together with the Vice-President, chosen for the same term, be elected as follows:

✓ Executive power is the power to carry out laws. This power is given to the **President,** who is the chief executive of the United States government. He or she serves a four-year term of office. The Vice-President is elected at the same time as the President and serves the same term.

Clause 2 Each state shall appoint, in such manner as the legislature thereof may direct, a number of electors, equal to the whole number of senators and representatives to which the state may be entitled in the Congress; but no senator or representative, or person holding an office of trust or profit under the United States, shall be appointed an elector.

The people do not elect the President directly. Electors of the President are chosen from each state in the way the state legislature decides. The number of electors from each state is equal to the total number of senators and representatives the state has in Congress. No senator or representative and no one holding a position in the national government may be an elector.

Together, the electors are known as the **electoral college.** In this case, college means "group," not "school." The electoral college votes the President and Vice-President into office.

Clause 3 The electors shall meet in their respective states, and vote by ballot for two persons, of whom one at least shall not be an inhabitant of the same state with themselves. And they shall make a list of all the persons voted for, and of the number of votes for each; which list they shall sign and certify, and transmit sealed to the seat of the government of the United States, directed to the president of the Senate. The president of the Senate shall, in the presence of the Senate and House of Representatives, open all the certificates, and the votes shall then be counted. The person having the greatest number of votes shall be the

President, if such number be a majority of the whole number of electors appointed; and if there be more than one who have such majority, and have an equal number of votes, then the House of Representatives shall immediately choose by ballot one of them for President; and if no person have a majority, then from the five highest on the list the said House shall in like manner choose the President. But in choosing the President, the votes shall be taken by states, the representation from each state having one vote; a quorum for this purpose shall consist of a member or members from two-thirds of the states, and a majority of all the states shall be necessary to a choice. In every case, after the choice of the President, the person having the greatest number of votes of the electors shall be the Vice-President. But if there should remain two or more who have equal votes, the Senate shall choose from them by ballot the Vice-President.

This clause describes the original way of electing the President and Vice-President. It was changed by the Twelfth Amendment.

The original method worked in this way. Electors met in their own states and voted for two persons for President. At least one of the persons they voted for had to live in a different state.

They then made a list of all the persons who had received any votes, and how many votes each had received. This list was signed, sealed, and delivered to the president of the Senate.

At a meeting attended by both houses of Congress, all of the lists were opened and the votes counted. The person having the most votes was President. However, that person had to receive votes from a majority of the electors. If two persons had more than a majority of the votes but were tied, the House of Representatives had to choose one of them to be President. If no one had a majority, the House of Representatives had to choose the President from the five candidates with the most votes.

Whenever the House of Representatives had to choose the President, each state had one vote and at least two-thirds of the states had to be present for the voting.

After the President was chosen, whether by electors or by the House, the Vice-President was chosen. The Vice-President was the person who came in second in the race for President. If there was a tie vote, the Senate would choose the Vice-President from the two or more candidates who were tied.

Clause 4   The Congress may determine the time of choosing the electors, and the day on which they shall give their votes; which day shall be the same throughout the United States.

Congress has the power to decide the date electors are chosen and the date they vote. That day must be the same throughout the United States.

Congress has set the Tuesday after the first Monday in November in every fourth year as the date for choosing electors. This is when the people have their chance to vote for President and Vice-President by voting for their electors. The electors cast their ballots on the Monday after the second Wednesday in December.

Clause 5   No person except a natural-born citizen, or a citizen of the United States at the time of the adoption of this Constitution, shall be eligible to the office of President; neither shall any person be eligible to that office who shall not have attained to the age of thirty-five years, and been fourteen years a resident within the United States.

✓   To be President, a person must have been born a citizen. The person must be at least thirty-five years old and must have lived in the United States for fourteen years. The only people eligible to be President who were not natural-born citizens were those who were citizens when the Constitution was adopted.

Clause 6   In case of the removal of the President from office, or of his death, resignation, or inability to discharge the powers and duties of the said office, the same shall devolve on the Vice-President, and the Congress may by law provide for the case of removal, death, resignation or inability, both of the President and Vice-President, declaring what officer shall then act as President, and such officer shall act accordingly, until the disability be removed, or a President shall be elected.

This clause describes the original method for the Vice-President to become President. It has been changed by the Twenty-fifth Amendment.

The original method was for the Vice-President to take on the duties of the President if the President died, resigned, or was unable to work. Congress still has the power to say who will be President if both the President and Vice-President are unable to serve. Under today's law, the Speaker of the House is next in line.

✓ **Clause 7**   The President shall, at stated times, receive for his services, a compensation, which shall neither be increased nor diminished during the period for which he shall have been elected, and he shall not receive within that period any other emolument from the United States, or any of them.

The President's salary cannot be raised or lowered during his or her term of office. Today the President makes a salary of $200,000 per year. Also, while in office, the President cannot receive any other salary from the United States or from any of the states.

This checks the power of Congress. Congress cannot bully the President by threatening to lower his or her salary. This clause also checks the President. He or she cannot try to influence the Congress to vote a raise. Any salary changes voted by the Congress do not take effect until after the next election.

Clause 8   Before he enter on the execution of his office, he shall take the following oath or affirmation:— "I do solemnly swear (or affirm) that I will faithfully execute the office of President of the United States, and will to the best of my ability, preserve, protect and defend the Constitution of the United States."

Before taking office, the President must take an oath of office. The President must promise to faithfully carry out the duties of the job and make sure that the Constitution is obeyed.

Section 2/Powers of the President

✓ **Clause 1**   The President shall be commander in chief of the army and navy of the United States, and of the militia of the several states, when called into the actual service of the United States; he may require the opinion, in writing, of the principal officer in each of the executive departments, upon any subject relating to the duties of their respective offices, and he shall have power to grant reprieves and pardons for offenses against the United States, except in cases of impeachment.

The President commands all the country's armed forces. The President even commands the state militias (national guard) when they are called into national service.

The writers of the Constitution made the President commander in chief because they wanted civilian control of the military forces. This control is the basis for much of the President's power today. Given our great military strength, this makes the President one of the most powerful individuals in the world today.

The President is in charge of all the department heads in the executive branch. He may call on the heads of executive departments, such as the Attorney General, for advice.

The President can grant a **reprieve,** or delay, in the sentences of those who have committed federal crimes. He or she can also **pardon,** or set free, these same people. However, the President has no power to do this in impeachment cases.

✓ **Clause 2**   He shall have power, by and with the advice and consent of the Senate, to make treaties, provided two-thirds of the senators present concur; and he shall nominate, and by and with the advice and consent of the Senate, shall appoint ambassadors, other public ministers and consuls, judges of the Supreme Court, and all other officers of the United States, whose appointments are not herein otherwise provided for, and which shall be established by law; but the Congress may by law vest the appointment of such inferior officers, as they think proper, in the President alone, in the courts of law, or in the heads of departments.

The President is the person who works out agreements with foreign countries. These agreements between nations are called **treaties.** These treaties do not go into effect unless they are approved by two-thirds of the Senate.

The Constitution does not specify anything about the content of treaties. The writers thought that by requiring the approval of two-thirds of the Senate, they would help ensure that treaties would be in the best interests of the nation.

This part of clause 2 is an important source of the President's power as maker of foreign policy. However, today, Presidents sometimes bypass this constitutional requirement by making **executive agreements** with foreign nations. An executive agreement simply means that the President and the head of another nation agree to certain things. Executive agreements do not require Senate approval before taking effect.

The President appoints persons to represent the United States in other countries. He or she also appoints justices of the Supreme Court and many other government officials. Many of these appointments must be approved by a majority vote of the Senate.

The requirement that the Senate must approve treaties and appointments is a check on the power of the President. The leaders of the executive departments—the **Cabinet**—are among the officials who must be approved by the Senate. However, the President alone has the power to fire them.

The jobs of many less important officials are not described in the Constitution. Congress may pass laws allowing the President, the courts, or heads of government departments to appoint people to these jobs without Senate approval.

Flexibility was built into the Constitution. The departments of the executive branch now have close to three million employees. Most of them are appointed through the Civil Service Commission. They are the cogs in the machinery of government.

✓ **Clause 3** The President shall have power to fill up all vacancies that may happen during the recess of the Senate, by granting commissions which shall expire at the end of their next session.

The President may temporarily appoint people to federal offices that become vacant while Congress is not in session. These appointments last until the end of the next meeting of the Senate.

Section 3/Other Presidential Powers

He shall from time to time give to the Congress information of the state of the Union, and recommend to their consideration such measures as he shall judge necessary and expedient; he may, on extraordinary occasions, convene both houses, or either of them, and in case of disagreement between them, with respect to the time of adjournment, he may adjourn them to such time as he shall think proper; he shall receive ambassadors and other public ministers; he shall take care that the laws be faithfully executed, and shall commission all the officers of the United States.

The President regularly speaks to Congress about the nation's condition (the state of the Union). The President recommends laws that will lead to changes or improvements that are either necessary or desirable.

Only Congress has the power to make laws. But the President's power to recommend new laws gives him or her an important part to play in the law-making process.

In times of emergency or necessity, the President may call a meeting of either or both houses of Congress. If the houses of Congress disagree about when to end their meeting, the President may decide when to end it. This allows the President to put pressure on Congress to take action.

The President is the official who meets with representatives of other countries. This power makes the President head of state. This role is partly ceremonial. But when the President decides to receive an ambassador, the President also decides whether to recognize a foreign government. The President is not checked by the courts or by Congress in performing this role.

It is the duty of the President to see that the laws

of the country are followed. The President must sign the papers that give officers the right to hold their positions.

Section 4/Impeachment

The President, Vice-President and all civil officers of the United States, shall be removed from office on impeachment for, and conviction of, treason, bribery, or other high crimes and misdemeanors.

The President, Vice-President, or other officers of the United States government can be removed from office for certain kinds of serious misconduct. This clause provides Congress with an important check on the other branches. As you may remember, it is the House of Representatives that first votes to impeach, or accuse, the officer whom it wishes to remove. Then he or she must be tried and convicted by the Senate. But an officer is not just removed because the House and Senate do not agree with the officer. The person must be guilty of "treason, bribery, or other high crimes and misdemeanors." **Treason** is defined as carrying on war against the United States and giving help to the nation's enemies. Nobody is sure exactly what "high crimes and misdemeanors" are, but the basic idea is that an officer can be removed for serious abuse of his or her power.

Article 3/Judicial Branch
Section 1/Federal Courts

The judicial power of the United States, shall be vested in one Supreme Court, and in such inferior courts as the Congress may from time to time ordain and establish. The judges, both of the supreme and inferior courts, shall hold their offices during good behavior, and shall, at stated times, receive for their services, a compensation, which shall not be diminished during their continuance in office.

The power to decide cases—**judicial power**—is given to the Supreme Court and to lower courts set up by Congress. Once appointed, judges hold office for life or until they have been found guilty of high crimes or misdemeanors. The salary paid to judges cannot be lowered as long as they hold office.

Section 2/Extent of Judicial Powers

Clause 1 The judicial power shall extend to all cases, in law and equity, arising under this Constitution, the laws of the United States, and treaties made, or which shall be made, under their authority, —to all cases affecting ambassadors, other public ministers and consuls; —to all cases of admiralty and maritime jurisdiction; —to controversies to which the United States shall be a party; —to controversies between two or more states; ~~between a state and citizens of another state~~; —between citizens of different states; —between citizens of the same state claiming lands under grants of different states, and between a state, or the citizens thereof, and foreign states, citizens or subjects.

Federal courts hear cases concerning the Constitution, laws of the United States, and treaties. They also settle disputes involving representatives of foreign countries and hear cases about ships and shipping. They hear any case in which the United States government is one of the two opposing sides, and they settle disputes between two or more states.

The courts originally heard cases involving a state and people from another state or foreign country. The Eleventh Amendment took away this power except when the state wants the case to be in federal court.

The courts also settle disputes between citizens of different states; disputes about certain claims to grants of land; disputes between a state and a foreign country; and disputes between an American and a person from a foreign country.

Clause 2 In all cases affecting ambassadors, other public ministers and consuls, and those in which a state shall be party, the Supreme Court shall have original jurisdiction. In all the other cases before mentioned, the Supreme Court shall have appellate jurisdiction, both as to law and fact, with such exceptions, and under such regulations as the Congress shall make.

The Supreme Court can act as a trial court in cases involving a representative of a foreign country or involving a state. All other cases must be tried in the lower courts first. The decision of the lower courts can then be appealed to the Supreme Court. Congress may decide that some kinds of cases cannot be appealed.

Jurisdiction is the power of a court to hear a certain kind of case. There are two kinds—original and appellate. If a court has **original jurisdiction,** it hears the facts of the case. The judge or jury decides which side wins the case. If the losing side thinks that the judge made mistakes in the trial, it can appeal the decision.

A court with **appellate jurisdiction** hears appeals. It does not decide the facts of the case. It judges how the law was applied in the original trial by the judge. If the appeals court finds serious mistakes that might have affected the decision, it can demand that a new trial be held. Sometimes the court reverses the decision

of the lower court. If so, it says that errors in the trial resulted in the wrong decision. In that case, the loser of the original trial is the winner.

Very few cases get beyond the Court of Appeals level. The Supreme Court must hear certain kinds of appeals, but it is not required to hear every appeal that comes up. It can choose which appeals it will hear. Still, the Supreme Court is extremely busy. In fact, some people have suggested establishing yet another appeals court to handle more of the workload of the Supreme Court.

Another way that appeals can reach the Supreme Court is through the state courts. Many cases are tried in state courts instead of federal courts. If a case in a state court involves federal law, or a treaty, or the Constitution, it too can be reviewed by the Supreme Court.

Clause 3 The trial of all crimes, except in cases of impeachment, shall be by jury; and such trial shall be held in the state where the said crimes shall have been committed; but when not committed within any state, the trial shall be at such place or places as the Congress may by law have directed.

Any person accused of committing a crime against the United States has the right to a trial by jury. The trial is held in the state where the crime was committed. Congress describes by law where trials are held in places that are not states (in territories, for example). The only exception to these rules are impeachment trials. They are tried in the Senate.

More requirements about the criminal jury were added by the Sixth Amendment, but this clause is still law.

Section 3/Treason

Clause 1 Treason against the United States, shall consist only in levying war against them, or in adhering to their enemies, giving them aid and comfort. No person shall be convicted of treason unless on the testimony of two witnesses to the same overt act, or on confession in open court.

Treason is defined here as carrying on war against the United States or helping enemies of the United States. Convicting a person of treason is difficult. At least two witnesses must testify in court that the accused person committed the same act of treason. Any confession by the accused must be made in open court. Confessions made elsewhere are not accepted as evidence.

Clause 2 The Congress shall have power to declare the punishment of treason, but no attainder of treason shall work corruption of blood or forfeiture except during the life of the person attainted.

Congress has the power to decide what the punishment for a person guilty of treason will be. It can punish only the guilty person. No punishment can be set for the heirs or the family of the guilty person. The guilty person's family cannot have their rights to family property taken away.

Corruption of blood is punishment of the family of a wrongdoer. It involves taking away a wrongdoer's right to pass an estate or title on to the family. **Forfeiture** involves taking away the goods and honors of the wrongdoer during his or her lifetime.

Article 4/Among the States

Section 1/Recognition of Each Other's Acts
Full faith and credit shall be given in each state to the public acts, records, and judicial proceedings of every other state. And the Congress may by general laws prescribe the manner in which such acts, records and proceedings shall be proved, and the effect thereof.

All states must accept the laws, records, and court decisions of other states as legal and binding. Congress has the power to make laws that force the states to respect each other's laws, records, and court decisions.

Section 2/Citizens' Rights in Other States
Clause 1 The citizens of each state shall be entitled to all privileges and immunities of citizens in the several states.

A citizen from another state has the same rights as the citizens of the state where he or she happens to be. He or she is not to be treated as a person from another country.

Clause 2 A person charged in any state with treason, felony, or other crime, who shall flee from justice, and be found in another state, shall on demand of the executive authority of the state from which he fled, be delivered up, to be removed to the state having jurisdiction of the crime.

People cannot escape justice by moving out of their state. Anyone accused of a crime in one state who escapes to another state is usually returned if the governor of the state where the crime was committed requests it. This process is called extradition.

Clause 3 No person held to service or labor in one state, under the laws thereof, escaping into another, shall, in consequence of any law or regulation therein, be discharged from such service or labor, but shall be delivered up on claim of the party to whom such service or labor may be due.

Slaves and indentured servants could not become free by escaping to another state. They had to be sent back to their owners.

A person held to service or labor was a slave, an apprentice, or an indentured servant. The Thirteenth Amendment ended slavery. Apprentices are no longer held to service as they once were. Indentured servants no longer exist.

Section 3/New States and Territories
Clause 1 New states may be admitted by the Congress into this Union; but no new state shall be formed or erected within the jurisdiction of any other state; nor any state be formed by the junction of two or more states, or parts of states, without the consent of the legislatures of the states concerned as well as of the Congress.

Congress has the power to add new states to the United States. No way is provided for a state to leave the Union.

Eleven states tried to leave, that is secede, in 1860-1861, but they lost the Civil War and had to remain part of the United States.

No state may be divided to make another state without the consent of the original state and Congress. Two states have been divided in this manner. Maine was split off from Massachusetts in 1820. West Virginia split off from Virginia when the Civil War started in 1861. West Virginia was admitted to the Union in 1863.

The consent of Congress and the states involved is needed for a new state to be made by putting parts of two or more states together. No states have been formed by joining two other states or their parts.

Clause 2 The Congress shall have power to dispose of and make all needful rules and regulations respecting the territory or other property belonging to the United States; and nothing in this Constitution shall be so construed as to prejudice any claims of the United States, or of any particular state.

Congress can sell or give away government lands and property. It has the power to make laws governing lands and other property. This clause is the source of power for Congress to decide how territories are governed before they become states.

Nothing in the Constitution is intended to favor

one state over another, or over the United States, in disputes over land claims.

Many states had claimed other lands. The writers of the Constitution worded this clause to avoid arguments over land claims that could hurt the chances of the Constitution being adopted.

Section 4/Guarantees to the States

The United States shall guarantee to every state in this union a republican form of government, and shall protect each of them against invasion; and on application of the legislature, or of the executive (when the legislature cannot be convened) against domestic violence.

The United States government promises that every state in the Union shall have a **republican form of government.** This is a government whose officials are elected by the people. The writers of the Constitution wanted to make sure that no state would turn into a monarchy.

The United States government also must protect each state from invasion. It promises to send help in putting down riots. This help must be requested by the state legislature, or if the legislature cannot meet soon enough, by the governor.

Article 5/Amending the Constitution

The Congress, whenever two-thirds of both houses shall deem it necessary, shall propose amendments to this Constitution, or, on the application of the legislatures of two-thirds of the several states, shall call a convention for proposing amendments, which, in either case, shall be valid to all intents and purposes, as part of this Constitution, and when ratified by the legislatures of three-fourths of the several states, or by conventions in three-fourths thereof, as the one or the other mode of ratification may be proposed by the Congress; provided that no amendment which may be made prior to the year one thousand eight hundred and eight shall in any manner affect the first and fourth clauses in the ninth Section of the first Article; and that no state, without its consent, shall be deprived of its equal suffrage in the Senate.

There are two ways of suggesting amendments to the Constitution. One way is for two-thirds of both the Senate and House of Representatives to vote for a specific amendment. The other way is for the legislatures of two-thirds of the states to ask Congress to call a special convention to suggest amendments.

All proposed amendments must be ratified by the states. An amendment can be ratified in one of two ways. The legislatures of three-fourths of the states can approve the amendment, or conventions in three-fourths of the states can approve the amendment. Congress chooses the method of ratification at the time an amendment is proposed.

No amendment proposed before 1808 could stop the slave trade or allow a different method of figuring direct taxes. No amendment can decrease the number of senators a state has unless the affected state agrees.

Amendments do not require the signature of the President nor can they be vetoed by the President. Therefore, the President has no official role in amending the Constitution. But he or she can play a political role by publicly supporting or opposing proposed amendments.

Article 6/National Supremacy

All debts contracted and engagements entered into, before the adoption of this Constitution, shall be as valid against the United States under this Constitution, as under the confederation.

This Constitution, and the laws of the United States which shall be made in pursuance thereof; and all treaties made, or which shall be made, under the authority of the United States, shall be the supreme law of the land; and the judges in every state shall be bound thereby, anything in the Constitution or laws of any state to the contrary notwithstanding.

The senators and representatives before mentioned, and the members of the several state legislatures, and all executive and judicial officers, both of the United States and of the several states, shall be bound by oath or affirmation, to support this Constitution; but no religious test shall ever be required as a qualification to any office or public trust under the United States.

All debts and treaties made by Congress under the Articles of Confederation were made binding on the United States under the Constitution.

This Constitution, laws made by Congress, and treaties made by the United States shall be the highest law of the land. State judges must follow this law, even if state laws or constitutions contradict it. This is one of the most important provisions in the Constitution.

All federal and state officials must promise to support this Constitution. However, no officials or public employees can ever be required to support or belong to any kind of religion in order to hold federal office.

Article 7/Ratification

The ratification of the conventions of nine states, shall be sufficient for the establishment of this Constitution between the states so ratifying the same. Done in convention by the unanimous consent of the states present the seventeenth day of September in the year of our Lord one thousand seven hundred and eighty seven and of the independence of the United States of America the twelfth. In witness whereof we have hereunto subscribed our names.

Government under this Constitution could begin after nine states had approved it at special conventions. This Constitution was signed on September 17, 1787, in the twelfth year of our country's independence. These were the signers.

George Washington— President and deputy from Virginia

Delaware
George Reed
Gunning Bedford, Junior
John Dickinson
Richard Bassett
Jacob Broom

Maryland
James McHenry
Daniel of St. Thomas Jenifer
Daniel Carroll

Virginia
John Blair
James Madison, Junior

North Carolina
William Blount
Richard Dobbs Spaight
Hugh Williamson

South Carolina
John Rutledge
Charles Cotesworth Pinckney
Charles Pinckney
Pierce Butler

Georgia
William Few
Abraham Baldwin

New Hampshire
John Langdon
Nicholas Gilman

Massachusetts
Nathaniel Gorham
Rufus King

Connecticut
William Samuel Johnson
Roger Sherman

New York
Alexander Hamilton

New Jersey
William Livingston
David Brearley
William Paterson
Jonathan Dayton

Pennsylvania
Benjamin Franklin
Thomas Mifflin
Robert Morris
George Clymer
Thomas FitzSimons
Jared Ingersoll
James Wilson
Gouverneur Morris

Amendments to the Constitution

The date given in parentheses is the date that ratification of the amendment was completed. Most of the amendments were added to meet specific needs as the country grew and changed. The first ten amendments make up the Bill of Rights. They were written by the First Congress at the request of the states. They limit the powers of the national government and protect the rights of individuals. All three branches of government are limited by the Bill of Rights.

Amendment 1 (1791)
Religious and Political Freedom
Congress shall make no law respecting an establishment of religion, or prohibiting the free exercise thereof; or abridging the freedom of speech, or of the press; or the right of the people peaceably to assemble, and to petition the government for a redress of grievances.

Congress cannot pass any laws that make any religion the official religion of the country. It cannot pass laws to stop people from following their own religion.

In some colonies, one religion had been the official or established religion. The First Amendment means that government and religion are separate from one another. The government may neither operate its own churches nor interfere with the religions that people choose for themselves.

Congress cannot make laws that stop people from speaking and writing what they wish. It cannot make laws that stop people from holding peaceful meetings or from asking the government to correct a wrong.

Freedom of speech is very important, but it does not mean that people can say anything they please. For example, the First Amendment does not protect the right to persuade other people to overthrow the government by force.

Amendment 2 (1791)
Right to Bear Arms
A well-regulated militia being necessary to the security of a free state, the right of the people to keep and bear arms shall not be infringed.

The people have the right to protect themselves by serving as armed citizens in the militia or national

91

guard, and Congress cannot prevent them from owning weapons.

However, Congress has restricted the possession of particular weapons. For example, private ownership of sawed-off shotguns, concealed weapons, and machine guns is prohibited by federal law. States, too, are free to regulate the use and sale of guns. People disagree as to whether the Second Amendment means that Congress and the states cannot make it illegal to own pistols.

Amendment 3 (1791)
Quartering of Soldiers

No soldier shall, in time of peace be quartered in any house, without the consent of the owner, nor in time of war, but in a manner to be prescribed by law.

In peacetime, citizens cannot be forced to **quarter** soldiers, that is, to give soldiers a place to sleep or meals to eat in their homes. In wartime, this may be done only in the way Congress describes in a law.

Amendment 4 (1791)
Search and Seizure

The right of the people to be secure in their persons, houses, papers, and effects, against unreasonable searches and seizures, shall not be violated, and no warrants shall issue, but upon probable cause, supported by oath or affirmation, and particularly describing the place to be searched, and the persons or things to be seized.

A person cannot be arrested, and his or her house cannot be searched, and his or her property or papers taken, except in ways that follow the law. Courts can issue search warrants and arrest warrants. But whoever asks for a warrant must explain why, exactly where the search is to be made, and who or what is to be taken.

A **search warrant** authorizes a police officer or sheriff to seize evidence that could prove who committed a crime. The purpose is to prevent evidence from being destroyed. An **arrest warrant** authorizes a police officer or sheriff to seize a person suspected of committing a crime.

Amendment 5 (1791)
Life, Liberty, and Property

No person shall be held to answer for a capital, or otherwise infamous crime, unless on a presentment or indictment of a grand jury, except in cases arising in the land or naval forces, or in the militia, when in actual service in time of war or public danger; nor shall

any person be subject for the same offense to be twice put in jeopardy of life or limb; nor shall be compelled in any criminal case to be a witness against himself, nor be deprived of life, liberty, or property, without due process of law; nor shall private property be taken for public use, without just compensation.

Before anyone can be tried in a federal court for a serious crime, a grand jury must formally accuse that person in an indictment. A **grand jury** does not decide cases. It examines evidence very carefully to decide if there is enough information to hold a trial. An indictment is the formal charge against a person by the grand jury. A **petit jury** is the trial jury that decides whether the person accused is guilty or not guilty. The petit jury is usually just called "jury."

Once a person is found not guilty of committing a particular crime, that person cannot be tried again for that crime by the federal government. Nor may the federal government punish a person more than once for the same crime.

To be tried twice for the same crime is **double jeopardy.** The protection against it is not absolute. If the offense is a crime under state law, the person can be tried in a state court, as well as in a federal court. Also if the offense hurts someone, the accused can be made to pay a certain amount of money called **damages** to the person or to the person's family.

No one can be forced to say anything that would help convict himself or herself of a federal crime. This provision was partly intended to prevent the use of torture in getting a confession.

The federal government cannot take a person's life, freedom, or property except in the exact ways written in law, and the law must give him or her a fair trial.

The Supreme Court has decided that this clause also means that some liberties cannot be taken away at all, for example, the right to go to a private school.

The Fourteenth Amendment applies this clause to the states as well.

The government can take a person's property for the benefit of the public. This power is called **eminent domain.** In exercising this power, the government must pay a fair price for the property.

Amendment 6 (1791)
Rights of the Accused

In all criminal prosecutions, the accused shall enjoy the right to a speedy and public trial, by an impartial jury of the state and district wherein the crime shall have been committed, which district shall have been previously ascertained by law, and to be informed of the nature and cause of the accusation; to be confronted with the witnesses against him; to have compulsory process for obtaining witnesses in his favor, and to have the assistance of counsel for his defense.

A person accused of committing a crime must be given a prompt trial in public. Guilt or innocence must be decided by a jury chosen from the state and the district where the crime was committed. The accused must be told what he or she is being tried for.

The accused must be present when witnesses speak in court, and the accused has the power to make witnesses come and speak in court in his or her favor. The accused also has the right to a lawyer to make a defense.

This amendment originally applied only to federal courts, but the Fourteenth Amendment has made it apply to state courts too.

Amendment 7 (1791)
Right to Jury Trial
In suits at common law, where the value in controversy shall exceed twenty dollars, the right of trial by jury shall be preserved, and no fact tried by a jury shall be otherwise re-examined in any court of the United States than according to the rules of the common law.

In many disputes that involve more than $20, either side in the dispute can insist on having a jury trial or both can agree not to have a jury. The second clause of the amendment limits the power of judges to interfere with a jury's decision.

Article III and the Sixth Amendment protect the right to jury trial in criminal cases. The Seventh Amendment provides for juries in other cases, such as those that have to do with auto accidents or unpaid bills.

Amendment 8 (1791)
Bail and Punishment
Excessive bail shall not be required, nor excessive fines imposed, nor cruel and unusual punishments inflicted.

This amendment forbids the courts to require an unusually large **bail.** Bail is the sum of money or property that the accused person gives to the court to hold as a guarantee that he or she will show up for the trial. People who are accused of crimes may be allowed out of jail on bail while they are awaiting trial.

Courts cannot fine persons too much for a crime or punish convicts in cruel or unusual ways.

Amendment 9 (1791)
All Other Rights
The enumeration in the Constitution of certain rights shall not be construed to deny or disparage others retained by the people.

The mention of certain rights in the Constitution does not mean that these are the only rights that people have and does not make other rights less important.

Some people were afraid that if they just listed some rights in the Bill of Rights it might take away any rights not listed. The Ninth Amendment was put in to show that this is not what the Bill of Rights means. It makes it clear that the federal government still can only do what it is authorized to do by the Constitution.

Amendment 10 (1791)
Rights of States and the People
The powers not delegated to the United States by the Constitution, nor prohibited by it to the states, are reserved to the states respectively, or to the people.

The states or the people have all the powers that have not been delegated to the central government or prohibited to the states.

Amendment 11 (1798)
Suits Against a State
The judicial power of the United States shall not be construed to extend to any suit in law or equity, commenced or prosecuted against one of the United States by citizens of another state, or by citizens or subjects of any foreign state.

Citizens of other states or foreign countries cannot sue a state in federal court without its consent.

Amendment 12 (1804)
Election of Presidents
The electors shall meet in their respective states and vote by ballot for President and Vice-President, one of whom, at least, shall not be an inhabitant of the same state with themselves; they shall name in their ballots the person voted for as President, and in distinct ballots the person voted for as Vice-President, and they shall make distinct lists of all persons voted for as President, and of all persons voted for as Vice-President, and of the number of votes for each, which lists they shall sign and certify, and transmit sealed to the seat of the government of the United States, directed to the president of the Senate;

The president of the Senate shall, in the presence

of the Senate and House of Representatives, open all the certificates and the votes shall then be counted;

The person having the greatest number of votes for President, shall be the President, if such number be a majority of the whole number of electors appointed; and if no person have such majority, then from the persons having the highest numbers not exceeding three on the list of those voted for as President, the House of Representatives shall choose immediately, by ballot, the President. But in choosing the President, the votes shall be taken by states, the representation from each state having one vote; a quorum for this purpose shall consist of a member or members from two-thirds of the states, and a majority of all the states shall be necessary to a choice.

~~And if the House of Representatives shall not choose a President whenever the right of choice shall devolve upon them, before the fourth day of March next following, then the Vice-President shall act as President, as in the case of the death or other constitutional disability of the President.~~

The person having the greatest number of votes as Vice-President, shall be the Vice-President, if such number be a majority of the whole number of electors appointed, and if no person have a majority, then from the two highest numbers on the list, the Senate shall choose the Vice-President; a quorum for the purpose shall consist of two-thirds of the whole number of senators, and a majority of the whole number shall be necessary to a choice.

But no person constitutionally ineligible to the office of President shall be eligible to that of Vice-President of the United States.

The electors meet in their own states, where they cast separate ballots for President and Vice-President. At least one of the candidates they vote for must live in another state. After the vote, the electors make a list of the persons voted for as President and another list of persons voted for as Vice-President. On each list they write the total votes cast for each person. They then sign their names, seal the lists, and send them to the president of the Senate in Washington, D.C.

In a meeting attended by both houses of Congress, the president of the Senate opens the lists from all the states, and the votes are counted.

The person having the most votes for President is President. However, the number of votes received must be more than half of the total number of all electors, now 270 or more. If no person has this many votes, the House of Representatives selects the President from the three candidates who have the largest number of electoral votes. Each state has one vote, no matter how many representatives it has.

Two-thirds of the states must be represented when this vote is cast. The candidate who receives a majority of the votes of the states is President.

If the House of Representatives does not elect a President before the date set for the new President to take office, the Vice-President acts as President. The date for this was changed to January 20 by the Twentieth Amendment.

The person who receives the most electoral votes for Vice-President becomes Vice-President. However, he or she must get more than half of the electoral votes. If no person has more than half, the Senate must choose the Vice-President from the two candidates with the most votes. Two-thirds of all the senators must be present when the vote is taken. To be elected Vice-President, the candidate must receive the votes of more than half, now 51 or more, of all the senators.

A person who does not have the qualifications for President of the United States cannot be Vice-President.

Amendment 13 (1865)
Abolition of Slavery

Section 1 Neither slavery nor involuntary servitude, except as a punishment for crime whereof the party shall have been duly convicted, shall exist within the United States, or any place subject to their jurisdiction.

Slavery is not allowed in the United States or in any lands under its control. No one may be forced to work unless a court has set that as a punishment for committing a crime.

Section 2 Congress shall have power to enforce this article by appropriate legislation.

Congress has the power to make laws that will put this amendment into effect.

The amendment had the effect of **emancipating,** or freeing, all remaining slaves in the United States. Some slaves had been freed during the Civil War, but slavery itself was not abolished until this amendment took effect.

Amendment 14 (1868)
Civil Rights in the States

Section 1 All persons born or naturalized in the United States, and subject to the jurisdiction thereof, are citizens of the United States and of the state wherein they reside. No state shall make or enforce any law which shall abridge the privileges or immunities of citizens of the United States; nor shall any state deprive any person of life, liberty, or property, without due process of law; nor, deny to any person within its jurisdiction the equal protection of the laws.

Everyone who has been born or naturalized in the United States and is subject to the country's laws, is a citizen of the United States and also of the state in which he or she lives. States cannot make or enforce laws that prevent any citizen from enjoying rights given by the federal government. They cannot take a person's life, liberty, or property without **due process of law,** or a fair trial. States must also guarantee **equal protection** of the laws to everyone. They cannot treat some people better or worse than others just because, for example, of the color of their skin.

Section 2   Representatives shall be apportioned among the several states according to their respective numbers, counting the whole number of persons in each state, excluding Indians not taxed. But when the right to vote at any election for the choice of electors for President and Vice-President of the United States, representatives in Congress, the executive and judicial officers of a state, or the members of the legislature thereof, is denied to any of the male inhabitants of such state, being twenty-one years of age, and citizens of the United States, or in any way abridged, except for participation in rebellion, or other crime, the basis of representation therein shall be reduced in the proportion which the number of such male citizens shall bear to the whole number of male citizens twenty-one years of age in such state.

All persons, except untaxed Indians, are counted in order to determine how many representatives in Congress each state is to have. A state's representation in Congress will be decreased if it keeps male citizens, who are 21 or older, and who have not committed crimes, from voting.

This section canceled the "three-fifths" clause of Article I, Section 2, clause 3 in which slaves were counted as three-fifths of a person. It also put the word "male" into the Constitution. This provision was intended to force states to allow black men to vote. If the states did not, this provision would decrease their representation in Congress. This was never enforced, but the Fifteenth Amendment has been used to enforce black voting rights.

Section 3   No person shall be a senator or representative in Congress, or elector of President and Vice-President, or hold any office, civil or military, under the United States, or under any state, who, having previously taken an oath, as a member of Congress, or as an officer of the United States, or as a member of any state legislature, or as an executive or judicial officer of any state, to support the Constitution of the United States, shall have engaged in insurrection or rebellion against the same, or given aid or comfort to the enemies thereof. But Congress may by a vote of two-thirds of each house, remove such disability.

People who had once been in state or federal government and who then fought against the United States in the Civil War were forbidden to hold office again or to be presidential electors. But Congress was allowed to change this by a two-thirds vote.

Congress worded the amendment so that only those Confederate leaders who had previously held state or national office were affected. This included most of the top leaders of the Confederacy. Congress removed this barrier on June 6, 1898.

Section 4   The validity of the public debt of the United States, authorized by law, including debts incurred for payment of pensions and bounties for services in suppressing insurrection or rebellion shall not be questioned. But neither the United States nor any state shall assume or pay any debt or obligation incurred in aid of insurrection or rebellion against the United States, or any claim for the loss or emancipation of any slave; but all such debts, obligations, and claims shall be held illegal and void.

The states or the federal government could not pay any part of the Confederate debt. The payment of the Union debt could not be questioned. No payment could be made for slaves who were emancipated.

Section 5   The Congress shall have power to enforce, by appropriate legislation the provisions of this article.

Congress has the power to make laws that will put this amendment into effect, such as laws punishing state officials who violate the amendment's other provisions.

Amendment 15 (1870)
Black Suffrage
Section 1   The right of citizens of the United States to vote shall not be denied or abridged by the United States or by any state on account of race, color, or previous condition of servitude.

Section 2 The Congress shall have power to enforce this article by appropriate legislation.

Neither the United States nor any state has the right to keep citizens from voting because of their race or because they were once slaves.

Congress has the power to make laws that will put this amendment into effect.

Amendment 16 (1913)
Income Tax

The Congress shall have power to lay and collect taxes on incomes, from whatever source derived, without apportionment among the several states, and without regard to any census or enumerations.

Congress has the power to put a tax on incomes without dividing the taxes among the states according to their population. **Income** is the money a person gets as payment for work done or from investments.

Amendment 17 (1913)
Direct Election of Senators

The Senate of the United States shall be composed of two senators from each state, elected by the people thereof, for six years; and each senator shall have one vote. The electors in each state shall have the qualifications requisite for electors of the most numerous branch of state legislatures.

When vacancies happen in the representation of any state in the Senate, the executive authority of such state shall issue writs of election to fill such vacancies: *Provided*, That the legislature of any state may empower the executive thereof to make temporary appointments until the people fill the vacancies by election as the legislature may direct.

This amendment shall not be so construed as to affect the election or term of any senator chosen before it becomes valid as part of the Constitution.

The Senate is made up of two senators from each state, elected by the people of the state for six-year terms. Each senator has one vote. Citizens entitled to vote for members of the largest house in the state legislature may vote for senators.

The governor of a state calls an election to fill a vacancy among that state's senators. But the state legislature may allow the governor to appoint someone to fill the Senate vacancy until the election is held.

This amendment did not affect any election that had been held or the term of any senator in the Senate at the time the amendment was adopted.

Amendment 18 (1919)
National Prohibition

~~**Section 1** After one year from the ratification of this article the manufacture, sale, or transportation of intoxicating liquors within, the importation thereof into, or the exportation thereof from the United States and all territory subject to the jurisdiction thereof for beverage purposes is hereby prohibited.~~

~~**Section 2** The Congress and the several states shall have concurrent power to enforce this article by appropriate legislation.~~

~~**Section 3** This article shall be inoperative unless it shall have been ratified as an amendment to the Constitution by the legislatures of the several states, as provided in the Constitution, within seven years from the date of the submission hereof to the states by the Congress.~~

One year after this amendment was ratified it became illegal in the United States and its territories to make, sell, or carry intoxicating liquors for drinking purposes. It became illegal to send such liquors out of the country and its territories or to bring such liquors into them.

The states and the federal government were to share enforcement duties.

Congress passed the Volstead Act to make this amendment effective. The act defined the percentage of alcohol in intoxicating liquors and provided penalties for violations. But the amendment was repealed after a few years by the Twenty-first Amendment.

Congress required this amendment to be approved by three-fourths of the states within seven years.

Amendment 19 (1920)
Woman's Suffrage

The right of citizens of the United States to vote shall not be denied or abridged by the United States or by any state on account of sex.

Congress shall have power to enforce this article by appropriate legislation.

Neither the United States nor any state can keep a citizen from voting because of one's sex.

Congress has the power to make laws that will make this amendment effective.

Amendment 20 (1933)
The "Lame-Duck" Amendment

Section 1 The terms of the President and Vice-President shall end at noon on the twentieth day of

January, and the terms of senators and representatives at noon on the third day of January, of the years in which such terms would have ended if this article had not been ratified; and the terms of their successors shall then begin.

The terms of office of the President and Vice-President end at noon, January 20. The terms of office of senators and representatives end at noon, January 3. Their terms end in the same years they would have if this amendment had not been approved.

Section 2 The Congress shall assemble at least once in every year, and such meeting shall begin at noon on the third day of January, unless they shall by law appoint a different day.

Congress must meet at least once a year. The meeting begins at noon on January 3 unless Congress selects another day by law.

Section 3 If, at the time fixed for the beginning of the term of the President, the President-elect shall have died, the Vice-President-elect shall become President. If a President shall not have been chosen before the time fixed for the beginning of his term, or if the President-elect shall have failed to qualify, then the Vice-President-elect shall act as President until a President shall have qualified; and the Congress may by law provide for the case wherein neither a President-elect nor a Vice-President-elect shall have qualified, declaring who shall then act as President, or the manner in which one who is to act shall be selected, and such person shall act accordingly until a President or Vice-President shall have qualified.

If the person elected President dies before **inauguration** day or the day the President is sworn into office, the Vice-President becomes President. If a President has not been chosen by January 20, or if the person chosen is not qualified to be President, then the person elected Vice-President acts as President until a President has qualified. Congress may pass a law to determine who shall act as President if no one has been officially elected President or Vice-President. This person will act as President until a President or Vice-President is officially elected.

Section 4 The Congress may by law provide for the case of the death of any of the persons from whom the House of Representatives may choose a President whenever the right of choice shall have devolved upon them, and for the case of the death of any of the persons from whom the Senate may choose a Vice-President whenever the right of choice shall have devolved upon them.

Congress has the power to make a law telling the House of Representatives what to do in case it must select a President and one of the candidates has died. Congress has the power to make a law that tells the Senate what to do in case it must select a Vice-President and one of the candidates has died.

Section 5 Sections 1 and 2 shall take effect on the fifteenth day of October following the ratification of this article.

Sections 1 and 2 of this amendment became law on October 15, 1933. Three-fourths of the states had to approve this amendment within seven years.

Amendment 21 (1933)
Repeal of Prohibition

Section 1 The eighteenth article of amendment to the Constitution of the United States is hereby repealed.

Section 2 The transportation or importation into any state, territory, or possession of the United States for delivery or use therein of intoxicating liquors, in violation of the laws thereof, is hereby prohibited.

Section 3 This article shall be inoperative unless it shall have been ratified as an amendment to the Constitution by conventions in the several states, as provided in the Constitution, within seven years from the date of the submission hereof to the states by the Congress.

This amendment repeals, or cancels, the Eighteenth Amendment. Prohibition is no longer a national law.

A state can forbid liquor for drinking purposes. Carrying liquor across state boundaries for use in a "dry" state is a crime against the United States as well as against the state.

Congress required this amendment to be ratified by assemblies especially elected for that purpose. They had to approve it within seven years. This is the only amendment so far to be ratified by conventions instead of by state legislatures.

Amendment 22 (1951)
Presidential Term of Office

Section 1 No person shall be elected to the office of the President more than twice, and no person who has held the office of President, or acted as President, for more than two years of a term to which some other person was elected President shall be elected to the office of the President more than once. ~~But this article shall not apply to any person holding the office of President when this article was proposed by the Congress, and shall not prevent any person who may be holding the office of President, or acting as President, during the term within which this article becomes operative from holding the office of President or acting as President during the remainder of such term.~~

Section 2 ~~This article shall be inoperative unless it shall have been ratified as an amendment to the Constitution by the legislatures of three-fourths of the several states within seven years from the date of its submission to the states by the Congress.~~

No person can have more than two terms as President. Holding the office of President, or acting as President, for more than two years will be considered as one full term.

Amendment 23 (1961)
Voting in the District of Columbia

Section 1 The district constituting the seat of government of the United States shall appoint in such manner as the Congress may direct:

A number of electors of President and Vice-President equal to the whole number of senators and representatives in Congress to which the District would be entitled if it were a state, but in no event more than the least populous state; they shall be in addition to those appointed by the states, but they shall be considered, for the purposes of the election of President and Vice-President, to be electors appointed by a state; and they shall meet in the district and perform such duties as provided by the twelfth article of amendment.

Section 2 The Congress shall have power to enforce this article by appropriate legislation.

The District of Columbia may choose electors in the election of the President and Vice-President. The number of electors is limited to no more than the number of electors from the state with the smallest population. The electors have to follow the rules for elections described in the Twelfth Amendment.

In 1980 the District's population was more than 637,000. The state with the smallest population was Alaska, with a little more than 400,000 people. Since Washington, D.C., can have no more electoral votes than the least populous state, it has the same number of votes as Alaska—three.

This amendment did not give the District a vote in Congress. Since 1971, Congress has allowed the District to send a non-voting representative to the House. This person is allowed to serve on committees and participate in debate, but is not allowed to vote.

Amendment 24 (1964)
Abolition of Poll Taxes

Section 1 The right of citizens of the United States to vote in any primary or other election for President or Vice-President, for electors for President or Vice-President, or for senator or representative in Congress, shall not be denied or abridged by the United States or any state by reason of failure to pay any poll tax or other tax.

Section 2 The Congress shall have power to enforce this article by appropriate legislation.

Neither the United States nor any state can make the payment of a **poll tax**, or a tax one must pay in order to vote, or any other tax a requirement for voting for federal officials. Both primary and general elections are covered. This rule applies to the election of the President and Vice-President, their electors, senators, and representatives in Congress.

A **primary election** is an election at which voters decide who their party's candidate will be. A **general election** is one at which the voters decide who will take office.

This amendment does not make poll taxes illegal in elections of state officials. However, as a practical matter, it makes them unlikely. If a state were to require a poll tax in state elections but not in federal elections, it would have to keep two different lists of voters and print two different kinds of ballots. This would be expensive and confusing.

Amendment 25 (1967)
Presidential Disability and Succession

Section 1 In case of the removal of the President from office or of his death or resignation, the Vice-President shall become President.

If the President dies or resigns, or is removed from office, the Vice-President becomes President.

Section 2 Whenever there is a vacancy in the office of the Vice-President, the President shall nominate a Vice-President who shall take office upon confirmation by a majority vote of both houses of Congress.

The President appoints a Vice-President if no one is serving in that office. The appointment must be approved by a majority vote in both houses.

Section 3 Whenever the President transmits to the president pro tempore of the Senate and the speaker of the House of Representatives his written declaration that he is unable to discharge the powers and duties of his office, and until he transmits to them a written declaration to the contrary, such powers and duties shall be discharged by the Vice-President as Acting President.

If the President notifies the Congress in writing that he or she is unable to perform official duties, the Vice-President takes over and serves as Acting President until the President is again able to serve.

Section 4 Whenever the Vice-President and a majority of either the principal officers of the executive departments or of such other body as Congress may by law provide, transmit to the president pro tempore of the Senate and the speaker of the House of Representatives their written declaration that the President is unable to discharge the powers and duties of his office, the Vice-President shall immediately assume the powers and duties of the office as Acting President.

Thereafter, when the President transmits to the president pro tempore of the Senate and the speaker of the House of Representatives his written declaration that no inability exists, he shall resume the powers and duties of his office unless the Vice-President and a majority of either the principal officers of the executive departments or of such other body as Congress may by law provide, transmit within four days to the president pro tempore of the Senate and the speaker of the House of Representatives their written declaration that the President is unable to discharge the powers and duties of his office. Thereupon Congress shall decide the issue, assembling within forty-eight hours for that purpose if not in session. If the Congress, within twenty-one days after receipt of the latter written declaration, or, if Congress is not in session, within twenty-one days after Congress is required to assemble, determines by two-thirds vote of both houses that the President is unable to discharge the powers and

duties of his office, the Vice-President shall continue to discharge the same as Acting President; otherwise, the President shall resume the duties of his office.

If a disabled President is unable or unwilling to notify Congress of his or her disability, the Vice-President may. In such a case, a majority of the Cabinet, or of some other group named by Congress, must agree. Upon making such a declaration, the Vice-President becomes Acting President.

When the President recovers from a disability, he or she may notify Congress of this recovery and resume the powers and duties of office. If the President's recovery appears doubtful, then the Vice-President may challenge the President's declaration. The Vice-President's challenge must be approved by a majority of the Cabinet or some other group designated by Congress. It must be sent to Congress before four days have passed. Congress must meet within forty-eight hours. Congress has 21 days to discuss the issue. If two-thirds or more of each house votes against the President, the Vice-President continues as Acting President. Otherwise, the President resumes office.

This amendment was put to use sooner than anyone had expected. In 1973 Vice-President Spiro Agnew resigned his office. Following the procedure outlined in Section 2, President Richard Nixon appointed Representative Gerald Ford of Michigan to the office of Vice-President. Congress confirmed the appointment in December, 1973.

In 1974 President Nixon, threatened with impeachment by Congress, resigned. Under the provisions of Section 1, Gerald Ford became President. Since the vice-presidency was again vacant, President Ford nominated former New York governor Nelson Rockefeller for the office. Congress confirmed the appointment in December, 1974. For the first time in our nation's history, neither the President nor the Vice-President had been elected to those offices.

Amendment 26 (1971)
Eighteen-Year-Old Vote

Section 1 The right of citizens of the United States, who are eighteen years of age or older, to vote shall not be denied or abridged by the United States or by any state on account of age.

Section 2 The Congress shall have power to enforce this article by appropriate legislation.

The United States and the state government cannot say that 18-year-olds are too young to vote. Congress can pass laws to enforce this amendment.

Chapter 5

Rights and Responsibilities of Citizenship

Introduction: The United States of America was born with a declaration of ideals concerning the rights of citizens. An **ideal** is a belief about the way something should be. Those who signed the Declaration of Independence in 1776 believed that government should protect the rights of citizens. They declared:

"We hold these truths to be self-evident: That all men are created equal; that they are endowed by their Creator with certain unalienable rights; that among these are life, liberty, and the pursuit of happiness.

"That to secure these rights, governments are instituted among men, deriving their just powers from the consent of the governed."

This then is the ideal: all American citizens should have an equal opportunity to enjoy certain rights. People are not born with the same abilities. However, it is hoped that all could have equal chances to develop their abilities. Laws and courts should treat everyone the same. People should each have an equal voice in the election of representatives in government.

Equality of opportunity and liberty did not exist for all Americans when the Declaration of Independence was written. Yet these ideals have influenced the thoughts and actions of Americans from 1776 until the present. The history of the nation has been marked by progress in the achievement of citizens' rights under the Constitution.

One purpose of this chapter is to show how the Constitution has been changed, or amended, to extend the rights of citizens. A second purpose is to teach about the responsibilities citizens must have if they are to preserve their rights under the Constitution.

A rally in Sacramento, California, held to protest educational budget cuts. Organized, peaceful protests can often encourage governments to change unpopular laws or decisions.

Section 1
Citizens' Rights and Liberties

Civil rights and liberties are freedoms guaranteed to United States citizens. They are spelled out in the main body of the Constitution and in the amendments.

Civil Rights and Liberties in the Main Body of the Constitution

Certain rights and liberties of citizens are protected in Article 1, Section 9, of the Constitution. For example, Congress does not have the power to suspend "the privilege of the writ of *habeas corpus . . .* unless when in cases of rebellion or invasion the public safety may require it." A **writ** is an order in writing, from a court of law, that requires the performance of a specific act. A **writ of *habeas corpus*** means that a person who has been accused of a crime has the right to appear before a judge in a court of law. The officials who are holding the person must convince the judge that there are lawful reasons for holding him or her. If the reasons for holding the accused person are not lawful, then the court must free that person.

Article 1, Section 9, also says that "No bill of attainder or *ex post facto* law shall be passed."

A **bill of attainder** is a law that punishes a person without a trial or fair hearing in a court of law. The person "attained," or punished, by legislative act could be forced by law

First Amendment Rights

Freedom of Religion

Freedom of the Press

Right to Petition Government

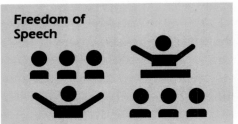

Freedom of Speech

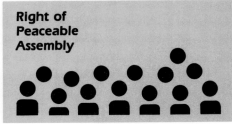

Right of Peaceable Assembly

How does this chart help to explain the First Amendment?

(the bill of attainder) to forfeit property, income, or employment. This would be a way for government officials to punish individuals who criticize them or who belong to an unpopular group. The United States Constitution protects individual rights and freedoms by denying to the government the power to pass a bill of attainder.

An *ex post facto* **law** would make punishable an action committed before a law prohibiting that action was passed. The Constitution protects individuals by denying to the government the power to punish them unfairly through the passage of *ex post facto* laws.

Another example of a legal right or freedom is in Article 6: "No religious test shall ever be required as a qualification to any office or public trust under the United States." This means that a person can hold a public office even if he or she holds unpopular religious beliefs, or expresses no interest in religion.

The Bill of Rights

Citizens primarily have amended the Constitution to expand their civil rights and liberties by limiting the power of the national government. The first ten amendments were added in 1791, only three years after the Constitution was ratified. These are called the **Bill of Rights.** They have been a symbol of freedom to Americans and to many others around the world.

The First Amendment. The First Amendment protects our freedom of speech. It says the government cannot make laws that stop people from speaking and writing their ideas. People have the right to criticize government decisions. If they believe that the President is doing a poor job, they are free to say so in speeches and in newspapers, books, and magazines. If citizens have ideas about how to improve their government, they may express their opinion to others, including government officials.

Freedom of speech and the press do *not* mean that people can say absolutely anything they want to, anywhere they want to. Courts have decided that if you print lies that damage a person's business or reputation, you can be sued for **libel** and made to pay for damages. Also, people cannot make speeches or print papers that urge the violent overthrow of government. You do not have the right to shout "fire!" in a crowded theater just to see what happens. People cannot abuse freedom of speech. Freedoms must be used responsibly.

The Second Amendment. The Second Amendment gives citizens the right to bear arms. The government cannot pass a law that stops people from having weapons. It can, however, restrict the possession of particular weapons. For example, it is against the law to own sawed-off shotguns. States are also free to regulate the use and sale of guns.

The Third Amendment. This amendment says that the government cannot force citizens to let soldiers live in their homes unless the country is at war. Even then, Congress must make a special law telling exactly how soldiers may or may not use the homes of citizens.

The Fourth Amendment. The Fourth Amendment gives citizens the right to privacy. A person's property cannot be seized. His or her house cannot be searched.

However, courts can issue a **search warrant** that allows police officers to enter a home when there is good reason to believe they will find evidence about a crime. The purpose of this legal kind of search is to prevent evidence of a crime from being removed or destroyed.

The Fifth Amendment. This amendment gives protection to people accused of crimes. First, a **grand jury** must decide that there is enough evidence against a person before he or she can be tried for a serious crime in federal court. (This right does not apply to members of the armed forces in times of war or public danger.) Also, the Fifth Amendment says a person found *not guilty* of a certain crime cannot be tried again for the same crime. Further, people can refuse to give evidence in court that could be used against them. And, the government cannot take away someone's life, freedom, or property without **due process** of law. This means government officials must deal with people according to law.

The Sixth Amendment. According to this amendment, people accused of crimes have the right to a prompt, public trial by jury. Accused persons have the right to be defended by a lawyer. They must be present when accused of a crime and when evidence is given against them. This amendment applies to federal courts, but the Fourteenth Amendment has made parts of it apply to state courts.

Serving a search warrant.

103

The Seventh Amendment. This amendment gives people the right to a trial by jury to settle conflicts over property rights. However, if both parties to the conflict agree, a judge may decide the case without a jury.

The Eighth Amendment. Courts cannot require an unusually high **bail,** according to the Eighth Amendment. Bail is the money or property that an accused person gives the court so that he or she may stay out of jail until the trial. The bail is a guarantee that the person will appear at the trial. After the trial, the money or property is returned. Fines and punishments, too, cannot be cruel or unusual.

The Ninth Amendment. According to this amendment, the civil rights stated in the Constitution are not the only rights that people have. And they are not necessarily the most important rights. This amendment recognizes the many other civil rights and liberties in state constitutions, state laws, and local laws.

The Tenth Amendment. The last amendment in the Bill of Rights says that if the Constitution does not give a certain power to the national government, then that power belongs to the states. For example, the Constitution does not give the power to make rules about marriage and divorce to the national government. The Constitution also does not say the states cannot have this power. Thus, according to the Tenth Amendment, the state governments may have it. Other examples of

A *Harper's Weekly* cover showing black voters at the polls. The Fifteenth Amendment gave blacks the right to vote.

powers "reserved to the states" are making rules about the establishment of schools, holding public elections for state and local offices, granting hunting and driving licenses, and many others.

Increasing Our Rights

Many of the amendments that have been made since 1791 have increased the rights or freedoms of citizens in one way or another. These amendments may be thought of as additions to the Bill of Rights.

The Thirteenth, Fourteenth, and Fifteenth amendments were made at the end of the Civil War to extend rights and liberties to blacks.

The Thirteenth Amendment. This amendment was passed in 1865. It ended slavery in the United States and lands controlled by it.

The Fourteenth Amendment. Passed in 1868, this amendment protects the rights of citizenship. A person is both a citizen of the state in which he or she lives and of the United States. No state government can take away any civil rights or liberties that belong to a citizen of the United States. All citizens have the right to equal protection of the law in all states.

The Fifteenth Amendment. This amendment, passed in 1870, says that no state may take away a person's right to vote on the basis of race or color.

The Seventeenth Amendment. Passed in 1913, this amendment says that senators shall be elected from each state by eligible voters from that state. Before this amendment, members of state legislatures, rather than eligible voters, picked the senators.

Four amendments passed in this century give more people the right to vote.

The Nineteenth Amendment. This amendment, passed in 1920, gave women the right to vote.

The Twenty-Third Amendment. Passed in 1961, the Twenty-Third Amendment says that residents of the District of Columbia may take part in the election of the President and Vice-President.

The Twenty-Fourth Amendment. Passed in 1964, this amendment says that payment of a **poll tax** may not be a requirement for voting. Thus, poor people cannot be kept from voting by making them pay a tax in order to vote.

The Twenty-Sixth Amendment. This amendment, passed in 1971, lowered the voting age to eighteen.

Section Review

Vocabulary:
bail, bill of attainder, Bill of Rights, due process, *ex post facto* law, grand jury, libel, poll tax, search warrant, writ, writ of *habeas corpus.*

(right, top) Suffragists demonstrating in 1919, one year before passage of the Nineteenth Amendment. (right) Young voters in Austin, Texas.

Reviewing the Main Ideas
1. Which amendments are part of the Bill of Rights?
2. Give at least five examples of civil rights or liberties protected by the Bill of Rights.
3. What rights are extended to citizens in the Thirteenth, Fourteenth, and Fifteenth amendments?

Skill Building
Read the Nineteenth Amendment. What is the main idea of this amendment?

Your Right to Free Speech

In the United States, the government is not supposed to take away a person's right to express ideas. The First Amendment says: "Congress shall make no law . . . abridging the freedom of speech. . . ." Each state constitution has a similar guarantee of free speech. Furthermore, guarantees of "liberty" and "due process of law" in the Fifth and Fourteenth amendments to the Constitution have been used to support the right of free speech against restrictions by state governments.

How Do Americans Use Free Speech?

Each person has an equal right to free speech. This right includes both popular and unpopular ideas. It applies to both wise and foolish statements. The right of free speech permits Americans to criticize government officials.

The constitutional right to free speech allows people in the United States to express different opinions in conversations, meetings, or public speeches to large groups. Both face-to-face discussions and broadcasts via radio and TV are covered by the guarantee of free speech.

The right to free speech means that a person may express views thought to be wrong by the majority of people. Thus, new ways of thinking or acting may be expressed in public. Some unpopular ideas may eventually prove to be acceptable to the majority of Americans.

Justice Louis Brandeis [bran'dīs], who served on the Supreme Court from 1916 to 1939, said that "freedom to think as you will and to speak as you think are means indispensable to the discovery and spread of political truth."

Justice Oliver Wendell Holmes, who served on the Supreme Court with Brandeis, also believed that the free exchange of ideas was necessary to the discovery of the truth. He said that "the best test of truth is the power of the thought to get itself accepted in the competition of the market," where opinions may be discussed freely.

What Are the Limits to Free Speech?

By and large, Americans are free to say what they want, where and when they want to say it. However, the courts have decided that the right to free speech has limits.

You are not free to ruin another person's reputation by spreading lies about him or her. If you do this, the offended person may seek compensation by suing you in a court of law. You do not have freedom, under the Constitution, to provoke a riot or other violent behavior. You are not free to speak or write in a way that injures other people or their property, that undermines public standards of right and wrong, that leads to criminal activities, or that calls for actions to overthrow the government by force.

Supreme Court Justice Edward Sanford described limits to free speech. In 1925, he wrote that the First Amendment does not protect "those who abuse this freedom by utterances inimical [harmful] to the public welfare, tending to corrupt public morals, incite to crime or disturb the public peace. . . ."

Citizens should use their freedom of speech responsibly, which means they should not interfere with the rights of others. For example, citizens may talk freely to others in the street, but they may not talk at a time or place that would block traffic. Citizens may criticize government officials in public, but they may not disrupt the operation of government. Citizens have the right to speak in favor of candidates for election to public office, but they may not use a loudspeaker to broadcast campaign messages so loudly that residents of a community are disturbed.

Disagreements About Free Speech

Americans believe strongly in free speech. They occasionally argue, however, about when and why this right should be limited. "All declare for liberty, and proceed to disagree among themselves as to its true meaning," wrote Justice Stanley Forman in 1951.

Sometimes it is very difficult to decide whether a person has exceeded the limits of free speech. For example, legal experts have argued about whether expression of certain ideas is harmful to the public or dangerous to the interests of the nation. In times of emergency, such as a war, people have often criticized laws made to limit speech critical of the government.

In general, judges try to weigh the interests of the community against the rights of the individual when making decisions about limits to free speech. They seek to balance a person's right to speak freely with the community's needs for order, stability, and safety. Deciding exactly how to balance an individual's rights with community needs is very difficult. It is possible for people with good intentions and vast knowledge to disagree about these decisions.

The Importance of Free Speech

Free speech is a precious constitutional right that is denied to many people of the world. In countries with communist governments, such as the Soviet Union and Cuba, people may not speak in public against their leaders. They are not free to oppose the ideas of the Communist party. There are also many non-Communist dictatorships where free speech is not allowed.

Most Americans believe that free speech is necessary for effective self-government. In 1948, Supreme Court Justice William O. Douglas explained that "it is only through free debate and free exchange of ideas that government remains responsive to the will of the people. . . . The right to speak freely and promote diversity of ideas and programs is therefore one of the chief distinctions that sets us apart from totalitarian regimes."

Review

1. Why is it sometimes difficult to decide whether a person has exceeded the limits of free speech?
2. What is the judge's role when making decisions about limits to free speech?

What statement is the cartoonist trying to make?

An overcrowded, segregated school in Tennessee in the 1940s.

Section 2
The Civil Rights Movement

For many years, black Americans were denied constitutional rights enjoyed by others in the United States. Until the end of the Civil War in 1865, most black Americans were slaves. Afterwards, they endured customs and laws that kept them from having the same opportunities and freedoms that most other Americans had. Black Americans, for example, were often kept from voting or running for public office. In some states, mostly in the South, they had to use separate and inferior public facilities. They were forced to go to separate schools, to use separate washrooms and drinking fountains, and to sit in separate cars on trains or in seats at the backs of buses. Blacks usually were not permitted to stay in hotels or eat in restaurants that served whites.

The social separation of blacks and whites was known as **segregation.** It meant that black citizens did not have rights and liberties equal to those of white citizens. In effect, blacks were forced, by traditions and laws, to be "second-class citizens."

Origins of the Civil Rights Movement

In 1909, a group of black and white Americans organized the National Association for the Advancement of Colored People (NAACP). The association was formed as a means to oppose laws and customs that denied constitutional rights and liberties to black Americans. In 1910, another group of concerned citizens formed the National Urban League, an organization that helps urban blacks find jobs and improve their opportunities to get ahead.

The NAACP and the Urban League are key organizations within the civil rights movement. Both organizations have long worked to remove blacks from "second-class citizenship status."

Gaining recognition and support for the aims of these two groups did not come overnight. At first, they had little success in their battle against segregation. Gradually, however, a small group of civil rights leaders built a movement involving millions of supporters.

A big gain for the civil rights movement came in 1948, when President Harry Truman ordered an end to segregation in the nation's armed forces. A bigger victory was won in 1954, when NAACP lawyers argued before the Supreme Court that segregation of blacks from whites in public schools was a violation of the Constitution. The Supreme Court agreed with the NAACP. Thus, a process was begun to provide equal opportunities in education to all citizens, black and white. (See the Case Study, *Brown* v. *Board of Education,* on page 116.)

The Leadership of Martin Luther King, Jr.

Martin Luther King, Jr., became one of the main leaders of the civil rights movement during the 1950s. He was a Baptist minister who had

earned a doctoral degree in theology at Boston University. King believed in peaceful protest as a way to change laws and customs that were unfair to blacks.

King became famous in 1955 as leader of a bus **boycott** in Montgomery, Alabama. (A boycott is the act of collectively refusing to buy or use the services or goods of a government or company.) The boycott started when a black woman, Rosa Parks, was arrested. Her "crime" was only that she said "no" when ordered to give up her seat on a bus to a white person. Blacks in Montgomery reacted by boycotting, or refusing to use, the buses in Montgomery. The bus company soon ran into financial difficulty—most of its riders were black. Meanwhile, King demanded an end to unfair treat-

ment of blacks by the bus company. The bus boycott ended after the Supreme Court ruled against the Alabama law that allowed segregation on buses.

After the victory in Montgomery, blacks across the nation turned to King for leadership in their efforts to achieve equality before the law. In 1957, King organized the Southern Christian Leadership Conference (SCLC) to support his civil rights activities. During the next few years, King led hundreds of peaceful protest demonstrations to win civil rights for all Americans.

On August 28, 1963, King spoke to more than 250,000 people at the Lincoln Memorial in Washington, D.C. These black and white Americans were taking part in the largest peaceful protest activity of the civil

(above, left) Members of an all-black air force unit. Segregation in the armed forces was ended in 1948. (above) Rosa Parks. Her refusal to give up her bus seat to a white was instrumental in rallying many people all over the nation to the civil rights cause.

Martin Luther King, Jr., addressing the more than 250,000 people who came to Washington, D.C. in 1963 to peacefully protest segregation laws.

rights movement. It was called "The March on Washington."

Martin Luther King called upon the federal government to ban the remaining segregation laws in the United States. He said:

"Five score years ago, a great American in whose symbolic shadow we stand, signed the Emancipation Proclamation. This momentous decree came as a great beacon light of hope to millions of Negro slaves who had been seared in the flames of withering injustice. It came as a joyous daybreak to end the long night of captivity.

"But one hundred years later, we must face the tragic fact that the Negro is still not free. One hundred years later, the life of the Negro is still sadly crippled by the manacles of segregation and the chains of discrimination. One hundred years later, the Negro lives on a lonely island of poverty in the midst of a vast ocean of material prosperity.

One hundred years later, the Negro is still languished in the corners of American society and finds himself an exile in his own land. So we have come here today to dramatize an appalling condition. . . . in spite of the difficulties and frustrations of the moment I still have a dream. It is a dream deeply rooted in the American dream.

"I have a dream that one day this nation will rise up and live out the true meaning of the creed: 'We hold these truths to be self-evident; that all men are created equal.' I have a dream that one day on the red hills of Georgia the sons of former slaves and the sons of former slaveowners will be able to sit down together at the table of brotherhood.

"I have a dream that my four little children will one day live in a nation where they will not be judged by the color of their skin but by the content of their character. . . ."

Congress and President Lyndon Johnson responded to the civil rights movement by passing the Civil Rights Act of 1964 and the Voting Rights Act of 1965. These laws gave blacks many of the rights King and others had been working for.

Martin Luther King was awarded the Nobel Peace Prize in 1965 in recognition of his leadership in the civil rights movement. King's triumph was followed in 1968 by the tragedy of his death at the age of thirty-nine. King was shot and killed in Memphis, Tennessee.

In 1983, Congress voted to honor the memory of Martin Luther King, Jr., with a national holiday in his name. He became the only American other than George

More Graduates

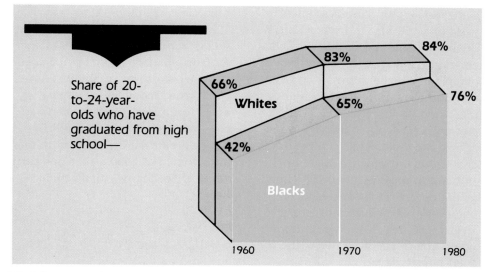

Share of 20-to-24-year-olds who have graduated from high school—

Whites
66% → 83% → 84%

Blacks
42% → 65% → 76%

1960   1970   1980

What conclusions can you draw from the graph?

Washington to be recognized in this way. Starting in 1986, the third Monday of January will be a holiday for all federal workers.

Achievements of the Civil Rights Movement

The primary achievement of the civil rights movement was to overturn segregation laws. Valuable new opportunities were opened to blacks in education, government, and private employment.

In 1960, only 42 percent of blacks, age 20–24, had graduated from high school. By 1981, the percentage had risen to 76. From 1960 to 1980, the number of black Americans in colleges or universities had increased by more than five times.

Black citizens made striking gains in their participation in government. By the 1980s, black public officials were prominent in many local and state governments across the nation. In 1984, eleven cities with populations of more than 200,000 were led by black mayors. Also in 1984, Jesse Jackson became the second black leader to seek the nomination for President via a major political party. Shirley Chisholm was the first in 1972.

By the 1980s, many black men and women had moved into jobs that provided prestige and higher incomes. Compared to 1960, there were twice as many blacks in professional and managerial jobs such as lawyer, medical doctor, engineer, and educator.

Jesse Jackson.

111

Ongoing Challenges

Various civil rights leaders and organizations have continued their work to fulfill Martin Luther King's dream of equal opportunity for all citizens. On August 28, 1983, they organized a celebration of the twentieth anniversary of the civil rights march on Washington, D.C. They met at the Lincoln Memorial to recognize the great achievements of the civil rights movement. They also pointed to ongoing challenges such as the need for jobs and higher incomes for many black Americans. In 1983, more than 30 percent of non-white Americans lived below the official poverty level.

President Ronald Reagan noted the progress of the civil rights movement and also the continuing challenges facing Americans who want equal rights for all citizens. The President made this statement on the twentieth anniversary of the "I Have a Dream" speech of Martin Luther King:

"But much remains to be done. America, mankind's last, best hope for freedom, is a special place, a place where so many dreams have come true. Today let us resolve anew to do everything we can in our time to continue to fulfill Dr. King's dream—a dream that all men and women of good will, black and white alike, share with all their hearts."

President Reagan discussing issues such as civil rights with students who were involved in a week-long program dealing with the government process.

Section Review

Vocabulary:
boycott, segregation.

Reviewing the Main Ideas

1. Name three forms of segregation endured by black Americans before the passage of civil-rights laws in the mid-1960s.

2. What is meant by the term "second-class citizenship"?

3. Describe Martin Luther King's methods for changing laws and customs that were unfair to black citizens.

Skill Building

1. Look at the graph on page 111. Write a paragraph summarizing the statistics shown.

2. Use an encyclopedia to find information about the civil rights movement. Write a brief report about your findings.

Section 3
Citizens' Responsibilities

Citizens of the United States have many rights. Citizens who want to keep these rights must assume the duty, or **responsibility,** for preserving, protecting, and defending them. They must act to preserve the Constitution.

Responsibilities of Knowing and Respecting the Law. The first duty of citizens is to respect and obey their laws. There can be no peace, cooperation, or progress where there is no **respect,** or high regard, for law.

Three main duties of citizenship are (1) to pay taxes for the services of government, (2) to serve, if called, as a member of a jury, and (3) to testify in a court of law if called as a witness.

Knowing About Rights. Citizens should also try to be informed. People who are ignorant of their rights are in a poor position to use or defend these rights. Part of being a good citizen is learning about the freedoms and rights provided by our federal, state, and local laws.

Citizens should know how their governments work and how public officials make decisions that affect them. They need to know how to use government and laws so as not to lose the benefits they deserve. Citizens should also keep informed by reading about proposed laws and Supreme Court decisions.

Respecting the Civil Rights of Others. You must respect the rights of others if you want to enjoy your

Can you think of other responsibilities that you could add to this chart?

Responsibilities of Citizenship

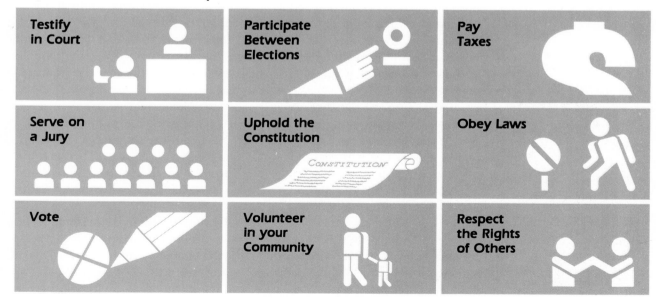

Testify in Court

Participate Between Elections

Pay Taxes

Serve on a Jury

Uphold the Constitution

Obey Laws

Vote

Volunteer in your Community

Respect the Rights of Others

own rights fully. By treating others with respect, you help create a climate of good feeling and cooperation. You also encourage others to treat you with respect.

If you want to respect the rights of others, you should remember this basic rule: Your freedom ends where the other person's freedom begins. For instance, your neighbor has the right to keep a dog as a pet. But she also has the duty of making sure her dog does not damage other people's property. Suppose her dog digs holes in your garden and barks all afternoon. Her right to a pet ends where your property rights begin. It is her duty to stop her dog from damaging your yard. Her right to a pet ends where your rights to peace and quiet begin. She has the duty to keep her dog from barking.

Our government has many laws that reduce areas of conflict. For example, many cities have a law that dogs must be leashed when outside. This is partly a health and safety measure. It is also aimed at reducing conflict when a pet becomes a nuisance to others. In the case of dog ownership, respecting the rights of others involves obeying the laws on dog ownership.

Respecting the rights of others means obeying the traffic laws that were passed to safeguard the rights of all highway users. It also means obeying a no-talking rule in study hall so that the rights of those who want to study are respected.

Acting to Defend Civil Rights and Liberties. Responsible citizenship in some countries involves only being obedient. The rulers expect passive followers who do not question their decisions.

Much more is expected of a responsible citizen in the United States. Of course, citizens are expected to obey laws and to respect leaders. They are also expected to think for themselves and to question what their leaders tell them.

In his Gettysburg Address in 1863, Abraham Lincoln said that we should preserve "government of the people, by the people, for the people." (The Gettysburg Address is in the Students' Resource Section of this text.) Citizens who rule themselves must be able to make their own decisions. They must know how to form their own opinions about their representatives in government.

In the United States, citizens have the right to speak freely against government actions they consider wrong or unwise. They can also defend the civil rights and liberties of citizens against government officials or others who might try to abuse them. It is not always easy for citizens to speak out and fight for their rights. Sometimes other people will try to punish them for their particular beliefs.

If citizens fail to use their legal rights, they risk losing them. Thus, citizens of the United States should be ready and willing to preserve, protect, and defend the Constitution —the legal source of citizens' rights.

Responsibilities to Participate in Civic Life. Choosing the leaders of government by voting is a basic right of citizens. Citizens who take the time to vote for good leaders may be rewarded with good government. A position in government carries much power. It is important to give this power wisely. Citizens should try to elect people who will serve the public interest.

Bad government often results when citizens do not bother to vote or when they vote without first finding out the strengths and weaknesses of the candidates. Citizens of the United States should be thoughtful voters in public elections.

Participating Between Elections. Citizens should try to influence government between elections as well as during elections. Leaders are more likely to respond to public needs if people are checking on their work between elections. Law makers need to know the views of the people they represent. Citizens of the United States should be as involved as possible in politics. One way of doing this is to be active in a political party or in a group that serves a citizen's interests.

Acting for the Good of the Community. Responsible citizens think about others as well as themselves. They are willing to give time, effort, and money to help others and to improve their own communities. They may volunteer their spare time to help needy people or to remove litter from public places. They may donate money to various charities.

The Citizens Committee for New York City is just one example among many groups of **volunteers** who help handicapped people, improve services in schools, libraries, and hospitals, and clean up parks.

Members of a volunteer fire department. Many small communities rely totally on volunteers to fight fires.

Section Review

Vocabulary:
respect, responsibility, volunteer.

Reviewing the Main Ideas
1. Why is it important for citizens to know about their rights?
2. What rule helps you balance your own rights with the rights of others?
3. Why should citizens take part in elections?
4. Name some ways in which citizens can be involved in civic activities between elections.

Skill Building
What does responsible citizenship mean to different people? You can find out by asking them. Interview at least five people to find out what their ideal of a good citizen is. Ask each person: What is your definition of responsible citizenship? Then write a report telling (1) what the people you interviewed said, and (2) your opinions of what they said.

115

★ ★

Case Study

Brown v. Board of Education

Brown v. *Board of Education of Topeka, Kansas,* is one of the most important Supreme Court decisions in this century. It overturned an earlier Supreme Court ruling and was a victory for black Americans.

In the late 1800s, about half the states passed laws that kept nonwhite people separate from white people in such public places as trains and theaters. A group of blacks formed a committee to test the constitutionality of these laws in the courts. In 1892, a member of the committee, Homer Plessy, was arrested for refusing to move to a railroad car for blacks only. He was convicted, and eventually his case reached the Supreme Court.

In 1896, the court announced its decision in *Plessy* v. *Ferguson.* It said that as long as the separate facilities for blacks were equal to the ones for whites, the Fourteenth Amendment was not violated.

After that, more segregation laws were passed. Blacks could not use the same schools, restaurants, telephone booths, and drinking fountains as whites. In one state, courtrooms had a separate Bible for blacks. These laws also kept American Indians and people of Mexican, Japanese, and Chinese descent from using facilities for whites.

There was no real challenge to the Plessy decision for forty years, even though in most cases the separate facilities for nonwhites were clearly not equal to those for whites.

In the late 1930s and early 1940s, the Supreme Court made some rulings requiring the separate facilities to be equal. Several states spent large amounts of money to improve the schools and universities for blacks. In 1954, Georgia spent $27.4 million of its $102 million school budget on its black schools.

(right) Linda Brown.
(far right) Thurgood Marshall, the main lawyer for the NAACP, congratulating two other lawyers on their victory in *Brown v. Board of Education.*

Some black schools became excellent places to get an education. However, very few Americans would have agreed that most black schools were equal to those for whites.

By 1950, seventeen states still had segregation laws. The National Association for the Advancement of Colored People (NAACP) began raising money and providing lawyers to fight these laws in court. Late in 1952, the Supreme Court agreed to hear five cases together. In each, black parents had sued a school district to let their children attend white schools. The cases came from district courts in Delaware, Kansas, South Carolina, Virginia, and Washington, D.C. Because Oliver Brown, father of eight-year-old Linda Brown, had the first name in the alphabetical listing of people who were suing the five school districts, the case now bears his name.

The lawyers who argued the case were highly respected men. The main lawyer for the NAACP was Thurgood Marshall, who later became a Supreme Court justice. He argued that separate schools could never be equal. There were many experts whose testimony was part of the **brief** he had given the Court. (A brief is a statement of the facts and the points of law of a case to be pleaded in court.) Marshall's brief showed that it hurt black children to keep them apart from whites.

On the other side was John W. Davis. He had been United States ambassador to Britain and the Democratic candidate for President in 1924. He said that the Supreme Court would be stepping into an area that should be decided by Congress or the state legislatures if it changed the segregation laws. The Supreme Court should not be in the business of drastically altering society, he argued.

The arguments ended on December 11, 1952. However, by June, when the Court recessed, no decision had been made. The Court said it would hear more testimony in fall.

All summer, the two sides prepared their new arguments. In addition, the Supreme Court invited the Department of Justice to give an opinion. The last testimony was heard on December 9, 1953.

The writing of the **opinion** took five months. An opinion is a statement by a judge of the reasons for the decision of the Court. On May 17, 1954, Chief Justice Earl Warren, speaking for the Court, handed down its unanimous opinion in the case of *Brown* v. *Board of Education of Topeka, Kansas*. It said in part:

"In the field of public education, the doctrine of 'separate but equal' has no place. Separate educational facilities are inherently unequal."

Review

1. What was the occasion for decision in this case?
2. What alternatives did the Court have?
3. What was Marshall's main argument? Davis's argument?
4. Do you agree with the Court's decision? Give your reasons.

Basic Social Studies Skills
Reading Graphs

Graphs, like tables, enable us to communicate detailed information in compact, easy-to-read formats. Two of the most commonly used graphs—line, and bar—are shown below.

Line graphs and **bar graphs** serve similar functions. They are both perfect for showing changes or trends that occur over periods of time. Either a line graph or a bar graph, for example, would be ideal for showing the win-loss record of a baseball team over a given number of seasons.

Study the graphs below and then answer the questions.

Skill Practice

1. During which two two-year periods did the number of registered black voters decrease?

2. Which state had less than ten percent of its black voting-age population registered in 1965 but almost sixty percent in 1967?

Number of Registered Black Voters 1966-1982

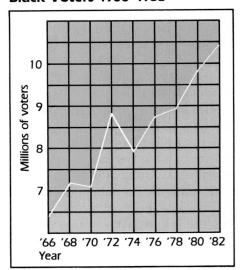

Effect of Voting Rights Act on Registration of Blacks in Four States

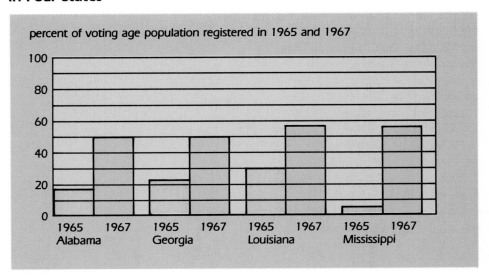

percent of voting age population registered in 1965 and 1967

Chapter 5 Review

Summary

Section 1: Citizens' Rights and Liberties

Civil rights and liberties are guaranteed in the Constitution. They are spelled out in the Bill of Rights and other amendments.

Section 2: The Civil Rights Movement

The civil rights movement opposed segregation laws that prevented blacks from enjoying the legal rights granted to all citizens of the United States. A great victory was in 1954. In *Brown* v. *Board of Education*, the Supreme Court decided that segregation of blacks from whites in public school is unlawful. In the 1950s and 1960s, Martin Luther King, Jr., emerged as one of the most powerful leaders of the civil rights movement. His peaceful, but forceful, influence helped bring about the passage of civil rights laws such as the Civil Rights Act of 1964 and the Voting Rights Act of 1965.

Section 3: Citizens' Responsibilities

Enjoyment of civil rights and liberties involves certain responsibilities. Citizens must not misuse their rights to trample upon the liberties of others. They should be ready and willing to participate in public activities to support their local, state, and national governments and to try to change these governments when they believe it is necessary. They should assume responsibilities to act for the good of their community. Finally, citizens have the responsibility to know and respect the law. In particular, they should act to preserve the Constitution, which is the legal source of citizens' rights and liberties.

Vocabulary

Define the following terms.

1. search warrant
2. libel
3. writ
4. Bill of Rights
5. bill of attainder
6. respect

Reviewing Main Ideas

1. True or false: A main purpose of the Bill of Rights is to protect your rights and liberties.

2. Each of the following is a guarantee of the First Amendment except

a. to be able to organize parades

b. to be able to establish schools

c. to be able to speak and write ideas

d. to be able to choose any religion

3. True or false: The Second Amendment gives a person the right to have a gun.

4. True or false: The Ninth Amendment guarantees that once found innocent you cannot be tried again for the same crime.

5. True or false: The Fourth Amendment says that your house cannot be searched without a warrant.

Thinking Critically

Finding Information

1. Find the Declaration of Independence in this book. On what page does it begin?

2. Find the Bill of Rights in this book. On what page does it begin?

Comprehending Information

Which document, the Declaration of Independence or the Bill of Rights, gives the basic freedoms the United States government guarantees to its citizens?

Communicating Ideas

Write a paragraph explaining the main ideas of this chapter. Use at least five of the words from the Vocabulary. Underline each vocabulary word that you use.

Unit Two Test

Vocabulary

Write *true* if the underlined word or phrase is used correctly. Write *false* if it is used incorrectly. Rephrase each false statement so that the underlined word or phrase is used correctly.

1. The <u>Federalists</u> wanted a strong central government, so they supported the Constitution.

2. The <u>Anti-Federalists</u> wanted a strong central government, so they supported the Constitution.

3. Changes made in laws are called <u>amendments</u>.

4. A <u>unitary government</u> is one in which powers are shared equally by federal and state governments.

5. The branch of government that makes laws is the <u>judicial branch</u>.

6. The branch of government that includes the federal courts is the <u>legislative branch</u>.

7. The branch of government that includes the President is the <u>executive branch</u>.

8. A <u>delegate</u> is a representative at a convention.

9. To <u>veto</u> a bill means to accept and sign it.

10. To gain entrance to someone's home, police must have a <u>writ of *habeas corpus*</u>.

11. A <u>bill of attainder</u> refers to a law that punishes a person without a trial or fair hearing in a court of law.

12. <u>Domestic tranquility</u> refers to peaceful life in all the states.

13. A <u>unanimous</u> vote means that everyone agrees.

14. To <u>ratify</u> a bill means to reject it.

15. <u>Bail</u> is money left with a court as a guarantee that a person will appear for trial.

Recalling Information

1. What rights can citizens of the United States expect their government to protect?
a. the right to help choose leaders
b. the right to live wherever they want
c. the right to be treated according to the laws
d. *a* and *c*

2. What responsibilities do citizens have toward the United States?
a. to be loyal
b. to uphold the laws
c. to vote wisely
d. all of the above

3. In 1787, leaders in the states wanted a convention to improve the Articles of Confederation because
a. the national government did not have the power to settle conflicts between states
b. the country had severe money problems and the national government did not have the power to solve them
c. there were disorders and riots in several states
d. all of the above

4. At the Constitutional Convention, the delegates decided to _____ the Articles of Confederation.
a. revise   **c.** ratify
b. throw out   **d.** approve

5. The Great Compromise settled an argument about
a. how much power the President should have
b. how many district courts there should be
c. how many legislators each state would have
d. what to do about a bill of rights

6. President Washington decided to put down the Whiskey Rebellion with force because
a. he wanted to show that the new government could enforce its laws
b. he wanted western Pennsylvania to separate from the United States
c. he was an Anti-Federalist
d. all of the above

7. True or false: The words "We the People" in the Preamble to the Constitution are important because they show that the government's authority comes from the people.

Skill Building
Below are some rights guaranteed by the Constitution. Following is a list of cases involving these rights. For each case, give the letter or letters of the rights involved.
a. freedom of speech
b. freedom of religion
c. freedom of the press
d. right of assembly and to petition government
e. right to keep and bear arms
f. protection from illegal searches and seizures
g. right to a grand jury hearing before being charged with a serious federal crime
h. once found innocent of a charge, protection from being tried again
i. protection from being required to testify against oneself
j. right to due process of the laws
k. right to know charges against oneself and to question the witnesses in court

l. right to a lawyer
m. protection from excessive bail
n. protection from cruel and unusual punishments

1. George Chow is tried and found innocent of the murder of his uncle. A year later, an eyewitness is found who agrees, finally, to swear in court that he saw George shoot the uncle. Can George be tried again?

2. Nancy Washington read in the paper that a man being questioned by a Senate investigating committee refused to answer when asked if he was connected with organized crime. Can he get away with this?

3. The leader of a gang suspected of bombing an airport was arrested. For three days she was questioned by the police. They did not let her call a lawyer because they said they weren't formally charging her, they were just questioning her. At the end of three days, she confessed. Then she was charged with a federal offense and bail was set at $3 million.

4. A certain state senator voted to spend government money because he had been bribed by a manufacturer who was sure to get much business from the vote. A group of citizens learned of the bribe and called a meeting to decide what to do. The senator phoned his friend the governor to call out the National Guard. The Guard broke up the meeting and arrested the leaders.

Unit 3
Making Decisions in the National Government

In 1787, when the Constitution was written, there were fewer than 4 million people in the United States. The government that was set up after the Constitution had been ratified was small. President Washington had only 780 people working for him in the executive branch in 1790. There were only 26 senators and 64 representatives.

In addition to being small in size, the national government was "small" in power during its first years. Problems that had to be dealt with by government were most often handled by state and local governments.

Today the national picture has changed. Currently, there are about a quarter of a billion people in the United States. They live very differently from the way people lived in the late 1700s. The problems people have in one part of the country are often tied to the problems people have in other parts of the country. Thus, the national government has taken on a larger role.

The rules laid down in the Constitution have allowed the national government to change as the nation as a whole has changed. Most noticeably, the national government has grown. Today, there are close to 3 million people working in the national government. In addition, rules and programs created by the national government touch many more areas of life than they once did.

You'll learn the details of how the national government is organized, and you'll learn more about the work it does today in this unit.

The United States Capitol decorated for the inauguration of President Ronald Reagan.

Chapter 6

Decision Making in Congress

Introduction. On a hot day in June, Representative Harold Jackson arrives at his office on Capitol Hill at 8:00 A.M. After a quick look at the newspaper, he meets with three members of his staff. They discuss bills ready for action in the House of Representatives and bills coming before the four committees on which Jackson serves. At 9:00, Jackson goes to a meeting of the Post Office and Civil Service Committee. The Postmaster General wants to raise the cost of first-class mail. Back at his office by 11:00, Jackson takes a phone call from a lobbyist representing the nation's steelworkers. The lobbyist wants Jackson to vote for an industrial-safety bill. An aide to the President then calls. He and Jackson talk about an education bill the President wants Jackson to introduce in the House. At 11:45, Jackson has lunch with an editor from his hometown newspaper.

By 2:00 P.M., Jackson is back in his office reading and signing outgoing mail. At 2:30, Jackson goes to the House floor. During the debate on a farm bill, he tells House members that farmers in his district want the bill passed. At 4:00, Jackson meets with officials from the Department of Defense. He tells them why his district would be a good place to build an army supply warehouse. At 5:00, Jackson rushes back to his office to have his picture taken with a group of mayors from his state. He promises to look into some problems they are having with the Department of Housing and Urban Development. At 6:00, the congressman meets with one of his administrative aides to discuss proposals to raise funds for his reelection campaign. Jackson then drives to a hotel for dinner with several members of Congress from his state who also belong to his political party. They discuss their plans for reelection. At home about 8:30, Jackson settles down to read several committee reports.

Such is a day in the life of a typical—but imaginary—member of Congress. In this chapter you will learn more about Congress.

The rotunda of the United States Capitol in Washington.

Section 1
How Congress Is Organized

Congress is the national legislature of the United States. Its basic job is to make laws. According to the Constitution, Congress has the power to tax and spend to promote the general welfare. It also has the power to regulate trade and to coin and borrow money. Congress can build post offices and highways. It can set up federal courts under the Supreme Court. It can declare war and raise and maintain an army and navy. And it can call on armed forces to put down rebellions or stop invasions. Congress can also make all laws necessary to carry out its other stated powers.

In part because they gave Congress so much power, the men who wrote the Constitution decided to make Congress a **bicameral legislature**—a legislature made up of two houses. Instead of giving all legislative power to one group of people, they divided legislative

The United States House of Representatives.

power between two groups. The two houses have to agree on a bill before it becomes a law. Each house can "check and balance" the other.

The House of Representatives

The House of Representatives has 435 voting members. After each ten-year census, Congress decides how the 435 representatives are to be divided among the states. Look at the map on page 142 to see how the representatives changed after the 1980 census.

Representatives are elected for two-year terms from **congressional districts** in their states. There is one representative for each congressional district. It is up to each state legislature to decide the boundaries of the congressional districts. However, state legislatures must draw the boundaries so that the districts are roughly equal in population.

Most powers granted to Congress in the Constitution are shared by the Senate and the House of Representatives. However, each of the two houses has some powers that are not shared. The House of Representatives has these special powers:
1. The House has the power to start all bills that raise money.

The men who wrote the Constitution believed that the members of Congress closest to the people should be the ones to tax the people. They designed Congress so that members of the House would be closer to the people than would members of the Senate. Representatives face election every two years, and they represent a smaller number of people than members of the Senate do. As a result, they are usually more concerned about local problems than senators are.
2. The House also has the power to start the impeachment process to remove the President and certain

The United States Senate.

other high officials. It was the House Judiciary Committee that drew up articles of impeachment against President Nixon in 1974.

3. If no candidate for President wins a majority of electoral votes, the House of Representatives picks the President. This happened with Thomas Jefferson in 1800 and with John Quincy Adams in 1824.

The Senate

The Senate has two members, or senators, from each state. Senators are elected for a term of six years. Each one represents his or her entire state.

Like the House of Representatives, the Senate has a number of powers that are its very own:

1. The Senate has the power to approve presidential appointments of Supreme Court justices, federal judges, cabinet members, ambassadors, and other officials.

2. The Senate holds trials for public officials impeached by the House. This has happened twelve times in the nation's history.

3. The Senate has the power to approve all treaties made by the United States.

4. If no candidate for Vice-President gets a majority vote, the Senate chooses the Vice-President.

Most senators are better known in Washington, D.C., and at home than are most representatives. This is partly because there are fewer senators. Also, a senator's term of office is three times longer than a representative's is.

Congressional Leaders

Within each house individuals and small groups take on special jobs. Congressional leaders have jobs that are especially important. They direct the activities of Congress.

Transportation Secretary Elizabeth Hanford Dole presenting her husband, Senator Robert Dole, with a new pet named Leader shortly after his appointment to the powerful position of Senate majority leader in late 1984.

House Leaders. The most powerful leader in the House of Representatives is the **speaker of the House.** The speaker directs business on the floor of the House. In addition, the speaker influences who gets other House leadership jobs. If anything happens to the President and Vice-President, the speaker becomes President. This is only true, however, if the speaker meets all of the qualifications for becoming President. The job of speaker has always gone to a member of the House **majority party,** the political party with most members in the House. Like other leaders in the House and the Senate, the speaker is usually a long-time member of Congress.

Both the House majority party and the House **minority party** elect a **floor leader** and a **party whip.** The floor leaders try to influence party members to vote the way the party wants. Working with other House leaders, the floor leaders also decide when bills will be introduced. The whips help the floor

leaders. They see that representatives are present for important votes. They keep track of how party members plan to vote on key issues.

Senate Leaders. The Constitution states that the Vice-President of the United States will serve as president of the Senate. The Vice-President acts as a chairperson of the Senate but votes only in case of a tie. The Vice-President does not have much influence on Senate decisions, however, and does not usually spend much time on this job.

The person who acts as chairperson of the Senate most of the time is an officer elected by the Senate called the **president pro tempore** [prō tem′pər ē], or pro tem, for short). This officer is usually a member of the majority party. As is true of the Vice-President, the president pro tempore has little influence over the Senate.

The real leaders in the Senate are the majority party leader and the minority party leader. These leaders are chosen by members of their parties. They steer bills through the Senate. They also set up the Senate's work schedule, or **agenda.** When the majority leader is in the same political party as the President, he or she usually tries to push the President's programs through the Senate. The two Senate leaders are assisted by whips, as in the House.

Committees: Little Legislatures
The real action in Congress is in the many House and Senate committees.

Standing Committees of Congress

House Committees

Agriculture
Appropriations
Armed Services
Banking, Finance and Human Affairs
Budget
District of Columbia
Education and Labor
Foreign Affairs
Government Operations
House Administration
Interior and Insular Affairs
Interstate and Foreign Commerce
Judiciary
Merchant Marine and Fisheries
Post Office and Civil Service
Public Works and Transportation
Rules
Science and Technology
Small Business
Standards of Official Conduct
Veterans' Affairs
Ways and Means

Senate Committees

Agriculture, Nutrition, and Forestry
Appropriations
Armed Services
Banking, Housing, and Urban Affairs
Budget
Commerce, Science, and
    Transportation
Energy and Natural Resources
Environment and Public Works
Finance
Foreign Relations
Governmental Affairs
Labor and Human Resources
Judiciary
Rules and Administration
Veterans' Affairs

Committees are small groups of senators and representatives who work in special areas, such as foreign policy or agriculture.

Most law-making work is done in committee rather than on the floor of the Senate or House. So many bills are introduced in Congress each year that few of them would be considered if the work weren't divided among many committees. Committee members and the staff hired to assist them work on the bills that will be voted on by the full House and Senate. They make the decisions about what is put in the bill and what is not.

When senators and representatives first come to Congress, they try to get on important committees that are of interest to them. Members of Congress from farm areas might want to serve on agriculture committees. Those with many factories in their districts might be interested in labor committees.

Representatives usually serve on four or five committees and subcommittees. A senator may serve on ten committees and subcommittees, and chair at least one subcommittee.

More Than Three Hundred Committees. There are several different kinds of committees in Congress. There are standing committees and their subcommittees, special committees, and joint committees. **Standing committees** are permanent committees that continue their work from session to session. Each standing committee covers a special area, such as education, veterans' affairs, or banking. The Senate has fifteen standing committees. The House has twenty-two standing committees.

Each standing committee is divided into **subcommittees.** Subcommittees deal with particular

(above) Former Senator Paula Hawkins of Florida was chairman of the Agricultural Credit and Rural Electrification subcommittee. She was also on numerous other Senate subcommittees. (chart) Why do you think the House and the Senate have committees dealing with some of the same subjects?

A House subcommittee
discussing aid for El Salvador.

problems and issues in the area handled by the "parent" committee. For example, the Senate Veterans Affairs Committee has subcommittees on health and hospitals, education and housing, and insurance. Some subcommittees are very powerful. Others are not.

Both the Senate and House also have **special committees.** These committees are set up to do a special job. In 1976, for example, the House Select Committee on Assassinations was formed. The committee's main job was to investigate the facts surrounding the assassinations of President John F. Kennedy and Martin Luther King, Jr. Like all special committees, the House Assassinations Committee disbanded when it finished its work.

Congress also has seven joint House-Senate committees. These **joint committees** are made up of both senators and representatives.

The Joint Committee on Atomic Energy, for example, is a group of members of both houses of Congress that considers problems and bills related to nuclear energy.

Committee Chairpersons. Every committee has a leader who acts as the chairperson. The chairperson controls the work of his or her committee. The chairperson normally decides when and if a committee will meet. He or she also decides what bills will be studied.

Because standing committees are important, the chairpersons of standing committees are important congressional leaders. They can have great influence on the lawmaking work of Congress. The knowledge they have on the subject of their committees adds greatly to their influence.

Chairpersons are almost always chosen by **seniority rule,** which is

not really a rule but a custom. Seniority rule means that the majority-party member with most years on a committee gets to be chairperson.

Some people think seniority rule is a good idea. They say it prevents fights over committee jobs. It ensures that those chosen to be chairpersons will have experience. It also allows members of Congress from small states to gain important jobs in Congress. Other people think seniority rule is a bad idea. They say that all a person has to do to become a leader is stay alive and be reelected. In fact, there has been so much criticism of seniority rule over the years that both political parties have moved slightly away from it. The senior majority party member on a committee still usually wins the role of chairperson, but it is no longer guaranteed.

Section Review

Vocabulary:
agenda, bicameral legislature, congressional district, floor leader, joint committee, majority party, minority party, party whip, president pro tempore, seniority rule, speaker of the House, special committee, standing committee, subcommittee.

Reviewing the Main Ideas
1. What are three special powers that the House has which the Senate does not have?
2. What are four special powers the Senate has that the House does not?
3. Who elects the floor leaders and whips in the House?
4. Why are committees important?
5. Define majority party and minority party.

Skill Building
1. According to the map on page 142, how many states lost seats in the House after the 1980 census?
2. List these three House jobs in the order of their importance and briefly describe the work of each: majority party floor leader, majority party whip, speaker of the House.
3. How does the work of a standing committee differ from that of a special committee?
4. Write a summary of this section. After you have completed it, compare it to the summary of the section on page 143.

Senator Edward Kennedy of Massachusetts serves on the Economic Joint Committee. Ten representatives and nine senators belong to this committee.

(top) Congressman Romano Mazzoli of Kentucky talking with constituents in Louisville. (above) New York Congressman Robert Garcia.

Section 2
The Job in Congress Today

Congress is more than formal rules and powers. It is people. About 20,000 people work full time in the Congress. This number includes senators and representatives and their assistants, secretaries, clerks, and many other workers. The most important people, of course, are senators and representatives.

Members of Congress

The legal qualifications for members of Congress are simple. They deal only with age, citizenship, and residence. However, as the chart on the next page shows, members of Congress have more in common than legal qualifications. Note that most members are white, male, and belong to one of the two major political parties. What does the chart show you about the educational level and occupational background of congressional members?

As you can see, some groups are not well represented in Congress. For example, about 12 percent of the population of the United States is black. Yet in 1985, less than 5 percent of the House members were black, and there were no black senators. What other groups are underrepresented in Congress?

People who are active in community organizations gain experiences and make contacts that help them get elected to Congress. Members of Congress tend to be "joiners." They are more likely than the average citizen to belong to such

groups as the Masons, Knights of Columbus, or Rotary Club. It is politically important for them to belong to these and other organizations. Important political allies may be gained through membership.

In addition, many congressional members have had previous political experience. One study showed that the average senator had held three public offices and had spent ten years in government service before being elected to the Senate.

Representing the People

What do people do once they are elected to Congress? The basic job of senators and representatives is to represent the people. In carrying out that responsibility, members of Congress do four major jobs.

Making Laws. The job of making laws is given to members of Congress by the Constitution. Members do this by writing and introducing bills, by taking part in committee work, by listening to the information and ideas of people for and against a bill, and by voting on the floor of the House or Senate.

Troubleshooting. Though lawmaking is important, most members of Congress are lucky if they can spend half their time doing that work. Much of their time is spent acting as troubleshooters for people from their home district or state who need help in dealing with the federal government.

Most requests for help reach members of Congress through the mail. A busy congressional office may get 6,000 letters every week.

Characteristics of the 99th* Congress

House	Party	Senate
252	Democrats	47
183	Republicans	53
	Sex	
413	Men	98
22	Women	2
	Race and Ethnic Background	
19	Blacks	0
10	Hispanics	0
2	Asians	2
1	Polynesian	0
403	Whites	98
	Religion	
263	Protestants	69
122	Roman Catholics	19
30	Jews	8
20	Others	4
49.4	**Median Age**	54.2

House	Profession	Senate
159	Lawyers	53
109	Business people	24
30	Educators	3
78	Government officials	8
15	Farmers and ranchers	4
12	Journalists	1
1	Dentists, veterinarians	1
2	Clergymen	0
0	Astronauts	1
1	Pro Athlete	1
10	Congressional Aides	0
2	Judge	1
0	Airline Pilot	1
0	Navy Admiral	1
0	Economist	1
16	Other	0

*Each Congress is numbered. The First Congress met after the Constitution was ratified. It was elected in 1788 and met from 1789 to 1791. Each Congress lasts for two years. The 98th Congress began meeting in 1983; the 99th, in 1985.

(chart) Which two professions do most senators belong to? Why do you think this is so?

The Congressional Black Caucus, an organization of black members of Congress with common legislative goals.

About 25 percent of these letters are written by people who want their senator or representative to vote a certain way on a particular bill. The rest are written by people who need help with special problems.

With what problems do people need help? One congressional aide put it this way: "Usually, it's a problem of some sort with the bureaucracy. A social security check doesn't come. Or a veteran's claim is held up. Maybe it's a slip-up by a computer . . . but getting action . . . is tough for the average person."

Some more examples follow:

- A woman in the Navy asks for a special transfer so that she can be near her sick father.
- A high-school student asks for information from the Library of Congress.
- A retired woman writes because the Social Security Administration has stopped sending her monthly check.

Most requests for help are handled by the senator's or representative's office staff. Staff members contact federal agencies, such as the Veterans Administration, to gather information and make requests. They then report back to the person they are trying to help. Often a question from a staff person is all that is needed to get things moving again. When a staff person cannot get action, the senator or representative usually steps in to help. Former senator Jacob Javits of New York once said, "My staff handles problems until the moment of truth. Then I'm called in to push a button, so to speak, to make a phone call at a crucial moment."

Most members of Congress accept this "troubleshooting" job. They know it will help them be re-elected. People they help are a source of support election after election.

Helping the District or State. Another part of a representative's or senator's job is to try to influence government decisions that will benefit his or her own district or state. The national government spends almost a trillion dollars a year. Business leaders, labor leaders, farmers, and other groups with interests expect their representatives in Congress to help direct some of that money into their state or district.

Business owners, for example, want federal contracts. One contract to make shoes for the army can bring a small business a lot of work. Labor leaders want their members to benefit from governmental actions. For example, the decision to build a dam in a district could create many jobs for workers.

The late Senator Robert Kerr once said, "I am a senator of the United States, but I want it fully understood that I represent the state of Oklahoma." Senator Kerr was very skillful at bringing federal money and projects into his state.

Keeping an Eye on the Executive Branch. Another job that members of Congress do is to watch over the executive branch. They try to make sure that executive branch departments carry out programs in a way that was intended by Congress.

Over the years, Congress has created many federal programs. The executive branch under the President is supposed to carry out these programs. Naturally, members of Congress have an interest in watching how these programs work. When laws are carried out poorly, members of Congress get complaints from voters and from interest groups. Factory owners in a state, for instance, may complain if they think the Environmental Protection Agency is unfair to them. Farmers will be angry if they think the Department of Agriculture is not carrying out a farm program in the way Congress intended.

Congress can do several things in carrying out its "watchdog" duties. Members of Congress can hold **committee hearings** to investigate special problems in an agency. They can also create or abolish federal agencies. In addition, senators can investigate federal agency leaders appointed by the President.

Congressional Staff—The Silent Helpers

During the early years of our history, Congress met only a few months each year. Today, serving in Congress is a full-time job. The duties are far too many for one person to handle. During each Congress between 10,000 and 20,000 bills are introduced. Members of Congress get millions of requests for help. There are thousands of committee hearings. And, of course, members of

Congress must run for reelection every two or six years. Reelection campaigns are often time-consuming and expensive.

One veteran of over thirty years in Congress described the increasing workload faced by lawmakers when he said, "This is another world from the time I came here. Then it was a picnic; now it's a treadmill."

To get help with their work, members of Congress hire a staff of clerks, secretaries, and special assistants. You may not hear much about these people in the news, but they are important. There are two main types of congressional staff. **Personal staff** work for individual senators and representatives. **Committee staff** work directly for House and Senate committees.

Personal Staff. The average senator has about thirty-six assistants and the average representative has sixteen assistants. These personal staff members are hired and fired by their senator or representative.

Personal staff members run their boss's congressional office in Washington as well as one or more offices in the home state or district. They gather information on new bills and issues that are to be discussed in Congress. They arrange for meetings and write speeches. They handle requests for help from voters. They deal with news reporters and **lobbyists**—people hired by private groups to influence government decision makers. And they work for their boss's reelection, even though the law requires them to do this work on their own time.

Committee Staff. More than three thousand people work directly as staff members for the various Senate and House committees. Many of

(below) House pages preparing copies of proposed bills for delivery to members of Congress. (chart) How large was the House staff in 1985? How large was the Senate staff in 1985?

Growth of Congressional Staff

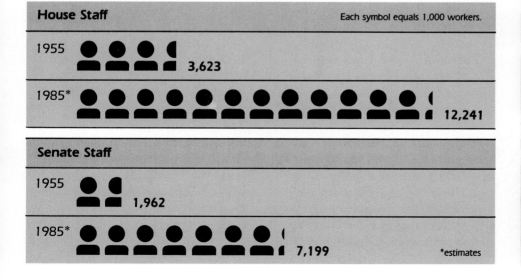

House Staff — Each symbol equals 1,000 workers.

1955 — 3,623

1985* — 12,241

Senate Staff

1955 — 1,962

1985* — 7,199

*estimates

135

these people are experts on special topics such as tax laws, military defense, and health-care policies. Committee staff members see their jobs as assisting members of the committee rather than as working for any one lawmaker.

Committee staff members do much of the day-to-day lawmaking work of Congress. They draft bills, investigate, gather information, plan and organize committee hearings, and negotiate with lobbyists. In short, they keep the complex lawmaking process moving.

Staff Agencies. Congress has also created four staff agencies to support its work. They are the Congressional Research Service, the General Accounting Office, the Office of Technology Assessment, and the Congressional Budget Office.

The Congressional Research Service (CRS) looks up facts and spells out arguments for and against proposed bills. CRS also uses computers to keep track of every major bill before Congress.

The General Accounting Office (GAO) investigates the work of federal agencies such as the FBI and monitors programs such as Medicare. GAO staffers work directly with congressional committees. They brief lawmakers on federal programs, prepare questions for use in hearings, provide legal advice about bills, and collect information requested by lawmakers.

The Office of Technology Assessment (OTA) is a small agency that studies technological developments that may require new laws.

Staff members investigate such matters as a plan to build a pipeline to carry oil or a new satellite telephone system.

The Congressional Budget Office (CBO) advises Congress on the possible economic impact of new programs. CBO staffers also provide information on the costs of new government programs.

Section Review

Vocabulary:
committee hearings, committee staff, lobbyists, personal staff, staff agencies.

Reviewing the Main Ideas
1. List the four main jobs that members of Congress perform.
2. List four staff agencies created to assist Congress and explain their functions.
3. List three duties of committee staff people.
4. Why is it necessary for members of Congress to watch the activities of the executive branch?

Skill Building
1. Look at the story of Representative Jackson on page 124. Find examples in his day of the four kinds of congressional jobs described on pages 132–134.
2. Look at the table on page 133 that shows characteristics of the Congress. There are many more workers and skilled tradespeople in the United States than there are lawyers. Which are there more of in Congress? Why?

Section 3
Making Laws

Congressional leaders, members, and staff work together to pass new laws. Sometimes an individual member of Congress will introduce a bill. However, most ideas for new laws start outside Congress. Eighty percent of all bills that become law begin in the White House. Other new bills are started by **special interest groups** working with one or more members of Congress. Special interest groups are organizations of people with some common interest who try to influence decisions of government officials.

How a Bill Becomes a Law
Just how do senators and representatives turn ideas into the law of the land? With 535 members of Congress (435 in the House, 100 in the Senate), many rules are needed to keep the lawmaking job fair and orderly. These rules make it hard for a bill to become a law. Of the 10,000 to 20,000 bills introduced in each term of Congress, only about 5 percent become law.

The numbered items below show the major steps a bill must follow to become a law.

1. Introduction. Any senator or representative can introduce a bill. However, many bills must start in the House because they involve money. Every bill is given a number when it is submitted. It is then sent to the standing committee that seems most qualified to handle it.

2. Hearings. In considering a bill, a committee may hold public hearings. Private individuals and people from different interest groups **testify** before the committee. They state their opinions about the bill and give facts to support their opinions. They may argue for or against the bill. People may also submit

(below left) President Ronald Reagan signing a social security reform bill at the White House. (below) Interest group presenting its views about a proposed bill to a House committee.

How a Bill Becomes a Law

Except for Money bills, a bill can be started in either house of Congress. This diagram shows a bill starting in the House of Representatives, but the same process would be followed for a bill started in the Senate. In practice, many bills are started in both houses at the same time.

1 A representative has an idea for a law or is asked to introduce a law.

2 His or her staff writes up the bill.

3 The representative introduces the bill in the House. The bill is sent to a committee.

4 House committee collects evidence, holds hearings, suggests amendments, votes.

5 If the committee approves it, the amended bill is sent to the whole House.

6 The House debates and votes.

7 If a majority favor it, the bill goes to the Senate. The bill is sent to a committee.

8 The Senate committee holds hearings, collects evidence, amends bill, votes.

9 A favorable vote sends the bill to the whole Senate.

10 The Senate votes. If a majority favor it, the bill is returned to the House.

11 The House considers the Senate amendments and votes.

12 A conference committee from both houses rewrites any unacceptable amendments.

13 Both houses vote on the amended bill.

14 A favorable vote sends the bill to the President.

15 If the President signs it, the bill becomes law.

A Vetoed bill

B If two-thirds of each house favors a vetoed bill, it becomes a law without the President's signature.

Study the chart above. Where must money bills start? What happens to a bill after it is passed by either house of Congress? What happens if a President vetoes a bill?

written statements. Sometimes committee members ask experts to present evidence for or against the bill.

3. Committee Decisions. Standing committees have life and death power over bills. After public hearings, often conducted by appropriate subcommittees, committee members make one of several decisions. The committee can (1) suggest that the bill be adopted with few changes, (2) change the bill almost completely, (3) ignore the bill and stop it by not acting on it, or (4) kill the bill by majority vote. The full House or Senate can overrule the decision of its committees, but this hardly ever happens. When a committee is against a bill, the bill almost never

becomes a law. This is why the committee chairperson and the committee system are so powerful.

4. Introduction to Full House or Senate. Bills that are approved in committee are ready for floor action in the House or Senate. In the House they go to the **Rules Committee** first. This group is the House "traffic cop." It decides the rules of debate when the bill goes to the floor of the House. The Rules Committee can kill a bill by not letting it get to the floor.

5. General Debate, Amendments, Vote. On the floor of the House or Senate, the bill is debated—reasons for and against the bill are stated.

Amendments may be added at this time. After amendments have been voted on, debate continues. Eventually, the bill is voted on as a whole. A simple majority is needed to pass a bill. If either the Senate or the House rejects a bill, it is dead. If a bill passes in one house, it is sent to the other.

6. Conference Committee. If either house of Congress makes changes in a bill after receiving it from the other house, the bill is sent to a **conference committee.** Five members from each house meet privately and work out differences between House and Senate versions of the bill. Only about ten percent of all bills go to a conference committee, but they are usually the most important bills.

7. Vote on Conference Report. Once a bill is released from the conference committee, the House and Senate must vote on the final version of the bill.

8. Presidential Action. When a bill is approved by both houses of Congress, it goes to the President. One of three things then happens. The President may sign the bill and declare it a new law. The President may veto the bill—refuse to sign it and send it back to Congress. Or the President may keep the bill for ten days without signing it. This is called a **pocket veto.** If the President keeps the bill while Congress is in session, the bill becomes law. If Congress is not in session, the bill does not become law.

When the President vetoes a bill, it is returned to the house where it was first introduced with a listing of his objections. Congress can override the veto with a two-thirds vote of the total membership of *each* house. If both houses vote to override, the bill becomes law without the President's approval.

The veto is a good example of the Constitutional principle of checks and balances and separation of powers. Congress makes laws but the President can check Congress' actions with the veto. As a balance, however, Congress can overturn the veto if two-thirds of the House and Senate support such an action.

Section Review

Vocabulary:
conference committee, pocket veto, Rules Committee, special interest group, testify.

Reviewing the Main Ideas
1. Where do eighty percent of all bills that become law begin?
2. About how many bills are introduced in each term of Congress?
3. What four things can happen to a bill after it is sent to committee?

Skill Building
1. List the steps an imaginary farm bill would have to go through before it could become law. (Make this a bill that goes to a conference committee and one that is signed by the President.
2. Why would a committee hold hearings on a proposed law?

Case Study

Moving a Bill Through Congress

As winter approached, the building industry began to run short of wood. A dry summer had caused logging to stop because of the danger of fire, and a boxcar shortage and dock strike slowed the delivery of what timber there was. Furthermore, much of the available timber was being exported to other nations.

Because wood is an important building material, the shortage slowed the building of houses. Home builders begged the timber industry for more wood. Naturally, the timber industry wished it had more wood to sell builders.

As a result, leaders from the National Forest Products Association, representing 1,500 forest product companies, and the National Association of Home Builders met in Houston, Texas. The two groups decided to work together to get Congress to pass a law allowing more trees in the national forests to be cut for timber. Other groups that thought a timber-cutting bill was in their interest also gave support.

The pro-timber cutting groups drafted a model bill. A timber-cutting bill based on their work was then introduced in Congress by a senator who supported the pro-timber groups and who, in turn, had received campaign contributions from several forest products and home building companies. The bill was sent to the Senate Agricultural Committee. The committee decided to do nothing with the bill until the House of Representatives acted on its own version of the bill.

Shortly after the timber-cutting bill was introduced in Congress, several different groups who were against the bill joined together. They called themselves the Conservation Coalition. Members of the Coalition objected to the bill for several reasons. They reminded people that the national forests were used for many things. Timber was only one use. If more trees were cut for timber, wildlife habitats, recreation areas, and watershed management would all suffer. They feared the legislation would bring protection of wilderness areas and scenic lands to a halt. Further, the Coalition believed that increased logging would not solve the housing shortage. They said the housing problem was caused by high interest rates, high labor prices, and high land prices.

Coalition members marshalled support for their views among sympathetic representatives. Some of the representatives had in the past received campaign support from Coalition members, including endorsements and contributions.

Action in the House then began. A House subcommittee held hearings on a House version of the bill. People from both the Conservation Coalition and the pro-timber group testified at the hearings. Each group presented information for its side. As a result, a revised House bill (called HR 12025) came out of the subcommittee, which in turn was approved by the Rules Committee. The bill would now go to the floor of the House, where it would be debated and voted on by all of the members.

As the time for the House vote neared, volunteers from the Conservation Coalition delivered information kits to members of Congress. The kits gave facts that supported the conservation view of the effects that HR 12025 would have on the national forests and the housing industry. In addition, four groups in the Coalition asked their members to write or send telegrams to their senators and representatives.

The pro-timber group was also hard at work. The group prepared a thirty-six-page booklet arguing in favor of HR 12025. The booklet was sent to all members of Congress and to 5,000 journalists across the country. Supporters of HR 12025 also talked directly with congressional staff and members. And pro-timber leaders sought the support of city groups concerned about housing and jobs. One response, a letter from the president of the National Urban League, was given to all members of Congress.

The showdown came on the floor of the House of Representatives. The House voted whether to pass HR 12025 or to reject it. The House voted 228 to 150 to reject the bill. HR 12025 was dead.

Review

1. Who first drafted a timber-cutting bill?
2. What did the Conservation Coalition see as the consequences of passing HR 12025?
3. What did the pro-timber group see as the consequences of passing this bill?
4. What is your judgment of the House's final decision? Give your reasons.

(below left) Harvesting a giant redwood. (below) Stacking timbers.

Basic Social Studies Skills
Reading a Representation Map

Changes in State Representation after the 1980 Census

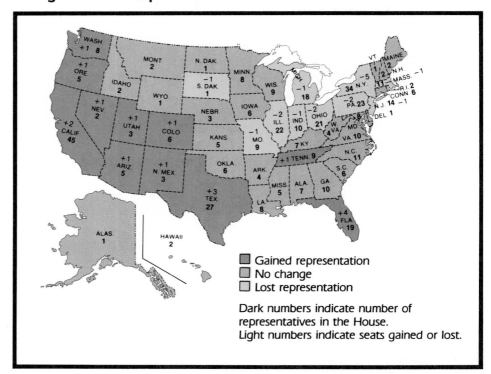

Gained representation
No change
Lost representation

Dark numbers indicate number of representatives in the House.
Light numbers indicate seats gained or lost.

The map above shows the number of representatives each state had in Congress after the 1980 census. Every ten years the government takes a census to find out how many people live in the United States and where they live. Then it changes the number of representatives a state may have in Congress. States that have gained population in relation to the other states get more representatives than they had before. States that have lost population lose representatives.

Study the map and its key very carefully, and then answer the following questions.

Skill Practice
1. Which geographical region of the United States made huge gains in congressional representation after the 1980 census?
2. Which three states gained the most representatives as a result of the 1980 census?
3. Did any state lose more than two representatives?
4. What general conclusions can you draw about the Midwest and the Northeast regions of the nation?

Chapter 6 Review

Summary

Section 1: How Congress Is Organized

The basic job of Congress is to make laws. Congress is divided into a House of Representatives with 435 voting members and a Senate with 100 members. Both houses of Congress must agree on a bill before it becomes law. Leaders in each house direct the work of Congress. Most lawmaking work is done in House and Senate committees. Committees are small groups of lawmakers who work on special topics such as farm policy or national defense.

Section 2: The Job in Congress Today

Senators and representatives represent the people and do four basic jobs. They make laws, solve problems for voters, bring federal projects to their district or state, and watch over the activities of the executive branch. Lawmakers are assisted by personal and committee staff members and by four staff agencies.

Section 3: Making Laws

To become a law, a bill must pass through many steps involving actions in both the House and Senate. Most work on bills is done in standing committees, which have the power to kill a bill or modify it as they see fit. Bills passed by both houses are sent to the President for approval. The President may veto any bill, but Congress can "check" that power with an override if it wants to.

Vocabulary

Define the following terms.
1. bicameral legislature
2. agenda
3. congressional district
4. subcommittees
5. testify
6. party whip
7. seniority rule

Reviewing Main Ideas

1. True or false: Congress is the national legislature of the United States.
2. True or false: The most important job of Congress is to make laws.
3. Which of the following does Congress have the power to do?
a. establish local voting rules
b. coin money
c. build churches
d. all of the above
4. The number of representatives from each state
a. never changes.
b. is equal for all states.
c. is larger for the original thirteen colonies.
d. varies according to the population.

Thinking Critically

Comprehending Information

1. Why are senators generally better known than representatives?
2. What is the difference between a standing committee and a special committee?

Organizing Information

Draw a diagram to show how a bill about energy conservation might become a law.

Evaluating Information

Do you think members of Congress are concerned about which committees they serve on? Why or why not?

Communicating Ideas

Write a paragraph telling how members of Congress make decisions.

Chapter 7

Paying for National Government

Introduction. "John, please get the calculator while you're up," Pat Stanowski called out from the kitchen.

Pat and John Stanowski were working on their family budget. "After paying taxes, my income this year should be $1,450 a month," John said returning with the calculator.

As they went to work, the Stanowskis found they were spending about $1,600 a month. "Well, we've got to cut back somewhere," Pat said. She and John wanted to balance their expenses with their income.

Nearly 2,000 miles away in Washington, D.C., the President of the United States and many advisers were planning the national government's budget. Like the Stanowskis, the President's advisers were considering expenses—how much money the national government would spend in the next year. They were also looking at government income—how much money was coming in from taxes and other sources.

The amounts the President and his staff were dealing with were quite different, however. The federal government would take in more than $745 billion next year. At the same time the government would spend about $925 billion. It would have to borrow $180 billion just to make ends meet.

Spending would include more than $264 billion for national defense and another $190 billion for Social Security payments. As with the Stanowskis, the President worried about matching income with expenses. However, in the President's case, there were no simple ways to do this.

Yet tough budget decisions could not be delayed. Each year the national government spends billions of dollars to provide services and benefits, such as building dams or highways, and to make and enforce rules. Where does the money to pay for the cost of government come from? How is the money spent? Who decides what the cost of government should be? You will learn the answers to these questions in this chapter.

Section 1
Where the Money Comes From

In 1790, when George Washington was President, 780 people worked for him in the executive branch of government. This small government served a nation of 4 million Americans and spent less than $10 million. Today, the yearly cost of government is close to $1 trillion! And this huge government serves a nation of almost a quarter of a billion people. Where does the government get the money it needs to serve so many people?

Taxes

The national government gets most of the money it needs from **taxes.**

Taxes are fees that citizens must pay to support the government. The government borrows the rest of the money it needs. The graph on page 146 shows the estimated proportions of government income from various sources for **fiscal year** 1985, the period from October, 1984, through September, 1985. A fiscal year is any year-long period that is set up for budget purposes. The federal government's fiscal year always begins on October 1.

Income Tax. The tax that brings in the most money to the national government is the **personal income tax.** This tax is charged on the income each person earns in a year. Personal income taxes amounted to

Internal Revenue Service (IRS) computer center in Martinsburg, West Virginia. Each reel can store records for up to 55,000 taxpayers.

145

(chart) Almost two-thirds of the government's income comes from what two sources? What is the third largest source of government income?

Sources of National Government Income*

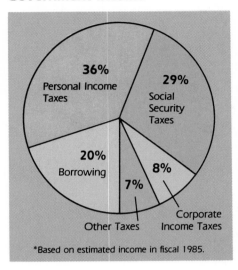

36%
Personal Income Taxes

29%
Social Security Taxes

20%
Borrowing

7%
Other Taxes

8%
Corporate Income Taxes

*Based on estimated income in fiscal 1985.

U.S. TREASURY DEPARTMENT

"Here it is, chief . . . the new simplified tax form and the rules explaining it!"

Our complicated tax system, with its ever-changing forms and rules, is often the target of political cartoonists.

about 36 percent of the money taken in by the government in fiscal 1985. This percentage represented more than $328 billion.

Not every dollar that a person earns is taxed. The tax laws passed by Congress allow people to deduct certain expenses from their income before figuring the tax. These amounts are called **deductions.** For example, if a person has children, he or she does not have to pay taxes on some of the money used to care for the children. People do not have to pay taxes on income given to charities. People can deduct part of the money they spend on doctor and hospital bills.

People do not all agree that the tax laws are fair. Deductions seem to favor some groups over others. Renters, for example, pay higher taxes than homeowners. So tax reform is something that many people want. Candidates running for office often promise to try to make the tax laws more fair. But they have a very hard time doing so because people cannot agree about what is fair. Is it fair to make the people who get the most benefits from government pay the highest taxes? Or should people who have the most income pay the most in taxes?

Our tax laws accept the second line of reasoning. After people have taken their deductions, the amount that is left is called **taxable income.** The tax rate on taxable income varies. People with more income pay a higher percentage of their income in personal income tax than others with less income.

Social Security Tax. The **social security tax** is another kind of income tax, but it is put into a special fund. Most of this tax money is used to give income to retired people. Everyone pays social security tax at the same rate up to a limit set by law. The limit changes often, but in 1985 it was $35,700. No one paid social security tax on any income over $35,700.

Each worker covered by the social security system is identified by a nine-digit number. As you earn money, social security taxes are held out of your paycheck and paid into the social security fund. On your paycheck, this amount is often labeled FICA—Federal Insurance Contribution Act—the law that set up the social security taxes. Your employer also pays a social security tax on the money you earn.

Social Security taxes deducted from your paycheck, as well as your employer's contribution, are sent to the Department of the Treasury. This department then distributes the money in the form of monthly checks to people who have reached the retirement age of 65. People who retire as early as age 62 may also collect monthly social security payments, but in a reduced amount.

FICA taxes are also used to provide retirement benefits to the families of workers who die and to disabled workers. In addition, FICA taxes are used to finance Medicare benefits, which include hospital and medical insurance for disabled and retired workers. Approximately one out of every seven people in the United States is currently collecting social security benefits.

Corporate Income Tax. Taxes collected from businesses accounted for about 8 percent of the federal government's income in fiscal 1985. This amounted to approximately $76.5 billion. Businesses pay more or less tax according to the amount of **profit** they make. Profit is the money left over after the cost of doing business has been subtracted from a company's income.

Like individuals, corporations may deduct certain expenses to lower their taxable incomes. For example, they may subtract money paid to buy new machinery or to build a new office building. And like the tax rate on individuals, the tax rate on businesses varies with their taxable income. Businesses with higher profits pay higher tax rates.

What is the point the cartoonist is trying to make in the cartoon below?

"*. . . plus Federal Tax, State Tax, City Sales Tax and a special tax we have here on 34th Street.*"

The law allows some organizations to pay no income taxes. These are nonprofit corporations or groups such as churches, universities, labor unions, and hospitals.

Other Taxes

Excise taxes, customs duties, unemployment-insurance taxes, and estate and gift taxes are also sources of income. Together, these taxes represented about 7 percent of the government's income in fiscal 1985. This amounted to about $69 billion.

Excise Taxes. Excise taxes are collected on certain goods made and sold in the United States. When people buy gasoline, liquor, and cigarettes, they must pay a small tax. There is also an excise tax on the purchase of certain services. People pay a small tax when they buy a ticket to travel on an airplane.

Excise taxes are placed on luxury goods or services. Excise taxes are not put on items that people need to live adequately, such as food and clothing.

Customs Duties. People must pay customs duties on certain products brought into the United States. For example, suppose you visit Germany. You buy a German camera, wristwatch, and radio to give to friends in the United States. When you return to the United States, you must pay a customs tax on the German products if their value exceeds a specific amount.

A **protective tariff** is a special kind of customs tax. Products from a foreign country that are made at a lower cost than similar goods in the United States are taxed with a protective tariff. This tax protects American companies against competition from low-cost foreign products. For example, auto makers in Japan produce their cars at a much lower cost than American companies do. To protect American auto makers, the United States government puts a protective tariff on the Japanese cars. This tax raises the price of Japanese cars in the United States, consequently making less expensive, American-made cars more appealing to some people.

Estate and Gift Taxes. Every year the national government takes in a few billion dollars from estate and gift taxes. An **estate tax** is paid on money, property, and other valuables left by a person who has died. (There is no tax on an estate that has a value below a certain sum fixed by law.) A **gift tax** is money collected on any gift, including cash, that is worth more than a certain amount set by law. These taxes prevent people from avoiding personal income taxes by giving money to family members or friends.

Presidential Election Campaign Fund. For the most part, individual taxpayers do not have the opportunity to determine precisely how their tax dollars are spent. That is the responsibility of the Congress, whose decisions on such matters are often heavily influenced by the President. But there is one exception to that practice. Taxpayers may indicate on their income tax forms

United States Customs inspectors checking for illegal shipments.

that they want one dollar of their taxes to go to the Presidential Election Campaign Fund. Under a law passed in 1971, money from this fund is used to help pay the costs of presidential general election campaigns, the presidential nominating conventions of the political parties, and campaigns by qualified candidates to gain their parties' presidential nominations. In recent years, between 25 and 29 percent of the income tax forms received by the federal government have indicated that one dollar (or two dollars on forms filed jointly by married couples) should go to the fund.

National Borrowing

When the government spends more money than it collects in taxes, it borrows money to make up the difference. Recently about twenty cents out of each dollar the government took in was borrowed money. The national government has had to borrow extremely large amounts of money in recent years in order to pay its bills. The amount of money the government owes is known as the **national debt.**

The government borrows money by selling government **securities** to citizens, banks, and businesses. These securities are treasury bonds, savings bonds, and treasury notes and bills. When you buy a United States savings bond, you are loaning money to the government. Let us say you go to buy a fifty-dollar bond. You pay $37.50. Then you hold the bond for ten years in a safe place. At the end of

this time we say the bond has reached **maturity.** At maturity, you turn it in for fifty dollars. The difference between what you paid for it and what you get at maturity is **interest.** Interest is the payment a borrower makes to a lender for the use of the money. At the time the government issues the security, it says how much it will pay in interest and over how long a period of time.

Section Review

Vocabulary:
corporate income tax, customs duty, deductions, estate tax, excise tax, fiscal year, gift tax, interest, maturity, national debt, personal income tax, profit, protective tariff, securities, social security tax, taxable income, taxes.

Reviewing Main Ideas
1. Where does most of the money for running the government come from?
2. Taxes do not pay all the costs of government. How else does the government get money?
3. Explain how social security works.

Skill Building
1. According to the graph on page 146, what percentage of federal government income was raised through personal income taxes?
2. What percentage came from taxes on corporations?
3. What percentage came from "other" taxes?

Defense spending accounts for a large part of the money spent by our government each year. Part of the defense budget in recent years has gone to the development of Trident submarines.

Section 2
How the Money Is Spent

The cost of national government is skyrocketing. In the early 1960s, government cost less than $100 billion per year. By 1985, it cost more than $900 billion. The graph on page 151 shows how the cost of government has increased since 1964.

Who gets the billions of dollars collected and spent by the national government each year? The greatest share is used for services and cash payments given directly to individuals who have some special need or special right to collect them. In fiscal 1985, forty-two cents of every dollar was spent for benefits to these people. Those who received funds included retired citizens, widows, orphans, veterans, and disabled and poor people.

The money that government spends on the military each year is also a very large sum. As you can see from the circle graph on page 151, twenty-nine cents of every dollar was spent on national defense in fiscal 1985. This amounted to almost $265 billion. Much of this money went toward salaries for members of the armed forces. Most of the rest was spent on weapons.

An increasingly larger part of the yearly cost of government is payment of interest on money that has been borrowed by the government. In fiscal 1985, thirteen cents of every dollar the government spent went for this purpose. This amounted to more than $164 billion.

The Cost of National Government

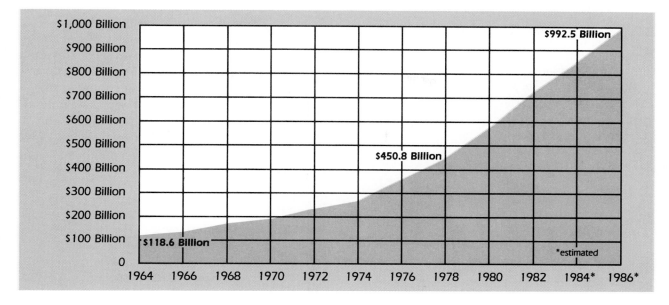

											$992.5 Billion

$1,000 Billion
$900 Billion
$800 Billion
$700 Billion
$600 Billion
$500 Billion
$400 Billion — $450.8 Billion
$300 Billion
$200 Billion
$100 Billion — *$118.6 Billion
0
*estimated

1964 1966 1968 1970 1972 1974 1976 1978 1980 1982 1984* 1986*

Eleven cents of every federal dollar spent in fiscal 1985 went to states and local governments in the form of **revenue sharing** and **grants-in-aid.** Revenue sharing is a plan in which the national government regularly turns over a certain amount of the taxes it collects to state and local governments. State and city governments spend the money for a variety of needs or programs. Grants-in-aid are payments made by the federal government to state or local governments for *specific* programs. For example, the federal government pays part of the costs of school lunch programs. State or local districts pay the rest.

Five percent of the fiscal 1985 budget was spent on operating the federal government. This amount included the salaries and benefits paid to the nearly 3 million civilian government workers.

How the National Government Spends its Money*

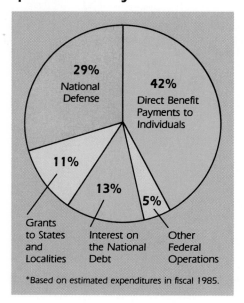

29% National Defense

42% Direct Benefit Payments to Individuals

11% Grants to States and Localities

13% Interest on the National Debt

5% Other Federal Operations

*Based on estimated expenditures in fiscal 1985.

According to the graph above, what is the estimated cost of government in 1986? What does the graph at left tell you about how most of the federal government's money is spent?

151

Through taxing, the government collects different sums of money from different people. Through spending for various services and programs, the government spreads this money among citizens with different needs. Through taxing and spending, the national government transfers billions of dollars each year from the pockets of some citizens to the pockets of others.

Section Review

Vocabulary:
grants-in-aid, revenue sharing.

Reviewing Main Ideas
1. What is the biggest area of government expenses?
2. Name five different reasons an individual might get payments from the national government.
3. Is national defense a large part of government costs? Explain your answer.
4. Is interest on the national debt a large part of government costs? Explain your answer.

Skill Building
Use the information presented in the graph on page 151, "The Cost of National Government," to support or deny this statement: The cost of running the government has not changed much in twenty years.

The government spends the money collected through taxes to pay for various federal services and programs. These services and programs benefit many people from many walks of life.

Section 3
Making the Federal Budget

The federal **budget** is the national government's plan for gathering and spending money. It covers a twelve-month period from October 1 to September 30.

The federal budget is a huge document. It is more than 1,000 telephone-book-size pages of small print. The budget shows the amount of money the government has available to spend. It lists both the sources of these funds and the expenses of government. See the chart below for a summary of the income and expenses listed in the fiscal 1985 national budget.

National Priorities. The government's budget reveals national priorities. **Priority** refers to what comes first. We give high priority to activities that we believe to be very important. We decide to do them before we do other things. Budget makers direct the largest amounts of money toward the programs that they have determined to have the most importance to the welfare of the nation. Programs that are perceived to be important, yet less crucial in nature than other programs,

Study the 1985 federal budget below. Where did most of the money come from? Where did most of it go?

1985* Federal Budget

Income

Taxes on individual incomes	$328.4 bil.
Social Security taxes	$236.7 bil.
Taxes on corporate profits	$ 76.5 bil.
Excise taxes	$ 30.1 bil.
Crude-oil excise taxes	$ 8.3 bil.
Unemployment-insurance taxes	$ 25.2 bil.
Estate and gift taxes	$ 5.6 bil.
All other revenue	$ 34.3 bil.
Total income	**$745.1 bil.**

Expenses

National defense	$264.4 bil.
Social Security benefits	$190.6 bil.
Interest on public debt	$164.7 bil.
Medicare, other health programs	$102.6 bil.
Public assistance, food stamps, other aid	$ 37.7 bil.
Education, manpower, social services	$ 27.9 bil.
Aid to veterans	$ 26.7 bil.
Aid to transportation	$ 27.1 bil.
Civil-service retirement	$ 23.2 bil.
Unemployment compensation	$ 20.1 bil.
International affairs, economic and military aid	$ 17.5 bil.
Energy	$ 3.1 bil.
Aid to communities, regional development	$ 7.6 bil.
General-revenue sharing	$ 4.6 bil.
Rivers, dams, natural resources	$ 7.2 bil.
Science, space, technology	$ 8.8 bil.
Pollution control	$ 4.2 bil.
Aid to agriculture	$ 14.3 bil.
Administration of justice	$ 6.1 bil.
Payment to the Postal Service	$ 0.7 bil.
Rents and royalties on outer continental shelf	−$ 7.4 bil.
Net interagency deductions and other spending	−$ 26.2 bil.
Total expenses	**$925.5 bil.**
Deficit	**−$180.4 bil.**

*estimated

153

receive smaller amounts of money. The priorities of various presidential administrations can be determined by examining national budgets.

Having a large and strong army, navy, and air force has been a very high national priority since World War II (1939-1945). During this postwar period, more money has been spent on national defense than on any other budget item.

When John Kennedy was President, the space program was given a high priority. The President had the goal of putting a man on the moon before the end of the 1960s. The government spent large sums of money for several years to reach this goal.

In 1978, President Carter's budget planning showed great concern for programs in education, health care, and public works to create new jobs.

During the 1980s, President Reagan prepared budgets aimed at decreasing spending for many government programs. At the same time, he called for increases in spending for national defense.

A Balanced Budget. When income is equal to expenses, we say a budget is balanced. Look at the budget on page 153. Is it a **balanced budget?**

When income is less than expenses, the difference is called a **deficit** [def'ə sit]. The government borrows money to make up the deficit, and interest on this borrowed money becomes an item in the budget. It has become very common for the government to have an unbalanced budget. As a result, the national debt is climbing. In 1985, the total national debt was more than $1.6 trillion.

As the graph shows, the national debt has climbed at an alarmingly fast pace in recent years.

Growth of the National Debt

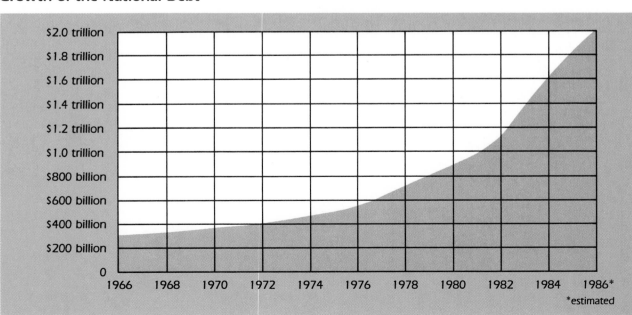

| | 1966 | 1968 | 1970 | 1972 | 1974 | 1976 | 1978 | 1980 | 1982 | 1984 | 1986* |

*estimated

Most of the national debt was caused by the wars in this century. The government borrowed money to buy the weapons and pay the troops needed to fight World War I, World War II, the Korean War, and the Vietnam War. Budget deficits have added to this already enormous debt. The chart on page 154 shows this growth. In what years did the debt decrease?

Many people worry about the national debt. All recent Presidents have promised to balance the budget by the end of their first term. This promise attracts many votes. A balanced budget would not get rid of the national debt, but it would keep it from growing.

Steps in the Budget-making Process. The first draft of the budget is created by the executive branch of government. The President, who has the overall responsibility for creating this first copy, sets the goals and general direction. The Office of Management and Budget (OMB) works out the details. (You will read more about the OMB in Chapter 8.)

Making the first draft of the budget requires many months of hard work. All government agencies and bureaus present yearly requests to the budget makers. The agencies try to get as much funding as possible so that they can carry out or expand their programs. Before making final decisions about the budget, the OMB and the President spend months studying and discussing the many requests. The end result is a compromise between what the various groups want and what decision makers think they ought to get.

Once the executive branch has completed its work on the budget,

David Stockman, President Reagan's budget director, telling the President how large the fiscal 1985 budget deficit would be.

155

the President sends a budget message to Congress. This message presents the President's budget proposal and urges Congress to pass it. Traditionally, the budget message has been delivered in January of each year to a joint session of Congress and a national TV audience.

According to the Constitution, all proposals approving government use of money must be passed first by a majority of the House of Representatives. Next, a majority of the Senate must give approval. In this manner, a majority of the members of Congress must approve the budget before any money can be spent.

In the course of the work it does, Congress almost always makes changes in the budget. The final budget is a compromise between what the President wants and what Congress wants.

Once the budget is approved, the President and other top officials of the executive branch are responsible for spending the money. They are expected to follow the budget approved by Congress.

The judicial branch also has a role to play in these money matters. It has power to settle arguments about collecting and spending government money. Suppose there is evidence that officials of the executive branch have not followed the approved budget. If these officials are taken to court, federal judges would decide whether or not they had broken the law.

Concerned citizens purchasing copies of the federal budget.

Making the budget involves important decisions about giving and withholding benefits from different citizens. A decision to cut back on defense spending would mean a loss of profits for companies that make weapons. It would also result in a loss of jobs and incomes for workers in these companies. A decision to spend more for health care for older people would not only aid senior citizens; it also would give more money to doctors, nurses, hospitals, and druggists. A decision to raise or lower income taxes for certain groups leads to more or less money in the pockets of different citizens. Thus, citizens should pay attention to important budget decisions in the national government.

Section Review

Vocabulary:
balanced budget, budget, deficit, priority.

Reviewing the Main Ideas
1. Which branch of government prepares the budget?
2. Which branch of government approves the budget?
3. How does a budget show national priorities?

Skill Building
1. According to President Reagan's budget for fiscal 1985, what three items have the highest priority for the national government?
2. How would you assign priorities to your own activities? What three things would you give most attention to?
3. How might citizens influence federal budget decisions?
4. What role does the judicial branch play in the development and implementation of the federal budget?
5. Imagine that you can make changes in the federal budget. List the sorts of programs that you would like to see the country give more money to. List the programs that you would like to see the country give less money to. Make a list of reasons that have influenced you to make these choices. Compare your list with others in the class to see whether it would take great or little effort for the class to agree on a budget.

Case Study

Federal Spending at Work

The national government today needs much more money than it did twenty years ago. The national government also provides more services and it makes more rules that affect our daily lives. Decisions made in the national government affect the food we eat, the cars we drive, the clothes we wear, the water we drink, the air we breathe, and the houses we live in.

Charlie and Betty Johnston's experience is a good example of how national government decisions affect individuals. The Johnstons are not experts on the national government. But they could tell you that national government programs, combined with action by private citizens, have recently made a big difference in their lives.

The Johnstons and their seven children live in Saul Hollow, Kentucky. For many years the Johnstons had lived in a crowded, four-room wooden shack. Like most of their neighbors, the Johnstons could not afford to move.

Charlie worked hard as a janitor at the local school, but he made only $4,000 a year. Like more than 50 percent of their neighbors in Clay County, the Johnstons' family income was well below the poverty level set by the national government. The Johnstons were too poor to buy a new home. They were too poor to qualify for a home loan from the national government.

The Reverend M. Dwayne Yost, a minister at a local church, decided to try to change things in the area. Yost took a six-month leave from his church to work for better housing in Clay County. Yost talked with other church leaders and with local business people. Many of them provided the money and volunteers to help Yost form an organization called the Kentucky Mountain Housing Development Corporation.

Once it had been formed, Kentucky Mountain Housing went to the national government to ask for money to start building new homes and fixing up old ones. They succeeded in getting a grant and started their program.

Today the Johnstons live in a new, three-bedroom, white frame house. Their new home has indoor plumbing, a new stove and refrigerator, a vegetable garden, and a nice lawn. Here's how the government program worked in the Johnstons' case:

Kentucky Mountain helped Charlie and Betty get a special $13,200 home loan from the Farmers Home Administration of the Department of Agriculture. At the same time, another federal government program provided the money to pay local workers to build the Johnston home for Kentucky Mountain. A third federal agency provided part of the money to run Kentucky Mountain Housing.

In addition to the federal government, private individuals and

The new house completed, a delighted home owner takes the title from an officer of Kentucky Mountain Housing as Reverend Yost looks on.

groups helped. A local coal company donated the use of its bulldozer. Within several years, Kentucky Mountain Housing had built sixty new homes. In addition, they had repaired hundreds of homes in Clay and Jackson counties.

Many of the people who moved into these homes had annual incomes that were even lower than the Johnstons'. One family had an income of just $1,100 per year. Yet not one family failed to make its loan payments. The program started by Reverend Yost and other citizens in Clay County was a success.

The homes now owned by the Johnstons and other families in eastern Kentucky could not have been built without federal money. However, the actions of private citizens were equally important. New homes were built because private citizens used government programs to help them reach their own goals. They were built because citizens like Reverend Yost and other community leaders worked together.

Review

1. Why were the Johnstons unable to qualify for a federal home loan?
2. How did Kentucky Mountain Housing and the national government change the housing alternatives facing the Johnstons?
3. Explain why this case study is an example of how the national government affects citizens' everyday lives.

Basic Social Studies Skills
Using an Almanac

You have just read about how the national government raises and spends money. You have explored some of the basics involved with preparing a national budget and collecting taxes and other revenue to meet expenses.

If you should ever find the need to explore these subjects further—for a term paper or simply for your own knowledge—an **almanac** would be a very good source.

Almanacs are reference books that are published annually. Some of the most widely used almanacs are the *World Almanac*, the *Hammond Almanac, Reader's Digest Almanac*, and *Information Please Almanac*. Each of these almanacs contains up-to-date information on subjects such as energy, education, manufacturing, economics, population, Congress, and presidential elections. Each also has important statistics about every nation in the world. If you wanted to find out the current population of France, for example, an almanac would have this information.

Before trying to locate specific information in an almanac, you should aquaint yourself with its organization. The *World Almanac*, for example, has its index in the front of the book instead of at the end.

A reproduction of a chart in the 1984 *World Almanac* appears below. It is typical of the type of information provided in an almanac. Study the chart and then answer the following questions.

Skill Practice

1. What were the total net receipts in fiscal 1982?

2. What was the largest outlay, or expense, in fiscal 1981?

3. What general conclusion can you draw by comparing net receipts and net outlays for the fiscal years on the chart?

4. Use an almanac to find information about the receipts and outlays of five nations for a given year.

Summary of U.S. Receipts by Source and Outlays by Function

Source: U.S. Treasury Department, Bureau of Govt. Financial Operations

(in millions)

Net Receipts	Fiscal 1980	Fiscal 1981	Fiscal 1982
Individual income taxes	$244,069	$285,551	$298,111
Corporation income taxes	64,600	61,137	49,207
Social insurance taxes and contributions	160,747	183,086	201,132
Excise taxes	24,329	40,839	36,311
Estate and gift taxes	6,389	6,787	7,991
Customs duties	7,174	8,083	8,854
Miscellaneous receipts	12,748	13,790	16,161
Total	**$520,056**	**$599,272**	**$617,766**
Net outlays			
National defense	$135,880	$159,736	$187,397
International affairs	10,472	11,052	9,983
General science, space, and technology	5,999	6,422	7,096
Energy	6,623	10,351	4,844
Natural resources and environment	14,130	13,764	13,086
Agriculture	4,951	5,598	14,808
Commerce and housing credit	7,795	3,995	3,843
Transportation	20,840	23,312	20,589
Community and regional development	9,917	9,538	7,410
Education, training, employment and social services	31,399	30,533	25,411
Health	58,165	65,984	74,018
Income security	192,133	225,599	248,807
Veterans benefits and services	21,167	22,937	23,973
Administration of justice	4,554	4,720	4,648
General government	4,641	4,759	4,833
General purpose fiscal assistance	8,306	6,621	6,161
Interest	64,564	82,590	100,777
Undistributed offsetting receipts	−21,933	−30,306	−29,261
Total	**$579,603**	**$657,204**	**$728,424**

Chapter 7 Review

Summary

Section 1: Where the Money Comes From

The cost of running the government is increasing every year. A major source of the money used to pay for government expenses is taxes. Personal income taxes, social security taxes, and corporate income taxes contribute a large share of the money Borrowing is another source of income.

Section 2: How the Money Is Spent

The money collected by the government from taxes and other sources is used to provide services and benefits to United States citizens. Retired people, widows, orphans, veterans, and disabled people receive the largest share of money. Another large share of the money goes to national defense. A considerable amount goes to state and local governments through revenue sharing and grants-in-aid. The government also must pay its own employees and pay interest on the national debt.

Section 3: Making the Federal Budget

The federal budget is the government's plan for collecting and spending money for a twelve-month period called a fiscal year. The federal budget is planned by the executive branch and modified and approved by the legislative branch. The judicial branch settles arguments dealing with the collecting and spending of money in the budget. Balancing a budget—making sure that expenses do not exceed income—has become an increasingly difficult goal to achieve in recent years. The nation has not had a balanced budget for several decades. This fact has contributed to a rapidly climbing national debt.

Vocabulary

Define the following terms.

1. interest
2. securities
3. tax
4. protective tariff
5. personal income tax
6. social security tax

Reviewing Main Ideas

1. The executive branch _____.
a. has nothing to do with the budget
b. approves the budget
c. makes up the budget
d. none of the above
2. True or false: Every dollar that a person earns during a year is taxed.
3. True or false: A cut in defense spending could put people out of work.
4. True or false: The largest expense in the federal budget is social security benefits.

Thinking Critically

Organizing Information

List the sources of national government income from largest to smallest. Then list five of the national government's expenses from greatest to smallest.

Evaluating Information

If the national budget were a balanced budget, what effect would it have on the national debt?
a. It would make the national debt grow larger.
b. It would make the national debt smaller.
c. The national debt would stay the same.

Communicating Ideas

Suppose someone asked you why the United States government spends so many billions of dollars a year. Describe three or four of the most expensive items in the national budget.

Chapter 8

The Presidency

Introduction. It is early morning in Washington, D.C. A telephone rings in one of the city's bedrooms. "Good morning, Mr. President," a voice says at the end of the line. "It is six o'clock, sir." The man who has been awakened gets up and begins another day as President of the United States.

What is it like to be President of one of the most powerful nations in the world? To be sure, the job of President is quite unlike any other job in the world.

The President lives and works in the White House. The first family does not have to bother with many things that take an average family's time. Grocery shopping, cooking, house cleaning, lawn cutting, and other chores are done for them by the White House domestic staff of more than eighty people.

There are plenty of ways to relax at the White House. A private movie theater is available. For exercise, there are tennis courts, a small gym, a one-lane bowling alley, and heated indoor and outdoor swimming pools. For reading, there is a private library.

When the President needs to travel, he commands a fleet of special cars, helicopters, and airplanes. For long trips, the President uses Air Force One, a specially-equipped Boeing 707 jet.

The President's life has another side. The presidency can be a life-threatening job. Four Presidents have been assassinated. Numerous attempted assassinations have also occurred. Consequently, the President and his family are always closely guarded by Secret Service agents.

The presidency can be life-threatening in another way. Most Presidents work long hours. They must make very important decisions. It is believed that the hard work and responsibility can shorten a person's life by several years. To help the President stay healthy, there is a medical staff and a small clinic inside the White House.

The President does not live like an average citizen. In this chapter you will learn about the person who leads such a special life.

Section 1
Getting Elected

The presidency is the top political job in the United States. The person who holds the job has the power to make decisions that affect people in all parts of the world. For these and other reasons, many people have tried for the office.

Requirements

People who have been elected President in the past have had many things in common. Naturally, all of them have met requirements stated in Article 2, Section 1, of the Constitution. Each has been (1) at least thirty-five years old, (2) a natural-born citizen, and (3) a resident of the United States for at least fourteen years.

Former Presidents have also had traits in common that are not formally required. For example, all have been white, and all have been men. All have been of European descent. Most have had previous political jobs. Most have had a college education. Many have been lawyers. Most have been from states that have large populations. And, for as long as national political parties have existed, all have been members of major political parties. Look at the chart on page 164.

At recent nominating conventions, women and nonwhites have challenged the idea that only white males can be President. To date, the major political parties have not been persuaded that a woman or a nonwhite could win a presidential election. However, a major step was taken in 1984. Geraldine Ferraro, a congresswoman from New York, became the Democratic party's candidate for Vice-President.

President Ronald Reagan shortly after his election to a second term of office in 1984.

163

Twentieth-Century Presidents

Name	Sex	College Education	Age Elected	Religion	Ethnic Background	State	Political Party	Early Career
Theodore Roosevelt (1901-1909)	Male	Yes	42	Protestant	Dutch & French	Large (New York)	Republican	Author & politician
William Howard Taft (1909-1913)	Male	Yes	51	Protestant	British	Large (Ohio)	Republican	Lawyer
Woodrow Wilson (1913-1921)	Male	Yes	56	Protestant	British	Medium (New Jersey)	Democrat	Teacher
Warren Harding (1921-1923)	Male	Yes	55	Protestant	British & Dutch	Large (Ohio)	Republican	Newspaperman & politician
Calvin Coolidge (1923-1929)	Male	Yes	51	Protestant	British	Medium (Massachusetts)	Republican	Lawyer & politician
Herbert Hoover (1929-1933)	Male	Yes	54	Protestant	Swiss-German	Large (California)	Republican	Engineer & businessman
Franklin D. Roosevelt (1933-1945)	Male	Yes	51	Protestant	Dutch & French	Large (New York)	Democrat	Lawyer & politician
Harry S. Truman (1945-1953)	Male	No	60	Protestant	British	Medium (Missouri)	Democrat	Storekeeper & politician
Dwight D. Eisenhower (1953-1961)	Male	Yes	62	Protestant	Swiss-German	Large Pennsylvania	Republican	Military leader
John F. Kennedy (1961-1963)	Male	Yes	43	Roman Catholic	Irish	Medium (Massachusetts)	Democrat	Author & politician
Lyndon B. Johnson (1963-1969)	Male	Yes	55	Protestant	British	Large (Texas)	Democrat	Teacher & politician
Richard M. Nixon (1969-1974)	Male	Yes	56	Protestant	British	Large (California)	Republican	Lawyer & politician
Gerald R. Ford (1974-1977)	Male	Yes	61	Protestant	British	Medium (Michigan)	Republican	Lawyer & politician
Jimmy Carter (1977-1981)	Male	Yes	52	Protestant	British	Medium (Georgia)	Democrat	Businessman & politician
Ronald W. Reagan (1981-1989)	Male	Yes	69	Protestant	Irish	Large (California)	Republican	Actor & politician
George Bush (1989-	Male	Yes	64	Protestant	British	Large (Texas)	Republican	Businessman & politician

Study the chart above. How many of the Presidents had college educations? How many were from large states?

Election of the President

A presidential election is one of the most exciting political events in the United States. Such elections are held every four years on the Tuesday after the first Monday in November. On this day, every eligible citizen who has registered may vote.

The entire election process, however, starts well before November of an election year. The election process includes three major steps: (1) the nomination of candidates, (2) the campaign, and (3) the vote.

Nomination. Presidential hopefuls start campaigning to be **nominated,** or named, as their party's candidate a year or more before the election. They meet voters in shopping centers and make speeches and radio and television commercials. They fly from state to state trying to persuade voters to choose delegates who will vote for them at their party's national nominating convention.

In summer of the election year, both major parties hold national conventions to nominate their candidate for President. Delegates come to these conventions from each state, the District of Columbia, and the territories of the United States. Convention delegates are selected in several ways. In many states, including almost all of the larger ones, delegates are elected by voters in a presidential **primary election.** In the remaining states, delegates are chosen by state conventions, party committees, or caucuses. A **caucus** is a meeting of political party leaders. The size of a state's delegation depends chiefly on its population. Large states have many delegates. Small states have few delegates. In addition, some elected and party officials are chosen by other officials as delegates.

The earliest primary is usually in New Hampshire in February or March. The last important ones are usually in Ohio, California, and New Jersey in June. As primaries and caucuses roll by, the hopefuls gain delegates and publicity.

The Democratic and Republican conventions are noisy, nationally televised affairs that last several days during the summer of an election year. The enthusiastic delegates wear buttons and carry signs promoting the people they hope will be nominated. There are many speeches. It is a time for party workers and party leaders to prepare for the election campaign ahead.

Presidential Election Process

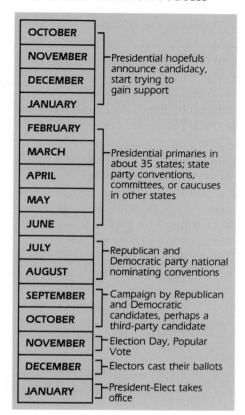

OCTOBER	
NOVEMBER	Presidential hopefuls announce candidacy, start trying to gain support
DECEMBER	
JANUARY	
FEBRUARY	
MARCH	Presidential primaries in about 35 states; state party conventions, committees, or caucuses in other states
APRIL	
MAY	
JUNE	
JULY	Republican and Democratic party national nominating conventions
AUGUST	
SEPTEMBER	Campaign by Republican and Democratic candidates, perhaps a third-party candidate
OCTOBER	
NOVEMBER	Election Day, Popular Vote
DECEMBER	Electors cast their ballots
JANUARY	President-Elect takes office

Study the chart. When are the national conventions usually held?

Senator John Glenn, a former astronaut, campaigned for the Democratic presidential nomination in 1984. He lost the bid to Walter Mondale. Here, Glenn is shown with members of Iowa's Marycrest basketball team.

165

(bottom) Democratic
presidential candidate Walter
Mondale and vice-presidential
running mate Geraldine
Ferraro at the Democratic
convention in 1984. (below)
Mondale-Ferraro backers.

The convention delegates vote to select the presidential nominee. In recent years, the convention's role in actually choosing the nominee has become less important than it was in the past. So much campaigning for the nomination now goes on in the primary elections that, by convention time, a clear leader with enough delegate support to guarantee the nomination has usually emerged.

Efforts have been made recently to give the delegates at the nominating conventions greater influence in the selection of a candidate than they had in the past. Thus delegates are no longer required by party rules to vote at the convention for the candidates they expressed a preference for when they were chosen as delegates through party primaries or conventions in their states. But most of them may be expected to support those candidates on the first convention ballot.

The presidential candidate picks the person to run for Vice-President. The delegates usually approve the choice by unanimous vote. This is possible because all of the debate concerning possible running mates is done beforehand by the candidate and his or her staff.

Campaign. Once the party conventions are over, the major candidates campaign to attract voter support. Presidential campaigns are usually in full swing by October. They go on until election day in November.

During the campaign, candidates travel across the country. They give speeches to many different groups. They appear on TV and hold press conferences. They meet state and local political leaders, and they urge members of their party to work for them. They may meet their opponents in televised debates. Party workers and other volunteers work for their candidate by passing out literature, making phone calls, and holding rallies.

It takes a great deal of money and energy to run a successful campaign. The hopefuls must choose wisely where they will concentrate their resources in order to make the best showing among voters.

Besides purchasing broadcast time on television and radio, and paying for air fare and other transportation, candidates must also pay salaries to campaign staff members and fees to professional campaign consultants. There are also telephone, postage, and printing costs.

In a recent presidential election year, $275 million was spent to elect a President. This figure includes the

costs of campaigns for presidential nomination by all candidates, the costs of the political parties' nominating conventions, and the costs of the general election campaigns.

The Vote. The Constitution does not provide for direct election of the President by the people. Instead, it provides that each state "shall appoint" electors who vote for one of the major candidates.

Thus, on election day in November, the voters are not selecting the President directly. Instead, they are actually voting for a group of presidential electors from their state. The electors meet in their state capitals in December to cast the state's electoral votes for President and Vice-President. The electors, who are collectively known as the **electoral college,** send their votes to Congress. There, they are counted. The winner is declared the President of the United States.

Each state has as many electors as its total of members in Congress. For example, in 1984, California had forty-five representatives and two senators. Thus, California had forty-seven electoral votes.

If the majority of the **popular votes** (those of the people) in a state go to the candidate of one party, then that person is supposed to get all of that state's electoral votes. This custom, which is rarely broken, is called **winner-take-all.** In a recent election one elector broke with custom. The elector voted for one candidate even though most of the popular votes in that state were cast for the other candidate. Nonetheless, the winner-take-all custom usually

means that the winner's margin of victory, as indicated by electoral votes, is larger than his popular vote margin. It is even possible for the candidate with the greatest number of popular votes to lose the election because he or she had fewer electoral votes.

The newly chosen President is called the President-elect until he or she takes office on January 20.

Section Review

Vocabulary:
caucus, delegates, electoral college, nominate, popular vote, primary election, winner-take-all.

Reviewing the Main Ideas
1. What three requirements must a person meet before he or she can be elected President?
2. Name three traits that are not required but that most Presidents have had in common.
3. How often are presidential elections held?
4. Why are presidential primary elections important?
5. What sorts of activities go on during a presidential campaign?

Skill Building
1. Why can the electoral college system be called a winner-take-all system?
2. According to the chart on page 164, who are the two youngest Presidents to be elected in the twentieth century?

President Reagan taking the oath of office on January 20, 1985.

Section 2
The President's Job

The President is the most powerful public official in the United States. Where does the President's power come from? What is the President's job today?

Constitutional Powers

The Constitution is the basis of the President's power. Article 2 of the Constitution says that the executive power shall be given to a President of the United States. Thus, the President's main job is to execute, or carry out, the laws passed by Congress.

The Constitution also gives the President the power to:

- veto laws proposed by Congress
- call Congress into special session
- serve as commander in chief of the armed forces
- receive leaders and other officials of foreign countries

- make treaties with other countries (These treaties must have Senate approval.)
- appoint heads of executive agencies, federal court judges, ambassadors, and other top government officials (These also must have Senate approval.)
- pardon people convicted of federal crimes, reduce their sentences, or lower their fines

Because the Constitution requires the President to give Congress information about the "state of the union," the President gives several speeches to Congress each year. The most important is the "State of the Union" speech, in which the President describes new programs he would like Congress to start.

The President's term of office, also stated in the Constitution, is four years. The Twenty-second Amendment limits the President to two elected terms in office, or ten years if the presidency was assumed during another President's term.

The Job Today

The President fills a number of different roles. Four of these roles come directly from constitutional grants of power. These roles are foreign-policy leader, commander in chief, chief executive, and chief legislator. Three other roles that have developed over the years are not established in the Constitution. These roles are head of state, economic leader, and party chief.

Foreign-Policy Leader. As **foreign-policy leader,** the President directs the foreign policy of the United States. It is the President who makes

President Jimmy Carter (center), Israel's prime minister, Menachem Begin (right), and Egypt's president, Anwar Sadat (left), signing the Camp David Accord in 1977. President Carter, in his role as foreign-policy leader, was credited with bringing about this historic peace treaty between Israel and Egypt.

the key decisions about how the United States acts toward other countries in the world. Presidents spend a lot of time working on foreign-policy problems.

Commander in Chief. The President's role as **commander in chief** is related to his foreign-policy role. The President is in charge of the Army, Navy, Air Force, Marines, and Coast Guard. All military officers take their orders from the President. The President also has the right to decide how weapons and troops will be used.

The power to make war is divided between the Congress and President. The Constitution gives Congress the power to declare war, but it is the President who really decides if there will be war or peace. Congress has declared war only five times: the War of 1812, the Mexican War, the Spanish-American War, World War I, and World War II. Presidents have sent troops into action overseas more than 150 times since 1789. In the 1960s and early 1970s, the Vietnam War was fought without a declaration of war.

Chief Executive. As **chief executive,** the President is responsible for carrying out the laws passed by Congress. To do this, the President is in charge of the nearly three million people who work for the national government. The President does not supervise all these people personally, but the President does appoint their supervisors. By appointing these leaders the President can influence the many parts of the executive branch.

Chief Legislator. The President can be considered **chief legislator** of the United States because most of the bills Congress considers each year are sent to Congress by the President's staff or by agencies in the executive branch. Congress has the power to pass laws, but the President largely determines what the business of Congress will be.

Every President has a **legislative program.** These are new laws that he or she wants Congress to pass. The President makes speeches to build support for this program. The President often meets with senators and representatives to try to convince them to support the proposed laws. In addition, the President appoints several staff members to work closely with members of Congress on new laws.

Historically, there has always been tension between the President and Congress over what new laws should be passed. One source of tension is that Presidents represent

Fulfilling the role of commander in chief involves frequent communications with top defense officials. Here, President Reagan confers with (left) Caspar Weinberger, Secretary of Defense, and (center) General John William Vessey, Jr.

people all over the United States while members of Congress represent only the people of their states or districts. To be elected or re-elected, the President must try to appeal to the entire country. No one group controls the President's attention. Individual members of Congress are not as free as the President to be concerned about nationwide problems.

Another source of tension is the difference in the length of time that Presidents and members of Congress can serve. Presidents can serve no more than two elected terms, while members of Congress can serve an unlimited number of terms. Therefore, many members of Congress do not want to move as quickly on programs as the President does. Presidents often complain that Congress is "dragging its heels" on new programs.

Head of State. As **head of state,** the President is the living symbol of the country. In this role, the President greets visiting kings and queens, prime ministers, and other leaders. The President meets with boy scouts and girl scouts, lights the nation's Christmas tree, and gives medals to the country's heroes. The President is expected to represent all United States citizens.

Economic Leader. As **economic leader,** the President tries to help the country's economy work well. Citizens want the President to take the lead in dealing with such problems as unemployment or high prices or high taxes. Business leaders, for example, may want the President to protect their industry from foreign competition. Labor leaders may want the President to start new job-training programs for people who are out of work. One job that the President must do each year as economic leader is to plan the budget.

Party Chief. As **party chief,** the President is regarded as leader of one of the major political parties. Members of the President's party work hard to elect the President. In turn, the President gives speeches to help party members who are running for office as mayors, governors, and members of Congress. The President helps the party raise money for its candidates, and the President works with other leaders to plan party activities.

As the head of state, the President presides over various ceremonies and meets with citizens from all walks of life. Here, President Reagan is watching the women's Olympic basketball team prepare for the 1984 summer Olympics.

Section Review

Vocabulary:

chief executive, chief legislator, commander in chief, economic leader, foreign-policy leader, head of state, legislative program, party chief.

Reviewing the Main Ideas

1. List three powers given to the President in the Constitution.

2. Name two presidential roles that are based on powers granted by the Constitution. Name one role that is not based on constitutional powers.

3. What does the President do that makes it appropriate to call him chief legislator?

Skill Building

1. Which of the seven presidential roles did the President assume in each of the following actions?

a. During the Korean War, President Truman fired General Douglas MacArthur. Truman later said, "I fired him because he wouldn't respect the authority of the President."

b. President Ronald Reagan named George Shultz to be his new Secretary of State.

c. In a major speech to Congress, President Lyndon Johnson called for a new government program to help poor people.

2. Find examples in your newspaper of the many roles and duties of the President as he fulfills the seven main job descriptions. Collect the articles for several weeks and then organize them on a bulletin board.

Section 3
Presidential Advisers

In 1801, President Thomas Jefferson (1801-1809) could do his job with the help of a few advisers, one messenger, and a part-time secretary. Today thousands of clerks, secretaries, and highly trained specialists assist the President. Most of these people work in the Executive Office of the President.

The Executive Office of the President

The **Executive Office of the President** (EOP) was created in 1939 to help the President do his job. It has been growing ever since. In a recent year, the EOP had nearly 2,000 employees and a budget of more than $100 million.

The men and women who work in the EOP investigate many different issues and problems. They

Study the chart below. Which offices deal with economic matters?

Executive Office of the President

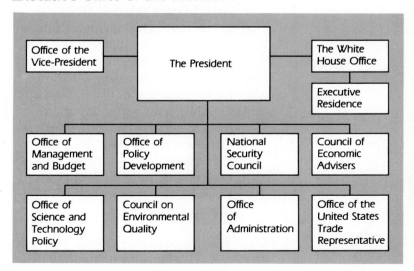

President Reagan conferring with members of the National Security Council.

prepare reports for the President on special topics, such as new taxes that might be needed. They help write bills for the President to send to Congress. They monitor the activities of the many different parts of the executive branch.

The chart on page 171 shows the organization of the EOP. Four of the units shown play important roles in advising modern Presidents. These are the **White House Office,** the **Office of Management and Budget,** the **National Security Council,** and the **Council of Economic Advisers.**

The White House Office. This unit consists of about five hundred people who work directly for the

President. Among them are ten to twelve people who serve as the President's closest political advisers.

These top advisers are often people who have known the President for years and have worked for his election. They have the President's trust. They are very loyal to the President and his policies. Most will only work at the White House as long as their President is in office. Each new President brings in his own group of top advisers.

Among the top advisers are the assistant for national security affairs, assistant for domestic affairs, counsel (lawyer) to the President, chief of staff, appointments secretary, assistant for public relations, assistant for

The President's top advisers also screen the flow of information and people trying to reach the President. A President could not possibly meet with everyone who wanted to see him. Nor could he read all the reports, memos, and letters sent to him. The White House Staff largely decides what information gets through to the President.

The White House Staff has a good deal of political power. This power comes from the staff's closeness to the President and its ability to act in the President's name. Lawmakers and other government officials know that to influence, or sometimes even to reach the President, they must deal with the White House Staff.

The Office of Management and Budget (OMB). This agency prepares the federal budget and monitors spending in hundreds of government agencies. The Director of OMB reports directly to, and works directly with, the President.

The National Security Council (NSC). This group helps the President coordinate United States military and foreign policy. The Council includes the President, Vice-President, the secretaries of State and Defense, and the Chairman of the Joint Chiefs of Staff. The President can also invite others to be a part of this group. Each President names an Assistant for National Security Affairs to direct the NSC staff.

The NSC recommends specific policies and decisions to the President. The President makes the final decision of whether or not to follow

legislative affairs, and press secretary. As a group, such advisers are known as the **White House Staff.**

The White House Staff advises the President in many areas. Will Congress accept a tax increase? Will business leaders oppose some new federal regulations? How can the President lower unemployment? What should our foreign policy toward the Soviet Union be?

The top advisers write speeches for the President, plan the President's trips, and try to make sure the President's orders are actually carried out by other government agencies. They work with local and state political leaders to build support for the President's programs.

Cabinet Departments

Department of State
Department of Defense
Department of Health and Human Services
Department of the Treasury
Department of Justice
Department of Labor
Department of Housing and Urban Development
Department of the Interior
Department of Agriculture
Department of Commerce
Department of Transportation
Department of Energy
Department of Education
Department of Veterans Affairs

Which of the Cabinet departments listed at right deals with farm programs? Which deals with employment programs?

the advice of the NSC. Some Presidents have relied heavily on the NSC for foreign policy advice, while others have not.

The Council of Economic Advisers (CEA). This group helps the President carry out the role of economic leader. The CEA consists of three members appointed by the President. The Senate must approve those members. The Council's job involves giving the President advice about complex economic matters such as employment, tax policy, and inflation. Along with the OMB and such officials as the Secretary of the Treasury, the CEA helps the President plan the nation's overall economic policy.

The Cabinet

Every President, from George Washington's time to the present, has had a **Cabinet**—a group of top-level advisers.

The Cabinet is currently composed of thirteen members, each of whom heads an important executive department and is appointed by the President and approved by the Senate. The Cabinet departments are listed at left.

The Cabinet was not created by the Constitution. It developed over the years through custom and usage. The Cabinet started when George Washington (1789-1797) began to meet regularly with the heads of the first four executive departments. These were the Attorney General, and the secretaries of State, War, and the Treasury.

The Cabinet meets whenever the President determines that it is necessary. This may be as often as once a week or hardly at all. Most Presidents have not relied heavily on their Cabinet and have felt free to ignore Cabinet advice. When his entire Cabinet was opposed to him on an issue, President Lincoln (1861-1865) once said: "Seven nays, one aye—the ayes have it."

There are several reasons why most Presidents do not rely on their Cabinet for advice on key decisions. Knowing these reasons helps explain why Presidents have come to rely so heavily on the White House Staff for advice.

First, Cabinet members are often more loyal to the department they direct and the interests their departments serve than to the President. The Secretary of Agriculture, for example, might oppose the President's desire to cut spending for farm programs. Second, Presidents want to discuss key problems in secrecy. With a dozen Cabinet members, it can be difficult to keep discussions secret.

The "Inner Cabinet." Most Presidents have several Cabinet members whose advice they depend upon on a regular basis. This group is sometimes called the **Inner Cabinet.** It is often made up of one or two secretaries the President has come to know well and trust. It might also include Cabinet members heading those departments of great concern to the President. These usually are the departments of Justice, State, Defense, and the Treasury.

The Vice-President

Vice-Presidents are usually not very visible to the public. The duties they perform often do not warrant front-page coverage in the daily newspapers. Yet, if the President dies, is removed from office, becomes ill, or resigns, the Vice-President becomes President. Nine Vice-Presidents have become President because of the death or resignation of a President. Four Presidents were assassinated, four Presidents died of natural causes, and one President resigned. John Adams, our nation's first Vice-President, described the role well. He said, "I am Vice-President. In this I am nothing, but I may become everything."

The Constitution gives little authority to the Vice-President. Article 1 states that the Vice-President presides over the Senate and votes in that body in the case of a tie. The 25th Amendment also gives the Vice-President a role in determining if a President is disabled and unable to do the job. Should that occur, the Vice-President would serve as Acting President until the President was able to go back to work.

Beyond this, what the Vice-President does is up to the President. Throughout the country's history, most Presidents have delegated little authority to their Vice-Presidents. Recent Presidents, however, have made some efforts to give their Vice-Presidents more responsibility. Recent Vice-Presidents have been appointed to serve as members of special presidential advisory groups. They have often been sent on visits to foreign nations as representatives of the President. In these and other ways they have sometimes served as advisers. However, no Vice-President has ever really become an important decision maker in any President's administration.

Section Review

Vocabulary:
Cabinet, Council of Economic Advisers (CEA), Executive Office of the President (EOP), Inner Cabinet, National Security Council (NSC), Office of Management and Budget (OMB), White House Office, White House Staff.

Reviewing the Main Ideas
1. What is the job of the White House Staff?
2. Who was the first President to have a Cabinet? Who served in it?

Skill Building
Would you say that people who work in the Executive Office of the President deal with many kinds of problems and many tasks or only a few? Explain your answer.

(above) President Jimmy Carter before signing a piece of legislation in 1977. (opposite, left) President Harry Truman at his desk in 1948. The sign on Truman's desk, ''The Buck Stops Here!'', emphasized that many crucial decisions are ultimately the sole responsibility of the President. President Carter kept President Truman's famous sign on his desk during his term of office.

Section 4
How Presidential Decisions Get Made

The decisions Presidents have to make are often difficult. President Eisenhower (1953-1961) put it this way. "There are no easy matters that will come to you as President. If they are easy, they will be settled at a lower level."

Moreover, Presidents cannot escape the tough decisions that come to them. President Truman (1945-1953) made this clear with a sign he kept on his desk. The sign said, "The Buck Stops Here!" The President may act or refuse to act on a certain problem. Either way, the President will be making a decision. The President is ultimately held responsible for both the good and the bad consequences of that decision.

Influences on a President's Decision

How do Presidents decide what to do? Many factors can shape a President's decisions. Six of the most important are: (1) historical circumstances, (2) public opinion, (3) Congress, (4) laws, (5) the President's personal beliefs, and (6) the President's leadership qualities.

Historical Circumstances. Not all Presidents face the same problems or opportunities. Perhaps the most basic force shaping presidential decisions is the nature of the times during which the President serves. Modern Presidents have served in times quite different from those faced by our earlier Presidents.

The events of the times bring each President special problems. George Washington, for instance, faced the unique task of getting a

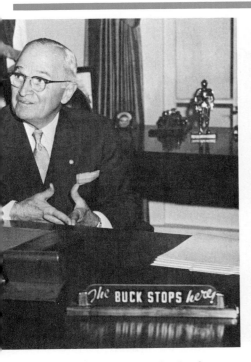

new government started. Abraham Lincoln faced terrible decisions coming from our greatest internal crisis—the Civil War. Woodrow Wilson (1913-1921) was the first President to lead the nation in a world war. Dwight Eisenhower faced many foreign policy decisions resulting from the fact that, after World War II, the Soviet Union created its own nuclear weapons.

Public Opinion. Presidents' decisions are also shaped by **public opinion**—the way voters feel about a particular issue. Presidents know they need the support of the public to carry out their programs. They also need the support of Congress, which is influenced by the President's public popularity. When elected officials see that the President has wide public backing for his

programs, they are more likely to accept them.

Understanding the public mood can also help Presidents time their decisions so they are most effective. Successful Presidents have a good sense of when the public is ready for a new idea and when it is not. Franklin D. Roosevelt (1933–1945) explained, "I cannot go any faster than the people will let me."

Presidents today closely monitor public opinion. Most Presidents have a specialist in the White House Office who regularly conducts public opinion polls. These polls measure the President's popularity or public attitudes toward a specific policy, such as a proposed tax increase.

Citizens' views also come to the President by letter, telegram, or phone call to the White House. Presidents receive from 35,000 to 80,000

President Reagan fielding questions from reporters at a press conference. Presidents often introduce new ideas at press conferences. Feedback from the public will then help the President determine if the ideas meet with popular approval.

letters a week. These communications rarely, if ever, reach the President directly. However, about twenty White House staff members regularly prepare summaries for the President of the opinions expressed in these messages.

Congress. Under the Constitution, the President and Congress have separate powers. At the same time, each branch shares certain powers through a system of checks and balances. Thus, Presidents must depend on Congress to pass laws they want, to approve money for their programs, and to approve their appointments of top officials.

As a result, Presidents care about what members of Congress think. Presidents often keep Congress in mind when making decisions. For example, if a President learns that many members of Congress oppose his plan for federal aid to cities, the President may change the plan to make it more acceptable to the lawmakers.

Modern Presidents often have difficulty getting support for particular programs from Congress. Usually Presidents receive more support in Congress from members of their own political party than from the opposition party. But this is not always true. Thus, as with public opinion, Presidents spend a great deal of time trying to win congressional support for their decisions.

Laws. No President is above the law. The Constitution and laws passed by Congress also limit or shape the President's decisions. In recent years, Congress has passed several

laws that put limits on the kinds of decisions Presidents can make.

In 1973, for example, Congress passed the **War Powers Act.** This law limits the President's power to send troops into combat without a declaration of war by Congress. In 1976, Congress passed the **National Emergencies Act.** This law requires Presidents to inform Congress before declaring a national emergency.

Personal Beliefs. A President's personal beliefs about people, other countries, government, and the presidency itself influence presidential decisions. President Gerald Ford (1974-1977) described the role of personal beliefs during his administration. He said, "I had a combination of . . . recommendations from people in the administration and my own background and personal convictions. It was a combination of the two—options that came to me and my own experience and convictions—that ended up in whatever decisions I made."

President Abraham Lincoln (1861-1865) talking to General George McClellan's troops during the Civil War. Many historians believe Lincoln was one of our strongest leaders.

Every President also has ideas about how Presidents should use their powers. Some have taken a limited view of presidential power. President William Howard Taft (1909-1913) expressed this view well: "The President can exercise no power which cannot be fairly and reasonably traced to some specific grant of power."

Other Presidents believed the President should try to exercise as much power as possible. President Theodore Roosevelt (1901-1909) expressed this point of view. He argued that, "it was not only [the President's] right but his duty to do anything the needs of the nation demanded unless such action was forbidden by the Constitution or by the laws."

Leadership Qualities. Finally, the kinds of decisions Presidents make are shaped by their own leadership abilities. Some Presidents are better leaders than others. Successful leaders are open to new ideas. They are willing to be flexible in their thinking and to settle disagreements through compromises. At the same time, they have the courage to do what they believe is right even if it may be unpopular.

Section Review

Vocabulary:
National Emergencies Act, public opinion, War Powers Act.

Reviewing the Main Ideas
1. Who must take responsibility for the most important executive-branch decisions?
2. List six important factors that can influence a President's decision making.
3. Give two reasons why public opinion is important to Presidents.

Skill Building
Rank the six factors that shape or influence a President's decisions to show which you think is most important and which is least. Explain your ranking.

The President's Veto Power

Glancing at a newspaper, you see the headline: PRESIDENT VETOES HOUSING BILL. If asked how the President's action relates to your rights and freedoms, you might find it hard to answer. Yet the President's power to veto—not sign—bills passed by Congress is one important way your rights may be protected by the Constitution.

What is the veto power? What does it have to do with your rights? How and why do Presidents use the power?

The Veto Power

The Constitution requires every bill passing the House of Representatives and the Senate to be sent to the President for signature before it can become law.

Article 1, Section 7, of the Constitution gives the President the power to veto a bill. The President may veto a bill in two ways. First, the President may send the bill back unsigned to the house of its origin. The President does this by simply writing "veto" (I forbid) across the front of the bill. The bill does not become law then unless both houses of Congress override the veto by a two-thirds majority vote.

The President may also use a pocket veto as a means of stopping a bill from becoming law. If the President does not sign a bill while Congress is still in session, the bill automatically becomes law after ten days. However, if Congress recesses before this ten-day period has passed, the bill is automatically killed.

Protecting Your Rights and Freedoms

How is the veto power related to your rights and freedoms? Individual rights can be abused by a powerful government. The veto is one key part of a system created by the Constitution to protect citizens against government abuses. This system is called checks and balances.

Checks and Balances. The system of checks and balances means each branch of the government has powers to "check", or "balance", the actions of the others. Under checks and balances, each branch is given some role, or share, in the actions of the others.

In addition to the veto, here are two other examples of checks and balances: 1) The Senate must approve all the people the President appoints to top jobs in government. 2) The Supreme Court may review laws passed by Congress and declare them unconstitutional. In short, checks and balances means no branch of the national government can do its job without some cooperation from the others.

Reasons for Checks and Balances. Why do we have a system of checks and balances? The Founders of our Constitution believed that people, if left unchecked, would seek power and try to dominate each other. Ben Franklin spoke for most of the Founders when he said, "There are two passions which have a powerful influence on the affairs of men: the love of power and the love of money." Alexander Hamilton added, "Men love power."

Given their views of human nature, the Founders faced a dilemma. How could they design a government run by the people and yet prevent abuses of power?

James Madison described the problem. He said, "In framing a government, which is to be

administered by men over men, the great difficulty lies in this: You must first enable the government to control the governed; and in the next place, oblige it to control itself."

Checks and balances were one answer. The Founders hoped that by creating separate branches that shared powers—executive, legislative, and judicial—they would help prevent the unjust use of power by the government.

The Veto Contributes to Checks and Balances

The veto contributes to checks and balances by giving the President an important tool to check the powers of Congress. Alexander Hamilton argued that the veto would allow the President to block what he called "improper laws." James Madison agreed. During the Constitutional Convention, he said the veto could prevent Congress "from passing laws unwise in their principle, or incorrect in their form" and from violating the rights of citizens.

How Presidents Use the Veto. Besides using the veto to try to block certain legislation, the President can also use a veto to try to get Congress to modify certain bills that it has passed. If the President vetoes a bill, and Congress does not have the votes to override the veto, it must modify the bill if it is ever to become law.

Sometimes the threat of a veto can be as effective as the veto itself. A President may threaten to veto a bill if Congress does not offer to make changes he wants in it. This often stops a bill from moving ahead in Congress.

Congress and the Veto. Congress is not powerless against the veto. However, it is very hard for Congress to overturn a veto with a two-thirds vote. Historically, only 4 percent of all vetoes have been overridden by Congress. Yet, the President's veto power has one limit. Presidents must veto an entire bill. They cannot veto only those parts of a bill they do not like. As a result, Congress uses two strategies to counteract the veto.

First, Congress often presents the President with bills that cover several topics. This prevents the President from considering (and perhaps vetoing) the bill as a single, neat package. Second, Congress may attach amendments, called **riders,** to money bills. These bills supply money for basic national government activities. Either the President must veto the entire money bill or veto none of it and let the rider, along with the rest of the bill, become law.

You and the Veto: Public Opinion

The veto is a limit on governmental power that has been built into our political system. Citizens share in the veto process indirectly through public opinion. Both Congress and the President pay attention to public opinion. Widespread public concern about an issue such as taxes can cause a President to veto a bill "because the public demanded it." At other times, Congress may have the votes needed to overturn a veto because of pressure by the public.

Review

1. How do checks and balances protect our rights and freedoms?

2. Why is the veto an illustration of checks and balances?

Case Study

The B-1 Bomber

During the summer of 1977, President Jimmy Carter had to decide whether or not the government should build a new fleet of bombers. The decision involved billions of dollars, thousands of jobs, and, eventually, Ronald Reagan, Carter's successor as President.

During the 1970s, the Defense Department had been planning a new bomber—the B-1. By 1977, the Department was ready to start building 244 of them. Each new B-1 would cost about $100 million.

The Air Force wanted the B-1 to replace the older B-52 bombers. They said the B-52s were no longer useful, and warned that the Soviet Union was building new bombers. Many citizens, military planners, and members of Congress said the B-1 was needed for national defense.

Some companies wanted the B-1. General Electric had a $744 million contract to make parts for the B-1. Rockwell International had a $1.37 billion contract to build the airframes for the bombers.

Many citizens, labor unions, religious groups, newspaper editors, and members of Congress were against the B-1. They argued that the plane was too costly, and that the new bomber had not been properly tested. They also said the Soviet Union's new bombers were no real threat to the United States.

During the 1976 presidential campaign, President Ford supported the B-1. His opponent, Jimmy Carter, was against the B-1. Carter said the B-1 "would be wasteful to taxpayers' dollars." Carter won the election. As

President, it was his decision: build the B-1 or not?

After the election, Carter gave himself time to make a decision. He collected information about his two alternatives. He talked often with the Secretary of Defense. He sought advice from White House staff members. He met with members of Congress. And he received reports from the Air Force.

On the weekend before his decision, the President reviewed the question. He asked the Vice-President, the Secretary of State, and several other top aides for written opinions. To help him decide, Carter made a list of the pros and cons.

It was clear that building the B-1 would be popular with the Air Force and with many Republican members of Congress. These people thought the B-1 was necessary for the defense of the country. Continued pressure was coming from business leaders who would make money from building the B-1. In addition, Japanese leaders said they hoped the B-1 would be built. Japan is geographically close to the Soviet Union. The Japanese were afraid that a decision to not build the bombers might encourage the Soviet Union to become more aggressive.

People against the B-1, many of whom had voted for Carter, continued to say that the B-1 was not necessary to the nation's defense. They said building the bombers would waste taxpayers' money. Some said that B-52s could be fitted with cruise missiles, which they claimed would make the B-52s as effective as B-1s. The cost of adding cruise missiles to the B-52s would be much less than the cost of building B-1s.

On June 30, 1977, President Carter announced, "My decision is that we should not continue with . . . the B-1, and I am directing that we discontinue plans for production of this weapons system." The President allowed some research on the B-1 to continue, and directed that B-52s be fitted with cruise missiles.

As it turned out, this research kept the B-1 program alive. Nearly four years later, it would give another President the chance to reconsider the project.

Reaction to President Carter's decision came quickly. One newspaper said: "We are disappointed by President Carter's action . . . he is taking a great gamble." But another paper said: "It took a lot of courage . . . Carter's move makes sense."

Rockwell International reacted to Carter's decision by announcing that 8,000 workers might have to be laid off. General Electric said 300 workers at an Ohio plant would probably be laid off.

Other companies were happy about Carter's decision. One such company was Williams Research Corporation. It began building a new factory to make parts for cruise missiles. Boeing Corporation, the manufacturer of the B-52s, would have plenty of work adapting the old planes to carry cruise missiles.

In the 1980 presidential election, Ronald Reagan defeated Jimmy Carter. As Reagan took office, plans were ready for a new version of the B-1. The new President now faced his own B-1 decision.

During his election campaign, Reagan called for strengthening the

The B-1 bomber.

national defense. In 1981, President Reagan announced that he had decided to go ahead with the production of one hundred new B-1 bombers. The new bombers would be more sophisticated than the version killed by President Carter. They would also cost more—at least $200 million each.

In the fiscal 1985 budget, President Reagan requested $8.2 billion for thirty-four additional B-1 bombers. He also called for Congress to approve $229.1 million for modernization of B-52s.

Review

1. How did Jimmy Carter feel about the B-1 bomber during the presidential campaign of 1976?
2. How did the Air Force and many Republican members of Congress feel about building the B-1?

Basic Social Studies Skills
Using Encyclopedias

With the exception of dictionaries, encyclopedias are the most widely used reference materials. This is because encyclopedias contain information on such a wide variety of topics. General encyclopedias such as *The World Book Encyclopedia* are useful not only at school and at work but at home as well.

Most encyclopedias come in sets, called volumes. *The World Book* has twenty-two volumes, the last being an index and research guide for the other volumes.

Each volume in *The World Book* has information about topics that begin with a particular letter or letters. Information about the United States presidency, for example, is found in Volume 15. This volume contains entries beginning with *P*.

Suppose you wanted to find information in *The World Book* about who would succeed the President in the event of his death or disability. You might choose to look up *President* in Volume 15 and then skim the content until you find the proper information. A better method, however, would be to locate *President of the United States* in the Index and Research Guide (Volume 22). Once you find this listing among the other alphabetical listings, simply skim the subtitles to find the reference to the appropriate articles. The reference will show you, in dark type, the letter of the volume and the page number.

Examine the reproductions of portions of pages 725 and 726 of

Volume 22 of the 1984 *World Book* and then answer these questions.

Skill Practice
1. Which subtitle under *President of the United States* would provide you with a reference to information about rules concerning the filling of a presidential vacancy?
2. If you were to turn to the *E* volume, page 115, what type of information would you find?
3. Where would you locate pictures of the Presidents?

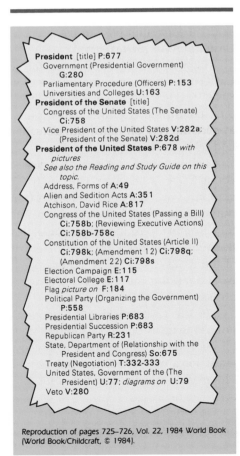

President [title] P:677
　Government (Presidential Government)
　　G:280
　Parliamentary Procedure (Officers) P:153
　Universities and Colleges U:163
President of the Senate [title]
　Congress of the United States (The Senate)
　　Ci:758
　Vice President of the United States V:282a;
　　(President of the Senate) V:282d
President of the United States P:678 *with pictures*
　See also the Reading and Study Guide on this topic.
　Address, Forms of A:49
　Alien and Sedition Acts A:351
　Atchison, David Rice A:817
　Congress of the United States (Passing a Bill)
　　Ci:758b; (Reviewing Executive Actions)
　　Ci:758b-758c
　Constitution of the United States (Article II)
　　Ci:798k; (Amendment 12) Ci:798q;
　　(Amendment 22) Ci:798s
　Election Campaign E:115
　Electoral College E:117
　Flag *picture on* F:184
　Political Party (Organizing the Government)
　　P:558
　Presidential Libraries P:683
　Presidential Succession P:683
　Republican Party R:231
　State, Department of (Relationship with the
　　President and Congress) So:675
　Treaty (Negotiation) T:332-333
　United States, Government of the (The
　　President) U:77; *diagrams on* U:79
　Veto V:280

Reproduction of pages 725–726, Vol. 22, 1984 World Book
(World Book/Childcraft, © 1984).

Chapter 8 Review

Summary

Section 1: Getting Elected
Presidential elections are held every four years in the United States. The qualifications for holding the position of President are written in the Constitution. The presidential election process involves three major steps: (1) candidates are nominated by their political parties; (2) candidates campaign for voter support; (3) the people vote for electors who select the President through the electoral college system.

Section 2: The President's Job
The President's main job is to execute, or carry out, laws passed by Congress. As Presidents exercise their powers they fill these roles: (1) foreign-policy leader, (2) commander in chief of the armed forces, (3) chief executive, (4) chief legislator, (5) head of state, (6) economic leader, and (7) chief of their political party.

Section 3: Presidential Advisers
Presidents rely on many advisers. The Executive Office of the President (EOP) assists the President. The White House Office in the EOP includes the President's closest political advisers. These people give the President advice, act for the President, and screen information coming to the President. Some members of the Cabinet may also become close presidential advisers.

Section 4: How Presidential Decisions Get Made
Presidents make many difficult decisions. Factors that influence a President's decisions include historical circumstances, public opinion, Congress, laws, the President's personal beliefs, and the President's leadership qualities.

Vocabulary
Define the following terms.
1. primary election
2. National Security Council
3. nominate
4. electoral college

Reviewing Main Ideas
1. True or false: A presidential nominating convention is a meeting to choose the party's candidate for President.
2. True or false: A candidate for Vice-President is also chosen at the presidential nominating convention.
3. The President has the power to _____.
a. call Congress into special session
b. appoint federal court judges
c. serve as commander in chief of the armed forces
d. all of the above

Thinking Critically
Evaluating Information
1. If you were to hear the following statement, would you agree or disagree? (Explain your answer.) Electing a President for four years is not a good idea.
2. What would you like best about being part of the "First Family"?
3. If you were President, which part of the job would you like best? Why?
Communicating Ideas
1. Imagine that you have a chance to influence a presidential decision. Write the President a letter, saying what you would like him to do.
2. Write a paragraph explaining the importance of decisions the President must make.

Chapter 9

Decision Making in Federal Agencies

Introduction. More than 2.8 million people work for agencies of the executive branch of the national government. They work in offices throughout the nation as well as in Washington, D.C. They are part of what is often called the federal **bureaucracy.**

Although you are probably not aware of it, federal agencies affect your life every day. For example, the Department of Transportation has set safety standards for the bus you take to school. When you are relaxing after school, the radio programs you listen to are broadcast on a frequency assigned by the Federal Communications Commission. The weather reports you hear use data from the National Weather Service.

Sometimes people resent the large role federal government plays in their lives. At other times, no one minds when the government steps in. When a storm hit eastern Pennsylvania, property damage came to $2 billion. In response, the Small Business Administration—a federal agency—loaned $725 million to 81,000 homeowners and 9,000 business people. At the same time, workers in the Department of Housing and Urban Development helped find housing for 20,000 people displaced by the storm.

In this chapter you will find out more about federal agencies and how they make decisions.

Section 1
The Work and Organization of the Federal Agencies

As part of the executive branch of government, **federal agencies** are set up to carry out laws passed by Congress. Federal agencies include thirteen executive, or Cabinet, departments and numerous independent agencies. Federal agencies perform three basic jobs. First, they turn new laws into action by deciding how to apply the laws to daily life. Laws passed by Congress are stated in very general terms. Federal agencies must develop specific rules and procedures to put the laws into practice. For example, a law may give benefits to "disabled" veterans.

But what does "disabled" mean? If it is not specified in the legislation, federal agencies decide upon a proper definition.

Second, federal agencies administer the day-to-day operations of the national government. Federal agencies deliver the mail, collect taxes, send social security payments to widowed, disabled, and retired people, patrol borders, run national parks, and perform thousands of other services.

Third, with authority of Congress, federal agencies regulate various activities. They **regulate,** or police, the activities of broadcasting companies, labor unions, banks, airlines, nuclear power plants, and many other organizations. They make sure that minimum standards are being met. One agency, the Federal Election Commission (FEC),

An experimental solar reflector. The Department of Energy, one of the thirteen Cabinet departments, devotes much of its time to the development of alternative sources of energy such as solar power.

(chart) Which branch has the most employees? Which branch has the fewest employees?

(chart, opposite) Which department operates the national parks? Which department operates the Weather Bureau?

Part of the EPA's job is to find ways to limit the amount of pollution that is emitted by automobiles.

Civilian Employees in the Federal Government

Total Employees:	**2,868,000**
Employees in Washington, D.C.:	347,000
Employees outside of Washington, D.C.:	2,521,000
Total Employees in Executive Branch:	**2,813,000**
Employees in Executive Branch Agencies:	2,811,000
Employees in the Executive Office of the President:	2,000
Total Employees in Legislative Branch:	**39,000**
Total Employees in Judicial Branch:	**16,000**

regulates the election campaign financing of congressional and presidential candidates.

In doing these jobs, federal agencies are helping to shape government policy. By deciding how to run a government program or what to do in a certain situation, federal agencies often determine what government policy will be. For example, the Environmental Protection Agency (EPA) is supposed to carry out the many laws dealing with pollution. When the EPA decides steel companies cannot dump certain chemicals into rivers, it is making government policy affecting the steel industry.

The executive branch includes many federal agencies that handle a variety of programs. Currently there are thirteen Cabinet departments, fifty-five major independent agencies, and more than two thousand other committees, boards, and advisory groups.

Cabinet Departments

The major executive agencies in the federal government are the thirteen **Cabinet departments.** Each department is responsible for a special area such as national defense, labor, or agriculture. Some of the major duties of each Cabinet department are described in the chart on the opposite page.

Independent Executive Agencies

The executive branch also includes more than fifty **independent executive agencies.** They are called independent because they are independent of the Cabinet. They are not, however, independent of the President. The President appoints the directors of these agencies with the approval of the Senate. The President may also fire these directors.

Most independent agencies are smaller than Cabinet departments. They are set up to do special jobs. The National Aeronautics and Space Administration (NASA) is an example. Created by Congress in 1958, it has responsibility for the United States space program. The Central Intelligence Agency (CIA) is another example of an independent agency. It was created after World War II to gather information about what is going on in other nations and to advise the President on foreign-policy matters.

Not all independent agencies are small. One such agency—the Veterans Administration (VA)—employs more than 250,000 people. It is the third biggest agency of the national government. The VA

Cabinet Departments

Department of State
- assists the President with foreign policy decisions
- arranges treaties and other agreements with foreign governments
- arranges economic, educational, and cultural programs with other nations
- represents the United States in the United Nations
- gives passports to United States citizens

Department of Defense
- directs and trains the military forces of the United States
- operates military bases in the United States and around the world
- collects information about other military forces around the world
- provides military aid and sells weapons to other nations

Department of Health and Human Services (HHS)
- administers social security, medical assistance, and medical programs
- operates many services for the poor and for the physically and mentally handicapped
- conducts research on the treatment of diseases
- checks food, drugs, and cosmetics for safety through the Food and Drug Administration (FDA)

Department of the Treasury
- collects taxes, manufactures paper money and coins, and carries out laws about banking
- controls taxes on alcohol, tobacco, and firearms
- carries out customs laws dealing with goods entering and leaving the nation
- directs the Secret Service, which guards the President and other top leaders

Department of Justice
- enforces all federal laws and prosecutes violators
- operates the Federal Bureau of Investigation (FBI) and federal prisons
- carries out the nation's civil rights, drug, and immigration laws
- represents the national government in legal matters

Department of Labor
- carries out laws related to safe working conditions, minimum wages, child labor, unemployment insurance, and workers' compensation
- operates job-training programs
- studies changes in employment and prices

Department of Housing and Urban Development (HUD)
- operates programs to help families buy houses
- provides money to build housing for low-income families
- grants money to communities to improve streets, sewers, and parks

Department of the Interior
- carries out laws on the use of public lands
- operates the national parks and historical places
- inspects mines and runs federally-owned dams
- operates programs for American Indians through the Bureau of Indian Affairs (BIA)

Department of Agriculture
- works to improve farm income and support American farm products
- helps farmers sell their products and teaches new farming techniques
- operates food-stamp and national school-lunch programs
- inspects food and controls crop and animal diseases

Department of Commerce
- provides economic information to businesses and government planners
- makes loans to small businesses
- conducts the census every ten years
- operates the Weather Bureau
- directs the United States Merchant Marine
- promotes American business opportunities in other nations

Department of Transportation
- administers programs for building and maintaining interstate highways, railroads, airports, and some waterways
- directs the Coast Guard during times of peace
- studies traffic problems and auto safety
- operates the Federal Aviation Administration (FAA)

Department of Energy
- explores new ways to use oil, gas, and coal resources
- develops new energy sources
- promotes energy conservation
- enforces governmental regulations affecting oil and gas companies

Department of Education
- sets up guidelines for granting financial aid to schools and colleges
- distributes financial aid to schools and colleges
- promotes research on educational problems

provides educational, medical, and housing benefits for veterans.

Some independent agencies are **government corporations.** In other words, they are businesses run by the government. The United States Postal Service, for example, is a government corporation. The Postal Service tries to make money by delivering the mail.

Regulatory Commissions

Regulatory commissions are also independent agencies. They are different from other independent agencies, however, in that they do not have to report to the President. Commission members are named by the President, but they cannot be fired by the President. They can only be removed from office by congressional impeachment.

Regulatory commissions make rules for certain industries or groups and make sure that they are followed. For instance, the Federal Communications Commission (FCC) makes broadcasting rules for the nation's television and radio stations. Many of the rules made by regulatory commissions fix the prices an industry may charge customers. Others place limits on how companies can operate. The purpose of such rules is to promote honesty and fair competition.

Regulatory commissions enforce their rules in several ways. First, they may wait for individuals or businesses to bring complaints to them. For example, the Interstate Commerce Commission (ICC) regulates the trucking industry. If one trucking company thinks another company is getting extra business

by violating a regulation, it may file a complaint with the ICC. The ICC will then settle the conflict.

Second, a commission may send inspectors into the field to look for violations of federal rules. The Occupational Safety and Health Administration often sends agents to factories to look for safety hazards.

In some cases, a commission may take violators into court. Other times the commissions themselves act as courts. The people who run a commission may bring charges against a business suspected of breaking one of the commission's rules. The commissioners will then hold hearings and collect evidence. Lawyers for the company and the commission may testify about the problem. If a violation is found, the commission may set a penalty.

Regulatory commissions may enforce their rules by requiring a business to get a license or permit in order to operate. This is one way the FCC regulates radio and television stations. To obtain a license, the station must meet federal regulations. To keep the license, stations must demonstrate that they are operating in ways that conform to the FCC's rules.

Deregulation. In recent years Congress and several Presidents have made efforts to **deregulate,** or cut back the federal regulation of business and industry. In 1978, Congress passed a law removing many federal regulations from the airline industry. Since then, Congress has deregulated other industries, including trucking, railroads, buses, and banking. In 1984, the FCC dropped some

Food and Drug Administration (FDA) workers enforce federal regulations pertaining to the quality and purity of food and medicines.

of the regulations it had imposed on the commercial television industry. Among the regulations dropped were guidelines requiring TV stations to broadcast minimum amounts of news and local programming.

Deregulated industries, such as the airlines, still must comply with many federal rules. For instance, federal regulations still require airplanes to carry special safety equipment such as fire extinguishers and life preservers. Deregulation is aimed at giving industries more freedom to set prices they charge their customers. It also aims to make it easier for new companies to enter an industry.

Section Review

Vocabulary:
Cabinet departments, deregulate, federal agencies, government corporations, independent executive agencies, regulate, regulatory commissions.

Reviewing the Main Ideas
1. What is the main job of the federal agencies?
2. How many Cabinet departments are there? Name six of them. What are their main functions?
3. Name one type of agency other than the Cabinet departments that is part of the executive branch.
4. Use the information in this section to tell whether these statements are true or false.
a. The job of government corporations is to make rules for certain industries.

b. The federal agencies are part of the executive branch of government.
c. Independent agencies are part of the Department of Defense.

Skill Building
1. The federal agencies are often called the federal bureaucracy. Look up the meaning of *bureaucracy* in the glossary. Tell why the word *bureaucracy* describes the workings of the federal agencies.
2. Which Cabinet department do you think would be responsible for the following:
a. the use of national forests
b. farm problems
c. enforcing civil rights laws
d. operation of passenger railroads

Section 2
Decision Makers in Federal Agencies

Decisions must be made at many levels in federal agencies. The decisions that get most public attention are made by agency leaders. However, many other agency workers make important decisions too.

Political Appointees
The top leaders in federal agencies are named by the President. These are the Cabinet secretaries, agency directors, deputy directors, and their assistants. These politically appointed leaders set overall policies and make key political decisions for the agencies.

Political decisions are those that interest Congress, news reporters, and strong interest groups. The Secretary of Defense, for example, may have to make important decisions about new weapons. The Secretary of Commerce may make decisions about creating business opportunities for minority groups and for women. The Secretary of the Interior makes key decisions about oil and gas pipelines, new dams, strip mining, and national parks.

Top agency leaders do not make key decisions alone. The alternatives from which they choose are often set by people working far below them in the agency. When considering the alternatives, leaders will usually talk with some of these people. They may also talk with the President or members of Congress. They may study facts collected by staff people and interest groups affected by the decision.

Presidents, of course, want the decisions of agency leaders to reflect their own ideas. As a result, Presidents try to appoint leaders with whom they share political views. Presidents need to do this to get some control over the huge federal bureaucracy.

Where do the top leaders come from? Who are they? Most top leaders are successful people in business or the professions. Almost all have a college education. Some have advanced college degrees. They are usually not experts in the work of the agency they head, but they often have some experience in the same area. Many have served in government before. Some have been elected officials.

Civil Service Workers

A former Cabinet secretary said, "A Cabinet member does not run a Cabinet department [alone]." Indeed, many important decisions, as well as the day-to-day operation of federal agencies, are handled by career **civil service workers.** These are people, ranging from clerks to doctors and lawyers, employed by the federal government through the **civil service system.** Unlike the political appointee, whose job usually ends when a new President is elected, the civil service worker's job may be permanent. About 90 percent of all federal government employees are civil service workers.

The Civil Service System. Before 1883, a great many jobs in the federal agencies were filled by the **spoils system.** Under this system, government jobs were given to people as a reward for their political support. Each newly elected President would replace federal workers with his own political supporters and friends. The idea was: "To the victor belong the spoils [jobs]."

Public dissatisfaction with the spoils system, and public outrage over the assassination of President Garfield in 1881 by a man who was refused a job under the spoils system, led Congress to pass the **Pendleton Act.**

The Pendleton Act, also known as the Civil Service Reform Act of 1883, limited the spoils system and created the federal civil service system. The **Office of Personnel Management** (OPM) directs the civil service system today. It sets standards for federal jobs, and it gives tests to people who want those jobs. People who are hired are chosen from lists of those who have passed the tests or otherwise met civil service standards. The civil service system is a **merit system.** It is not "who you know" but "what you know" that is supposed to count in getting a civil service job.

The Decision Makers. Those civil service workers who make important decisions about day-to-day agency business are managers and specialists. Most civil service managers have worked for the government fifteen years or more. They have usually worked their way up from low-level jobs to the top career jobs. Many have never worked in Washington, D.C. Instead, they work in one of their agency's local offices.

In carrying out their agency's program, career managers wrestle with decisions such as these: What kind of cancer research project should we give money to? How should we set up the new school lunch program passed by Congress? Most of these decisions do not make headlines, but the decisions are important nonetheless. In many ways, the policy of the national government is formed by these decisions.

Study the chart below. What are the highest paying jobs? Which jobs are the most plentiful?

Average Salaries of Full-time Federal Civilian Employees

Occupation Blue Collar	Men No. of employees	Men Average salary	Women No. of employees	Women Average salary
Baker	188	$18,514	17	$18,580
Barber	28	18,381	—	—
Beautician	—	—	6	20,034
Boiler operator	4,852	21,355	21	17,326
Carpenter	8,155	20,869	73	18,194
Cook	3,728	20,258	1,033	18,001
Electrician	12,835	21,600	261	17,956
Elevator operator	57	13,472	109	13,926
Forklift operator	2,114	18,461	114	16,864
Janitor	14,396	14,630	5,585	14,446
Laborer	14,575	14,344	1,274	14,125
Locksmith	274	19,852	9	18,859
Locomotive engineer	125	21,354	—	—
Machinist	13,571	22,207	315	18,029
Mechanic, A/C	5,304	21,329	46	16,451
Mechanic, aircraft	15,409	22,289	243	19,109
Mechanic, general	9,965	20,322	107	17,178
Painter	9,423	20,231	326	17,648
Pipefitter	15,719	22,626	156	18,573
Plumber	2,417	20,190	19	17,153
Pressman	2,305	21,341	274	19,327
Sheet metal	12,638	21,203	649	18,695
Store worker	2,529	16,753	1,353	12,859
Toolmaker	994	24,903	6	20,533
Tractor operator	2,248	17,349	35	16,569
Vehicle operator	14,104	18,461	449	17,105
Warehouseman	22,534	17,715	2,296	16,500
Welder	8,883	20,946	147	17,741

Occupation White Collar	Men No. of employees	Men Average salary	Women No. of employees	Women Average salary
Accountant	18,110	$31,261	3,555	$24,593
Architect	1,513	32,775	106	28,588
Attorney	13,056	40,092	4,062	34,578
Chaplain	521	31,948	10	16,789
Chemist	6,479	33,684	1,490	27,310
Clerk/Typist	3,575	11,703	59,679	11,593
Dental assistant	201	13,653	2,769	13,560
Editor/Writer	857	29,000	1,344	23,418
Editor, technical	1,085	28,278	691	24,038
Engineer, civil	15,731	33,197	480	24,417
Engineer, electrical	4,504	33,084	108	26,482
Engineer, mechanical	10,221	33,121	187	25,082
Law clerk	261	23,164	246	23,187
Librarian	1,117	30,728	2,296	27,473
Messenger	525	10,277	71	10,906
Nurse	2,598	21,498	32,931	22,840
Paralegal	815	30,042	1,288	23,501
Personnel mgmt.	5,356	33,306	4,053	26,868
Pharmacist	2,063	27,286	527	24,960
Public relations	1,878	33,531	1,122	26,654
Purchasing	1,172	17,022	3,844	15,723
Secretary	842	14,825	85,091	15,836
Social work	2,030	28,675	1,607	27,164
Statistician	1,889	33,817	755	28,770
Technician, medical	1,144	17,011	1,527	15,819
Therapist, occupational	81	23,274	597	21,943
Therapist, physical	245	23,842	437	21,748

Section Review

Vocabulary:

civil service system, civil service workers, merit system, Office of Personnel Management, Pendleton Act, spoils system.

Reviewing Main Ideas

1. What sorts of positions do presidential appointees hold in the federal agencies?
2. Who usually makes the federal agency decisions that get most public attention—political appointees or career workers?
3. What led to the Pendleton Act?
4. What is the civil service system?

Skill Building

1. Use an encyclopedia to find additional information about one of these topics: the Pendleton Act, the Office of Personnel Management, President Garfield's assassination. Write a summary of your findings.
2. Refer to the chart on page 193, and then answer the following questions:
a. Which white-collar job pays the most?
b. Which blue-collar job pays the most?
c. What conclusion might you draw after comparing the average salaries of men and women in both white- and blue-collar jobs?

Section 3
Influences on Federal Agencies

Federal agency workers face many pressures when making decisions. The Congress, the President, the clients whom federal agencies serve or regulate, other agencies, and the mass media, all have an influence on the decisions they make.

Congress

Congress can influence agency decision makers in several ways. First, Congress has the power to set up agency programs. The House or Senate Armed Services Committee, for instance, can start or stop programs in the Department of Defense.

Second, Congress has the power to pass or not pass laws an agency wants. The Environmental Protection Agency may study pollution in rivers and draft a new bill to deal with it, but only Congress can turn that bill into law.

Third, each agency depends on Congress for money. Without money from Congress, agencies would have to go out of business. Every year when it passes the federal budget, Congress decides whether to approve the money for each agency.

The President

As head of the executive branch, the President has several ways of influencing agency decisions. First, the President names the top leaders in most federal agencies. These leaders will try to influence others in their agency to carry out the President's policies.

Second, the President can use the budget to get some control over federal agencies. Congress approves each agency's budget, but it is the President who decides how much money to request for each agency.

Third, the President may set up new agencies to work on programs that deserve special attention.

There are also several limitations on the President's influence. Although the President can appoint and fire top agency leaders, the jobs of civil service workers are protected by complex rules. It is difficult to fire them.

Another limitation on presidential influence is the fact that Presidents come and go, while many civil service workers hold their jobs for twenty years or more. The decision makers among this group have their own ideas about how things should be run. They are often more interested in their agency's programs than in any new ideas the President may have.

Client Groups

Client groups are composed of citizens who work with and are most affected by the decisions of federal agencies. Every agency has its own set of clients. The Department of Agriculture, for example, works with farmers and others in the farming business. The Federal Communications Commission makes decisions that involve telephone and telegraph companies and radio and television stations. These client groups are a third source of influence on agency decisions. The groups are often represented by lobbyists. The lobbyists write letters, testify at agency

Lobbyists waiting to see federal agency representatives about problems that concern their clients.

Investigations conducted by the mass media often affect the decisions made by federal agencies. (right) Pam Zekman, a newswoman for Channel 2 in Chicago, conducted an investigation that may lead to tighter regulations in the dispensing of prescription drugs.

hearings, and do other things to get their group's ideas across to an agency. Sometimes a client group does not get the results it wants. Then its members may try to get help from a member of Congress, who may have received campaign contributions from the group's political action committee, or even from the President.

It is normal for agency officials and clients to work together. Indeed, agency officials must often work closely with client groups if they are to get anything done. Working closely with a client group, however, may cause special problems for the regulatory commission. Regulatory commissions are often called **watchdog agencies.** They are supposed to regulate industries for the public good. They set and enforce safety standards for products and enforce laws against unfair business practices.

Over the years these watchdog agencies have developed close associations with the industries they regulate. Commissioners often come to their government jobs from these industries. And after they work for the government, they often go back to the same industries again. Some observers say these close ties are quite natural. They say that if watchdog agencies are to make fair rules, they must know a lot about the industries they regulate. Critics say that such close ties make it hard for the regulatory commissions to do their job. They charge that the watchdog agencies protect the industries that they are supposed to regulate.

Other Federal Agencies

A fourth source of influence on federal agencies is other agencies. Sometimes programs or rules in different agencies conflict with each other. For example, rules about hiring members of minority groups made by the Department of Justice may conflict with policies set by the Office of Civil Rights in the Department of Health and Human Services. Decision makers in each agency may try to influence the others to accept their programs or rules.

The Mass Media

The **mass media**—television, radio, and newspapers—can shape federal agency decisions in several ways. First, the media can influence the government's decision-making agencies by calling public attention to certain problems. For instance, a television network might broadcast a special television report on illegal drugs in big cities. A lot of publicity on the "drug problem" can put pressure on agencies such as the Federal Bureau of Investigation or the Drug Enforcement Administration to "crack down."

Second, the media provide useful information to agency decision makers. Most top Washington leaders pay close attention to the media. They read the *New York Times*, *Washington Post*, and other newspapers every morning. The media present fresh information about current problems, often before information is available from government agencies. The media also give decision makers an idea of the public's attitude toward current events.

Finally, the media give agency leaders a chance to test the public's reaction to new ideas before making a final decision. Agency leaders will often unofficially give, or "leak," information about a new program or a possible decision to the media. If the public reacts favorably, the decision will be made officially or the new idea put into practice. If the public reaction is negative, the decision or new idea may be dropped.

There is a natural and healthy tension between the mass media and federal agencies. There is tension because each usually wants something different.

Government officials want public support for their agencies and programs. They want the media to show their agencies as hard-working and successful in serving the public. The mass media often see themselves as critics of government. They want to expose government waste, corruption, and wrongdoing. By so doing, the media hope to present exciting news stories that will attract a big audience.

Section Review

Vocabulary:
client groups, mass media, watchdog agencies.

Reviewing the Main Ideas
1. List five individuals or groups that have influence on federal agency decisions.
2. Describe how client groups may try to influence agency decisions.

Skill Building
Write a paragraph that lists and explains three ways that the media can shape agency decisions.

Case Study

The *Concorde*

In the winter of 1976, Secretary of Transportation William Coleman faced a tough choice. He had to decide whether or not to let *Concorde* jetliners land at Dulles Airport near Washington, D.C., and at Kennedy Airport near New York City. The Secretary of Transportation has the power to grant or deny landing rights at United States airports to new kinds of aircraft. Usually this is a routine decision. *Concorde*, however, was no ordinary plane. *Concorde* was a supersonic transport, an SST, a jet that could fly at twice the speed of sound. It had been built by Britain and France at a cost of $3 billion over 13 years.

In January, the Secretary held hearings. Many groups tried to influence Coleman's decision.

The British and French testified that the *Concorde* would cut flying time between the capitals of Europe and New York City or Washington, D.C., in half. They said the *Concorde* was safe and not much louder than regular jets. Further, they argued that the decision was important to their governments. Billions of dollars and the jobs of thousands of workers were involved.

Major opposition to the *Concorde* came from the Environmental Protection Agency (EPA). Roger Strelow of the EPA testified that jet exhaust from many *Concordes* could put a layer of gases, dust, and water vapor in the upper air. This could ruin the weather on earth by

The *Concorde* can travel at twice the speed of sound. That's more than 2,000 feet per second.

heating or cooling the planet. Further, some studies had shown that exhaust from the *Concorde* might damage the ozone layer.

Finally, Strelow was worried that the *Concorde* would be much louder than other jet planes. He said it would be in direct conflict with government programs aimed at lowering noise levels.

The National Aeronautics and Space Administration (NASA) disagreed with EPA's position. It agreed that the new plane might be a little noisier than others, but it said that it would not seriously damage the ozone layer or change the world's weather. They noted that fighter planes had flown higher and faster than the *Concorde* for years.

Finally, the Secretary of State expressed the State Department's concern about how the decision would affect foreign policy. He urged the Secretary of Transportation to decide "yes." He argued this would show friendship for France and Britain.

Other non-government groups were interested in the problem. Environmental groups were against the *Concorde*. In addition to the reasons given by the EPA, these groups argued that the *Concorde* was a gas guzzler. It would use about four times more fuel than other jets.

The New York Port Authority was against letting the *Concorde* land. The Port Authority runs Kennedy Airport in New York. New Yorkers living near the airport had been fighting jet traffic at Kennedy Airport since the 1960s. They did not like the noise jets made, and were very much against the *Concorde*.

After the Department of Transportation hearings, the Secretary studied the evidence. He talked with staff members and others. In February, he announced his decision to let the *Concorde* land on a limited basis. His permission was for one year only, after which the decision would be reviewed. Only two flights a day could land at Kennedy; only one a day at Dulles. All flights could be cancelled at any time.

The New York Port Authority refused to let the *Concorde* land, in spite of the Secretary of Transportation's ruling. In 1977, however, a federal court overturned the ban and *Concordes* began landing in New York. One year later, the Department of Transportation said that the *Concorde* would be permitted to use airports in eleven other United States cities as long as it met local noise requirements.

In the early 1980s, the *Concorde* controversy faded considerably. However, rising fuel costs pushed the price of a ticket out of the reach of most passengers.

As of early 1985, both of the airlines and the French and British governments were busy trying to discover ways to make the *Concorde* a profitable means of transportation.

Review

1. Make a decision tree to study the Secretary's decision.
2. Do you think the decision the Secretary made was a good one? Explain your thinking.

199

Basic Social Studies Skills
Thinking Inductively

Inductive thinking involves using information about parts of a whole to draw general conclusions about the whole.

The Bureau of the Census, for example, conducts a "Current Population Survey" every month to obtain important population statistics. This survey involves interviewing members of 65,000 households across the nation. This sample of Americans is only a small percentage of the total population, which includes more than 80 million households. And yet the information obtained from this sample is used to draw conclusions about the entire population.

The "Current Population Survey" concluded in April, 1984, that the national unemployment rate was 7.8 percent. The following statements show the three basic steps involved in drawing this conclusion:

Step 1: Sixty-five thousand households were selected to represent, as accurately as possible, the total population of the nation.

Step 2: The survey showed that there was a 7.8 percent rate of unemployment among the 65,000 households.

Step 3: Based on the survey, the Bureau concluded that the nation had an unemployment rate of approximately 7.8 percent.

General conclusions drawn from samples are not always accurate. A conclusion drawn by the Bureau of the Census, for example, might be inaccurate if it is based on a sample that does not accurately represent the entire population.

Although conclusions drawn by using inductive reasoning may not always be accurate, you can generally have great confidence in conclusions that are based upon carefully selected samples. The table below illustrates this clearly.

Skill Practice
What are some of the advantages of drawing conclusions based on inductive thinking? What are some of the disadvantages?

Population Comparisons

	March 1980 Census Survey	April 1980 Complete Count
Number of households	65,000	80,389,673
All Family Households	73.9%	73.2%
Those Headed by Married Couples	60.9%	60.2%
Those with Single Female Head	10.8%	10.5%
Those with Single Male Head	2.2%	2.6%
All Nonfamily Households	26.1%	26.8%
Persons Living Alone	22.5%	22.7%
Persons Living Together	3.6%	4.1%

Chapter 9 Review

Summary

Section 1: The Work and Organization of the Federal Agencies

Federal agencies are part of the executive branch. They apply new laws to daily life, administer the day-to-day operations of government, and regulate important activities such as banking. The major agencies are the thirteen Cabinet departments.

Section 2: Decision Makers in Federal Agencies

Top leaders in federal agencies are appointed by the President. They are responsible for overall direction of their agency and for major political decisions. The top leaders are chosen because their appointments serve the President's interests. They usually leave government when a new President is elected. Most federal workers are hired through the civil service system. This system provides for the selection of people for jobs based on merit.

Section 3: Influences on Federal Agencies

The President, Congress, client groups, the mass media, and other agencies influence federal agency decision making. Congress has considerable influence because it controls money for the agencies, can pass or not pass laws the agency wants, and can create or kill agency programs. The President also has considerable influence because he names the leaders of the agencies.

Vocabulary

Define the following terms.

1. regulatory commissions
2. client groups
3. government corporations
4. independent executive agencies
5. Cabinet departments
6. civil service system

Reviewing Main Ideas

1. True or false: There are many federal agencies other than Cabinet departments.
2. More than _____ people now work for federal agencies.
   a. 200,000
   b. 500,000
   c. 1,000,000
   d. 3,000,000
3. Federal agencies are part of the _____ branch(es) of government.
   a. executive
   b. legislative
   c. judicial
   d. three national
4. Congress does *not* have the power to
   a. create a federal agency program.
   b. select federal agency leaders.
   c. approve the money an agency asks for.
   d. pass the laws an agency wants.

Thinking Critically

Organizing Information

Outline Section 3 of this chapter. Use the section heads and subheads as the heads on your outline.

Evaluating Information

Do you think the civil service system is a good system for hiring government employees? Why or why not?

Communicating Ideas

Imagine that you have a chance to suggest a new Cabinet department to the President. Write a paragraph stating what the department will be, what its main jobs would be, and why you think it is needed.

Chapter 10

Decision Making in the Federal Courts

Justice Sandra Day O'Connor
and Chief Justice Warren
Burger.

Introduction. Working in her Phoenix, Arizona, office in July, 1981, Sandra Day O'Connor was interrupted by a telephone call from Washington, D.C. It was President Ronald Reagan.

The President informed O'Connor that he had selected her to fill a vacancy on the United States Supreme Court. Would she accept the job? O'Connor, an Arizona appeals-court judge, said "yes."

With that phone call, the last major barrier to America's most exclusive "men's club" finally fell. After 192 years and 101 male justices, a woman had been nominated for a seat on the Supreme Court.

Shortly thereafter, the United States Senate approved O'Connor's appointment. She had risen to the very top of the United States legal system.

As the nation's highest court, the Supreme Court decides some of the toughest and most controversial issues facing the nation. In this chapter, you will learn about some of these issues and decisions.

Section 1
How Laws and Courts Serve the People

There are four different kinds of laws in the United States. Laws made by lawmaking bodies such as Congress, state legislatures, or city councils are **statutory laws.** For example, a state law that says a driver must signal before making a left turn is a statutory law.

Another type of law, called **common law,** has developed from common practice and customary ways of dealing with problems. For example, having twelve people on a jury is part of common law. It is traditional. The decisions of judges also make up common law. When a judge is deciding a case, he or she looks at the ways other judges have decided similar cases.

Administrative laws are those laws made by government agencies. The Department of Transportation ruling that all passenger cars must have seat belts is an example of an administrative law. As federal and state governments have grown, the number of administrative laws has grown too.

Finally, there is **constitutional law.** Constitutional law is based on the Constitution and the interpretations of the Constitution described in Supreme Court decisions.

Courts use these different kinds of law to settle disputes. Whether the dispute is between people or between a person and the government, the parties to the dispute come before a court. Each argues for its side. The court then applies the law to the facts that have been presented, and a decision is made in favor of one or the other.

Equal Justice for All

Our legal system is based on an important ideal—**equal justice** *for all* under the law. The goal of the legal system is to treat every person the same. Under the Constitution, every person accused of breaking the law has the right to a public trial. Every accused person has the right to a lawyer. If an accused person cannot afford a lawyer, the courts will appoint one and will pay the lawyer's

(below) Lawyer consulting with her client. (bottom) The lawyer asking her client questions during a jury trial.

203

The Hoosier Dome, the new home of the Indianapolis Colts, formerly the Baltimore Colts of the National Football League. The owner of the Colts moved his team to Indianapolis in March, 1984, much to the surprise of many Colts fans including the mayor of Baltimore. Baltimore attempted to force the team to return by filing suit against the team. Baltimore's suit claimed that the doctrine of eminent domain gave the city the right to claim ownership of the team.

fee. Every person is considered innocent until proven guilty. And a person has the right to ask for a review of his or her case if, in that person's view, the courts have made a mistake.

The ideal of equal justice is a difficult goal to reach. Judges and juries are not free from the prejudices of their communities. Poor people do not have the money to spend on legal help that wealthy citizens or large companies do. Nonetheless, Americans believe in the ideal. There are some countries in the world where prejudice is legal and where there are different laws for different groups of people. In the United States, all people are equal before the law. If injustice occurs, citizens have the right to speak out and correct it.

The Cases Heard in Federal Courts

The federal courts are the third branch of the national government. They have authority to hear certain kinds of cases.

Cases Involving the Constitution. Federal courts have **jurisdiction** over cases involving the Constitution. Jurisdiction is the authority to judge and administer the law. If the law in question is the Constitution, including the amendments, the case must be heard in a federal court.

Cases Involving Federal Laws. If a person is accused of breaking a federal law, such as kidnapping, tax evasion, or counterfeiting, the case is heard in a federal court. Disputes that involve issues over which the national government has constitutionally granted control—such as patent rights or bankruptcy—are also heard in federal courts.

Disputes Between States or People from Different States. Any disagreement between state governments is brought to trial in a federal court. Lawsuits between citizens of different states also come under the federal courts. For example, Mrs. Armand of Nebraska may bring suit in a federal court against Mr. Duvall of New York for not fulfilling his part of a business agreement. Such suits must involve a minimum amount.

Disputes Involving the Federal Government. The United States government may sue someone. For example, the Defense Department might sue a company that had contracted to build missile parts if the job was not completed on time. The suit would be heard in a federal court. Also, the government can be sued. For instance, if you were hit by a Postal Service truck, you could sue the United States Postal Service to pay for your medical expenses.

Disputes Involving Treaties or Admiralty or Maritime Law. Disputes between the United States and other governments are heard in federal courts. A treaty case might involve a dispute over the way the State Department interpreted a trade agreement. Admiralty and maritime laws have to do with rules on the high seas. Disputes involving shipping commerce, collisions, or crimes committed at sea are all heard in federal courts.

Section Review

Vocabulary:
administrative laws, common law, constitutional law, equal justice, jurisdiction, statutory laws.

Reviewing the Main Ideas
1. Name and describe the four major types of law in the United States.
2. Describe the job of the courts in our legal system.
3. Explain in your own words what is meant by "equal justice for all."

Skill Building
Read Article 3, Section 2, clause 1, of the Constitution and Amendment 11 to answer these questions:
1. Can a citizen of Ohio sue the state of Alabama in a federal court?
2. If a citizen of France sues the state of New York, will the case be heard in a federal court or in a New York state court?
3. If a ship owned by a woman from Delaware collides with a ship owned by a man from South Carolina, what kind of court will decide who was at fault?

Section 2
How the Federal Courts Are Organized

There are three main levels of federal courts: district courts, courts of appeal, and the Supreme Court. In addition, there are several special courts. The chart on page 208 shows the relationships among courts in the federal court system.

United States District Courts. Most federal cases are handled in the ninety-one United States **district courts.** Every state has at least one district court. Some states have two, three, or four such courts. In all, there are eighty-nine district courts in the fifty states, one in the District of Columbia, and one in Puerto Rico. Each has from one to twenty-seven judges, depending on need.

Almost all federal court cases begin with a trial in a district court. District courts are the only federal courts where juries are used and witnesses are called. Many cases do not end in the district courts. Cases may go on to the next level of the court system—the appeals courts.

United States Courts of Appeals. The job of the **appeals courts** is to review decisions made in the district courts. There are twelve federal appelate courts. Each one covers an area called a **circuit.** There are eleven circuits in the fifty states. The twelfth circuit is in the District of Columbia.

Sometimes mistakes are made in district courts. Thus, every person has the right to ask for a review of his or her case in a United States court of appeals. Appeals are usually made when lawyers think the law was not correctly applied in a case or wrong procedures were used. An appeal can also be made if new evidence turns up.

There are no trials in a court of appeals. Instead, a panel of three or more judges reviews the record of the case being appealed from the district court. The judges also listen to arguments from lawyers for each side. The judges then meet and make a decision by majority vote.

When an appeals court decision is made, one judge writes an opinion for the court. The opinion explains the reasons for the decision. If the appeals court finds a mistake,

A cartoon from the late 1800s showing an avalanche of cases waiting to be reviewed by the Supreme Court. Today, the Supreme Court faces a similar avalanche of cases. In 1985, Chief Justice Warren Burger asked that certain types of cases be transferred to lower courts to ease the Court's case load.

it sends the case back to the district court for a new trial. If the appeals court finds that justice was done, the decision made in the district court is upheld. In the vast majority of cases, the decision of the appeals court is final.

The United States Supreme Court. The Supreme Court stands above all other courts in the land. The main job of the Supreme Court is to decide whether or not laws are in agreement with the Constitution. Although many people do not know it, citizens do not have the right to have their cases heard in the Supreme Court. The Constitution gives Congress the power to decide which kinds of cases may be appealed to the Supreme Court. Except for certain kinds of cases involving the Constitution, the Supreme Court decides which cases it will hear. When the Court refuses to review a case, the decision of the lower court remains unchanged.

Other Federal Courts. From time to time, Congress has created special courts. The chart on page 208 shows these special courts. They are the Temporary Emergency Court of Appeals, the Court of Claims, the Court of Customs and Patent Appeals, the Customs Court, the Territorial Courts, the Court of Military Appeals, and the Tax Court.

The Temporary Emergency Court of Appeals has been in operation since 1972. In 1971, Congress passed certain laws aimed at keeping the country's economy stable. It set up this special court to handle appeals from the district courts in cases having to do with these laws.

The Court of Claims handles cases involving suits against the national government. If the court rules against the government, the person suing the government is usually granted a sum of money.

As you can tell from its name, the Court of Customs and Patent Appeals is an appeals court. It reviews cases decided in the Customs Court. It also settles disputes between inventors and the national government Patent Office. The Customs Court settles disputes between merchants from other countries and the United States officials who tax their goods.

The Territorial Courts are like district courts for the territories of the United States. There is one each in Guam, the Virgin Islands, the Canal Zone, and the Northern Mariana Islands. These courts handle both the kinds of cases federal courts hear and the kinds state courts hear. (The Commonwealth of Puerto Rico also has a federal court, but it is classified as a district court.)

The Court of Military Appeals is the appeals court for the armed services. It reviews court-martial decisions. The judges on this court also have responsibility for recommending improvements in the country's system of military justice.

Tax Court is the final decision maker for disputes about federal taxes. Citizens who believe that the government has not figured their taxes correctly may argue their case before this court.

The Judicial Branch

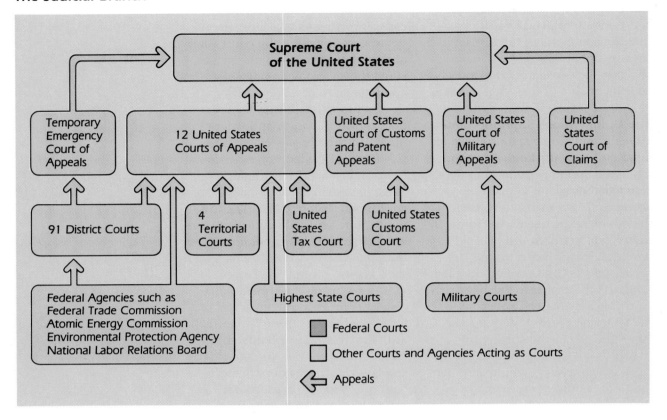

Study the chart. Which two courts handle appeals from the district courts?

Decision Makers in the Judicial Branch

The chief decision makers in the judicial branch are the **federal judges.** They are appointed to their jobs by the President, and approved by the Senate.

Senators play a key role in selecting federal district court judges. By a tradition called **senatorial courtesy,** the Senate allows any senator of the President's political party to "veto" a person nominated for judge in his or her state. If the senator objects to the candidate, the Senate will reject the nominee.

Presidents want to appoint judges who will share their ideas about politics and justice. They also want to reward their own political party. Thus, Presidents usually appoint judges who belong to their own political party. About 90 percent of the federal judges appointed by recent Presidents have belonged to the same party as the President.

Once appointed, a federal judge has a job for life if he or she wants it. A judge can be removed from office only through impeachment. The writers of the Constitution gave federal judges this sort of job security because they wanted judges to be able to decide cases without interference from others.

Judges do not work alone. They have help from many others. Judges appoint clerks, secretaries, court reporters, probation officers, and United States **magistrates.** Magistrates take care of much of a judge's routine work. They issue search and arrest warrants in federal cases. They also decide whether people who have been arrested should be held in jail or released on bail.

The Executive Branch in the Courts

Each district court has a **United States attorney** and one or more deputies. United States attorneys are government lawyers who prosecute people accused of breaking federal laws. They look into complaints of crime, prepare formal charges, and then present evidence in court. United States attorneys are appointed to a four-year term by the President with consent of the Senate. They are members of the executive branch. Their boss is the Attorney General of the United States, the head of the Justice Department.

Each district court has a United States **marshal** too. Marshals and their staffs make arrests, collect fines, and take convicted persons to prison. They protect jurors, serve legal papers, and keep order in federal courts. Like the United States attorneys, the marshals are members of the Department of Justice.

Section Review

Vocabulary:
appeals court, circuit, district court, federal judge, magistrate, marshal, senatorial courtesy, United States attorney.

Reviewing the Main Ideas
1. What are the three main types of federal courts?
2. What is the job of a United States court of appeals?
3. Name two of the special federal courts that Congress has created and tell what kinds of cases each hears.

Skill Building
Read the chart on page 208 to answer these questions.
1. If you do not agree with the Internal Revenue Service about how much tax you have to pay, which court would hear the case and make the final decision?
2. Suppose you were in the army and were mistakenly accused of helping the enemy. In your court-martial a witness lies, and you are convicted and jailed. Then evidence is finally found that proves you could not have done the crime. To what court would you appeal your case?
3. Suppose you own a business regulated by the Federal Trade Commission and you don't agree with a ruling the Commission makes against you. To what court could you appeal the commission's decision?

Section 3

What the Supreme Court Does

The Supreme Court is in Washington, D.C., but the Court's influence is felt all across the United States. Supreme Court justices are important political decision makers. Their decisions often affect citizens as much as do the decisions made by Congress or the President.

Justices of the Supreme Court

The Supreme Court is made up of eight associate justices and one chief justice. The justices work in Washington from October through June. Each month during this time, they spend two weeks listening to oral arguments on cases and then two weeks in recess. During recess the justices write opinions and study new cases. During the summer they take their "homework" with them. They study applications for review, write opinions, and catch up on other legal work.

The President appoints Supreme Court justices with the consent of the majority of the Senate. The Senate has approved a vast majority of the Supreme Court nominations sent to it. Senators have usually felt that the President should have a fairly free hand in picking new Supreme Court justices.

Supreme Court justices are always lawyers. They have had successful careers practicing or teaching law, serving in lower courts, or holding other public positions.

Political support and agreement with the President's ideas are important factors in who gets appointed. Presidents want justices who agree with their own political ideas. Of course, once appointed, a justice may make decisions that the President does not like.

Judicial Review

The main job of the Supreme Court is to decide whether laws or actions by government officials are allowed by the Constitution or are **unconstitutional.** It does this by using a power called **judicial review.** This is the power to say that a law or action of government goes against the Constitution. The Constitution does not say that the Supreme Court has the power of judicial review. However, Americans agree that if the Constitution is to be upheld as the highest law in the land, then the highest court in the land must have the power to decide if governmental laws and actions go against it. If the Court decides a law is unconstitutional, then it is no longer in force.

John Marshall, who served as chief justice from 1801 to 1835, wrote the first opinion about the constitutionality of a federal law in 1803. The case was between William Marbury, who had been promised a justice-of-the-peace appointment, and Secretary of State James Madison. All cases are called by the names of the parties to the dispute; this one is called *Marbury* v. *Madison.* (The *v* stands for the Latin word *versus,* which means "against.")

Marbury said that the Judiciary Act passed by Congress in 1789 allowed the Supreme Court to write a special kind of court order that would force the Secretary of State to give him his appointment. In the Supreme Court's opinion, Marshall wrote that the Judiciary Act of 1789 went against the Constitution. The Act gave the Supreme Court powers it should not have.

Opinions of any court set **precedents.** A precedent does not have the power of law, but it is a very powerful argument in court. Ever since 1803, *Marbury* v. *Madison* has been the precedent for the Supreme Court's power of judicial review in regard to federal laws and actions by the President or federal agencies.

How Cases Reach the Supreme Court

The Supreme Court is both a trial court and an appeals court. Three types of disputes have their original trials in the Supreme Court: (1) cases involving the official representatives of other nations, (2) suits between states, such as an argument between California and Arizona over water from the Colorado River, and (3) cases involving a state and the national government. Most cases, however, are appealed from a lower court, federal court, or state court.

No matter where they start, all cases submitted to the Supreme Court must be real legal disputes. To test whether or not a law is constitutional in the Supreme Court, someone must actually break the law, or someone must show that he or she was directly affected by the

(top) Supreme Court justices. (above) Justice Thurgood Marshall conferring with his law clerks.

law. A person cannot simply ask the Supreme Court to decide whether or not a law is constitutional. This way of determining what the Supreme Court can and cannot review is called the **real case rule.**

The Court at Work

Every case reviewed by the Supreme Court goes through a series of steps. These steps are (1) acceptance, (2) written arguments, (3) oral arguments, (4) conference, (5) opinion writing, and (6) announcement. Let's look at each step.

Acceptance. The thousands of cases sent to the Court each year go first to the Office of the Clerk of the Court. Staff members summarize each case and send copies to each of the nine justices. From the many cases submitted to them, the justices make a list of cases they want to discuss more carefully. Once a week the justices meet to pick from this list the cases the Court will actually review. The Court can accept for review just about any case it wants.

Written Arguments. Once a case is accepted, the lawyers for each side are asked to prepare a brief. A brief is a written document that explains one side's position on the case. The justices study the briefs given them by the lawyers.

Oral Arguments. The next step is for lawyers for each side to present oral arguments to the Court. The lawyers stand facing the nine justices to make their arguments. The justices often question the lawyers about the case.

Conference. On Fridays the justices meet in a large conference room to make their first decisions about the cases they have been studying. Each justice has one vote. If, as usually happens, all nine justices vote on a case, five votes are required to decide a case.

Opinion Writing. Once a decision is made, one justice is given the job of writing a majority opinion for the five or more justices who voted the same way on the case. This is an important step, for there is still time for justices to change their minds about a case. A well-written opinion may influence a justice to change his or her vote.

A member who disagrees with the majority's decision may write a **dissenting opinion.** Sometimes two, three, or even four members write dissenting opinions. A justice who agrees with the majority, but for different reasons, may write a **concurring opinion.**

Announcement. When the opinion writing is finally completed, the Court makes a public announcement of its decision. Printed copies of the opinion are given to waiting news reporters. The written opinions are used by the Supreme Court and other courts around the country to guide decisions in new cases.

What Influences Supreme Court Decisions?

In the United States, the law is supposed to be the most important influence on a justice's decisions. Justices look at the Constitution when

The press receiving copies of a Supreme Court opinion at a public announcement.

making decisions. The Bill of Rights has been the focus of many important Supreme Court decisions.

The Law. Here is one example of how the Supreme Court interprets the law: In early December of 1965, Chris Eckhardt and John and Mary Beth Tinker decided to wear black armbands to school to protest American involvement in the Vietnam War.

On December 14, officials of the school system heard about the students' plan. They feared the protest would cause disruptions in the schools, so they made a special rule. Any student wearing an armband to school would be asked to remove it. Students who refused would be suspended until they came to school without an armband. A few days later Mary Beth, Chris, and John wore black armbands to school and were suspended.

The students' parents sued the school officials in a United States district court. Their lawyers argued that the school's armband rule violated a student's constitutional right of free expression of ideas.

The First Amendment applies not just to Congress but also to state officials such as school principals because of the Fourteenth Amendment. That Amendment says: "No state shall make or enforce any law which shall abridge the privileges . . . of citizens of the United States; nor shall any state deprive any person of . . . liberty . . . without due process of law. . . ."

School officials argued that the armband rule was necessary because wearing armbands might cause disturbances in school.

The district court agreed that the school officials' action was reasonable in order to prevent disturbance of school discipline. The Tinkers appealed to a United States Court of Appeals. In 1967 the appeals court upheld the decision of the district court. The Tinkers then appealed their case to the Supreme Court. In 1968 the Supreme Court agreed to hear the case.

It was now up to the Supreme Court to interpret the Constitution. Did the Constitution give students the right to free speech while in school? Under what conditions, if any, could students express their opinions?

The Supreme Court made its decision on February 24, 1969. The Court supported the students. It declared the action of the school officials to be unconstitutional. The Court decided that the "armband rule" violated the First Amendment. In stating the Court's opinion, Justice Abe Fortas wrote:

"First Amendment rights . . . are available to teachers and students. Students in schools as well as out of school are 'persons' under our Constitution. They are possessed of fundamental rights which the state must respect, just as they themselves must respect their obligations to the state . . . In the absence of a specific showing of constitutionally valid reasons to regulate their speech, students are entitled to freedom of expression of their views."

However, the Supreme Court also said that students' free-speech rights had certain limits. The Court

Mary Beth Tinker and her mother.

Landmark Decisions of the Supreme Court

MARBURY V. MADISON (1803)
Provided the constitutional base for the Supreme Court's power of judicial review.

MC CULLOCH V. MARYLAND (1819)
Declared the Constitution gives Congress "implied powers" to pass all laws "necessary and proper" to do its job. This greatly expanded Congress' power.

GIBBONS V. OGDEN (1824)
Defined the power of Congress to regulate interstate commerce such as shipping very broadly. Laid the foundation for later interpretations giving Congress control over nearly all business activity.

DRED SCOTT V. SANFORD (1857)
Ruled Congress did not have authority to prohibit slavery and blacks could not be citizens. The decision angered many people and contributed to the coming of the Civil War. The ruling on blacks was overturned by the 14th Amendment in 1868.

EX PARTE MILLIGAN (1866)
Established the principle that neither the President nor Congress could legally deny to an accused person a civilian trial by jury and due process of law, as guaranteed by the Constitution.

MUNN V. ILLINOIS (1877)
Ruled the Constitution allowed state governments to regulate private businesses. Established a principle both Congress and state legislatures use today to regulate many business activities.

PLESSY V. FERGUSON (1896)
Declared that "separate but equal" facilities for blacks were not a violation of the Constitution. Served as justification for discrimination against blacks in many states for the next half century.

MULLER V. OREGON (1908)
Established that information on social conditions such as the effect of long working hours on people as well as strictly legal arguments could be considered when making court decisions.

SCHENCK V. UNITED STATES (1919)
Set forth the principle that when spoken or written words "create a clear and present danger" to the nation the government may limit speech. Established that the 1st Amendment guarantee of free speech is not absolute.

GITLOW V. NEW YORK (1925)
Ruled the 1st Amendment protection of free speech applied to the states as well as the national government. First of a long line of decisions holding the 14th Amendment extended the guarantees of the Bill of Rights to the states.

UNITED STATES V. CURTISS-WRIGHT EXPORT CORP. (1936)
Distinguished between the powers exercised by Congress and the President in "external" (foreign) affairs and "internal" (domestic) affairs. Recognized the President as having the key role and great freedom in directing the nation's foreign affairs.

BROWN V. BOARD OF EDUCATION OF TOPEKA (1954)
Declared that separate public schools for blacks and whites were inherently unequal thus violating the constitutional guarantee of equal rights for all. Reversed *Plessy* v. *Ferguson* and destroyed the constitutional foundation of all forms of state-supported segregation in the United States.

GIDEON V. WAINRIGHT (1963)
Ruled that all persons charged with serious crimes have a constitutional right to a lawyer in state trials and that the state must provide a lawyer if the accused person cannot afford to pay for one.

REYNOLDS V. SIMS (1964)
Established the principle of "one person, one vote." Ruled that state legislatures must set up their legislative districts in both house and senate so the districts represented nearly equal numbers of people.

MIRANDA V. ARIZONA (1966)
Ruled the 5th Amendment requires police to inform suspects in their custody of their right to remain silent, that anything they say can be held against them, and that they have a right to a lawyer.

UNITED STATES V. NIXON (1974)
Ruled the President must give a court confidential material needed for evidence in a criminal trial.

said schools could stop students from expressing their views if their speech would seriously disrupt the work and discipline of the school. The Supreme Court decision applied to all schools in the country.

Precedents. Justices also look at earlier court decisions when settling a case. The Court's decision in the Tinker case was based on the idea that students have constitutional rights like adults. One precedent the Court used to support the majority opinion in the Tinker case was in the case of *West Virginia State Board of Education* v. *Barnette*. In that case the board of education required students to salute and pledge allegiance to the flag each day or be expelled. The Court said this rule violated students' rights under the First and Fourteenth Amendments.

Sometimes there are precedents that support opposite sides in a case. In the Tinker case, for example, Justice Black dissented from the majority. To support his argument that students' constitutional rights to free speech could be limited in school, he referred to the case of *Cox* v. *Louisiana*. In it the Supreme Court had ruled that the rights of free speech "do not mean everyone with opinions or beliefs to express may address a group at any public place and at any time."

Social Conditions. The social situation in the country can also influence Supreme Court decisions. When social conditions change, the Court may make new interpretations of the law. Justices, like all citizens, are affected by what other people around the country believe about important social issues. Further, their thinking on legal problems can be influenced by social science research and by the writings of legal scholars.

Personal Beliefs. Finally, the personal beliefs of the justices influence Supreme Court decisions. Some members, for example, believe that the Court should be very active and hear many different kinds of cases. Others believe that the Court should be careful not to involve itself in issues the public disagrees about.

Section Review

Vocabulary:
concurring opinion, dissenting opinion, judicial review, precedent, real case rule, unconstitutional.

Reviewing the Main Ideas
1. Why is *Marbury* v. *Madison* an important case?
2. List and briefly describe the steps a case goes through after it is appealed to the Supreme Court.
3. List the factors that can influence Supreme Court decisions.

Skill Building
1. What qualifications do you think a Supreme Court justice should have? Explain your reasons.
2. Why would a President want to appoint justices who agreed with his or her political ideas?
3. Explain what it means for the Supreme Court to interpret the law. Use the Tinker case as an example.

(chart, opposite) Which of the landmark cases dealt with an interpretation of the Bill of Rights?

215

Gideon v. Wainwright

The services of a lawyer are often expensive. Poor people who are accused of crimes may not have money to pay a lawyer to defend them in a court of law. In such cases, does a state government always have the duty to provide a lawyer?

In 1942, the U.S. Supreme Court considered this question in the case of *Betts* v. *Brady.* Four years earlier, Smith Betts had been charged with robbing a country store in Carroll County, Maryland. He pleaded "not guilty" and asked the judge to appoint a lawyer to help him because he could not afford to pay for a lawyer himself. The judge refused. Smith Betts was found guilty and sent to jail for eight years.

Betts appealed his conviction, and the case went to the U.S. Supreme Court. Betts argued that he had been denied his constitutional right to a lawyer guaranteed by the Sixth Amendment. Furthermore, he claimed that his conviction also violated the Fourteenth Amendment to the Constitution, which says: "No state . . . shall deprive any person of life, liberty or property without due process of law." Betts claimed that being without a lawyer was a denial of due process (fair legal procedure). He pointed out that the state government had used a lawyer to prosecute him. It seemed only fair that he should have a lawyer to defend himself, even if the state government had to pay for the lawyer.

A majority of the Supreme Court justices decided that "the Sixth Amendment to the Constitution applies only to trials in federal courts." The Court concluded that Smith Betts had a fair chance to defend himself during his trial. In cases that did not involve the death penalty, the states did not have to supply a lawyer to a defendant too poor to employ his own attorney.

Justice Hugo Black disagreed with the majority decision in *Betts* v. *Brady.* Having failed to change the minds of the majority during discussions behind closed doors, Black, joined by two other justices, wrote a dissenting opinion. He argued that the due-process clause of the Fourteenth Amendment applies to those rights spelled out in the Bill of Rights, which includes the Sixth Amendment guarantee of the right "to have the assistance of counsel. . . ." Thus, Justice Black concluded that the state of Maryland had denied Smith Betts one of his constitutional rights.

Black also argued that no person should "be deprived of counsel merely because of his poverty." To do so, said Black, "seems to me to defeat the promise of our democratic society to provide equal justice under the law."

In 1963, twenty-one years after the Betts case, Hugo Black was still a member of the Supreme Court. He had another opportunity to consider the question about constitutional rights that had been presented by *Betts* v. *Brady* in 1942. The case of *Gideon* v. *Wainwright* had come before the Supreme Court.

Two years earlier, Clarence Earl Gideon had been arrested and accused of breaking into the Bal Harbour Pool Room in Florida. Gideon was too poor to hire a lawyer, so he asked the state court to provide one for him. The judge refused and told Gideon either to obtain a lawyer on his own or to defend himself. Gideon conducted his own legal defense. However, he was no match for the prosecuting attorney. Gideon was found guilty and sent to prison for five years.

Gideon appealed to the U.S. Supreme Court. His handwritten petition said: "The question is very simple. I requested the court to appoint me an attorney and the court refused." He argued that the state court's refusal to appoint a lawyer for him violated his rights under the Sixth and Fourteenth amendments.

The Supreme Court agreed to accept Gideon's case for review. An excellent lawyer, Abe Fortas, was appointed to represent Gideon before the Supreme Court.

The case of *Gideon* v. *Wainwright* was decided unanimously in favor of Gideon. The decision in *Betts* v. *Brady* was overruled. Chief Justice Earl Warren asked Hugo Black to write the Court's opinion. Justice Black said that "The Bill of Rights . . . is made obligatory upon the States by the Fourteenth Amendment. . . . The Sixth Amendment's guarantee of counsel is . . . one of those fundamental rights. . . . In our . . . system of criminal justice, any person . . . who is too poor to hire a lawyer, cannot be assured a fair trial unless counsel is provided. . . . This seems to us to be an obvious truth."

One consequence of the Supreme Court's decision was a new trial in Florida for Clarence Earl Gideon. This time, helped by a lawyer that the court provided, Gideon was found innocent. Another consequence of the Gideon case was a review of many similar cases around the country. New trials were held for people who had been found guilty without the help of a lawyer. Finally, it became customary for state courts to provide poor people with **public defenders—**lawyers paid with government funds.

Clarence Earl Gideon and his hand-written petition to the Supreme Court.

Review

1. Describe the rights provided by the Sixth Amendment.
2. What is "due process"? Was Smith Betts correct in claiming that he was denied due process? Why or why not?

217

Basic Social Studies Skills
Thinking Deductively

Deductive thinking is the process of using **premises**—statements assumed to be true—to arrive at specific conclusions, or **deductions.**

Here is an example of deductive thinking:

Premise 1: All people are mortal.

Premise 2: George Smith is a person.

Deduction: Therefore, George Smith is mortal.

The conclusion, or deduction, is a specific statement that is implied by the two premises. The conclusion follows logically from the two premises.

Deductive thinking does not always lead to sound conclusions. Consider this example:

Premise 1: All people are immortal.

Premise 2: George Smith is a person.

Deduction: Therefore, George Smith is immortal.

The judges you read about in this chapter often use deductive thinking when making decisions about the law. Here is an example of a Supreme Court decision that was based on deductive thinking.

In 1796, the case of *Ware* v. *Hylton* came before the United States Supreme Court. The issue before the court was whether or not the government of Virginia could make and enforce a law that violated a treaty signed by the federal government.

In 1783, the United States and Britain signed the Treaty of Paris, a treaty which formally ended the Revolutionary War. A part of the treaty stated that the United States would not interfere with the efforts of British citizens who wanted to collect debts owed to them by United States citizens. Virginia, however, passed a law that contradicted this promise. It said that citizens of Virginia did not have to pay their debts to the British.

The Supreme Court overturned the Virginia law because it violated the Constitution. Article VI says that "all treaties made, or which shall be made, under the authority of the United States, shall be the supreme law of the land; and the judges in every state shall be bound thereby, anything in the Constitution or laws of any state to the contrary notwithstanding."

The deductive thinking of the Supreme Court justices in this case is shown below:

Premise 1: All state laws that violate treaties of the United States are invalid, or illegal.

Premise 2: The Virginia law at issue violated a treaty between the United States and Britain.

Deduction: Therefore, the Virginia law is invalid, or illegal.

Skill Practice

1. State two premises from which you could make a deduction.

2. Review "Thinking Inductively" on page 200. What are the differences between these two types of thinking processes?

Chapter 10 Review

Summary

Section 1: How Laws and Courts Serve the People

Our legal system involves four different kinds of law: statutory law, common law, administrative law, and constitutional law. Courts use these kinds of law to settle disputes. The ideal behind our legal system is equal justice for all under the law. This means treating each person the same.

Section 2: How the Federal Courts Are Organized

There are three levels of federal courts. District courts are trial courts and handle most federal cases. United States Courts of Appeals review decisions made by district courts. The Supreme Court, the highest court in the land, decides whether laws and government actions are in agreement with the Constitution.

Section 3: What the Supreme Court Does

The Supreme Court is made up of nine justices. The Court has the power, called judicial review, to declare a law or action of government unconstitutional. Although the Court acts as both a trial court and an appeals court, most cases reach the Court as appeals from decisions in lower courts.

Vocabulary

Define the following terms.

1. precedent
2. public defender
3. statutory law
4. unconstitutional
5. common law
6. judicial review
7. administrative law
8. constitutional law
9. senatorial courtesy

Reviewing Main Ideas

1. True or false: Most federal cases are handled in the Supreme Court.
2. The Supreme Court is made up of eight associate justices and one chief justice.
3. Federal judges are appointed by _____.
a. the Senate
b. the House of Representatives
c. the President
d. the attorney general
4. In which of these federal courts would you see a jury?
a. a district court
b. the Supreme Court
c. an appeals court
d. all of the above

Thinking Critically

Comprehending Information

1. How are Supreme Court opinions used?
2. What is the "real case rule"?
3. Explain what "equal justice under the law" means.
4. What is the Supreme Court's most important job?

Organizing Information

1. Make a diagram that shows how the federal court system works.
2. Explain how a case is handled in the Supreme Court by listing and explaining the steps each case goes through.

Evaluating Information

1. Is it important that the Supreme Court has the power of judicial review? Why or why not?
2. Federal judges can have their jobs for life unless they are impeached. Do you feel this is a good idea? Why or why not?

Unit Three Test

Vocabulary

Write *true* if the underlined word or phrase is used correctly. Write *false* if it is used incorrectly. Rephrase each false statement so that the underlined word or phrase is used correctly.

1. A <u>tax</u> is a fee that a person pays to support his or her government.

2. <u>Congressional district</u> is a term that refers to the place where Congress meets in Washington, D.C.

3. <u>Seniority rule</u> is the tradition of selecting the majority party member with fewest years on a congressional committee to head the committee.

4. Members of Congress can hold <u>committee hearings</u> to create or abolish federal agencies.

5. A <u>lobbyist</u> is a person who tries to influence decisions in government.

6. To be <u>nominated</u> at a presidential nominating convention means that someone has been elected President.

7. The <u>electoral college</u> is made up of those people who vote directly for the President.

8. The <u>Cabinet</u> is a group of Congressional members who advise the President.

9. The <u>civil service system</u> is a system for hiring government workers.

10. A federal agency's <u>clients</u> are those people who work for the agency.

11. A law is <u>unconstitutional</u> if it does not agree with the Constitution.

12. The power of <u>judicial review</u> is the power to decide whether or not laws are unconstitutional.

13. A <u>precedent</u> is any court decision that serves as a guide in later decisions.

Recalling Information

1. True or false: The United States Congress is made up of two houses—the Senate and the House of Representatives.

2. True or false: The President heads the legislative branch of government.

3. True or false: The personal income tax is used to provide income for retired people.

4. Each state has _____ senators.
a. 2   **c.** 6
b. 4   **d.** 8

5. The number of House members that each state has is determined by _____.
a. the amount of taxes a state pays
b. the number of square miles in the state
c. the number of people in the state
d. the year in which the state entered the union

6. Which of these is a power of the Senate but not of the House?
a. the power to start the impeachment process
b. the power to approve presidential appointments of Supreme Court justices
c. the power to start all tax bills
d. the power to choose a President if no candidate receives a majority of votes

7. True or false: The party whips in the House assist the floor leaders.

8. True or false: The most powerful leader in the Senate is the president pro tempore.

9. A standing committee _____.
a. chooses the leaders of all the other committees in Congress
b. is a committee that handles a particular problem and disbands when the problem is solved
c. meets to settle differences of opinion when the Senate and the House cannot agree on a particular bill
d. is a permanent committee that deals with one particular kind of legislation

10. According to the Constitution, the President has power to _____.
a. create federal courts
b. make treaties with other countries
c. impeach the Chief Justice of the Supreme Court
d. all of the above

11. The Constitution requires that in order to be elected President a person must _____.
a. be a lawyer
b. be fifty-five years old
c. be a natural-born citizen
d. be a member of a major political party

12. The President's term of office is _____ years.
a. 2   **c.** 6
b. 4   **d.** 8

13. Most of a Vice-President's duties are created by _____.
a. the Congress   **c.** the President
b. the Constitution   **d.** none of the above

14. Which Cabinet department is in charge of collecting taxes?
a. the Department of Defense
b. the Department of Housing and Urban Development
c. the Department of the Treasury
d. the Department of Transportation

15. Federal agency decisions are influenced by
a. the President   **c.** client groups
b. Congress   **d.** all of the above

16. A law made by a government agency is called _____.
a. a common law
b. a statutory law
c. a constitutional law
d. an administrative law

17. The federal court in which you would have a jury trial is _____.
a. a district court
b. an appellate court
c. the Supreme Court
d. none of these courts

18. What is a federal judge's term of office?
a. two years   **c.** twenty years
b. ten years   **d.** life

Building Skills

You are a member of Congress who has been asked to vote on a bill that would provide more money for space exploration. Tell how you would vote. If you were to vote for the bill, where would you plan to get the money to pay for it? Who do you think would support your decision? How might they support it? Who would oppose it? What information might the opposition be able to provide that would convince you to change your mind? What goals or values do you have that would explain your final decision?

Unit 4

How Citizens Influence Government

Voting is an important right of citizenship in the United States. Without this right, which is guaranteed in the Constitution, citizens would not be able to elect the people who run their government. They would have no guaranteed say in governmental decisions that affect them.

Voting is also an important responsibility of citizenship in the United States. Citizens who neglect to vote lose a chance to take part directly in their government.

Citizens also have the responsibility of using their vote carefully and wisely. Every voter should try hard to judge the competing candidates so that only the best ones are elected. Citizens who fail to vote, or who vote carelessly, may help inferior candidates gain office. Edmund Burke, a famous eighteenth-century statesman, warned of the consequences of irresponsible citizenship. "The only thing necessary for the triumph of evil is for good men to do nothing," Burke said.

Voting is not the only way that Americans can be involved in government. They can also influence government decisions by participating in political parties or interest groups.

Through responsible participation in political parties, interest groups, and elections, citizens exercise their right to self-government under the Constitution. President Franklin D. Roosevelt reminded Americans of their precious rights and important responsibilities of citizenship. "Let us never forget that government is ourselves. The ultimate rulers of our democracy are . . . the voters of this country."

Voting in elections, participating in interest groups, and participating in political parties are three important ways that Americans can use their right to self-government.

(opposite) Part of a long caravan of tractors that farmers formed in Sacramento, California, to protest government farm policies. Many other farmers across the nation staged similar demonstrations during the mid-1980s. The farmers called for state and federal land reforms that would allow them a better chance to make a profit on their farms. Thousands of farmers have lost their farms in recent years due to bank foreclosures.

Chapter 11

Taking Part in Interest Groups

Introduction. People who have the same goals and opinions often join forces as members of a group. The Sierra Club, for example, is a group of people who are interested in preserving the natural environment. They want to stop pollution of the air and water, to protect wildlife, and to conserve natural resources.

Many groups try to influence decision makers in government to support their goals. Such organizations are called interest groups. The Sierra Club is an interest group because its members try to persuade government officials to act in favor of the group's goals.

In the United States, people are free to take part in interest groups. The First Amendment to the Constitution protects this right. It says that "Congress shall make no law . . .

abridging [limiting] . . . the right of the people peaceably to assemble and to petition the Government for a redress of grievances." This means that people have the right to act peacefully in groups to try to get the government to respond to their concerns.

A group of citizens often is more likely to have influence on the government than is a citizen acting alone. By joining forces in an interest group, people with the same goals and values may increase their power. If it has good leadership and organization, an interest group can have an effect on decision makers in government.

The main purposes of this chapter are to help you learn about interest groups and their influence on government in the United States.

Environmentalists with stacks of petitions demanding the resignation of Secretary of the Interior James Watt. Watt's environmental policies were much criticized by environmental groups. Pressure exerted by these groups and by Congress resulted in Watt's resignation in October, 1983.

Section 1
Why Citizens Join Interest Groups

Interest groups are organizations of people that have common goals and interests. They try to influence government decisions. Citizens join or support interest groups because they believe that by pooling their resources—time, money, and skills —they will increase their chances of influencing decision makers.

Different Interest Groups

There are thousands of interest groups in the United States. The National Association of Manufacturers, for example, is one of the largest interest groups. It works on behalf of business owners and managers who want to attain common goals.

The American Federation of Labor and Congress of Industrial Organizations (AFL-CIO), an alliance of labor unions, is another large special interest group. The AFL-CIO works to protect and promote the economic interests of workers. Other examples of interest groups include the American Farm Bureau Federation, the American Legion, and the American Medical Association. These groups support the goals and interests of farmers, veterans, and medical doctors.

Interest groups with different values and goals sometimes clash. One group may have goals that conflict with the goals of another group. Members of each group try to influence government officials to support their point of view. For example, there has often been conflict between groups about how much

(top) Showing support for a development project in the Florida Keys. Supporters claimed the project would create many jobs in the area. (above) Expressing disapproval of the development plan. Critics claimed the project would seriously damage the coral reef.

money government should spend on public education. In one state, the teachers' association tried to influence lawmakers to pass a larger school funding bill. "If the state doesn't spend more, it will end up providing poor education," the president of the association said. "Our state ranks very low in the amount of public funds spent on each pupil," he reminded the lawmakers.

However, some other groups in this state opposed spending more money to improve public schools. One wanted any available funds to be used to improve public transportation. Another wanted more money for welfare programs. Still another wanted the government to cut back all spending and lower taxes. Each

group tried to influence decision makers in government to support its interests.

Public Interest Groups

Whereas some interest groups support the goals of only select groups of people in specific businesses or professions, **public interest groups** support causes that affect the lives of citizens from many different walks of life.

Common Cause is one example of a public interest group. It was founded by John Gardner in 1970 to help ordinary citizens get a better deal from government decision makers. Gardner argued that citizens with many resources—for example, those with great wealth—have a better chance than others to influence government officials. He believed that government officials should serve the common needs of all citizens rather than the interests of a few.

Common Cause has grown tremendously since it was started. It now has more than 200,000 members and a budget of several million dollars a year. It has influenced the passage of laws to control pollution, to reform election campaign practices, and to protect consumers.

The League of Women Voters is another example of a public interest group. It was founded in 1920 by Carrie Chapman Catt. The primary purpose of the League was to help women learn to vote responsibly and effectively. (Women gained the right to vote in 1920, when the Nineteenth Amendment was passed.)

The League's main goal today is to promote responsible citizenship through informed and effective participation in government. The League aims to educate voters about candidates, public issues, and participation in elections. League members study problems at the local, state, and national levels. After the members agree on how a problem should be solved, they work to influence legislation. The League does not endorse candidates or back any particular political party.

Deciding Which Groups to Support

If at some time you join an interest group, you will want the decision to be a good one. The following five questions may help you decide whether or not a group deserves your support:

1. Does the group support programs, goals, and values with which you agree?

2. Do people that you respect belong to the group?

3. Does the group try to accomplish its goals in a legal and honest way?

4. Does the group set goals that it can achieve or does it try to achieve impossible goals?

5. Is decision making within the group in the hands of a few leaders or is decision making shared by all members?

If the answers to these questions meet with your approval, then giving support is probably a good idea.

President Ronald Reagan debating presidential hopeful Walter Mondale in 1984. The debate was sponsored by the League of Women Voters.

Section Review

Vocabulary:
interest group, public interest group.

Reviewing the Main Ideas

1. Why do people join interest groups?

2. What ideas should guide your thinking when you are trying to decide whether or not to join a particular interest group?

3. Name one public interest group.

Skill Building

1. Find one of the interest groups described in this section that has an office in your city or in the nearest large city. Use the telephone books at your public library to get this information. Write the office and ask for information about the organization.

2. Locate an article in your daily newspaper about a public interest group. Summarize the article for the rest of the class.

Section 2
How Interest Groups Influence Government

In order to be able to influence political decisions, interest groups must have **political resources**—the time, money, skills, or information needed to help achieve their goals. Groups with the most resources tend to have the most influence.

Using Resources to Influence Election of Government Officials

Some groups use political resources to support certain candidates at election time. The League of Conservation Voters and the Sierra Club back candidates who support laws to protect the environment. They oppose candidates who disagree with their goals and beliefs about how people should use their natural surroundings. In New Mexico, for example, the League of Conservation Voters campaigned against United States Senator Harrison Schmitt, a Republican. They worked for his opponent, Jeff Bingaman, a Democrat. With the help of several environmental interest groups who gave money, time, and energy as campaign workers, and skill in organizing campaign activities, Bingaman won election to the United States Senate.

In Vermont, the League of Conservation Voters and similar interest groups backed a Republican senator, Robert T. Stafford, in his successful bid for re-election.

The League of Conservation Voters does not regularly back the candidates of one political party. Rather, it identifies candidates from both major parties—the Democrats and the Republicans—who either agree or disagree with League goals and beliefs. The League expects to have influence on the decisions and actions of government officials whom it helped to elect to office.

The National Rifle Association (NRA) is against laws that would ban or severely limit the use of guns. It supports candidates for election to local, state, and national office who agree with NRA views about the right of citizens to own guns.

The NRA, the League of Conservation Voters, and many other interest groups, including most labor unions and a large number of business corporations and trade associations, have formed **political action committees (PACs).** More than 3,500 PACs are now active in federal election campaigns. These PACs collect contributions of money from the members of their groups. The

Terry Dolan, chairman of the National Conservative Political Action Committee.

(far left) Advertisement promoting membership in the National Rifle Association, a powerful interest group. (left) Demonstrators calling for a law that would outlaw handguns. Gun control has been one of the most hotly debated issues of recent years.

PACs then use the money to back certain candidates and issues and oppose others. In a recent congressional election year, for example, all PACs together contributed about $83 million to congressional candidates, almost 25 percent of all the money the candidates received. Among the largest interest group PAC contributors were the Realtors Political Action Committee, which gave candidates more than $2 million; the American Medical Association PAC, which gave about $1.7 million; and the United Auto Workers PAC, which gave about $1.6 million.

Interest groups also have been active in state election campaign funding. Recently, for example, the California Medical Association, the United Farm Workers, and the State Employees Association were major sources of funding for state legislative campaigns in California.

Using Resources to Influence Voting About Initiatives and Referendums

Interest groups also try to influence voters during campaigns involving initiatives and referendums. The **initiative** is a way for citizens to propose new laws. Citizens who want a new law gather signatures of qualified voters on a petition. If a sufficient number of citizens sign the petition, the proposed law is placed on the ballot at the next general election. If a majority of voters approve of the proposal, it becomes a law. Citizens may use the initiative in twenty-three states and the District of Columbia.

The **referendum** is a way for citizens to vote on laws that have been passed by the state legislature or city council. Citizens in more than half of the states have the right to petition to have a law referred, or sent back, to the voters for their

229

Campaign Contributions from Political Action Committees

Political Action Committees (PACs) contributed more that $83 million to congressional candidates during the 1982 election campaign. This spending accounted for almost 25 percent of the total of congressional campaign contributions. In 1982, there were more than 3,000 PACs in the United States.

The top ten PAC contributors to federal candidates are listed below. Most of the money they contributed was given to congressional candidates.

1. Realtors Political Action Committee (National Association of Realtors)	$2,115,135
2. American Medical Association PAC	$1,737,090
3. UAW-U-CAP (United Auto Workers)	$1,623,947
4. Machinists Non-Partisan Political League (International Association of Machinists and Aerospace Workers)	$1,444,959
5. National Education Association PAC	$1,183,215
6. Build Political Action Committee (National Association of Home Builders)	$1,005,628
7. Committee for Thorough Agricultural Political Education (Associated Milk Producers)	$962,450
8. BANKPAC (American Bankers Association)	$947,460
9. Automobile and Truck Dealers Election Action Committee	$917,292
10. AFL-CIO COPE Political Contributions Committee	$906,425

Name the professions and trades that are represented in the table at right. Why do you think PACs believe it is important to contribute money to political candidates?

approval. If enough citizens sign a petition for a referendum, the law is put on the ballot at the next general election, and the voters may either approve or reject it.

In forty-nine states, amendments to state constitutions must be approved by the voters. (The exception is Delaware.) Recently, for example, the legislature of New Hampshire proposed that the governor's term of office be changed from two to four years. Less than two-thirds of the voters in New Hampshire approved this proposal. Thus it could not become an amendment to the state constitution.

Interest groups across the country have been very involved in recent years in campaigns about initiatives and referendums. The NRA, for example, has campaigned actively in general elections in California, New Hampshire, and Nevada. In California, the NRA spent $2.4 million to help defeat a proposal for strict regulation of handguns. In New Hampshire and Nevada, the NRA supported citizens wishing to vote in favor of their right "to keep and bear arms."

Opposing interest groups have clashed several times in recent years over propositions to limit smoking in public. An example was the California election of November, 1978. The issue that voters had to decide was whether or not smoking should be restricted in some public places. The smoking restriction was listed on the ballot as Proposition 5.

The interest group that organized support for Proposition 5 was a California citizens' group called the Campaign for Clean Indoor Air. They collected the 600,000 signatures needed to get the issue on the ballot. They also collected about $625,000 to run the campaign. Groups giving support included the California Medical Association, the California PTA, the California division of the American Cancer Society, the American Association of Retired Persons, and the California Lung Association. The Campaign for Clean Indoor Air argued that the health of nonsmokers was endangered when they were forced to breathe the smoke of other people's cigarettes.

The main opposition to Proposition 5 came from the American Tobacco Institute and some of the nation's largest cigarette makers. The opposition campaign was paid for almost wholly by the cigarette makers. They spent more than $5 million in their attempt to stop Proposition 5. They argued that the law would be hard to enforce and would greatly limit the freedom of smokers.

The difference in resources available to the two sides seems to have had a clear effect on voter attitudes. In August, about two and a half months before the election, a survey of voters showed that Proposition 5 was supported by 58 percent of the California population and opposed by 38 percent. At that point the cigarette companies had spent about $1 million to fight the measure. During the next two months the cigarette companies

spent an additional $4 million—much of it on television and radio advertising. By election day, the cigarette makers' advertising campaign had apparently influenced many voters—Proposition 5 was defeated, 54 percent to 46 percent.

How Lobbyists Use Resources to Influence Government Decision Makers

Interest groups often use political resources to influence government decision makers. They try to convince lawmakers to pass or reject certain laws. They also try to influence the government officials who carry out or enforce laws.

To help get what they want, special interest groups hire lobbyists. Lobbyists serve as a link between interest groups and government decision makers. Lobbyists give information about their group's position. They sometimes write bills for members of Congress to consider. They suggest solutions to problems and issues.

Lobbyists get their name from a practice that they once used. They would stand in the lobby outside legislative meeting rooms waiting for lawmakers to come out. Then they would try to influence the lawmakers' opinions.

Today, lobbyists usually phone government officials to make appointments. They talk with officials or their staff members in government offices. They also may discuss business over lunch or dinner in a restaurant or private club.

Supporters of Proposition 5.

Lobbyists sometimes ask influential people such as mayors and business leaders to visit or call members of Congress in support of a position. They also try to get the general public to pressure members of Congress.

Information is one of the lobbyist's most important resources. Lawmakers need up-to-date information about public issues. The most effective lobbyists are able to supply useful information to lawmakers that helps their own case. For example, leaders of the Committee on Political Education (COPE) of the AFL-CIO regularly give facts to government officials about working conditions in factories, mines, and offices. These facts help influence official thinking and win support for the labor point of view.

The top lobbyists in Washington, D.C., are well educated. They have great skill in presenting information. But most of all, the top lobbyists represent important interest groups with many resources. Those with the most resources have the best chance to be effective.

Using Resources in the Courts

Interest groups also use political resources in state and federal courts. When a law is on the books, but is—in the opinion of an interest group—not being properly enforced, the group may sue the party who is breaking the law. A group may also use the courts to show that an existing law is unconstitutional. Before going to court, however, the interest group must have knowledge of the problem, the time and skills to

NAACP member conducting a campaign to increase black voter registration in Atlanta, Georgia.

investigate the problem, and money for legal help. The National Association for the Advancement of Colored People (NAACP) is one group that has often used its resources in this way. By so doing, it has improved the legal rights of blacks.

Section Review

Vocabulary:
initiative, political action committees, political resources, referendum.

Reviewing the Main Ideas
1. What are four different kinds of political resources?
2. How can political resources be used to influence elections?
3. How do interest groups try to influence members of Congress?
4. What is a lobbyist's job?

Skill Building
1. Find an example of interest-group activity in the newspaper. Describe the activity in a brief report. Tell whether or not you think this interest group can be effective. Give your reasons.
2. Find a newspaper article that includes an example of people using political resources. Write a paragraph that describes how the resources were used to influence government.

Section 3
How Citizens Can Take Part in Interest Groups

Why are some citizens and groups more effective than others when they take part in political activities? As you have seen, one answer is that some have many more resources than others. There is a second answer, too. Citizens who know how to make the best use of their resources, whatever those resources may be, are more effective than citizens who do not.

Guidelines for Effective Group Action

The guidelines that follow should help citizens make better use of group resources. Those who follow the guidelines are more likely to have influence than those who ignore them.

Guideline 1: Use Resources Wisely. Some people with many resources fail to have much influence because they waste their resources or use them foolishly. In contrast, some people with few resources achieve their political goals because they use their resources wisely. They do not try to achieve impossible goals.

To use resources wisely, a group should find out what it has. Who are the good speakers? The good writers? The organizers? The poster-makers? Who might be able to donate money? How many people will take part in a demonstration? It is wise to use people's talents. The group's spokesperson should be a good speaker, not necessarily its most well-known member.

Knowing what it has to use can help a group decide which political activities to take part in. A group that has plenty of money can donate to an election campaign. It can buy ads and hire skilled publicity people. A group that has little money and few other political resources will need to use a different approach. Often such groups find that they can be effective by organizing marches or public meetings to draw attention to their cause.

Guideline 2: Pool Your Resources. Citizens form groups because they realize that groups are usually more effective than people working alone. Groups, too, can be more effective by joining and pooling resources. When interest groups join together to reach a goal, they are said to have formed a **coalition** [kō'ə lish'ən]. By forming coalitions, groups increase their chances of reaching their common goal.

Guideline 3: Do Not Try to Do Too Much. Some groups try to do too much at one time. They usually achieve little or nothing. They spread their resources too thinly across too many different political activities and goals. People who stress one or two goals at a time increase their chances of success.

Guideline 4: Do Not Give Up Easily. Some persons and groups get excited about a cause. They put on a whirlwind campaign to reach their goal. When they do not see progress right away, however, they

Members of the American Association of Retired People preparing mailings urging people to protest federal budget cuts that would reduce benefits for retired people.

quit. They do not realize that reaching goals is almost always a slow and hard process. The cost of victory is a large pay-out of time and energy. Some groups work for years to reach their goals. It took the National American Women's Suffrage Association decades to win what they wanted—women's right to vote. Those who stick with a cause raise their chances for success.

Guideline 5: Try to Influence Public Opinion to Support Your Goals. A group is more likely to succeed if many citizens agree with its beliefs and goals. Therefore, it is useful to try to influence public opinion to favor the group's cause. Public opinion refers to beliefs a large number of people hold about issues and government.

One way to influence public opinion is to write letters to be printed on the editorial pages of a newspaper or magazine. A well-written letter can inform and persuade readers about a group's point of view. Another, more expensive way to inform and influence the public, is to pay for advertisements of the group's views on radio or TV.

Government Regulation of Interest Groups

Although the Constitution guarantees Americans the right to participate in interest groups, interest group activities may be regulated by laws of state and national governments. For example, the Federal Election Campaign Act of 1971 and its amendments limit the amount interest group PACs may contribute to candidates for national office. A PAC may give no more than $5,000 to any single candidate during an election cycle. An election cycle is two years for the House and six years for the Senate. PACs also may contribute a maximum of $5,000 to a presidential hopeful during a four-year cycle.

The Federal Regulation of Lobbying Act says that any person hired as a lobbyist to influence Congress must register with the Clerk of the House of Representatives and the Secretary of the Senate. Lobbyists are required to tell who hired them, how much they are paid, and how they spend money related to their work. State governments have passed similar laws to regulate the activities of lobbyists.

In 1983, there were about 6,500 organizations and individuals registered with Congress as lobbyists. Some of these lobbyists work

Lobbyists Registered With Congress

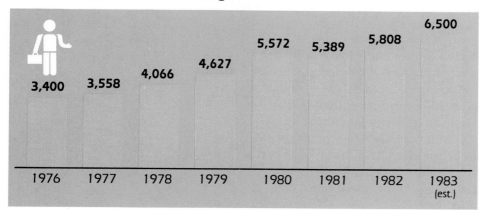

Year	Lobbyists
1976	3,400
1977	3,558
1978	4,066
1979	4,627
1980	5,572
1981	5,389
1982	5,808
1983 (est.)	6,500

Study the graph. What general conclusion can you draw from the statistics?

individually for different groups who might want to hire them. These "professional lobbyists" are really in business for themselves. They sell the service of lobbying to any organization or person willing and able to pay for it.

Most lobbyists work for interest groups. Political interest groups, such as the American Conservation Union or the Americans for Democratic Action, are represented in Washington, D.C., by their own lobbyists. Likewise, businesses, labor unions, and trade associations have their own lobbyists who work full time to represent their groups in the federal and state governments.

Effective interest groups and lobbyists often have a great deal of influence on government decisions. Some citizens have argued that they have too much say in government. They have claimed that interest group campaign contributions give the interest groups undue influence over officeholders. Others, however, have defended the role of interest groups and lobbyists. They point

out that, by themselves, typical citizens usually can have little effect on government officials. But as members of an effective interest group, with skilled lobbyists to represent them, citizens can magnify their influence in government.

Section Review

Vocabulary:
coalition.

Reviewing the Main Ideas
1. What are five guidelines to effective political participation?
2. Define public opinion.
3. What is one way in which you can influence public opinion?

Skill Building
1. Write a letter to the editor of your local newspaper expressing a viewpoint about a local issue.
2. Volunteer to help a local interest group. Report to the class on your "job" for the day.

Case Study

The Bottle Controversy

Each year Americans throw away 40 billion bottles and cans, 4 million tons of plastics, 100 million tires, 30 million tons of paper, and millions of worn-out gadgets. Much of this waste clutters our landscape.

Ellis Yochelson, a scientist living in Bowie, Maryland, had researched this problem. His research showed how waste products damaged the environment.

In the spring of 1970, the principal of a high school in Bowie asked Yochelson to be the main speaker at an "Earth Day" program the school was holding. When the day arrived, Yochelson gave a stirring talk. He showed how throwaway cans and bottles littered the community and how they could scar the landscape of the Bowie area in the future.

Yochelson ended his talk with a rousing call to action. He passed out petition forms to the students. The forms asked that the Bowie City Council pass a law banning the sale of throwaway bottles. He asked the students to sign the petitions and to ask their parents, friends, and neighbors to sign.

The students responded enthusiastically. In a short time they had more than 2,000 names on the petitions, and they presented them to the city council. They also took a poll of city residents about the ban-the-throwaways issue. They found that seventy-six percent favored a law against throwaways. This finding appeared in local newspapers and on radio and television.

Bowie's mayor saw the petitions

'. . . For Purple Mountain Majesties . . .'

and read about the students' poll. He sent the students a note to say that he supported their work.

Several local groups backed Yochelson and his student followers. The groups included the Jaycees and the Parent-Teacher Association. A national group also gave support. It was the National Resources Defense Council, a group of lawyers who support environmental causes.

Opposition to the ban-the-throwaways proposal came from various business and industrial groups—the nearby Bethlehem Steel Company, the United Brewers Association, liquor dealers, the local merchants' association, container manufacturers, and a soft-drink group. These groups warned that a ban on throwaway bottles would be costly. The price of soft drinks would go up, and many jobs would be lost.

In July, 1970, the city council voted unanimously to pass a law banning nonreturnable bottles. In the following months the city council continued to study the issue. In 1971, the council passed a new law which required a deposit on all beverages sold in bottles and cans. The deposit was meant to motivate citizens to return the bottles.

However, the throwaway-bottles conflict continued in Bowie. The Washington, D.C., Soft Drink Association and the local liquor dealers' association sued the city of Bowie for passing the bottle law. The Natural Resources Defense Council helped the city of Bowie prepare its defense. In March, 1974, the suit came to trial in the County Circuit Court. The court ruled in favor of the Bowie law.

The Bowie law got nationwide publicity. City officials got more than 6,000 letters asking for copies of the law and details about how it was passed. Officials from all over the United States and Canada asked Yochelson to help them prepare similar laws.

Today, some states have laws requiring a deposit on beer and soft-drink containers. Government officials in Oregon reported that roadside litter was reduced by 83 percent within the first two years of its bottle-deposit law. In Michigan, litter has been reduced in state parks by 90 percent since passage of a bottle-deposit law. Officials in Maine said that they have saved about $100,000 a year in cleanup costs because citizens are motivated to return bottles to get the deposit.

Despite the success stories in a few states, there has been continuing opposition to passage of bottle-deposit laws in most parts of the country. In Maryland, for example, there is no state law similar to the bottle-deposit law in Bowie. Opponents of bottle-deposit laws have included soft-drink businesses and labor unions. These interest groups have argued that the increase in prices of soft drinks or beer, caused by the deposit laws, leads to declines in sales, profits, and jobs.

Opponents of bottle-deposit laws campaigned against them in four western states in 1982. Referendums were held on bottle-deposit laws in Arizona, California, Colorado, and Washington. In California, for example, a proposition on the ballot called for a five-cent deposit on all soft-drink and beer containers. Opponents, including the Glass Packaging Institute and the Can Manufacturers' Institute, spent more than $5 million to campaign against the bottle-deposit proposition. The 1982 bottle-deposit propositions were defeated in all four states.

Review

1. What was the occasion for decision in Bowie, Maryland?
2. What were the alternatives?
3. Which individuals and groups supported each alternative?

237

Using a Time Line

A **time line** is a chart that shows **chronology,** the order in which events happened. A time line can help you see the relationship of events in the past. For example, look at the time line on this page. It shows important events of the black civil rights movement.

In this chapter you read about interest groups that attempt to influence government decision makers. Several interest groups have worked to increase the civil rights of black Americans. The time line on this page helps you to see the sequence of selected major achievements of the civil rights movement, a movement that continues today.

All time lines are drawn to scale. This means that the unit of measurement, or distance between intervals on the scale, is the same. On the time line on this page, for example, the distance between 1900 and 1920 is the same as the distance between 1940 and 1960.

Time lines may be drawn vertically or horizontally. The time line on this page is vertical. The period of time shown on this chart extends from 1900 to 2000.

The time line does not include all of the important events of the civil rights movement. Rather, the events shown were considered important by the person who made the time line. Another person might have chosen to list other events.

Selected Events of the Black Civil Rights Movement

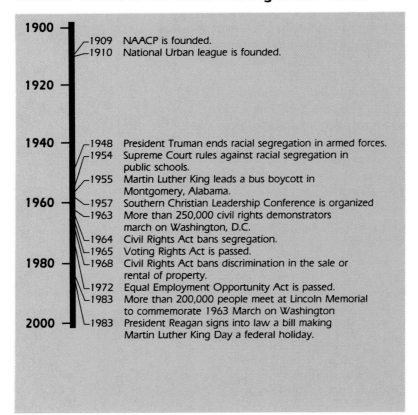

1900	
1909	NAACP is founded.
1910	National Urban league is founded.
1920	
1940	
1948	President Truman ends racial segregation in armed forces.
1954	Supreme Court rules against racial segregation in public schools.
1955	Martin Luther King leads a bus boycott in Montgomery, Alabama.
1960	
1957	Southern Christian Leadership Conference is organized
1963	More than 250,000 civil rights demonstrators march on Washington, D.C.
1964	Civil Rights Act bans segregation.
1965	Voting Rights Act is passed.
1980	
1968	Civil Rights Act bans discrimination in the sale or rental of property.
1972	Equal Employment Opportunity Act is passed.
1983	More than 200,000 people meet at Lincoln Memorial to commemorate 1963 March on Washington
2000	
1983	President Reagan signs into law a bill making Martin Luther King Day a federal holiday.

Skill Practice

1. What event on the time line occurred in 1963?

2. In which year did the Supreme Court rule against racial segregation in public schools?

3. Construct a time line that will show some of the major events in the history of your school. Interview teachers to obtain the information you will need.

Chapter 11 Review

Summary

Section 1: Why Citizens Join Interest Groups
Interest groups are organizations formed to influence government decisions about the goals and interests of group members. Members of interest groups have common goals. They try to increase their chances of influencing government decisions by pooling resources of time, money, information, and skills.

Section 2: How Interest Groups Influence Government
Interest groups with the most resources tend to have the most influence on government. Interest groups try to convince people to vote for particular political candidates. They also try to influence the outcomes of initiatives and referendums. Interest groups hire lobbyists to influence government decision makers. Sometimes an interest group may try to influence the government by taking part in court cases.

Section 3: How Citizens Can Take Part in Interest Groups
Effective interest groups use resources wisely. They pool their resources to form coalitions that try to influence public opinion in support of group goals. Citizens have a constitutional right to take part in interest groups. The federal and state governments may regulate interest group activities to protect the general interests of the public. There are currently more than 3,500 PACs registered with the Federal Election Commission and about 6,500 lobbyists registered with Congress.

Vocabulary
Define the following terms.
1. interest group
2. public interest group
3. political resources
4. political action committee

Reviewing Main Ideas
1. Common Cause has been involved in all but which of the following?
a. controlling pollution
b. collecting taxes
c. changing election campaign practices
d. protecting the rights of consumers
2. True of false: People join interest groups to support things that they value.
3. The League of Women Voters would not
a. try to educate voters.
b. try to improve local government.
c. endorse a political party.
d. do any of the above.
4. Which of the following is a point that the authors say should be considered before you join an interest group?
a. the group's programs and goals
b. how decisions get made in the group
c. the type of people who are members
d. all of the above

Thinking Critically
Organizing Information
List four political resources. Under each write a statement telling why the resource can be useful in achieving political goals.
Evaluating Information
1. Do you think that citizens with limited resources can influence government decisions? Why or why not?
2. Do you think groups are usually more effective than individuals? Why or why not?
3. What do you think is the cartoonist's attitude toward throwaway containers?

Chapter 12

Taking Part in Political Parties

Introduction. Joe Molina is the owner of a small insurance agency. His job keeps him very busy. However, because he is a loyal supporter of the Republican party, Joe makes time for political party work. Here is what Joe said about his activities during an interview with Janice Karlson, a local reporter:

Karlson: Why do you give so much of your time and energy to political party work?

Molina: I have beliefs that are important to me. Working in politics gives me a chance to do something about them.

Karlson: What are your most important party contributions?

Molina: Winning elections is the name of the game in politics. So, I do my bit to turn out Republican voters.

Karlson: What do you do to win voters to your side?

Molina: First of all, I keep tabs on who the loyal Republicans are

around here. I try to persuade as many as possible to take an active part in election campaigns. Another thing I do is to talk to voters who might want to switch to my party.

Karlson: How does your political party work contribute to good government in this town?

Molina: I've tried to help good people get elected—not only people who have ideas like mine, but also leaders who'll be honest and fair. I feel that we get the government we deserve. If we want better government, we have to work for it.

Karlson: Does your party work give you influence with candidates you've helped to elect?

Molina: When I've done a good job for them, yes, they help me out. When I ask them to help people in my neighborhood, they often listen to me.

This chapter tells you more about political parties and citizens who take part in them.

University of Wisconsin-Madison students showing support for their candidates prior to the 1984 presidential election.

Section 1
Political Parties in the United States

A **political party** is an association of voters who wish to influence and control decision making in government by recruiting, nominating, and electing members to public office. Party members usually share many ideas about government. They pick candidates who support their ideas to represent the party in public elections. They try to persuade voters to back the party's candidates.

A Two-Party System

During most of the nation's history, there have been two major parties. Other parties have sometimes competed in elections, but they have seldom won them. For these reasons,

the United States is said to have a **two-party system.**

Major Parties. The Republican and the Democratic parties have been the two major parties for many years. The Republican party was formed in 1854. The Democrats can trace their roots to Thomas Jefferson, who was President from 1801 to 1809.

Although the Democratic party is the larger of the two major parties, both the Republicans and the Democrats have many supporters in all parts of the country. In fact, they have so much strength that since the 1860s one or the other has always held the presidency. They have held most seats in Congress as well.

Minor Parties. The Socialists, Populists, Progressives, and Prohibitionists are examples of the many minor

Wisconsin's Robert M. La Follette was the Progressive party's candidate for President in 1924. Although he received almost 5 million popular votes, La Follette was only able to win the electoral votes of his own state.

parties in United States history. Minor parties sometimes last a long time. The Prohibitionist party was started in 1869; the Socialists in 1901. However, minor parties have few supporters compared with the major parties. Thus, they win few elections. Some have won seats in Congress. Others have held local office such as mayor.

Some minor parties hope to grow into major parties someday, but most want only to gain acceptance for certain ideas. The Prohibitionist party, for example, wants to ban the sale of alcoholic drinks. The party's candidates don't expect to win elections; they use election campaigns to try to influence citizens to accept the party's ideas about drinking. They hope to influence government officials to make laws against the sale of alcoholic beverages. They have achieved this goal in some parts of the United States.

Third Parties. Some minor parties become temporary challengers to the two major parties. Thus, they are called **third parties.** Third parties appear to have growing support for a short period of time. A third party may win many votes and even influence the outcome of a national election. One third party that did exactly that was the Progressive party.

The Progressive party was formed in 1912 to challenge the Democrats and Republicans in the presidential election of that year. The Progressives ran Theodore Roosevelt, who had already served as President, as a Republican, from 1901 to 1909. When the election was

over, Roosevelt had received more votes than the Republican candidate, William Taft, but fewer votes than the Democratic candidate, Woodrow Wilson. Although Roosevelt lost, his candidacy had an important effect on the election. Roosevelt had many supporters who might otherwise have voted for Taft. Thus, Roosevelt and his Progressive party helped Wilson to win.

Independent Candidates. Not all candidates for office run as members of political parties. Occasionally candidates run as independents. They build their own campaign organizations but do not form parties as such. In 1976, for example, Eugene J. McCarthy, a former Democratic senator from Minnesota and former Democratic presidential candidate in 1968, ran as an independent presidential candidate. He received less than 1 percent of the popular vote. In 1980, John B. Anderson, who was a Republican congressman from Illinois, conducted an independent presidential campaign. He received about 6.6 percent of the votes, enough to qualify him for $4.2 million in public funds after the election. He used the money to help pay his campaign debts.

Roots of the Two-Party System. The Constitution says nothing about political parties. Many delegates to the Constitutional Convention were against them. George Washington warned that parties would be the source of conflicts that could disrupt the nation.

In spite of Washington's warning, rival political groups did form a short time after Washington became President. Thomas Jefferson and Alexander Hamilton became leaders of the two groups. Jefferson was the Secretary of State and Hamilton the Secretary of the Treasury under President Washington. They disagreed strongly about what the government should do.

Hamilton wanted to make the national government stronger. He especially wanted the President to have stronger powers. His group was called the Federalist party.

Jefferson wanted to limit the power of the national government. He argued for stronger protection of civil rights and liberties. He favored more power for the state governments because they were closer to the citizens. At first, Jefferson's group was called the Democratic-Republican party. In 1828, under the leadership of Andrew Jackson, the name was shortened to the Democratic party.

From 1800 to 1816 the party of Jefferson grew stronger as the party of Hamilton (the Federalists) grew weaker. In fact the Federalists lost so much support during those years that from 1816 to 1828 the party of Jefferson and Jackson faced no serious challenges. In 1830, the Whig party rose up to challenge the Democrats. The Whigs and the Democrats remained rivals until 1850.

In 1854, the Republican party was formed; it soon replaced the Whigs. In 1860, the first Republican President, Abraham Lincoln, was elected. Since the 1860s, Republicans and Democrats have competed as the major parties in our system.

Party Organization

Political parties are organized at the local, state, and national levels. The diagram on page 244 shows the main features of the Republican and Democratic party organizations.

The national committee includes one man and one woman from each state and territory. One of its jobs is to raise money for the party. Its other main jobs are to conduct the party's national convention and to help direct the presidential election campaign every fourth year.

The second level in the diagram shows the congressional campaign committees. Both major parties have a campaign committee in each house of Congress. The committee's main job is to help members of Congress get re-elected.

Each party also has state committees made up of leaders who represent lower level organizations. State committees oversee and regulate party activities within the state.

Members of the Democratic National Committee discussing campaign strategies for the 1984 election.

Major Political Party Organization

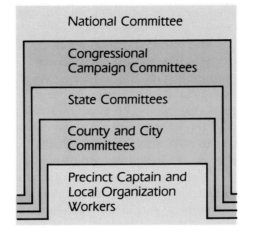

National Committee

Congressional Campaign Committees

State Committees

County and City Committees

Precinct Captain and Local Organization Workers

Which level of party organization is considered the "grass roots" level?

Counties and cities have party committees too. Each committee is headed by a chairperson, who usually is a very important party leader. The main job of these committees is to see that party candidates for local offices win elections.

Cities and counties are often divided into **precincts,** or neighborhood election districts. Each precinct has from 200 to 1,000 voters who cast their ballots at the same polling place. A precinct leader is elected or appointed by each party.

Higher-level party leaders depend on precinct leaders to build the party at the "**grass roots,**" or neighborhood, level. Where the precinct organization is strong, precinct leaders work throughout the year to win converts to the party, to register voters, and to bring the party's supporters to the polls on election day. The precinct organization often is the key to the party's success on election day.

There is no chain of command that enables the national committee to control the state and county committees. The head of the national committee, the national chairperson, does not direct the activities of the various state and local party leaders. Rather the national, state, and local party committees are only loosely tied together. One common bond is a loyalty to similar political beliefs. The committees are also held together by the desire to win public office for the party's candidates.

Section Review

Vocabulary:
"grass roots," major party, minor party, political party, precinct, third party, two-party system.

Reviewing the Main Ideas
1. Why are political parties formed?
2. Describe our two-party political system.
3. What are the aims of a minor party in a two-party system?

Skill Building
1. What level of political party organization do you think is most important? Why?
2. Use an encyclopedia to find information about one of the minor political parties in American politics. Write a brief report on the purposes of the party and its contributions to American politics and government.

Section 2
Deciding Whether to Give Support

Which party should you support? Should the Democrats have your loyalties? Should you back the Republicans? Should you belong to some minor party? Or should you be an **independent voter,** supporting no party all of the time, or even most of the time. How should you decide about party loyalties?

What's the Difference?

The first step in making your decision is to know what the two major parties stand for. What's the difference between Democrats and Republicans? "Not much," say some people.

Both major parties have tried to appeal to as many voters as possible. To ignore large numbers of voters may mean defeat at election time. Thus, the leaders of both parties often seem to be saying the same things. Leaders of both the Democrats and Republicans declare the need to keep our military forces strong, to spend money to help handicapped people, to support the United Nations, to promote full employment of workers, and so on. However, there are differences between Democrats and Republicans.

Different Beliefs. One major difference has to do with the duties of government. In recent years Democrats have been more likely than Republicans to want the national government to deal with various kinds of social problems. For

Labor union volunteers canvassing for Walter Mondale, the Democratic party's candidate for President in 1984.

example, Democrats have tended to favor programs that give aid to poor people. They have also been more likely than Republicans to support the taxes needed to pay the costs of these services. Republican leaders, on the other hand, have tended to urge less responsibility for the national government in dealing with various social problems. They have urged that private groups do more to help needy people. They have also stressed the role of state and local governments in dealing with the needs of citizens.

Both parties support the interests of labor unions and business organizations. However, the Democrats more often seem to be a closer ally of labor. The Republicans are more often viewed as boosters of business goals. (The use of words such as *tend to* and *often* in discussing differences between Democrats and Republicans reminds us that various points of view can be found in the ranks of both parties. These

245

Vote by Groups in Recent Presidential Elections

	1968		1972		1976		1980		1984	
	Democrat percent	Republican percent	Democrat percent	Republican percent	Democrat percent	Republican percent	Democrat percent	Republican percent	Democrat percent	Republican percent
Total	43.0	43.4	38	62	50	48	41	51	41	59
Race										
White	38	47	32	68	46	52	36	56	37	63
Non-white	85	12	87	13	85	15	86	10	78	22
Education										
College	37	54	37	63	42	55	35	53	37	63
High School	42	43	34	66	54	46	43	51	44	56
Grade School	52	33	49	51	58	41	54	42	42	48
Occupation										
White Collar	41	47	36	64	50	48	40	51	38	62
Blue Collar	50	35	43	57	58	41	48	46	49	51

Study the table. What voting trends can you detect?

words also should alert us to changes in opinions of party leaders from time to time.)

One easy way to find out how the parties differ at a particular time is to read the **party platforms.** The platforms are written at the presidential nominating conventions that are held every four years. Each platform is a series of statements on election issues. Each important statement is called a **plank.** The Democratic platform tells what the Democrats think about the issues. The Republican platform tells what the Republicans think.

Different Kinds of Supporters. There is another way to look at differences between Democrats and Republicans. We can look at the tendencies of various social and economic groups to support one party or the other. The table above gives some facts.

Keep in mind that what is true of the past may not be true in the future. Political conditions change from time to time. What is true about voter preferences today may not be true tomorrow.

Making a Choice

Deciding where to give your political support can be difficult. The guidelines that follow may help.

Guideline 1. Choose the party that stands for political beliefs with which you agree. If no one party seems to represent your ideas, you might prefer to be an independent.

Guideline 2. Choose the party that tends to nominate candidates who appeal to you. Think about the people that each party nominates. Do you agree with their ideas? Do they have the ability to be good leaders and decision makers? Would you be proud to be represented by them? If neither major party tends to nominate appealing candidates, then you might want to be an independent or a minor party member.

Guideline 3. Choose the party that seems most open to changes that you, and those like you, might suggest. Good citizens are constructive critics; they offer ideas for changes that seem likely to improve their society. Once again, if neither major party is open to reforms that you support, then maybe you should be a political independent or a minor party supporter.

Section Review

Vocabulary:
independent voter, party platform, plank.

Reviewing the Main Ideas
1. What are two differences between the Democratic and Republican parties?
2. Define "independent voter".

Skill Building
Look at the table on page 246. Which groups or individuals have been more or less likely to support Democratic or Republican candidates in the presidential elections shown?

Section 3
The Role of Political Parties

Political parties play an important role in our system of government. They select candidates for public office. They keep people informed and interested in the issues and the candidates. They try to see that those party members who are elected to office do a good job. They keep an eye on the opposition, calling the public's attention to actions that they don't approve. They also act as a link between different branches and levels of government.

The parties carry out these activities during every month of every year. Their activities are most obvious, however, at election time.

Parties Nominate Candidates
Political parties are the only organizations that select and offer candidates for public office. They do this through the **nomination** process. In the United States, candidates are nominated in one of four ways: (1) direct primary, (2) party convention, (3) self-nomination, (4) petition.

Direct Primaries. Most nominees at all levels of government are chosen in **direct primaries.** The direct primary is a preliminary election in which voters choose candidates to represent each party in a general, or final, election to public office.

There are two main forms of the direct primary: the closed and the open primary.

The **closed primary,** used in most states, is an election in which

Participating in a primary.

247

only the declared members of a party are allowed to choose the party's nominees. In many closed primary states the voters go to the **polling place** on primary election day. They tell their party choice to a polling place clerk. Then they choose among candidates of this party to represent them on the general election day. (Candidates usually get their names placed on the primary ballot simply by announcing the desire to run and by paying a filing fee.) If a voting machine is used, the machine will be set so that the voter can vote only for candidates of the chosen party. If a paper ballot is used, voters receive a ballot with candidates of their party only.

The **open primary,** used in a few states, is a nominating election in which qualified voters may take part without telling their party preference. In most open-primary states, the voter chooses a party in the privacy of the voting booth. Where written ballots are used, a polling-place clerk gives the voter the ballots of all political parties involved. The voter marks one ballot and discards the others. Where voting machines are used, the voter moves the levers of only one party and the other ballot is locked automatically.

In three states—Alaska, Louisiana, and Washington—the voter may vote for anyone on the ballot regardless of party.

People who favor the closed primary say that it helps keep the members of one party from crossing over into the other party's primary to try to name weak candidates. (Weak candidates are desirable from the opposition's point of view,

because they are easy to defeat.) An argument against the closed primary, on the other hand, is that it doesn't permit a truly secret ballot, since voters must declare a party preference. It also discourages independent voters from taking part in the primary election.

Other Methods of Nomination. In a few states **party conventions** are used to nominate candidates for elective state offices. Members of the party from all parts of the state pick delegates to represent them. These delegates then meet at a convention to nominate the party's candidates through majority vote.

Another way of getting nominated is **self-nomination.** It is used by write-in candidates as a way of putting themselves before the public in a general election. The candidate simply announces that he or she is running and then encourages voters to write his or her name in the appropriate place on the ballot. In some states a write-in candidate may distribute stickers that show his or her name. The voters can then paste the name on the ballot.

Independents and minor party candidates are nominated in most states by **petition.** This means that a certain number of qualified voters must sign papers declaring support in order for a candidate to get his or her name on the ballot. In 1980, John Anderson successfully petitioned to have his name placed on the ballot in all fifty states as an independent presidential candidate. It was a difficult and expensive undertaking, costing his campaign $2 million.

Parties Campaign for Their Candidates

Once a party has nominated its candidates for office, it begins to campaign for them. The party's goal during the campaign is to gather support for its candidates, but it also helps inform the voters about public issues and about the way government works.

The types of activities that party workers and other interested people engage in at election time vary greatly, but most have to do with gathering information or getting information out to the voters. Party workers and volunteers **canvass** neighborhoods, visiting homes to give out information and to find out who is and who is not supporting their candidates. Many also work at party headquarters. They stuff envelopes with information about the candidates and send the material out to voters. They answer telephones and type letters. They arrange for rallies and dinners that will help raise the money needed to pay for advertising and other campaign costs. Supporters hold meetings in their homes so that candidates or their representatives can meet the voters and try to persuade them to help the campaign. On election day they "get out the vote." That is, they try to make sure that as many party members as possible go to the polls.

Campaign Workers

Working in an election campaign is one good way to influence government. There are indoor jobs and outdoor jobs in every campaign. There are jobs that require much experience and others that require no experience at all.

The campaign manager oversees all the work of the campaign. Since winning is the goal of the campaign, the campaign manager must come up with a plan that will help reach that goal.

Most campaigns have a publicity chairperson. This person is responsible for creating posters and ads, for writing information that will appear in letters and leaflets, and for getting information out to the press.

The campaign treasurer keeps track of money that comes in (donations) and money that goes out. Usually campaigners must pay for office space, telephones, the printing of posters and campaign literature, and sometimes advertising time on radio and television.

A coffee coordinator is in charge of "coffees" held in the homes of supporters. In a local election people who attend coffees may get to meet the candidate. One goal of the coffees is to find additional workers.

Within the office there are other jobs to do as well. Every campaign needs people to handle telephone calls. Workers use phones to ask for donations, to contact people about coffees, and to line up workers. Envelope addressers and stuffers are a must as well. These people send out fund-raising appeals and information about the candidate. Still other people put together poll lists, leaflets, and other materials for workers to use when they go into the neighborhoods to contact voters. The person who is in charge of these indoor activities is the office manager.

President Reagan's campaign headquarters in New Hampshire was a busy place for months prior to the 1984 election.

(top and above) Campaign workers encouraging voters to register and to support their candidates.

The jobs that need to be done "on the streets" are just as important as those done in the office. The people in charge of neighborhood workers are the area chairpersons. Each area chairperson is responsible for a particular area within the candidate's district. An area chairperson sees that the neighborhood workers are organized and informed.

Many neighborhood workers go out weeks in advance of election day. Some pass out campaign literature to people they meet on the street. Others go to the homes of voters. They encourage people to register and they try to find out who is supporting their candidate.

When election day arrives, some campaign workers become "poll watchers." They work at the polls to see who has and who has not voted. Other workers called "runners" go to the homes of people who have not voted to remind them that there is still time. Some runners help voters get to the polls by offering rides or by sitting with children.

Parties Help to Manage Government

Party activities are less noticeable once an election is over, but they are important nonetheless. In fact, parties are involved in one of the first tasks that come up after an election—the appointment of people to government jobs.

Many government jobs are filled according to civil service rules. However, chief executives in national, state, and local government have the power to appoint their trusted supporters to many jobs. These supporters will usually be party members. In addition, when the chief executive has jobs to fill and no names in mind, he or she often seeks advice from party leaders.

Party ties are also important in forming links between different levels of government and between different branches of government. For example, a Democratic President may have more influence with a Democratic governor than with a Republican governor. Likewise, when a majority of legislators are of the same party as the chief executive, cooperation between the two branches is likely to be better than if they are not of the same party.

Finally, the parties play an important "watchdog" role after an election. The party that is out of power (the party not in control of the presidency, the governor's office, the Congress) watches for any mistakes or misuse of power by those who are in power. The party out of power tries to find issues that can help its candidates win control of the government in the next election. In this way, competition between political parties can serve the cause of good government.

Party Decline. For some years many observers have drawn attention to the decline in political party influence on elections and legislation. Parties no longer demonstrate the ability to marshal the support of voters or maintain the loyalty of candidates and officeholders which they once had. There are many reasons for this. Over the years voters have become more educated and independent-minded. They are less likely to follow the lead of party officials in casting their votes. The population in general has become more mobile; citizens change residences more frequently, moving from city to city, state to state. That makes it more difficult for political party organizations to attract members and establish a stable following. The growth of television as a medium of communication means many candidates may now appeal to voters directly; the candidates are no longer dependent on the parties to gather an audience for them. Finally, the development of the direct primary system for choosing political candidates has decreased the importance of the party organization in the nomination process.

There is no doubt that the role of the political parties is changing. The direction of that change will become clearer in the years ahead as party officials and elected officeholders try to adjust to changing times.

Section Review

Vocabulary:
canvass, closed primary, direct primary, nomination, open primary, party convention, petition, polling place, self-nomination.

Reviewing the Main Ideas
1. How do the open and closed primaries differ?
2. What is the chief reason for having a closed primary?
3. What is one advantage of the open primary?
4. Describe three nomination methods other than primaries.
5. What is the most widely used method for nominating candidates in the United States?
6. What role do political parties fill at election time?

Skill Building
Team up with one other person and conduct a canvass of one block in your neighborhood. Try to find out (1) if the people voted in the last election, (2) which party they backed, and (3) whom they intend to vote for in the next election, and (4) their opinions on a local issue that you have researched. Tell people you are students conducting a canvass for your civics class. If people don't want to answer your questions, that's their right. Thank them for their time and go on to the next door. Summarize your findings in a brief report. Refer to the Writing and Research Skills section at the back of your text if you need help with your report.

Case Study

The Election of Mayor Goode

More than three thousand people crowded the splendid hall of the Academy of Music in Philadelphia, Pennsylvania, on January 3, 1983. They were there to observe the inauguration of Philadelphia's new mayor, W. Wilson Goode.

The crowd clapped and cheered as Goode stepped forward to be sworn in as the city's 126th mayor. Mayor Goode said that his achievement might have, at one time, seemed impossible, "a dream which could never come true."

"But in America, dreams can come true," said Philadelphia's first black mayor.

As a child in North Carolina, Goode's chances to become famous seemed slight. His father and mother worked hard as farm laborers, but the family was poor. However, Goode did well in school and began to dream of a successful career in business or government. He was determined to overcome all obstacles. Through hard work, Goode became the first in his family to go to college. After finishing college, he continued his education and graduated with a master's degree in public administration from the highly rated Wharton School of the University of Pennsylvania.

Goode gradually built a solid reputation as an excellent bureaucratic official. His skill as chairman of the Pennsylvania Public Utility Commission attracted a lot of attention and led to his appointment as City Managing Director of Philadelphia in 1980.

For three years, Goode managed city government under Mayor William Green. Goode did an outstanding job and won the praise of community leaders.

In 1983, Goode decided to run for election to become mayor of Philadelphia. He entered the Democratic primary election. His opponent was Frank Rizzo, who had served as mayor for the eight years before William Green's term of office.

Goode and Rizzo competed for nomination as the Democratic party's candidate. At the same time, three Republicans campaigned to become their party's candidate.

In May, 1983, each political party held its primary election. From among those listed on the ballot, party members were to nominate one person to be their candidate for mayor.

Goode won the Democratic party primary election. The Republican winner was John J. Egan, chairman of the Philadelphia Stock Exchange. A third candidate for mayor in the November, 1983, general election was Thomas Leonard, who ran as an independent candidate. Leonard was a Democrat who had served as City Controller under Mayor Green. He had entered and then dropped out of the Democratic party primary election.

The winner of the Democratic primary election has usually been the favorite to be elected mayor in Philadelphia. The Republican party had not won a mayoral election since 1947. Furthermore, the

Democratic voters in Philadelphia outnumbered the Republicans by about four to one.

Goode, however, faced a stiff challenge. The Republican candidate, John Egan, was a popular and able rival. Thomas Leonard, the independent candidate, was certain to take many Democratic party supporters away from Goode. Finally, Goode was the first black person to win nomination as a candidate for mayor. Would many white voters, who usually backed the Democratic party, vote for one of the white candidates? Or, would they back their party's nominee, W. Wilson Goode?

Goode and his supporters campaigned vigorously. He visited every neighborhood in the city to make speeches and meet with voters. Goode's campaign workers went door to door to canvass voters and urge them to vote for the Democratic candidate. They also scheduled regular political ads on radio and TV. Again and again, the Democratic party leaders emphasized Goode's outstanding record as City Managing Director under Mayor Green.

Goode's campaign was boosted by Frank Rizzo, his rival for the Democratic party nomination in the primary election. Rizzo was a loyal member of the Democratic party. He joined forces with his fellow Democrat, Goode, to oppose the other candidates. Rizzo urged his followers to vote for Goode, and he made several public appearances and speeches for the Democratic party candidate. Most important, Rizzo influenced the Building and Trades Council, a powerful labor organization, to support Goode.

Black Mayors

Cities Over 200,000, 1990	Mayor	Population in thousands	% Black
New York	David Dinkins	7,071	25%
Los Angeles	Tom Bradley	2,966	17%
Philadelphia	W. Wilson Goode	1,688	40%
Detroit	Coleman Young	1,203	63%
Wash., D.C.	Marion Barry	638	70%
New Orleans	Sidney Barthelmy	558	55%
Seattle	Norman Rice	487	10%
Atlanta	Andrew Young	425	67%
Oakland	Lionel Wilson	339	47%
Newark	Sharpe James	329	58%
Birmingham	Richard Arrington	284	56%
Richmond	Geline Williams	219	51%

On election day, Goode was the winner with 55 percent of the votes. He pledged his best efforts to provide excellent leadership.

W. Wilson Goode became one of twelve black mayors of cities with more than 200,000 in population. In 1990, four of the nation's largest cities—New York, Los Angeles, Detroit, and Philadelphia—had black mayors.

Review

1. Why did Goode's chances to become famous appear remote?
2. Why is it sometimes advantageous to be a member of one major political party rather than the other?
3. Summarize Goode's campaign activities after his victory in the Democratic party primary election.

(above) W. Wilson Goode in Philadelphia after his victory. (chart) Blacks make up less than 50 percent of the population in which two cities? Who are the mayors of these cities?

253

Basic Social Studies Skills
Asking Good Questions

Political party leaders, as you discovered in this chapter, always need accurate, up-to-date information about voters. How do they get this important information?

Two of the most effective ways of obtaining important voter information are questionnaires and interviews. Interviews are conducted either in person or on the phone. Questionnaires are usually filled out in the home by the voter and then mailed back to the person who designed the questionnaire.

Obtaining accurate, useful information from questionnaires and interviews is directly dependent upon the quality of the questions asked. Good questions have three major qualities. They are (1) relevant, (2) clear, and (3) unbiased.

A **relevant** question is one that gets directly to the point. It asks *only* for the information that is needed. **Irrelevant** questions, those that stray away from the point, will only serve to confuse the person being interviewed.

Good questions are clearly written. Clear questions are neither confusing nor misleading and are likely to mean the same thing to all who respond to them. Here is an example of a clear question: "Did you vote for John Jones or Jennifer Wells in the election last week for mayor of Sun City?"

Sometimes one word will make an otherwise clear question into an unclear one. Here is an example. "Did you participate frequently in the election campaign for mayor last May?" This question is unclear because of the likely confusion about the meaning of *frequently*. Words such as *frequently*, *often*, and *usually* are likely to mean different things to different people. A better way to phrase the above question would be: "Did you participate in the election campaign for mayor last May (a) more than ten times, (b) between five and ten times, (c) less than five times, or (d) not at all?"

Good questions are also **unbiased.** A **biased** question is "loaded" with words that favor a certain answer. Here is an example of a biased question: "Do you agree with the governor that Tom Brown is the best candidate for mayor of Zenith City?" The question is structured in a way that "encourages" respondents who respect the governor's opinion to answer "yes." It also "encourages" people who dislike the governor to answer "no."

Skill Practice

Design a questionnaire titled "Participant Sports" for your classmates to fill in. Structure your questions in a manner that will enable you to find out the class's favorite sport, the average amount of time spent playing the sport, the average amount of money spent on the sport (equipment, fees, etc.), and where the sport is played.

Chapter 12 Review

Summary

Section 1: Political Parties in the United States

A political party is a group of citizens organized to influence the government by electing members to public offices. The two major political parties in the United States are the Democratic party and the Republican party. The two major parties are organized at the local, state, and national levels. However, there is no chain of command that enables the national leaders to control the state and local party organizations.

Section 2: Deciding Whether to Give Support

Knowing how the Democrats and Republicans differ is the first step in deciding which party to support. One way to find out how the parties differ is to read party platforms, which are statements on election issues made by each party at the presidential nominating conventions. Citizens should support the party that tends to stand for their beliefs. Citizens should back the party that tends to nominate candidates who appeal to them. And, citizens should support the party that seems most likely to work for changes in government that they want.

Section 3: The Role of Political Parties

Political parties select candidates for offices in government. Each party conducts election campaigns for its candidates. The parties try to keep the public informed and interested in elections and government decisions. Political parties also help to manage local, state, and national governments through the officials they nominate and elect.

Vocabulary

Define the following terms.

1. political party
2. major party
3. minor party
4. third party
5. canvass
6. petition

Reviewing Main Ideas

1. The first political parties formed because
a. Hamilton and Jefferson differed in their ideas about government
b. Washington directed Hamilton and Jefferson to form them.
c. the Constitution required them
d. Washington and his opponent needed parties to help them campaign
2. True or false: The Republican party is the older of the two major political parties.
3. True or false: The Constitution tells how to organize and run political parties.
4. Which of the following is *not* a way that political cal parties get involved in government?
a. Government officials appoint party supporters to government jobs.
b. The party out of power plays a "watchdog" role.
c. The party out of power runs the Justice Department.
d. Party ties link levels of government.

Thinking Critically

Organizing Information

List the various ways that people are nominated for public office. Write a short description next to each method.

Evaluating Information

Which do you think is the better method of nominating candidates—the *closed primary* or the *open primary?* Explain your answer.

Chapter 13

Voting

Introduction. At 4:45 A.M. Susan Sertich walked into the large room at the front of Markham Elementary School. She was bursting with pride. It was election day and she was to be in charge of the polling place in her neighborhood. Within minutes, other poll workers began to arrive. The polls were to open in little more than an hour and there was work to be done first.

At five o'clock Susan called the workers together and reminded them of their duties for the day. Then she added, "Don't forget, only election officials and voters are allowed in the polling place. No one can try to influence voters within fifty feet of the polling place."

The workers checked the two voting machines to make sure they were ready. Then they marked the entry way to the polling place and posted voting instructions.

When the preparations had been completed, Susan called the group together and asked them to take an oath to carry out the election laws faithfully. Then—promptly at six—Susan let the first voters in.

By late afternoon over four hundred people had voted. The day had passed without a serious problem. At 6:00 P.M. Susan closed the polls.

When the last voter was finished, Susan and two helpers read and recorded the vote totals from the counters on the back of the machines. Susan locked the machines and then opened a package of absentee ballots. They had been marked prior to election day by voters who knew they would be out of town on that day. Susan added these votes to the totals.

After finishing the tally of the precinct votes, Susan thanked the other workers. As she prepared to leave, she was still feeling excited about her part in the election. Now she was anxious to hear the results from other parts of the city and state.

In this chapter you will read about the rules that govern voting and about voter decisions.

Section 1
Rules for Voting

During our nation's early years, the only people who had the right to vote were white male property owners. The many people who were not eligible to vote included all women, black males, Indian males, persons under twenty-one, and white adult males who did not own property.

In a democracy, all—or nearly all—adults should be eligible to vote. Today the rules are quite different from what they were in 1790.

Qualifying to Vote

The Constitution grants states the right to decide who is qualified to vote. However, the Constitution also says that no state can deny the right to vote because of race, color, sex, non-payment of a poll tax, or age—if the person is at least eighteen. (See amendments 15, 19, 24, and 26 on pages 95–99.)

Most states today have similar voting qualifications. With only a few exceptions, a person may vote if he or she is (1) at least eighteen years old, (2) a resident of the state in which he or she wants to vote, and (3) a citizen of the United States. People who have been convicted of serious crimes are the most common exception to the general rules. Most states deny them the right to vote—at least until they have served their sentences.

In most large communities, people who meet the personal qualifications must complete a

Voting in Columbus, Ohio.

257

voter registration form before they can take part in an election. Voter registration is a procedure citizens must follow to prove that they are qualified to vote. Rules that require people to register in person in a government office can make it hard for some people to qualify to vote. Many people may find it difficult to get to the office during the hours when it is open. To help solve this problem, some states permit registration by mail, and at more convenient times and places.

Like other rules covering registration, registration deadlines affect the number of people who qualify to vote. In more than half the states, it is too late for people to register if they wait until the last few days before an election. In these states the deadline for registration is thirty or more days before election day. In a few states, the deadline is much later—ten or fewer days before the election. In states where the deadline is near election day and where voters can register in convenient places, both registration and voter turnout tend to be higher than in other states.

Casting a Vote

On election day, voters go to the polling place in their neighborhood. Once inside, they follow rules passed by the state government. The rules are very similar from one state to another.

The following example describes what happens at one

County election day in a small town in the mid-1800s. The painting is by George Caleb Bingham.

precinct polling place. This polling place may not have the same rules as polling places in your state. However, the example will give you a general idea of what goes on when people vote.

When voters first arrive at the polling place, some study the sample **ballot** posted on the wall of the entry way. Once inside, voters go to the clerk's table. Here, each voter writes his or her name and address on an application form. The clerk reads the name aloud and passes the form to a challenger's table.

The challenger (there are challengers representing each party) locates the voter's registration form and compares the signature on it with the signature on the application form. If the two do not appear to match, the challenger may require further identification. A voter whose registration form is not on file will be required to get proof of registration.

When the challenger is convinced that the voter is eligible to vote, he or she initials the application form and returns it to the voter.

A voter's last stop is the voting booth. The voter hands the application form to a judge and the judge provides whatever further help is needed.

The judges do a number of different jobs on election day. Judges make sure that everyone can vote in secret. They watch to see that no one tries to tell anyone else how to vote inside the polling place. They help voters who are handicapped, elderly, or who can't read. They also

make certain that the vote totals are recorded accurately at the end of the day. When people finish, judges make sure that the voting machines are ready for the next person.

When a new voter enters the booth, the first thing he or she does is to close the curtain. This ensures privacy and prepares the machine to record a new vote. In a general election, the voter chooses among major party candidates, minor party candidates, and independents. The voter picks one person for each office. If the voter chooses some candidates from one party and some from another, he or she is said to be voting a **split ticket.** Of course, the voter may decide to vote a **straight ticket,** voting for all the candidates in one party. He or she may also vote for someone who is not on the ballot. In that case the voter fills in the spot under **write-in candidate.**

When finished, the voter opens the curtains and steps away from the machine. When the curtains open, the vote is recorded.

Section Review

Vocabulary:
ballot, split ticket, straight ticket, voter registration, write-in candidate.

Reviewing the Main Ideas
1. What are the main qualifications for voting in most states?
2. Why is voter registration usually required?
3. How can rules about where and when to register make it easier or

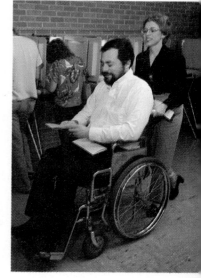

Voters in Austin, Texas.

harder for a person to qualify to vote?

4. Who are the officials at a polling place and what jobs does each do?

Skill Building

Find the voter registration laws for your state in your local library. Then answer these questions for the people described below: (a) Which of these people would be allowed to vote, according to your state laws? (b) Which persons must update their registration forms or fill out new forms to be able to vote? (c) In your opinion, should rules be changed to permit any of the unqualified people to vote?

1. Larry is nineteen and out of work. He is a high-school dropout and can barely read. He has never held a job longer than six weeks. He was born and raised in your community and lives with his parents.

2. Janet, age thirty, is a skilled secretary. At age nineteen she went to prison for a serious crime, but everyone who knows Janet today sees her as a model citizen.

3. Mirko, age twenty-two, moved from Yugoslavia to your town two years ago. He wants to become a citizen of the United States soon. Mirko speaks English very well. He is well educated and seems bright. He also has a good job. He likes politics and wants to vote in the next election.

4. Paul and Margie are married and have lived in your town for the past twenty years. They enjoy politics and have voted in every election. Last month they bought a new home in a different precinct about two miles from their old one.

5. Anne is a registered voter. She was married last month.

6. Judy was a registered voter in 1980. However, she has not voted since 1982.

7. Martha, a seventeen-year-old high-school senior, has not registered. The next election takes place in five days.

Section 2
Deciding How to Vote

People have different reasons for choosing one candidate over another. Many people vote a straight party ticket. The party a candidate belongs to has more influence on these voters than anything else about the person. Other voters are interested mostly in the issues. They tend to vote for candidates who have opinions similar to their own. Still other voters are most influenced by the candidate's personality and appearance. They tend to be attracted or put off by the way a candidate looks or the way he or she speaks.

How about you? Do party labels mean more to you than the issues or the personalities of the candidates? If you are more interested in the person than the party, are you always able to judge what the candidates are really like and where they really stand on the issues? This section will provide some help in judging candidates and their campaign appeals.

Choosing the Best Candidate

Why would you vote for one candidate over another? Thoughtful voters consider a number of points when making that decision. Knowing what qualities others look for may be helpful to you.

Goals and Values. Many experienced voters look for candidates who tend to support programs, goals, and values with which they agree. They do so in hopes that these candidates will make political decisions of which they approve.

How does a person learn about a candidate's goals and values? The most common sources of information are newspapers, news magazines, TV, radio, and such publications as the *Congressional Quarterly Reports* and *The Congressional Record*. All these sources report on the decisions and beliefs of candidates.

Many interest groups also provide information. Some give out regular reports that rate members of Congress on their support of the group's programs and values. Five of those groups are (1) Americans for Democratic Action, (2) the AFL-CIO Committee on Political Education, (3) the League of Conservation Voters, (4) the United States Chamber of Commerce, and (5) the American Conservative Union. If you agree strongly with one of these groups, you might use the group's ratings of your representatives in Congress to help you decide whether or not to support them.

Reliability and Honesty. Many voters also look for candidates who are reliable and honest. Does the candidate live up to campaign pledges and other public statements? Can the candidate be trusted to do a good job? Some voters look at a candidate's record of public promises and compare these against the candidate's actions. When the candidate fails to live up to pledges, the voters expect a good explanation. Voters also look for willingness to answer questions openly.

Effectiveness. Experienced voters also try to judge how effective a candidate will be. If two candidates are acceptable in other respects, many voters ask themselves who would better be able to get the most done. One way to answer this question is to make a rough account of the person's resources. How much experience does the candidate have? What are the candidate's political connections? Is the candidate respected by other political leaders?

Chances for Election. Many voters think carefully before voting for candidates who have no real chance to be elected. Voters are faced with a difficult problem when their favorite candidate seems to be a sure loser. Should they be loyal to the person they believe to be the best candidate even if the person cannot win?

When faced with this problem, many people vote for the person having the best chance of beating the candidate they like the least. Other people, however, may be willing to support a sure loser just to register a protest vote. For example, suppose that candidate Smith calls for the development of three new

(above) Paul Newman, a popular movie actor, campaigning with Walter Mondale, the Democratic presidential nominee in 1984. (above right) Filming a spot commercial for a political candidate.

city swimming pools, an idea that you support. You might hope that a large minority will vote for Smith with you. Even though Smith loses, the winner may take notice of the strong support for the new pools. This showing might convince the winner to support the pools too.

Detecting Propaganda in Campaign Appeals

The goal of an election campaign is to influence as many voters as possible to vote for a certain candidate. Various methods are used to persuade the voters. Billboards, bumper stickers, posters, leaflets, speeches, and newspaper ads have all been used for a long time. In recent years, however, candidates have relied more and more on television and radio to "sell" themselves to voters.

The spot commercial is the most common method for advertising candidates on television or radio. These are sixty-second

commercials aimed at increasing the candidate's appeal to voters. Spot commercials are usually designed to appeal to voters' emotions. Campaigners also create filmed documentaries to be shown on television. These films highlight the candidate's best qualities.

An important purpose of any election campaign is to educate voters about public issues, candidates, political parties, and government. Unfortunately, not all campaigns are as straightforward as they should be. Appeals to emotions may be used more often than appeals to reason. Clever **propaganda techniques** may be used to influence voters.

In order to vote wisely, you should avoid being swayed by propaganda. To do that, you must know how to spot propaganda techniques when you see them. They include the following: name-calling, glittering generality, transfer, testimonial, plain folks, card-stacking, and bandwagon.

Name-calling. To name-call is to give a candidate a bad label. The aim is to influence voters to reject the candidate without looking at the evidence. Suppose Jones and Smith are running for mayor. Jones makes speeches in which he calls Smith "un-American." However, Jones does not give evidence to convince voters that Smith is not a good American. Rather, he tries to bias voters against Smith by calling him a bad name.

A particular danger of name-calling is that it can damage the reputation of the person accused. The mere accusation is enough to get many people to believe the worst. Whenever name-calling is used to influence our opinions, we should look for evidence to support the accusation.

Glittering Generality. Many candidates use glittering generalities during their campaigns. These are general statements that almost no one would disagree with. An example is: "I'm for peace and prosperity." Candidates who consistently rely upon glittering generalities may be trying to avoid taking a stand on a particular issue. Or, they may be trying to hide the fact that they are not very informed about particular issues.

Transfer. The technique of transfer is to associate something everyone thinks is good with a candidate. The purpose is to influence voters to transfer their good feelings for that thing (such as the American flag) to the candidate. This is why some candidates use patriotic slogans or songs at their campaign rallies. For example, when Senator Stone ran for President, he used the slogan, "A Vote for Stone Is a Vote for America." Senator Stone was trying to get voters to transfer their feelings of patriotism to him.

Testimonial. A candidate who gets a famous, well-liked person to say good things about him or her is receiving a testimonial. The purpose is to suggest that if this person supports the candidate, other voters should support the candidate too. For example, Governor Green may get a famous movie star to say, "I'm for Green. He's the best candidate for governor." Governor Green hopes that this testimonial will influence voters to support him.

The person who hears or sees a testimonial should ask these questions: Is this well-known person really qualified to express such an opinion? Was the testimony purchased? Was the well-known person quoted correctly and fully?

Plain Folks. When the "plain folks" technique is used, a candidate tries to convince voters that he or she is just like them—just an ordinary person. The candidate hopes to get support in this way. For instance, candidate Mike Murphy may say that he is the workingman's friend. He may appear on a speaker's platform wearing a "hard hat" to show

President Reagan eating lunch at a McDonald's restaurant in Tuscaloosa, Alabama, during the 1984 presidential election campaign. Which of the seven campaign techniques do you think the President was utilizing here?

Bandwagon. When candidates say, "Most people in your group are voting for me; you should too," they are using the bandwagon propaganda technique. They are trying to create the impression that the majority of people you care about are for them. Thus, you should go along with the others and be for the candidate too. When candidates "leak" a private poll to the press reporting that they are favored by a large majority of the voters, they are trying to create the impression of a "bandwagon." They are suggesting that others ought to be with the majority and vote for them too.

that he identifies with construction workers. Another candidate may have her picture taken while mowing the lawn, milking a cow, or eating pizza at the corner restaurant. She is just "plain folks" like the rest of the people. The important thing to remember is that these pictures are meant to create images in your mind. Ask yourself, what is the candidate really like?

Card-Stacking. When candidates present only the facts that are favorable to them, they are using the propaganda technique of card-stacking. They are presenting only one side of an issue—their side. For example, a state senator may say that he helped defeat tax increases. Thus, the voters should support him. However, he does not report that several programs to help handicapped people train for jobs had to be ended because of lack of money that would have been provided by new taxes.

How Voters Learn the Facts. To avoid being taken in by the exaggerated claims of the propagandist we must try to get all the facts. There are a number of solutions. For one, public debates can be held during a campaign. Candidates who present their cases can be questioned by the audience. For another, people can get information about candidates from both parties and from newspapers. When the candidates disagree on an issue, facts and opinions are usually available from interest groups who are affected by the issue. The more we insist on hearing all sides, the less we will be influenced by the exaggerations of the persuader.

Candidates who depend on propaganda tend to rely on controlled communications with voters. They present themselves through radio and television commercials, documentaries, and set speeches rather than through spontaneous interactions with voters or other candidates. The kind of communication they use is controlled because the candidate has complete command over what is said or done. In contrast, when a candidate faces unrehearsed questions and criticisms of voters or other candidates, he or she is not completely in control of the situation.

It is easier to use propaganda techniques during controlled communications. It is easier to "smoke out" the real beliefs and behaviors of candidates when they cannot control the questions they are asked. Voters should be suspicious of any candidate who usually appears in situations where communication with voters is totally under his or her control.

Section Review

Vocabulary:
bandwagon, card-stacking, glittering generality, name-calling, plain folks, propaganda techniques, testimonial, transfer.

Reviewing the Main Ideas
1. Explain why many voters believe that each of the following points should be considered before voting: (1) a candidate's goals and values, (2) a candidate's honesty and reliability, (3) a candidate's potential effectiveness, (4) a candidate's chance of being elected.
2. How can a voter get the information he or she needs to judge each of the first three points mentioned in question 1?

3. What is *controlled communication?* Why do some candidates use it?

Skill Building
Can you spot the examples of propaganda in the list below? Identify the method that is being used in each example.
1. "My opponent has taken part in public protest demonstrations. He is a dangerous radical and agitator who probably is in sympathy with communist causes."
2. "A majority of the people in the community are supporting Stonewall Smith for governor. Where do you stand?"
3. Brock Jones makes a campaign appearance in a small town. He begins his talk by telling the audience that he was born in a small town and thinks of himself as a "small-town boy."
4. "If you believe in freedom, justice, and equality of opportunity, then you should vote for Stonewall Smith."
5. Stonewall Smith travels around the state in a bus decorated with American flags and pictures of bald eagles. A sign painted on both sides of the bus says, "Stonewall Smith believes in America."
6. A newspaper ad tells how Stonewall Smith saved thousands of tax dollars during his first term as governor. But the ad says nothing about the enormous cutback in services to the poor, sick, and elderly that resulted from his budget cuts.

Your Right to Fair Representation in Government

The 1793 constitution of Vermont guaranteed one seat in the state's House of Representatives to each town. This seemed fair, because each town had about the same number of people. By 1960, however, there were great differences in the populations of towns in Vermont. Nonetheless, each town was still represented by one member of the state legislature. For example, the town of Stratton, with 24 people, elected 1 representative, as did Burlington, with a population of 35,531. Less than 12 percent of the people in Vermont were able to elect a majority of the state's House of Representatives. This seemed extremely unfair.

The Issue of Fair Representation

Across the United States in 1960, voters in rural areas were overrepresented in their state legislatures. A minority of voters in rural areas were able to elect more representatives to their state legislatures than could the majority of voters in urban areas. Thus, a minority of voters in rural areas had more influence in state governments than the urban majority had. Was this fair or should each member of a state legislature have been represented by an equal number of people?

Origins of the Fair Representation Issue

During the nineteenth century, when most Americans lived in rural areas, there were few concerns about fair representation of different legislative districts. By 1920, however, there were slightly more Americans in urban than in rural areas. By 1960, most people lived in cities and suburbs.

Legislative districts—the areas of each state represented by lawmakers in Congress and in state legislatures—had not been changed to reflect changes in population. Rather, the districts remained, for the most part, as they were in the nineteenth century.

People's votes are equal when each member of a legislative body represents about the same number of people. Clearly, the people in more populous urban districts were not equally represented with voters in less populous rural districts. As a result, city and suburban problems did not receive the attention in state legislatures that farming and rural concerns did.

State legislatures, dominated by the influence of rural votes, refused to change legislative districts to fit the growth of urban and suburban population. People from the rural areas did not want to lose representatives and influence. Some state governments refused to change their districts. Others changed their districts only in ways that continued to favor rural interests.

Urban Voters Turn to the Courts for Help

Citizens pointed to the Fourteenth Amendment to the Constitution to support arguments for equal representation. It says: "No state . . . shall deny to any person within its jurisdiction the equal protection of the laws." Did Alabama, California, Vermont, and other states violate the equal-protection rights of voters by setting up legislative districts with unequal numbers of people?

In 1946, a majority of the U.S. Supreme Court decided that the "equal protection" clause of the Fourteenth Amendment could not be applied to the issue of fair representation in a state legislature *(Colegrove* v. *Green)*. Three justices disagreed with the majority opinion. One dissenter, Hugo

Black, said that a voter's right to "equal protection of the laws" was violated by legislative districts with unequal numbers of people. "What is involved here is the right to vote guaranteed by the federal Constitution," said Justice Black. "It has always been true that where a federally protected right has been invaded the federal courts will provide the remedy to rectify the wrong done," he concluded.

In the 1960s Justice Black's dissent became the majority opinion of the Supreme Court. *Reynolds* v. *Sims* (1964) was the key case in a series of Supreme Court decisions that established the rule of "one person—one vote" in the drawing of legislative districts.

The "one person—one vote" rule means that every person's vote should be of equal weight and importance. States that set up legislative districts with unequal populations gave more weight to rural voters than to urban voters. Thus, urban voters were denied their right to "equal protection of the laws" under the Fourteenth Amendment. The Supreme Court decided that plans for setting up legislative districts could not discriminate against people on the basis of where they live (city residents in this case) any more than they could on the basis of race, sex, occupation, or income.

Chief Justice Earl Warren concluded that "the basic principle of representative government remains, and must remain, unchanged—the weight of a citizen's vote cannot be made to depend on where he lives . . . A citizen, a qualified voter, is no more nor no less so because he lives in the city or on the farm. This is the clear and strong command of our Constitution's Equal Protection Clause."

Consequences of the "One Person-One Vote" Rule

The Reynolds decision had a major effect on state legislatures. After the decision, forty-nine state governments changed their legislative districts on the basis of equal population. Oregon had already done so in 1961. The decision ended control of state legislatures by rural minorities. The "one person—one vote" rule had to be used in elections of members of a state legislature.

Congressional districts, from which members of the U.S. House of Representatives are elected, also had to be redrawn to fit the "one person—one vote" rule. The U.S. Senate is the only legislative body to which the "one person—one vote" rule does not apply. The U.S. Constitution says that each state, regardless of population, shall have two senators. The only way to change the unequal representation of voters in the U.S. Senate is by an amendment to the Constitution.

The Supreme Court has provided state governments leeway, or room for minor variations, in drawing legislative districts. The legislative districts in a state do not have to be exactly equal. There must, however, be a clear and obvious effort to create districts that do not conflict with the "one person—one vote" rule.

Review

1. Why were the voters in rural areas overrepresented in their state legislatures in 1960?
2. What is a legislative district?
3. What is the "one person—one vote" rule?

Case Study

The Twenty-Sixth Amendment

At what age does a young person become an adult? Age twenty-one has been the usual answer to this question. From the earliest days of our country, it has been a tradition that people become adults on their twenty-first birthday.

According to the Tenth Amendment to the Constitution, the power to make voter eligibility laws is reserved to the states. And in line with tradition, twenty-one became the minimum voting age in every state in the country.

Then, in 1943, Georgia lowered the voting age to eighteen. In 1955, Kentucky followed Georgia's example. In 1959, Alaska set the voting age at nineteen and Hawaii at twenty. Still, the other forty-six states kept twenty-one as the minimum voting age.

During the 1960s there was much debate about whether to lower the voting age to eighteen throughout the country. The Supreme Court ruled that it was necessary to amend the Constitution in order to change the voting age all at once in every state.

Those who favored giving the right to vote to eighteen-year-olds used the following arguments:

1. Males were at that time drafted into the armed forces at age eighteen. They were fighting and dying in Vietnam but they could not vote. Somehow this seemed wrong.

2. Young people, at age eighteen, seemed to be more educated and mature than they were in previous times. They seemed as qualified to vote as older people.

3. Younger people would be more responsible citizens if they had the right to vote. It is easier to learn how to be a responsible citizen by taking part in government than merely by reading about it.

4. Eighteen-year-olds seemed motivated. They seemed to want to take part in elections.

Those who were against giving eighteen-year-olds the right to vote used these arguments:

1. What had been good in the past was still good. Why change when the old law has worked?

2. Eighteen-year-olds do not know enough to vote wisely. They seemed too immature to make sound judgments.

3. Citizens who were settled and who had steady jobs were more responsible. Most eighteen-year-olds did not seem to be settled yet. They did not have enough of a stake in society to make wise judgments about voting.

4. Eighteen-year-olds did not seem to care enough to take part. Why give them the right to vote? Most would not bother to use the right.

These arguments reached a peak in 1970. Early in 1971, an amendment was put before the Congress: "The right of citizens of the United States, who are eighteen years of age or older, to vote shall not be denied or abridged by the

Who Turned Out to Vote (1988 Presidential Election)

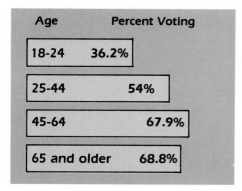

Age	Percent Voting
18-24	36.2%
25-44	54%
45-64	67.9%
65 and older	68.8%

United States or by any state on account of age."

More than two-thirds of the members of Congress voted for this amendment. At least three-fourths of the fifty states had to approve the amendment in order to make it part of the Constitution. At the end of June 1971, Ohio's legislature became the thirty-eighth to ratify the proposal. So, it became the Twenty-Sixth Amendment to the Constitution.

More than 11 million new citizens, from ages eighteen to twenty-one, were added to the lists of eligible voters. However, their impact on most elections has been slight. In 1976, the youngest voters were the least likely to take part in elections. The general turnout of young voters during the 1970s was a disappointment to those who had worked to extend to them the right to vote.

The low turnout of young voters continued during the 1980s. In the 1982 congressional election, for example, only 25 percent of people aged 18 to 24 voted. By contrast, 64 percent of the people 55 to 64 years of age turned out. (See the graph above. Compare groups that voted in the 1988 Presidential election.)

Some groups of young voters have been active in a few local elections around the country. These small groups of younger citizens have shown that they can have an impact on election outcomes. Will you accept the responsibility of voting? If so, you might be part of a movement to increase the turnout of young voters in the elections of the future.

(above) Student registering to vote for the first time. (above left) Which group in the chart had the highest percentage of its voters participate in the election?

Review

1. Why was it necessary to amend the Constitution in order to make a decision in this case?
2. Describe the amendment process used in this case.
3. What in your opinion are the reasons younger Americans do not vote in large numbers?

Basic Social Studies Skills
Making and Testing Hypotheses

Whether you are aware of it or not, you often form hypotheses (hī poth'-ə sēz') to explain things or answer questions. A **hypothesis** (hī poth'-ə sis) is simply a reasonable, or educated, guess about the answer to a question.

Hypotheses cannot always be proven to be true or false. Evidence, however, can be collected and used to support a hypothesis. Likewise, evidence can be found that strongly indicates that a hypothesis is incorrect.

Study the following three hypotheses. Each is a response to this question: Is the percentage of men who vote in national elections higher than that of women who vote in national elections?

Hypothesis 1: The percentage of men who vote in national elections is *higher* than that of women.

Hypothesis 2: The percentage of men who vote in national elections is *lower* than that of women.

Hypothesis 3: There is *little* or *no difference* in the percentage of men and women who vote in national elections.

Skill Practice

1. Study Figure 1. Based on the evidence, which hypothesis would be the most correct for the 1968 election? Which hypothesis would be the most correct for the 1976 and 1980 elections?

2. Study Figure 2. Write two hypotheses that the facts in Figure 2 would

support, and two hypotheses that the facts in Figure 2 would dispute.

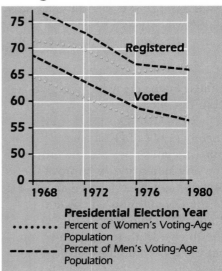

Percent of Men and Women Who Reported Registering and Voting in Presidential Elections

Presidential Election Year

.... Percent of Women's Voting-Age Population
– – – – – Percent of Men's Voting-Age Population

Percent of Voting Age Population NOT Registered

Presidential and Congressional Election Years	18-20	21-24	25-34	All Ages
1972	41.9	40.5	31.6	27.7
1976	52.9	45.2	37.8	33.3
1980	55.3	47.3	38.0	33.1
Congressional Election Years				
1974	63.6	54.7	45.4	37.8
1978	65.3	54.9	44.5	37.4
1982	65.0	52.2	42.9	35.9

Chapter 13 Review

Summary

Section 1: Rules for Voting

The Constitution grants state governments the power to decide who is qualified to vote in elections. However, the Constitution also says that no state can deny the right to vote because of race, color, sex, non-payment of a poll tax, or age—if the person is at least eighteen. On election day, qualified voters go to the polling places in their neighborhood. Once inside, they follow rules for voting that have been made by their state government.

Section 2: Deciding How to Vote

Careful voters consider a number of points when deciding for whom to vote. They back candidates who tend to support programs, goals, and values with which they agree. They support candidates who are reliable and honest. Careful voters also try to judge how effective a candidate will be if elected. Voters should be careful to avoid being misled or confused by clever propaganda in an election campaign. Careful voters know how to spot propaganda techniques such as name-calling, glittering generality, and transfer.

Vocabulary

Define the following terms.
1. ballot p.
2. straight ticket vote
3. propaganda
4. glittering generality
5. write-in candidate
6. name-calling
7. split ticket vote
8. voter registration
9. bandwagon
10. card-stacking
11. plain folks
12. transfer
13. testimonial

Reviewing Main Ideas

1. True or false: In 1790 Indians, blacks, and women could not vote.
2. The Constitution says that no person can be denied the right to vote on the basis of
   a. color.
   b. race.
   c. sex.
   d. all of the above.
3. Who is responsible for making election rules?
   a. Congress
   b. the President
   c. the state governments
   d. the federal agencies

Thinking Critically

Comprehending Information

1. On election day you must show that you are a qualified voter in order to vote. Explain what this means.
2. Why do many voters look for candidates (1) with whom they share goals and values (2) who are honest and reliable (3) who are able to get things done?

Evaluating Information

1. Tell why you think this statement is true or not true: The more we insist on learning all sides of an issue, the less likely we are to be influenced by propaganda.
2. Do you think that the government should make it easy or difficult for people to register to vote? Why do you think so?

Communicating Information

Draw two cartoons—one illustrating the use of *transfer*, and the other illustrating the use of *plain folks* in a campaign appeal.

Unit Four Test

Vocabulary

Write *true* if the underlined word or phrase is used correctly. Write *false* if it is used incorrectly. Rephrase each false statement so that the underlined word or phrase is used correctly.

1. The time, money, skills, and information needed to help achieve political goals are called <u>political resources</u>.

2. An <u>interest group</u> is an organization that tries to influence government decisions and that is made up of people who share common interests and beliefs.

3. A <u>coalition</u> is a series of statements that tell a political party's position on public issues.

4. People hired by interest groups to try to influence government decision makers are called <u>lobbyists</u>.

5. A <u>polling place</u> is a city office where opinion polls are filled out.

6. A neighborhood election district is often called a <u>precinct</u>.

7. <u>Independent voters</u> are voters who support only minor party candidates.

8. A <u>major party</u> is a party that has a long history of winning many important elections.

9. A group formed to nominate and support candidates for public office is called a <u>political party</u>.

10. In a <u>two-party system</u> only two political parties are allowed to exist.

11. The form that people mark when they vote is called a <u>petition</u>.

12. A preliminary election in which voters choose candidates to represent a political party in a final, or general, election is called a <u>direct primary</u>.

13. A <u>party platform</u> is the place to which a person goes to vote.

14. An area in a state that is represented by lawmakers in Congress and state legislatures is a <u>legislative district</u>.

Recalling Information

1. The authors suggest that you ask some questions about an interest group before joining it. Which question below is <u>not</u> one of those suggested?
a. Does the group work toward goals in an honest and legal way?
b. Do you share the group's goals?
c. Is the group able to accomplish what it sets out to do?
d. Has the group received national recognition in a widely-read news magazine?

2. Which of the following is one of the "guidelines for effective group action" that were suggested by the authors?
a. Use resources wisely.
b. Do not try to do too much at once.
c. Do not give up easily.
d. All of the above.

3. True or false: Political parties were formed in the early years of United States history because political leaders had ideas about government that differed from one another.

4. Which of the following is a major political party?
a. the American Legion   **c.** the Progressive party
b. the Republican party   **d.** the Prohibition party

5. The main purpose of political parties is to
_____.
a. get people to vote
b. win elections
c. raise money
d. get new party members

6. True or false: The Republicans and the Democrats became the two major political parties in the 1930s.

7. True or false: Voter turnout is highest in states where it is relatively easy to register.

8. Which of the following are ways political parties work after an election?
a. National committee members operate the Department of the Treasury.
b. Party members are appointed to some government jobs.
c. The party out of power plays "watchdog" over the party in power.
d. Party ties link various levels of government.

9. True or false: In the past, the Republicans have been more likely than the Democrats to urge that the national government try to solve social problems.

10. Which of the following is a way of being nominated for public office?
a. a party convention
b. a direct primary
c. a national committee meeting
d. *a* and *b*

11. Which of the following is a major party in the United States?
a. Socialist   **c.** Progressive
b. Populist   **d.** none of the above

12. When candidates say that they support "love, peace, and justice," but never talk about specific actions they will take if elected, the candidates are using a propaganda technique called _____.
a. glittering generality   **c.** testimonial
b. bandwagon   **d.** plain folks

13. If candidates distort the truth by presenting only one side (their side) of an argument, the candidates are using a propaganda technique called _____.
a. plain folks   **c.** glittering generality
b. card-stacking   **d.** name-calling

Building Skills

1. Explain how an interest group could use time, money, information, and skills to influence voters.

2. Write a letter to one of your U.S. senators expressing your opinion on a current issue.

3. Write a paragraph describing the ideal candidate. Base your description on the "points that many experienced voters consider before selecting a candidate."

4. Make a Decision Tree that shows what is involved in deciding whether or not to join a political party.

5. Assume that you have decided to try to influence government decision making. Name three ways you might be able to do so. After each method, tell what resources you would need.

Unit 5
State Governments

We live in a nation of states. The states and state governments existed before we had a national government. It was delegates from the thirteen states who met in Philadelphia in 1787 "to form a more perfect union." Since 1790, thirty-seven more states have joined the Union. Each has a place in the Union equal to that of all other states.

As new states entered the Union, they planned their governments after those of the older states. They also borrowed ideas from the federal Constitution. The fifty state governments differ in many ways, yet they are also alike.

Although you are probably not always aware of it, your state government affects you almost every day. The public elementary schools, high schools, colleges, and universities in your state are partially funded by your state government. Even the subjects you learn in school, if you are in public school, are determined in part by your state government. Your state decides how much money to spend on each student, and sometimes which textbooks will be used. And it determines which kinds of taxes will pay for public schools.

Your state also pays for the building and maintaining of many roads. Although there are more than 2 million miles of paved roads in the nation, the federal government provides less than one-third of the money needed for them. Most of the money comes from state government. Consequently, states have much to say about where to build new roads, how to maintain old roads, how to patrol the highways, and how to levy taxes for the payments needed to provide these important services.

Your state government is also responsible for operating welfare and health-care programs. Most states operate foster homes, homes for the aged, hospitals, and homes for the mentally ill. Funds for these facilities are generally shared by the states and the federal government.

In this unit you will see how the decisions of people in state governments affect life in the states and how citizens, in turn, affect state government decision makers.

(opposite) The Georgia state capitol in Atlanta.

Chapter 14

States and State Legislatures

Introduction. You must pay sales taxes. When driving, you must observe speed limits. You must have a license to operate a beauty parlor.

Who decides these things? Legislators do. They are the men and women who make up the legislature, or lawmaking body, in your state government.

Altogether, voters elect more than 7,500 men and women to serve in state legislatures. Their duties often require hard work and long stays away from home. In many states the pay is not very high, although it has been getting better in recent years.

Why would anyone want the job? Here is what four state legislators had to say:

Stanley Sivinski: "They need people down here who will represent the average worker. The state legislature needs people who aren't lawyers, who are for the common people."

Sheila Greenberg: "For eight years I worked in the county treasurer's office. During that time I visited the state legislature often on business, and I provided the legislature with information on several laws affecting county government officials. I decided I had some good experience and that I should run for the legislature."

James Robbins: "I own my own business. Many people asked me to run for the legislature. I didn't want to spend time away from my factory, but my friends convinced me the business point of view needed to be represented in the legislature."

Jean Shepard: "I am a lawyer. I have always been interested in state government. Being a state lawmaker was a good way to expand my knowledge of the law. Also by working here, I have met many people who can help me improve my own law office at home."

As you have read, people serve in state governments for many reasons. In this chapter you will discover more about state governments.

Interior of Boston's State House, where Massachusetts state representatives meet.

Section 1
The Powers of State Government

The United States has a federal system of government. In our federal system, the powers of government are divided between the national government and the fifty state governments. The Constitution defines the place of state governments in the federal system. The diagram on page 278 shows how powers are divided. The left side shows those powers that only the national government has. The right side shows some of the many powers reserved for the states. In the middle are powers shared by both the national government and the states. For example, both levels of government make and collect taxes, borrow money, pay debts, set up courts, protect health and safety, and so on. However, the federal Constitution, laws, and treaties are supreme over state constitutions and laws.

State Constitutions

All fifty states have their own constitutions. Each state constitution describes how its government shall be organized. It gives the powers and duties of various officials and agencies. It names the rights of citizens. It deals with voting and elections, the means of making laws, and the way to change the constitution itself.

State constitutions vary a great deal in length. They range from Vermont's 6,600-word document to some that are five or six times longer. The average state constitution is more than three times longer than

Division of Powers in Our Federal System

Powers of National Government

To coin money; regulate foreign and interstate commerce; pass naturalization and immigration laws; establish post offices; grant patents and copyrights; declare war and make peace; admit new states and govern territories; maintain military establishments; fix standards of weights and measures; provide for the common defense; govern the District of Columbia; conduct foreign relations; do anything "necessary and proper" for carrying out the delegated powers.

Powers Common to Both (Concurrent powers)

To tax; borrow money; charter banks; pass bankruptcy laws; establish courts; promote agriculture, industry, and science; protect the health, safety, and morals of the people; take property for public purposes; pay debts.

Powers of State Governments

To provide for local governments; conduct elections; ratify Constitutional amendments; make laws about wills, contracts and domestic relations; regulate commerce within the states; provide for and supervise schools; care for handicapped and mentally ill; assume power not granted to the United States nor prohibited to the states (reserved powers).

(above) Why do you think the division of powers in our federal system is organized in such a way? Why do the two governments share certain powers?

the federal Constitution with all its amendments. The short constitutions deal only with the basic rules for state government. They give the state legislature the power to make changes in the rules to keep up with the times. Long state constitutions include many details about running state government on a day-to-day basis.

Nineteen states are still using their original constitutions. That of Massachusetts dates from 1780, but, of course, it has been amended many times. Many states have had two or three new constitutions over the years. Louisiana has had 11; Georgia, 8; South Carolina, 7; and three other states, 6 each. Many

changes have taken place in state constitutions since 1950 as the states have sought to modernize their governments.

In spite of how they vary in length, content, and age, all state constitutions have some common features. They all begin with a preamble. Most start out like the federal Constitution, "We the people," and then list purposes that the government is to serve. All state constitutions have a Bill of Rights that lists basic freedoms like those in the federal Constitution.

As with the national government, state constitutions also assign powers and duties of government to three branches. The diagram above

State Government Organization

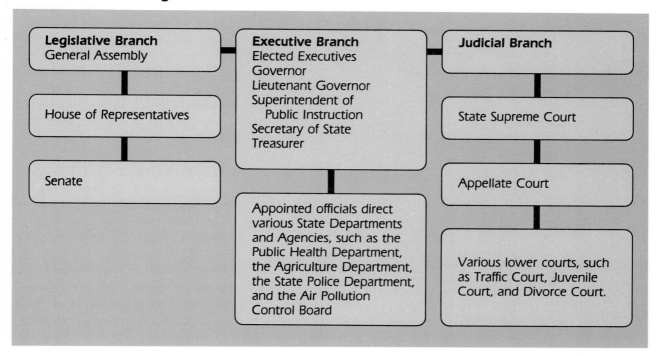

Legislative Branch
General Assembly

House of Representatives

Senate

Executive Branch
Elected Executives
Governor
Lieutenant Governor
Superintendent of
  Public Instruction
Secretary of State
Treasurer

Appointed officials direct
various State Departments
and Agencies, such as the
Public Health Department,
the Agriculture Department,
the State Police Department,
and the Air Pollution
Control Board

Judicial Branch

State Supreme Court

Appellate Court

Various lower courts, such
as Traffic Court, Juvenile
Court, and Divorce Court.

shows the basic pattern of organization of state governments. Your state government may be organized a bit differently, but, in general, it should resemble this diagram.

State constitutions give each branch of government power to check the other branches. This is to keep the powers of the three branches in balance. For example, the state legislature has the power to make laws. A governor can check the legislative branch with a veto of any law he or she may oppose.

State Legislatures

The legislative branch is known as the State Legislature in a little over half the states. It is called the General Assembly or Legislative Assembly in twenty-one of the states. In New Hampshire and Massachusetts, it is called the General Court.

All but one of the states has a **bicameral legislature.** This means that it is divided into two houses: a house of representatives (or assembly) and a senate. Nebraska has a one-house, **unicameral legislature,** called the Senate.

Regardless of name, the legislature is the state's chief lawmaking body. Legislatures may enact any law that does not conflict with the state constitution, the United States Constitution, or federal laws and treaties.

State Legislatures Pass Laws on Taxes and Spending. One of the state legislature's important tasks is

How does state government organization compare to federal government organization?

Environmentalist Marjory Stoneman Douglas and former Florida Governor Bob Graham on the banks of the Kissimmee River. A huge canal system built in the 1960s changed the area from marshland to dry plain. The change killed much of the wildlife that had lived in the area. Now, because of the efforts of environmentalists such as Douglas, the area is being returned to its natural state. State governments often pass laws to protect and manage the environment.

to pass laws providing for the collection of money to pay for government. State and local governments use this money to provide for firefighters and police; roads, bridges, and dams; care for the poor; and many other services. Money also goes for state employees' salaries.

Where does a state government get money? Your state gets most of its money from taxes. These include state sales and income taxes, death and gift taxes, sometimes property taxes, and fees for various licenses. States also receive money from the federal government.

Legislatures tax and allot money according to a plan called the state budget, which the governor's office prepares. The budget usually covers a specific period of time, in many states a two-year period.

No money from the state treasury can be spent unless the legislature approves. It does this by passing laws called **appropriations.** For instance, in order for the

schools to get the money they need to operate, the state must pass an Education Appropriations bill. Each legislature must appropriate money every year or every other year.

Much conflict arises over how much money to spend on various programs. During legislative sessions, the halls of state capitols are filled with individuals and groups urging legislators to allot money for programs they support.

State Legislatures Pass Laws to Guide Behavior. These laws spell out what people and businesses must and must not do. Many of these laws aim to protect health and safety. All criminal laws are in this category. They set penalties for such acts as theft, murder, arson (setting fire on purpose), and vandalism. Other health and safety laws may require inspection of restaurants. They might provide for truck weight inspection or set speed limits on state and county roads.

As times change there is often a need for new laws. Laws regulating nuclear power plants, for example, were not needed until recently. Now state legislatures may make such plants pass safety inspections.

State Legislatures Pass Education Laws. Each state provides some funding for public schools. As a result, a large portion of a state budget goes for education. Legislatures also pass laws affecting school operations. Such laws may set qualifications for school bus drivers as well as for principals. They may require schools to have fire drills twice a month or to teach the metric system in grades seven and eight. State legislatures also provide money for and regulate state colleges and universities.

State Legislatures Create Local Governments. The power of local governments in a state is set by the state legislature. When a community believes it needs its own government, it asks the state legislature for a **charter.** All cities, towns, and villages have charters, or plans for government. The charter says where the city boundaries are and what laws it is free to pass. It will say how the city may raise money.

State laws set up districts to provide certain services. These districts are usually run by a local board, either elected or appointed. Thus school districts, park districts, airport districts, hospital districts, urban mass transit districts, and cemetery districts are all examples of local governments.

State lawmakers pass laws that regulate the jobs of such local officials as mayors, sheriffs, police chiefs, fire chiefs, and county engineers. They may also regulate local government operation, for example, by requiring county offices to stay open one night each week.

Other Legislative Activities. Usually the legislature, or at least the state senate, must approve many of the governor's appointments to state jobs. In some states, the legislature itself has the power to appoint certain high-ranking officers. Most legislatures can impeach state officials and remove them from office upon conviction. Legislatures also vote on proposed amendments to the United States Constitution.

Section Review

Vocabulary:
appropriations, bicameral legislature, charter, unicameral legislature.

Reviewing the Main Ideas
1. Describe our federal system.
2. How does a state government get money?
3. Give five examples of different kinds of things state legislatures pass laws about.

Skill Building
1. Read the diagram on page 279 to find out in which branch of government each of these state officials works:
a. governor
b. judge of the Appellate Court
c. state senator
d. Superintendent of Public Instruction
2. What is the state legislature called in your state? Where is it located? Is it bicameral or unicameral?
3. Name five different local governments with which you come in contact.
4. Read Article 1, Section 10 of the United States Constitution and list the powers states do *not,* have.
5. How old is your state constitution? When was it last amended?

Section 2
How State Legislatures Work

Once elected to a state legislature, a person becomes part of a large, well-organized group. The new member works with others to make decisions and create laws. The rules of the legislature guide his or her behavior.

Committees

Most of the work of a state legislature is done in committee. There are between twenty and thirty **standing committees.** Each considers a certain area of legislation. The Rules Committee decides on the procedures for submitting bills, when they will come to the floor for a vote, how bills can be amended, under what conditions a roll-call vote is needed, and so on. The Appropriations Committee decides which state projects will get how much money. These two committees are very powerful. The decisions these committees make are important ones—ones that often directly affect the lives of every state resident.

At the beginning of a session, each legislator lets party leaders know which committees he or she is interested in being on. Usually, those who have been in the legislature the longest get their choices first. Leaders, however, try to give each new member at least one of his or her choices.

Committee members read through all the bills proposed in their area. They choose the ones they favor most, or they may put parts of several together. They may also work out a bill on their own. Then they put the bill before the house for a vote. If a committee does not approve a legislator's proposed bill, it has no chance of becoming law. Legislators want to be on the committees that matter most to the people in their district.

The governor of Georgia addressing a joint session of the state's general assembly.

How a Bill Becomes a Law

A bill becomes a law in a state legislature in much the same way as in Congress. Once a bill is introduced in one house, it goes to a committee. The committee can hold hearings on the bill.

If the committee approves the bill, it is then placed on the calendar. At a certain time, the entire house considers it. Members may agree on amendments, and they eventually vote on the bill. If that house passes the bill, it goes to the other house. There the committee, calendar, amendment, consideration, and voting procedure is repeated. If the second house approves a different version of the bill, a **conference committee** of members of both houses irons out the differences. The bill then goes to the governor. He or she may sign it into law, or veto it. The legislature can override a veto by a two-thirds majority of both houses or, in Nebraska, the one house.

Leaders

Not every legislator has equal influence on what happens in a legislature. Leaders who organize and guide legislative work have the most influence.

Both houses have leaders. In most states the lieutenant governor serves as **president of the senate.** Members of the house elect a leader, usually called the **speaker of the house.** These leaders are a legislature's **presiding officers.** As a rule, they appoint committee members and chairpersons, refer bills to proper committees, and conduct

sessions of the two houses. They also help set the legislative calendars and take part in debates. The speaker votes on all bills. The lieutenant governor votes only in case of a tie.

In most legislatures each political party has **floor leaders.** These leaders try to pass bills their political parties want passed. They make certain that all party members know how their leaders want them to vote on key bills. They also remind lawmakers when important bills are coming up for consideration so they can be present. In addition, floor leaders help the presiding officers decide which people to assign to which committees.

Section Review

Vocabulary:
conference committee, floor leaders, president of the senate, presiding officers, speaker of the house, standing committees.

Reviewing the Main Ideas
1. What do standing committees do?
2. How do floor leaders help their parties pass legislation?
3. What is the difference between *legislator* and *legislature?*

Skill Building
With classmates, find out the names of your state legislators in both houses. Find their addresses at the state capitol. Then divide into groups to write letters and find out on which committees each serves. Ask for information about the legislation each has introduced in the most recent session.

Section 3
State Lawmakers

Traditionally, being a state lawmaker has been a part-time job. In the past, most state legislatures met only every other year. In recent years, however, the job has become more time consuming. Today, nearly all state legislatures meet annually. Lawmakers in some of the larger states stay in session nearly as long as Congress.

Legal training is useful to legislative work, and many state lawmakers are lawyers who have their own law practices at home. For some lawyers, service in the legislature is a step toward such other public jobs as judge or attorney general. Many other lawmakers own their own businesses, or are teachers, farmers, or homemakers.

State lawmakers represent citizens of their districts. They know their people's problems and needs. Most lawmakers come from the district they represent. In a recent year in New Jersey, for example, 83 percent of the legislators were born in the district they represented or had lived there at least thirty years. Even in California, where people change residences frequently, 56 percent of the lawmakers were born or raised in their districts.

The Job Today

The job of state lawmaker is often a brief one. Many legislators serve only one term of two or four years. Usually this is because lawmakers are not well-paid and they find the job takes too much time from other duties. One legislator put it this way:

"Any way you look at it, the job means a sacrifice to you, your home, your business. Lawmaking duties take time enough. Doing special jobs for the voters also takes time. Why, yesterday my phone rang 68 times. It's a problem of time."

Some lawmakers remain in office many years. This is especially true in California, where many lawmakers consider their jobs as professions. As one said, "I enjoy being a legislator. I am interested in government. I like solving problems with people at home and working on new laws here."

Making Decisions. The primary task of lawmakers is to make decisions about laws. To do this they study bills. They listen to individuals or groups interested in certain legislation. In committees they listen to witnesses. They might testify on bills themselves. They offer amendments. Unlike national legislators, they have small staffs to help with their work. A considerable burden is placed on the individual legislator and his or her time.

A lawmaker may vote on hundreds of bills during a session. Deciding whether to vote "yes" or "no" will be more difficult in some cases than in others.

Many of the bills a lawmaker must consider affect only a few people. For example, a bill might provide special medical benefits for two state workers hurt in an accident. Such bills do not call for great change and usually do not involve great sums of money. Not many people outside the legislature will care about them.

On the other hand, a bill might affect many people's income, property, health care, or education. The lawmaker who must vote on such a bill finds citizens swamping his or her office with letters. Interest groups try to influence legislators' decisions. At those times, the state legislature becomes an arena of action and pressure. Decisions about such bills can be difficult to make.

Helping Citizens. Another part of the lawmakers' job is to help citizens and groups who come to them with problems. Legislators know that such help may earn them votes in the next election. Many also believe that it is their duty to help. One legislator put it this way: "A good lawmaker should serve as a contact between the voters and the departments of state government. A lawmaker should be a sort of walking directory who can refer citizens to the right person or department when they have a problem with state government."

A legislator might help a builder learn about environmental regulations. He or she might help a trucker get required licenses. A lawmaker might help a set of parents learn about state college scholarships. Examples of legislators aiding people of their districts are endless.

Overseeing State Agencies. Lawmakers also review, or oversee, the work of state agencies, such as the highway department or the department of public health. Lawmakers may ask agency leaders to report on certain programs, or they may re-

Members of Georgia's house of representatives conferring about and lobbying for a proposed bill.

Posting bills on the agenda of the New Jersey Assembly.

Who Influences Lawmakers?

Many people try to influence lawmakers' decisions. Chief among these are the governor, interest groups, and individuals.

The Governor. Lawmakers and citizens expect the governor to suggest legislation on taxes, pollution, education, health services, and the like. During every session many bills are written in the executive branch of the state government. Lawmakers who belong to the governor's political party introduce these bills and the governor tries to influence their passage into law.

In addition, the governor prepares the state budget. He or she tries to influence legislators to accept it. Each legislator has an interest in at least certain items in the state budget.

The veto power is also a way in which a governor can influence legislation. Every state legislature can override a governor's veto, but in most states this requires a two-thirds majority of both houses. In fact, sometimes the mere threat of a veto can influence legislators' decisions.

Governors may also call legislatures into **special session.** This is a series of meetings of the legislature at a time when it usually does not assemble. Many legislators do not like having to return to the capital to consider special problems or bills. Governors sometimes use this dislike for special sessions to force legislators to act on a proposal during a regular session.

Governors can also rely on **prestige.** The news media and

quire agency leaders to explain and defend their agency's budget. By doing this lawmakers keep a watch over the agencies in the executive branch of state government.

citizens pay attention to what a governor says. Governors can use media publicity more easily than lawmakers. They can use their prestige as the state's highest elected official to build public opinion in support of their legislative programs.

Another political resource governors have is **patronage.** It is the power to give jobs or favors. A governor can often arrange to have new roads, parks, or hospitals built in a lawmaker's district, or grant state jobs or business to friends of lawmakers. In return, a governor expects the lawmaker's support for his or her programs.

Finally, as leaders of their political party, governors can use party leadership to influence legislators from their own party. As party leader, a governor can appeal to a lawmaker's party loyalty, asking for support of a bill for "the good of the party." At times a governor may offer a lawmaker a good party job in return for support.

Interest Groups. Many different interest groups seek to influence lawmakers' decisions. These groups include such business and labor organizations as chambers of commerce and particular unions. They also include organizations representing teachers, farmers, and government employees.

Groups with an interest in legislation often contribute money to their candidates' election campaigns. They also support lobbyists who work in the state capital and attend legislative sessions. Lobbyists provide lawmakers with useful information about bills, and they seek to

Lobbyist speaking with a representative about a proposed bill.

influence votes just as lobbyists in Congress do. State legislators often depend more on lobbyists for information than do members of Congress. This is because they work only part-time as lawmakers. And, unlike members of Congress, they do not have large staffs to collect information for them.

Consider, for example, this state legislator's comment: "I think lobbyists are usually helpful. They can study issues and present information we have no time to get for ourselves. In ten minutes a lobbyist can explain what it would take you hours to learn by reading bills."

Individual Citizens. Unless you are a lobbyist, you will not be able to spend much time trying to influence lawmakers. There are things, however, individual citizens can do to

287

communicate their interests to various legislators.

Citizens can contact them. Although few people write or call their lawmakers, this is not hard to do. Legislators like to keep in touch with **constituents,** the citizens who live in the legislator's district. It is not easy for lawmakers to know what their constituents think about proposed legislation.

In addition, citizens can find groups working for goals they are interested in. A person might join an interest group, or at least contribute money to one.

Finally, every citizen has the right to vote and to join a political party. By working with a party, citizens may help elect to state legislatures candidates who support their ideas.

Section Review

Vocabulary:
constituents, patronage, prestige, special session.

Reviewing the Main Ideas
1. Why do many state legislators hold other jobs?
2. Describe three key parts of the lawmaker's job.
3. Name the ways citizens might try to influence lawmakers' decisions.

Skill Building
1. Write a paragraph describing what you think is the most important part of a legislator's job. Give your reasons.
2. What political resource is each

governor in the stories below using? Be prepared to defend your answers.

Governor 1: State Senator Alice Irwin answered the phone. The governor was calling. "Alice," the governor said, "you are a loyal party member. I hope you will vote for the new tax bill I want. It's important for our party that we pass that bill."

Governor 2: Governor Hill was a guest on a TV interview show. The governor answered questions about his legislative program. He explained why the public should support it.

Governor 3: Representative Ed Kolski had been a loyal supporter of Governor Kauffman for many years. Kolski had almost always voted for the governor's programs. Last week the governor named Kolski to be the state director of public works.

Section 4
Lawmaking By Popular Vote

State lawmakers are elected to represent the people in making laws for their state. Some states, however, have also given power directly to the people themselves to make their own laws.

The Initiative
An initiative is a procedure that allows interested citizens to propose a law or state constitutional amendment for approval by voters during an election. Twenty-three states and the District of Columbia allow the

Examples of Propositions Voted on in Selected States in Recent Years (simple majority needed for passage)

Proposition	State	For	Against	
Limit property tax to one percent of full value	California	63%	37%	↑
Eliminate sales tax on food and medicine	Arkansas	45%	55%	↓
Tie state spending to growth in economy	Texas	84%	16%	↑
Mandatory minimum sentences for crimes	Idaho	70%	30%	↑
Open more land for homesteading	Alaska	55%	45%	↑
Allow technicians to fit dentures without dentist	Oregon	78%	22%	↑
Allow state police union	Michigan	56%	44%	↑

The propositions in the chart are only some of the initiatives that voters have proposed and voted on in recent years. Has your state voted on any initiatives in recent years? What were the initiatives? Were they passed?

making of laws by initiative. In California, Oregon, Washington, North Dakota, Arizona, and Colorado the initiative has become a common way to pass laws. On November 6, 1984, forty initiatives were considered by voters in sixteen states.

In most states the initiative works like this. Supporters of a particular policy, such as reducing taxes or eliminating the death penalty, draft a proposed law or constitutional amendment. They must then get signatures from a certain percentage of registered voters to get their proposed measure on the ballot in the next general election. The number of signatures needed varies from state to state. Recently in California, for example, more than 393,000 signatures were required to get a proposed new law on the ballot. More than 630,000 signatures were needed to get a constitutional amendment on the ballot. Once on the ballot, the voters decide "yes" or "no" on the proposed measure.

The initiative bypasses the legislature. It puts citizens directly in the role of lawmakers. In recent years the number of initiatives put on the ballot by citizens has been increasing. Most states call initiatives **propositions.** When more than one is put on the ballot, the so-called propositions are numbered. A famous initiative to limit property taxes in California was called "Proposition 13." (See page 346.)

The Referendum
The referendum is also a powerful tool of the people. A referendum

allows a majority of voters to veto legislation or reject constitutional amendments. About half the states use some type of referendum procedure for legislation. A referendum is required in all states, except Delaware, for approval of constitutional amendments. As with initiatives, most states call a referendum a proposition once it is on the ballot.

There are several kinds of referendums dealing with legislation. Some states use a **mandatory referendum.** This requires that certain bills, often those dealing with taxes, must be referred to the voters before they become law.

An **optional referendum** allows the legislature to specify that a bill will not become law until approved by voters at an election. This method may be used when lawmakers want to shift decision-making responsibility on some controversial issue to the people.

The most common type of referendum is a protest, or **petition referendum.** This allows voters to change or reject a bill after it has been passed by the legislature and signed into law by a governor. Groups protesting a law must obtain a certain number of signatures on a referendum petition to place the issue on the ballot. Voters then have a chance to vote for or against the law in a general election.

The Recall

The **recall** is a procedure through which the voters may remove elected public officials before the end of their term in office. Fourteen states permit recall of state government officials. Many other states provide for recall of local officials.

A recall begins by getting the signatures of voters on a recall petition. Usually, signatures equaling 25 percent of the number of votes cast for the official in the last election are needed. An election is then held. In some recall elections, people simply vote for or against the official. In others, people may also vote for competing candidates for the office. The elected official is removed or kept in office by a majority vote.

Officials do not have to be accused of wrongdoing to be recalled. People may start a drive to recall a governor or state lawmaker or mayor because they do not like the official's position on issues such as taxes or school busing.

The recall is used much less often than the initiative and the referendum. Recall elections are called more frequently at the local level than at the state level. Only one governor has ever been recalled. Recently in Michigan, however, several state lawmakers were recalled by voters angered by the lawmakers' support for higher taxes.

Tools for Direct Democracy

Our national government is organized as a **representative democracy.** This means the people elect representatives to act for them in making laws and decisions. There are no provisions in the U.S. Constitution for initiative, referendum, or recall.

Our state and local governments are also organized as representative

democracies. However, those states that allow initiative, referendum, or recall also provide a means for **direct democracy.** In a direct democracy, political decisions are made by the people directly rather than by their elected representatives.

In the early 1900s, opponents of these procedures challenged them in the Oregon Supreme Court. They claimed that the initiative and the referendum destroyed the representative nature of state government and, thus, violated the Constitution. The court upheld the initiative and referendum as constitutional. It ruled that in a state with the initiative and referendum, "the representative character of the government still remains. The people have simply reserved to themselves a larger share of the legislative process."

Section Review

Vocabulary:
direct democracy, mandatory referendum, optional referendum, petition referendum, proposition, recall, representative democracy.

Reviewing the Main Ideas
1. Describe the purpose of the initiative.
2. List three types of referendums.
3. Why is the recall used?
4. Why would an optional referendum be used?

Skill Building
Write a paragraph describing the information presented in the table on page 289.

Instructor explaining voter registration procedures to Hispanic voters in Los Angeles. In a democracy, the power to change existing laws or create new ones is in the hands of the people.

Equality Before the Law—A Fundamental Right

All people are entitled to equal treatment and equal rights before the law. This is one of our greatest democratic ideals.

The Fourteenth Amendment brings this idea to life. It declares that no state shall deny to any person "the equal protection of the law." The **equal-protection clause** has become the key guarantee of your right to be treated fairly and to be given equal opportunities by state laws.

The equal-protection clause also limits the national government. The courts have ruled that the Fifth Amendment applies the clause to national as well as state laws.

The Meaning of Equal Protection

The equal-protection clause prohibits government from making unreasonable distinctions among groups of people when passing laws. For example, a law that does not allow blacks to vote is unreasonable because there is no relationship between the ability to vote and the color of a person's skin.

The equal-protection clause fights discrimination. Discrimination exists when laws treat people unfairly solely because of their race, sex, ethnic group, religion, or age.

The equal-protection clause, however, does not require the government to treat all groups of people exactly the same. Laws may reasonably classify people into different groups. For example, the state may require people who make a lot of money to pay more taxes than people with small incomes. A law may require that only people sixteen years or older can get a driver's license. Such classifications are reasonable. There is a relationship between income and the ability to pay taxes, and between age and the ability to drive safely.

Whenever a law is challenged as violating equal protection, the constitutional question is not whether the law may classify or make distinctions among groups of people. The question is whether the classification being made is reasonable or not.

The Courts Interpret Equal Protection

If citizens believe a law violates their right to equal protection, they may challenge the law in court. It is the court's job to distinguish between reasonable and unreasonable classifications.

The Supreme Court may use one of several tests or guidelines to decide whether a law unfairly discriminates against a group. These are called (1) the rational basis test, (2) suspect classifications, and (3) fundamental rights.

Rational Basis Test. Your right to equal protection is usually not violated when a law makes a reasonable classification that is "rationally related" to an acceptable goal of government. For instance, a law prohibiting people with certain types of medical problems from working in restaurants would not violate the equal-protection clause.

The Supreme Court uses this guideline in deciding most cases. It gives states wide discretion in making laws that treat some groups differently from others. This allows states to get on with the necessary business of making laws. It puts the burden of proving discrimination on the person challenging the law.

Suspect Classifications. The right to equal protection is almost certainly violated when a law classifies people on the basis of race or national origin. The Court has said such laws are immediately "suspect" of violating the equal-protection clause. Thus, a law prohibiting Hispanics but not others from holding a government job, such as police officer, would involve a "suspect" classification. The Supreme Court would strike down such a law unless the state could clearly prove the law somehow benefits the public interest.

The Court has not been as tough on laws that classify people by sex. As a result, lawyers have called sex an "almost suspect" classification. Recently, the Court has ruled that treating women differently from men (or vice versa) is forbidden when such distinctions are based only on "old notions" about women's roles in society.

Fundamental Rights. Any laws that classify people in a way that interferes with their fundamental rights guaranteed by the Constitution will be struck down. Thus, a law denying some groups the right to travel freely or to vote or to engage in free speech violates the equal-protection clause.

Fighting Discrimination

The equal-protection clause gives all citizens an important tool to fight discrimination. Here are two examples of how citizens have used this right to protect themselves.

Racial Discrimination. In the early 1950s a group of black parents asked the courts to strike down laws that required black children and white children to go to separate schools. These parents charged that such laws violated the equal-protection clause of the Fourteenth Amendment.

Eventually these challenges were heard together in 1954 by the Supreme Court in the landmark case of *Brown* v. *Board of Education of Topeka* (see page 116). The Court ruled that segregated schools violated the equal protection clause and that this was unconstitutional. This decision helped spark the civil rights movement in the United States.

Sex Discrimination. Women have worked long for equal rights and opportunities in our society. Women gained the right to vote in 1920 after a difficult struggle. Since the early 1970s, the equal-protection clause has often been used to challenge discrimination based on sex. As a result, using the "almost suspect" guideline, the Court has ruled that:

● Employees cannot require women who are pregnant to take a leave of absence from work (*Cleveland Board of Education* v. *LaFleur*, 1974).

● A state cannot set different ages at which men and women legally become adults (*Stanton* v. *Stanton*, 1975).

● A state cannot set different ages at which men and women are permitted to buy beer (*Craig* v. *Boren*, 1976).

● Women cannot be prohibited from jobs by arbitrary height and weight requirements (*Dothard* v. *Rawlinson*, 1977).

Review

1. What is the purpose of the equal-protection clause?
2. Which test used by the Supreme Court gives states the benefit of the doubt when passing laws?
3. Why is sex an "almost suspect" classification?

Our Changing State Legislatures

Our Constitution created a federal system. Federalism divides power between two levels of government—the national government and the fifty state governments.

Where does the balance of power in this federal system lie? For nearly 150 years after the national government was created in 1787, state legislatures were the key source of political power and action. They built highways, set standards for education, regulated utility companies, established banks, and performed countless other jobs.

During this period, state legislatures often took the lead in social progress. Wyoming already had women's suffrage when it became a state in 1890. That was thirty years before the national government gave women the right to vote. North Dakota passed one of the nation's first child-labor laws just after World War I.

Throughout our nation's early years, the national government's role was very narrow. The national government mainly provided military defense, conducted foreign policy, and delivered mail.

In the early 1930s, however, the balance of power and political action began shifting toward the national government in Washington. The Great Depression was underway. Millions were out of work and hungry. Chaos threatened. States by themselves were unable to solve these severe economic problems.

In 1933, President Franklin Delano Roosevelt took office with the promise to put people back to work.

FDR's "New Deal" policies launched many national government programs to deal with the nation's economic crisis. A trend had started.

During the late 1950s and into the 1960s, the national government's power continued to grow at the expense of state legislatures. State legislatures were unable, or unwilling, to deal with pressing social problems. The national government stepped in. For example, continuing voter discrimination against blacks by some states led the Congress in Washington to pass the Voting Rights acts of 1965, 1970, 1975, and 1982. These laws weakened state authority over voting in favor of uniform national control.

State legislatures also lost power because they did not keep up with the growth of the national government. Unlike Congress, most state legislatures did not meet every year. Legislative staffs were small, and legislators were paid very low salaries. Committee work was not well planned. Committees did not keep good records. In short, state legislatures did not develop smooth procedures for passing laws and dealing with complex modern problems.

Then, in the early 1970s, just as state legislatures were being called "do nothing" and "sometime" governments, they started to modernize. The process continues today.

Many legislatures have added full-time staffs to assist lawmakers. As a result, lawmakers no longer depend so much on the governor or lobbyist for information. One leader of the Kansas legislature recalls that before staff were added, "we were so handicapped we didn't even know what questions to ask."

Many legislatures have also increased lawmakers' salaries. Higher salaries are making it possible for people other than well-to-do lawyers and business people to take part in lawmaking.

State legislatures are also working longer. In 1966, only twenty state legislatures met every year. Now most do. An Iowa lawmaker explains that one result of longer sessions has been to close a "void in lawmaking" that Congress filled in the past.

Modern technology has also come to state legislatures. In Kansas, for example, computers are used to draft and keep track of all legislation. As a result, bills are printed daily with amendments. This helps lawmakers to follow the movement of bills through the legislature.

Finally, many legislatures have passed laws to open up state government to the public. In 1967, Florida passed a "sunshine law" allowing citizens to attend committee meetings and hearings. Since then thirty-seven other states have passed similar laws. Many legislatures have also passed laws that regulate election campaign funding and lobbying activities.

Modernization costs. Many state legislatures have been spending more money to do their jobs. In a recent seven-year period, the Kansas legislature increased its budget from $1.7 million to more than $6 million per year.

Thus, after decades of decline,

state legislatures are reclaiming powers they had let slip to Washington. In recent years, the states have actually moved ahead of Washington in developing new approaches to some problems.

California passed a clean air act many years before the national government enacted such a law. California's law remains tougher than the federal law. Pennsylvania enacted strict regulations for strip-mining long before Congress passed a national law.

In 1978, Colorado passed a law that protects taxpayers from paying extra taxes because of inflation. Since then, at least eight other states have passed similar laws. The national government still has not adopted such a law.

The states have moved faster than Washington on other subjects, and state lawmakers think this trend will continue. The president of the Oregon senate recently explained: "As opposed to the snail's pace of Congress, anything is possible at the state level. We can see the problems, make inquiries, and bring about change. We're manageable."

Heavy cloud of smog shrouding Los Angeles.

Review

1. Describe the role of state legislatures in the federal system at the start of our history.
2. What caused power to shift from state legislatures to the national government?
3. Describe three steps state legislatures have taken to modernize.

Basic Social Studies Skills
Interpreting Political Cartoons

Political cartoons represent a unique, often humorous way of expressing ideas and opinions about government leaders, policies, and important issues.

Most political cartoons appear in daily newspapers, usually on the editorial page. Millions of people read political cartoons every day. Because of this fact, political cartoons are one of the most effective means of communicating political thoughts.

Learning how to interpret political cartoons is not difficult if you are aware of some of the devices used by cartoonists.

One such device is the use of symbols. Political cartoons often include symbols that are familiar to many of us. A donkey, for example, is often used to represent the Democratic party. An elephant is used to represent the Republican party. These symbols were popularized by Thomas Nast, a cartoonist whose most famous cartoons appeared in *Harper's Weekly* in the 1860s and 1870s.

Another basic device used by political cartoonists is the caricature. Caricature is the art of picturing people, places, or events in exaggerated form. Caricatures are used to ridicule or focus special attention on some aspect of a person or thing. For example, a cartoonist who wants to show the domination the Soviet Union has over its satellite nations might choose to draw the Soviet Union proportionately much larger than the satellites. A cartoonist who

"The more I feed him, the bigger he gets."

Don Hesse
St. Louis Globe-Democrat
Los Angeles Times Syndicate

wants to emphasize the age of a particular political candidate might choose to draw exaggerated wrinkles on the person's face.

Study the cartoon above and then answer the following questions.

Skill Practice

1. What is the main idea of the cartoon?
2. How is exaggeration used to drive across the artist's point?
3. Do you agree with the viewpoint of the cartoonist?
4. Draw a political cartoon that expresses the same ideas as shown in the cartoon.
5. Use library resources to find out about the history of political cartoons. Prepare an informative report.

Chapter 14 Review

Summary

Section 1: The Powers of State Government

Our federal system divides power between the national government and the fifty state governments. Each of the fifty states has its own constitution that spells out the plan of government for that state. Each state also has its own legislature to pass laws. State legislatures may enact any law that does not conflict with the state constitution, the United States Constitution, or federal laws and treaties.

Section 2: How State Legislatures Work

Bills become law in state legislatures through steps similar to those used in Congress. Most legislative work is done in committees. A typical state legislature has between twenty and thirty standing committees. Bills passed by the legislature go to the governor for approval. Leaders in both the house and senate play key roles in lawmaking.

Section 3: State Lawmakers

Being a state lawmaker remains a part-time job for many legislators. In recent years, however, the time demands of the job have increased and some lawmakers now consider their jobs as their chosen professions. Key responsibilities include making decisions about proposed laws, helping citizens with problems, and overseeing the work of state agencies. The governor, interest groups, and individual citizens all influence lawmakers' decisions.

Section 4: Lawmaking by Popular Vote

Several states have procedures that allow people to take part directly in passing laws. The initiative allows people to propose and vote on laws or constitutional amendments. The referendum allows voters to veto legislation. In addition, some states permit the recall of public officials by majority vote. These procedures are examples of direct democracy.

Vocabulary

Define the following terms.
1. appropriations
2. bicameral legislature
3. mandatory referendum
4. petition referendum
5. unicameral legislature

Reviewing Main Ideas

1. True or false: After the thirteen states signed the Constitution, there was no need for states to have their own constitutions.
2. True or false: States can pass laws that punish people for crimes.
3. Both the national government and the states have power to _____.
a. conduct elections
b. establish post offices
c. establish courts
d. make treaties with foreign governments

Thinking Critically

Comprehending Information

1. Write a short paragraph on what you think is the most important way a governor can influence legislation.
2. Explain in a short paragraph or diagram how a bill becomes a law in a state legislature.

Communicating Ideas

Your legislature is considering a bill to raise the age at which one can get a driver's license to nineteen. Write a letter to your state senator explaining why you are for or against this bill.

Evaluating Information

If you were trying to make a judgment about your state legislator before voting to reelect, what questions would you want answered to help you make up your mind?

Chapter 15

Governors and State Agencies

Introduction. The **governor** is the highest elected public official of a state. Look over the news flashes below to see some of the powers and duties a governor has:

Jefferson City, MO—Missouri's governor today ordered 3,500 National Guard troops to the state's flood-ravaged areas along the Mississippi River. The troops are stacking sandbags along the river to prevent further flooding.

Lansing, MI—Warning that Michigan was facing financial disaster, the governor called for a 38 percent increase in the personal income tax.

Springfield, IL—The governor today signed a bill that sets stiff penalties for certain crimes. The governor also announced that the state will build two new prisons.

Along with the governor, the executive branch of state government is made up of many agencies and departments. Here are some examples of their work:

Atlanta, GA—Georgia is going to get a new system of hiking trails in state parks. The state Department of Natural Resources announced it would start building the new trails shortly.

Richmond, VA—The Department of Highways and Transportation said that new markers would be placed along dangerous curves on state roads. It is hoped that the markers will reduce highway accidents.

Columbus, OH—The Department of Education will suggest new objectives for citizenship education in grades eight and twelve. Educators from around the state will be asked to give their advice on the project.

In this chapter you will discover more about governors and state agencies.

New York's governor, Mario Cuomo, giving the keynote address at the Democratic National Convention in 1984.

Section 1
The State Executive Branch

The executive branch enforces laws. This branch includes the governor, six to ten other executive officers, such as the lieutenant governor, state treasurer, and attorney general, and numerous agencies.

The Office of Governor

Voters in each state elect governors directly. Each state constitution sets the requirements for becoming governor. Generally, a candidate must be an American citizen, a resident of the state for a certain number of years, at least thirty years old (in some states, twenty-five), and a qualified voter in the state.

In forty states, governors have four-year terms. The other ten elect them to terms of two years. In twelve states, governors cannot run for election for a second term in a row. In ten states, the limit is two terms in a row.

Every state except Oregon provides for the impeachment of the governor and other state officials. As a rule, in a case of wrongdoing, the house brings a "bill of impeachment" against the governor, and the senate tries the individual. If found guilty, a governor must leave office and usually cannot hold any public office in the state again.

Shared Powers. Some governors can be stronger leaders than others. One reason is that some state constitutions grant governors more power than others. In some plans for state government, the governor can be a strong leader because he or she can appoint the heads of state agencies. This allows governors to choose people loyal to them. Such people are likely to try to carry out the governor's programs.

In other states, voters elect the heads of key state agencies. In addition, appointed officials serve long terms in office. Officials elected by the people or appointed to long terms do not owe as much support to the governor as those a governor can hire and fire at will. The governor has less influence over them.

Some people believe the governor should have power to appoint

Kentucky's former governor, Martha Layne Collins (seated), observing a computer class. Collins, a Democrat, was elected in 1983. She became the state's first woman governor.

and remove state officials who serve in the executive branch. One reason is that voters seldom know much about the different state offices or the candidates seeking those offices. Another reason is governors are unable to tie state activities together if they lack authority over those who carry out the activities.

In any state, a governor's power also will depend a great deal on his or her leadership skills. Strong governors are those who can command support from their legislature, political party, citizens, and interest groups in the state. They are leaders who can persuade others to support their decisions.

Personal Background. Who becomes a governor? About half of all governors elected over the past one hundred years have been lawyers. Most governors also have had experience in other state or local elected offices. Some have previously served in Congress. Many have held such state posts as lieutenant governor or secretary of state. A great number have also been state legislators.

Campaign Costs. An additional qualification to run for election as governor in many states is the ability to raise substantial amounts of campaign money. Over the last decade, the cost of becoming governor has increased notably. For example, in 1978 candidates for governor in 36 states spent more than $99 million on their campaigns. Four years later candidates for governor in those same states spent $185 million.

Inflation, or the rise in general costs, accounted for a large portion of the increase. But several other factors have contributed to increased costs. Among them are the rise in the use of mass media advertising— particularly television advertising— in campaigns as well as the use of sophisticated and expensive public opinion polls and large-scale appeals for votes and campaign funds through mailings and telephone. Candidates for other state offices also have experienced an increase in campaign costs. This has led some states to enact public funding measures, as we have seen. Other states have sought to control campaign spending by limiting contributions and by requiring all state candidates to make public the sources and uses of their campaign money.

Other Executive Officers

No governor alone can carry out the laws of a state. Every state has several other important executive officials. They are responsible for managing the services and duties of the various state agencies. In many states they are elected. In some the governor appoints them.

Lieutenant Governor. Elected directly in thirty-eight states, this official is the "vice president" of state government. It is not uncommon for the lieutenant governor to belong to the opposite party from the governor. The lieutenant governor in most states becomes the governor should the governor be unable to serve. In some states the lieutenant governor has the governor's authority whenever the governor is traveling out of the state. Lieutenant governors also serve as presiding officers of state senates and on many boards and commissions dealing with state services or problems.

Attorney General. This official is elected in forty-two states. The attorney general serves as legal adviser to the governor and other state officials and represents the state in legal proceedings. People expect the state's attorney general to go after serious crime problems by gathering evidence and prosecuting suspects.

Secretary of State. The secretary of state is elected in thirty-nine states. In most states, he or she is in charge of elections, official state records, and various licenses and permits.

State Treasurer. Treasurers are elected in forty-one states. The state treasurer's main duties are to supervise collection of state funds and to pay the state's bills.

State Auditor or Comptroller. Thirty-one states elect a person to this office. This officer serves as a watchdog over state funds. He or she makes sure that money is spent according to law and that state funds are accounted for.

Chief School Officer. This official is called the superintendent of public instruction or the commissioner of education. He or she is the leader in carrying out state laws and providing services related to schools.

Section Review

Vocabulary:
attorney general, chief school officer, lieutenant governor, secretary of state, state auditor, state treasurer.

Reviewing the Main Ideas
1. What is the job of the executive branch of state government?
2. Describe the requirements for a governorship.

Skill Building
1. Which state executive official would be responsible for:
a. Paying a construction company for work on a state building.
b. Making arrangements for an election in the state.
c. Serving as the presiding officer in the state senate.
d. Advising the governor on how a decision would fit state laws.
2. Decide whether the following statements are true or false. Rewrite each false statement to make it true.
a. The lieutenant governor shares a great deal of power with the governor in most states.
b. Top state officials are elected in most states.
c. The secretary of state is mostly busy with keeping official state records and supervising state elections.
3. Find the names of the people in your state who have the jobs of governor, lieutenant governor, attorney general, secretary of state, state treasurer, state auditor or comptroller, and chief school officer.

Section 2
The Governor's Job

The governor has several leadership roles. He or she is expected to be (1) a ceremonial leader, (2) the executive leader, (3) the chief legislator, (4) the commander in chief, and (5) the political party leader.

Ceremonial Leader. A governor's weekly schedule is filled with ceremonial duties. He or she meets groups of people, leads parades, dedicates new buildings, welcomes official visitors, and travels to make speeches and hand out awards. The governor also represents the state at governors' conferences.

Executive Leader. The governor must work with many other officials in the executive branch to carry out state laws. And as most governors are leaders in shaping state budgets, they can influence the goals and actions of state agencies.

Governors and their staffs prepare a plan for income and spending. This goes to the legislature which, after some changes, usually approves it. The governor then oversees spending by the various agencies, departments, and commissions in the state.

Chief Legislator. Governors are leaders in lawmaking even though they are not part of the legislative branch. The governor sends messages to the legislature proposing new laws or changes in existing ones. In addition, every governor except North Carolina's has veto power.

Governors can also issue executive orders. An **executive order** is a rule issued by a governor that has the effect of law.

Commander in Chief. The governor is commander in chief of the state's unit of the National Guard. The governor can order the Guard out to help with such disasters as floods. Governors have also used the Guard to control riots and to keep order.

(bottom right) Aftermath of prison riot. (bottom left) Illinois' governor, James Thompson, and President Reagan at a political rally. (below) The State of Illinois Building in Chicago. The modern building is a workplace for 3,000 state employees as well as the governor. Which of the roles listed at left do you think are represented in the photos?

Political Party Leader. The governor usually is the head of a major political party in the state. As party leaders, governors support and campaign for party candidates. The governor also names key party supporters to some top-level state positions. If a state's United States senator dies or resigns, the governor must choose a party member to fill out the term.

Factors in a Governor's Decision Making

When governors make decisions, they must consider many factors. Among them are time, legal authority, other decision makers, and public opinion.

Time. Governors sometimes face such disasters as floods and such emergencies as prison riots. These demand fast action. A governor has life and death decisions to make, and quickly.

Decisions concerning new goals or changes in policies can be made more leisurely. For example, a new state tax plan presented to the legislature will have undergone months of careful consideration by the governor, the state tax collector, and budget officials.

Legal Authority. State constitutions set limits on the appointment and removal powers of governors. They also spell out procedures and rules a governor must follow. State legislatures pass laws concerning what a governor can or cannot do. And state courts further limit governors' powers.

The Constitution and federal laws also affect the power of a governor. He or she is also responsible for enforcing federal laws and the Constitution.

Other Decision Makers. Governors seek advice and support from many other officials. A governor will often consult with agency heads, state legislators, and leaders of his or her political party. He or she will meet with interest groups affected by a decision. Local and federal officials

Mississippi legislators conferring about an important piece of legislation proposed by their governor.

may need to be contacted in decisions affecting highways or pollution control, for example.

Personal Beliefs. No two governors agree exactly on what is best for their state. Some governors want to attract new industries and more people to their states. They believe in growth. Other governors may not want industrial growth or more people as much as they want a high quality of environment.

A few years ago the governor of one eastern state was able to limit the growth of industries and housing along the state's coastline. He said his state needed to preserve some of its natural beauty for future generations. The governor of a western state made a different choice. He urged the building of a huge hydroelectric plant near the state's most scenic parklands. The coal-burning plant would provide much needed jobs and income for the state.

Some governors favor state spending for the poor and needy. They strongly support programs in welfare, education, and health care. Other governors may believe the state government should not try to take on heavy spending programs. They may prefer instead low taxes, low-cost public service programs, and more government activity in creating a climate for business growth. Thus, personal beliefs are an important factor in a governor's decision making.

Public Opinion. Governors gain their position through election. So, before making decisions, they consider the public opinion factor. Governors who ignore public opinion may not be elected again to public office. And governors with strong public support stand a good chance of being able to carry out programs.

Section Review

Vocabulary:
executive order.

Reviewing the Main Ideas
1. What are a governor's leadership roles?
2. List and briefly explain the factors that can affect a governor's decision making.

Skill Building
1. Which two factors do you think are the most important in a governor's decision making? Give reasons for your answer.
2. Identify the governor's leadership role in each of the following examples:
a. The governor gave several speeches supporting members of her political party campaigning for the state legislature. She called on all party members to work together.
b. New York's governor greeted the Queen of England at the pier when the royal yacht docked. The queen began an official visit to New York City.
c. The governor asked the state legislature to approve his new tax program. It called for a state income tax and for cutting the sales tax on such items as food and medicines.

Section 3
State Agencies

A governor works with the many agencies that are a part of the executive branch. A **state agency** is a unit of government that provides a certain service. Agencies are called departments, boards, or commissions. For example, the Public Health Department in Illinois is a state agency that enforces laws concerning health and sanitation. Among its functions, the agency licenses and inspects nursing homes and hospitals, educates the public on health matters, and inspects restaurants and other food service businesses. Other agencies might include the Racing Commission, the Department of Children and Family Services, and the state Library Board.

Among the nearly three million people who work in agencies of the fifty state governments, only a few have top-level executive jobs. These administrators are called **bureaucrats** [byùr'ə krats]. Bureaucrats are government employees who supervise or carry out government regulations and programs.

Those who work at the top levels of decision making are usually appointed to their jobs. Some are chosen for certain skills. Others get their positions as a reward for supporting the elected official who named them.

As in the federal government, lower-level state employees often get their jobs through the civil service system. Thirty-three states have civil service. Most of the other seventeen states are moving toward some form of civil service or merit system. Under a civil service system, government employees are hired and promoted for their ability and length of service. Jobs are filled by people who score highest on tests. Pay is based on levels of employment. The people at higher levels earn higher salaries.

Factors in a State Agency Official's Decisions

State agency officials carry out laws. Frequently they interpret laws. The officials in a state environmental protection agency, for example, make rules about how much air or water pollution is acceptable. The state's antipollution laws guide the officials in making rules. State agencies also act like courts. They make

State agencies provide a variety of valuable services. One of them is administering nutrition programs for many nursing homes.

decisions to settle disputes about the enforcement of laws.

When state agency officials make decisions, they usually consider the same factors as governors do. Time, legal authority—other decision-makers, and public opinion.

Features of a Bureaucracy

State agency officials work in a **bureaucracy** [byù rok′ rəsē]. A bureaucracy is a collective term for government agencies. All bureaucracies in local, state, and federal government have these same things: (1) a chain of command, (2) formal rules to guide their actions, (3) a division of work, and (4) resources.

Chain of Command. A bureaucracy is organized into ranks or levels. The agency chief holds the top rank, and has the authority to direct those below that position. Department heads usually hold positions just below the agency chief. These leaders rank second in command. They have the authority to give orders to those lower in the organization, and so on down the line.

Conformity to Rules. The chain of command in a bureaucracy works according to written rules. There are rules for hiring and firing workers, for promoting people, for dealing with citizens, and for managing day-to-day business. Bureaucrats and other workers who do not go along with the rules might lose their jobs.

Division of Work. In a bureaucracy, work is divided into different depart-

ments. For example, a state department of agriculture deals only with matters related to farming. The state education agency handles educational services and problems.

Each agency hires experts. The department of health hires medical doctors and nurses. Agronomists, who are experts in farming, work for the state agricultural agency. Lawyers work in the office of the attorney general.

Resources. The resources available to reach a goal will influence state agencies' decisions. An agency cannot accomplish much without money, and without workers having knowledge and skills.

Holding back funds from a state agency *checks* it. When the governor and the legislature make up the budget, they can help or hurt an

Public Health Department workers.

State agency decisions are influenced by many different groups, including (above) citizens' groups and (above, right) the media.

agency by giving it more or less money. They often will reward an agency when its officials are doing things they approve. They can cut the funds of agencies doing things they disapprove.

Tips for Influencing State Agencies

Suppose the state insurance commission approved a 45 percent increase in car insurance rates for drivers under twenty-one. Many teenagers would think the state insurance commission's decision was unfair. When they took driver's education they were told that it would help them get less expensive auto insurance. What could they do? How can citizens influence the decisions of state agencies? Here are some ideas that can help citizens act effectively.

Approach the Agency. If you think you've been wronged, tell someone about it. Lower-level bureaucrats are normally quite available to citizens. If you're not happy with the response, move to higher levels of the agency. Try to contact the department chief at the highest level. (Your state publishes a directory, often called a "Blue Book," that lists all the state officers, legislators, agencies, and agency heads. Most public libraries carry it.) Teenage drivers could contact the head of the state insurance commission. Some top officials are easily approached. Others are almost impossible to see. But the citizen owes the agency at least the chance to hear a complaint directly.

Contact an Elected Official. Sometimes the agency or its staff is unable or unwilling to solve a problem, or the citizen still feels he or she is being treated unfairly. The next step is to write or telephone a state senator or representative. They usually will try to be of help if a complaint or problem really deserves a hearing.

Appeal to the Governor's Office.
Governors receive hundreds of letters from citizens with complaints or problems. Most appeals are given to staff aides, who then forward the letters to the proper agencies or officials. Sometimes agencies are quicker to act when the request comes by way of the governor's office.

Organize with Others. Citizens who share the same problem or complaint will be more effective if they work together. When a large number of citizens complain, public officials are more willing to listen. Citizens can also contact an interest group concerned with their kind of problem. The interest group may use its resources to help.

Use the Press. Citizens can contact the local newspaper or a television station. They can try to get a reporter interested in their problem. Some newspapers carry regular "hotline" or action columns that seek out such problems. Citizens may also write a letter to the editor with the facts of their problem.

Tell the Ombudsman. An **ombudsman** [om budz′mən] is a high government official with the power to investigate citizen complaints against public officials. The word *ombudsman* is Swedish. It means *grievance man*. Sweden appointed the first ombudsman in the world in 1809. In 1969, Hawaii became the first state to have an ombudsman. Since then other states have followed suit.

Five states have ombudsmen for their state penitentiary systems. The officials hear complaints from prisoners about prison guard treatment, food, and medical care.

North Carolina's Department of Transportation and Department of Human Resources each have an ombudsman. They can be called toll free from anywhere in the state.

Section Review

Vocabulary:
bureaucracy, bureaucrat, ombudsman, state agency.

Reviewing the Main Ideas
1. Explain the jobs of three agencies in your state.
2. Describe four factors that affect decision making in agencies.

Skill Building
1. Find information in Section 3 to support this statement: State agency officials cannot make simply any decision they wish.
2. The *Thorndike Barnhart Advanced Dictionary* gives the following as one definition of *bureaucracy:* "excessive insistence on rigid routine, resulting in delay in making decisions or in carrying out requests; red tape." How do the features of a bureaucracy help explain why this has come to be a meaning of the word?
3. Find the "Blue Book" discussed in this chapter at your local or school library. What are its call numbers? In which section of the library was it located? Summarize the types of information found in the book.

Case Study

Governor Dukakis's Roadblock

Governor Dukakis.

It was not exactly another Boston Tea Party, but the roar of anger that greeted the governor of Massachusetts's order could be heard all over the Bay State.

Governor Michael Dukakis had ordered a halt to some $57 million worth of highway projects. He called the proposed highway work a "waste of taxpayers' money."

The governor's order meant that the secretary of transportation and the commissioner of public works were not to apply for federal highway grants-in-aid, amounting to about $51 million. The governor said that the planned highway projects did not meet the real transportation needs of Massachusetts. Furthermore, he said, the projects would slow down traffic and cause tie-ups on many sections of the state's interstate system. And, he added, Massachusetts would have to put up $5 million of its own funds to get the federal money. He preferred to spend state money on mass transportation.

Reaction to the governor's decision was swift. "Massachusetts will lose 4,000 construction jobs," said the owner of one of the companies expecting to work on the projects. Another construction official predicted that 4,700 jobs would be lost.

"For a year and a half, the governor has been telling us he wants jobs and federal funds," said an official. "Now at his first opportunity, he puts thousands of construction workers out of jobs and gives away $50 million to other states!"

Labor union officials were also angry. One labor leader said that Massachusetts already had as many as a third of its construction workers unemployed.

In further explaining his refusal to take the federal money and continue the projects, Governor Dukakis said he believed that the projects might damage the state's environment. He also pointed out that he had a duty to see that state and federal tax dollars were "spent wisely and well."

Other state officials did not agree with the governor. One was Lieutenant Governor Thomas P. O'Neill III. Another was the commissioner for public works. He refused to answer any questions. He referred all calls to the governor's office. The transportation secretary was also silent. Environmental Affairs Secretary Evelyn Murphy said she had no objection to the highway projects. Even so, several environmental groups had protested against some of them.

Perhaps the most important opposition came in the Massachusetts legislature. Both Republican and Democratic leaders, in a rare show of unity, proposed a resolution asking the governor to reconsider. Republican leader Francis Hatch said of the governor's decision: "It was just one more example of a long list of things the governor has done to lose our confidence." The lawmakers approved the resolution by a 219 to 1 vote.

Construction on one of the highway projects approved by Governor Dukakis.

Most newspapers opposed the governor's decision. Said one editorial: "The governor's action . . . will not save the taxpayers here or anywhere else a dime. If Massachusetts fails to participate in the program, the federal government will simply give that $51 million to other states where it will be spent for the same purpose, whether or not it is spent 'wisely and well.'"

The angry public reaction and the state legislature's action were consequences Governor Dukakis had not expected when he made his decision. He held a press conference. Said Governor Dukakis, "I have concluded that the economic arguments to proceed with the program outweigh the dubious values of the projects themselves." He ordered the appropriate state agencies to get the federal money and complete the highway construction programs.

House leader McGee said: "I'm pleased with the governor's decision. It means money and jobs for our state. And we need both badly."

The leaders of construction companies scheduled to work on the projects were also happy. They thanked the governor for his decision. They promised to get started quickly on the work in order to provide new summer employment for workers.

Review

1. Draw a decision tree to show the alternatives and consequences involved in the governor's decision to stop the highway projects.
2. What goals moved the governor to halt the projects?
3. What caused the governor to change his mind about halting the projects?
4. Do you think the governor should have changed his mind? Why or why not?

Basic Social Studies Skills
Clarifying Public Issues

An issue is a dispute about a question. Should the state government pass a law to prevent construction of nuclear power plants? This question is an example of an issue. It is controversial. Many different groups and individuals disagree about how to respond to it.

There are at least two sides or positions to an issue. Some people, for example, might favor the use of nuclear energy. They would respond "yes" to the issue of whether or not to build nuclear power plants. People against the use of nuclear energy would be on the opposite side of this issue.

You cannot respond to an issue unless you clarify it. Stating an issue as a controversial question is the first step in clarifying it.

A second step in clarifying an issue is to define ambiguous or difficult words in a controversial question. For example, suppose you are faced with the issue of whether or not to prevent construction of nuclear power plants within your state. You cannot respond intelligently to this issue unless you know the meaning of key words, such as nuclear power plant. You need to define and understand the terms of an issue before you can deal with it.

A third step in clarifying an issue is to identify alternative positions or opinions about the controversy. Sometimes there are only two sides to an issue. If possible, you should try to identify several alternatives. By identifying more than two

reasonable options, you increase your chances of finding the best response to an issue.

Finally, you should know the difference between public and private issues. Public issues are controversies that may be settled by government decisions. They have consequences for many or all people living under the authority of a government.

Private issues are controversies within a family or group of friends. They involve only personal concerns that affect a few people, and the government does not become involved in settling them. For example, suppose your family is trying to decide where to take a vacation. There is a disagreement about whether to travel to a seaside resort or to camping grounds in a wilderness area. The controversy about the family vacation is a private issue. It is settled within the family.

Skill Practice

1. Can you state clearly a public issue having to do with one of the following items?
a. pollution
b. government spending
c. minimum wage laws
d. conservation of natural resources
2. Identify at least two sides or positions to the issue stated in response to question 1 above.
3. Identify and clarify at least one public issue in your weekly or daily newspaper.

Chapter 15 Review

Summary

Section 1: The State Executive Branch
The governor heads the executive branch of state government. Governors are elected directly by voters in their state. Governors in most states serve a four-year term and can run for re-election. Some governors are given more power by their state constitution than other governors. Other important executive officials are lieutenant governor, attorney general, secretary of state, state treasurer, state auditor, and chief school officer.

Section 2: The Governor's Job
Governors fill several leadership roles. These are ceremonial leader, executive leader, chief legislator, commander in chief, and political party leader. As executive leader, the governor works to carry out laws and manage the work of state agencies.

Section 3: State Agencies
State agencies are part of the executive branch. Agencies provide services such as enforcing health laws and inspecting buildings. Administrators in state agencies are called bureaucrats. State agencies have four organizational features in common: (1) a chain of command, (2) the use of rules in making decisions, (3) the division of work into different departments, and (4) the use of resources, such as money, to accomplish their job. There are numerous strategies citizens can use to influence state agency decisions. Among them are contacting ombudsmen, appealing to the governor, and using the press.

Vocabulary
Define the following terms.

1. lieutenant governor
2. executive order
3. secretary of state
4. state auditor
5. bureaucracy
6. ombudsman

Reviewing Main Ideas

1. When the governor travels across the state to make a speech urging the reelection of a certain state senator, he or she is acting in the role of
a. ceremonial leader.
b. executive leader.
c. chief legislator.
d. political party leader.

2. True or false: A state in which the voters elect most state agency heads has a stronger governor than one in which these people are appointed.

3. True or false: A chain of command is a feature of bureaucracies.

Thinking Critically

Finding Information
1. How can you find the name of the person who heads up a state agency, if you need to contact that person?
2. What state government office would you contact if you had information about serious crime taking place?
3. What state office would you go to to get information about the requirements for a driver's license?

Evaluating Information
In the case study, what seemed to be the main factor that changed the governor's mind? Do you think this should have been a main factor in the decision? Why or why not?

Communicating Ideas
The governor of your state has vetoed a bill removing food from state sales taxation. Write a letter to the editor of your newspaper explaining why you agree or disagree with the governor's action.

Chapter 16

State Courts and the Law

Introduction. Most people do not realize it, but most of the legal disputes that occur in this nation are settled by only twelve hundred state and local courts. These courts handle millions of cases each year. The news items below show some of the legal problems they deal with.

Castel Found Innocent—A criminal court jury today found Joe Castel innocent of the armed robbery of a Los Angeles jewelry store. Castel had claimed he was at a movie at the time of the robbery. After the decision, Castel's lawyer said, "The state never had enough evidence to prove Joe guilty."

Court Rules for Resort Owners—A state court today ordered the Drake Chemical Company to stop dumping chemical waste into nearby Moon Lake. The dispute began when resort owners on the lake sued the company. They claimed that if the dumping continued, the lake would be ruined and they would all lose their businesses.

State Supreme Court Overturns Suspension Case—The state supreme court ruled today that a lower court decision allowing teachers to suspend students without a hearing violated the state constitution. In other action, the court agreed to review a lower court decision that allowed state police to search a person's house without a warrant. Lawyers for the state say the case involves the Fourth Amendment to the United States Constitution.

The news flashes show that state courts handle cases such as Joe Castel's, in which a crime had taken place. State courts settle lawsuits between individuals, such as the dispute between the resort owners on Moon Lake and the chemical company. Some state courts review the meaning of the state constitution, as when the court declared teachers could not suspend students without a hearing. Finally, in handling cases, state courts may also have to interpret the federal Constitution. In this chapter you will learn more about state courts.

General trial court judge instructing jurors before the start of a civil case.

Section 1
Organization of State Courts

Each state constitution provides for a state court system. However, the state legislatures spell out the courts' actual organization.

Four Levels of Courts
All states have at least four kinds of courts: (1) lower or local courts, (2) general trial courts, (3) appellate courts, and (4) a state supreme court. The chart on page 317 shows how most state court systems are organized.

Lower Courts. The lower courts in most states hear only special cases. Usually these are minor violations of state law or lawsuits involving small amounts of money. Some of these courts hear only cases involving traffic violations and are called traffic courts.

General Trial Courts. The job of the general trial courts is to handle all major criminal and civil cases. **Criminal cases** always involve the government as one party to the dispute. The other party is an individual accused of a crime. In state courts, the criminal cases involve the breaking of state or local laws. The least serious crimes are called **misdemeanors.** Driving through a red light is a misdemeanor. More serious crimes are called **felonies.** Armed robbery and murder are felonies. Each state has a criminal code that determines the classifications

315

Judge listening to testimony at the Tioga County Courthouse in Wellsboro, Pennsylvania.

of, and punishments for, various crimes.

Civil cases involve disputes between people over their legal rights and duties. Civil cases often involve a dispute over property, money, or damages of some kind. For example, suppose you buy a bottle of soda pop. When you start to open it, the bottle explodes and injures your eye. You ask the soft-drink company to pay you $50,000 in damages. You claim the injury was their fault. They say it was your fault and refuse to pay anything. You go into court to try to collect from them. In other words, you sue them. This is a civil case.

Appellate Courts. These courts hear appeals from trial courts. Appeals are made when lawyers think the law was not correctly applied in the original trial, or if they believe illegal procedures were used. Suppose a judge would not allow an important witness to testify, and the accused person was found guilty. His or her lawyer might appeal the case hoping the apppeals court judge would agree that the witness's testimony was allowable.

State Supreme Court. This is the highest court in the state. It is made up of three to nine judges. The state supreme court reviews cases appealed from general trial courts and the appellate courts. Unless a case involves some aspect of the United States Constitution, there is no further appeal from the decision of a state supreme court. It is final.

State Courts Are Crowded

Even though many new courts have been set up over the years, cases move slowly. In big cities, people accused of crimes often must wait a year or more for their cases to be heard. In Massachusetts, a man charged with armed robbery was set free because the state had failed to try his case within the two-year limit the state constitution set.

Long delays have caused riots. One hot August about 4,500 prisoners in New York City's five largest jails rioted. The prisoners had many complaints. One of the most important was the long delay in city courts. Many of these prisoners were too poor to afford bail. They were in jail awaiting their trials. They had not been found guilty yet. Even so, most had been in jail about ninety days. Some had been waiting a year. One prisoner, charged with murder, had been waiting three years for a trial.

Why does it take so long? There are five reasons. First, a huge number of cases go through state courts. The Florida Supreme Court heard about 1,000 cases in a recent year. Florida circuit courts deal with almost 100,000 cases every year. Other trial courts in Florida handle over 400,000 cases in a typical year.

Second, often there are not enough judges. In New York City, for example, each judge may face as many as 200 serious criminal cases each day.

Third, most states do not spend enough money to hire enough clerks, secretaries, and other people to help judges do their work. In

Organization of State Courts

In the chart at left, which is the court of last resort?

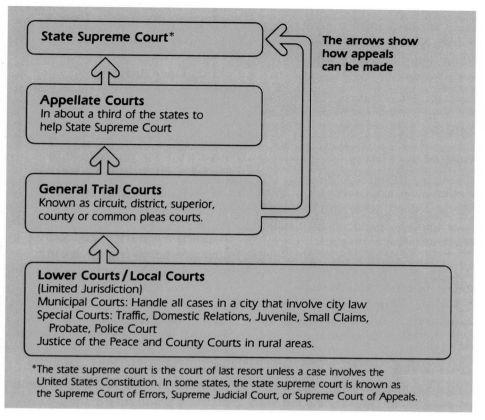

State Supreme Court*

The arrows show how appeals can be made

Appellate Courts
In about a third of the states to help State Supreme Court

General Trial Courts
Known as circuit, district, superior, county or common pleas courts.

Lower Courts / Local Courts
(Limited Jurisdiction)
Municipal Courts: Handle all cases in a city that involve city law
Special Courts: Traffic, Domestic Relations, Juvenile, Small Claims, Probate, Police Court
Justice of the Peace and County Courts in rural areas.

*The state supreme court is the court of last resort unless a case involves the United States Constitution. In some states, the state supreme court is known as the Supreme Court of Errors, Supreme Judicial Court, or Supreme Court of Appeals.

addition, many state courts have yet to adopt modern management practices to speed up justice.

Fourth, there are many steps to follow in legal cases. Many state court systems are not set up to help cases move smoothly and quickly. In some states the defendant is first brought before a judge to plead "guilty" or "not guilty." In another step, a trial date is set. The trial itself is another step. Defendants, lawyers, police and witnesses must return to court six to ten times before a case is completed.

Finally, delays are caused in many cases because the lawyers involved ask for a **continuance.** When a lawyer is not ready to defend a case, he or she goes into court and asks to have the trial date changed. Most judges allow a case to be continued once or twice. Many allow it to be delayed more often than that. Continuances give lawyers time to gather evidence and prepare a defense.

Small Claims Courts

Today every state has **small claims courts.** These were developed as one answer to overcrowding in other state courts. To ease the workload, small claims courts handle cases involving small amounts of money. No lawyers are needed. Suing someone is fairly simple in such courts.

Section Review

Vocabulary:
appellate court, civil case, continuance, criminal case, felony, general trial court, lower courts, misdemeanor, small claims court, state supreme court.

Reviewing the Main Ideas
1. Why are state courts so crowded?
2. In what ways are small claims courts different from other courts?

Skill Building
Prepare a chart similar to the one on page 317 for your state court system.

Section 2
Procedures in Criminal and Civil Cases

How do state courts handle criminal and civil cases? This section tells what actually happens in court.

Steps in a Criminal Case
Criminal cases begin with the arrest of a suspect. If the crime is a misdemeanor, the accused is simply brought before a judge. The judge listens to the evidence, decides whether the accused is guilty or innocent, and what penalty to hand out. If a felony is involved, there are many more steps.

Preliminary Hearing. Whenever the arrest takes place, the suspect must be brought before a judge as quickly as possible to hear why he or she is being held. The judge decides whether the person should be released or be "held to answer." At this time, bail may be required. Sometimes a person is released on his or her "own recognizance." This happens when the judge decides that a person is a good risk to return to court for the trial. He or she is released without bail.

Indictment. After the preliminary hearing, the **prosecutor** (prosecuting attorney) must bring a formal charge called an indictment [in dīt' mənt] against the accused. In some states, a **grand jury** of from six to twenty-three persons hears evidence and decides whether the person should be indicted.

Arraignment. After indictment, the accused comes before a judge. The charge is read and the judge asks, "guilty or not guilty?" This step is called the arraignment [ə rān' mənt]. If the person pleads guilty, the judge pronounces sentence.

Trial. If the accused pleads innocent, then the case goes to trial, usually before a **jury.** A jury is a group of citizens who hear evidence and decide guilt or innocence in a trial. Defense and prosecuting attorneys choose jurors from a large group of people. They try to avoid seating any juror who might be unfavorable to their side. Both lawyers can turn down a number of would-be jurors without explanation.

Once a jury is chosen, the prosecutor presents the case against the accused. Witnesses are called, sworn in, and questioned. They may be cross-examined by the other side. Next the defense presents its case. The attorneys for both sides then summarize their arguments before the judge and jury.

Before the jury determines the verdict, the judge instructs them in the proper legal procedures. Then the jury retires to reach a "guilty" or "not guilty" verdict. The vote must be unanimous. If a jury is unable to reach a decision, it is declared a **hung jury** and dismissed. Depending upon the wishes of the prosecutor, a new trial with new jurors may be scheduled.

Sentencing. If the verdict is guilty, the judge must decide on a sentence. Usually the law sets minimum and maximum penalties, and the judge chooses a sentence within that range. The judge may ask for special reports on the defendant's background before making a decision. The judge may also choose to suspend the sentence. This means the person does not have to pay any penalty. Usually a person who gets a suspended sentence has never been in trouble with the law before.

Plea Bargaining

Most criminal cases in state courts today do not go through all the

As this cartoon humorously suggests, witnesses to a crime do not always agree with the descriptions of accused criminals.

steps you have just read about. In fact, 90 percent of all criminal cases never come to trial. Instead, they are settled by **plea bargaining.** In plea bargaining, the prosecutor, the defense lawyer, and the police work out an agreement. In many courts, the judge is also part of the plea bargaining process.

How does it work? Sam Carver was charged with armed robbery. If Carver was found guilty, he could be sentenced up to twenty years in prison. The prosecutor had hundreds of cases to deal with. He thought the evidence showed that Carver was clearly guilty. To avoid the time and money involved in a trial, the prosecutor would agree to reduce the charge to unarmed robbery if Carver would agree to give up his right to a trial and plead guilty to this lesser charge. The lesser charge would carry a much lighter sentence.

Convicted criminal in jail cell.

People have widely differing views about plea bargaining. Here are the views of two people who are against it:

1. "In the United States, people are supposed to be considered innocent until proven guilty in a fair trial. Plea bargaining treats people as if they were already proven guilty. It encourages people to give up their right to a trial."

2. "It's not a good idea because it lets real criminals get off lightly. People who fully deserve to spend twenty years in jail are back on the streets inside a year. No wonder there's so much crime!"

Here are the views of two people who are for plea bargaining:

1. "The system works well. It gives the defendant a chance to save himself. It allows him to bargain with the court to get a fair break, even if he can't afford a fancy lawyer."

2. "Like it or not, plea bargaining is necessary. If every person charged with a crime were given a full-scale trial, we would need thousands more judges and courts."

The Supreme Court has ruled that plea bargaining is constitutional. That means states that want to do away with it must pass laws making it illegal. Chief Justice Warren Burger has said he believes that when done properly and fairly, plea bargaining is necessary and should be encouraged.

Steps in a Civil Case

Civil cases settle disputes between parties. Civil cases are known as **lawsuits.** In a lawsuit, one party believes it has suffered injury at the hands of the other. Lawsuits follow these steps.

Hiring a Lawyer. Lawsuits begin when a person hires a lawyer to file a suit. Lawyers may work for an hourly wage or a **contingency fee,** usually one-fifth to one-half of the total money won in the lawsuit. With a contingency fee, if no money is won, no fee is paid. The person suing is called the **plaintiff.** The person being sued is called the **defendant.** The plaintiff pays the costs of the suit, such as for investigators or for copies of interviews with witnesses.

Filing Charges. The plaintiff spells out his or her charges against the defendant in a complaint filed with the court. State courts handle most civil suits. Cases go to federal court only when an issue involving the Constitution is at stake or under other special circumstances. The complaint is delivered to the defendant who has from ten to sixty days to answer. Failure to answer means victory by default for the plaintiff.

Pretrial Discovery. Before a trial each side gathers testimony from the other. Lawyers for the plaintiff question the defendants and vice versa. Evidence such as documents or photos is gathered as each side prepares its case. The purpose of discovery is to uncover the facts of the case. This allows both parties to assess the strengths and weaknesses of their case. Discovery may take weeks, months, or in complex cases, even years.

Settlement Talks. The parties to a civil lawsuit can settle their dispute at any time before, or even during, a trial. A great many cases do not end in a trial. Going through a trial is costly and time-consuming. Often, during or after the discovery phase, both parties work out a deal.

For example, Alice Moy suffered a back injury after a traffic accident. She hired a lawyer. Her lawyer filed charges against the driver of the car that hit her and against his insurance company. Alice sued for $100,000 in damages. During the discovery phase, an exam proved Alice did have a back injury but doctors disagreed on its severity. After much bargaining, Alice's lawyer agreed not to go to trial if the insurance company paid Alice $10,000. The case was settled out of court.

Trial. If not settled beforehand, a lawsuit eventually gets to trial. Courts are so crowded with lawsuits that it may take up to four years for a case to come to trial. Civil trials are similar to criminal trials. A trial usually has between six and twelve jurors. The plaintiff presents his or her case and examines, or questions, the two parties and any witnesses. Then the defendant does the same. Both sides sum up their cases. The judge gives the jury instruction, and then the jury decides the verdict.

The Award. If the plaintiff wins, the jury awards damages. These may equal the amount the plaintiff asked for or be more or less. Once in a while, a judge may reduce a damage award if it appears the jury's award is out of line.

After all of these steps, the case may not be over. The loser may appeal to a higher court. Should the defendant refuse to pay damages, the plaintiff has to get a court order judgment. This will direct the police to seize and sell the defendant's property to pay the damages.

An Equity Suit

An **equity suit** is one type of lawsuit. In an equity suit, a plaintiff is trying to stop some action before suffering damages that would probably result from the action. The news story about the resort owners on Moon Lake at the beginning of the chapter told about an equity suit.

A judge makes the decision in equity cases. No jury is used. In the Moon Lake case, the lawyer for the resort owners tried to show that they would be harmed if the chemical company continued dumping. The company's lawyer tried to show that this was not true. The judge listened to the arguments and finally decided in favor of the owners.

The judge ordered the company to stop dumping waste into Moon Lake. This order is called an **injunction.** An injunction orders a person or a group to stop doing something that does or might do harm.

As the result of an equity suit, a court may order a person or group to *do* something. This order is called a **writ of mandamus.** For example, Mary, a good basketball player, wants to play on the high-school team. School rules do not allow girls on this team, so Mary goes to court to get a writ of mandamus that

Many equity suits involving the issue of whether girls should be allowed to try out for boys' sports teams have been filed in recent years.

forces the school authorities to let her try out for the team.

Section Review

Vocabulary:
arraignment, complaint, contingency fee, defendant, equity suit, hung jury, indictment, injunction, lawsuit, plaintiff, plea bargaining, preliminary hearing, prosecutor, writ of mandamus.

Reviewing Main Ideas
1. List and describe the steps in a criminal case.
2. List and describe the steps in a civil case.
3. How are equity suits and lawsuits alike? How are they different?

Skill Building
Write several well-constructed paragraphs giving your view of plea bargaining. Is it fair? How does it affect you and others?

Section 3
The Judge's Role

Judges are the heart of state court systems. Every day judges help to settle thousands of disputes across the country. They preside over most of the criminal trials. They settle most of the lawsuits between individuals. As part of their duties, judges also interpret their state constitution and the United States Constitution. When the legislature passes a law, it is the judges who may eventually say exactly what the law means.

Selection of Judges
In the early days of our nation, most judges were chosen by governors or legislatures. By the 1830s, however, there was growing concern that the people had no direct say in selecting judges. As a result, over the next several decades, most states changed to popular election of judges. Along with popular election came criticism that judges were being controlled by the political party machines that elected them. By the early 1900s some states began to experiment with merit systems for choosing judges. Today judges are selected in five different ways.

Five Methods of Selection. The table on page 323 shows the methods various states use to select judges.
1. *Partisan Election:* Judges run for office as candidates of a political party. People vote for judges just as for other public officials.
2. *Nonpartisan Election:* Judges run for office but not as the candidate of a political party. However, in several states, political parties will campaign for their favorite candidate.
3. *Selection by Legislature:* Judges are chosen by the state legislature.
4. *Appointment:* Judges are appointed by the governor, usually with consent of the state senate.
5. *Missouri Plan:* Judges are selected by merit. The plan was named after the state where it was first used in 1940.

Methods of Selecting State Supreme Court Judges

1 Partisan election	**2** Nonpartisan election	**3** Selection by legislature	**4** Appointment	**5** Missouri plan
Alabama	Florida	Connecticut	Arizona	Alaska
Arkansas	Idaho	Rhode Island	Delaware	California
Georgia	Kentucky	South	Hawaii	Colorado
Illinois	Louisiana	Carolina	Indiana	Iowa
Mississippi	Maryland	Vermont	Maine	Kansas
New Mexico	Michigan	Virginia	Maryland	Missouri
New York	Minnesota		Massachusetts	Nebraska
North	Montana		New	Oklahoma
Carolina	Nevada		Hampshire	Tennessee
Pennsylvania	North Dakota		New Jersey	Utah
Texas	Ohio			
West Virginia	Oregon			
	South Dakota			
	Washington			
	Wisconsin			

(above) Voters have the responsibility of electing judges in many states. (chart) Which method of selecting judges does your state use?

The Missouri Plan. This plan combines election and appointment to choose judges. Under the plan, a special committee nominates three candidates for judge. The committee is made up of three lawyers, three citizens appointed by the governor, and the chief justice of the state's highest court. The governor then appoints one of three candidates.

The newly appointed judge then serves for at least one year. At the next general election the judge's name is placed on the ballot. The voters are asked: "Shall judge X be retained in office? Yes _____ No _____."

If a majority vote "yes," the judge then serves a full term of office. If the voters vote "no," the governor must pick another name from those listed by the special committee. The entire process then starts over again.

Removal of Judges

Federal judges may hold office for life. State judges are elected or appointed for fixed terms. These terms vary. They may range from four to fourteen years. Once in office, judges have great power. Yet, there are several ways citizens can remove or discipline judges who abuse their powers. First, of course, judges may be defeated if they run for reelection. Second, some states make it possible to recall judges. Third, state constitutions provide means for impeaching judges. Impeachment is a long process and it is rarely used. However, judges, sometimes resign if they are faced with a serious threat of impeachment.

Because impeachment is so difficult to use, most states have created other procedures to review and discipline judges. Today, forty-seven states have a board, a commission, or a court to deal with complaints about judges. These commissions are usually made up of both lawyers and non-lawyers. They may also include other judges.

The commissions investigate charges of wrongdoing against judges and sometimes hold special hearings. They have the power to remove judges or to recommend their removal to the governor or the state supreme court.

Judges at Work

Trial-court judges fill three important roles. They serve as (1) administrators of their court, (2) umpires during a jury trial, and (3) final decision makers on key legal questions.

Administrator. Judges in most states are responsible for administering their own court. This involves two kinds of work. First, judges are in charge of court "housekeeping." They prepare their court's budget and appoint clerical assistants. They also make certain the court has the rooms and other facilities it needs.

Second, each judge controls the flow of cases through his or her court. This is an important responsibility. People evaluate a court and its judge by how well the court keeps up with cases brought to it. Long delays can be expensive and may interfere with justice.

Every case coming to a court is put on a **calendar.** The calendar lists cases in the order that they were filed with the court. Most courts have separate calendars for different types of cases. Divorce cases, for instance, might be listed on one calendar and personal injury cases on another.

Judges can control the flow of cases in several ways. First, they may regularly call up cases on their calendar. When a case is called, the attorneys must be prepared or the judge will dismiss the case. Second, judges may refuse to grant many delays or continuances in a case. Third, judges may limit how many cases one lawyer or law firm can handle at one time in their court. This stops delays caused by lawyers who have too many cases to handle at once.

Skillful judges also move civil cases along by encouraging the parties to settle before a trial. One judge explained: "I think that judges are problem solvers at a personal level. A judge must be active in trying to get lawyers to settle without waiting until the investment in a case is so great that the parties feel they must have a trial."

Umpire. The judge serves as legal umpire when a case goes to a jury trial. As the trial proceeds, the judge interprets and enforces the rules. The judge decides whether certain evidence can be used. The judge also gives instructions to the jury when all the evidence has been presented. This is a key phase in a trial.

When giving instructions, judges may tell the jury which issues should be ignored. They summarize the evidence for the jury. They rearrange the testimony to form a clearer story. Judges determine which legal rules apply to the case. They explain what the rules mean, and they tell the jury the range of decisions it may make in the case.

Judges recognize the importance of this role. As one judge put it: "Judges, unlike lawyers, are in a special position; they are under an obligation to do the right thing in every case, to determine, as best they can, the truth in a case and to apply the law."

Final Decision Maker. In trials without a jury, the judge alone makes the decision. Even in jury trials judges have great decision-making power. In criminal trials, the judge often decides what the punishment will be for those found guilty by the jury. In civil cases, judges have the final power to reduce the amount of damages awarded by a jury.

In appeals court, there is no jury at the hearing. A panel of judges alone makes the decision. Appeals-court judges work privately in their own offices, called **chambers.** They review the records of a case. Often there are **precedents**—legal decisions made in previous cases—and evidence supporting both sides of cases that come to the appeals court. The final outcome in such cases may depend on how the judge chooses to interpret the law or the constitution.

When judges use their legal decision-making powers, they often shape public policy. A judge ruled, for example, that a state insurance law must apply equally to men and women. The judge's decision not only settled the dispute. The decision also spelled out what the government's policy is toward such an issue.

Judge encouraging two lawyers to settle a case out of court. Many costly, time-consuming trials are averted in this manner.

Section Review

Vocabulary:
calendar, chambers, Missouri Plan, precedent.

Reviewing the Main Ideas
1. List and define five methods used to select judges.
2. How does the Missouri plan combine appointment and election?
3. Describe ways judges can be removed.
4. What are three roles judges fill?

Skill Building
1. Which of the three roles filled by judges do you think is most important? Why?
2. Study the chart on page 323. Do southern states favor one plan for selecting judges more than other plans? Explain your answer.
3. How does your state select judges?

325

Case Study

You Be the Jury

Joe Hill left his office for home. As he drove his car out of the parking lot, turning left onto Washington Street, another car collided with his. The other driver was Louise Milton.

Not long afterward, Joe developed back trouble. Ms. Milton's insurance company refused to pay the $100,000 damages Joe's lawyer demanded. It said the accident had been Joe's fault. As a result, Joe's lawyer filed a lawsuit against the company.

The trial opened about two years later before a judge and jury. Joe's lawyer first called Joe's doctor. The doctor testified that the accident had caused the back trouble. Joe's lawyer then questioned Joe:

Q. Will you describe the circumstances of the accident, Mr. Hill?

A. Well, it was raining. I was going home from work. I pulled up to the entrance to the parking lot at my office. I intended to turn left onto Washington Street.

Q. Did you clear yourself?

A. Both ways. There was a car approaching from the left. It had the right turn signal blinking. I assumed it would turn into the lot, so I pulled out. The car collided with mine.

On cross-examination Louise Milton's lawyer questioned Joe:

Q. Have you ever had the experience of a car not turning even though a signal was on?

A. Well, once or twice, I guess.

Q. But you still trust turn signals?

A. I certainly did in this case! They're supposed to indicate a driver's intentions.

She then questioned Louise Milton:

Q. Please explain the circumstances of the accident.

A. I turned right from Bush Road onto Washington to go east. I saw a car waiting at the parking lot entrance. As I approached, it suddenly pulled out and we collided.

Q. Did you apply your brakes?

A. Oh yes, but the distance was short and the road was wet.

Q. Was your right turn signal on?

A. No. I'm sure it was not.

Q. Had you used it when you made a right turn from Bush?

A. Yes. I always use signals when making turns.

Q. And the signal was in good working order?

A. Yes, it was.

Joe's attorney then cross-examined Louise:

Q. Have you ever had a turn signal on and not noticed it?

A. Well, yes. I guess everybody does that some time or other.

Q. Might that have happened on the occasion in question?

A. No. I'm sure not.

Q. Would you agree it was possible that the signal malfunctioned, and because of the weather and so on you didn't notice it was on?

A. Well . . . that could have happened, I suppose. But no, I don't think so.

Q. How fast were you going, Ms. Milton?

A. About twenty-five miles per hour.

Q. Did you check your speed?

Traffic Accident Map

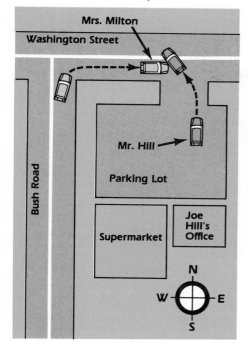

Mrs. Milton

Washington Street

Bush Road

Mr. Hill

Parking Lot

Supermarket

Joe Hill's Office

N
W —⊕— E
S

Exchanging insurance information after an auto accident.

A. I don't remember doing so. But I'm a cautious driver, and it was raining. I'm sure I was not over the speed limit.

Q. And did you try to avoid the accident?

A. Yes. I braked, but it was too late.

When the testimony was over, the judge instructed the jury as to the facts and the law. The judge said:

"You have heard conflicting testimony here as to the facts in the case. Your task is to decide just what the facts are.

"As to the law, this is a negligence case. *Negligence* is carelessness. It means not taking reasonable care to avoid an accident or to avoid causing harm. According to law, if negligence on the part of one party causes harm or injury to another,

the negligent party must make amends for the harm done. Mr. Hill claims that Ms. Milton's negligence caused him injury and he asks $100,000 damages as a result.

"You must decide. If you find that Ms. Milton was indeed negligent, then you must award damages to Mr. Hill. If, on the other hand, you find that Ms. Milton was not negligent, then you must deny the award of damages.

"Ladies and gentlemen of the jury, you may now retire to consider your verdict."

Review

Suppose you were a member of the jury. Consider the following questions:

1. How would you vote?

2. How did you arrive at your decision?

3. What role did the lawyers play in this case?

4. Was this a civil or a criminal case?

Basic Social Studies Skills
Reading a Diagram

A diagram can be used to clarify legal relationships in judicial decision making. The diagram on this page, for example, shows relationships at different levels of American government—national, state, and local. Look at the lines and arrows that connect the last three boxes in this diagram. They show relationships of courts within a state to the state constitution.

Lines and arrows show the flow of authority from the top to the bottom levels of this diagram. Boxes are used to indicate constitutions and courts at different levels of government.

Remember that the United States has a federal system of government. This means that power is divided and shared between the federal government and the state governments. The United States Constitution and federal government are supreme. However, certain powers and duties are reserved to the states. Thus, state courts are not controlled directly by federal courts. However, judicial decision making in state courts should not violate or go against the United States Constitution and laws and decisions made under it.

Levels of Judicial Decision Making

Constitution of the United States
The Supreme Law of the U.S.A.

United States Supreme Court
- Decisions should agree with the Constitution.
- Decisions apply to the entire nation.

Lower Federal Courts
- Decisions should agree with
  —the Constitution
  —standing decisions of the Supreme Court

Constitutions of Each State
- State constitutions should not contradict the Constitution of the United States.
- Each state constitution applies only to people within the state.

Courts Within Each State
- Decisions should agree with
  —The Constitution of the United States
  —Standing decisions of the federal courts
  —The state constitution
- State court decisions apply only to the state.

Local Courts Within Each State
- Decisions should agree with
  —The Constitution of the United States
  —Standing Decisions of the federal courts
  —The state constitution
  —Standing decisions of higher courts in the state

Skill Practice

Use the diagram on this page to answer the following questions.
1. What is the relationship of judicial decision making in state courts to the state constitution?
2. What is the relationship of judicial decision-making in state courts to the Constitution of the United States?

Chapter 16 Review

Summary

Section 1: Organization of State Courts

All states have at least four levels of courts. Lower, or local courts, hear special cases such as traffic violations. General trial courts deal with all major civil and criminal cases. Appellate courts hear appeals from trial courts. The state supreme court is the highest court. State courts today are very crowded and there are often long delays before cases come to trial.

Section 2: Procedures in Criminal and Civil Cases

Criminal and civil cases follow a series of steps. Criminal cases begin with the arrest of a suspect. Many criminal cases end before trial with plea bargaining. Civil cases begin when one person or group believes they have been injured by another. The injured party hires a lawyer to file a lawsuit. Many civil cases are also settled before they go to trial.

Section 3: The Judge's Role

Judges play a key role in the state court system. States use one of five methods to select judges. Once chosen, state and local judges serve for fixed terms. As administrators, judges manage their own court. As umpires, judges make sure trials follow certain procedures. As final legal decision makers, judges determine guilt or innocence as well as set sentences.

Vocabulary

Define the following terms.
1. felony
2. arraignment
3. plea bargaining
4. jury
5. defendant
6. indictment
7. misdemeanor

Reviewing Main Ideas

1. The four main types of state courts are lower courts, _____, appellate courts, and the state supreme court.
   a. tax courts
   b. general trial courts
   c. customs courts
   d. federal courts

2. State courts are overcrowded because:
   a. there are not enough judges
   b. states don't spend enough money on courts
   c. there are too many steps in bringing a case to trial
   d. all of the above

Thinking Critically

Evaluating Information

You are a member of a jury. The case is a civil case growing out of a two-car accident at a street intersection. Several people are called to testify on how the accident happened. Which person's or persons' testimony do you think would be most accurate? Which would be least accurate? Rank the persons on that basis from 1 to 6:
   a. policeman called to the scene
   b. drivers of the cars
   c. a person waiting to cross the street
   d. passengers in the cars
   e. a person who saw the accident from a block away
   f. a person who heard the crash and came out of a store to investigate

Communicating Ideas

Hold a class discussion to discover why members of the class assigned numbers above as they did.

Unit 5 Test

Vocabulary

Write *true* if the underlined word or phrase is used correctly. Write *false* if it is used incorrectly. Rephrase each false statement so that the underlined word or phrase is used correctly.

1. If state legislators want to be reelected they should listen to the views of their <u>constituents</u>.

2. The United States has a <u>unitary</u> government.

3. A governor can use <u>patronage</u> as a political resource.

4. The people in Oregon voted "no" to a state <u>sales tax</u>.

5. <u>Floor leaders</u> help keep order in state courtrooms.

6. In the governor's role of <u>political party leader</u>, the governor may work to get other members of the same party elected.

7. The state's <u>attorney general</u> is the "vice-president" of state government.

8. State agency officials are part of the bureaucratic <u>chain of command</u>.

9. If people in the state have trouble with the <u>bureaucracy</u>, they should elect someone else in the next election.

10. When a governor wants something done, he or she issues a special order called an <u>ombudsman</u>.

11. A <u>civil case</u> is when the crime is not very serious.

12. A <u>felony</u> is a serious crime.

13. If you want a court to make someone stop hurting you, you ask for an <u>injunction</u>.

14. <u>Plea bargaining</u> is a practical solution to overcrowding in state courts.

15. A person guilty of a <u>misdemeanor</u> who had never been in trouble with the law before might get a suspended sentence.

Recalling Information

1. State and federal governments share all of the following powers <u>except</u> power to _____.
a. tax
b. set up courts
c. control health care programs
d. admit new states

2. Which of the following powers do <u>not</u> belong to state governments?
a. establish a post office
b. establish police protection
c. provide for public health
d. control education

3. Which of the following services are provided by state government?
a. schools and grocery stores
b. police and firefighters
c. churches and recreation centers
d. all of the above

4. State legislators can pass laws that regulate all the following <u>except</u> _____.
a. jury duty
b. other states
c. highway speeds
d. gambling

5. State legislatures usually have all the following parts <u>except</u> _____.

a. a senate
b. a house of representatives
c. committees
d. courts

6. Which of the following influence the decisions a governor makes?
a. personal values
b. public opinion
c. other decision makers
d. all of the above

7. Which of the following is <u>not</u> a state agency?
a. board of health
b. district court
c. highway commission
d. state police department

8. Which of the following have to do with civil cases?
a. equity suits
b. injunction and writ of mandamus
c. felonies
d. indictment

9. True or false: Unlike the federal government, state governments do not attempt to regulate campaign financing.

10. State governments get money from _____.
a. the federal government
b. state taxes
c. license fees
d. all of the above

11. To spend state money, state legislatures must _____.
a. amend their constitutions
b. pass appropriations bills
c. issue executive orders
d. ask the national government

12. State legislatures can _____.
a. prosecute criminals
b. set up local governments
c. appoint ambassadors
d. none of the above

Skill Building

1. What are the four guidelines for using a small claims court?
2. Read the graph below to answer these questions:
a. What does the graph show?
b. In 1985, what did Illinois spend most of its money on?
c. True or false: In 1985, most of the state money went to public protection and justice.
d. Does the graph give information to help you judge if Illinois spent enough money on state courts?

Projected Illinois State Expenditures in 1985

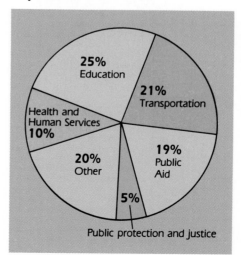

25% Education
21% Transportation
Health and Human Services 10%
20% Other
19% Public Aid
5%
Public protection and justice

Unit 6

Government in Our Communities

The governments that affect all of us the most are often the ones that are closest to home. Is it safe to walk outside after dark? Are there bad traffic snarls every day at five o'clock? Is there a safe place for small children to play outdoors? Can people find employment? Is the city wasting taxpayers' money fighting the county over who has the power to decide about park land? Is it cheaper to buy gasoline in the next county? Is it cheaper to live in another county? The answers to these questions lie in the decisions local government leaders make.

This unit explores the many different local governments we have in the fifty states. You will read what some of these governments are, how they are governed, what services they provide, and what problems they try to solve.

You will learn how local officials deal with state and national officials as well as with officials from nearby local governments.

Mayor Sharon Greene is a good example. Greene is the mayor of a medium-size city. Recently, the city began a project to build bike paths around the city. Mayor Greene worked with national government officials to obtain grants of money from the national government to help build the bike paths. She also worked with state government officials to get permission to build the bike paths next to some state roads. She also bargained with county government officials. County officials wanted some of the new bike paths to go to nearby parks operated by the county.

This unit also explores how local officials deal with problems facing the cities today. These problems include air and water pollution, crowded streets and highways, and poor housing.

Evanston, Illinois, city council in session.

Chapter 17

Local Governments

Introduction. About a half million people serve as elected officials in local governments. They perform many important services for citizens in cities, towns, counties, and townships across the nation.

Juan Hernandez has been a county sheriff for ten years. Last year, Sheriff Hernandez and six deputies handled 465 traffic violations, 90 cases of assault, 75 fishing and hunting violations, 69 robberies, and 15 drug violations. "In addition to crime, we deal with lots of other problems," says the sheriff. "This week," he adds with a smile, "we rounded up a bunch of cows that had gotten loose and were blocking the county highway."

Maria Vasquez is serving her second term on a city council. Recently, the city council had to decide where to build a new trash-burning plant. "Everyone agreed we needed the plant," she recalls, "but they didn't want it in *their* neighborhood. It was a tough decision."

In addition to elected officials, more than eight million people work for local governments in the United States. These people include clerks, secretaries, construction workers, administrators, and scientists.

Laura Jones, a city sanitation engineer, helps to plan garbage collection services. "And right now," she explains, "I am planning a collection center where people can bring paper, cans, and bottles to be recycled."

Tony Amatto is a doctor in a county health department. He wants all children in the county to have physical checkups and the shots that prevent diphtheria, polio, tetanus, and measles.

People such as those above bring the services of local government directly to citizens.

The purpose of this chapter is to introduce local government to you.

Local governments create many types of special districts to handle a wide variety of tasks. At left is a section of Chicago's Deep Tunnel, a $12.5 billion project run by the Metropolitan Sanitary District of Greater Chicago. Scheduled for completion sometime around the year 2000, the project has been termed the nation's most ambitious public works project ever. When it is completed, the city will have a 131-mile network of tunnels and reservoirs beneath its streets and rivers. Engineers hope the system will control overflow sewage that had been polluting Lake Michigan, the main source of drinking water for Chicagoans.

Section 1
Kinds of Local Governments

There are about 80,000 local governments in the United States. These include counties, townships and towns, cities and suburbs, special districts, and school districts. Illinois alone has 6,467 local governments. Pennsylvania has more than 5,000. Texas has more than 4,000.

Local governments are part of state government. They are created by the states to help them carry out laws and provide services. Local governments must operate according to state law. They can do only those jobs authorized by state law or the state constitution.

State government officials influence the decisions of local officials in several ways. They require reports from local governments. They give advice and technical help to local governments. They also issue orders and make rules for local governments. For example, the states can

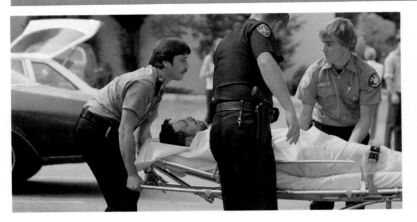

Local Governments in the United States

Government	Number
National	**1**
State	**50**
County	3,041
Cities & Suburbs	19,076
Townships & Towns	16,734
Special Districts	25,962
School Districts	14,851
Total	**79,715**

(above) Paramedics treating an accident victim. Many local governments provide their citizens with the services of highly trained paramedic teams. Sometimes, several communities will share the services and costs of paramedics. (above right) Which of the governments listed in the chart do you think affects you the most on a daily basis? Why?

order a local government to build a sewage-treatment plant. They appoint and remove certain local officials. They can withhold money from local governments if they do not obey state laws or meet state standards.

Local governments are also influenced by officials in the national government. More than one hundred federal agencies supply services to local governments.

The FBI, for example, works with city and county police officers. FBI agents will help local police identify handwriting, fingerprints, tire treads, hairs and fibers, and shoe prints.

What are the main types of local government? Chief units of local government are counties, townships, cities and towns, and special districts. The chart on this page shows how many local governments there are in the United States.

Counties

Each state is divided into parts called **counties.** In Alaska such units are called **boroughs.** Louisiana calls them **parishes.** The

number of counties ranges from three in Delaware and Hawaii to 254 in Texas. Connecticut and Rhode Island have counties but no organized county government. In the other New England states, the counties exist chiefly as court districts.

States set up counties to help carry out state law. In the early days, it made no sense to try to administer state law from the capital city. Also, from the start, Americans liked the idea of local control. They set up county courts with sheriff, prosecuting attorney, and judge to deal with people breaking state laws or having legal disputes. Other county officials took care of such state duties as issuing marriage licenses, keeping records of property deeds, and collecting taxes.

Over the years the states took on more and more activities. Often the states would direct the counties to handle the programs. Thus, aid to poor people might be handled by a county welfare department.

Townships

In twenty states, the counties are divided into **townships** to handle certain jobs. In horse-and-buggy days even the county seat was a great distance from many residents. Thus a township constable and a justice of the peace took care of small problems and everyday needs.

In some states today this unit of government is losing ground. Most of its jobs have been taken over by other local units, especially the county. But in other places, township government is very much alive.

Municipalities

Cities, towns, villages, and many suburbs are **municipalities.** This means they operate under a **municipal charter** granted by the state. The charter is a kind of constitution. It tells what form of government the community will have.

Why do states create municipalities when there are already counties (and sometimes townships) to provide public services? The answer is that where many people are crowded close together in an area, they need more services than rural people need. City residents often want extra police and fire protection, garbage collection, public water supply, sewage disposal, parks, playgrounds, libraries, and museums.

When a community reaches a certain size, state governments usually permit it to become a municipality. The city, town, suburb, or village can then make some laws for local use and provide services beyond those required by the state.

Special Districts

A fourth kind of local government is the **special district.** It is organized

State Special Service Districts

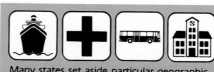

Many states set aside particular geographic areas in which they administer a single service. This list includes some of the most common districts.

Air Pollution Control	Parks
Alcohol Rehabilitation	Port Authority
Ambulance Service	Recreation
Animal Control	Sanitation
Fire Service	School
Flood Control	Sewer Service
Forest Preserve	Soil Conservation
Hospital	Street Lighting
Mental Health	Transportation Authority
Mosquito Abatement	Water Pollution Control
Noise Abatement	Water Supply

How do the special districts in your area compare to those listed in the chart at left?

to supply the people of a given area with one or a few special services.

The school district is a kind of special district. It usually has the same boundaries as some other local government: county, township, or city. In some places, one or more cities in the county each has its own school district, and the rest of the county makes up another school district. In another case, three or four townships may each have their own school district for operating elementary schools. But the townships set up a separate district to operate a consolidated high school.

Over the past twenty years, the number of school districts has dropped sharply because of school consolidations. But there has been a big rise in the number of other special districts. One reason is that within a special district, a service can be given only to an area that

337

needs and wants it. Another reason is that local units such as cities or counties can support a service jointly that would be too costly if each had its own department. A third reason is that state law often puts a limit on the amount a local government may tax and borrow. If a city or county is near this limit, people may ask the state to set up a special district to raise money and pay for some needed service.

Decision making for a special district is usually in the hands of a board of three to five members. They make policy, set the tax rate needed to support the service, borrow money, and hire people to run the program.

Section Review

Vocabulary:
borough, county, municipal charter, municipality, parish, special district, township.

Reviewing the Main Ideas
1. Give at least three ways that state government officials influence the decisions of local officials.
2. How are local governments affected by the national government?
3. What are four kinds of local governments?

Skill Building
1. Why does a state set up special districts to offer services?
2. How many local governments affect your daily life? Name them.
3. What county do you live in? What municipality do you live in?

Section 2
How County Governments Provide Services

Citizens get more services from local governments than from any other governing unit. This means that the government decisions that affect your daily life are most often made by people close by.

How are local government services provided and who make the decisions? First, we will look at local government in action by visiting a typical county. Second, we will see how local governments are facing the problem of providing services in growing urban areas.

A Visit to Franklin County
Half the states in the nation have a county named after Benjamin Franklin. Franklin is a very popular name for a county. The largest Franklin County is in Ohio. It has more than 900,000 people living in it. Nebraska's Franklin County is the smallest, with 4,500 people. Most have a population between 10,000 and 40,000—a typical size for American counties. Farming is likely to be a chief source of income in many of the Franklin counties.

State law says what officials a county shall have and what their powers and duties are. The Franklin County we will visit is governed by a board of commissioners. The board's five members are elected by voters in the county. In some counties, the governing board is called a board of supervisors.

The Board of Commissioners. The Franklin County board acts as a legislative and an executive body. As a legislative body, the board levies taxes, votes how money will be spent, and borrows money—all subject to state limits. Some states let counties pass local laws, called **ordinances.** For example, a board might pass ordinances about waste disposal, land use, or public health. The board may also have power to issue licenses for such things as drive-in movies, eating places, and junkyards.

As an executive body, the county board sees that various state and county programs are put into effect. In most cases, the board has the power to appoint certain other county officials and to hire county workers.

During a regular Franklin County board meeting, the members may spend some time going over next year's budget. They might hear a report on plans for the upcoming county fair. At tonight's meeting they appoint a new member to the Board of Health. They approve plans for building an addition to the county nursing home, and they act on requests for road repair.

In most counties, the voters also select six to twelve other county officers. Let's tour the Franklin County Court House and see how some of them bring services to the citizens of the county.

County Judge. Judge Sheila Mc-Nabb is winding up a divorce case. This week she has handled three other civil cases. Friday she'll preside at a trial of three persons charged with auto theft. In addition to handling adult criminal cases, McNabb is judge of the juvenile court. A larger county might have a separate person holding this office. In a juvenile court, young offenders get special treatment different from a formal criminal trial.

Prosecuting Attorney. The office of Prosecutor Wayne Bender is next to the judge's chambers. Bender brings formal charges against persons accused of crimes. In court, he presents evidence against such persons.

Bender is also county attorney, which is a separate job in some counties. He gives legal advice to other county officials. He also represents the county whenever it is involved in a court case.

Sheriff. Sheriff Juan Hernandez and his deputies are the county police force. They patrol areas not covered by city police. The sheriff is in charge of the county jail. Hernandez is also an officer of the court. He delivers court orders. For instance, recently the Brown Hotel won an injunction from the county court. The court ordered the Hanson Construction Company to stop drilling in the lot next door after ten at night. Hernandez delivered the injunction to Mr. Hanson and got his signature on a receipt.

Coroner. From time to time Dr. Elaine Lydon, the county coroner, gets a call to investigate a death if the cause is unknown or foul play is suspected. Lydon works closely with Bender to get the facts on murders and suicides. Then she presents the

View of Wrigley Field, the home of the Chicago Cubs baseball team. City and state ordinances banning the use of lights at the stadium have been the subject of much controversy in recent years. The owners of the team want the ban lifted. They believe playing night games would make more money for the team. People who live in the Wrigley Field neighborhood want the ordinances to stand. They claim the lights and traffic would seriously disrupt the neighborhood.

evidence before a jury to get a decision about the cause of death—murder, suicide, or death by natural causes. In some states this job is done by an appointed medical examiner or the prosecuting attorney.

Treasurer, Auditor, and Assessor. As we go to Treasurer Edgar Cash's office, we see a few people in line to pay their property tax bills. He deposits county income in selected banks and writes checks when money is to be paid out. Before writing any checks, he must have auditor Charles King's approval. To protect against misuse of public money, the auditor examines and approves all claims for payment. About a third of the states have county auditors.

Assessor Jim Todd's job is to keep track of the value of all property on which property taxes are levied. His office prepares tax bills.

Clerk and Recorder. As county clerk, Kim Okawa holds one of the top jobs in Franklin County. She is clerk of the county court, keeping all court records. She also serves as secretary for the county board. Clerk Okawa is also chief election officer in charge of registering voters, printing and distributing ballots, and setting up polling places. In addition, she issues various licenses and keeps records of births, deaths, marriages, and divorces.

County Recorder Martha Alexander keeps public records of the sale and transfer of real estate. In some states her title would be Register of Deeds.

Appointed Boards and Officials. Other officials in Franklin County

(below) Coroners sometimes are thrust into the national spotlight. Such was the case when several coroners were called in to investigate the sudden death of Swale in 1984. Swale had won the Belmont Stakes, a major horse race, only eight days prior to his death. He had also won the Kentucky Derby. The coroners did not find any evidence of foul play. (below, center) A couple receiving a marriage license from a Register of Deeds.

MARRIAGE LICENSE

are not elected. They get their jobs through the state civil service system or are appointed by the governor, state legislature, or state agency heads. The head of the county board of health and the superintendent of the county highway department are two examples.

In some places an official county surveyor conducts land surveys and determines boundary lines. A county engineer may supervise the building of roads and bridges. In Franklin County, the commissioners simply hire experts for these jobs on a part-time basis.

Like most counties, Franklin County has a county agricultural agent and a home demonstration agent. These agents, who are employees of the federal-state Agricultural Extension Service, give advice and support to farmers and

organizations such as the 4-H Club. The 4-H Club teaches agriculture, home economics, community service, and personality development to young people in rural areas.

Providing Services in Urban Counties

Seven out of every ten Americans today live in an **urban area.** The Census Bureau calls cities, suburbs, and all other towns with a population of 2,500 or more urban areas.

People have moved steadily from rural to urban areas. This has meant the growth of urban areas in counties which used to be mostly rural. For example, Howard County, Maryland, had a 70 percent increase in population over a ten-year period. Johnson County, Iowa, had a large, but more typical, 34 percent increase in population.

The urban areas in some counties have expanded to the county boundaries. Many urban areas spill over into two or three counties. Kansas City lies in two states—Missouri and Kansas. The urban area around New York City spreads from the state of New York to parts of New Jersey and Connecticut.

Urban growth has made it hard for some local governments to provide services effectively. Within one urban area there may be one large city, several suburbs, and parts of two counties, each with its own local government. The entire area, tied together with a network of roads and commuter trains, has the same needs for government services. There can be waste and inefficiency when too many local government units are trying to do the same things.

One answer to the problems of urban counties has been for several communities to cooperate in setting up a special district for one service or another. However, some people believe that special districts merely add to the confusion. They urge **consolidation** to solve the problem of too many local governments in urban counties.

City-County Consolidation. When governments consolidate, they put their different departments together and become just one government. Since 1947, about twenty-five mergers have taken place. Usually these mergers are brought about by voters in a public referendum. Some examples are the city of Jacksonville and Duvall County, Florida; the city of Indianapolis and Marion County, Indiana; the city of San Francisco and San Francisco County; the city of Nashville and Davidson County, Tennessee; and the city of Lexington and Fayette County, Kentucky.

Merging Services. City-county consolidation never totally merges all small units of government into one regional, county-wide system. Rather, only certain services are merged and others remain separate. In Indiana, for example, consolidation of Indianapolis and Marion County created one unit of local government called UNIGOV. UNIGOV provides services such as county-wide health care. However, the city and county school systems, as well as the police and sheriff's departments, remain separate.

Buying Services. Another way to end overlapping is for one unit of government to contract with another to buy a certain service. For example, suburbs may ask the city to provide fire protection. A contract will be made to pay the city for fire protection. Since 1954, Los Angeles County has provided various services to communities by contract.

Section Review

Vocabulary:
consolidation, ordinance, urban area.

Reviewing the Main Ideas
1. What official would handle each of the following matters in Franklin County?
a. a complaint about a tax bill
b. an application for a marriage license
c. paying a bill for painting the courthouse
d. deciding what to do with three youths who admit to vandalism
e. investigating the death of a body found in the woods
2. What kinds of government problems are caused by urban growth?

Skill Building
1. Name three services that city and county governments might merge to provide.
2. Name three services one government might buy from another.

Section 3
Paying for Local Government

The services provided by local governments cost a lot of money. In a recent year, local governments spent more than $113 billion. Where does the money come from?

Local governments get most money from the **property tax.** They also get money from the national and state governments, and from non-tax sources such as parking meters and vehicle stickers.

With few exceptions, local governments have no power to tax on their own. If a city finds its property tax does not bring in enough money, city council members cannot decide to put a tax on liquor sold in the city or to have a city income tax. They must ask the state legislature to let them add a tax.

Property Taxes

About 84 percent of all local tax revenue comes from the property tax. This is a tax on the value of the property a person or business owns. The usual items on which people pay property tax are land, houses, and other buildings. In some states, people also pay a property tax on such things as cars and boats.

The property tax is usually paid to the county treasurer and then given to the various units of local governments. Property owners pay the property tax directly. Others pay it indirectly. Renters pay it as part of the rent, and businesses pass on the cost of property taxes in the prices they charge to customers.

Other Taxes

The need for more money has led local governments to look for new ways to get money beyond the property tax. States have allowed large

COOK COUNTY COLLECTOR				**REAL ESTATE TAX BILL**	
118 N. CLARK STREET CHICAGO,ILLINOIS 60602					
1500 MAYBROOK SQUARE MAYWOOD,ILLINOIS 60153				HOURS 9AM TO 5PM MONDAY THRU FRIDAY	
VOLUME 105	PERMANENT REAL ESTATE INDEX NUMBER		05-31-112-018-0000	TOWN 23005 NEW TRIER	
1981 TAX RATE	1981 AMOUNT OF TAX	1982 TAX RATE	1982 AMOUNT OF TAX	TAXING AGENCIES	
2.664	463.86	2.627	478.80	SCH DISTRICT 37	
				NORTH SUBURBAN MASS TRANSIT DIST	
.852	148.35	.860	156.74	VILLAGE OF GLENVIEW	
.343	59.72	.357	65.07	GLENVIEW PARK DISTRICT	
.213	37.09	.213	38.82	OAKTON COMMUNITY CLG DIST 535	
2.801	487.71	2.907	529.83	NEW TRIER TOWNSHIP HIGH SCHOOL 203	
.010	1.74	.010	1.82	NORTH SHORE MOSQUITO ABATEMENT DISTRICT	
.643	111.96	.664	121.02	METROPOLITAN SANITARY DIST OF GREATER CHGC	
.002	.35	.007	1.28	GENERAL ASSISTANCE NEW TRIER	
				ROAD AND BRIDGE NEW TRIER	
.057	9.92	.053	9.66	TOWN NEW TRIER	
.038	6.62			CONSOLIDATED ELECTIONS	
.013	2.26	.012	2.19	SUBURBAN T B SANITARIUM	
.107	18.63	.117	21.32	FOREST PRESERVE DISTRICT OF COOK COUNTY	
.379	66.00	.470	85.66	COUNTY OF COOK	
.324	56.41	.350	63.79	COOK COUNTY HEALTH FACILITIES	
8.446	1,470.62	8.647	1,576.00	TOTAL TAX	

Analyze the real estate tax bill at left. What were the two costliest services this taxpayer paid for?

cities to tax all kinds of things. If you take a look at a phone bill or bill for gas or electricity, you are likely to see a charge for taxes. This kind of tax is a utility tax. Some cities have city sales taxes—another percent or so on top of the state sales tax. Cities often tax visitors and tourists. New York and Atlantic City, for example, have a hotel room tax. And Mount Clemens, Michigan, a resort center, taxes every mineral bath taken within the city limits. Some cities, such as Detroit, have local income taxes.

State and National Money

State governments prefer to pass money on to local governments rather than letting them create their own taxes. States give money to local governments through **grants** and **shared taxes.** A grant is a direct payment from the state to the local government. Shared taxes means the state creates and collects a tax. Then the state shares part of the revenue from that tax with local governments in the state. The amount each local government gets depends on how much tax is collected. State taxes on gasoline, automobiles, liquor, and income are most often shared with local governments.

Local governments also get money directly from the national government. The amount of national government aid to local governments varies from year to year. In one recent year, the national government gave more than $11 billion directly to local governments. In other years, it gave much less.

Money from the national government comes from the federal

Many of the dams around the nation were built with the help of federal funds.

income tax paid by citizens and businesses. In the national budget, the money given to local governments is called **revenue sharing** and **grants-in-aid.** Grants are usually given for a specific job, like building a health clinic, that national government decision makers think is important. Grants have become one way these officials influence the decisions of local government leaders.

For example, suppose the national government wants to build low-cost housing for poor families. The national Department of Housing and Urban Development (HUD) will offer grants to local governments to do the job. Local decision makers may not think the project is a high priority, but they will do the job because the national government is putting up all or most of the money.

Other Sources

Local governments have several other ways to raise small amounts of money. Cities and counties earn money from licenses and fines. They charge a small amount for marriage licenses, building permits, and traffic tickets. In many counties, lawyers, doctors, plumbers, morticians, and others have to buy a license to work in the county.

Local governments also borrow money by selling **bonds.** A bond is a certificate stating that the government has borrowed a certain amount of money from the owner of the bond. Bonds are used to raise money for special projects like building a bridge or a school. When people buy bonds, the local government gets the money it needs right

away. In return, the government promises to repay the full amount it borrowed plus interest by a certain date.

Some cities and counties also issue **service charges.** Individuals or businesses may get separate bills for water supply, garbage collection, street lighting, snow removal, weed cutting, schoolbook rental, and other services. Local governments often use service charges to avoid raising taxes.

Section Review

Vocabulary:
bond, grant, grants-in-aid, property tax, revenue sharing, service charge, shared tax.

Reviewing the Main Ideas
1. What is the largest source of money for local governments?
2. How do state governments help support local governments?
3. How does the national government help pay for local services?

Skill Building
1. If your community needed more money to give people the services and protection they want, how would you suggest the money be raised?
2. How would your answer affect yourself?
3. How is your answer fair?
4. How is it a practical solution?
5. Study your family's gas, telephone, or electric bill. How much was the utility tax?

345

Voting on Taxes for Local Government

Case Study

Californians, like most other citizens, support their local governments with property taxes. In the late 1970s, the property tax became a major political issue for voters in California.

Discontent with property taxes developed when the value of land and houses went up rapidly. Within the space of a few years many Californians found their homes nearly doubling in value. Because the amount of property tax is a percentage of a house's value, this caused property taxes to go up a great deal. During the same time, however, most peoples' income did not rise nearly enough to help pay the new taxes.

As a result, large numbers of Californians began to support a campaign to lower property taxes. The campaign was led by Howard Jarvis, a long-time foe of property taxes. Jarvis's group, the United Organization of Taxpayers, got 1.4 million people to sign petitions putting a special issue on the ballot in the next election. The Jarvis initiative, called Proposition 13 on the June, 1978 ballot, would roll the taxable value of business and residential property back to the 1975-1976 valuation of the property by each county's assessor. It would then limit property taxes to one percent of that taxable value. Property could be revaluated by county assessors, however, when it changed ownership, and newly constructed property would be valuated upon completion of the construction. If it won, this proposal would cut property taxes by nearly 60 percent in California.

Support for Proposition 13 came from apartment owners, homeowners, and real estate groups. They argued, "It's time we cut back on property taxes." Many believed taxes could be cut and there would still be enough money for important government services. They thought that government officials should look for ways to cut out waste and increase efficiency.

Opposition to Proposition 13 came from educational leaders, teachers, labor unions, renters—especially those who planned to purchase homes after the new law would go into effect—and many state and local government officials. Local officials realized taxes were high, but they argued that the cost of local government was going up. Trucks and gasoline cost more. New buildings and parks were more costly to build. Plus, many citizens were asking for better services or new ones—better mental health care, a new sports center. Proposition 13 would mean an enormous cut in revenue provided by the property tax. Where was the money for government services going to come from?

The mayor of San Francisco was clearly worried. "Our police, our fire department, and our schools would be crippled," he said. In Berkeley, the city manager said he might have to lay off seventy-six police officers

★ ★

and fifty firefighters. In Oakland, Alameda County officials warned they could lose $115 million in revenues. And school district officials were telling teachers across the state that many could lose their jobs.

In response to such concerns, the state legislature came up with an alternative. It passed a bill cutting property taxes on homes and apartments by 30 percent. However, this new law would only go into effect if Proposition 13 were turned down by the voters. The governor signed the bill.

The state legislature's bill would not save homeowners as much money as Proposition 13. But the state's plan would leave more money for local governments. However, the legislature's bill was apparently too little too late.

California voters passed Proposition 13 by a two to one margin. In states across the nation political leaders viewed the California vote as a general "taxpayers' revolt" and a demand for lower taxes. They began to look for ways to cut the costs of government and prevent taxpayers' revolts in their own states. In the year following Proposition 13, about forty-five states made some reductions in their taxes.

In California, state and local officials began to cut expenses and services. As it turned out, the immediate effects of Proposition 13 were not as harsh as some opponents of the initiative had predicted. Over the years the state government had accumulated a $5 billion surplus. The state began using that money to maintain vital services.

Despite the additional state funds, however, many local governments in California have been forced to raise various fees for services to make up for the lost property tax revenues. Many local services, such as special summer school programs, library hours, and park maintenance, have been cut.

Review

1. What caused California homeowners to put Proposition 13 on the ballot?
2. What alternatives for tax relief did California voters have?
3. What was the voters' decision?
4. Do you think they made a wise choice? Explain your answer.

Howard Jarvis celebrating the passage of Proposition 13.

Look at the organization chart on this page. It uses lines and arrows to show the sources and flow of authority in a typical county government.

Units of the county government are connected by horizontal and vertical lines to show their level of responsibility or authority. Horizontal lines connect units on the same level or row of the chart. Vertical lines connect the higher and lower levels or rows of county government units. Units on the top row have more authority and responsibility than those on the bottom row.

Each unit of county government on the top level has distinct powers and duties. The County Board, however, is shown to have the broadest duties and powers. All units on the second row of the chart are either appointed or administered by the County Board.

Skill Practice

1. Which officials of this county government are elected by the voters?
2. Which unit of county government has more authority and responsibility, the Board of Commissioners or the Zoning Commission?

Organization of County Government

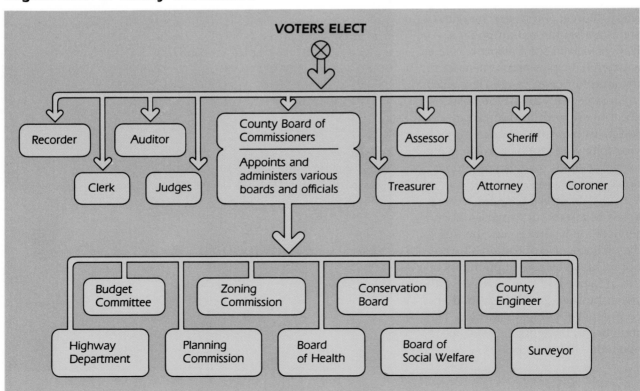

VOTERS ELECT

Recorder | Auditor | County Board of Commissioners — Appoints and administers various boards and officials | Assessor | Sheriff

Clerk | Judges | Treasurer | Attorney | Coroner

Budget Committee | Zoning Commission | Conservation Board | County Engineer

Highway Department | Planning Commission | Board of Health | Board of Social Welfare | Surveyor

Chapter 17 Review

Summary

Section 1: Kinds of Local Governments

Local governments are created by state governments to carry out laws and provide special services. The county is a basic unit of local government. Counties in some states are divided into townships. Municipalities, which include cities, towns, villages, and many suburbs, are other key units of local government. In addition, special districts supply special services such as fire protection to specific areas.

Section 2: How County Governments Provide Services

County officials deliver government services to the people. A typical county is governed by a board of commissioners, or supervisors, elected by voters in the county. The county judge may handle both criminal and civil cases. The county prosecutor brings charges against people accused of crimes. The county sheriff enforces laws within the county. Other officials may include a coroner, a treasurer, and a county clerk. In some growing urban areas, city and county governments have merged to provide better services.

Section 3: Paying for Local Government

Local governments have several sources of income. The property tax is the most important. This is a tax on the value of property a person or business owns. Local governments must gain permission from the state legislature to create additional taxes. Today, most local governments tax many different things including telephone, gas, and electric services. Local governments also receive a good deal of money from state governments and the national government.

Vocabulary

Define the following terms.

1. borough
2. municipal charter
3. parish
4. special district

Reviewing Main Ideas

1. True or false: The main role of local government is to help state government by enforcing laws and providing services.
2. True or false: The only rules a local government has to follow are the ones it sets up for itself in its constitution.
3. The major source of money for local governments is the _____.
   a. federal government
   b. state government
   c. property tax
   d. fees for drivers' licenses

Thinking Critically

Comprehending Information

1. Look at the property tax bill on page 343. What services are paid for in part by this property tax?
2. Which community service receives the largest amount of this property tax?
3. Are there any services shown here you think should *not* be paid for out of property taxes? Explain your answer.

Organizing Information

Make a diagram to show how local, state, and national governments are related to each other.

Evaluating Information

1. If you read that your community was trying to get state approval to add a one-half percent sales tax, what would you think? How would such a tax affect you?
2. What in your opinion would be the best way for local governments to get money to provide needed services? Explain your answer.

Chapter 18

City Government

Introduction. The people on Myrtle Avenue in Chicago could not agree. Martin Sosin spoke for many when he said, "I want the tree down." Tom Bowler spoke for others when he said, "I've fought for five years to keep that tree."

The cause of this disagreement among neighbors was a giant cottonwood that stood at the edge of an alley. It was more than 135 years old, and the largest tree in the northwest part of the city. Experts said it was healthy and had historical value.

The people on Myrtle Avenue had paid a special fee to have the dirt alley behind their houses paved. The city planned to cut the tree down before paving the alley so its growing roots would not crack the new pavement. Many wanted to keep the old giant. Some wondered who would pay for the tree's removal if it died later.

The giant cottonwood created a situation which required a decision by Alderman Roman Pucinski [pü-chin'skē], who represented the Myrtle Avenue area in the Chicago City Council. After considering the alternatives, Pucinski said, "We're going to save the tree." His choice was influenced by the experts who said the tree was healthy.

The mayor and commissioner of streets agreed. They canceled the order to cut down the tree. They said the city would pay for its removal if the tree later died. Nearly everybody was satisfied with the decision.

The daily lives of most citizens are affected by decisions of city government officials like those you have just read about.

There are about eighteen thousand towns and cities in the United States. Three out of every four Americans live in a city or town. In this chapter you will learn more about city government.

The mayor of Los Angeles, Tom Bradley, at opening ceremonies of the 1984 Summer Olympics. The position of mayor often requires the performance of ceremonial duties.

Section 1
Plans for City Government

Cities are not mentioned in the United States Constitution. They are created by state governments. They have only those powers given them by their states. The city or municipal charter granted by the state is the authority for a community to have its own government. No two cities are the same, but most use one of the following plans for government.

Mayor-Council Plan

The diagram on this page shows the **mayor-council plan** for government used by 51 percent of all American cities. All cities with populations over 1 million use this plan.

The **mayor** is the main executive official, and is elected by the citizens of the city. The mayor has the duty of enforcing and carrying out laws.

The **council** is the legislative branch of the government. The city is divided into wards, or districts, and each is represented in the council by one member. Council

Mayor-Council Plan

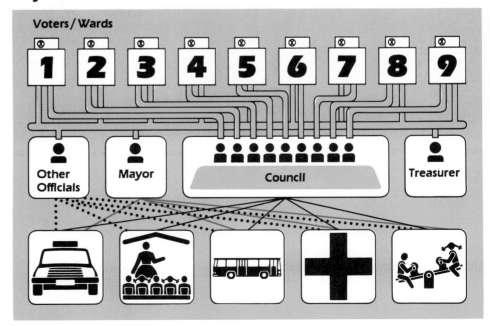

members are called councilors, councilmen, aldermen, or supervisors. The council makes ordinances for the city by majority vote. In most states, the mayor can veto bills passed by the council. Often the council can override the mayor's veto with a two-thirds majority.

In the mayor-council plan, the voters elect a treasurer and other executive officials such as a clerk and a city attorney. The mayor and other executive officials appoint the heads of the city departments that provide city services—the police department, the fire department, the department of sanitation, the department of public health, and others.

Council-Manager Plan

About 43 percent of American cities use the **council-manager plan** shown in the diagram on this page. The voters elect a council whose presiding officer is often called "mayor." The council hires (and can fire) a **manager,** who appoints the other executive officials.

The council's job is to make rules and set goals. The manager's job is to carry out the rules and conduct the day-to-day business of the city. The manager hires the heads of the various city departments. The manager is responsible to the council, and the heads of the city departments are responsible to the manager.

The council-manager form of government was first used in the early 1900s. It was created because many city government officials had

Council-Manager Plan

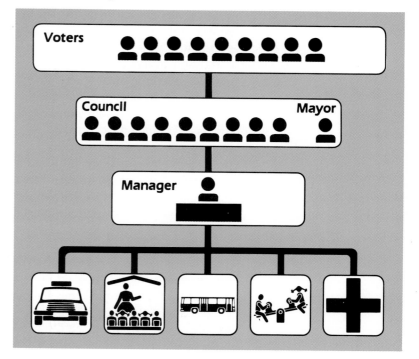

Commission Plan

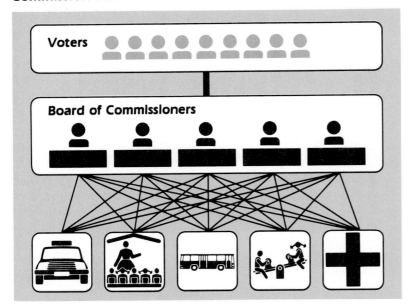

What are the city departments shown in the chart? Who heads them?

become dishonest, and citizens were not getting the services they wanted. People wanted city government taken out of the hands of corrupt political leaders and run instead by people trained in the skills of management. It was thought that a city could be run like a business. Many people called for putting city government on a "businesslike" basis.

More and more cities and towns have turned to council-manager government in recent years. Some twenty-eight hundred cities now have city managers. Most rapidly growing cities in the South and Southwest have such a plan.

Commission Plan

The diagram on this page shows the **commission plan.** It is used by only about 6 percent of cities in the United States. The commission is usually a body of five elected officials who make local laws. Each

commissioner also heads a city department. A mayor is elected from among the commissioners.

Cities have moved away from the commission plan because often it did not work well. Few commissioners had the skills or training to run city departments. In some cities, commissioners developed separate areas of personal power and influence. As a result, the commission, as a body, was often unable to agree on decisions. Only a few large cities have a commission form of government today. They include Memphis, Tennessee; St. Paul, Minnesota; Omaha, Nebraska; and Tulsa, Oklahoma.

Section Review

Vocabulary:
commission plan, council, council-manager plan, manager, mayor, mayor-council plan.

Reviewing the Main Ideas
1. List and describe three plans for city government.
2. For each plan write one sentence that tells how this plan is different from the others.

Skill Building
1. Which plan for city government do you think gives citizens the most voice in their government? Explain your answer.
2. What form of city government does your city have? Prepare an organization chart that clearly shows how your city government is structured.

Section 2
City Decision Makers

City governments have several key decision makers. The mayor, the city manager, city council members, and other city bureaucrats—all make decisions that affect citizens.

Mayors

President Lyndon Johnson once said, "Things could be worse, I could be a mayor." Mayors are in the "hot seat" of American politics. They must keep important city services working well. They must also deal with such urban problems as housing, racial tension, unemployment, crime, and deteriorating business districts. They must find the money to keep their cities going.

Some mayors have more power to do these jobs than others, depending on which of the different plans for government a city or town has. In cities with a council-manager plan, the mayor does not usually have many administrative duties or much power. The job may be mostly ceremonial. A city manager once compared his role to that of the city's mayor in saying, "The mayor cuts ribbons while I cut costs!"

Even in cities with a mayor-council plan, mayors may have to share power with other city officials and the city council. Mayors with little formal power are called "**weak mayors.**" They have only limited power to appoint or remove officials. They have little formal control over the city council and city budget. Weak mayors often have to rely on bargaining and persuasion to influence others to go along with their programs.

Mayors with more formal power, especially those in our largest cities, are known as "**strong mayors.**" Strong mayors oversee the operation of most, if not all, city agencies and departments. They can appoint and remove many top city officials. They play an important role in shaping the city budget. They can suggest legislation to the city council. They also have the power to veto bills passed by the council.

In city government, mayors have several leadership roles to play. They handle these roles differently from city to city. It depends on whether the mayor is strong or weak.

Ceremonial Leader. The mayor leads parades and dedicates new

The Pope speaking to a large crowd in Chicago in 1979. As ceremonial leaders, mayors often welcome important and famous people to their cities.

355

parks. The mayor digs the first shovelful of dirt at a groundbreaking ceremony for an important new project. The mayor welcomes famous visitors and issues proclamations. Weak or strong, all mayors do these things. The role is important; the mayor stands as the symbol of the city.

Executive Leader. Strong mayors are chief executives. They have power to run the executive branch. Weak mayors have far fewer executive powers and duties.

The mayor's most valuable executive power is to appoint and remove people from important government posts. Strong mayors are able to appoint many city officials. The appointment power gives a mayor control over day-to-day business. If a mayor does not like the way a certain department is being run, or the way a program is being administered, he or she can do much more about it with the power to get rid of the department head.

Legislative Leader. All mayors can recommend legislation to city or town councils. Strong mayors often have a great deal of influence in setting goals for the council.

In cities where the mayor is elected by the other members of the city council, the mayor may propose legislation and vote just like any other council member. In other cities, the mayor may not be on the council but can vote on legislation in case of a tie vote in the council. Strong mayors have the power of veto. About two-thirds of America's mayors have veto power.

Political Leader. The mayor is the head of his or her political party in the city. The mayor often has much influence over council members who belong to the same party.

However, city politics in many American cities is **nonpartisan.** This means that people who run for mayor or for city council do not identify themselves to the voters as either Republicans or Democrats. Often they represent local political groups that might have such names as the Good Government party, the Urban Reform movement, or the Independent ticket. As with the major political parties, the mayor elected from a local political group is recognized as the leader of that group.

Promotional Leader. Mayors represent their cities or towns in dealings with business, labor, and government leaders. Most cities want to attract new businesses to their communities both to increase the city's income from taxes and to give jobs to city people. The mayor works with leaders to make the community attractive to business.

Often the mayor must compete with other mayors and public officials for funds from state and federal government. A great deal of today's city budget comes from state and federal programs. The mayor is the city's representative in dealing with these important sources of money.

City Manager

City managers are important decision makers in cities with a council-manager plan of government. They set the agenda for council meetings, prepare the city budget, write reports on city problems, and supervise the heads of city departments. Let's look at how a typical city manager influences decisions.

Mike Arredondo is a city manager hired by the city council. He works in a city of about 85 thousand people in south Texas. Mike is an expert in administration and management.

One of Mike's first duties after he was hired was to decide whether to keep the heads of the various city departments or to hire new people to work for him. He decided to hire a new police chief and a new city planner. He kept the rest of the city department heads. He fired the police chief because the crime rate was rising, and most city leaders thought police protection needed to be improved. He fired the city planner because she had goals for the future of the city that were quite different from Mike's. He decided they could never agree.

During his first weeks on the job, Mike developed a smooth working relationship with the council members. He knew that his ability to get things done depended on his being able to work with the city council.

One of Mike's best skills is managing money. He did an outstanding job of preparing the annual city budget. He worked closely with the city budget director and city tax collector to find out how much money the city could take in and what each different department's history of spending was.

Mike influenced the council through his budget management. He knew that his planning determined how the city would distribute its resources to its citizens. When the council approved his budget proposal with next to no change, they let him decide "who gets what" from the city.

Mike also influenced the council's decisions about technical matters. For example, the council was trying to decide whether to allow a nuclear energy plant to be built within city limits. Mike asked technical experts whom he trusted to provide the council with facts about the need, costs, benefits, and possible dangers involved in having the plant within city limits.

A city manager (standing) discussing zoning changes with city planners.

Mike Arredondo keeps a low profile. "I'm not running for any public office," he says. "I don't need to shake a lot of voters' hands or make a lot of speeches to civic groups. I leave politics to the politicians." But in his own way Mike is a first-rate politician. He knows how to use influence to gain his goals.

City Council Members

Every city and town in the United States has a legislature. Most are called city councils. They vary greatly in size. Chicago's fifty-member council is the nation's largest. Several small town councils have only two members. Many average between seven and nine members. Terms of office differ from city to city as well. Four-year terms are the most common.

Within the limits of the city charter, councils make ordinances. Two of the most important legislative duties they perform have to do with taxation and spending.

Councils decide who is to be taxed and how. They decide how the city's money is to be spent.

People who serve on city councils are chosen in one of two ways. The **ward system,** once the most common, today is mostly found in larger cities such as Chicago, Philadelphia, Los Angeles, Cleveland, Baltimore, and Houston. Here, the city is divided into sections called wards. Each ward elects a representative to the council. Each voter chooses only one representative. The other system of choosing city council members is through at-large elections. In this system, voters choose all the council members. If the council has seven members, each voter votes for seven representatives.

Other City Officials

In larger cities, many officials make decisions. Heads of key city departments and the city attorney and city planners all make important decisions that affect citizens' lives.

Water commission worker examining a sample of water that the city provides its residents. Most cities have a water commission that oversees the distribution and quality of the water supply.

Many city departments are run by boards or commissions. The city officials who serve on these boards make decisions about important city services. The library board may choose a location for a new library. The city water commission often decides how much people will have to pay for water.

The city attorney handles legal matters affecting the city. The city attorney advises other city officials on what they can and cannot do within their charter.

Thus when the headlines read: "Mayor Announces New Park Program" or "City Council Cracks Down on Gambling," many unnamed officials may be involved in planning and carrying out these decisions.

Section Review

Vocabulary:
nonpartisan, "strong mayor," ward system, "weak mayor."

Reviewing the Main Ideas
1. What is the difference between a "strong mayor" and a "weak mayor"?
2. Compare the manager's role and the mayor's role. Which leadership roles do both play? Which belong only to the mayor? To the manager?
3. Describe the job of city council members.

Skill Building
1. Which form of city government does the city nearest to you have?
2. What is the name of the mayor? If it has a manager, what is the manager's name?

Section 3
Who Influences City Politics?

Many groups influence the decisions of city government officials. One city council member put it this way: "Pressure groups are probably more important in local government than they are nationally or in the state because they are right here. You see them and they see you, and what you do affects them."

Business Groups
People doing business in the city have a big stake in the decisions made by city officials. City government decisions may affect how much money a business makes, what taxes it pays, and how easy it is to conduct business in the city.

In New York, for example, the city council passed an ordinance permitting a parade on Fifth Avenue during a regular business day. Store owners tried to influence the mayor to veto the ordinance. They said closing off the street for the parade would cost them $1 million in sales.

Many businesses are concerned with city government decisions. Department stores usually want low taxes, plenty of parking spaces near their stores, and good highways and public transportation to bring customers in. Banks are interested in the growth of the city and in rising property values because they lend money for mortgages. City building codes give rules about how plumbing, electricity, driveways, garages, elevators, and so on have to be put into buildings. These determine business costs for builders.

Most cities have a **chamber of commerce.** This is an organization of businesses in the city. The chamber of commerce usually supports lower taxes and efficiency in government operations. Chambers of commerce may also support civic improvements such as new street lighting or new playgrounds.

City Employees

Police, firefighters, teachers, street crews, bus drivers, welfare workers, sanitation workers, clerks, and secretaries work for the city government. They all have a personal stake in decisions about their wages, working hours, and working conditions. They frequently try to influence the decisions of city officials.

In larger cities, workers often belong to labor unions. In other cities, city workers do not have unions, but they may form interest groups such as the Fraternal Order of Police.

City workers are **public employees.** They work for a government. Most state laws give public employees the right to organize unions and bargain with city officials about wages and working conditions. State laws usually make it illegal for public employees to go out on strike.

However, in recent years, many teachers, police, firefighters, garbage collectors, and others have ignored no-strike laws. Strikes by police or firefighters threaten the safety of the city. Strikes by bus drivers or garbage collectors greatly inconvenience citizens. These strikes put great pressure on city officials to meet the city workers' demands. Handling strikes by public employees requires some of the toughest political decisions faced by city government officials.

Newspapers

Newspapers are an important influence in local politics. **News stories** tell what's going on around town. These stories are supposed to give straight facts that explain: Who did something? What happened? Where? When? How? and Why?

In addition to factual news stories, **editorials** interpret and judge the things going on in the city. An editorial might start by stating, "The city council's vote to build a new library is a good idea." It would go on to explain why the editor felt this way. Editorials often support candidates. The day or so before an election, a newspaper prints a list of the candidates it recommends. In communities where there are many elected officials and more names on the ballot than most voters have ever heard of, voters often take their favorite newspaper's recommendations into the polling place to help them decide how to vote.

In addition to the official views of the paper given in editorials, newspaper columnists give their personal opinions in the **columns** that usually carry their names and pictures. A local columnist might begin a column with: "There is a rumor around city hall that some members of the council who opposed the new sports arena made a deal with the mayor." The column might then go on to give the columnist's opinion of what happened.

Columnists often are active supporters of one or the other political party. They do not try to be objective. Rather, their columns are interesting because they contain strong views. Columnists, too, are influential with those readers who share their general views.

In the **letters-to-the-editor** section of the paper, citizens have an opportunity to use the newspaper to influence others. If you glance at this part of the paper for a few days, you can get a good idea of what is on some people's minds.

articles about some issue in your city that is "hot."

2. Find news stories about the issue.

3. Find an editorial about it. What is the newspaper's view of it?

4. Find a columnist who has a viewpoint different from yours. How do you disagree with him or her?

Columnists such as Mike Royko and TV commentators such as Walter Jacobsen have a great deal of influence over city politics. Royko writes a daily column for the *Chicago Tribune*. Jacobsen appears on Chicago's Channel 2.

Section Review

Vocabulary:

chamber of commerce, column, editorial, letters-to-the-editor, news story, public employee.

Reviewing the Main Ideas

1. What three groups influence city decision makers?

2. Name four or five programs business groups would like to see their city provide.

3. What are two or three reasons city employees might threaten to strike?

Skill Building

1. Bring in newspapers and look for

Case Study

Solving a City Crisis

San Francisco police officers walking the picket line in front of police headquarters.

One evening in August, some tourists were dining in a Chinese restaurant in San Francisco. Silence suddenly fell as one of two men with guns shouted, "This is a stick-up! Hand over your money."

The two robbers left the restaurant with their pockets stuffed with money. A few people started to call the police. Then it dawned on them —there were no police to be called!

The day before, San Francisco's police force and firefighters had gone on strike. These public employees were bitter because they felt they were not being paid enough for the important, often dangerous jobs that they did. They had demanded a 13 percent pay raise. San Francisco's council, the Board of Supervisors, offered only 6.5 percent, so the public employees went out on strike.

After the strike began, several small fires were put out by fire department officers. But if a really big fire started, the city would have been in deep trouble.

Small bands of youths broke shop windows and took merchandise. There was no way of knowing how much crime was going on. There was no one on duty to receive calls from victims.

★ ★

The strike took place at the busiest time of the tourist season. Many visitors left the city. Others canceled their visits.

San Francisco's mayor said the strike could not go on much longer. However, the mayor refused to call in the state police to provide the missing services. That would make the city look like an armed camp. Furthermore, such action would make it harder to bargain with the striking workers.

Instead the mayor met with strike leaders and arranged a wage settlement that the police and firefighters accepted.

The Board of Supervisors voted unanimously (9-0) against the mayor's plan. "We do not wish to negotiate with outlaws," argued one supervisor. The strike was illegal. Board members did not want to make any agreement until the strikers went back to work.

Also, board members feared taxes would have to go up sharply to pay for the big salary increases. They believed the city could not afford the mayor's plan.

The mayor checked with the city attorney to see what alternatives he had. He learned that the San Francisco city charter clearly gave the mayor power to take action without board approval if he declared an emergency existed.

The mayor declared a state of emergency. He granted the strikers a 13 percent wage increase. The strikers accepted and began returning to their jobs.

Board members were furious with the mayor's decision. One supervisor called the mayor a "dicta-

tor." Another said the mayor's settlement was a "sellout."

Newspaper editorials supported the supervisors, saying the mayor's "decision to give in to striking firefighters and police ended the strike, but San Francisco residents will be paying for it soon."

A columnist wrote that the mayor "was a willing 'fall guy' in the recent strike settlement. As he is not up for reelection in November, he was in a good position to take the heat from city taxpayers. The board, most of whom are facing the election, get to look like public heroes."

Anxious to prevent a mayor from overruling them again, the Board of Supervisors added three propositions to the November ballot: (1) future mayors cannot declare emergencies without board approval, (2) strikes by police or firefighters will be grounds for dismissal, and (3) future police and firefighters' salaries will be based on the average salaries for those jobs paid in the five largest cities.

San Francisco voters overwhelmingly accepted all three of the propositions.

Review

1. Why did city workers go on strike?

2. What is your judgment of the mayor's decision to pay the striking workers the full amount they were demanding?

3. What is your judgment of the way the Board of Supervisors handled the entire situation?

Basic Social Studies Skills
Distinguishing Fact from Opinion

What is a fact? What is an opinion? Do you know how to tell the difference between statements of fact and opinion?

The American Heritage Dictionary of the English Language defines a "fact" as "something known with certainty." The dictionary gives this definition of "opinion": "A belief or conclusion held with confidence, but not substantiated [supported] by positive knowledge or proof."

It is a fact that the Sears Tower in Chicago is 1,454 feet high and has 110 stories. It is a fact that Richard J. Daley was mayor of Chicago from 1955 until 1976. How do we know these two statements about Chicago are facts? There is evidence that shows these statements to be true beyond doubt. The Sears Tower has been measured, and there are public records that reveal exactly when Richard J. Daley served as mayor.

It is an opinion that the Sears Tower is the best office building in the world. This statement is a judgment about the worth or value of the Sears Tower. It is reasonable for different people to disagree about this judgment.

Here is another opinion: The main reason for Mayor Daley's success in politics was his skill as an organizer of election campaigns. This statement is an interpretation or explanation of what happened during Daley's career as mayor. There may be evidence to support the statement. However, there may also be contrary evidence to support

other explanations about the main reason for Daley's success. Thus, it is possible for people to have different opinions about this matter. There is a lack of solid evidence to settle the disagreement.

Ability to distinguish facts from opinions is a very important skill for a student of civics. This skill is also very useful in the daily life of citizens. It can be used when reading articles in newspapers or magazines and when watching and listening to news broadcasts on television.

Skill Practice

Read each of the following statements carefully. Then decide whether each statement is a fact or opinion. Be prepared to support each decision.

1. Chicago's fifty-member city council is the largest in the United States.

2. San Francisco's mayor is an inspirational leader.

3. Residents of Chicago enjoy a higher quality of life than do the residents of New York City.

4. In 1981, the income per person in Chicago was $12,510.

5. In 1995, the income per person in Chicago will be $15,000.

6. The Sears Tower of Chicago is taller than the two towers of the World Trade Center in New York.

7. A great fire burned most of Chicago in October 1871.

8. Residents of Chicago had an easier life in the 1920s than they do today.

Chapter 18 Review

Summary

Section 1: Plans for City Government

Cities are created by their state government. Most cities use one of three plans for government. Under the mayor-council plan, the mayor is elected by voters and has responsibility for carrying out the law. Under the council-manager plan, a city council makes rules, sets goals, and hires a manager to handle everyday city business. Under the commission plan, a group of elected commissioners makes laws and runs key departments.

Section 2: City Decision Making

Mayors have important leadership responsibilities. These include being a ceremonial leader, legislative leader, executive leader, political leader, and promotional leader. City managers need both political skills and expertise in administration and management. City council members often make key decisions regarding taxation and spending city money.

Section 3: Who Influences City Politics?

Three major groups try to influence the decisions of city government officials. They are business groups, city employees, and newspapers. Business groups generally support proposed laws that will lower taxes and improve the efficiency of government. City employees generally want laws that will give them higher wages and better working hours and conditions. Newspapers, through news articles, try to give readers the facts about certain issues. They also give personal opinions on certain issues through editorials and columns. And they give readers a chance to react to their stories and opinions through letters-to-the-editor sections.

Vocabulary

Define the following terms.

1. council
2. mayor
3. manager
4. ward system
5. nonpartisan

Reviewing Main Ideas

1. True or false: City governments are set up in Article III of the Constitution.
2. Most American cities use the _____ form of government.
   a. commission
   b. council-manager
   c. mayor-council
3. Which form of city government is growing most rapidly?
   a. commission
   b. council-manager
   c. mayor-council

Thinking Critically

Comprehending Information

1. In your own words, describe the difference between a "strong mayor" and a "weak mayor." Include at least two differences in their powers.
2. Draw a diagram or cartoon to show what is meant by "mayors are in the 'hot seat' of American politics."

Evaluating Information

Suppose you could interview your mayor or manager about city government in your community. Write up the questions you would ask. Write at least five.

Communicating Ideas

Write a brief summary of the main ideas of this chapter. Include at least five words from the vocabulary section of this test. Underline each vocabulary word you use.

Chapter 19
City Challenges

Introduction. Thomas Jefferson once wrote to his good friend James Madison, "When our governments get piled upon one another in large cities, as in Europe, they will become corrupt as in Europe." Jefferson, like many others of his time, thought life on the farm was better than life in the city.

Today many Americans still criticize life in our big cities. They point with alarm to urban problems that never seem to go away. These include violent crime, high taxes, crowded expressways, dirty air, poor housing, and troubled public schools. They argue that cities are a cold, impersonal, brutal environment where people have no sense of community. A familiar saying is: "The city is a great place to visit and work in but I sure wouldn't want to live there."

Other people ask: "If life in the city is really so bad, why do millions of Americans insist on living in cities?" Cities often supply economic opportunity. People come to our cities because cities provide greater numbers of jobs as well as greater freedom in choosing careers. City living can mean a higher income. Cities are a meeting place for talent from all over the nation and the world: dancers, musicians, writers, actors, business leaders.

Cities also offer opportunities for the "good life." City dwellers are better educated on the average than non-city residents. Cities have better hospitals and health care. They have more entertainment. They have more cultural attractions—libraries, museums, symphonies, live theater, and ballet.

Life in our cities is constantly changing. In this chapter you will learn about both the problems and the progress of our cities.

Section 1
How Cities Have Grown

When Miami police officer Ed Kezar retired, he thought of the many changes he had seen in the large Florida city.

Expressways now cut through and around the city. A rapid transit system was in the works. Tall new office buildings lit up the skyline at night. The people had changed too. Thousands of immigrants from nearby Cuba had added variety to the city's cultural life. And every year, more and more "snowbirds," people from the north, kept moving to the Miami area. In recent years the area's population had jumped by nearly 16 percent. This growth had brought some problems, too. More cars jammed the roads. Housing prices went up. Crime increased.

Like Miami, every American city has seen new people, new buildings, and new problems. Our cities have always been changing.

The City in Our History

The United States began as a rural nation. At the time of the American Revolution, 95 percent of the colonists were farmers. In 1790, the first census showed that New York, with

Aerial view of Miami, Florida. Like many other cities in the South and Southwest, Miami has grown tremendously in recent years.

367

Chicago's Sears Tower (background) towering above Chinatown, a nine-square-block area on Chicago's near south side. The area was settled by Chinese immigrants in the early 1900s. About 2,500 people of Chinese descent live in Chinatown today.

33,000 people, and Philadelphia, with 28,000, were our biggest cities. Baltimore and Boston were towns with fewer than 20,000 people each.

When the Civil War ended in 1865, cities began to grow rapidly. By 1900, New York had more than 3 million people. Chicago had 1.5 million people. Boston and Baltimore had more than 300,000 each.

The growth of factories and industry had brought many people into the cities. There was work in the city for newcomers. By the late 1800s and early 1900s, millions of immigrants from such countries as Ireland, Italy, Germany, Poland, and Russia had arrived.

The cities also offered jobs to Americans from the farms. The invention of new machinery had changed farming, so fewer farmers and farm laborers were needed. Farm workers and younger members of farm families moved to the cities for work.

Cities were exciting places to be. The growing cities had gas lighting and running water. They had new theaters, restaurants, museums, and libraries. There were people to see and know. And fortunes could be made in the city.

By 1920, more Americans were living in the city than in rural areas. During this century, our cities have continued to grow. Now we have nearly 400 cities with more than 50,000 people. We have more than 50 cities with 250,000 or more people. And 6 cities have populations of more than 1 million.

A Pattern in City Growth

Most American cities have grown from the inside out. They started as small towns near a river, fort, waterfall, or crossroads. Then they grew out from the center in bigger and bigger circles. If you start at the center of a typical city, you see tall buildings, stores, banks, and theaters. The traffic is heavy. This is the original section of the city. Next you come to a run-down area that surrounds the central city. Here you find old warehouses, vacant lots, junk cars, and slum buildings.

After this is a ring of small homes, grocery stores, and apartment buildings. Most of the houses are old. Many are built side by side with little or no space between them. Signs in foreign languages tell that different ethnic groups are part of this circle.

As the traffic gets lighter, you move into the next circle. Here you'll find newer shops, banks, and a big modern shopping center. If you turn into the smaller, side streets, you'll see larger one-family homes with yards and garages. There are fewer apartment buildings here than nearer in. The ones you do find are quite new.

Soon you'll be out of the city and into the next community—a suburb. Since the 1950s, many people have been moving from the city to the suburbs. In recent years, nearly twenty million Americans moved to suburbs.

Families moving to suburbs seek to get away from city problems. They want cleaner air, more living space, less traffic and crowding, and better schools. Many businesses,

How American Cities Have Grown

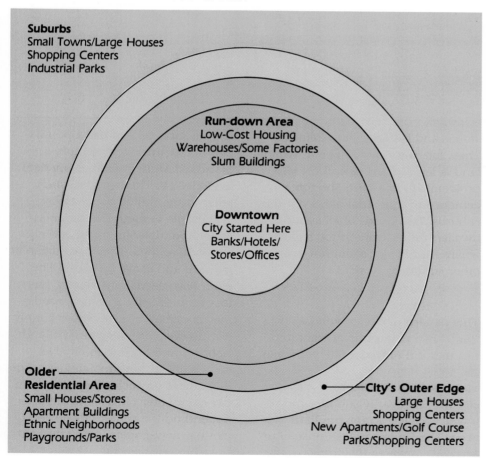

Suburbs
Small Towns/Large Houses
Shopping Centers
Industrial Parks

Run-down Area
Low-Cost Housing
Warehouses/Some Factories
Slum Buildings

Downtown
City Started Here
Banks/Hotels/
Stores/Offices

Older
Residential Area
Small Houses/Stores
Apartment Buildings
Ethnic Neighborhoods
Playgrounds/Parks

City's Outer Edge
Large Houses
Shopping Centers
New Apartments/Golf Course
Parks/Shopping Centers

(above) Residents of a Harlem neighborhood in 1939. Harlem is a primarily black community north of Central Park on New York City's Manhattan Island. Many rural blacks settled in Harlem during the early part of the century. (left) Does the pattern shown fit the pattern of growth for the city you live in?

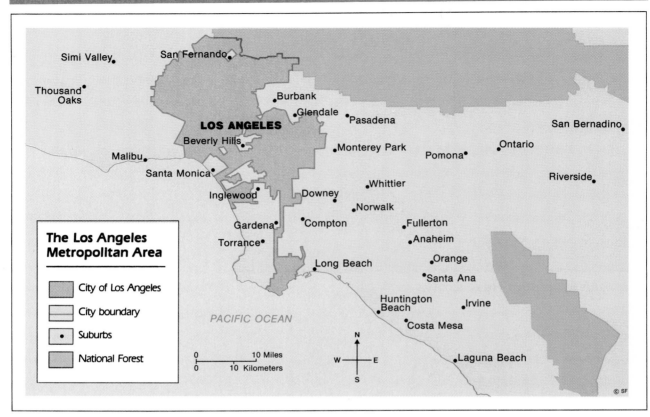

The Los Angeles Metropolitan Area

Legend:
- City of Los Angeles
- City boundary
- Suburbs
- National Forest

PACIFIC OCEAN

0   10 Miles
0   10 Kilometers

N W E S

© SF

Study the map above. How many suburbs does Los Angeles have? About how many square miles is the Los Angeles metropolitan area?

stores, and factories have followed. They, too, want to go to areas where land is less expensive and big city problems do not exist. Shopping centers and industrial parks dot the suburbs. Two-thirds of all suburban dwellers either work in the suburb where they live or commute to another suburb to work.

Supercities

This pattern of city growth has produced two new kinds of communities that did not exist fifty years ago.

Metropolitan Areas. Today, a large city with its nearby suburbs and towns is called a **metropolitan area.** The United States Census Bureau calls any area including a city

and its suburbs that has a population of fifty thousand or more a **Standard Metropolitan Statistical Area** (SMSA). There are 243 such areas in the United States today.

People in metropolitan areas come from different racial and ethnic backgrounds. They have different political and social attitudes. They often have needs for different services from the city and their needs may conflict. The differences among city dwellers are the source of both richness and conflict in city life.

People in metropolitan areas are dependent on each other. People in the city's outer circles and suburbs depend on the center city for food, clothes, newspapers, entertainment, hospitals, jobs, and many other things. The center city looks to the rest of the area for its workers, managers, and customers. Everyone looks to the city government to provide key services.

Megalopolis. As metropolitan areas have grown, the space between gets smaller and smaller. New housing built on the outer edge of the city pushes further and further into the country. An area where large cities have started to overlap is called a **megalopolis.** The word means "very great urban area." We have three in the United States.

One is an area about 100 miles wide and 500 miles long. It includes New York City, Boston, and Washington, D.C. About 50 million people live in this megalopolis—called Boswash, Boshington, or Bosnywash.

The area along the shores of the Great Lakes from Chicago, Illinois, to Buffalo, New York, is another megalopolis. The third is in California, spreading out from Los Angeles.

Section Review

Vocabulary:
megalopolis, metropolitan area, Standard Metropolitan Statistical Area (SMSA).

Reviewing the Main Ideas
What are some advantages of living in a city? What are some disadvantages of living in a city?

Skill Building
Draw a diagram showing how cities have grown.

Section 2
City Problems

Juliet Hazen is the mayor of a mid-size, typical American city. Recently, she was interviewed by Allan Hernandez, a local reporter.

Hernandez: In your opinion, has city life been getting better or worse?

Hazen: Most city dwellers today live more comfortably than ever before. Cities are cleaner than, say, in the 1920s. There are more schools and more people go to school. And the treatment of racial and ethnic minorities has improved.

Hernandez: What problems face local government leaders today?

Hazen: Major problems include poor housing, slums, crime, traffic problems, and pollution.

Hernandez: Can local governments solve all these problems?

Hazen: They have to try. One of the toughest problems is deciding how much local government can do and how much citizens and private businesses must do for themselves.

This section considers some of the problems Mayor Hazen is talking about, and which apply to many American cities.

Housing

Jean Palmer lived in Apartment 2W. Forty other families lived in the small building. Most tried to keep the building clean, but it was just no use. The owner did not live there and did not care. The owner only wanted the rent.

The building was a mess. There was no janitor to fix things. The

A public housing project in the Bronx, New York.

fight slums and improve housing. Some have worked better than others. One idea that has not worked so well is **public housing projects.** These are apartment buildings built with public funding. Usually slums are torn down to make way for these projects. The rents are kept at a level most of the housing project families can afford.

Although the idea behind housing projects is a good one, the end result has often been failure. Poor management is often the culprit. Insufficient planning and inadequate maintenance has often given birth to new slums where old ones were. Many public housing projects have high crime rates and many of the other problems that were in place before the projects were built.

Another plan, which has been more successful, is called **urban renewal.** Under this plan, huge areas of a blighted area are torn down. The land is then used for light industry, civic centers, modern hotels, or offices. The idea is to attract new economic life to areas that were once considered dead.

Some existing houses, many of which are historically valuable, are allowed to stand. These properties are then sold, often through public auction, to people who make a commitment to the city to restore and then live in the property. Some cities have experienced much success with this type of plan.

The properties are sold at low prices and usually low interest rates. This attracts a committed buyer. Then the buyer improves the property, moves in, and brings to the community an income that benefits

toilets didn't work, the sinks were cracked, windows were broken. The walls had holes in them. Many times the furnace broke and there was no heat. And there were rats.

Slum buildings like Jean Palmer's are one of the toughest problems facing cities. A **slum** is an old, dirty, run-down part of a city. People in slums may live crowded together in a few small rooms. Slums are found mainly in the circle next to the downtown area. But, slums can develop in any area of the city where buildings are neglected and there is overcrowding.

Slums develop as some people move out to more desirable neighborhoods and poorer people move in. Often the only housing newcomers can find or afford is in already run-down buildings left behind by others. These areas then get worse as landlords take advantage of the poor who need housing. The rents are high. Few, if any, repairs are made on buildings.

City government decision makers have used several programs to neighborhood stores and other businesses. Everyone benefits.

Most city governments have special departments that work on slum problems. The federal government has provided much of the money for such projects. The Department of Housing and Urban Development (HUD) grants billions of dollars to cities for housing aid.

All these efforts have helped improve urban life. But most city officials agree that much more needs to be done to solve the housing problem in cities.

Transportation

The auto population in our country is growing faster than the human population. In 1921 there were 20 million cars. Today there are more than 160 million cars, buses, and trucks. These vehicles burned 115 billion gallons of fuel in 1984.

Cars helped cities and suburbs grow. With cars, people could live away from the downtown center and still get around the city. But now cities are choking on cars.

Most cities were not planned for the automobile. City traffic is often a mess. There are not enough parking spaces. During "rush hours," traffic moves at a snail's pace.

In addition, giant expressways and parking garages take up valuable space in the city. This space could be used for buildings that pay property taxes. In Los Angeles people were shocked to learn that more than two-thirds of the downtown area was used in one way or another for automobiles.

Miami's Metro Rail.

Urban experts agree that trains are the best way to move people around the city. Such trains are called **rapid transit systems,** or **subways** when they run under the ground. In recent years Miami, Atlanta, San Francisco, Baltimore, and Washington have built rapid transit and subway systems. Building such systems is expensive. It also requires planning and cooperation by many local government decision makers.

Miami is an example. By the mid-1970s, the city was swamped with cars. Downtown Miami was surrounded by parking lots. U.S. Highway 1, a main north-south road, was designed to carry 1,800 cars an hour; instead it carried 3,000.

To help solve the problem, city and Dade County government officials began planning for a $795 million, 21-mile rapid transit system. The county, which includes Miami, would provide $132 million. The rest would come from the federal government. The Metropolitan Dade County Office of Transportation Administration was set up to design and operate the system. Hundreds of meetings with local residents were held to plan the system. Sometimes the spots for stations were moved when residents objected to them. Dade County voters approved the county's plans in a special election. Soon afterward, work on the system started.

City officials hope new, fast, clean rapid transit systems such as Miami's will encourage city dwellers to get off the expressways and onto trains.

Pollution

Air and water pollution have been problems for cities for a long time. Dirty air and dirty water can make city life unpleasant.

Clean Air. Air pollution hurts plants and trees. It makes clothes dirty. It can ruin the paint on cars. And it can and does cause lung disease. Some doctors maintain that almost every city dweller today has some damage to the lungs as a result of air pollution.

About 60 percent of the air pollution in large cities is caused by fumes from cars, trucks, and buses. A second major cause of air pollution is the smoke and gases from factories. Every year factories spray tons of dirt and gases into the air.

City governments have fought air pollution for many years. The first air pollution law in the United States was an ordinance passed by the Chicago City Council in 1881. The problem is tough to deal with. Even when one city cleans up its air, winds can bring dirty air from a nearby city or factory. Each local government makes its own decisions about air pollution.

In 1955, Congress passed the first federal law on air pollution. Others have followed. Federal laws provide money to help cities and counties clean up their air. They also limit the amount of pollutants factories and autos can emit.

Clean Water. As cities have grown, water pollution has become a serious problem in some areas. One source of water pollution is sewage. Cities have spent billions of dollars on sewage treatment plants.

A dangerous source of water pollution is waste from factories and from farms. Animal wastes, fertilizers, and farm chemicals drain into nearby rivers and lakes. This pollution is carried by rivers past many cities. Each city then adds more pollution to the river.

Planning for the Future

Most cities today have official planning agencies. Almost every large city employs full-time, professional planners. In a large city, planners include traffic engineers, population specialists, economists, political scientists, landscape architects, and many other types of scientists.

Many city problems have come from lack of planning. As cities grew no one gave much thought to protecting the environment. Nor were streets, parks, businesses, hospitals, and public transportation planned to best fit people's needs. Instead cities grew by chance.

Today there is a real need for planning. Here are the kinds of problems planners deal with. Where should a new rapid transit system go? How will it affect people who live along the route? How many newcomers to the city are expected in the next ten years? What kinds of services will they need? Does the city need more parks or more land for factories?

Planners have no legal powers to make other city officials and citizens accept their plans. They report on their plans to the mayor or city manager and to the city council. It is up to these officials to put the plans into action and make them legally binding upon others.

Thus planners may influence the decisions of city officials with their ideas for the future. Real estate developers, builders, property owners, and citizens also try to influence city officials. They may or may not agree with the planners.

One way city officials enforce new plans is through **zoning ordinances.** Zoning divides the city into different "zones," or areas, for industry, homes, apartment buildings, and stores. Owners of land in each zone may use the land only as called for in the ordinance. Planners often help write zoning ordinances for the city council to vote on.

Today the federal government requires cities to develop a plan before it will give federal money for public housing, urban renewal, airports, sewage systems, highways, parks, or even hospitals. This rule has led many cities to set up planning agencies.

(top) Chicago's Navy Pier as it looked in 1985. (above) An architect's plan for a new Navy Pier.

Section Review

Vocabulary:
public housing project, rapid transit system, slum, subway, urban renewal, zoning ordinance.

Reviewing the Main Ideas
1. What are slums and how do they develop?
2. What problems have automobiles created for cities?

Skill Building
Using what you know about overlapping local governments, tell in several paragraphs why pollution is a hard problem for local governments to deal with.

375

San Francisco mother protesting new meal guidelines for the federally-funded Child Care Food Program in 1982. The guidelines called for catsup to be considered a vegetable, and therefore a legitimate substitute for other vegetables.

Section 3
Federal Aid for Cities

Dealing with urban problems takes a lot of money. Many large cities today are short of money. Services such as rapid transit are becoming more and more costly. Controlling pollution is expensive for businesses and for government. And clusters of poor people who need special services place a further burden on city governments. Where does the money to pay for these services come from?

During the Depression of the 1930s and early 1940s, the national government began granting money to cities for child welfare, public welfare, public housing, and employment programs. After World War II, federal money was also available for schools and expressways.

As their money problems got worse, cities in the 1960s turned to the national government for even more money. Washington responded with many new aid programs.

Federal money became a big part of the budget of many cities. In a recent year, for example, money from Washington made up 36 percent of Baltimore's budget and 25 percent of Cleveland's budget.

Most city officials would agree with Detroit's mayor: "I don't apologize for the federal aid we get. For a long time the property tax was a fine way to finance city government. But it's very obvious now that it's not enough."

Cities have gotten money from Washington in three ways: (1) federal grants-in-aid, (2) revenue sharing, and (3) block grants.

Federal Grants-in-Aid

Federal grants-in-aid, also known as categorical grants, are the single biggest source of federal money for cities. More than 75 percent of federal money going to state and local governments comes through these grants.

Grants-in-aid can be used only for special purposes that are named by the federal government. All have different requirements that cities must meet to obtain the money. There are more than six hundred federal aid programs. Cities may get federal grants to assist in everything from draining swamps to buying milk for school lunch programs.

Federal Control. City officials have learned that along with federal aid comes a lot of federal control. The national government gives money to cities only if cities are willing to meet conditions set by Congress. For example, Washington may grant a city money for a new library. But city officials must agree to build special ramps for the handicapped, hire members of minority groups to work in the library, and use certain types of building materials.

Red Tape. To get aid from Washington, city officials must find the right program. They must learn how to apply for aid. They must fill out forms correctly. Once they get the money, city officials must make regular reports to federal agencies in Washington.

All the paperwork takes time and costs money. One official figured her city needs 20 percent of the federal aid it gets just to pay for the paperwork.

Supporters of federal aid point out that it helps cities provide important services they could not afford alone. They add that federal guidelines have helped improve local programs. These guidelines have helped to ensure that cities do not engage in discrimination.

Revenue Sharing

When the national government takes part of the money it collects from federal taxes and gives it back to city governments, this is revenue sharing. The money comes with few strings attached. It can be spent for nearly anything the city needs. Most cities use this money to help pay for such services as police and fire protection, sewage and garbage disposal, air and water cleanup, and parks. About 10 percent of all federal aid comes from revenue sharing.

Many big city mayors think the national government is better at collecting taxes than local governments. But, they say, local officials are closer to the people and better able to spend the money from Washington to meet local problems.

Many national government officials do not like revenue sharing. These officials argue that decisions about spending should be made by the same people who have the burden of collecting the tax money. Many people also consider revenue sharing to be unjust because many rich communities get money to spend on things such as tennis courts or swimming pools. These people believe money should be allocated on the basis of true need.

Block Grants are another attempt to cut the federal controls linked with grants-in-aid. Under this program the federal government identifies a broad area such as "community development" or "law enforcement." Cities may then obtain federal money to conduct whatever specific project they want as long as it fits within the broad federal category.

Block grants give cities more freedom to do what they want than grants-in-aid. However, they do not give as much freedom as revenue sharing. About 15 percent of federal aid comes through block grants.

Members of the Youth Conservation Corps building log steps at a Pennsylvania state park. Federal programs are sometimes geared to providing teenagers with summer work.

Section Review

Vocabulary:
block grants.

Reviewing the Main Ideas
1. Give three reasons cities need money from Washington.
2. What is one argument city officials give for why the money should come from Washington?
3. What is one argument national government officials make against giving money directly to cities?

Skill Building
Use library resources to help you locate a recent budget for your city or community. How much money did your city receive in the form of revenue sharing? About what percent was this of the total amount of money taken in?

Your Right to Privacy

As you have read in this unit, your local government serves you in many ways. It creates many laws and services that affect you in many beneficial ways every day. It has the power to make many decisions concerning the operation and well-being of your community.

But along with this power, your local government also has the responsibility to see that your rights as an American citizen are never infringed. One of these rights is the right to privacy.

Fourth Amendment Protections

Many of your rights regarding privacy are rooted in the Fourth Amendment. That amendment says: "The right of the people to be secure in their persons, houses, papers, and effects, against unreasonable searches and seizures, shall not be violated, and no warrants shall issue, but upon probable cause, supported by oath or affirmation, and particularly describing the place to be searched, and the persons or things to be seized."

The Fourth Amendment protects you from unfair actions by police and other officials. However, the amendment does not forbid all searches and seizures (arrests), only "unreasonable" ones. What makes a search or seizure unreasonable?

The second part of the Fourth Amendment, the "warrant clause," provides one answer. Most searches and arrests are unreasonable unless the police have a valid warrant. A warrant is a written order from a court authorizing the search of a specific place or the arrest of a person.

When is a warrant valid? The amendment says, "no warrants shall issue, but upon probable cause, supported by oath," and describing the "persons or things to be seized." In short, there must be good reason, "probable cause," for a

warrant and the warrant must be specific.

Even with such guidelines, it is often hard to determine when some searches or seizures are reasonable. As a result, courts deal with Fourth Amendment issues on a case-by-case basis. Here are some major conclusions.

Protections Against Unfair Arrest. The police have no right to simply arrest you in a public place. They must have an arrest warrant unless they have "probable cause" to believe you have committed or are about to commit a crime.

Protection against unfair arrest while in your home is even greater. Except for an emergency—such as when someone's life is in danger—the police have no right to enter a house without a warrant to make an arrest. This holds even if the police have probable cause to believe the person inside has committed a felony.

Protection Against Unfair Searches. Despite the detective shows you may see on television, the police have no general right to invade homes and break down doors. Except for special circumstances such as frisking an armed person, the police have no constitutional right to search without a valid search warrant.

Your right to privacy is protected in any place a person has a reasonable "expectation of privacy." This includes not only your own home, but a hotel room, a rented house, a friend's apartment, or even a telephone booth.

Protection Against Wiretapping. The government cannot tap your phone or eavesdrop in other ways without a search warrant. Telephones and wiretaps were, of course, unknown to the Founders. But the Supreme Court has ruled that a conversation can be seized electronically. Thus, it is tangible evidence just like books and other documents protected by the Fourth Amendment.

The Exclusionary Rule. What if the police seize evidence illegally? The courts have used the **exclusionary rule** to enforce Fourth Amendment protections. This rule was announced by the Supreme Court in a 1914 case, *Weeks* v. *United States*. The rule says that evidence obtained in violation of a person's Fourth Amendment rights may not be used in court as evidence.

The exclusionary rule applied only to the federal courts until 1961. In that year, in the landmark case of *Mapp* v. *Ohio*, the Court ruled illegal evidence must also be excluded from state trials.

In 1984, an opinion by Chief Justice Warren Burger eased restrictions imposed by the exclusionary rule. In essence, the Supreme Court ruled that certain illegally obtained evidence *can* be used in court as long as prosecutors can prove that such evidence would have "ultimately or inevitably" been discovered through lawful means.

New Protections for Personal Privacy

The Constitution does not *directly* mention a right to personal privacy. However, as far back as 1927, Supreme Court Justice Louis Brandeis [bran′dīs] argued that the Founders wanted citizens to have "the right to be left alone—the most comprehensive of rights and the right most valued by civilized men."

Since the 1960s, the Supreme Court has made several decisions dealing with citizens' rights to personal privacy in their everyday lives. These decisions have been concerned with protecting peoples' rights to live their personal lives as they choose and to have their own ideas, thoughts, and secrets free from government interference.

A Constitutional Basis. The Supreme Court's rulings have established that the right to personal privacy has a constitutional basis. According to the Court, "various guarantees" in the First, Third, Fourth, Fifth, and Fourteenth amendments spell out "zones of privacy" for citizens. The Ninth Amendment also supports this right. That amendment says that the list of our rights in the Constitution is not exhaustive and that other rights are "retained by the people." These other rights include the "right to privacy."

Action by Congress. Congress has also acted to protect your right to privacy by passing two laws. These laws aim to prevent information about your personal life collected by public officials from being misused.

The Privacy Act of 1974 gives all citizens the right to examine and copy most information about them stored by federal government agencies. It also allows citizens to challenge and correct any inaccurate information about them in federal files.

The Family Educational Rights Act of 1974 applies to schools and universities. It opens your school files to your parents. This law permits parents to check test scores, guidance counselor reports, and any other information in their children's school records. Students who are eighteen years old or older can check their own files.

Review

1. What is a warrant?
2. What makes a police search or seizure "unreasonable"?
3. "Zones of privacy" are found in amendments one, three, four, five, nine, and fourteen. What do these amendments deal with specifically?

Case Study

Improving City Life

Despite the serious problems they face, American cities are staging a comeback. In many cities billions of private and government dollars are being used to build new shopping malls, fix up waterfronts, and put up stylish hotels, apartments, and office buildings. "Cities," as one mayor put it, "are entering an era of quality."

Evidence of new life for our cities is everywhere. In the early 1970s Seattle's major employer was the Boeing Company. When the aircraft maker became financially troubled, unemployment rose dramatically. People fled the city. Things were so bad that one billboard in town read, "Will the last person leaving Seattle please turn out the lights?"

Seattle has recovered. City officials accomplished this recovery by raising taxes, cutting services, and offering incentives to companies that moved their operations to the city. Officials also encouraged increased trade. Today, Seattle is one of the world's busiest ports.

Baltimore is another stunning example of the comeback of our cities. The Charles Center, a $180 million hotel, office, apartment, and shopping complex, has given new life to the downtown area. The city's greatest pride, however, is in redevelopment of the decaying waterfront area once called "Inner Harbor."

"Ten years ago Inner Harbor was a real disaster," says Baltimore's Mayor, "with rotting wharves, abandoned warehouses, sunken boats, rats, and dirt." Today that's all gone. In its place is Harborplace, a beautiful complex of restaurants, shops, a convention center, apartments, office buildings, and hotels. All are on or near the once decaying waterfront.

Why all the improvements in urban areas? Observers give at least three reasons. First, many cities are becoming more efficient. Mayor Dick Eardley of Boise, Idaho, says, "I think most cities are better run today than they were in the 1960s and early '70s. We are under more scrutiny because people are so conscious of costs. We're forced to run a better operation."

Tight budgets have often meant cuts in services. But they have also forced other changes. Mayor Eardley says, "Cities are also looking for better ways to do things, to do them more efficiently and at less cost."

Baltimore's Harborplace.

City officials have been facing up to the fact that city governments cannot do everything for everybody. Mayor Margaret Hance of Phoenix explains: "Cities have to return to basics. Our responsibilities are to provide police and fire protection, deliver good clean water, pick up garbage, and provide adequate sewage and transportation systems."

A former San Diego mayor agrees: "Abraham Lincoln once said that the legitimate object of government is to do for people what needs to be done but which they cannot by individual effort do at all or do so well for themselves. Lincoln instinctively knew that government could grow too large and spend too much. More officials are coming to that viewpoint."

Cities are also improving because city officials have worked hard to get help from private industry. General Motors is leading a $20 million effort to rebuild slums around its headquarters in Detroit. Control Data Corporation has built plants in urban ghettos of San Antonio, St. Paul, Minneapolis, and Washington, D.C. These plants hire and train local residents.

Finally, cities are rebounding because of the hard work of average citizens. The people of the Morris Park section of the Bronx in New York City are a good example.

Not long ago about two hundred houses were up for sale in the 154-block area making up Morris Park. Worried residents and merchants were running to the suburbs as crime increased and decay set in. Things looked bad for the community of Morris Park.

Then many of the 10,000 Morris Park families decided to work together rather than run away. They formed the Morris Park Community Association to stop the decline of their neighborhood. Association members demanded the city start cleaning the streets and parks regularly. The association told real estate agents to stop badgering established homeowners to sell.

Residents also set up a volunteer anticrime patrol. The volunteers helped make the parks safe for sports and summer concerts. The local business association planted trees along the main street.

Things began to change. Longtime residents decided to stay put. Some people living in the suburbs began to move into Morris Park. The value of vacant land in the community rose dramatically. And new businesses began to move in. In one twelve-month period, twenty new firms began operations in Morris Park.

Barbara Fried, secretary of the community association, says proudly, "We're not running now." Morris Park, she says, is becoming like a pleasant small town in the middle of a big city. "We're holding our ground and making it good." The same can be said for an increasing number of cities across the land.

Review

1. Describe evidence that American cities are making a comeback.
2. What are three reasons for improvements in American cities?

Basic Social Studies Skills

Interpreting Photographs

In this chapter you learned about the growth of cities. Over the years, our cities have developed and changed. You can get a great deal of information about cities, or other subjects, from photographs.

Here are guidelines for studying a photograph to gain information about the past.

1. Identify the topic or subject of the picture. What events, people, places, or objects are shown in the picture?

2. Determine the time and place of the photograph. When was the picture taken? Where was it taken? How do you know this information?

3. Interpret the main idea or point of view of the photograph. What is the main message conveyed by the picture? Is a point of view or bias of the photographer revealed by the picture?

4. Judge the effect of the photograph on viewers. How do you feel about the subject of the picture? What general effect does the picture have on you?

5. Find information about the past from the photograph. What information can you gain from the photograph about events, objects, people, or places? What does the picture indicate about how life was different in the past?

Skill Practice

1. What information can you gain from this photograph about life in a city in the past?

2. What impressions do you have about how cities have changed from the time of this photograph?

New York's Mulberry Street in the early 1900s.

Chapter 19 Review

Summary

Section 1: How Cities Have Grown

We began as a rural nation. By the 1860s, our cities were beginning to grow rapidly. By the 1920s, more Americans were living in cities than in rural areas. Most cities have grown from the inside out. Today, large cities and their suburbs are called metropolitan areas. A huge, sprawling metropolitan area is called a megalopolis.

Section 2: City Problems

Cities face a continuing set of problems. Slum areas are marked by poor housing and high crime rates. Automobiles crowd the streets. Air and water pollution are serious problems. Urban renewal, rapid transit systems, and laws controlling pollution are some of the solutions cities have developed to cope with their problems. Careful planning is a must for all cities that hope to avoid future problems.

Section 3: Federal Aid for Cities

Cities need money to deal with their problems. The federal government is an important source of money for many local governments. Federal money comes to cities in three ways: Grants-in-aid, revenue sharing, and block grants. Most federal aid to cities comes through grants-in-aid.

Vocabulary

Define the following terms.

1. metropolitan area
2. megalopolis
3. block grants
4. SMSA
5. rapid transit system
6. slum
7. urban renewal
8. public housing project
9. exclusionary rule
10. zoning ordinance

Reviewing Main Ideas

1. Most cities have grown
   a. from the inside out.
   b. from the outside in.
   c. only in the middle.
   d. with no pattern.
2. A Standard Metropolitan Statistical Area is a city and surrounding area with a population of
   a. 20,000 or more.
   b. 30,000 or more.
   c. 40,000 or more.
   d. 50,000 or more.
3. Which of the following is not an example of a megalopolis?
   a. Chicago to Buffalo
   b. Washington, D.C., to Boston
   c. Minneapolis to Chicago
   d. Los Angeles to San Diego

Thinking Critically

Evaluating Information

Thomas Jefferson felt life on the farm was better than life in the city. Using your own experiences and things you have read and seen, tell whether you agree or disagree and why.

Communicating Ideas

Express your ideas about city problems. You may write a paragraph, compose a song, paint a mural, make a stand-up picture in a box, draw a cartoon, or use any other art form you choose.

Comprehending Information

1. Explain why cities grew rapidly in the late 1800s.
2. Name three problems most large cities face today.
3. How has the federal government influenced cities to have city planners?

Unit Six Test

Vocabulary
Write *true* if the underlined word or phrase is used correctly. Write *false* if it is used incorrectly. Rephrase each false statement so that the underlined word or phrase is used correctly.

1. A <u>municipal charter</u> is a "constitution" for a city or town.

2. In some New England states, <u>counties</u> are mainly court districts.

3. There are large farms in <u>urban areas</u>.

4. The city of Lexington and Fayette County <u>consolidated</u> their governments.

5. In order to get more money to provide services, a city can sell <u>ordinances</u>.

6. California voters did not want to pay high <u>property taxes</u>.

7. The <u>council-manager</u> plan is a way some cities are governed.

8. Politics in many local governments is <u>nonpartisan</u>.

9. In Alaska, counties are called <u>boroughs</u>.

10. A <u>chamber of commerce</u> is an organization of local government officials.

11. States are divided into sections called <u>wards</u>.

12. A <u>city manager</u> could suggest ordinances.

13. The council voted to begin a <u>megalopolis</u> to help solve the problems of slums in the city.

14. <u>Revenue sharing</u> is a way that county and state governments can merge into one government.

15. A city planner could recommend that a <u>rapid transit system</u> would help solve traffic problems.

16. If the city council did not want to have a bowling alley in a certain district of houses and apartments, it could pass a <u>zoning ordinance</u>.

17. A <u>metropolitan area</u> is a rural area.

18. Federal <u>grants-in-aid</u> are the single biggest source of federal money for cities.

19. The courts are not allowed to use the <u>exclusionary rule</u> to enforce Fourth Amendment protection.

20. Some counties are divided into <u>townships</u>.

Recalling Information
1. Which governments are mentioned in the United States Constitution?
a. local governments
b. state governments
c. the federal government
d. all of the above

2. All states have the following types of local government <u>except</u>
a. special districts   **c.** cities
b. states   **d.** townships

3. Which form of government provides you the most services?
a. state government
b. local government
c. federal government
d. all of the above equally

4. Which form of city government do most cities over 1 million in population have?
a. township
c. council-manager
b. commission
d. mayor-council

5. True or false: The national government has been able to get many communities to use city planners.

6. Where in a city would you usually expect to find government offices?
a. downtown
b. in the run-down area
c. in the older residential area
d. at the outer edge

7. An enclosed shopping mall and a zoo would most likely be found _____.
a. downtown
b. in the run-down area
c. in the older residential area
d. at the outer edge

8. The run-down area would most likely include
a. large homes, golf courses, and new apartments
b. factories, warehouses, and low-cost housing
c. banks, hotels, and offices
d. all of the above

9. Your right to privacy is protected in
a. your home
c. a hotel room
b. a telephone booth
d. all of the above

10. Which amendment protects you from unfair police searches?
a. First Amendment
b. Tenth Amendment
c. Fourth Amendment
d. none of the above

Skill Building

People have many roles. Match the following people to the local government job each performs.
1. sheriff
2. prosecuting attorney
3. county judge
4. coroner
5. treasurer
a. Mary Ellis made the formal charges in a murder case.
b. Perez decided a juvenile court case.
c. Sam Jones delivered a summons for a witness to appear in court.
d. Sherman is the person to pay property taxes to.
e. A woman drowned and Johnson was called in.

6. Name three services provided by local government.

7. Name three local officials that are elected. Which job do you feel is most important? Why?

8. What is the main way a local government gets the money it needs? Name two other ways.

9. Divide your paper into two columns. Label one column "mayor-council." Label the other "council-manager." Compare the two forms of city government.

10. Name three leaders in city government. Explain the role of each.

11. Name three groups that try to influence city governments.

12. Name at least three major problems cities are facing today.

Unit 7

Community Citizenship

You are a citizen of the United States and of your own state. You are also a citizen of your local community.

Citizenship in a community brings both rights and responsibilities. Community members have the right to participate in governing their community. They may, for example, vote on local issues and for candidates for such offices as city council, mayor, or the school board.

Citizens also have a responsibility to contribute to their community. Volunteer work is one important way to help your community. Every year millions of teenagers and adults spend some of their time and energy helping meet important needs in their community.

In a Connecticut town, high-school students have helped to run the town's volunteer ambulance service during the daytime. In a New York community, a senior Girl Scout troop organized a summer day camp for the children of migrant workers. In a western city, teenagers and adults worked together to clean up some land donated by a local business for use as a park.

Volunteer work makes a vital contribution to democracy. When citizens give their time to work on community problems they are taking responsibility for dealing with community needs that otherwise might have to be taken care of by government. Volunteer work allows citizens in each community to decide for themselves how to handle their own problems.

Community citizenship also involves respect for the law. Unfortunately, every community must deal with crime. The police play a key role in keeping order in a community. Citizens can help make their community safer by cooperating with the police and by following simple precautions.

Nearly every community has special juvenile courts to deal with young people who are neglected or in trouble with the law. The job of these courts is to help youngsters, not simply punish them.

In this unit you will learn how citizens improve their communities by working together and how every community protects itself against crime.

**Chapter 20:
Taking Part in
Community Life**

**Chapter 21:
Law in Your Community**

Raising the Stars and Stripes at a one-room school in South Dakota.

Chapter 20

Taking Part in Community Life

Introduction. Every year more than 37 million citizens do volunteer work to help make their communities become better places to live. More than 20 percent of these volunteers are between the ages of fourteen and seventeen. These Americans volunteer to work in health clinics, little leagues, nursing homes, animal welfare shelters, and many other places. They may be neighbors working to clean up a vacant lot, or grandparents teaching nursery-school children, or students giving up weekends to organize a bowling tournament for handicapped children.

The United States has always been a nation of volunteers. More than 150 years ago, Alexis de Tocqueville [də tôk'vil], a French political writer, visited America to see how the young country was doing. He was amazed to find Americans volunteering to work on all sorts of problems that government handled in other countries. In this chapter you will learn about voluntary group activities.

Section 1
Voluntary Groups

"I like the way the kids feel toward me when I come in each day. For weeks I worked really hard with one boy. Then, one day, he put his hand out and shook mine."

Barb Ferris, a high-school junior, was describing her volunteer work with a mentally retarded child at Sonoma State Hospital. Every day, groups of teenagers visit the hospital to work with patients. These young volunteers spend hours taking patients out for walks, helping with physical therapy, reading to patients, playing with children, starting arts and crafts projects, and much more.

Many students also spend part of their summer vacations working at the hospital. The volunteers took over an old barn on the hospital grounds. They fixed it up and turned it into a living quarters they call Volunteer Village.

To **volunteer** is to offer to work or help without pay. **Voluntary groups** are spare-time organizations whose members·are mostly unpaid volunteers. Working with a voluntary group is one important way citizens in America help meet needs in their community.

Large Groups

There are many different kinds of voluntary groups working on solving community problems. Some groups are very large. The American Red Cross, for example, has 30 million members spread across the United States, and the Girl Scouts has more than 3 million members. Examples of other large groups are the

Voluntary groups often help people help themselves. Such is the case with the many Special Olympics contests that volunteers sponsor for mentally and physically handicapped young people each summer. The athletes shown above won medals at the Baton Rouge, Louisiana, Special Olympics.

A blind woman and her guide dog, which was provided by the Lions Club.

American Cancer Society, the League of Women Voters, the Kiwanis Clubs, and the General Federation of Women's Clubs. Large groups usually work on many different activities. They sponsor sports projects, provide food baskets, cut wood, and give other help to the poor. They also support medical clinics and research.

The Lions Club is one very large voluntary group that carries on many important services. The group has more than a million members. These members belong to more than 27,500 local Lions Clubs in cities all over the world.

Lions Club members pay a small dues each year and go to regular meetings, usually once a week. They use their spare time to work on many local projects. Some attend an annual convention of the entire group.

The motto of the Lions Club is "We Serve." At a 1925 convention, Helen Keller, a blind and deaf woman who did much to promote the interests of the blind, asked the Lions Club to work to help the blind. Since then group members have worked on many projects for the blind. They set up eye clinics and eye banks. They hold workshops and help pay scholarships for blind students. They introduced the white canes used by the blind. They provide guide dogs for many blind people. Some other Lions Club projects include repairing hearing aids for the needy who are hard of hearing, sponsoring career night at local high schools, building playgrounds, and starting local clean-up campaigns.

Small Groups

Many voluntary groups are small and locally organized. They often work on one or two projects, such as collecting toys for needy children at Christmas time.

The Worthington Historical Society, for example, is a group of citizens working to preserve the heritage of the city of Worthington, Ohio. Members collect antiques, old pictures, and other items that show what frontier life in the Ohio town was like.

The Orange Johnson House is one of the group's biggest projects. Built in 1816, the house is a good example of early life in Worthington. Hundreds of people each year tour the beautiful old house. To raise money for their projects, historical society members hold an annual flea market, an antique show, and a summer concert.

Many high-school students in Fall River, Massachusetts, have volunteered to help their community in another way. They work in the Youth Elderly Services (YES) program. In YES, the student volunteers work with elderly people in Fall

River's nursing homes. The students spend one or two hours a week meeting with their elderly friends. They write letters, run errands, help with odd jobs, and provide companionship. The YES program is a way students can help their community. It also gives the elderly a sense that young people care about them.

In Atlanta, Georgia, public high-school students perform a variety of community services after school and on weekends. Students in Atlanta are required to perform at least seventy-five hours of unpaid community service during their four years in high school. This service is a requirement for high-school graduation and enables students to earn academic credit.

Most students in the Atlanta schools do not object to such a requirement. According to one school official, the "students think it's a neat idea, and for many of them it is nothing new." Many of the students already had been actively involved in community service projects.

Helping by Giving

Using your time to work with a voluntary group such as the Red Cross is the heart of volunteerism. However, there is another way Americans support worthy causes. This is by contributing money. In a recent year, Americans gave about $60 billion to charity.

Much of this money comes from small donations by average citizens. The typical American donates nearly 2 percent of his or her income to charity. A working couple with two young children explain,

Danny Thomas, a popular comedian, is the founder of St. Jude Children's Research Hospital in Memphis, Tennessee. The hospital, which treats children with leukemia and other forms of cancer, relies heavily upon contributions from individuals and businesses.

"With the kids it's hard for us to give time, so we try to help our community by giving money."

Many wealthy Americans donate large amounts of tax-deductible money to hospitals, universities, youth programs, and other worthy causes. An oil man recently donated $3 million to create a children's diabetes center in Denver, Colorado. The owner of a computer company pledged $20 million to help pay for a new children's hospital in California. In Greensboro, North Carolina, an insurance executive gave $100,000 to the city to hire seventy-five people, mostly teenagers, to fix up city parks during the summer.

Some large businesses also contribute to community projects and to voluntary groups. In Minnesota, a food company gave more than 400,000 pounds of food to the public through food pantries. In Los Angeles, a soft drink company gave $500,000 to the city for youth basketball, public swimming pools, and other recreational activities.

Private donations like these provide support for many social services and activities. They show, as one official put it, that "the spirit of volunteerism lives in America."

Section Review

Vocabulary:
voluntary group, volunteer.

Reviewing the Main Ideas
1. Define *voluntary group.*
2. Why are the Lions an example of a voluntary group?
3. How is a voluntary group different from a business?

Skill Building
1. Make a list of as many voluntary groups in your community as you can. Add your list to the lists of classmates, eliminating duplicates.
2. What services are not being provided in your community that could be handled by a voluntary group?
3. Contact a local group and ask if it needs teenage volunteers. Volunteer your services and then report on your experiences.

Section 2
How Voluntary Groups Are Governed

Like any group, voluntary groups must govern themselves in order to get things done. This involves making rules, setting goals, and planning projects to meet the goals. Many voluntary groups have **bylaws** that serve as a written constitution for the group. Such groups run their meetings according to a set of rules called **parliamentary procedure.**

Let's look closely at how one voluntary group works.

Sheila McCreary was president of the Parent Teacher Association (PTA) at her son's school. As president, it was her job to be the leader of the group. "Good evening," Sheila began. "I would like to call the meeting to order. I'm glad everyone could be here. We have some important business to discuss."

Alan Greenbaum was the secretary. His job was to keep formal notes of what happened at business meetings. These notes are called the **minutes.** Alan began the meeting by going over the minutes from the last meeting.

Next the group heard from Lucy Shaefer, the treasurer. The treasurer is in charge of the group's money. The treasurer pays the group's bills, collects dues, and deposits the group's money in a bank. Lucy reported that the group had $985 in its account. She also reported that a bill of $20 for printing new membership forms was paid last week.

Tony Rossi was the vice-president. The vice-president takes charge of meetings if the president cannot attend. Often he supervises the work of the group's committees. Tony asked Hugh Falbo to report on the membership committee's work.

Hugh said that the members of his committee were planning several projects to get new members. On Monday, for example, all the students were going to bring a membership form home to their parents.

The PTA also had a committee for special projects and a publicity committee. Committees are one way voluntary groups carry on projects.

After hearing reports, the officers of Sheila's PTA group discussed plans for the spring bike safety rodeo. Sheila suggested they set up a new committee to plan the rodeo. The others agreed. Sheila said she would contact Mike Stamborski, a PTA member, to see if he would be chairperson of the bike rodeo committee. Then she said, "If there is no further business, the meeting is adjourned."

Group Leaders and Members

How do people become voluntary group officers? In most groups the officers are elected by members. Often there is a **nominating committee** that meets to talk over possible candidates. The nominating committee will talk to the various individuals it wants for offices. The committee wants to make sure these people have the time, energy, and commitment the leadership jobs require. Then they will suggest a **slate** of candidates. Most of the time, candidates for office in voluntary groups are unopposed. However, most groups' bylaws allow nominations to be added by anyone at election time. Then all the members vote.

In most cases, committee chairpersons are chosen by the president. Members of committees may be selected by the president or by the committee chairperson. Often members may choose which committees to serve on based on their interests.

Voluntary groups need good officers. The officers must act as leaders if the group is to be successful. It is the leader's job to govern the group, to keep projects going, to

Student council conducting a meeting in a member's home.

Students and their teacher planning a community clean-up project.

officers in a typical voluntary group? Describe their main responsibilities.
2. Why do voluntary groups have committees?
3. How are officers chosen in most voluntary groups?

Skill Building

What ways of governing a voluntary group are similar to the ways our other governments are run? Find at least five points of comparison.

raise money, to plan and follow through on new projects, and to find new members.

Voluntary groups also need good followers. No group can be successful without members who pay their dues, go to meetings regularly, support the goals of the group, and work hard on group projects. Not every person may have the chance or want to be a group leader. But every member can have a chance to be a good follower and contribute to the success of the group.

Section Review

Vocabulary:
bylaws, minutes, nominating committee, parliamentary procedure, slate.

Reviewing the Main Ideas
1. What are the jobs of the different

Section 3
Volunteers Help Make Democracy Work

Volunteer work and voluntary groups make an important contribution to democracy. In every community, citizens working in voluntary groups take responsibility for meeting important community needs that otherwise might have to be taken care of by government.

Here is an example. Every year thousands of voluntary groups in local communities across the country provide useful services for the sick and the poor. Volunteer members of these groups collect money for new medical equipment, run clinics for the deaf and blind, collect food and clothes, run sports programs for handicapped youngsters, help with physical therapy programs and much more. Without these volunteers, many of these needs simply would not be met—or the government would have to do the job.

Volunteer groups are one of the most important differences between a **totalitarian society** and a democracy. In totalitarian societies, such as many communist countries, almost all areas of life are controlled by the government. There are no voluntary groups of the kind we have in our society. Instead, citizens must look to the government for guidance in meeting all community needs.

Citizen participation in most totalitarian societies is controlled by the government or a ruling political party. It is the government, not the individual, who decides how and when citizens should take part in community projects such as building a new well or repairing a school building. In the People's Republic of China, for example, many services are provided by citizens working in their spare time. But this work is planned and controlled by the government. Citizens have little or no freedom to decide for themselves whether or not to participate.

In a democracy, the government and citizens share responsibility for meeting the community's needs. For example, we expect the government to provide police service and roads in our communities. But it is up to citizens to volunteer their time to help run the libraries, hospitals, nursing homes, sports programs, historical societies, and museums in their communities. In a democracy, there is a limit to the services a government provides. Thus, along with being a free citizen comes the responsibility of taking part in solving community problems.

One political leader put it this way, "In every community and every state we need a program for voluntary action by the people, not just

Raising funds for the American Cancer Society.

government action for the people." The idea in a democracy is that many community needs can best be met through local voluntary groups.

Section Review

Vocabulary:
totalitarian society.

Reviewing the Main Ideas
1. Why are voluntary groups important in a free society?
2. Why is there little place for voluntary groups in a totalitarian society?

Skill Building
1. Summarize in a paragraph the main idea of Section 3.
2. Find the People's Republic of China on the world political map in your text's atlas. What is its capital?

395

Case Study

Teenage Volunteers Save a City

On a stormy March afternoon a Fort Wayne, Indiana, radio station broadcast an urgent message. The message was from the student-council president of one of the city's high schools. He was appealing to all the students of Fort Wayne to help fight a major crisis that threatened the usually peaceful city of 178,000.

Fort Wayne was in grave danger. Fed by melting snow and heavy March rains, the city's three rivers were flooding. On Sunday, the rising, dirty brown water had forced 3,000 people from their homes. By Tuesday nearly 10,000 more families had to flee.

Adult volunteers had filled and stacked thousands of sandbags along the riverfront. But it was not enough. The rivers kept rising. The earth dikes built to hold them back were soaked with rain. From the city's east side came frightening news: the five-block-long Pemberton dike could give way at any time.

Tuesday night, Fort Wayne's mayor turned to the city's high-school students for aid. The mayor asked the school superintendent to close all city schools so that the students could help. The superintendent agreed. But insurance regulations prevented him from asking students to help fight the flood. The students would have to volunteer.

City officials were counting on the students. To survive, Fort Wayne needed thousands of volunteers to work on the dikes. Some people believed the students would not show up.

There was no need to worry. By Wednesday morning hundreds of teenagers started pouring into the city's exhibition hall. They began shoveling mountains of sand into bags, tying the bags, and tossing them into waiting dump trucks. Soon they were filling 20,000 bags an hour. But still it was not enough.

By Wednesday afternoon two hundred new students an hour were volunteering. When floodwaters blew up a sewer, students built a wall of sandbags to contain the water. At the Spy Run dike, an army of teenagers repaired a dangerous leak. Near State Boulevard, students helped an elderly woman save her belongings from the rising waters.

The students were tireless. Student volunteers were supposed to leave the dikes and work inside every two hours. But trucks and buses were coming back from the work sites nearly empty. The students refused to let the rising waters get the best of them.

The students' greatest moment came at Pemberton Dike. Soon after midnight on Thursday, the water-soaked dike began to give way. The huge dike held back a wall of muddy water ten feet deep and two miles long. If the dike broke, the water could destroy everything in its path for nearly three square miles.

Police supervisors, fearing for the safety of the volunteers, ordered everyone out of the area.

The mud-soaked teenagers refused to leave. They voted to keep working despite the danger.

The students worked all night.

With aching backs and arms they passed the huge, bulging sandbags up the dike. Slowly, a wall of sandbags began to form.

Thursday morning brought thousands of student reinforcements to the exhibition hall. On Pemberton dike, 1,500 students continued piling up sandbags made at the hall. Everyone knew that the battle would be won or lost at Pemberton.

By Thursday evening, the dike had grown taller, but so had the raging river. Early Friday morning a new dam was finished. Within twenty-seven hours the students had built a dam twelve feet high, thirty feet across, and five blocks long. They had filled, tied, and carried into place 300,000 sandbags.

Everyone watched and waited. Would the new dam hold? Rain fell Friday morning. The volunteers added even more sandbags. On Friday evening the river finally began to drop. The crisis was over. The dam had held.

The students could go home. Many had been working for more than a day with only a short break.

About fifty thousand people had volunteered to fight the flood in Fort Wayne. Nearly thirty thousand of them were students. Everyone agreed that the teenagers had pulled off an extraordinary feat, one that the people of Fort Wayne would not soon forget.

Review

1. Why did the city of Fort Wayne need volunteers?
2. What did the students do at Pemberton Dike?
3. What would have been the consequences had the students not volunteered?

Fort Wayne students taking a needed break from their exhausting duties.

Basic Social Studies Skills
Identifying Main Ideas and Supporting Details

Main ideas are the themes, or most important points, in a body of information. A newspaper article, for example, has one or more main ideas or major points. Main ideas are also presented in speeches, graphs, charts, tables, and pictures.

Supporting details are facts used to clarify, justify, or elaborate upon main ideas. Suppose that the main idea of a newspaper article is the amount of money raised for charity by different groups of volunteers. The supporting details in this article would tell how much money was raised by different groups, how it was raised, and how it would be used.

Main ideas hold together a body of information. They make up the framework that gives form or order to the details. The main ideas are the keys to the meaning of a message. You show understanding of a message when you pick out the main ideas and supporting details.

The chapters and sections of this textbook have main ideas and supporting details. Before reading a textbook chapter, you should look at the list of section titles that follows the introduction. The three section titles of Chapter 20, for example, are clues to the main ideas of the chapter. They tell you that this chapter emphasizes the organization, activities, and importance of voluntary groups in American communities.

Skill Practice

1. After identifying a main idea in Section 2, find details that support the idea.

2. Identify one main idea and the supporting details in Section 3 of Chapter 20.

3. Study the graphs below. What is a main idea in this pair of graphs? What details support the main idea?

Sources of Charitable Giving

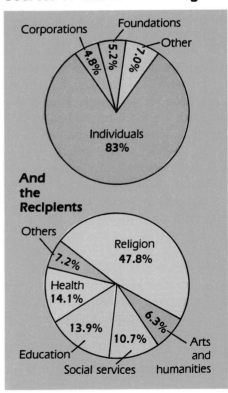

Chapter 20 Review

Summary

Section 1: Voluntary Groups

The United States has always been a nation of volunteers. Performing volunteer work is one way people fulfill their responsibilities as citizens. Some voluntary groups, such as the Red Cross, are very large. Others are small and organized locally. Americans also contribute to worthy causes by donating money.

Section 2: How Voluntary Groups Are Governed

Like other groups, voluntary groups must govern themselves to get things done. Voluntary groups usually have written constitutions called bylaws. They also have officers such as a president, vice-president, treasurer, and secretary. In most groups, the members elect their officers. Successful voluntary groups require good leadership and hard-working members.

Section 3: Volunteers Help Make Democracy Work

Volunteer work and voluntary groups are one of the most important differences between a democracy and a totalitarian society. In the United States, citizens working in voluntary groups take responsibility for meeting important community needs. This gives citizens opportunities to shape their own lives and to help their community.

Vocabulary

Define the following terms.
1. volunteer
2. voluntary group
3. bylaws
4. nominating committee
5. minutes
6. totalitarian society
7. slate

Reviewing Main Ideas

1. The group treasurer does all the following *except*
a. pay bills
b. collect dues
c. take notes on the meeting
d. put money in the bank
2. True or false: In most voluntary groups, the officers volunteer for their positions.
3. True or false: In order for any group to work well it needs both leaders and followers.
4. Voluntary groups meet needs that otherwise would have to be met by
a. businesses
b. government
c. wealthy citizens
d. students

Thinking Critically

Evaluating Information

1. The authors have said that voluntary groups help a democratic form of government. What reasons do they give?
2. Do you agree or disagree with the reasons given by the authors in number one above? Give your reasons.

Communicating Ideas

1. Choose a voluntary group in your community whose work you feel is worthwhile. Design a poster to get more people to help.
2. You want to convince a friend to join a voluntary group. List your key arguments.

Comprehending Information

1. How are voluntary groups like the national government?
2. How are voluntary groups different from the national government?

Chapter 21

Law in Your Community

Introduction. "Many people believe that police work involves one shoot-out after the other. The television police shows are much to blame," says Julio Sanchez, a veteran police officer.

Unlike the television shows, police work in Sanchez's district rarely includes a shootout. According to Sanchez, a lot of police work involves helping someone solve an everyday problem. Sometimes this may involve finding someone's social security check, locating a street address, or helping settle a family quarrel.

Sheila Seltzer, one of a growing number of young women doing police work, agrees with Sanchez. "This is not a Wyatt Earp-type job," she says. "Although I have been in a number of pretty dangerous situations, most of my time is spent solving simple community problems." On a recent night, for example, Seltzer dealt with a minor traffic accident, drove home several teenagers who were out after curfew, and talked with a store owner whose burglar alarm had been tripped accidentally.

Both Seltzer and Sanchez also devote much of their time toward crime prevention. This includes talking to local groups about ways to discourage burglaries and lecturing drivers' education classes on the abuse of alcohol.

Police officers such as Seltzer and Sanchez are typical of police officers in cities all over the nation. They are dedicated people who perform a wide variety of community services.

Section 1
Dealing with Crime

Dealing with crime is a major task for most communities today. In a recent year, almost 13 million serious crimes were reported to police across the country. There were more than three million burglaries and more than one million stolen cars reported. Put another way, on the average, a burglary was committed every nine seconds, a rape every seven minutes, a robbery every fifty-nine seconds, a murder every twenty-five minutes, and a car or truck stolen every thirty seconds.

Role of the Police

Every community looks to its police officers to enforce the law and help keep order. New York City organized the first paid police force in 1844. As our society has grown more complex, the police officer's job has become more difficult. One big-city police chief explains, "Policing used to be a fairly simple job. It was organize the posse, jump on the horses, and go after the bad guys. Now it requires much greater response to the human condition."

Police officers do three kinds of jobs. These are: (1) enforcing the law, (2) settling disputes, and

Police officers in large cities must be prepared to handle a wide variety of problems and situations. These two Chicago policemen are asking the driver of a passing car if she has information regarding a robbery in the neighborhood.

Crime Clock

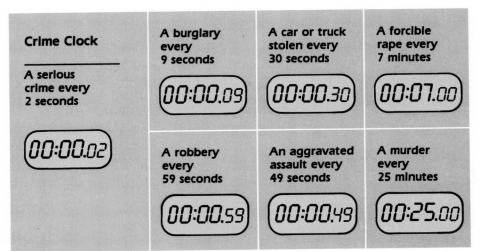

Crime Clock			
A serious crime every 2 seconds `00:00.02`	**A burglary every 9 seconds** `00:00.09`	**A car or truck stolen every 30 seconds** `00:00.30`	**A forcible rape every 7 minutes** `00:07.00`
	A robbery every 59 seconds `00:00.59`	**An aggravated assault every 49 seconds** `00:00.49`	**A murder every 25 minutes** `00:25.00`

Which of the crimes in the chart at right occurs more frequently than all other serious crimes?

(3) providing useful services. All three jobs require police officers to continually make tough, on-the-spot decisions. Should the group of noisy teenagers be left alone or warned to move along quietly? Should the driver of a suspicious-looking car be stopped and questioned? Did the angry young father really hit the screaming baby or did the child fall from its crib as the father claims?

Enforcing the Law. Police have the duty to prevent crime, and to find and arrest those who violate the law. The government gives police the legal power to use force if necessary to enforce the law.

When the police arrest someone for a crime, their work has just begun. The arresting officer must prepare reports for the courts. And the officer must appear in court as a witness.

Although important and often dangerous, law enforcement actually takes up a fairly small amount of most police officers' time every day. Police usually spend more time on the other two parts of their job.

Settling Disputes. Police officers play a key role in keeping peace. They are often called upon to break up family fights, quiet noisy parties, deal with gang problems, or settle neighborhood quarrels. In such situations most police officers are careful. They try to use good judgment and patience in dealing with people. It can be difficult to determine who is to blame. Most officers try reestablishing order rather than simply arresting everyone involved.

Providing Useful Services. Finally, the police carry out many day-to-day jobs. They handle traffic accidents, help stranded motorists, give first aid to injured people, search for lost children, and even get cats down out of trees. Some experts say police spend as much as 30 percent of their time on service jobs.

Property Crimes Versus Violent Crimes

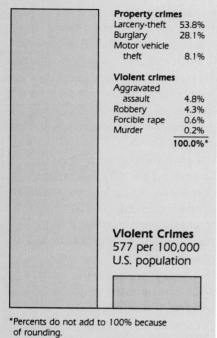

Property crimes outnumbered violent crimes by 9 to 1

Property crimes
5,223 per 100,000
U.S. population

Property crimes	
Larceny-theft	53.8%
Burglary	28.1%
Motor vehicle theft	8.1%

Violent crimes	
Aggravated assault	4.8%
Robbery	4.3%
Forcible rape	0.6%
Murder	0.2%
	100.0%*

Violent Crimes
577 per 100,000
U.S. population

*Percents do not add to 100% because of rounding.
Source: FBI Uniform Crime Reports, 1981.

Guidelines for Citizens

Citizens can help control crime. In communities where people work with the police and follow some simple safeguards, crime rates tend to go down. Here are guidelines you can follow to help protect yourself and your neighborhood.

Protecting Yourself at Home. Most burglars are not "pros." Most often they take advantage of an easy mark —someone who leaves their door unlocked or windows open. To stop burglars follow these tips:

- Use "deadbolt" type doorlocks with a strong metal bar that extends one inch into the door frame.
- When it is too hot to close and lock windows, put nails in window frames so the windows cannot be opened more than a few inches until you take the nails out.
- Protect sliding glass doors by putting a small wooden beam or broom handle in the door track. This keeps the door shut even if the lock is pried open.
- When you take a trip, stop newspaper and mail delivery or ask a neighbor to collect things so they do not pile up outside your door.
- When you take a trip, use automatic timers to turn lights and radios on and off. Set lights to go on in different rooms at different times.
- Engrave things, such as your television, stereo, or tools, with a personal identification number. Announce that fact by sticking a warning sign on your door or window. In Phoenix, Arizona, people who followed this practice had burglary rates eighteen times lower than neighbors who did not mark their valuables.

Protecting Yourself on the Street. Unfortunately, snatching purses, mugging, and picking pockets are big business. Pickpockets average $124 a "take" and purse snatchers about $98. Follow common sense to protect yourself on the street.

(above) Most counties have law enforcement units that patrol areas within county borders. When necessary, they lend support to local police departments. (chart) How many property crimes occur in a one-year period? Use 250 million as the total population of the United States when figuring your answer.

- Be alert and walk confidently. Notice who passes you and who is behind you.
- At night, avoid shortcuts through parks, tunnels, alleys, or parking lots.
- Women: hold your purse tightly, in front of your body. Men: put your wallet in your front pocket or button your hip pocket.
- Carry as little cash as possible.
- Carry a whistle or other noisemaker. If you are in trouble, use it.
- Finally, if someone does grab your purse or wallet, let it go! It is not worth risking your life to save it.

Protecting Yourself Against Fraud. **Fraud** is any deliberate misrepresentation of the truth or a fact used to take money or rights away from someone. Con artists use lies and smooth talking to take your money. They may seem like "nice," ordinary people. They make a living convincing you to pay your money for products or services they will never deliver.

- When somebody offers you something for nothing, be very suspicious—usually you will wind up with nothing.
- Deals that are "too good to be true" usually turn out to be no bargain.
- Never pay large sums in cash until you have the goods or services you are paying for.
- Do not let yourself be pressured into signing a contract. Wait a while and read it carefully. If a lot of money is involved, take the contract to a lawyer.
- If you sign a contract, but later change your mind, cancel it. Most states give you three days to cancel a newly signed contract.

Protecting Your Neighborhood. People can work together to prevent crimes in their neighborhood. Here are examples of steps people have taken to control crime:

(above) Police officers apprehending two robbery suspects. (right) Officer and his sidekick. The two visit schools to teach young children safety rules.

- Neighbors can exchange work and vacation schedules so they can keep an eye on each other's homes.
- In some communities, neighbors get together to patrol their streets for suspicious activities. If they see trouble, they report it to the police, who then deal with the problem.
- Neighbors can volunteer to accompany an elderly person to the store, bank, post office, or anywhere so the senior citizen won't have to walk alone.
- In apartments, neighbors have formed tenant patrols to look out for suspicious activities in their buildings.
- In some apartments, neighbors volunteer to take turns with other tenants to screen visitors to the building.
- Always check with the police before starting any community crime prevention program. The police may be able to offer help and suggestions on getting organized.

Report a Crime. If a crime occurs, report it to the police immediately. A five-minute delay reduces the chances of catching the criminal by two-thirds. You contribute to the crime rate if you fail to report a crime. At least half the crimes committed in the United States are not reported. As a result, the police never get a chance to arrest the criminal.

(left) Officer posting a Neighborhood Watch sign. The sign is a warning to potential lawbreakers that the people in this neighborhood are on the lookout for crime in the area and will report any suspicious activity to the police.

Section Review

Vocabulary:
fraud.

Reviewing the Main Ideas
1. Name three jobs that police officers perform for the community.
2. Give two examples of how you can protect yourself from burglary.
3. Give two examples of how you can protect yourself on the street.
4. Give two examples of how you can protect yourself from fraud.

Skill Building
1. Which of the three jobs performed by police officers do you think is most important?
2. Design a chart that will show the major ways a citizen can help control crime. Use ideas from the chapter as well as your own.
3. Write a report about crime prevention in your community. Interview police officers or crime prevention groups to get your information.

Section 2
Juvenile Justice

Young people commit a large number of the nation's crimes. Juvenile crime costs about $16 billion a year. In a recent year, young people were responsible for 43 percent of the burglaries, 29 percent of the robberies, 15 percent of the rapes, and 20 percent of the total crime in the United States.

At the same time, many children and young people are victims. In a recent year, there were over 750,000 official reports of child abuse involving more than 1.2 million children. Even larger numbers of young people found themselves in homes where parents took little responsibility for them. Young people who come from such homes are more likely to commit crimes than youngsters from good home situations.

Juvenile Delinquency

Juvenile delinquency is a violation of the law by a young person. Each state sets the age at which a person is legally considered to be a juvenile. In most states, a juvenile is anyone under eighteen years of age. A few states set the age as low as sixteen or as high as twenty-one.

Juvenile delinquency includes actions, such as bank robbery, which would be a crime if adults committed them. It also includes those acts only illegal for juveniles, such as staying out past curfew or drinking beer. In addition, for many people, "juvenile delinquency" has come to mean repeatedly bad behavior by young people, whether illegal or not. This might include constantly causing trouble at school, running away from home, or regularly disobeying parents.

Juvenile delinquency is a serious problem in many nations, including the United States. Unhappy home conditions, membership in street gangs, alcohol and drug use, and unemployment are some of the causes of juvenile delinquency.

Purpose and Organization of Juvenile Courts

All fifty states have special courts to deal with juvenile delinquency. These **juvenile courts** exist side by side with our federal and state courts. Some juvenile courts are called "family courts." All were created by special laws describing what cases the juvenile courts will handle and how they will work.

Origins and Purposes. Juvenile courts are a fairly new idea. Cook County, Illinois, set up the first juvenile court in 1899. Denver started one in 1903. By 1925, nearly every state had created juvenile courts.

Before the establishment of juvenile courts, anyone over fourteen who committed a crime was treated as an adult. Young people were tried in regular criminal courts. They could be, and often were, sentenced like adults to long prison terms. Occasionally children were even sentenced to death, usually by hanging.

Juvenile courts were created to stop such harsh treatment of young people. They are based on the idea that young people sometimes make mistakes because of a lack of experience rather than criminal intent. They also recognize that the proper care of youngsters is the concern of all people in the community. The government, acting for the people, has a responsibility for children in need of help.

Thus, the purpose of juvenile courts is to aid, rather than punish, young persons. The procedures and decisions in juvenile courts are supposed to help youngsters by giving them needed care, treatment, discipline, and supervision.

Cases Heard in Juvenile Courts. Juvenile courts handle cases involving youngsters accused of breaking the law. In some states, young people over fourteen charged with very serious crimes, such as murder, must be tried in regular criminal courts. In many states, the government decides which court will deal with young people over the age of thirteen.

Juvenile courts also handle cases involving children or young people who are neglected or in need of supervision. Neglected children are those whose families are not caring properly for them. Young people in need of supervision are youngsters who constantly misbehave. These young people may not have violated a criminal law. Rather, they are youngsters whose behavior is impossible for parents and teachers to control.

Court Officials. Judges make the key decisions in juvenile courts. Juries are not used in most juvenile courts. The judge's job is to help

young people, rather than simply punish them. The judge will study information about the offender's case and will talk with parents and others about the best treatment.

In many busy juvenile courts, **referees** assist judges by listening to facts and making decisions on cases. The judge then reviews their work. However, most cases are decided on the basis of the referee's recommendation.

Judges are assisted by **probation officers.** These officials do several important jobs for the juvenile courts. They investigate the family life and activities of young people for the court. They also supervise offenders released by the court on probation. Being on **probation** means the offender is free to live at home and go to school under certain conditions. The conditions may include restrictions, such as not being allowed to drive a car

Members of the controversial Guardian Angels, an organization of young people who patrol public transportation in an attempt to prevent crimes. The Angels, who have branches in many cities across the nation, have been both criticized and praised. Critics say law enforcement should strictly be in the hands of the police. Those in favor of the Angels say the group is needed because there aren't enough police officers in high-crime areas.

407

or to loiter near certain trouble spots. Finally, probation officers have the authority to bring young people who violate the conditions of their probation back to court.

Steps in Juvenile Court

Juvenile courts follow special procedures to handle cases. These procedures are similar to regular trials but there are some differences. Here are the basic steps.

Custody. When the police take a juvenile into custody, they must promptly make an effort to call his or her parents. The police must then take the juvenile "without delay" to a juvenile officer. At this point the young person may be released by the police to his or her parents. This often happens for a first offense. This release is called a **station adjustment.**

If the young person is not released, the juvenile officer must take him or her before a judge, again "without delay." The judge then decides on the next steps. These usually involve two hearings.

Hearings. Juvenile courts hold **hearings** instead of trials. The first is the **adjudicatory hearing.** This hearing determines the facts of the case. The judge reviews the case with the young person, his or her parents and possibly their lawyer, and court officials, including a prosecutor. The judge then decides whether the juvenile is delinquent, neglected, or in need of supervision.

If a youngster is found guilty or neglected, a **dispositional hearing**

is held. At this hearing the judge decides what shall be done with the young person. Several alternatives are available. These include: (1) sending the young person to a foster home if he or she is neglected, (2) releasing the delinquent on probation, or (3) sending the delinquent to a reformatory, or training school.

Action by the Court. Juvenile courts usually place children who are neglected with foster families. A foster family is a family willing to care for a neglected young person for a certain period of time. Juveniles in need of supervision or found guilty of violating the law may be placed in foster homes, community-based group homes for youth, or, in some cases, a **reformatory.** A reformatory is an institution, much like a prison, that is occupied only by young people.

Juvenile court judges usually take a young person away from his or her family only when absolutely necessary. Some states have laws which say that a child should be cared for in his or her own home whenever possible. Some of these laws state that a child cannot be considered neglected or be removed from home simply because the family lacks money.

To protect youngsters, the laws discourage publicizing the names of juvenile delinquents. Further, juveniles do not receive a criminal record by going to juvenile court or by being sent to reform school. A criminal record can follow people through life. It can make it difficult for them to change their ways because society has labeled them as "criminals." Juvenile court procedures seek to prevent such labeling.

The laws state that juvenile court records cannot be inspected without a court order. In addition, juvenile records cannot be used later in life for other purposes, such as denying a person an application for a license or disqualifying a person from holding public office.

Constitutional Rights In Juvenile Court

Young people in juvenile court have the same constitutional protections given to adults. In 1967, in a case called *In re Gault*, the Supreme Court ruled that juveniles have the right to: (1) be informed of the specific charges against them, (2) be represented by a lawyer, (3) confront and question all witnesses, and (4) refuse to testify against themselves. At the same time, the Court said that juveniles did not have the right to bail or a jury trial. Today, however, sixteen states give juveniles the right to be tried before a jury.

Other Supreme Court decisions since *Gault* added to juveniles' rights. As a result, many juvenile court proceedings today are very similar to regular trials. As this has happened, new questions about juvenile rights are continually being raised. Are there instances when juveniles should not be protected from pretrial publicity? Should a young rape victim be protected from reporters during her testimony? Do

the police have to stop questioning a juvenile who asks to speak with his father or his probation officer, rather than to a lawyer? The meaning of juveniles' constitutional rights will continue to be spelled out as the courts deal with such issues.

Section Review

Vocabulary:
adjudicatory hearing, custody, dispositional hearing, foster family, hearing, juvenile courts, juvenile delinquency, probation, probation officer, referee, reformatory, station adjustment.

Reviewing the Main Ideas
1. What is the purpose of juvenile courts?
2. What is the judge's job in juvenile court?
3. List the main steps in juvenile court proceedings.
4. What constitutional rights did the Supreme Court give juveniles in the case of *In re Gault*?

Skill Building
Draw a chart comparing the steps in a juvenile court proceeding and the steps in a criminal trial described on pages 318-319. What are the main similarities and differences?

Juvenile in a detention cell awaiting a hearing.

Jury Duty: Your Right and Responsibility

"It was a great big mystery that had to be solved," said Ruth Yudkoff. "It would have been perfect for the movies, only the mystery was real, and we had to solve it."

Yudkoff was describing her service on a jury in a murder trial. A **jury** is a group of citizens who hear testimony in legal disputes and decide what it believes is the truth.

The right to a trial by jury is one of the basic constitutional rights in our democracy. Like freedom of speech, it is part of every American's legal birthright.

Serving on a jury is also an important duty for citizens. Jury service can be hard work. It can interrupt our daily lives. Yet, jury service can be one of the most important ways citizens contribute to democracy and law in their community.

Constitutional Guarantees and Importance

The Constitution provides for juries in several ways.

- Article 3, Section 2, Clause 3 states: "The trial of all crimes, except in cases of impeachment, shall be by jury. . . ."
- The Fifth Amendment declares: "No person shall be held to answer for a capital . . . crime, unless on . . . indictment of a Grand Jury."
- The Sixth Amendment guarantees criminal defendants "the right to a speedy and public trial by an impartial jury."
- The Seventh Amendment states that in common law cases "the right of trial by jury shall be preserved."

The use of juries helps put important constitutional ideals into practice in daily life. Juries can protect against government oppression by letting people be judged by fellow citizens. Juries promote equal justice under the law; rich and poor alike may have a jury trial. Juries give citizens a chance to participate in applying the laws in their own community.

Thomas Jefferson saw the importance of juries. He said the jury system was "the only anchor ever yet imagined by which a government can be held to the principles of its constitution."

The Jury System at Work

How do you get to be a juror? How does the jury system work today?

All citizens of sound mind who have not been convicted of a major crime may be called for jury duty. State and federal courts usually select people randomly from master lists of registered voters. Doctors, lawyers, and those who can demonstrate hardship are excused from jury duty.

Once called for jury duty, you must wait with other citizens to be chosen to serve on a case. Juries in criminal cases are made up of twelve members. In some states other cases may use juries of from five to eight members.

Selection of a Jury. Choosing twelve jurors is an important step. Lawyers for both sides question each juror. Each lawyer may reject any number of possible jurors "for cause." This means the lawyer explains why an individual should not serve as a juror. For example, the person being considered as a juror might be a relative of someone involved in the case.

Lawyers may also disqualify a limited number of people with a **peremptory challenge.** This is

410

excusing a juror without giving a reason. As one juror said, "It can be upsetting to get bounced." Yet being excused from a case does not reflect badly on a person. It is simply part of the process.

Once accepted to serve on a jury, you will be given an oath by the judge. The judge will then give the jury instructions about court procedures and the trial begins.

Listening to Testimony. During the trial jurors must listen carefully to all the testimony from both sides. Trying to take notes can be distracting. Thus, jurors are not allowed to take notes. From time to time the judge may ask the jury to leave the courtroom while the lawyers argue about legal fine points. Finally, the lawyer for each side summarizes the case and the jury is ready to decide.

Sometimes during the middle of a trial the jury may be told the case has been settled and its job is over. This happens when one side decides the case is going against it. The side that fears it is losing may compromise rather than let the case go to the jury for decision.

Reaching a Verdict. The jury meets in a private room, the jury room, to make its decision. In civil cases one party is suing another. The jury will usually decide who is at fault and how much money should be paid in damages.

In a criminal trial, the jury decides whether the defendant is guilty or innocent. The jurors must be convinced "beyond a reasonable doubt" that the defendant is guilty in order to convict him or her. Usually a **unanimous vote**—all jurors in agreement—is needed for conviction.

A **hung jury** is one in which the jurors can-

not agree on a verdict. When that happens a new trial with new jurors is held.

After the jury reaches its decision, it comes back into the courtroom. The jury announces its decision, or verdict, and the case is closed. Jury members are free to go. In most communities jurors will not be asked to serve again for at least two years.

All in all, jury duty can be dull, long, and just plain hard work. Yet one juror described the experience in a way that would surely have pleased the Founding Fathers. He said, "Twelve strangers meet by chance in this process, learn to work together, reason together, and finally reach a conclusion that may be crucial in the lives of others. When you achieve this, you feel you have really accomplished something. It brings out the best in most people."

Review

1. List four ways the Constitution provides for juries.
2. Define these terms: unanimous vote, peremptory challenge, hung jury.

Case Study

Volunteers Fight Crime

Seventy-two-year-old Dorothy Olmstead explained why she joined the Sheriff's Posse as she strapped on her .38 police revolver. "Basically," Olmstead said, "I just hate stealing."

Member of the Sun City Posse on patrol.

Dorothy Olmstead is one of 400 members of the Sun City Sheriff's Posse. The Posse is an all-volunteer police force for Sun City, Arizona, a retirement community outside Phoenix. Senior citizens, like those living in Sun City, are too often easy targets for criminals. The crime rate in Sun City, however, has been steadily going down ever since the all-volunteer Posse was formed more than a decade ago.

Posse members average nearly eighty years of age. Of the four hundred members, thirty are women. Sixty-nine-year-old Madelyn Stroud is typical. A retired computer programmer from Indiana, Stroud volunteers an average of two hundred hours per month to the force. Walking her beat in a shopping center, she explains, "What we really are is a deterrent." Simply having Posse members around, Stroud maintains, "helps cut down purse snatching, things like that."

The Sun City Posse works in close cooperation with the Maricopa County Sheriff's Department. County Sheriff Jerry Hill supports the Posse. Posse members go through the same training program given regular police officers by the county sheriff. Training includes learning basic police procedures, how to handle communications equipment, and the use of weapons. Gun-carrying members of the volunteer Posse take marksmanship tests twice a year.

The Sun City Posse pays for itself. It receives no government assistance. It receives nothing from the federal government, nothing from the state, nothing from the county. Its entire budget comes from community donations. Most donations come during a yearly fund-raising drive run by members of the Posse themselves.

Recently, donations were large enough to pay for a new headquarters building. In addition, the Posse maintains a fleet of eight squad cars equipped with two-way radios. The posse also uses electric golf carts to patrol certain areas, such as shopping centers.

Posse members buy their own uniforms. The brown uniforms look like the county sheriff's outfits. Posse members also buy their own boots, handguns, holsters, and hats. Chuck Fisher, 71, figures he spent nearly $600 on his complete uniform.

"I don't count the money," Fisher says. "I work about twenty-five hours per week, and I get no pay at all. But the fact is, I'm active, I'm out and about, I'm among people, and I'm doing something that I think is necessary and worthwhile."

Fisher and other Posse members think the uniforms and squad cars improve the image of the Sun City Posse. In turn, that image helps build the community's confidence in the Posse.

The Posse's main job is not the thrill-a-minute stuff you see on police TV shows. Rather, it is to regularly patrol the community and be a visible source of help. Ed Johnson explains that Posse members are citizens trained in law enforcement. As such, they act as "the eyes and ears" of the county sheriff's department.

Member Bill Moore agrees. As the eighty-three-year-old Moore looks at it, "Showing the colors is 90 percent of law enforcement." Dorothy Olmstead has said: "I think we are a deterrent to crime, very much so. What we're doing is making people conscious that if they see anything irregular or suspicious, they can report it to us, and we'll check it out."

Posse members are in direct contact with the county sheriff's office should serious trouble arise. "What would I do if I walked in on a bank robbery?" Ed Johnson does not think twice about his answer: "Well, I would radio for assistance from the county sheriff's department."

Posse members do more than patrol. They also engage in search and rescue work. Sometimes the results are tough to handle. Bill Moore says, "One of the things that gets to you is when you have to break into someone's house and you find somebody dead. I've had four of them, four little widows who died all alone." Moore adds, shaking his head, "That really gets to you."

Sometimes, however, the results are better. The Posse also helps with a local hospital call-for-help program. "Quite frequently," Chuck Fisher says, "we have arrived just in time to save somebody's life."

Review

1. What is the main job of the Sun City Posse?
2. Who pays for operating the Posse?

413

Basic Social Studies Skills
Analyzing a Judicial Decision

In 1984, the United States Supreme Court decided the case of *Schall* v. *Martin*. This was a major decision about the rights of juveniles accused of crimes. What was involved in this decision? How did it affect you and other young citizens?

You need to know how to analyze judicial decisions in order to understand how they might affect you and others. You can divide a judicial decision into five parts. You can use these categories to analyze the judicial decision in *Schall* v. *Martin*.

1. Background of the Case

In 1977, the Family Court Act of New York was challenged in a lawsuit by two juveniles who had been held in New York City's Spofford Juvenile Center. The act permits the pretrial detention of a juvenile charged with a criminal offense for up to seventeen days. The law states that a judge may order confinement of a suspected juvenile offender who presents a "serious risk" of committing another criminal act before trial.

2. The Legal Issue

A legal issue is a dispute over a question about the law. In this case, the question was about the "due process" clause of the Fourteenth Amendment. (See Section 1 of the amendment on pages 94-95.) Did the Family Court Act violate the "due process" clause of the Fourteenth Amendment?

3. The Court's Majority Opinion

Six of the nine members of the Court decided that the Family Court Act did not violate the "due process" clause. Justice William H. Rehnquist, who wrote the majority opinion, said that it is the state's duty to protect the community from crime. The "preventive detention" permitted by the Family Court Act succeeds in doing this, Rehnquist said. He added that this type of detention is not intended as a punishment.

4. The Dissenting Opinion

Justice Thurgood Marshall wrote the dissenting opinion of the three judges who disagreed with the majority opinion. He said that the Family Court Act permits detention of juveniles without "due process" of law. He also said that the law gives power to judges to treat different juveniles unequally and unfairly.

5. The Legal Consequences

The judicial decision in this case permits pretrial confinement of juveniles in all parts of the United States. The fifty states and the District of Columbia have laws permitting "preventive detention" of juveniles under certain conditions. However, legal rights established in the Constitution must not be violated.

Skill Practice

1. What is the main idea of the majority opinion?
2. What is the main idea of the dissenting opinion?

Chapter 21 Review

Summary

Section 1: Dealing with Crime

Crime control is a challenge for all communities. Crime is misconduct forbidden by law. The police have a major responsibility for dealing with crime. Police officers today perform three types of jobs for their community. They enforce the law, settle disputes, and provide needed services. Citizens can also help control crime by following certain safeguards and working together. Citizens also have a responsibility to report crimes to the police immediately.

Section 2: Juvenile Justice

Juvenile delinquency, crime, or misbehavior by young people, is a serious problem. Juvenile courts deal with juvenile delinquents and with neglected children. These courts aim to help, rather than simply punish, youngsters. Judges and probation officers are key officials in juvenile courts. These officials deal with offenders through hearings instead of trials. Juvenile delinquents have basically the same constitutional protections given adults.

Vocabulary

Define the following terms.
1. peremptory challenge
2. fraud
3. custody
4. dispositional hearing
5. adjudicatory hearing
6. reformatory
7. juvenile delinquency
8. referee
9. probation
10. station adjustment

Reviewing Main Ideas

1. Police officers do three kinds of jobs. These are providing useful services, settling disputes, and
   a. enforcing the law.
   b. interpreting the law.
   c. judging the law.
   d. making the law.
2. True or false: If you sign a contract, but change your mind the next day, you are still committed to the contract.
3. True or false: Juvenile courts are a fairly new idea.
4. True or false: Juvenile courts hold hearings instead of trials.

Thinking Critically

Comprehending Information

Look at the diagram and the graph on pages 402 and 403. What are two conclusions that can be drawn from the statistics shown?

Organizing Information

Make a chart showing various ways that ordinary citizens can fight and prevent crimes. Use information in Section 1 and any other information that you can find from library resources.

Communicating Ideas.

Write a well-organized report about crime or crime prevention in your community. Refer to the Writing and Research Skills section of the Students' Resource Section in your text for help in preparing your report.

Unit 7 Test

Vocabulary

Write *true* if the underlined word or phrase is used correctly. Write *false* if it is used incorrectly. Rephrase each false statement so that the underlined word or phrase is used correctly.

1. Voluntary groups are spare-time organizations whose members are mostly unpaid.

2. A jury is a group of lawyers who hear testimony in legal disputes and decide what they believe is the truth.

3. A reformatory is a place where convicted adult criminals are sent.

4. Lawyers may disqualify a limited number of jurors with a peremptory challenge.

5. A hung jury is a jury that has declared a person guilty by unanimous vote.

6. Fraud is an unintentional misrepresentation of the truth.

7. Communist countries have totalitarian societies.

8. Usually a unanimous vote—three-fourths of the jurors—is needed to convict a person in a criminal trial.

9. Many groups have bylaws that serve as a written constitution.

10. Many voluntary organizations have a nominating committee that meets to discuss possible candidates for office.

11. A person who is put on the slate is prohibited from running for office.

12. Juvenile courts and "family courts" are the same things.

13. Juvenile courts hold hearings instead of trials.

14. An adjudicatory hearing is held to determine the facts of a case involving a juvenile.

15. Dispositional hearings are jury trials for juveniles.

Recalling Information

1. The group treasurer does all the following except
a. pay bills
b. collect dues
c. take notes on the meeting
d. put money in the bank

2. Voluntary groups meet needs that otherwise would have to be met by
a. businesses
b. government
c. wealthy citizens
d. students

3. The President of the local PTA could not attend the meeting. Who took charge of the meeting?
a. treasurer
b. secretary
c. vice-president
d. special projects chairperson

4. True or false: Juries are not used in most juvenile cases.

5. True or false: A five-minute delay in reporting a crime to police reduces the chances of catching the criminal by two-thirds.

6. Which of the following is not considered a voluntary group?
a. Chicago Police Department
b. Kiwanis Club
c. Lions Club
d. Sun City Posse

7. Approximately what percent of volunteers are high-school students?
a. 5 percent
b. 20 percent
c. 50 percent
d. 70 percent

8. Which of the following organizations introduced the white canes that are used by the blind?
a. PTA
b. Lions Club
c. Kiwanis Club
d. Red Cross

9. Which of the following people may be excused from jury duty?
a. doctors
b. lawyers
c. people who can demonstrate hardship
d. all of the above

10. True or false: Juveniles have the right to refuse to testify against themselves.

11. True or false: Juveniles have the right to a jury trial.

12. True or false: Juvenile offenders who are on probation are allowed to live at home and go to school.

13. True or false: State and federal courts usually select jurors randomly from lists of registered voters.

14. Of the following jobs, which takes up the least amount of the average police officer's time?
a. enforcing the law
b. settling disputes
c. providing useful services

15. The juvenile court judge was extremely busy last week. Who assisted her in listening to facts and making decisions about several juvenile court cases?
a. a probation officer
b. a referee
c. a parole officer
d. a jury

Building Skills

1. Write a short essay for one of the following two activities:
a. How are voluntary groups like the national government? How are they different?
b. The authors have said that voluntary groups help a democratic form of government. What reasons do they give? Do you agree or disagree? Give your reasons.

2. Give examples of three large voluntary groups and three small voluntary groups. Ask a representative of one of these groups to speak to your class about the group's goals and accomplishments in your community.

Unit 8

Our Free Enterprise System

Have you ever had ten dollars to spend? If so, you undoubtedly have had to face the problem of making an economic choice. Should you use the money to buy a new record album? Perhaps a pizza would be better? Since you only have ten dollars, you cannot afford both of them. You will have to make a choice between the two.

Nations are no different. They too have to make choices. Consider the land a country has within its borders. The people in that country must somehow decide how the land should be used. Should a one-hundred-acre plot of land be used for growing food, for a new shopping center, or perhaps for houses? If it is used for new homes, it cannot be used for growing food or that new shopping center. Just as you cannot buy everything you want with ten dollars, a society cannot produce everything people want. It has only a limited amount of resources available to it. Somehow, choices must be made. The way these decisions are made varies from nation to nation depending upon the type of economic system the country has adopted.

As a citizen of a democratic country such as the United States, it is important that you understand our economic system. You are an important part of the economy. You make economic choices every day. Deciding how to spend that ten dollars is just one example. In addition, you will help determine the type of economy we have by the people you vote for in local, state, and national elections. They will determine the amount of control the government will have over the economy, how much it will spend, and how high taxes will be. It is therefore impossible to separate a nation's political system from its economic system. When citizens like you understand how the economy works, they can make wiser decisions as buyers, sellers, producers, and voters.

(opposite) The New York Stock Exchange on a busy day of trading.

Chapter 22

The American Economy

Introduction. During the summer, Don Fraser worked part time as a lifeguard at his school's swimming pool. This enabled him to save $200 for his college fund and another $200 that he would like to spend on something nice for himself. Although there are many things he would like to buy with the money, he has narrowed down a long list to a new stereo or a new bicycle. Each costs a little less than $200.

A stereo would be nice to listen to when friends come over or to provide some background music when Don does his homework. On the other hand, Don recently acquired an interest in bike racing. A new bike would enable him to be more competitive in some of the local races. Unfortunately, he does not have enough money to buy both. What should he do? Should he buy the stereo or the bike? Only Don can decide which would be best for him.

In choosing between the bike and the stereo, Don is making an economic decision. He has to choose between two things that he wants because he has a limited amount of money to spend. In this chapter, you will learn about the economic problems that nations as well as individuals face and the various ways they are solved.

Section 1
Making Economic Decisions

People throughout the world use goods and services every day. **Goods** are products such as shoes, automobiles, and food. **Services** are what people do for someone else in exchange for something of value. Car dealers sell goods—automobiles. Auto mechanics sell services—car repairs.

All of the goods and services people consume are made from the resources available to them. **Natural resources** come from the earth. They include water, soil, trees, and minerals. **Human resources** come from people. They are the skills, knowledge, energy, and physical capabilities of human beings.

Unfortunately both human and natural resources are limited. There are simply not enough resources available to produce all of the goods and services that people want. This is the economic problem of **scarcity** —only a limited amount of resources are available to satisfy unlimited wants.

Because of the problem of scarcity, people must make choices about the production and distribution of various goods and services.

What Should Be Produced?

It is important to realize that every decision to produce one thing is also a decision not to produce something else. The steel, glass, and rubber used to make a car cannot be used to make a bus, train, plane, or motorcycle. This is similar to the decisions you make as a consumer. If you spend your ten dollars on a pizza, you cannot buy the record album you want. Every time a

Economic decisions of one kind or another face all of us.

421

society decides what products will be produced, it is also deciding which ones will not be produced.

Sometimes people decide to do without certain goods and services in the present so that they can prepare for the future. This is what happens when people use resources to produce capital goods. **Capital goods** are products that are used to make other goods. Tools and machines are capital goods. In contrast, **consumer goods** are consumed directly by people. Clothing, food, furniture, and houses are examples of consumer goods. If people decide to produce more capital goods, they will have fewer consumer goods in the present.

How Many to Produce?

Closely related to the decision of what to produce, is the second question of how many to produce. If a nation decides it wants to use trains for transportation instead of cars, it must then decide how many

This computer tester is involved in producing goods for market.

trains to make and how many miles of track to lay. If a person with a 125-acre farm decides to grow corn and strawberries, he or she must then decide how many acres will be devoted to each.

How Should Goods and Services Be Produced?

The third type of economic decision concerns how things are produced. What resources will be used to produce the desired goods and services? How will they be made? Who will make them?

In the American economy, producers try to use scarce resources as efficiently as possible. They try to avoid or limit waste. In an effort to earn a profit they attempt to produce the good or service for the least possible cost by using resources efficiently. This tends to increase the wealth of the producers. The total wealth of the country also grows when its resources are used efficiently.

Who Gets the Goods and Services Produced?

The fourth kind of economic decision is concerned with the distribution of goods and services among the people. Once a society has decided what to produce (cars for example), how many of them to produce, and how to produce them, it must decide who gets the cars. Should they go to the workers who made them, the political leaders of the country, low-income families, the rich, or to anyone who is willing to pay the price being asked for them? Some of these ways of deciding who gets the cars may seem strange to Americans. In this country, the distribution of goods and services is determined in the market place. As a result, people who make the most money are able to buy the most. But this is not true in all countries.

Section Review

Vocabulary:
capital goods, consumer goods, goods, human resources, natural resources, scarcity, services.

Reviewing the Main Ideas
1. What four decisions must be made when people try to satisfy unlimited wants with limited resources?
2. Why does increased production of capital goods result in decreased production of consumer goods (at least for the present)?

Skill Building
Suppose your teacher has a small pizza. Because it is not large enough for everyone to have some, the class must find a way of determining who will get to eat the pizza. Begin by making a list of the different ways this could be decided. As a class, choose which method you will adopt (majority rules). What would happen if this method were used in the economy as a whole?

Section 2
Economic Systems

The basic economic questions— what goods and services to produce, how many to produce, how to produce them, and who gets them— must be answered in every nation. The way in which these questions are answered is determined by each country's economic system. An **economic system** is a nation's way of finding answers to the four economic questions.

In any economic system the answers to the four basic questions can be the result of decisions made either by the people or by the government. One way to compare economic systems is to look for differences in who makes the economic decisions. Should the government or the people decide what will be produced and who gets it?

What is the proper role of government in a nation's economy? This has almost always been a controversial topic in the United States. Economics cannot tell you the answer. However, it can describe different economic systems and what is likely to happen under each one.

To compare economic systems, one can focus on the amount of control the government has over the economy. A good place to begin is with two systems which are exact opposites—a **pure market system** and a **pure command system.**

Comparing Two Extremes
As the name suggests, the government makes all economic decisions in a pure command economy. It

Five Countries on the Economic Continuum

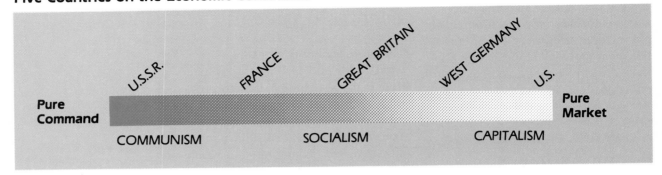

Pure Command — COMMUNISM — SOCIALISM — CAPITALISM — Pure Market

U.S.S.R.   FRANCE   GREAT BRITAIN   WEST GERMANY   U.S.

(chart) What other countries can you think of that belong in the center of the economic continuum? (above) In a command type of economic system, the government determines the kinds of goods that will be produced and where they will be distributed. This means that consumers often face shortages of certain types of goods. In the photo above, people line up to buy scarce food products during a recent shortage in communist Poland.

decides what types of products will be made, how many will be made, how they will be made, and who gets them. The government can do this under this type of system because it owns everything. Property that is owned by the government is called **public property.** Under this type of system, individuals in society have very little to say about what happens in the economy.

In contrast, government makes no economic decisions in a **pure market economy.** In this type of system, answers to the four economic questions are the result of **voluntary exchanges** between individuals. Sellers produce goods or services which they think will sell at a profit. Buyers purchase only those items they feel are worth the price being asked. Thus both the buyer and seller must feel they will be better off or the voluntary exchange will not take place. In addition, everything would be owned by individuals. This is known as **private property.**

Does either type of pure system exist in the real world? No. Every economic system is a mixture of governmental and individual control.

But the two pure systems can be viewed as opposite ends of a continuum. Each country can be viewed as being somewhere between the two endpoints. With this in mind, it is convenient to divide economic systems into three types—communism, capitalism, and socialism.

Communism. For the most part, **communism,** as practiced in the Soviet Union, is a command type of economic system. The government owns the land, the factories, and the stores. The Five-Year Plan tells each factory what it will produce and which store it will send its products to. Because the government owns all of the stores, there is no competition between them. In fact, the government sets the prices for all of the items they sell.

Because the government is making the decisions, consumers have very little to say about the types of goods that are produced. Things such as blue jeans, rock records, stylish clothes, and gum are hard to find. Whenever a store does receive a shipment of a popular item, a long line quickly forms.

424

The quota system used in the Five-Year Plan often creates problems for consumers. Many Russians keep their car's windshield wiper blades in the glove compartment of the car. Why? Because it is very difficult to get new ones. The quotas for automobile factories are set in terms of weight. Since the factory managers can choose the type of parts that will be made, factories produce a lot of heavy parts to make it easier to meet their monthly quota. As a result, very few lightweight parts, such as wiper blades, are made.

Housing in the Soviet Union is provided by the government. Each Soviet citizen is entitled, by law, to one hundred square feet of living space. Ten people are therefore assigned to a one thousand-square-foot apartment. As a result, it is not unusual for several families to end up sharing an apartment.

The government takes care of its citizens in many other ways. It provides everyone with free medical care and a free education. There is no unemployment; everyone is guaranteed a job. Prices of items considered necessities are set low by the government. The government takes care of people in their old age.

Under this type of system, factories and stores are not run for a profit. Their major goal is to meet their quotas. This creates a situation where there are no incentives to use resources efficiently. This type of system is also very slow to respond to consumer demands. This is made worse by the fact that Soviet citizens cannot use the political process to influence the decisions the government makes.

Capitalism. A market economy, such as the one in the United States, is called **capitalism,** or **free enterprise.** In this type of economy, the four economic questions are answered as a result of voluntary exchanges between buyers and sellers. Kristen O'Neal, for example, might decide that her home town needs a new fast-food restaurant. She will try to determine what type of food people want and what price they are willing to pay. If Kristen thinks the money she will receive for selling the food will be greater than the costs of doing business, she will open up the restaurant.

Are there any guarantees that Kristen will make a profit? No, not in a capitalist system. She will face competition from other restaurants. If her prices are too high, people will eat somewhere else. If this happens, she will lose money and go out of business. This is the punishment under capitalism for making bad decisions. Thus, competition encourages Kristen to keep her prices as low as possible. To do so, she will try to use resources as efficiently as possible to keep costs down.

Competition will also encourage Kristen to produce a high quality product. Have you ever bought something because its price was really low? Perhaps you discovered afterward that it was poorly made. If so, you probably did not buy that item again. Competition also results in a wide variety of goods being offered for sale. If Kristen can find a

In a capitalist economy, competition results in a wide variety of goods being offered for sale.

In Sweden, a socialist country, the government provides its citizens with many benefits. These include day care, guaranteed income, and, as pictured below, government-subsidized health-care centers.

type of food people want but not currently available, that will increase the chances of her being successful. It will also give consumers a wider choice for eating out.

In the United States, the government is more active in the economy than the very limited role it would play in a pure market system. For example, it provides Americans with roads, public schools, fire protection, and public parks. Half of the federal government's annual budget is devoted to social programs. It has passed laws designed to protect the environment. To provide these services for its citizens the government must tax them. In these and other ways the governments in capitalist countries such as the United States, Japan, Hong Kong, and South Korea, influence the economy.

Socialism. As the diagram on page 424 shows, **socialism** fits in between capitalism and communism. It therefore has some characteristics of each. Under socialism, major industries such as steel, coal, and communications are owned and operated by the government. As a result, there is no competition in these industries. Smaller industries, however, such as those that produce food, clothing, and household items, are privately owned and operated. Businesses in these industries must compete with each other. They are therefore more responsive to the wishes of the consumer.

In a socialist country, such as France or Sweden, the government does not have a detailed Five-Year Plan. Instead, it influences the economy through its spending and taxing decisions and by the way it runs the publicly-owned businesses. A major difference between capitalism and socialism occurs in the way the major businesses are run. Because the businesses are owned by the government, they are usually not operated to make a profit. If the company is losing money, the government may decide to continue operating at the current level of production just to keep all of its workers employed. To do this, it must use tax money to cover the loses. Under capitalism, businesses cannot do this.

Section Review

Vocabulary:
capitalism, communism, competition, economic system, free enterprise, private property, public property, pure command economy, pure market economy, socialism, voluntary exchange.

Reviewing Main Ideas
1. Compare a pure market system to a pure command system.
2. What has to be true for a voluntary exchange to take place?
3. Name the three types of economic systems. Give an example of each. Describe the basic characteristics of each system.

Skill Building
Identify three successful businesses in your community. What contributed to their success?

Section 3
Judging an Economy's Performance

During the past few years, newspaper headlines such as these have appeared frequently: *U.S. Economy Is on the Upswing, U.S. Economy Dips, Inflation Rises to 6 Percent.* People read articles with headlines like these because they want to know what's happening with the nation's economy. They know that whatever is going on will personally affect them sooner or later.

Finding Out Where the Economy Stands

When people want to find out how an economy is doing, these are some of the questions they ask: How productive is the economic system? In other words, how many goods and services are being produced? How much wealth does it provide for each citizen? How well do people live?

Gross National Product. One way to answer these questions is to look at **Gross National Product** (GNP). GNP is the total value of the goods and services produced in a country during a year.

When economists calculate the gross national product, they count only final goods and services. They count goods that are ready for people to buy, such as bicycles and typewriters. They count services that are provided directly to consumers, such as the services of a doctor or teacher.

Population and GNP in the Fifteen Most Populous Nations

	Population*	GNP*
China, People's Republic	21%	5%
India	15	2
USSR	6	11
United States	5	24
Indonesia	3	Under 0.5%
Japan	3	8
Brazil	3	2
Bangladesh	2	Under 0.5%
Pakistan	2	Under 0.5%
Nigeria	2	Under 0.5%
Germany, Federal Republic of	2	7
Mexico	1	1
United Kingdom	1	4
Italy	1	3
France	1	5
Rest of world	32	27
Total	**100%**	**100%**

*Percent of world's total

The United States is considered very productive because it has 24 percent of the world's total GNP in spite of the fact that it has only 5 percent of the world's population. What other nations do you think are considered productive?

Once the GNP has been calculated for a specific year, it can be used to make comparisons. Sometimes the United States' GNP is compared with the GNP of other countries. The table above shows that in a recent year the United States had 24 percent of the world's total GNP in spite of the fact that it had only 5 percent of the world's population. This shows that its economy is very productive. One reason for this is that the United States has a large amount of capital goods. These machines help workers produce goods and services in large quantities very quickly.

Another fact you should know when looking at GNP is that goods and services which are traded, volunteered, or otherwise given free of charge are not counted in the GNP. This is true in the United States, and it is true in all other countries. In a country like the United States, people buy most goods and services with money. In some countries that is not true. In countries such as Nigeria many people grow some of their own food and make some of their own clothing and tools. What they do not make themselves, they may get without using money. Trading one good or service directly for another without using money is called **bartering.** Because bartered goods and services are not included in the GNP, the GNP figures make it look as if the people have fewer goods and services than they really do.

Recent United States GNP figures can also be compared with earlier United States figures. In 1983, for example, GNP in the United States was more than $1.5 trillion. This means that, taken together, all the final goods and services produced in 1983 were worth that much. Figures for the thirty years prior to 1983 show a steady increase of GNP in the United States. People like to see the GNP rise, or at least stay about the same, from one year to the next. If the GNP goes steadily down year after year, it means that fewer and fewer goods and services are being produced (at least those that are counted in the GNP). That can mean that more and more people are out of work.

Nations such as the United States have a very high technology. The plant pictured below manufactures sophisticated robotics machinery.

Output Per Hour Worked. The hourly output of workers is another sign of productivity in an economy. Workers who are able to produce more goods in one hour this year, as compared to last year, have increased their productivity. Growth in the hourly output of a worker means that resources are being used more efficiently.

Many factors affect a nation's productivity. One factor is the work force—both how hard people work and how skilled they are. Advances in **technology** are also very important to improving productivity. Technology refers to the capital goods—tools, machines, factories—that workers use to produce goods and services.

During most of the 20th century, American workers, using the latest technology, have been very productive. From 1947 until 1965, for example, their output per hour of work grew steadily. The average increase per year during this period was about 2.5 percent. In recent years, however, the productivity of American workers has increased at a slower rate than that of workers from Japan and certain countries of western Europe. In spite of this, in most industries Americans are still the most productive in the world.

Income. Another way to judge an economy is to look at **personal income.** Personal income is the amount of money a person earns during the year. A nation's personal income is the sum of all the personal incomes of its people. The United

States consistently has one of the highest yearly incomes per person in the world.

Available Goods and Services. You can also judge an economy by looking at what people buy with their money. Americans have a wide variety of goods and services available to them. In 1982, Americans purchased almost $2 trillion worth of goods and services. The quality and abundance of these goods and services indicate that, in this respect, Americans have a very high **standard of living.**

Figures on a nation's gross national product, personal income, and the products available do not tell everything about an economy. They tell about the quantity, or amount, that is produced, earned, and purchased. However, they cannot tell much about the quality of the goods and services produced.

The Ups and Downs of a Market System

During the 1930s, millions of Americans were out of work. Many others had their wages cut. People found it difficult to buy what they wanted. Businesses had trouble selling what they made. Many went out of business. Times were so bad, in fact, that the period is called the Great Depression.

In any country, the level of economic activity varies over time. There are times when businesses are producing at full capacity and very few people are out of work. At other times factories may be producing at only 60 percent of their full capacity and many people are unemployed. These ups and downs in economic activity are called the **business cycle.** (See the diagram on page 430.)

There are four parts, or phases, of the business cycle. During the **expansion phase,** business activity is increasing. Factories are beginning to produce more of their products. To do so, they need more workers. As it becomes easier for people to find new jobs, the unemployment rate begins to decline. Stores notice that people are starting to buy more. They place larger orders with their suppliers.

This increasing activity continues until the economy hits the **peak phase** of the business cycle. During this phase, factories are working at full capacity. They have probably added an extra shift or have their regular employees working overtime. The unemployment rate is very low. Stores are experiencing record sales.

The next phase of the business cycle is called the **contraction phase.** Stores notice that things are not selling quite as quickly. As their storerooms begin to fill up, they order less from their suppliers. Factories start cutting back on production by eliminating that extra shift or begin cutting back to a regular forty-hour work week. As it becomes more difficult to find a job, the unemployment rate gradually begins to increase. This slowdown in economic activity is often referred to as a **recession.** If things really get bad as they did in the 1930s, it may even be called a **depression.**

This decline in economic activity continues until the business cycle hits the **trough phase.** At this point,

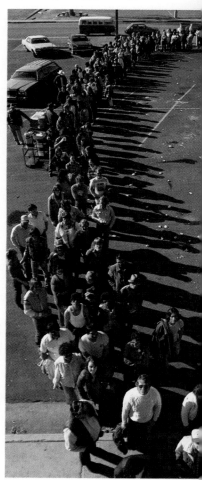

During the contraction and trough phases of the business cycle, many people are out of work. Many unemployed people must often wait in long lines to just get the opportunity to apply for a job.

Economic Activity: The Ups and Downs

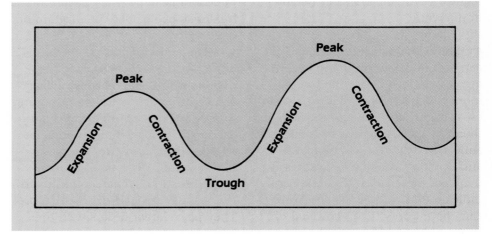

What are the four phases of the business cycle?

factories are operating well below their full capacity. They may be forced to lay off some of their regular employees. The unemployment rate hits its peak. Stores are finding it very difficult to sell their products. People just do not have much money to spend.

In the real world, the business cycles are not as smooth and regular as those shown in the diagram. Some have lasted little more than two years. In contrast, the business cycle which occurred during the 1960s lasted almost ten years. While there is a great deal of variation in the length of business cycles, the expansion phase generally lasts longer than the contraction phase.

In the past, economists believed that the general level of prices tended to follow the business cycle. As people tried to buy more goods and services during the later stages of the expansion phase, prices for most things increased. This increase in the general level of prices is called **inflation.** As economic activity declines during the contraction phase, prices for most items may even decline. This is called **deflation.**

The recessions which occurred in 1974, late 1979 to early 1980, and in 1982, changed the minds of many economists. They were quite different from previous recessions. During these, the American economy experienced not only a high rate of unemployment but also a high rate of inflation. To find the cause of inflation, economists turned their attention to the amount of money in circulation compared to the amount of goods and services being produced.

To see how this works, suppose everyone wakes up tomorrow morning with twice as much money as they have today. Thinking they were twice as rich, they would rush to the stores to buy all of the things they could not afford before they had all this extra money. What would happen if the amount of goods in the stores had not doubled? Customers who get to the store late in the day would find empty shelves. Rather than be stuck with a hand full of money, they might be willing to pay a higher price. Outbidding other customers would be the only hope they have of getting the things they want. The end result would be prices twice as high as they are today. That is inflation. According to this theory, if the amount of money in circulation increases more rapidly than the increased production of goods and services, inflation will result. This helps explain how inflation can occur during a recession.

What can be done to smooth out the ups and downs of the business cycle? Since the 1930s, many economists have felt the federal government could do this by properly adjusting its spending and taxing decisions. During a recession, the government might try to increase economic activity by spending more. Congress may decide to build some new roads, a new dam, or begin some other new construction project. This helps create new jobs. Or Congress could increase spending on social programs such as unemployment compensation. Another approach would be to decrease taxes. That would leave people with more money to spend for themselves on goods and services they want. This commonly results in a budget deficit.

During the expansion phase, the government could do just the opposite. By reducing its spending, it would decrease the demand for the goods and services being produced. Increased taxes would leave people with less money to buy the things they want. This should result in a budget surplus.

How well has Congress done at following this advice? If the budget is any indication of their success, it has not done very well. For almost ten of the fourteen years between 1970 and 1984, the economy was in the expansion phase of the business cycle. During the entire fourteen-year period, the federal budget ran a deficit every year. In addition, government spending increased in each of those years.

Section Review

Vocabulary:
barter, business cycle, contraction phase, deflation, depression, expansion phase, gross national product, inflation, peak phase, personal income, recession, standard of living, technology, trough.

Reviewing the Main Ideas
1. Name three types of figures used to determine how well a nation's economy is doing.
2. Name the four phases of the business cycle. Describe each one.

Skill Building
Describe the actions the government can take to slow down the expansion phase of the business cycle. What can it do to increase economic activity during a recession? How successful has Congress been at following this economic policy in recent years?

Case Study

Competing for Survival

In the early and mid-1960s people who wanted to travel by air from one point in Texas to another used one of two airlines—Braniff International or Texas International. Because of decisions made by government regulatory agencies, these were the only airlines allowed to compete for the business of local consumers.

In 1968 another airline, Southwest Airlines, joined the competition. After years of trying, it had finally received permission from the Texas Aeronautics Commission (the state agency that regulated air travel) to provide air service between Houston, Dallas, and San Antonio.

When the two existing airlines learned of their new competition, they reacted. They went to court to try to prevent the change. They said that there was no need for a new airline in Texas. They argued that the Texas Aeronautics Commission had made an error in allowing Southwest to begin operations.

Southwest fought back. It took its case all the way to the United States Supreme Court. In 1971 Southwest won. The Supreme Court decided that it did have the right to operate in Texas.

Once Southwest began operating, its primary goal was to attract enough customers to stay in business. There were two sources of passengers: (1) people who were flying Braniff or Texas International and (2) people who were not using any airline service. Southwest had to find a way to attract these people.

The Southwest owners identified three possible plans of action. One choice was to charge less for air fare than either Braniff or Texas International. Perhaps customers would come to Southwest to save money. A second choice was to provide services that the other airlines did not offer. Perhaps customers would come to Southwest to enjoy a more comfortable flight. The owners could survey passengers to find out what services they wanted. Then Southwest might provide them. A third choice was to offer gifts. Consumers might fly Southwest to get gifts that were not offered by Braniff or Texas International.

Southwest decided to lower the price of air fare. They charged $20 to travel between the cities of Houston, Dallas, and San Antonio. The other airlines charged $27.

At first the decision to cut prices worked. Customers flocked to Southwest. When Braniff and Texas International realized the success of Southwest's plan, they fought back by lowering the price of their fares to $20. In addition, they offered extra services such as hot towels, free telephone calls at the check-in gate, free beverages, and free newspapers. Most passengers returned to Braniff or Texas International.

After one year Southwest Airlines was in trouble. They could not make a profit by charging only $20 for tickets. As a result the air fare was raised to $26. Braniff and Texas International quickly raised the price of their tickets to $26 too.

Southwest's next move was to offer service to Houston's Hobby Airport instead of to the Houston International Airport. A customer survey had revealed that most passengers wanted that service because Hobby is closer to downtown Houston. This decision attracted many passengers back to Southwest. In response, Braniff also switched its flights to Hobby.

Southwest's owners then decided to offer gifts. In addition, they offered a bonus plan in which a person could win a free flight after purchasing a certain number of tickets.

Braniff and Texas International continued to compete vigorously with Southwest Airlines, but the new company continued to attract enough passengers to survive. There seemed to be enough customers to support three local airlines. Although increased competition caused those who were producing a service to work harder for customers, it brought benefits to consumers. They had better service and lower prices than they would have had without it.

On the national level, Congress deregulated the airline industry in 1978. This meant that the Civil Aeronautics Board no longer set air fares or decided which airlines would fly which routes. New companies were allowed to enter this industry. For the airlines already in the industry, all of this meant increased competition. What had happened in Texas during the early 70s occurred nationwide. Price wars became commonplace. The lower fares forced airlines to become more efficient in an effort to reduce costs. To attract new customers, the airlines made every effort to improve the quality of their service.

What was the end result of deregulation? Consumers benefited through lower fares and improved services. Some airlines were able to adjust to the increased competition. Southwest, for example, earned a profit of $40.9 million during 1983 on revenues of $448.2 million. In contrast, Braniff had a much more difficult time in this newly competitive market. After several years of heavy losses, it filed for bankruptcy in 1982. New investors took over Braniff and resumed operating the airline. In 1989 Braniff again filed for bankruptcy.

Review

1. What was Southwest's main problem when it first began operating in Texas?

2. What decisions did Southwest make in attempting to solve its problem? Why?

3. What were the consequences of these decisions?

433

Basic Social Studies Skills
Making Comparisons

Making comparisons is identifying similarities and differences of two or more things.

Suppose you want to compare the output of farmers in the Soviet Union and the United States. You might look at differences in three things: (1) farm workers as a percentage of the total work force, (2) grain production, and (3) meat production.

Here are three ideas to remember when making comparisons:
1. Clarify your purpose in making a comparison. Know exactly what you want to compare.
2. Be certain that the items you want to compare are comparable. It makes no sense, for example, to try to compare voting in public elections with the production of grains. You should try to compare similar types of things.
3. Make significant comparisons. Do not waste your time and energy thinking about trivial comparisons. Instead, try to make comparisons that help you come to a conclusion about something that helps you prove a significant point.

Skill Practice
Use information in the graph and the table at right to complete the following activities.
1. Compare labor productivity in the non-farm sector of the American economy in two different periods of time—(a) 1948–1965 and (b) 1979–1983.

2. Compare manufacturing productivity in the United States and six other countries listed in the table. (a) In what country was the rate of productivity most unlike that of the United States from 1970–1980? (b) In what country was the rate of productivity most similar to that of the United States from 1970–1980? (c) Which nation experienced the highest increase in productivity?

Productivity of the American Labor Force

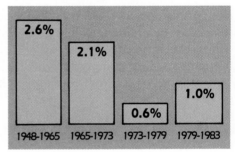

2.6%	2.1%	0.6%	1.0%
1948-1965	1965-1973	1973-1979	1979-1983

Productivity Comparisons

Annual Changes in Manufacturing Output Per Hour of Work	
	10-Year Average (1970-1980)
Canada	+1.4%
U.S.	+1.5%
Britain	+2.5%
Italy	+3.7%
West Germany	+4.2%
France	+4.6%
Japan	+6.2%

Chapter 22 Review

Summary

Section 1: Making Economic Decisions

The basic economic problem is that human wants are greater than the resources available to satisfy them. People make four kinds of economic decisions in response to this problem of scarcity—limited resources and unlimited wants. They decide (1) what goods and services to produce, (2) how many of them to produce, (3) how to produce them, and (4) how to distribute them.

Section 2: Economic Systems

An economic system is a nation's way of finding answers to the four economic questions. Two different kinds of economic systems are the pure command economy and the pure market economy. Economic decisions are made very differently in these two types of systems. In a pure command economy, the government makes all economic decisions. In a pure market system, buyers and sellers make the economic decisions through voluntary exchanges.

Every country is a mixture of the two economic systems. Capitalism is basically a market economy while communism is mostly a command economy. Socialism has characteristics of both capitalism and communism.

Section 3: Judging an Economy's Performance

Several different types of figures can be used to help you judge how well an economic system is doing. Gross National Product (GNP) tells the total value of the goods and services produced in a country during the year. Output per hour worked tells how much one worker produces during one hour on the job. Personal income reveals how much money is earned by workers during the year. Information about the products available to people can also be used.

Vocabulary

Define the following terms.

1. goods
2. services
3. voluntary exchange
4. socialism
5. scarcity

Reviewing Main Ideas

1. True or false: The basic economic problem of all nations is having too great a supply of resources.
2. True or false: Every time we buy something, we make an economic decision.
3. True or false: Consumer goods are products used to make other products.

Thinking Critically

Finding Information

All countries make economic decisions. In doing so, they answer four important questions. Find the section in which the four questions are discussed. What is the section title? What are the four questions?

Evaluating Information

Look back to the decision the government had to make about Southwest Airlines. Did the government make a wise decision? How did you decide?

Communicating Ideas

List two or more questions you would ask to find out what kind of economic system a country has.

Chapter 23

Production Decisions

Introduction. Lee Wong is a great mechanic. His special interest is old cars. He thinks all cars should have a very long life and likes to help people keep them running.

Lee's interest in cars first developed when he was seventeen. He bought an old car himself. Then one part after another had to be replaced or repaired. Lee quickly learned how to "do it himself."

By nineteen Lee was getting regular offers of money to work on the cars of friends and relatives. At first Lee said "no." He already had a job in a factory. Finally, Lee decided to give it a couple of hours a night. That is how Lee Wong's car-repair business was born.

During the first six months, Lee worked by himself in his parents' garage. He didn't have to pay for space, but he did have to buy some new tools.

Business was so good from the very first weeks that Lee soon got back every penny he had spent. As word spread of Lee's skill and fair prices, requests for his services became far greater than he could provide. He simply couldn't work faster or work more hours.

Finally, Lee decided to make his part-time business a full-time business. He would give up his factory job, rent a large garage that he knew about, equip it with necessary tools, and hire one or two mechanics to help him.

First, Lee went to a nearby bank to get a loan. He had some money saved, but not enough to pay for all the equipment he would need. Then Lee hired two helpers. One was a beginner. The other was a skilled mechanic.

Lee took a risk when he opened the business. He couldn't be sure that he would get enough customers to pay his bills and himself. Lee decided to take that risk in order to become a full-time producer and seller of car-repair services. In this chapter you will learn more about the decisions of people who produce goods and services.

Section 1
Organizing and Managing Businesses

In a market economy, the owners and managers of businesses make important decisions. They decide what to produce, how to produce it, and what price to charge for finished products. If there are any **profits** (money made over and above expenses) they decide how much to save, and how much to spend on capital goods.

Organizing a Business

Anyone who runs a business must first decide how to organize it. There are three main kinds of business organizations: (1) the single proprietorship, (2) the partnership, and (3) the corporation. In addition, cooperatives and other nonprofit organizations are sometimes organized to meet special needs.

Single Proprietorship. A business owned by one person is a **single proprietorship.** This is the most common form of business in the United States.

Lee Wong's auto-repair business is an example of single proprietorship. Lee is the single owner; he is the only boss. You may know of such businesses in your community. Many drugstores, beauty shops, grocery stores, shoe-repair shops, and restaurants fit this category.

One important advantage of a single proprietorship is that the owner gets all the profits. A second advantage is that the owner does not have to check decisions with anyone else. Thus, the single proprietor has a great deal of freedom to act as he or she thinks best. Finally, the single proprietor can take special pride and satisfaction in business ownership.

Single proprietors often take special pride and satisfaction in ownership. They frequently work long hours and personally supervise the work in their businesses to make certain it meets their standards of quality.

437

Business in the United States

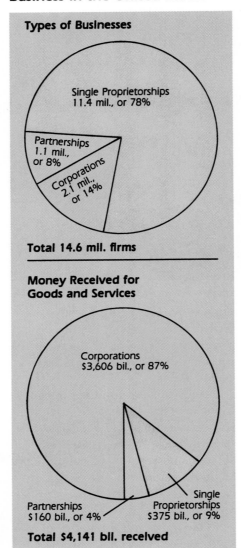

Types of Businesses

Single Proprietorships
11.4 mil., or 78%

Partnerships
1.1 mil.,
or 8%

Corporations
2.1 mil.,
or 14%

Total 14.6 mil. firms

Money Received for Goods and Services

Corporations
$3,606 bil., or 87%

Partnerships
$160 bil., or 4%

Single
Proprietorships
$375 bil., or 9%

Total $4,141 bil. received

(above) Partners in an architectural firm look over plans together. (graphs) What kind of business is most common in the United States? What kind of business sells the most goods and services?

business than it is for one person to do so. Another advantage is that partners can take charge of different parts of the business. One partner might make decisions about production while the other makes decisions about selling. By sharing the responsibilities of management, the partners can often do better together than either could do alone.

The Corporation. The type of business that has the largest sales in the United States is the **corporation.** (See the graph on this page.) Corporations sell about 87 percent of all goods and services produced in this country each year.

Ownership in a corporation is determined by who owns **shares of stock.** The number of shares that a person owns represents his or her portion of the ownership. For example, suppose a corporation sells 100,000 shares of stock. A person who buys 10,000 shares owns 10 percent of the company.

People who own stock, the **stockholders,** usually do not operate the business themselves. Instead, they elect a **board of directors** to do so. The board of directors appoints the top managers of the corporation. They include the company's president, vice-presidents, secretary, and treasurer. These top managers direct the day-to-day business.

A primary advantage of the corporation is **limited liability.** This means that the owner's risk is strictly limited to the amount of money paid for the shares of stock he or she owns. If the business fails, the

Partnership. A business owned by two or more people is called a **partnership.** The partners share the costs, profits, and responsibilities of the business.

A major advantage of the partnership is that it is easier for two or more people to raise the money needed to start or expand a

438

stockholders can lose the money they paid for stock, but they do not have to pay the company's debts.

A second advantage of the corporation is that a very large sum of money can be raised by selling stock. Some corporations have thousands of stockholders.

A third advantage of a corporation is unlimited life. A single proprietorship ends when the owner dies. Likewise, a partnership dies when one partner dies; it must be reorganized if the business is to continue. However, the life of a corporation is not tied to the lives of stockholders, who are the owners. Upon the death of a stockholder, the shares can be willed to other people, or they can be sold.

Cooperatives. A **cooperative** is a business association that provides services for its own members. Producer cooperatives, for example, help members sell goods that they have produced. Many farmers are members of producer cooperatives. Consumer cooperatives offer savings to members on the purchase of certain goods. Sometimes consumers set up their own grocery stores. By purchasing food in large quantities, the cooperative is able to buy items at reduced rates. These savings are eventually passed on to members.

The **credit union** is another type of consumer cooperative. Credit unions provide banking services to members. Members can deposit money and earn interest on their savings. Often the rate of interest is higher than at a bank because the credit union is not run for profit.

Top Ten Industrial Corporations in the United States

1988	Total Number of Employees	Sales
1. General Motors	817,000	$121.1 Billion
2. Ford Motor	350,000	$ 92.5 Billion
3. EXXON	102,000	$ 79.6 Billion
4. IBM	389,000	$ 59.7 Billion
5. General Electric	302,000	$ 49.4 Billion
6. Mobil	120,000	$ 48.2 Billion
7. Chrysler	145,000	$ 35.5 Billion
8. Texaco	50,000	$ 33.5 Billion
9. E.I. duPont de Nemours	140,000	$ 32.5 Billion
10. Philip Morris	114,000	$ 25.9 Billion

Source: Dun's Business Rankings, 1989

Managing the Factors of Production

A business must have four resources in order to produce goods or services. First, someone must start the business and accept the risks of operating a business in a market economy. This is a special kind of labor called **entrepreneurship.** A business must also have natural resources, labor, and capital goods. Economists call these four resources the **factors of production.**

Entrepreneurship. Entrepreneurs are the people who take the risk of starting a business in a market economy. If the business is successful, they receive the rewards—profits. Lee Wong is an example of an entrepreneur. He is also a manager. People who run businesses are called managers. They decide how to produce goods and services. They also decide how to sell their products, what price to charge, and what to do with the profits.

Managers need skills in decision making. Lee Wong is one of the

According to the table above, which corporation is the nation's largest employer?

mechanics in his own business, but he is also the manager. If he makes the right decisions, such as what workers to hire, what tools to buy, and what prices to charge, he will be successful. In many cases, the managers of corporations are hired by the stockholders. These types of managers do not bear the risks of ownership, and are therefore not considered to be entrepreneurs.

Natural Resources. Natural resources are important to all businesses. Minerals such as oil, coal, and iron ore make up one important group of natural resources. Minerals are used in making most manufactured goods. For example, iron ore is used to produce many of the automobile parts that Lee Wong uses in his car-repair business.

Because natural resources and the products created from them are scarce, they are costly. One must pay a price to get them. For instance, part of the rent that Lee Wong pays every month is for the land under his building. When he moved his business out of his parents' garage into a bigger building, he picked a building located at the edge of town. Land prices are lower there than they are in the center of town. Lee decided that keeping his prices down was more important than locating his business in the most convenient place possible. His customers seem to agree.

All business owners must make decisions that involve the use of natural resources. Like other business decisions, these are important because they help make the business succeed or fail.

Labor. A person who offers his or her services in exchange for wages is part of the labor force. No business can succeed without capable employees. The more skilled the employees are, the better off the business will be.

Labor, which is a collection of many human resources, is scarce, just as natural resources are. As a result, labor is not free. Lee Wong, for instance, must pay his two workers a certain amount of money for each hour they work.

Workers who get the highest wages are often those who have special skills or special knowledge. They can do jobs that most others can't do. Lee Wong hired two people. One is a skilled mechanic. The other is unskilled; he is being trained by Lee. Lee pays the skilled worker higher wages for two reasons: First, the skilled worker can do more jobs and do them faster and better than the other worker can. Therefore, she is more valuable to the business. She helps bring in more income. Second, the supply of skilled mechanics is rather small and the demand for their services is great. This tends to increase the price of their services—their wages. When the supply (the amount) of any good or service is small and the demand (by consumers or employers) is great, prices tend to be high. On the other hand, when supply is great and demand is small, prices are low.

Capital Goods. Equipment, machines, and tools needed to produce goods and services are capital goods. For example, the wrenches, jacks, and other tools in Lee Wong's auto shop are capital goods.

Capital goods help workers produce goods and services. Businesses with good equipment and workers who can use the equipment skillfully are likely to be successful.

Government Regulation of Business

When one company controls all or most of the supply of a particular good or service, a **monopoly** is said to exist. If there were only one company that produced automobile tires, for example, consumers would be forced to deal with that company if they wanted tires for their cars.

This lack of competition places buyers at a disadvantage. Monopoly owners know that their customers have no choice but to buy from them. As a result, a monopoly may produce goods or services of poor quality, or the monopoly may charge more than it could if it had competitors. In order to keep monopolies from forming, Congress has passed antimonopoly laws.

Antimonopoly Laws. The most important antimonopoly laws have been (1) the Sherman Antitrust Act, (2) The Clayton Antitrust Act, and (3) the Federal Trade Commission Act.

The Sherman Act was passed in 1890 to give government the right to break up businesses that had established monopolies by forming trusts.

John D. Rockefeller, head of the Standard Oil Company in the 1800s, formed a trust in the following way: He began by getting stockholders from several oil companies to turn over their voting rights to a group of men called trustees. The trustees then acted as a single board of directors to manage all the companies as if they were one. Such a trust could gain enough power to wipe out competition. The Sherman Act said that the government could stop the formation of trusts. Because the law was rather vague, however, it was not easily enforced.

In 1914 both the Clayton Antitrust Act and the Federal Trade Commission Act were passed to strengthen the government's ability to control monopolies. The Clayton Act was easier to enforce than the Sherman Act because it listed a number of specific activities as being monopolistic and, thus, illegal. The Federal Trade Commission Act created a government agency called the Federal Trade Commission (FTC). The Federal Trade Commission was created to help enforce antimonopoly laws and protect consumers against other unfair business practices.

Legal Monopolies. In some industries, monopolies are allowed to exist. Take the case of electricity. Some people feel it would be a waste of our scarce resources if three or four electric companies ran separate lines down each street in town. In cases such as this, laws have been passed that allow only

A worker removes an AT&T sign and replaces it with a new American Bell sign. In 1982, the United States Justice Department won an antitrust suit against AT&T. The Justice Department argued that allowing competing companies to offer phone services would benefit consumers by improving services and lowering prices. As a result of the Court's decision, AT&T was forced to give up its local telephone operations by January, 1984. It was allowed to keep its long distance service, however.

441

one company to provide a service.

The attitudes of some people toward this type of legal monopoly began changing in the early 1980s. The telephone monopoly, for example, was broken up in 1984. Today there are probably several companies in your area that offer long distance telephone service. It was argued that allowing competitors in this market would benefit consumers by improving the quality of service and by keeping prices as low as possible. When the law went into effect, however, not everyone's rates went down. This happened because, prior to 1984, some customers had been paying rates well below the cost of providing them telephone services.

Legal monopolies are allowed to exist mainly in **utilities,** such as water, sewage disposal, electricity, and gas. Because these companies could take advantage of consumers, government officials have the authority to control, or regulate, the utilities' activities. Government officials must first give approval before important company decisions are made, such as raising prices or changing services.

Deregulation. Most Americans agree that if a legal monopoly is allowed to exist, the government should have some power to regulate it. There is considerable disagreement, however, about how much power the government should have over decisions of private businesses.

In recent years, the federal government has acted to **deregulate,** or decrease the amount of government control over, some industries. For example, Congress acted in 1978 to reduce federal regulation of airline companies. (Review the Case Study in Chapter 22.) Decisions about prices and services no longer had to be made according to the rules of a government agency. During the 1980s, several other major businesses were deregulated. Financial institutions are just one example. Before 1980, there were very strict rules on the types of services banks, savings and loan associations, and credit unions could offer. Today, they offer identical services and compete directly with each other.

A water treatment plant. Utilities, like water, gas, and electricity, often are legal monopolies.

Section Review

Vocabulary:
board of directors, cooperative, corporation, credit union, deregulate, entrepreneur, entrepreneurship, factors of production, limited liability, monopoly, partnership, profits, shares of stock, single proprietorship, stockholders, utilities.

Reviewing the Main Ideas
1. What are the advantages of each of these kinds of business organizations? (a) single proprietorship, (b) partnership, (c) corporation, (d) cooperative
2. What are the four factors of production?

Skill Building
1. Write a paragraph that summarizes the information in the graphs on page 438.

Section 2
How Labor Unions Affect Business Decisions

Before 1800, most Americans were self-employed as farmers, shopkeepers, and skilled craftsmen. Very few people worked for wages. Those people who did work for wages usually saw such jobs as short-term work. They planned to work only long enough to save the money they needed to set up households or businesses or to buy farms of their own. After 1800, all that began to change.

The Growth of Unions

During the nineteenth century, manufacturing developed rapidly in the United States. Factories were built and equipped with expensive machinery. Many people were hired to help run the machines.

Working conditions in the factories were, by today's standards, often unpleasant and dangerous. The men, women, and children who worked in the factories labored ten to fifteen hours a day and six, sometimes seven, days a week. Often, all family members had to work to make a living.

Several congressional committees looked into working conditions in factories, but little was done. Government officials were generally friendly to the interests of business owners. In addition, it was a widely held view in the late 1800s that government aid for workers was

interference in the economy.

In an attempt to improve their economic position, some workers decided to form **labor unions**. They felt that business leaders had increased their power in the marketplace by forming giant corporations and business organizations. Union members felt that the only way they could offset this power was to combine to increase their strength. Once the employees of a particular company united, the employer would have to improve conditions or be faced with a **strike.** When union members strike, they stop working. They know that a company cannot make profits during a strike. Unions hope that a loss of profits will influence the employer to give in to their demands.

To make a strike successful, union members must do more than simply stop working. They must be able to prevent other workers who do not belong to the union from

The United States Cavalry clears the way for a train to pass through strikers' lines during an 1894 strike at the Pullman Palace Car Company. The Chicago company was the leading manufacturer of sleeping cars and parlor cars for railroad trains.

offering to work for the employer for less than what the union is demanding. In other words, unions must be able to keep their competitors from selling their labor for less than union wages.

Differences between those who supported unions and those who opposed unions widened greatly between 1880 and 1890. During that decade there were more than one thousand strikes per year. Some of the strikes produced bloodshed. The issues were almost always the same. Unions wanted higher wages, better working conditions, and shorter hours. Employers resisted this because it would increase the cost of producing their products. This might force them to raise the price of their products and make them less competitive.

The union movement grew slowly in the late 1800s and early 1900s. In the 1930s, however, it began to grow quickly. In the early and mid-1930s Congress made it legal for workers to form unions, to strike, and to bargain collectively with employers. The right to **collective bargaining** meant that employers were required to talk to individuals from the union about wages, hours, and working conditions. Employers had to try to come to some decision that would satisfy both sides.

In the late 1930s workers organized unions in the steel and automobile industries. These victories gave a boost to unions in other industries. By the early 1940s, after many strikes, most big manufacturing industries were unionized.

This telephone worker is a union member.

Unions Today

In the United States today about 20 percent of all workers belong to labor unions. The number is down from a high of 36 percent in 1945. Workers in the big manufacturing industries such as steel and automobiles usually belong to unions, as do workers in the clothing industry. Craft workers such as electricians, plumbers, bricklayers, and carpenters tend to belong to unions. Many teachers, police officers, firefighters, and government employees also belong to unions.

Union Goals. One important union goal has always been higher wages. Labor leaders generally have been successful in reaching this goal.

A second union goal has been shorter working hours. Most workers today spend about eight hours per day, five days per week on the job. This is many fewer hours per week than workers labored in the late 1800s. In some unions the push for fewer hours has become a more important goal than higher pay.

A third union goal has been job security. That is why unions favor the **seniority system.** Under this system, workers who have held their jobs for the shortest time have the least seniority. Thus, they would be the first to lose their jobs if the company decides to lay off workers. Those who have the most seniority have the most job security.

A fourth union goal has been to protect its members against dangers to health and safety in the work place. Unions have cooperated with businesses to try to create the best possible working conditions.

Finally, unions have tried to get better **fringe benefits** for members. Fringe benefits include medical care plans, life insurance plans, paid vacations, and retirement programs. Companies pay for all or part of these benefits.

Bargaining Power. Union bargaining power is greatest when all workers in a company are union members. When this is so, a strike will completely stop production. To increase bargaining power, union leaders in the past tried to force companies to have closed shops. In a **closed shop,** the company agreed to hire only union members.

Unions were becoming powerful in the late 1940s; some people thought that they had become too powerful. In 1947, the Taft-Hartley Act was passed to place limits on their power. One thing it did was to ban closed-shop agreements for any company doing business in more than one state. The closed shop was soon replaced by the union shop. In a **union shop,** the company can hire nonunion workers, but workers must join the union within a certain period of time. If they do not, they lose their jobs.

The Taft-Hartley Act also allows the President to stop, for eighty days, any strike that would be a threat to national security or well-being. In addition, the act gives state governments the right to pass **right-to-work laws.** In 1984, twenty states had such laws. If a state has a right-to-work law, both closed shops and union shops are illegal. These states allow only the open shop. In an **open shop,** a worker does not have to join a union in order to keep his or her job. Both union workers and nonunion workers may be employed in the same company. Labor union leaders are against the open shops because it weakens their power during collective bargaining.

Unions do more than bargain with employers. Political activities are a particular interest. At election time, unions may try to influence union members to support candidates who support union goals. Between elections, unions hire lobbyists to try to influence government decision makers. Whatever activities a union takes part in, however, its central purpose remains the same. That purpose is to improve the economic condition of its members.

Section Review

Vocabulary:

closed shop, collective bargaining, fringe benefits, labor union, open shop, right-to-work laws, seniority system, strike, union shop.

Reviewing the Main Ideas

What are five goals that labor unions have worked for?

Skill Building

Write a paragraph that supports one of these statements:
a. The union shop should be required by law in every state.
b. Every state should have a right-to-work law.

Not all workers want to join a union. These waitresses feel that their employer provides good employee benefits and working conditions.

445

Case Study

Mass-Produced Meals

More than twenty-five years ago, the two McDonald brothers of California went into business for themselves. They put their money into a small restaurant in San Bernardino. They decided to sell only hamburgers, French fries, and milk shakes.

For a time, the McDonald brothers ran a successful small-scale business. Then they met Ray A. Kroc.

Ray Kroc owned a small business that made fast-working milk-shake machines. Kroc got together with the McDonalds because he wanted to make some sales.

The McDonalds liked the machines. They bought eight. Kroc liked the McDonalds' restaurant. In fact, it was the restaurant that set Kroc to thinking. Why not a chain of McDonald restaurants—all making use of the special milk-shake mixers?

Kroc presented his ideas to the McDonald brothers. Kroc would put up the money for several new McDonald restaurants. Kroc would manage them, too, and pay a share of the profits to the McDonald brothers. All Kroc wanted in return was the McDonald name. The brothers accepted the offer.

Ray Kroc's goal was to produce the best hamburgers at the lowest price. Kroc believed that efficient production methods would lead to his goal. Efficiency means producing goods as cheaply as possible. By keeping costs low, Kroc could sell hamburgers for the lowest possible price and still make a good profit.

Ray Kroc.

Kroc decided that three keys to efficiency were (1) specialization, (2) standardization, and (3) division of labor.

Specialization meant limiting the menu to only a few items, such as hamburgers, cheeseburgers, and French fries. Kroc could buy large amounts of the ingredients needed to make the few products. By buying large quantities, he could save money.

Standardization meant making each product in exactly the same way. For example, each McDonald's hamburger would be a 1.6 ounce patty, .221 inches thick and 3.875 inches wide when uncooked. The patty would fit in a 4.25-inch bun. By standardizing products, waste would be limited. This, too, would help to keep production costs as low as possible.

Division of labor meant that the restaurant work would be divided into several different jobs. Each worker would be required to do only one job. For example, one person would make only French fries. Another would make only shakes. The job of grilling hamburgers would be done by one worker, and so on. A manager would make sure that each job was done efficiently and in harmony with other jobs. Division of labor could result in fast food production. Each worker would have to do only a few tasks and thus should be able to do them quickly and do them well. The end result was to be mass-produced meals—

the making and selling of very large amounts of each item.

Ray Kroc's production decisions were aimed at keeping costs as low as possible. Savings on production costs could be passed on to customers in the form of lower prices. Prices could be kept low as long as the business attracted a large number of customers. A small amount of profit would be made on each sale, but a very large number of sales would add up to a large profit.

Kroc's mass-production system worked. Customers flocked to the restaurants. In fact, profits were so large that Kroc soon had enough money to build more stores. It wasn't long before the McDonald name had spread across the United States.

Eventually Kroc bought the McDonald brothers' share of the business. Then he went on to expand the business even more.

By 1984 the McDonald's chain had sales of more than seven billion dollars, and its symbol, the golden arches, had become familiar around the world. Kroc's business decisions had led to the goal he had hoped for. By carefully managing the factors of production, Kroc was selling more hamburgers each day than anyone else in the world.

Ray Kroc died in January, 1984. He was eighty-one. The McDonald's restaurant business, however, continued to thrive. Mr. Kroc had built a strong foundation for his company, which seems likely to endure for a long, long time.

Review

1. What decisions did Ray Kroc make about the four factors of production?
2. What were the consequences of Kroc's decisions?

McDonald's has been so successful that the company has restaurants all over the world. This McDonald's is on the Ginza in Tokyo, Japan.

447

Basic Social Studies Skills

Reading Stock Tables in a Newspaper

Stockholders usually follow the ups and downs of stock prices. They read the stock market reports that are printed daily in major newspapers. See the following segment.

New York Stock Exchange Issues

Consolidated Trading
Monday, May 21, 1984

52-Week High	52-Week Low	Stock	Div	Yld %	PE Ratio	Sales 100s	High	Low	Last	Chg.
10	6	Jewlcr		....	16	2	6⅞	6¾	6⅞	......
49¾	33⅜	JohnJn	1.20	3.6	13	x3569	34¾	33⅜	33½	- ⅝
49⅜	40¼	JohnCn	1.66	4.0	9	41	42¼	41¾	42	......
29½	16	JonLog s	.54	2.0	10	27	27⅜	27¼	27¼	......
30⅜	25⅞	Jorgen	1.00	3.6	22	11	28	27¾	27¾	- ½
29⅞	23⅜	Josten	1.12	4.4	11	64	25⅞	25¼	25½	- ¼
32⅝	24⅜	JoyMfg	1.40	5.4	68	136	26	25⅝	26	+ ¼
10¼	5⅝	KDI	.15e	1.9	9	34	8⅛	7⅞	7⅞	- ¼
74	47	KLM		....	9	62	54	53⅝	53¾	+ ½
39¼	26¾	K mart	1.24	4.5	7	1228	28	27¼	27⅜	- ⅛
40	21¼	KN En		....	14	172	35⅜	35	35	......
22⅝	14⅛	KaisrAl	.60	4.3	...	771	14⅜d	13¾	14	- ¼
79	62	Kai 66pf	4.75	7.5	...	2	63	63	63	+ 1
28	18¾	KaisCe	.20	1.0	...	213	20¾	20½	20⅝	+ ⅛
22½	17¼	KaiC pf	1.37	7.2	...	3	19	19	19	......

The names of different companies are listed under the label "Stock" in the third column from the left. The company names are usually abbreviated. Notice that the "K-Mart" company is listed tenth.

The first column, at the left side of the report, is labeled "High." It shows the highest price paid for a share of stock during the past 52 weeks. The next column, "Low," shows the lowest price paid for a share during the past 52 weeks. The 52-week high price for a share of K-Mart stock was 39¼, or $39.25.

"Div." is the label of the fourth column from the left. This column shows the most recent dividend per share of stock paid by the corporation. For example, K-Mart paid a dividend of $1.24 per each share of common stock.

Column five, "YLd.%," stands for the percentage yield of a share of stock. It shows the dividend as a percentage of the current stock price. As of May 21, 1984, the yield for a share of K-Mart common stock was 4.5%.

Column six, "PE Ratio," is the price earnings ratio. This means the price of the stock over the earnings. The price-earnings ratio for K-Mart was 7 as of May 21, 1984.

Column 7 shows the total shares that were traded during the day in 100s. The volume of trading for K-Mart shares was 122,800.

Column 8 shows the highest price paid for a share of stock on that day. The "High" for a share of K-Mart stock, on May 21, was $28.

Column 9 shows the lowest price paid for a share of stock on that day.

Column 10 shows the price of a share of stock when the market closed for the day.

Finally, column 11 shows the "Net Change." This is the difference in price of a share of stock from the end of the previous day of trading to the end of this day.

Skill Practice

1. Which company on the table was the one with the highest volume of trading in its shares?

2. What was the 52-week high for KLM?

Chapter 23 Review

Summary

Section 1: Organizing and Managing Businesses

The three main kinds of business organizations are (1) the single proprietorship, (2) the partnership, and (3) the corporation. The success of any business depends on wise decisions about use of the four factors of production. These are (1) entrepreneurship, (2) natural resources, (3) labor, (4) capital goods. The government regulates decisions about production in order to protect the public from unfair practices. In recent years, however, the federal government has deregulated some major businesses to stimulate efficiency and productivity, and to lower prices for consumers.

Section 2: How Labor Unions Affect Business Decisions

A labor union is an organization of workers that seeks to improve working conditions and wages through collective bargaining. The union movement in the United States began during the nineteenth century. It followed development of the factory system and a modern industrial technology. During the 1930s, the membership and power of labor unions increased greatly. The federal government helped by making laws that made it easier for workers to form unions, bargain collectively, and use the strike to influence employers. In recent years, union membership has declined.

Vocabulary

Define the following terms.

1. single proprietorship
2. corporation
3. partnership
4. cooperative
5. monopoly
6. labor union
7. shares of stock
8. seniority system
9. strike
10. profits
11. utility
12. union shop

Reviewing Main Ideas

1. True or false: The most common form of business in the United States is single proprietorship.
2. The type of business that takes in the most money each year is the _____.
a. single proprietorship.
b. partnership
c. corporation
d. cooperative
3. True or false: There are about as many single proprietorships as partnerships.
4. True or false: A credit union is an example of a cooperative.

Thinking Critically

Comprehending Information

Pretend that you are the owner of a bakery. Tell how you would make use of the four factors of production.

Evaluating Information

A monopoloy is never of value. Do you agree? Why or why not? Use information in the chapter to help support your answer.

Communicating Ideas

Create a questionnaire to be used to interview the owner of a single-proprietorship business in your area. Review what Lee Wong did before you decide what to ask.

Finding Information

Skim the chapter heads and subheads to find the advantages of organizing a business as a corporation. How were the heads and subheads helpful? What are the three advantages that you were looking for?

Chapter 24

Consumer Decisions

Introduction. Juan Gonzalez and his sister Maria live on a small farm in Texas. Juan is sixteen and Maria is fifteen. To earn money, they take care of a flock of fifty chickens. They sell the eggs their chickens produce to their neighbors and people in town for slightly less than the local grocery stores charge.

They do not get to keep all of the money they receive for the eggs. The feed is their only major expense, though. Just like any other business, they must keep track of their expenses and deduct these from the money they receive from their customers. They get to keep what is left.

While they are not getting rich, selling eggs provides them with weekly spending money. Deciding what to spend it on is not always easy. There are so many different things they would like to buy. But they do not make enough from their egg business to buy everything they want. So Juan and Maria try to get the most for their money.

Most of the time they are happy with what they buy. But sometimes,

like the time Juan bought a game he saw advertised on TV, they make mistakes. The kids in the commercial were having a great time playing it. When he got home from the store and started playing it, Juan found out it was boring. He wished he hadn't rushed out and bought it.

There are many things to be considered when deciding how to spend your hard-earned money. You might even want to save some of it for the future. Maria, for example, is already thinking about going to college. Her father has a good job in town. But she knows the only way her family will be able to afford college is if she helps pay some of the expenses. So she is trying to save some money for that. Of course that means she has less to spend today. And Juan would like to have a car. But he has not been able to save any money yet. There always seems to be something that he wants to buy right now.

The main purpose of this chapter is to help you learn about consumer decisions.

Consumers can save money at the grocery store by taking the time to compare prices and read labels.

Section 1
Buying Goods and Services

American consumers spend billions of dollars each year on various goods and services. The chart on page 464 shows how much they spend on major categories of goods and services.

Most of the time consumers are satisfied with their purchases. Everyone, however, has been disappointed by some purchase they have made. Careful buying may make the difference. The careful consumer plans ahead, examines products, and knows where to get information about products, producers, and sellers. Careful consumers try to get the most for their money.

Plan Before Buying

What do you want? When do you want it? How much money can you afford to spend on a particular item? The consumer who plans before buying thinks carefully about these questions.

Thinking About What You Want. If you were a millionaire, what would you like to have? Could you make a list of what you would want? It would probably be a very long list. Would your list look exactly like the lists of your classmates? No. No two people have the same likes and dislikes. Everyone has a different set of values. As a result, something that is very valuable to you may be of no value to someone else.

Many things affect what people want. A person's age, sex, and marital status are three important factors. Juan, for example, was saving for a car while his sister was saving her money for college.

Making a Budget. Consumers have only so much money to spend. Every time Juan or Maria decides to spend money on one thing, they are giving up the chance to spend that money on something else. If Maria decides to buy a new dress, she will have less money to help pay her college expenses.

Consumers can make budgets to help them decide how to use their money. A **budget** is a plan for both spending and saving. It helps consumers make sure that money gets used for the things they want the most. It also helps them avoid buying more things than they can afford. For example, if you have a budget, a quick look will tell you whether you can afford a new record. The budget may show that if you buy the record, you will have no money for a movie on Friday night. In this way a budget helps you make choices.

When people make a budget, they begin by comparing their income and expenses. They write down the total amount of money they expect to receive during a certain period. Then they list all the things they feel they have to buy as well as the cost of each item. If the amount of money that goes out is greater than the amount that comes in, they must borrow.

The first step in making a budget is to write down **fixed expenses.** Fixed expenses are costs to which you are already committed. In most cases they stay the same from month to month. For example, a family pays $400 per month to rent an apartment.

The next step is to estimate **flexible expenses.** These are costs that change from month to month. The cost of food and clothing change somewhat from month to month. So do amounts spent on recreation, gifts, medical bills, and household needs.

When planning a budget for the first time, it is important to know how much you are spending on flexible expenses. To find out, write down everything you buy in a small notebook. At the end of each week,

Which items in the budget below are fixed expenses? Which are flexible expenses? Is this a balanced budget? Why?

Monthly Budget

Budget for March	
Income before taxes	$1,916.00
Taxes	425.00
Income after taxes	$1,491.00
Fixed Expenses	
Housing	$380.00
Flexible Expenses	
Food, household supplies	$420.00
Electricity, gas telephone, water	84.00
Gifts, contributions insurance	65.00
Reading, recreation, education	70.00
Medical care	80.00
Clothing	80.00
Transportation	205.00
Savings	107.00
	$1,491.00

record these purchases in a larger notebook. The large notebook should have one column for each type of expense—clothing, food, recreation, and so on. At the end of each month add up the columns. In this way you will be able to find out exactly how much you are spending on each item.

The final step in making a budget is to try to balance estimated expenses with income. If expenses are more than income, consumers must either decide where to cut down or how much to borrow. Money borrowed today must be paid back, plus interest, in the future. Unless the person's income increases, this will mean less money available in the future.

Look Before Buying

Wise consumers plan ahead. They think, they save, and they budget. They also look before buying.

Looking for a Home Computer. Imagine for the moment that your family is interested in buying a home computer. You have a vague idea of what you want and know about how much you can afford to spend.

Now you are ready to gather information. Go to your public library. Magazines of all sorts describe and rate products. The best kind of magazine is a consumer magazine such as *Consumer Reports* or *Consumer Bulletin.* Consumer magazines are published by organizations that test products for quality. When the organization rates a group of products, it tells what the tests showed. If a

consumer magazine has rated home computers, it will tell you what features come on each brand tested and how much they cost.

Once you have gathered information, begin to shop around. Find the stores that carry the computers that come closest to having what you want. Then compare prices. One store may charge less for a particular computer than other stores. Also, see if they will demonstrate it for you. How easy is it to operate? What kind of accessories are available? How much do they cost? Finally, make sure that you can return the computer if you find something wrong with it when you get it home.

Researching products in consumer magazines is often well worth the effort. Not only can you save money, but you can avoid purchasing inferior or poorly made products.

What types of things should you consider before purchasing clothing? Does higher price always mean better quality? Why?

Tips for Smart Shoppers. The steps to follow in buying other items are much the same as those you followed in buying a home computer. They are

(1) Plan ahead. Know exactly what you want. Don't buy just because you're in a "buying mood."

(2) When you're buying something expensive, get as much information as you can. Check the consumer magazines.

(3) Shop around. Buy where you get the best price (as long as the dealer is honest, of course). When you're buying food, check the **unit price.** Check to see how much you are paying for each ounce, each quart, each pound, or each piece.

(4) Examine the item to make sure that all parts are working.

(5) Ask about **warranties** and **guarantees.** These are promises that the seller or producer makes to repair, replace, or refund if a product doesn't do what it's supposed to do. Make sure that warranties and guarantees are put in writing, and make sure that you save them. Also save **sales receipts.** You'll need them if you have a complaint.

(6) Read **labels** on food. Make sure you know what you're eating. Also check the freshness dates. If an item is still on the shelf and the date has passed, don't buy it.

(7) Read the labels on clothing too. Are the pants you just bought likely to shrink? What do you have to do to keep them clean? If it takes great effort or expense to keep the pants looking good, you may decide not to buy them.

(8) Don't give in to salespeople. Most salespeople try to treat customers fairly. But once in a while you'll meet those who do not. Don't let a salesperson persuade you to do something you don't want to do.

454

(9) Be a critical watcher and reader of ads. Some advertisements give useful information. Newspaper ads and catalog ads often tell size, price, and so on. Other ads, particularly television ads, do not tell much at all. Instead, they use propaganda techniques to appeal to your emotions.

(10) If you buy records or books through the mail, make sure you know what you're agreeing to do. If you accept a number of almost-free items, you will probably have to follow up with a certain number of purchases. Be sure to read all letters that you get from the seller. Otherwise, you may receive books and records that you didn't order.

(11) Beware of **"bait and switch."** If you go into a store to buy an item that has been advertised at a very low cost and the salesperson tries to sell you a more expensive version of the same item, he or she may be doing something illegal. The store has offered "bait" in the form of the ad and you have been "switched" to another item. Such activity is against many state or local laws.

Section Review

Vocabulary:
bait and switch, budget, guarantee, fixed expense, flexible expense, label, sales receipt, unit price, warranty.

Reviewing the Main Ideas
1. Describe the main steps in making a budget.
2. Why should consumers make budgets?

Skill Building
1. Look at the budget on page 452. Which three items does this family spend most on? If this family had to cut its budget by $50, where would you suggest this be done?
2. Write instructions for someone who wants to buy a television set. Keep "Tips for Smart Shoppers" in mind as you give advice.

Section 2
Saving and Borrowing

Consumers regularly make decisions about saving and borrowing money. When people save, they put money aside for a certain time so that it can be spent later. When people borrow, they use someone else's money with the promise to pay it back, with interest, at a certain time.

When Should Consumers Save or Borrow?
People can always find ways to spend what they earn. Why, then, is it wise to save?

Reasons for Saving. Many people save in order to prepare for emergencies such as getting sick or losing a job. People also save for retirement. Finally, people save so that they can buy certain costly items. It almost always takes planning and saving if a person wants to pay cash for such items as pianos and vacation trips.

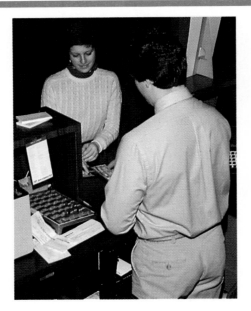

Banking Industry In Profile 1983

National banks	
Commercial banks	4,586
Mutual savings banks	418
State banks	10,445
Savings & loan associations	
Federal	1,671
State	2,072
Credit unions	20,000

(right) Check-cashing privileges are a service most financial institutions provide to their customers. (chart) Which financial institution has the most organizations?

Reasons for Borrowing. Many consumers borrow money. In 1985, American consumers owed more than one trillion dollars to various lenders. These consumers were buying goods and services on **credit.** To buy on credit means to pay later for what you get now.

The main reason that people use credit is so that they can buy high-priced items such as cars and houses sooner than if they had to save enough to buy them. Consumers also borrow money during emergencies. Illnesses or accidents can result in unexpected expenses. Loss of a job may leave a person short of money until a new job is found. Because there is always a charge for borrowing money, it helps to save for emergencies.

Where to Go to Save or Borrow

There are various places where a person can save or borrow money. It is useful to know how services differ from one place to another.

Banks. Banks provide services to people who want to save as well as to those who want to borrow. When people save in a bank, the bank pays them interest. The amount of interest earned depends on the amount of money put in the bank, the interest rate, and the length of time the money is left there. When people borrow, they pay interest.

Other Places to Borrow and Save. People also borrow and save at savings and loan associations and at credit unions. In the past **savings and loan associations** generally specialized in large loans such as the kind given when people buy houses. In 1980, however, they began offering many of the same services that banks offer. For example, today you can have a checking account at a savings and loan.

Credit unions, are nonprofit organizations formed to serve members. Interest rates charged for loans often are lower than rates charged elsewhere. Interest rates paid on savings accounts often are higher. Credit unions can do this because they are not run for profit.

Buying bonds and buying shares of stock in corporations can

also be ways of saving. Even buying insurance can be a form of saving; it helps prepare for emergencies. Some kinds of life insurance policies can be used for borrowing. A policyholder can borrow part of the money he or she has paid in premiums. The interest charged on these loans is usually low.

Other Sources of Credit. There are several other ways to borrow. One source of credit is the finance company. It is sometimes easier to borrow from a finance company than it is from a bank. However, the amount of interest that finance companies charge can be very high.

Some stores provide credit to consumers by offering **charge accounts.** A person with a charge account can buy now and pay later. If a bill is paid very quickly, the store may charge no interest at all. However, if payments are made over months or years, a high rate of interest is charged.

Credit cards, such as Master-Card, Visa, and American Express, also allow consumers to buy now and pay later. **Credit cards,** like other charge cards, offer convenience. The credit-card owner can buy without carrying large amounts of cash. However, interest is charged on overdue accounts.

Buying on credit is sometimes necessary. Few consumers would be able to buy houses if they couldn't get loans. Buying on credit, as you have seen, can also be convenient. However, buying on credit can be expensive. Always find out how much you must pay for the use of someone else's money.

Section Review

Vocabulary:
charge account, bank, credit, credit card, savings and loan association.

Reviewing the Main Ideas
1. Why do people save money?
2. Why do people borrow money?
3. Where and how can people save money?
4. Where and how can people borrow money?

Skill Building
1. If Janet wanted to buy a tape player, would you suggest that she use cash or credit?
2. If you had to borrow money, would you go to a credit union, a bank, or a finance company? Why?

Section 3
Protecting Consumer Rights

Most of the time, the free market does a good job of providing what consumers want. Sometimes, however, a consumer buys a product that doesn't work right and the seller won't take the product back. What can consumers do when this happens? How can consumers protect themselves when a producer makes goods that are a danger to health and safety? What can consumers do if a seller labels products falsely, so that buyers are misled? In other words, what can consumers do when producers or sellers treat them unfairly?

457

Government Agencies That Help Consumers

There are agencies at all levels of government that aid consumers. The work that some of them do is described below.

Federal Trade Commission (FTC).

The FTC hears complaints about false advertising. The commission enforces laws that prohibit misleading or dishonest information in guarantees, warranties, ads, or product labels. Consumers may bring problems to any one of twelve FTC regional offices.

Food and Drug Administration

(FDA). The FDA inspects certain food products to make sure that they do not threaten the health of consumers. For example, the FDA examines chemical additives that are put in food products to preserve or color them. The FDA decides whether these additives are dangerous to health. If so, the FDA has the power to ban them—to say that they cannot be used. The FDA also inspects drugs and cosmetics to make sure they are safe.

Consumer Product Safety Commission (CPSC).

The CPSC can investigate and control the sale of all products that might be unsafe. The CPSC requires producers to report information that shows their products might be unsafe.

The main goal of the Consumer Product Safety Commission is to help prevent injuries related to the use of consumer products. The Commission works toward that goal in several ways. It sets and enforces safety standards for many products. It looks into the causes of product-related illnesses and accidents. It tries to find ways of preventing those illnesses and accidents in the future. And it carries out educational programs to make consumers aware of product safety.

The Postal Inspection Service.

The Postal Service handles complaints about products or advertisements that have been sent through the mail. For example, a consumer may see an ad that tells how to order a product through the mail. The consumer may send money with an order but never receive the product. Or the consumer may receive a product that is different from the one described in the ad. When this sort of thing happens, the consumer should complain to postal inspectors.

State and Local Agencies.

Each of the fifty state governments, as well as many local governments, have

Food and Drug Administration worker testing food for nutritional value.

agencies that protect consumer rights. For example, most states have set up consumer protection agencies within the state attorney general's office. The main purpose of these agencies is to investigate false advertising or misleading claims on product labels. Many state and local governments also have bureaus to deal with complaints about repair shops.

Private Groups That Aid Consumers

Many private groups also try to protect consumer rights. The following are only a few examples.

Consumer Interest Groups. Consumer interest groups have been organized at both the national and local levels. Ralph Nader's Public Citizen, Inc., is a widely known national interest group that backs consumer causes. The leader, Ralph Nader, is a well-known **consumer advocate.** He speaks out about consumer problems and tries to correct them.

The National Consumer League is an interest group that helps local consumer groups in all parts of the country. It is based in Washington, D.C., and gathers information about consumer issues that come up in Congress, the federal courts, and agencies of the federal bureaucracy. The National Consumer League provides information to local consumer groups and tries to represent their interests to decision makers in the federal government.

An example of a group that works at the state level is the Louisiana Consumers' League. This group brings legal action against producers and sellers who break consumer-protection laws. The group also lobbies in the Louisiana state legislature on behalf of consumer goals.

Better Business Bureaus. The National Better Business Bureau was founded in 1912 to work for fair business practices and to protect consumer rights. Today, there are local Better Business Bureaus in communities all over the United States. The Bureau provides shopping tips, information about local businesses, and warnings about dishonest business practices. The Bureau also investigates written consumer complaints about false or misleading advertising. The Bureau tries to persuade businesses to follow the law. If the Bureau fails to influence a business to change its ways, the Bureau may take the business to court.

Section Review

Vocabulary:
consumer advocate.

Reviewing the Main Ideas
1. Name three government agencies that aid consumers. What are their roles?
2. What is one private group that aids consumers?

Skill Building
Find a newspaper or magazine article about consumer interest group activities. Summarize the article.

Making a Contract—Your Rights and Responsibilities

Roseanne Gutierrez received a form letter from the publisher of a magazine. The publisher offered a special low price to anyone who wished to order a six-month subscription to the magazine. Roseanne decided to accept the offer. She signed her name to a card that stated the terms of the publisher's offer. The card described the price of the magazine, the period of time covered by the offer, the number of magazines that would be sent to new subscribers, and so forth. Roseanne mailed the card to the magazine publisher's office. The publisher responded to the card from Roseanne by sending her a new copy of the magazine she had ordered.

Roseanne Gutierrez and the magazine publishing company had made a **contract.** Any voluntary agreement between two or more parties, which may be enforced legally, is a contract. A contract is made when one party (a person or business) offers something that is accepted by another party.

Legal Foundations of Contracts

The rights and responsibilities of parties to a contract are based on state and national laws. Any adult who is considered legally competent has the right to make a contract. Insane persons are not considered to be legally competent. They are not supposed to make contracts. If they do, they are not bound by the obligations called for by the contract. The same is true for a minor. Any contract made with a minor cannot be enforced.

The responsibilities of parties to a contract are recognized in the Constitution. Article I, Section 10 says: "No State shall . . . pass any . . . law impairing the obligation of contracts."

All contracts, however, are subject to certain legal limitations. A contract may not violate laws that protect the health and safety of the public.

Breach of Contract Suits

A contract is fulfilled when all parties to it carry out the obligations that they accepted when agreeing to the contract. A **breach of contract** occurs when one party fails to act as promised by the terms of the agreement. The other party may take legal action by initiating a breach of contract suit. The dispute is settled in a court of law. A judgment against the defendant may require payment of damages to the plaintiff. If Roseanne fails to pay for the magazines she has agreed to buy, the publishing company could take her to court.

In breach of contract suits, evidence is presented about the terms of the agreement. Usually, the contract is made in writing, and the parties to it sign the agreement. If so, it is easier to prove whether someone has failed to carry out an obligation assumed by signing the contract.

Many contracts are only verbal. The parties agree among themselves in a conversation about the conditions of the contract. They may shake hands after making their agreement. But they do not sign their names to a written contract. In these cases, it is more difficult to prove breach of contract, especially if there were no witnesses to the verbal agreement.

Laws require some types of contracts to be made only in writing. For example, agreements to buy and sell real estate must be put in writing and signed by the parties named in the contract. Long term agreements, which cannot be carried out in less than a year, also must be in writing.

One general rule to follow is to make all contracts in writing. This provides the greatest protection against breach of contract.

A second rule is to read very carefully every word in a contract before signing it. If you are not sure about the meaning of any words, ask a person you trust for help. You may need to hire a lawyer to explain a complicated contract. Careful reading and interpreting of a contract, before signing it, may help you to avoid taking on obligations you are neither willing nor able to fulfill.

Defenses Against Breach of Contract Suits

A person who has broken, or breached, a contract is not necessarily liable to pay damages to the other party. There are defenses against breach of contract suits. For example, one party to a contract may intentionally mislead the other party to influence him or her to make the agreement. Intentionally falsifying information in an effort to deceive a party to a contract is known as **fraud.** Persons who find out that they have been misled or deceived may have cause to breach a contract. If fraud can be proved, then the party who breached the contract is not liable for damages.

Duress is also a defense against a breach of contract suit. **Duress** means that a party to a contract was unduly pressured into making an agreement. For example, one person might be forced to sign a contract at gunpoint. Later on, the person forced to make the agreement breaches it. He or she is not liable for damages in a breach of contract suit if duress can be proved.

Another defense against a breach of contract suit involves non-performance of an obligation by the plaintiff. What if the party who is suing for damages did not do what he or she promised? If so, damages may not be collected from the other party, who also did not perform his or her part of the bargain.

In every state, there is a statute of limitations that might be used as a defense against a breach of contract suit. A statute of limitations provides that one may sue another for breach of contract only within a certain number of years after making the contract. If the period of time has passed, then the defendant can use the statute of limitations to defend the breach of contract suit. Anyone with a claim against a party to a contract must take legal action within a period of years established by state law. If the statute of limitations is overlooked, a person with a solid claim for damages will not gain satisfaction in a court of law.

The Value of Contracts

Individuals who decide to make a contract gain legal protection concerning the agreement. As long as the contract involves lawful actions, the parties to it are protected against interference by the government. Any contract that is made according to the law protects the parties to it against breaches of the agreement. This gives people who make contracts confidence that they will get what they expected from the bargain.

Review

1. Who has the right to make a contract?
2. Why is it wise to make all contracts in writing?
3. What prevents a state from making a law impairing the obligation of contracts?

461

Case Study

Consumer Advocate

Ralph Nader and his assistants try to influence government decision makers to pass laws they feel will help consumers. Several federal laws can be traced to Nader's work.

Nader began his work as a consumer advocate in 1963. He had graduated a short time before from Harvard Law School. Nader was practicing law in Hartford, Connecticut, specializing in automobile accident cases.

Nader believed that unsafe cars, not poor drivers, caused many accidents. He was disturbed. Should he try to inform consumers about his findings? Should he try to influence government officials to do something about auto safety?

Nader was faced with an important decision. He had a promising

career as a lawyer. Giving a great deal of time to auto safety might interfere with his job. Furthermore, Nader would be taking a risk. Some important people might become angry if he reported embarrassing facts about the production and sale of unsafe autos. They might try to hurt Nader in some way.

However, Nader believed in assuming citizenship responsibility. He thought that auto companies were not treating consumers fairly and believed that something had to be done. Nader decided to defend consumer rights no matter what the personal risks might be.

Nader continued to study the problem of unsafe autos. The result was a best-selling book, *Unsafe at Any Speed*, which pointed out safety hazards in cars. Members of Congress and federal agency workers read Nader's book. People inside and outside the automobile industry read the book too.

After the book came out, Nader gave many speeches about the need to pass laws requiring safer autos. He was asked to share his ideas with congressional committees.

The auto makers were worried that Nader's activities would hurt car sales. They tried to persuade him to stop his consumer-protection campaign. First, they tried to influence public opinion. They tried to make Nader seem to be an irresponsible troublemaker. When this tactic failed, auto makers hired private detectives to investigate Nader's private

Ralph Nader, founder of Public Citizen, Inc., a group dedicated to solving consumer problems.

life. They hoped to find embarrassing information that could be used against Nader.

The private investigators uncovered no embarrassing facts about Nader. Rather they found that Nader was dedicated totally to his work. He sometimes worked as long as sixteen hours a day seven days a week. He spent little money. His friends and neighbors praised him.

The outcome of Nader's auto-safety campaign was a new federal law, The Motor Vehicle Act (1966). The law required auto makers to add seat belts, dashboard padding, and other safety features to their cars.

Nader became a public hero. Many young citizens began to work with him. Together they started new projects to try to improve the way government and businesses serve the public. Nader's career as a consumer advocate had begun.

In 1971, Nader organized Public Citizen, Inc., an interest group that works on behalf of consumer interests.

In 1972, Nader and his followers influenced Congress to pass the Consumer Product Safety Act. This law created the Consumer Product Safety Commission (CPSC). It sets safety standards for many consumer products and helps to protect the public against the use of unsafe products.

Nader achieved many of his goals, but he did not always win. Nader suffered a big setback in 1978 when Congress voted against a consumer-protection law he had worked for.

Nader has continued to work on solutions to consumer problems. Public Citizen, Inc., has kept up its activities in support of consumer interests. A main goal of Nader and his assistants is to arouse public interest in specific areas so that citizens will ask for and get better quality products and services from businesses.

Ralph Nader has made a career of acting as a public citizen. His full-time job is keeping a watch on government officials and businesses so that they might do better in serving all citizens.

Review

1. An important occasion for decision was described in the early part of this case. What was it?

2. What were Nader's alternatives?

3. What decision did Nader make? Why?

4. What were the consequences of his decision?

5. Read *Consumer Reports* or some other consumer magazine. Find a report on a product that you might consider buying in the near future. Read the report carefully and then prepare a summary of your findings for the class.

6. Use library resources to find current information about the activities of Ralph Nader and Public Citizen, Inc. Prepare a short report. See the Writing and Research Skills section at the back of your book for help with your report.

Basic Social Studies Skills
Using Evidence to Support a Generalization

A generalization is a comprehensive statement. It refers to many details or pieces of information. It is a conclusion that sums up and connects various specific facts.

Here is an example of a generalization: Younger adults in the United States tend to save less money annually than older adults do.

Evidence is the information or data on which a generalization is based. The generalization about younger adults, older adults, and savings is based on data about the American people that have been collected by the federal government.

There may be exceptions to a generalization. For example, there are young adults who manage to save large amounts of money. There are some older adults who save little or no money each year. These individuals, however, are exceptions to the generalization stated above. This generalization is a tendency statement. The majority of relevant information supports it. By contrast, there are no exceptions to a universal conclusion. Here is a universal statement: No Americans under 18 years of age are eligible to vote in public elections.

A generalization is no better than the evidence used to support it. If the evidence is faulty then the generalization based on it will be incorrect.

Be careful to check the sources of evidence that you use in making or supporting a generalization. Some sources are more reliable and valid than others.

Skill Practice

Which of these three generalizations is supported by evidence in the table on this page?

a. American consumers have tended to spend more money per year for non-durable goods than for durable goods.

b. Total expenditures for personal consumption declined each year from 1977 to 1982.

c. Most American consumers spend more money on motor vehicles and parts than they spend on food.

Personal Consumption Expenditures for the U.S.

Source: Bureau of Economic Analysis, U.S. Commerce Department (billions of dollars)

	1979	1980	1981	1982
Durable goods	213.4	214.7	236.1	244.5
Motor vehicles and parts	96.6	90.7	101.6	109.9
Furniture and household equipment	81.8	86.3	93.3	93.5
Other	35.1	37.7	41.2	41.1
Nondurable goods	600.0	668.8	733.9	761.0
Food	311.6	345.1	375.9	396.9
Clothing and shoes	99.1	104.6	115.3	119.0
Gasoline and oil	66.6	84.8	94.6	91.5
Other nondurable goods	122.8	134.3	148.1	153.5
Fuel oil and coal	16.1	18.6	20.7	20.0
Other	106.6	115.7	127.4	133.5
Services	693.7	784.5	887.1	986.4
Housing	236.0	266.2	302.0	334.1
Household operation	99.3	113.0	128.4	144.3
Electricity and gas	47.8	57.6	66.8	76.3
Other	51.5	55.4	61.6	68.0
Transportation	56.3	61.1	65.5	68.4
Other	302.0	344.3	391.3	439.6
Total personal consumption expenditures	1,507.2	1,668.1	1,857.2	1,991.9

Chapter 24 Review

Summary

Section 1: Buying Goods and Services

Consumers are not able to buy everything they want. They have a limited amount of money to buy the different goods and services being offered for sale. Thus, consumers must plan carefully before making decisions about what to buy and what to do without. Careful consumers make budgets to help them plan the use of their money. They also take the time to shop around carefully before deciding what to buy.

Section 2: Saving and Borrowing

Consumers are faced with decisions about saving and borrowing money. People save money to prepare for emergencies, for retirement, and for costly purchases in the future. Consumers borrow money when they buy goods or services on credit. People also borrow money to pay for costs in an emergency, such as a serious illness or accident.

Section 3: Protecting Consumer Rights

Government agencies and private groups help protect the rights of consumers. For example, the Consumer Product Safety Commission, a federal agency, investigates and regulates the sale of all products that might be unsafe. The National Consumer League, an interest group, also works to protect consumers.

Vocabulary

Define the following terms.

1. budget
2. fixed expense
3. contract
4. flexible expense
5. fraud
6. consumer advocate
7. duress
8. guarantee
9. credit

Reviewing Main Ideas

1. The Better Business Bureau is an organization that _____ .
   a. helps businesses locate in new cities
   b. lobbies in state legislatures on behalf of business interests
   c. works for consumer rights
   d. helps business people sell their products
2. True or false: Public Citizen, Inc., is a government agency that works for consumer rights.
3. The FTC is mostly concerned with _____ .
   a. health
   b. safety
   c. false advertising
   d. loaning consumers money

Thinking Critically

Comprehending Information

When people buy cars, how do their car choices show something about their values?

Organizing Information

Write the three steps in making a budget in the order that you would do them.

Evaluating Information

1. According to what you have read, is it ever wise to borrow money? Why?
2. Marty must borrow money to buy a car. She can borrow from a bank or a credit union. Which would you recommend? Why? If you wanted to be sure that you were making the right recommendation, what additional information would you need?

Communicating Ideas

Make up a set of instructions to follow when a person makes a major purchase such as a TV, car, or dishwasher.

Chapter 25

Career Decisions

Introduction. Rosalyn Yalow is a physicist. She does laboratory research at the Veterans Administration Medical Center in New York. In 1977, Yalow won the Nobel Prize. This honor was awarded in recognition of her many achievements during her career in physics research.

Phil Knight has achieved excellence in a very different career. Knight started a business in Beaverton, Oregon, during the 1970s. He had a new idea for a special type of running shoe. Knight and a partner used their savings to start a company to produce the shoes. The new product became very popular among joggers and runners. Knight's small business soon grew into a large company that sold more than $500 million worth of shoes a year. A new idea plus some very hard work led to a very successful career in business for Phil Knight.

William Raspberry also has achieved excellence in his career field—journalism. He writes a column that appears daily in one of the nation's top-rated newspapers, *The Washington Post.* Raspberry has won many awards for excellence during his career as a journalist. His articles are carried in many other papers across the country.

Rosalyn Yalow, Phil Knight, and William Raspberry have different talents, interests, and jobs. They each have achieved excellence in their particular field.

Not everyone can expect to reach the standard of excellence achieved by these three people. Yet there are certain preparations people can make that will enhance their chances of achieving their highest potential in a career. This chapter will help you to start thinking about some of these preparations.

Steven Jobs (left) and partner Steve Wozniak, two self-taught electronics wizards, had a wonderful idea in 1975: create a "user friendly" computer that ordinary people could use in their homes. The result of their idea was the creation of an almost instantly successful computer and the beginning of Apple Computers, Inc., which is now one of the world's largest computer manufacturers. Do you know of any other similar success stories?

Section 1
Your Opportunities for a Career

An important characteristic of a market economy is freedom to choose. In the United States, people are free to choose jobs that suit their talents and interests. They have the opportunity to use their talents to produce goods and services that contribute to their own well-being and that of their community, and the nation as a whole.

Different Kinds of Careers

What kinds of careers can a person choose? People need to know as much as possible about alternatives to make informed career decisions. They need to know the kinds of jobs that are available today and how to prepare for them. They also need information about career trends—the kinds of opportunities that are likely to be important in the future.

Careers, or occupations, may be grouped in many different ways. The Federal Bureau of Labor Statistics divides occupations into ten categories. These groups are (1) professional and technical, (2) managers and administrators, (3) sales, (4) clerical, (5) craft workers, (6) factory operatives, (7) transport operatives, (8) laborers, (9) service workers, and (10) farm workers.

Professional and Technical. Many years of education are required to prepare for professional jobs such as lawyer, medical doctor, teacher, and minister. Professional occupations require mental ability and advanced knowledge of special career fields.

467

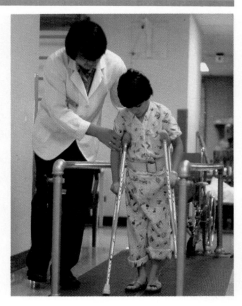

(above) Medical technicians recording information on a computer. (above right) Physical therapist helping a young patient walk. Which of the ten occupations groups do these workers fit into?

Professionals in science, for example, prepare for their jobs by completing advanced courses at a university. Chemists, physicists, geologists, botanists, and geneticists are a few of the professional occupations in the field of science. Writers, painters, and musicians are examples of professionals in the arts.

Technical occupations require special training and skills that may be gained in school or on the job. Technical workers usually have completed special courses in a college or vocational school. Television camera operators, dental hygienists, medical laboratory technicians, and computer technicians are examples of technical occupations.

Managers and Administrators. People in charge of businesses or other organizations, such as government agencies, are called managers or administrators. They are responsible for making and carrying out major decisions. In addition,

managers and administrators supervise or direct the work of others in their business or agency.

Most managers and administrators work for large corporations. Some, however, are self-employed and manage their own businesses.

Many managers and administrators work in the local, state, or federal governments. They direct or carry out the work of various public agencies or bureaucracies.

Sales. People who sell goods or services are involved in a sales occupation. Some people sell goods over the counter in a retail store. Others may sell products to other businesses or government agencies. Still others go from door to door in neighborhoods to sell directly to consumers.

Most sales workers learn their skills on the job. Some, however, need knowledge and skills gained from special courses or training

programs. Sellers of real estate or insurance, for example, usually have completed programs to prepare them for their jobs.

Clerical. Typists, secretaries, stenographers, and other office workers are included in the clerical category of occupations. Clerical workers do the daily paperwork required in the operation of businesses, government agencies, and other organizations. Clerical workers increasingly make use of computers, photocopiers, and other modern office equipment.

Craft Workers. Plumbers, bricklayers, electricians, carpenters, and printers are examples of craft workers. The craft worker is highly skilled in a trade. These skills are learned through special programs in vocational schools and at places of work. **Apprentices,** or beginning workers, learn skills on the job from masters of the craft.

Factory Operatives. Machine operators in industrial plants or mills are called factory operatives. Many work on assembly lines. Some operate various kinds of factory equipment such as blowtorches, cranes, and punch presses. In contrast to skilled craft workers, the work of factory operatives is called semiskilled.

Transport Operatives. Most transport operatives are also semiskilled workers. They drive buses, trucks, taxicabs, and other vehicles. In contrast to the jobs of craft workers, semiskilled jobs usually can be learned in a shorter time without special training outside of the workplace.

Laborers. Jobs that require little or no training or special skills are filled by laborers. These workers usually are required to do physical labor, such as handling heavy loads, digging ditches, or collecting garbage.

Which of the ten occupations groups would the postal employee fit into? Which occupations group do the firefighters belong to?

Study the graph at right. What trend does the graph show?

Service Workers. Many workers provide services of one kind or another. Firefighters and police officers, for example, provide protection to the public. Workers in restaurants, hotels, beauty salons, and barbershops are other examples of service workers. There are many different service occupations that call for various types and levels of knowledge and skill.

Farm Workers. Anyone who earns a living by the practice of agriculture is a farm worker. This category includes owners and managers of farms plus farm laborers. Some farmers specialize in producing certain kinds of crops. Others produce dairy products or raise livestock for sale to plants that process and market meat products.

Career Trends

Career trends indicate the growth or decline of opportunities in different job categories. In recent years, for example, the need for farm workers has declined greatly. By contrast, the demand for certain professional and technical workers has increased.

In general, job opportunities have been decreasing for "blue-collar" workers, such as factory laborers. There are, however, growing opportunities for workers in four "white-collar" job categories: (1) managers and administrators, (2) professional and technical, (3) clerical, and (4) service.

There are two types of production: (1) the production of goods and (2) the production of services. Since the 1950s, there has been a steady growth of service-producing jobs

Percentage of Employment in Services

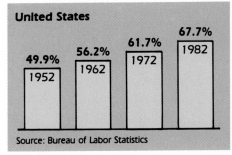

United States

49.9% 1952
56.2% 1962
61.7% 1972
67.7% 1982

Source: Bureau of Labor Statistics

and a decline of goods-producing jobs. By 1980, more than two-thirds of all jobs were involved in the production of services. Less than one-third were goods-producing jobs. The United States Department of Labor predicts that in the 1990s an even greater percentage of people will be employed in service-type jobs.

The continued growth of the service sector of the economy means that some types of white-collar jobs will increase more than others. The opportunities for managers and administrators, for example, are likely to be better in businesses providing services of one kind or another than in factories, which manufacture goods. Likewise, professional, technical, and clerical workers are more likely to find job openings in businesses that produce services.

Careers related to the use of computers will be plentiful in the coming years. Some of these jobs will involve the production of goods. Others will be in the service sector of the economy. Demand will remain high for people to fill jobs such as computer programmers, operators, and technicians. The employment outlook for systems analysts is very good and will

Employment In Computer Occupations, 1970, 1980, and Projected 1990

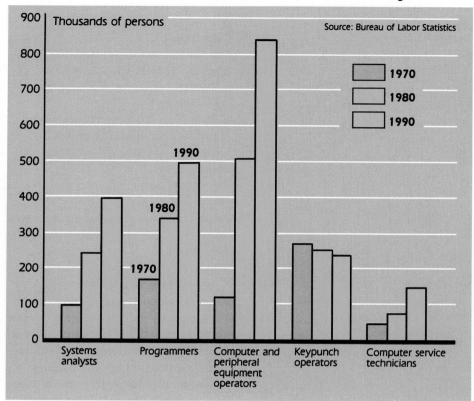

Thousands of persons

Source: Bureau of Labor Statistics

Legend:
- 1970
- 1980
- 1990

Categories (x-axis): Systems analysts, Programmers, Computer and peripheral equipment operators, Keypunch operators, Computer service technicians

(above, left) Which computer occupations will experience growth between now and 1990? (top) An architect designing a building. (above) Dr. Sally K. Ride, an astronaut, talking with ground controllers from the flight deck of the space shuttle *Challenger*.

become even better during the 1990s. A systems analyst develops and directs a company's use of computers and other data processing equipment. Jobs dealing with the production of computers and other information-processing equipment should also increase.

New Career Opportunities for Women

In 1980, more than 45 million adult women worked outside the home. This was about half of the adult female population. Women can now be found working in all of the job categories listed by the Federal Bureau of Labor Statistics.

About 40 percent of all jobs in the nation were held by women in 1970. The Department of Labor reported that in 1984 more than 50 percent of all employed people were women.

During the 1970s and early 1980s, many new job opportunities were opened to women. Before this time, few women held executive-level positions in businesses or government. From 1972 to 1982, however, the number of female managers and administrators rose from 1.4 million to 3.2 million. This trend is reflected in the undergraduate enrollment in colleges of business across the country. Texas A&M

Women Bosses

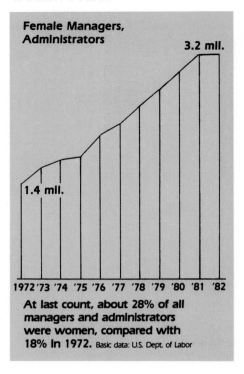

Female Managers, Administrators

3.2 mil.

1.4 mil.

1972 '73 '74 '75 '76 '77 '78 '79 '80 '81 '82

At last count, about 28% of all managers and administrators were women, compared with 18% in 1972. Basic data: U.S. Dept. of Labor

University, for example, has the fifth largest college of business in the nation. Half of its students are women. Opportunities for women in professional and technical jobs also have increased greatly in recent years.

Section Review

Vocabulary:
apprentice.

Reviewing the Main Ideas
1. What are the main categories of occupations as listed by the Federal Bureau of Labor Statistics?
2. How will the continued growth of the service sector of the economy affect the availability of managerial and administrative jobs? How will it affect the availability of factory jobs?

Skill Building
Use the bar graph on page 471 to answer the following questions:
a. In 1990, how many programmers will there be?
b. Based on the projections, which computer occupation will have fewer jobs available in 1990 than it had in 1980?

Section 2
Selecting Your Career

Children often dream about what they want to do when they grow up. They usually think of many different possibilities, some more realistic or practical than others. Teenagers, however, should begin to think carefully and realistically about careers. Soon they will be young adults faced with the responsibility of finding, and keeping, a full-time job.

Learning About Your Career Interests and Aptitudes
A primary step in choosing a career is self-examination. You need to know as much as possible about yourself in order to select a career that is best for you. You need to assess your interests, capabilities, and possibilities for self-development. You should try to choose a career that fits your personality. A shy person, for example, should not pursue a career as a salesperson.

Your interests provide clues about careers that might suit you. Most people will do better work in jobs that they like. For example, someone who likes to play musical instruments might enjoy working as a high-school music teacher. However, if a musically inclined person does not care to work with young people, then a career in teaching would not suit him or her.

No matter how interested you are in a career, you should not choose it unless you have the necessary aptitude. **Aptitude** is the potential to develop a talent or ability to do something.

You can learn about your aptitudes and interests through experiences in school or in organizations for young people. For example, you might explore interest in a business career by taking part in Junior Achievement. This is an organization that teaches young people how businesses are managed.

Your preferences for certain school subjects reveal interests related to a career choice. For example, if you like courses in mathematics, then you might want to consider careers in engineering, accounting, data processing, or scientific research.

Learning About Careers That Might Suit You

There are many books that can help you learn about careers that might fit your interests and aptitudes. Three good references are published by the United States Department of Labor: (1) *Dictionary of Occupational Titles*, (2) *Occupational Outlook*

Handbook, and (3) *Guide for Occupational Exploration.* These books describe the various occupations open to Americans. There is information about qualifications for different careers, working conditions, earnings, and career trends.

Another way to learn about careers is through part-time jobs. More than half of all teenagers in the United States have jobs. A high-school student can learn the nature of a sales career, for example, by working part-time as a clerk in a clothing store. Various kinds of part-time work can be a means for teenagers to explore career goals.

Experiences in school can help you learn about careers. For example, writing for the school newspaper is a way to explore career goals in journalism. Participating in the student council can help you explore political interests and aptitudes that are related to careers in government.

Preparing for Careers

You need at least a high-school education to qualify for most occupations in the United States. In recent years, a growing percentage of Americans have completed high school. For example, in 1960, only 41 percent of American adults, age 25 and over, had completed high school. Today, over 70 percent have finished their high-school education.

Those who drop out of school usually are the last to be hired and the first to be fired. They have high rates of unemployment and low levels of earnings. High-school graduates earn, on the average, almost

What types of interests and aptitudes do you think would be essential for someone wanting to become a teacher?

473

What type of job training do you think the people on this page had to go through?

How Education Raises Income

Heads of Family (age 25 or older)	Median Family Income, 1982
5 or more years of college	$41,587
Finished college	$35,778
1 to 3 years of college	$27,440
Finished high school	$23,837
1 to 3 years of high school	$17,517
Finished grade school	$15,251
Did not finish grade school	$12,047

twice as much yearly as those who quit school.

An increasing percentage of Americans seek a college education or vocational training after completing high school. Most of the best paying jobs require some kind of education beyond high school. The average lifetime earnings of college graduates is about $200,000 more than those who have graduated only from high school.

Many people have neither the interest nor the aptitude to succeed in college. They prefer to enter vocational schools or apprenticeships.

Vocational schools offer training for specific jobs. Many technical occupations, for example, require one or two years of courses in a vocational school. Community colleges or junior colleges usually have vocational-training programs.

An apprenticeship is the usual way to train for a career in a particular craft. Apprentices learn necessary skills at the workplace from masters of the craft. Apprenticeship programs may also involve classroom work at a trade school. The

typical apprenticeship program is completed in about three or four years. Apprentices earn a modest income while learning their craft or trade. A big increase in earnings is usually possible after finishing the apprenticeship.

Higher education or vocational training does not guarantee success in a career. However, those with more education or training have a big advantage.

People who achieve good records at school usually have an advantage in competing for their first jobs. Employers are impressed by job-seekers who have achieved success in school. They believe that good students are more likely to follow the rules and get along satisfactorily at the work place than poor students.

Section Review

Vocabulary:
aptitude, vocational school.

Reviewing the Main Ideas
1. Describe the connection between aptitudes and interests in making a career choice.
2. What are some of the ways a person can learn more about a specific career?
3. Identify a trend that has been taking place in education during the last twenty-five years.

Skill Building
Use information provided in this section to investigate two careers that interest you.

Case Study
The Successful Career of Mary Hudson

In 1934, Mary Hudson faced a difficult decision. She had an opportunity to lease a gas station in Kansas City, Kansas, and go into business for herself. She needed several hundred dollars to pay the costs of starting the business. Should she borrow the money?

After careful thought, Mary decided to take the risk of borrowing money to invest in her own business. She installed two gas pumps and opened her service station.

Friends and neighbors worried about Mary Hudson. It was unusual in those days for a woman to own and manage her own business. They feared she would fail, lose all her money, and acquire a large debt.

Mary Hudson had risked everything she had in the hopes of achieving success in business. However, she had realistic hopes of becoming a successful entrepreneur. She had helped her husband to manage a service station before he died, so she knew how to run a business.

Within three years, Mary Hudson had acquired five service stations. She was on the way to fame and fortune. By 1941, she was head of a company with more than one hundred stations.

The Hudson Oil Company gained a reputation for providing high-quality service and products for a fair price. Satisfied customers were the company's best advertisements. They spread the news that Mary Hudson's service stations were good places to do business.

In 1977, Mary Hudson paid more than $20 million to purchase an oil refinery in Oklahoma. This refinery produced 500,000 gallons of gasoline per day. Thus, Mary Hudson was able to supply gasoline to her own service stations, which helped make her company more competitive.

During her long, successful career, Mary Hudson won many honors. Her oil company became famous all over the world. In 1977, Mary was the first woman to win admission to the American Petroleum Institute's Twenty-Five-Year Club. This group of leading business executives changed its bylaws to admit Mary Hudson.

Mary Hudson achieved a remarkable career through hard work, intelligence, and discipline. She was willing and ready to take risks in competition with other businesses. By providing better services and products for lower prices, she was able to compete successfully.

Review

1. Why was Mary Hudson called an entrepreneur?
2. What personal qualities helped Mary Hudson become successful?

Basic Social Studies Skills
Identifying Trends and Making Forecasts

A trend is a direction of movement or a tendency. The following two statements describe career trends in the United States.

1. Employment in computer occupations has been increasing rapidly since 1970.

2. The number of women working at jobs outside the home has increased steadily since 1920.

Trends show how aspects of our current way of life have developed in the past. By identifying trends, you increase your understanding of relationships between the past and present.

Knowledge of trends is also useful in making forecasts. A forecast is an estimate about what seems likely to happen. It is a reasonable guess about the future. The following two statements are forecasts made by the U.S. Department of Labor in 1980. They are guesses about the future based on trends, developments from the past to the present.

1. Employment in computer occupations is likely to increase by more than 150,000 persons from 1980 to 1990.

2. The number of women employed outside the home is likely to increase from 45.5 million in the United States in 1980 to more than 55 million in 1990.

Both of these forecasts, made in 1980, were based on trends that have been developing for many years. These are hypotheses about the future. Facts collected by the Census Bureau and others in 1990 can be used to support or reject the forecasts made in 1980.

Skill Practice
Use information in the following three graphs to identify trends and make forecasts.

Trends in Farming, 1940–1980

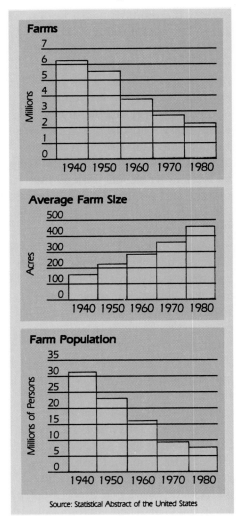

Farms

Millions — 7, 6, 5, 4, 3, 2, 1, 0

1940 1950 1960 1970 1980

Average Farm Size

Acres — 500, 400, 300, 200, 100, 0

1940 1950 1960 1970 1980

Farm Population

Millions of Persons — 35, 30, 25, 20, 15, 10, 5, 0

1940 1950 1960 1970 1980

Source: Statistical Abstract of the United States

Chapter 25 Review

Summary

Section 1: Your Opportunities for a Career

Americans have freedom to choose their careers. They have many choices. The Federal Bureau of Labor Statistics divides careers into these ten categories: (1) professional and technical, (2) managers and administrators, (3) sales, (4) clerical, (5) craft workers, (6) factory operatives, (7) transport operatives, (8) laborers, (9) service workers, and (10) farm workers.

The trend has been for jobs in the service sector of the economy to increase. In contrast, goods-producing jobs have been declining. Career opportunities for women have been steadily growing in many job categories. The majority of married women hold jobs outside their households.

Section 2: Selecting Your Career

Choices about careers should be based on knowledge about your interests, aptitudes, and potential for self-development. Knowledge is also needed about careers that might fit your interests, aptitudes, and potential. You also need to know how to qualify to enter various careers.

You should select a career that offers many advantages that match your career goals. In general, you should select a career that interests you, fits your personality, offers pleasant working conditions, provides opportunities for advancement, offers a satisfactory income, and requires talents that you can develop.

Vocabulary

Define the following terms.
1. aptitude
2. apprentice
3. vocational schools

Reviewing Main Ideas

1. Most managers and administrators work for _____.
   a. small companies
   b. large corporations
   c. partnerships
   d. craft workers
2. Most transport operatives are also _____.
   a. semiskilled workers
   b. craft workers
   c. managers
   d. clerical workers
3. True or false: You need at least a high-school education to qualify for most occupations in the United States.

Thinking Critically

Communicating Information

1. Collect newspaper and magazine articles that deal with careers and career opportunities. Post the articles and accompanying photos, graphs, and other illustrations on the bulletin board.
2. Constuct a chart that shows some of the major steps involved in choosing a career.

Evaluating Information

1. Do you think career preparation should start in high school or at an earlier time? Why?
2. Tell why you think this statement is true or false: The highest-paying jobs are usually the ones that require the most career preparation.

Unit 8 Test

Vocabulary

Write *true* if the underlined word or phrase is used correctly. Write *false* if it is used incorrectly. Rephrase each false statement so that the underlined word or phrase is used correctly.

1. <u>Goods</u> are products such as cars, refrigerators, and shoes.

2. Food, clothing, houses, buses, tools, and books are types of <u>services</u>.

3. <u>Natural resources</u> are the skills and knowledge of human beings.

4. In recent years, the federal government has acted to increase, or <u>deregulate</u>, the amount of government control over business.

5. A nation's <u>economic system</u> determines how economic decisions get made in the country.

6. <u>Inflation</u> is a time of rising prices.

7. After economic activity reaches a peak, <u>the contraction phase</u> of the business cycle begins.

8. <u>Depression</u> is a time of full employment, high personal income, high GNP, and high business profits.

9. <u>GNP</u> stands for Gross National Product.

10. Under <u>communism</u>, most economic decisions get made by consumers and producers.

11. In a <u>capitalistic system</u>, most economic decisions are made by government.

12. <u>Consumer goods</u> are never used up.

13. A <u>monopoly</u> exists when only one company makes a product.

14. <u>Single proprietorship</u> is the most common form of business in the United States.

15. In an <u>open shop</u> you don't have to join a union, but in a <u>union shop</u> you do.

16. <u>Corporations</u> usually have one owner.

17. During <u>collective bargaining</u>, employers and workers try to reach decisions that will satisfy both sides.

18. A <u>labor union</u> is an organization of business owners.

19. <u>Flexible expenses</u> may occur each month but the amount spent changes.

20. What a person pays in rent each month is a <u>fixed expense</u>.

21. A <u>budget</u> is a plan for spending and saving money.

22. <u>Credit unions</u> are stores that sell on credit.

Recalling Information

1. True or false: The problem of scarcity is the problem of too many resources and too few wants.

2. True or false: During the 1970s and 1980s, many new job opportunities were opened to women.

3. In a capitalistic system _____.
a. the government makes all major economic decisions
b. there is private ownership of property
c. everyone works for the government
d. all of the above

4. True or false: In a market economy, producers who fail to offer what consumers want will probably go out of business.

5. True or false: A communist country usually has free enterprise.

6. In a market system, prices _____ when there is a large supply of some item and a very small demand for the item.
a. go up
b. go down
c. stay the same
d. none of the above

7. True or false: In the United States most economic decisions are made by the command system.

8. Gross national product tells _____.
a. the value of final goods and services produced during a certain period of time
b. the number of cars built during a certain period of time
c. the income earned by workers during a certain period of time
d. the value of services bought by consumers during a certain period of time

9. You and a friend want to form a business. You would most likely form a _____.
a. single proprietorship
b. partnership
c. corporation
d. none of the above

10. Which of the following people could be called producers?
a. the owner of a bakery
b. a manager of a can company
c. an assembly worker for Ford
d. all of the above

11. Capital goods are _____.
a. workers
b. machines and tools
c. natural resources
d. all of the above

12. Which of the following has been a goal of labor unions in the past one hundred years?
a. to improve working conditions
b. to increase wages
c. to get more fringe benefits
d. all of the above

13. Which of the following should a person do when making a budget?
a. List fixed expenses.
b. Estimate flexible expenses.
c. Balance estimated expenses with income.
d. all of the above

Skill Building

1. Explain the difference between producers and consumers.

2. How do consumers influence producers in the United States?

3. Why are people hurt by inflation?

4. Describe conditions in the 1800s that led to the rise of labor unions.

Unit 9

The United States and the World

The United States is linked to the world in many ways. Government leaders in the United States make decisions about the relationships between our country and others. Some of these decisions involve American troops and weapons. Such decisions can affect millions of lives.

At the same time, our business activities take us all over the world. Americans buy and sell raw materials and finished goods in places as far away as China. Decisions made by American business people affect other people the world over.

Likewise, our lives are affected by the business decisions of others in the world. The decision by a German company, for example, to sell cameras in the United States, gives us new choices as consumers. It also means American camera-manufacturing companies will have more competition. The decision of the Organization of Petroleum Exporting Countries (OPEC) to raise the price of crude oil affects the price of our gasoline and the cost of heating our homes.

Our farmers also link the United States to the world. American farmers are some of the best farmers in

the world. Through technology, our farmers can get more food out of an acre of land than most farmers in any other nation. As a result, private farmers and government officials often make decisions about selling or giving food to others in the world. Many individuals come to the United States to study our farming techniques.

Our students and teachers also link the United States to others in the world. More than fifty thousand American students go to school in other countries. Nearly four times that number of foreign students study in the United States.

In this unit you will learn about foreign policy. You will read about the decisions of national government leaders that affect how the United States behaves toward other nations in the world. And you will discover what some major concerns of our foreign policy have been over the years.

You will also learn about new foreign-policy challenges facing citizens of the United States. And you will discover how the daily lives of ordinary citizens link them to others around the world.

(opposite) Thousands of card-holding spectators created these flags during the opening ceremonies of the 1984 Summer Olympics in Los Angeles. Do you recognize any of the flags?

Chapter 26

Making Foreign Policy

Introduction. Thousands of United States government officials work full-time on international relations. One of these officials is the Secretary of State. Here's a recent day in the life of a Secretary of State.

7:30 A.M. The Secretary wakes up in his hotel room in Cairo, Egypt. He showers, dresses, and has breakfast. While eating, he reads messages from Washington.

8:30 A.M. An assistant enters the room. They discuss the Secretary's plans for the week. The Secretary decides to meet with the Soviet foreign minister later in the week.

10:00 A.M. The Secretary meets with the foreign minister of Egypt. The two officials make final plans for a loan of $80 million from the United States to Egypt. News reporters take pictures.

11:08 A.M. The Secretary rushes to the airport. His government jet is waiting.

1:05 P.M. In Syria, the Secretary and the Syrian president discuss peace in the Middle East.

6:10 P.M. The Secretary is back on his plane and flying to Israel. He talks with American news reporters who are traveling with him.

9:00 P.M. In Tel Aviv, the Secretary and the prime minister of Israel have dinner. The Secretary explains why the United States has loaned money to Egypt. The prime minister and several of his aides request more military aid.

11:30 P.M. The Secretary returns to his hotel, writes a report to the President, issues orders to his assistants, and goes to bed.

This chapter looks at how the United States government develops plans for dealing with other nations.

Soviet Foreign Minister Andrei Gromyko (left) and United States Secretary of State George Shultz leaving a meeting at which the two officials discussed the possibility of limiting nuclear weapons.

Section 1
American Foreign Policy

Look at these recent headlines. What do they have in common?

- President to Meet with Mexican Leaders
- Congress Gives Aid to Czechoslovakia
- Agriculture Department Announces New Trade Policy with Japan
- U.S. Watches Apartheid in South Africa
- Soviet Union and U.S. to Discuss New Reductions in Nuclear Weapons

All these actions deal with our relations with the rest of the world. They involve American foreign policy. What is foreign policy? How has American foreign policy developed since our nation's founding?

What Is Foreign Policy?

The general plan a national government makes about how to act toward another nation is called its **foreign policy.**

Today, the United States, like many other nations, has many foreign policies. For example, the national government has policies about how much trading American business should do with other countries around the world. It also has policies about which nations can buy American weapons and bombs. And it has policies about which countries the United States will help to defend if they are attacked.

American foreign policy, in many respects, has stayed the same for many years. For instance, the

President Nixon talking with Chinese officials in Peking in 1972. Nixon's visit signaled a dramatic change in United States policy toward communist China. It paved the way for new trade agreements between the two nations and for the formal recognition of the People's Democratic Republic of China in 1979.

United States has given military support to Western European nations for decades and plans to continue to do so for the foreseeable future. Likewise, the United States has supported and continues to support some poor nations around the world through food donations and other assistance programs.

Foreign policy does change, however. For example, the United States made a dramatic change in foreign policy when, after thirty years, it formally recognized the communist government of the People's Republic of China in 1979. This change of policy did not happen overnight. It evolved over the years and involved the resolution of many complicated issues.

Key Developments in American Foreign Policy

Our foreign policies have changed over the years as the nation's needs have changed. Here are some key stages in the development of American foreign policy.

Isolationism. In the early 1800s the United States was a small and weak nation. Our foreign policy was aimed at protecting the new nation from the strong European countries. We wanted to avoid becoming involved in European affairs. Thus, our foreign policy at this time was called **isolationism.**

President George Washington first set forth this idea. He declared that it was the nation's policy "to steer clear of permanent alliances with any portion of the foreign world." Thomas Jefferson agreed. In 1801, he said that America wanted peace with all nations and "entangling alliances with none."

The Monroe Doctrine. In 1823 President James Monroe acted to further protect the United States and Latin America from outside interference. In a message to Congress, Monroe set forth two ideas. First, America intended to stay out of the internal affairs of Europe. Second, Europe—including Russia—should stay out of internal affairs in North and South America. This policy has been known ever since as the **Monroe Doctrine.**

Over the years the Monroe Doctrine has become a key principle of American foreign policy. It seeks to promote our self-defense by keeping "America for the Americans." Every Congress and President since Monroe have supported this policy. In recent years, the Monroe Doctrine has been challenged by the development in Cuba of a communist government supported by the Soviet Union, and by Cuban efforts to promote revolution in Central and Latin American countries.

Growth of Power and Territory.
By the mid- and late 1800s our nation's needs were changing. The United States was growing stronger. New foreign policies were aimed at adding more territory and helping to protect our growing industries. In 1846, we acquired Texas in a war with Mexico. In 1898, the United States won the Spanish-American War and gained control of Cuba, Puerto Rico, Hawaii, and the Philippines.

World War I and Isolationism. In 1917, the United States joined France and England in World War I against Germany and its allies. American troops, equipment, and other resources tipped the balance and led to victory.

After the war, however, the United States retreated into isolationism. The United States refused to join the League of Nations—an organization of nations aimed at promoting world peace. Americans wanted no part of Europe's problems. The United States pulled back from many of its international involvements.

World War II and Great Power.
American attempts to isolate itself from the world ended with World War II (1939–1945). During the war, the United States and its allies defeated Nazi Germany and Japan. The United States emerged from the war as the world's strongest nation.

In 1945, the United States helped create the United Nations (UN) in the hopes of preventing further world wars. It soon became clear, however, that the Soviet Union and the United States would become

great rivals. As a result, we created new foreign policies designed to hold back the spread of Soviet communism. Today Japan and West Germany have become important allies of the United States. Even the Soviet Union is seen as less of a rival today because of the new policies of Mikhail Gorbachev.

The U.S.S. *Maine* exploding in the harbor of Havana, Cuba, in 1898. The *Maine* had been sent to the Spanish-held island to protect Americans whose lives were in danger because of a revolution. Although Spain was cleared of any involvement in the sinking of the *Maine* and the deaths of 260 crewmembers, public outrage over the incident was one of the reasons why President McKinley declared war on Spain.

Section Review

Vocabulary:
foreign policy, isolationism, Monroe Doctrine.

Reviewing the Main Ideas
1. What is foreign policy? Give an example.
2. What are the key ideas of the Monroe Doctrine?
3. Should modern nations have isolationist foreign policies? Why?

Skill Building
1. Find political cartoons in magazines and newspapers that deal with United States foreign policy. Categorize the cartoons into

President Reagan and Japanese Prime Minister Yasuhiro Nakasone. The two officials held a series of meetings in Los Angeles in early 1985 to discuss ways to open new Japanese markets for American products, especially telecommunications equipment. In recent years, the United States has had huge trade deficits. It was hoped that the development of new markets for American goods would help decrease the deficit.

two groups—those that are critical of U.S. policies and those that are in favor of U.S. policies. Post the cartoons on a bulletin board and discuss.

2. Find an article in the newspaper concerning U.S. foreign policy. Read the article and summarize it for the class.

Section 2
From Cold War to Coexistence

The most important concern of American foreign policy since World War II has been our security against the expansion and competition of the Soviet Union. The years from 1947 to the 1980s have been called the **Cold War.** During that time the United States and the Soviet Union did not fight each other directly. But they competed in many ways. Each country built many weapons to defend itself against the other. Each country threatened the other. Each country gave aid to either communist or noncommunist groups fighting in other countries. How did the Cold War start?

Communism and Cold War

Karl Marx (1818–1883) developed the ideas behind communism. Marx, a German writer, believed that workers in all nations were treated unfairly by the capitalists, or factory owners and business leaders. In a book, *Das Kapital*, Marx argued that the workers, called the **proletariat** [prō′lə-ter′ē ət], should take over factories

and businesses in all nations. Marx called for the proletariat to take control of government by force if necessary. Under communism there would be no private property or businesses. Instead, the government would own everything and run factories in the name of the workers.

In a democracy, individuals are free to own property and seek their fortunes. Under communism, the state owns nearly everything and individuals come to have much less freedom.

In 1917, Russia became the first country to accept communism. Under the leadership of a man called Lenin, workers, soldiers, and peasants overthrew the Russian czar and took over the government. In 1924, Joseph Stalin became the leader of Russia—now called the Union of Soviet Socialist Republics, or the Soviet Union. Stalin made the Soviet Union into a world power. He also created a dictatorship that took complete control of Russian life.

In World War II, the Soviet Union and the United States fought together against Germany. But shortly after the war, they began to disagree. Perhaps neither government ever really trusted the other. The Russians believed they had done most of the fighting against Hitler. Their military casualties were fifteen times those of the United States. Seven and one-half million Russian soldiers lost their lives in World War II. Stalin wanted to keep control of Poland and other Eastern European countries to protect Russian borders against future attacks.

So, at the end of World War II, the Russians kept their troops in the countries of Eastern Europe. They did not permit free elections. In each country they created communist governments under their control. In 1946, Winston Churchill, Britain's prime minister, described what happened to Eastern Europe. He said, "An iron curtain has descended across the continent."

By 1947, President Truman and others were convinced the Russians wanted to take over Europe and then the rest of the world. They believed World War II had started because Hitler was not stopped when he began taking over other countries. They did not want to make the same mistake with the Soviets.

In a 1947 speech before Congress, President Truman announced a new foreign policy toward the Soviet Union. The President said it was necessary for the United States to help countries all over the world fight off the expansion of the Soviet Union and communism.

The policy came to be known as **containment.** The policy of containment meant the United States would use money and military power to contain the Soviet Union, that is, to keep it from expanding the territory it controlled, and to prevent countries from developing governments friendly to communism. This policy has been followed by all Presidents since Truman.

Tools of Containment

Here are some of the more important foreign-policy tools the government has used to carry out the policy of containment.

Recipients of U.S. Foreign Aid

Who Gets U.S. Economic Aid?		Who Gets U.S. Military Aid?	
1. Israel	$1,200 mil.	1. Israel	$1,800 mil.
2. Egypt	$ 820 mil.	2. Egypt	$1,302 mil.
3. El Salvador	$ 414 mil.	3. Turkey	$ 494 mil.
4. Pakistan	$ 276 mil.	4. Greece	$ 344 mil.
5. Philippines	$ 253 mil.	5. Pakistan	$ 314 mil.
6. Honduras	$ 175 mil.	6. El Salvador	$ 112 mil.
7. Costa Rica	$ 161 mil.	7. Spain	$ 108 mil.
8. Guatemala	$ 154 mil.	8. Philippines	$ 103 mil.
9. Jordan	$ 111 mil.	9. Honduras	$ 61 mil.
10. Turkey	$ 102 mil.	10. Thailand	$ 52 mil.

Estimates, 1987   Source: Statistical Digest, 1989

Foreign Aid. This involves giving economic or military goods to other countries. Aid has been given to try to strengthen countries against communism. It has included loans of money and gifts of food, technical help, road building, education programs, and weapons. Since the end of World War II, the United States has given more than $220 billion in aid to over ninety countries.

Security Treaties. The United States has made six major treaties that pledge us to defend forty-one nations. Countries that have signed

(top) Which two nations were the biggest beneficiaries of United States military aid? (above, left to right) Britain's Prime Minister Winston Churchill, President Harry Truman, and Soviet Premier Joseph Stalin at Potsdam in East Germany in 1945. The nations agreed to allow free elections in the nations that had been occupied by Germany in World War II. The Soviet Union soon broke the agreements, however, and set up communist governments in Poland and other eastern European nations. The United States responded with its policy of containment.

487

East Berlin's Conciliation Church toppling to the ground in early 1985. Berlin was divided after World War II, with the Soviet Union occupying East Berlin, and the Western Allies—Britain, France, and the United States—occupying West Berlin. In the years after World War II, thousands of East Germans fled to freedom in West Berlin. In 1961, the East German government countered by building the Berlin Wall, a 26-mile wall of concrete and barbed wire around East Berlin. East German officials razed Conciliation Church in an effort to stop escapes from the area around the church. In December, 1989, the East German government stunned the world by opening up the Berlin Wall.

these mutual defense treaties have promised to protect each other from communist aggression. If a country is attacked, others that have a treaty with it are supposed to come to its aid. The chart on page 493 shows these treaties and the countries protected by them.

These treaties allow the United States to place its military forces around the world. Recently the United States had over 530,000 troops stationed overseas. Experts argue this helps contain Soviet power in two ways.

First, the presence of U.S. troops limits Russia's military moves around its own borders. Second, having American troops in foreign countries allows the U.S. to respond more quickly to military threats in distant lands.

Secret Operations. These involve secret, or **covert, activities** in another country. These operations include such things as spying, giving money to political groups, or helping one political party fight another. Some of our secret operations have been aimed at changing the government of another country to get someone in power favorable to our national interests.

Using the Armed Forces. Small numbers of American troops have sometimes been sent into other countries to act as police. They may stop rioting or help governments the United States wants to keep in power. For example, in April 1965 rebels attacked the government of the Dominican Republic. This government was supported by the United States. President Lyndon Johnson sent several thousand American troops to keep order and protect the government. Johnson said that the rebels were communists. In recent years, United States troops have been called upon to stop a communist takeover of Grenada, to maintain peace in Lebanon, and to overthrow a dictator in Panama.

Massive Retaliation. This is the threat to use our large and small nuclear weapons. The United States invented the atomic bomb during World War II. Atomic bombs were used in 1945 to end the war with Japan. Since then America has not used such weapons but it could. This threat really stands behind all the other "tools" of containment.

However, the Soviet Union also has many nuclear weapons. A war between our two countries would destroy life as we know it. The most important goal of foreign policy is to prevent an all-out nuclear war.

Fighting Limited Wars

Limited wars have been another tool of containment. A **limited war** does not involve nuclear weapons and is fought for specific objectives other than total victory over the enemy. American troops have fought costly limited wars against communist-supported armies in Korea and Vietnam.

The Korean War. In June, 1950, communist North Korea attacked South Korea, a noncommunist country. President Truman sent American troops to fight on the side of the South Korean army. Communist Chinese troops soon entered the war to help North Korea. The major goal of the United States was to drive the Chinese and North Koreans back into North Korea. When General Eisenhower became President in 1952, he threatened to use nuclear weapons against China to stop the war. In July of 1953 a truce was signed and the fighting stopped.

Over 36,000 Americans were killed in Korea and more than 103,000 were wounded. The war cost 54 billion dollars.

The Vietnam War. In the 1950s it looked as if a communist group in North Vietnam was going to take over all of Vietnam. President Eisenhower sent money and a small number of military advisers to help the noncommunist government in South Vietnam. But the communists grew stronger. Under President Kennedy, the United States sent more money, weapons, and military advisers to help South Vietnam. By 1963 there were 15,000 American advisers helping the South Vietnamese government. Russia and China, in turn, were helping North Vietnam.

A Vietnam War Memorial in Constitution Gardens in Washington, D.C. features these seven-foot sculptures of Vietnam soldiers in battle. More than 58,000 soldiers were killed or were missing in action as a result of the conflict.

(top) El Salvador's former President José Napoleón Duarte [dwär'tä]. El Salvador, which is in Central America, has been plagued by internal political conflict in recent years. This conflict has often flared into full-scale civil war. (above) United States military adviser instructing El Salvadoran soldiers in the operation of a rocket launcher. The United States has from time to time offered advisory aid as well as military supplies to the government of El Salvador to help fight off rebels. These rebels claim that the government of El Salvador is undemocratic and controlled by the military and rich landowners. The election of Duarte was viewed as a hopeful sign that Salvadorans might settle their differences. In late 1984 Duarte met with rebel leaders in the first of a series of peace talks.

There was no formal declaration of war between the United States and North Vietnam. But, in 1964, Congress passed the Gulf of Tonkin Resolution giving President Johnson power to take emergency action in Vietnam. During 1964 and 1965, the total of United States troops in Vietnam jumped to 185,000. By 1968, more than one-half million Americans were fighting in Vietnam.

In spite of these large numbers of American helpers, the South Vietnamese were not able to win. The war dragged on for eight more years. Many Americans became very unhappy with a foreign policy that involved the United States in a long, drawn-out war. Finally, in 1973, a truce was signed, and President Nixon withdrew all American troops from Vietnam. In April 1975, the South Vietnamese government surrendered and Vietnam became one communist nation.

The Vietnam War was a bitter experience for the United States. More than 46,000 Americans gave their lives in the war. Another 304,000 were wounded. Between 1965 and 1973, the United States spent more than $107 billion to fight the war. The war caused many people during the 1970s to seriously question the policy of containment. They thought that wars like that in Vietnam showed that such a policy could be a mistake. Yet, by the 1980s, Soviet actions led to new concerns about the need to contain Soviet ambitions.

Uneasy Coexistence

Today the two superpowers—the United States and the Soviet Union—are locked in a kind of uneasy coexistence. The Soviet Union appears as determined as ever to expand its worldwide influence. At the start of the 1980s, for example, Soviet troops invaded the nation of Afghanistan. The president of Afghanistan was killed and the Soviets put in their own leader.

For its part, the United States still follows a policy of containment. President Carter denounced Soviet actions in Afghanistan, stopped grain sales to the Soviet Union, and asked Congress to reinstate registration for the military draft. President Reagan greatly increased national defense spending.

American concerns about the Soviet Union are deeply rooted in our distrust of Soviet political ideas. The Soviet government is a powerful dictatorship that gives little freedom to its citizens. Such a government is seen as a continuing threat to American ideals of liberty, equality, and freedom.

Section Review

Vocabulary:
Cold War, containment, covert activities, limited war, massive retaliation, proletariat, secret operations.

Reviewing the Main Ideas
1. Explain the term "Cold War" and describe how the Cold War started.
2. What is the policy of containment?

3. Describe the foreign-policy tools used by the United States to carry out the policy of containment.

Skill Building

Find information to answer the following questions.

1. What is the name of the current Secretary of State?

2. What foreign-policy problems concern decision makers today?

3. Read a recent news-magazine article about a foreign-policy problem to find out which people and ideas are influencing foreign-policy decision makers.

4. Use *Readers' Guide* to find an article about the Vietnam War. Was your article "for" or "against" United States involvement in the war?

Section 3
Making Foreign-Policy Decisions

Who decides how the United States should act toward others in the world? Many people and groups in government help make foreign policy.

The President

"I make American foreign policy," President Truman declared in 1948. The President is indeed a very important foreign-policy decision maker. President Kennedy once said that in world affairs, "the President bears the burden of responsibility. . . . The advisers may move on to new advice."

Presidents must often choose among conflicting advice when making foreign-policy decisions. President Lyndon Johnson once complained, "The State Department wants to solve everything with words, and the generals, with guns." President Reagan explained, "You try to figure out in your mind what is best . . . then you go forward."

The Constitution gives the President the power to: (1) make treaties with other nations (two-thirds of the Senate must approve the treaty), (2) appoint diplomatic officers (subject to Senate approval), and (3) recognize the legal existence of a nation and its government. As a result, the President is the nation's chief **diplomat.** (Diplomats are the officials who manage relations between countries.) Americans and others in the world look to the President to represent our country in foreign affairs.

In addition, as commander in chief of the armed forces, Presidents can use troops and weapons to carry out foreign-policy decisions. This is a great power. Presidents throughout history have made use of it. For example:

- Thomas Jefferson ordered the navy to deal with the Barbary pirates in 1801.
- James K. Polk sent troops into Mexico to defend Texas in 1845.
- Abraham Lincoln blockaded southern ports and declared martial law in 1861.
- President Ford sent the Marines to free an American merchant

cargo ship seized by Cambodians in 1975.

- President Reagan sent troops to stop a communist takeover in Grenada in 1983.

The Foreign-Policy Bureaucracy

The President and assistants in the White House do not make foreign-policy decisions alone. They work with a large foreign-policy bureaucracy. This bureaucracy is made up of the Department of State, the Department of Defense, the Central Intelligence Agency, and the National Security Council.

Where did this bureaucracy come from? At the end of World War II (1945) many Americans feared the United States could not stop the Soviet Union from taking over other countries. They believed foreign-policy decisions had to be made quickly as problems arose. In 1947, Congress created the Department of Defense, the Central Intelligence Agency (CIA), and the National Security Council. It put these agencies in the executive branch of government under the authority of the President. The idea was to give the President the information and advisers he needed to respond quickly to foreign-policy problems.

These agencies have helped make the President very powerful in foreign affairs. They give the President valuable information. They can carry out presidential decisions around the world. Today key foreign-policy decisions about war and peace, nuclear weapons, and national defense are made in the executive branch by the President and the foreign-policy bureaucracy.

Sometimes, the foreign-policy bureaucracy can be hard for a President to control. Many of the people in the bureaucracy had their jobs long before the President took office and they will be there long after he leaves. President Truman once complained, "Those fellows in the State Department, who stay there no matter what happens in elections, can't be trusted to carry out a President's policies."

The Department of State. This is a major agency for government foreign-policy decision making. The Secretary of State is the President's official adviser on foreign-policy matters. Most secretaries work closely with the President on foreign-policy decisions.

The State Department's job is to make decisions about how the United States should act toward other countries and toward global problems such as hunger or pollution. The State Department is supposed to carry out decisions made by the President. The Department arranges treaties and other agreements with foreign governments. It helps American citizens who get in trouble in foreign countries, and it gives information about the United States to foreigners.

The Department of Defense. The Department of Defense is directed by the Secretary of Defense. The Defense Department shares directly in making foreign-policy decisions. The Secretary of Defense and the Joint Chiefs of Staff advise the President about military aspects of foreign policy and other defense matters. Presidents rarely make important decisions without consulting their military advisers.

In addition, many foreign-policy decisions about military affairs are made in the Defense Department. The Department is in charge of hundreds of American military bases in all parts of the world.

See the chart at right. It shows the nations the United States was committed to defend in 1984.

The Central Intelligence Agency.
This agency finds out what is going on in other countries. The **CIA** was set up to gather information, evaluate it, and pass it on to the President and other foreign-policy decision makers. It gets its information from its own secret agents, from paid informers, from foreign news sources, and from the information agencies of foreign governments friendly to the United States. All large nations have information-gathering agencies like the CIA.

Information-gathering agencies are necessary to a country's security. In 1962, when the Soviet Union sent nuclear missiles into Cuba, in striking distance of our nation, we needed to know it. Our President was able to take action to make the Soviet Union remove the missiles. But information-gathering agencies are troublesome in a democracy because they work in secret. Americans have always been suspicious of the things a government does in secret. In the mid-1970s, Congress investigated the CIA and called for stricter control of its activities.

U.S. Defense Treaties

The United States is a party to six treaties that pledge this country to defend 41 nations—

NATO
North Atlantic Treaty Organization
Signed in 1949

Belgium, Britain, Canada, Denmark, France, Greece, Iceland, Italy, Luxembourg, Netherlands, Norway, Portugal, Spain, Turkey, West Germany

ANZUS
Signed in 1951

Australia, New Zealand

South Korea Mutual Defense Treaty
Signed in 1953

Rio Treaty
Inter-American Treaty of Reciprocal Assistance
Signed in 1947

Argentina, Bahamas, Bolivia, Brazil, Chile, Colombia, Costa Rica, Dominican Republic, Ecuador, El Salvador, Guatemala, Haiti, Honduras, Mexico, Nicaragua, Panama, Paraguay, Peru, Trinidad and Tobago, Uruguay, Venezuela

Japan Mutual Defense Treaty
Signed in 1951

Philippines Mutual Defense Treaty
Signed in 1951

The National Security Council.
This is an advisory group for the President. The Council brings officials from the foreign policy bureaucracy together. The Vice-President, the secretaries of State and Defense, and the Chairman of the Joint Chiefs of Staff are members along with others invited by the President. When a crisis erupts anywhere in the world the President may call the Council into session. The Council's job is to collect military and other kinds of information in order to give advice to the President. The director of the Council staff, who is called the National Security Adviser, usually serves as a top adviser to the President.

Study the chart. Which treaty commits the United States to defend nations in western Europe? Which treaty commits the United States to defend some of the nations in South America?

United States marines guarding their compound in Beirut, Lebanon in 1983. Civil unrest in Lebanon due to religious differences and conflicts with Syria and Israel, prompted the United Nations to send special peace-keeping forces to Lebanon in the late 1970s and early 1980s. In 1983, peace-keeping forces from the United States and France became victims of terrorist attacks by groups who wanted them to leave the nation. The United States lost 241 soldiers and France 54 in two separate attacks by terrorists in 1983. The peace-keeping force was withdrawn in 1984.

Other Government Agencies

Almost all government agencies are involved to some degree in foreign affairs. Three of the most important government agencies are the departments of Treasury, Commerce, and Agriculture.

The Treasury Department makes decisions about money problems and international loans. The Department of Commerce makes decisions related to foreign trade. The Department of Agriculture makes decisions related to technical assistance to other countries and to selling American food products.

Congress and Foreign Policy

The Constitution divides the power to conduct foreign and military affairs between the President and Congress. The President is chief diplomat and commander in chief, but Congress has the power to declare war, to approve certain actions, and to spend money for defense.

The Constitution does not clearly spell out how the legislative and the executive branches can use their powers. As a result, there has always been a built-in struggle between Congress and the President over foreign policy.

In this struggle, one branch or the other has dominated at various times in our history. After World War II, Congress lost much of its control over foreign policy to the President. Then, in the late 1960s and early 1970s, dislike of the Vietnam War led Congress to try to restore some of its war powers. Today the struggle continues. Here are the three tools Congress uses in foreign policy:

War Powers. The Constitution (Article 1) gives Congress alone the power to declare war and maintain an army and navy. But, from the beginning, Presidents have ignored this authority. In 1798 President Adams ordered American warships to fight French ships. Since then, Presidents have sent American troops to fight more than forty times without a declaration of war.

In 1973, Congress passed the War Powers Act over a presidential veto. Congress wanted to limit the President's power. The law requires the President to consult Congress "in every possible instance . . . before introducing U.S. armed forces into hostilities or into situations where . . . involvement" of troops is likely. The War Powers Act also prohibits the President from keeping troops in combat for more than ninety days unless Congress declares war or passes a joint resolution extending the time.

Approval Powers. The Constitution also requires the Senate to approve all treaties the President arranges with other countries. Two-thirds of the Senate must vote in favor of a treaty before it becomes law. Presidents often avoid this step by making executive agreements with other countries. An executive agreement is made directly between the President and the leader of another country.

Ambassadors, ministers, consuls —all members of the foreign service —must also be approved by the Senate. The Senate usually accepts the President's choices in these matters.

Money Powers. The President and other government agencies cannot spend money for foreign-policy activities unless Congress gives it to them. When the President submits the national budget every year, committees in the House and Senate must approve his requests for foreign policy and military defense. During the year, the President may submit bills about foreign policy that call for special funding.

Section Review

Vocabulary:
diplomat, Department of State, Department of Defense, Central Intelligence Agency, National Security Council.

Reviewing the Main Ideas
1. Describe the agencies that make up the foreign-policy bureaucracy. What is the relationship of these agencies to the President?
2. How can Congress check the President's foreign-policy actions?

Skill Building
Label each statement below as true or false. Support your choice with evidence from this section.
1. The President has to work with many people when making foreign-policy decisions.
2. Only the President and State Department actually make foreign-policy decisions.
3. The National Security Council sells military equipment to foreign countries.
4. The Department of Defense has little influence on the President's foreign-policy decisions.
5. The President can send American troops into combat without a declaration of war by Congress.

Case Study

The Panama Canal Treaties

The Panama Canal cuts across the narrow Isthmus of Panama. (Locate the canal on the map on the next page.) Before the canal was built, it took many weeks for ships to sail around South America from the Atlantic to the Pacific. American business needed a shorter water route to transport goods. And during the Spanish-American War, when it took an American battleship 68 days to reach Cuba, American interest in building a canal grew even stronger.

At that time the Isthmus was under the control of Colombia. In 1903, the United States Secretary of State and the Colombian representative in Washington negotiated a treaty. The United States Senate ratified the treaty, but the Colombian government did not.

The people in Panama wanted the canal to be built. It would bring much business to their land. They revolted against the Colombian government—some historians say the United States aided their revolution. President Theodore Roosevelt arranged a treaty with the new Panamanian government.

The treaty gave the United States complete authority forever over a ten-mile-wide strip of land across Panama. This was called the Canal Zone. Panama got $10 million and yearly payments.

The Canal was built by the United States from 1903 to 1914. It cost $387 million. More than 6,000 workers died from malaria, yellow fever, and other diseases while working on the canal.

Over the years the people of Panama came to believe the 1903 treaty was unfair. They did not like the idea that the United States would control forever a strip of land that split their country from ocean to ocean. Some Panamanians were angry because the better jobs at the Canal went to Americans living in the Canal Zone. For many years young people in Panama were taught that Americans were causing many of their country's problems.

In 1964 anger at the Americans finally boiled over. There was rioting in Panama. Four Americans and twenty-one Panamanians died. There was fear that the canal might be damaged by even more violence.

President Lyndon Johnson decided it was time to change American foreign policy toward Panama. State Department officials

(below) The Culebra Cut, the deepest excavated portion of the Panama Canal, as it looked during construction in 1913. (opposite) President Carter and General Omar Torrijos signing the Panama Canal treaties.

began to work with the Panamanians on a new treaty.

Work on the treaty continued under Presidents Nixon, Ford, and Carter. Finally, in 1977, two new treaties were ready. One called for the United States to give Panama control of the canal by the year 2000. The other gave the United States the right to defend the canal even after 2000.

The treaties represented a new foreign policy toward Panama. On September 7, 1977, President Jimmy Carter and General Omar Torrijos [tôr hē′ yōs], the leader of Panama, signed the treaties in Washington. President Carter said it was the start of a new era of friendship between the United States and the people of Latin America.

Now all eyes turned to the U.S. Senate. Two-thirds of the senators had to vote yes before the treaties would become law. For seven months opponents and supporters of the treaty waged a battle to influence the Senate's decision. The opponents' beliefs were summed up by former California Governor and future President Ronald Reagan, who said, "We bought the canal; we paid for it; it's ours."

Opponents said that Panama would not run the canal well, it would be more expensive for us to pay tolls to Panama than to run it ourselves, and Panama might turn communist. They ran ads in newspapers. They urged citizens to write their senators and tell them to vote no. Some formed a "truth squad" that traveled and gave speeches.

At the same time President Carter worked to gain support for the

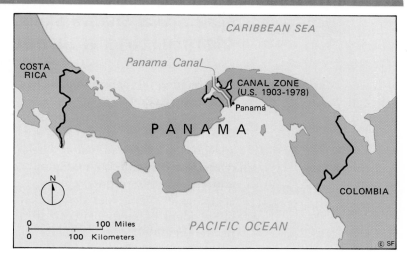

treaties. He sent the Secretary of Defense and the Secretary of State to give speeches to the Senate. He talked personally with many senators.

Supporters of the treaty argued that a no vote on the treaties could cause rioting in Panama and serious damage to the canal. A yes vote would show other Latin American countries that the United States was fair. A no vote would weaken the President's ability to carry out other important foreign-policy decisions.

The Senate debated the treaties for a long time. Finally in the spring of 1978, the Senate approved both treaties by 68 to 32.

Review

1. What were the views of the supporters of the canal treaties?
2. What were the views of the opponents of the canal treaties?
3. What is your judgment of the Senate's decision? Why?
4. How does this case study illustrate the role of Congress and the President in making foreign policy?

497

Basic Social Studies Skills
Memorizing a Speech

After reciting the oath of office, new Presidents give their inaugural addresses. A few inaugural addresses have been ranked among the best speeches in American history. President John F. Kennedy's inaugural address was one of these great speeches. The final four paragraphs of President Kennedy's speech are printed below.

"In the long history of the world, only a few generations have been granted the role of defending freedom in its hour of maximum danger. I do not shrink from this responsibility—I welcome it. I do not believe that any of us would exchange places with any other people or any other generation. The energy, the faith, the devotion which we bring to this endeavor will light our country and all who serve it—and the glow from that fire can truly light the world.

"And so, my fellow Americans: Ask not what your country can do for you—ask what you can do for your country.

"My fellow citizens of the world: Ask not what America will do for you, but what together we can do for the freedom of man.

"Finally, whether you are citizens of America or citizens of the world, ask of us here the same high standards of strength and sacrifice which we ask of you. With a good conscience our only sure reward, with history the final judge of our deeds, let us go forth to lead the land we love, asking His blessing and His help, but knowing that here on earth God's work must truly be our own."

Skill Practice

You can learn the excerpt from President Kennedy's famous speech by following these seven guidelines.

1. Read the entire excerpt slowly and silently. Then read it aloud.

2. Identify the main idea or theme of this excerpt from President Kennedy's speech.

3. Read the first paragraph again silently. What is the main point of this paragraph? How is the main point of this paragraph related to the main idea or theme of the entire excerpt?

4. Recite the first paragraph aloud. Think about the main point President Kennedy is making in the paragraph.

5. Follow the same steps with the second, third, and fourth paragraphs.

6. You may need to repeat these procedures several times before you memorize this excerpt from President Kennedy's inaugural address. Practice for no more than 15 or 20 minutes at any one time.

7. Finish this activity by writing this portion of President Kennedy's address from memory.

8. Use these steps to memorize another speech. A good selection is the "Gettysburg Address" by President Abraham Lincoln, which can be found in the Students' Resource Section of this book.

Chapter 26 Review

Summary

Section 1: American Foreign Policy
Foreign policies are the plans a government makes about how to deal with other nations. American foreign policy seeks to protect the United States and promote trade and peace. During its early history the United States tried to isolate itself from European politics. After World War II, the United States became a world power deeply involved in world affairs.

Section 2: From Cold War to Coexistence
Since 1947, the United States has been in global competition with the Soviet Union. This competition has been called the "cold war." To limit Soviet power, the United States developed a policy of containment. Tools of containment include foreign aid, security treaties, secret operations, use of the armed forces, limited wars, and the threat of nuclear weapons.

Section 3: Making Foreign-Policy Decisions
Many people are involved in making foreign policy. The President is a key foreign-policy leader. Presidents are assisted by a large foreign-policy bureaucracy. This includes the departments of State and Defense, the Central Intelligence Agency, and the National Security Council. The Constitution also gives Congress foreign-policy powers. There is often tension between Congress and the President over the control of foreign policy.

Vocabulary
Define the following terms.

1. foreign policy
2. isolationism
3. covert activities
4. CIA
5. Cold War
6. containment
7. foreign aid
8. diplomat
9. massive retaliation

Reviewing Main Ideas

1. The Constitution gives the President power to do which of the following?
a. appoint diplomatic officers with Senate approval
b. acknowledge the existence of a nation and its government
c. make treaties with Senate approval
d. all of the above
2. True or false: The President makes all foreign-policy decisions alone.
3. True or false: All large nations have groups like the CIA.

Thinking Critically

Comprehending Information
1. Explain the main goals of United States foreign policy.
2. What branch of government makes foreign policy?
3. What checks are there on this branch's foreign-policy powers?

Organizing Information
Make a time line for the years 1900–1990. Include at least ten important dates and events relating to foreign policy.

Evaluating Information
Since 1903, the people of Panama felt the original treaty was unfair. Were they right? Give evidence to support your answer.

Communicating Ideas
Suppose you were Secretary of State. List 5–10 goals you would have for American foreign policy. Explain which of these goals are the most important and why you have chosen these goals.

Chapter 27

Global Issues

Introduction. Stanley and Helen Carson know very little about Japan. Yet their lives were recently affected by a decision made by some Japanese business leaders.

The Carsons own a small farm in southern Wisconsin. Owning the farm has meant hard work for them. It also has brought the Carsons in touch with the wider world around them.

Like most of their neighbors, the Carsons raise soybeans. Things have gone pretty well for them since Kikkoman Shoyu, a Japanese company, opened a modern processing plant in nearby Walworth, Wisconsin. The Kikkoman plant buys soybeans from local farmers to make soy sauce. The plant has meant that the Carsons have a steady customer for their crops.

The Carsons are one example of the many ways our lives are becoming more connected to others around the world. Other examples of our links to the world can be found on almost any airplane flight. Peggy Robinson recently left Cleveland, Ohio, on a business trip. She was traveling to Europe to buy bicycles for a store in Cleveland. Also on the plane were a university president, a group of ministers, and Governor Richard Celeste of Ohio. The university president was going to Paris to arrange a student exchange program between several French universities and her university in Ohio. The ministers were going to represent United States churches at a meeting of the World Council of Churches. Governor Celeste was going to visit several European countries in hopes of convincing several automobile manufacturers to build factories in Ohio. These factories would create many new jobs for Ohio residents.

As our links to the world increase, new foreign-policy problems arise for the United States and for individual citizens.

Harvesting soybeans on a Walworth, Wisconsin, farm. The beans will be sold to the Japanese-owned Kikkoman Shoyu processing plant less than a half mile away.

Section 1
Our Shrinking World

People today say "the world is growing smaller." By this they mean that there have been many changes in the modern world that are bringing people closer together. Travel, for example, is faster than ever. And through satellites, words and pictures can be flashed around the globe instantly. One of the most important changes is a great increase in interdependence.

Global Interdependence

The world has become interdependent. **Global interdependence** means people and nations all over the world now depend more on one another for goods and services. It also means that what

happens in one nation or area of the world affects what happens in other places.

The simple candy bar provides one example of global interdependence. In Hershey, Pennsylvania, many Americans earn their living working in a candy factory. Chocolate, sugar, and nuts go into the candy bars they make. In today's world many things can affect the production of these candy bars and hence people's jobs.

Chocolate comes from cacao seeds. Many of these seeds are grown in central Africa. A good crop can lower the price of cacao and hence of chocolate. On the other hand, a war in central Africa could disrupt farming and affect the supply of cacao.

Nuts for the candy bar may come from Brazil. Dock workers in Brazil might strike for higher pay.

The strike could prevent the nuts from being shipped to North America.

Sugar for the candy bar may come from a Caribbean island. A revolution on such an island could change the government of the island. The United States might not recognize the new government and might refuse to trade with it. The candy factory would have to find a new source of sugar.

The fuel to power our cars, planes, trucks, buses, and factories is an important example of growing interdependence. This fuel comes from crude oil. Today the United States uses far more oil than it can produce by itself. As a result we import about 50 percent of the oil we need. One of the important goals of United States foreign policy is to maintain good relations with the oil-producing countries.

In addition, the United States imports many of the key minerals its industries need to keep working. For instance, 98 percent of the manganese, 93 percent of the bauxite, 81 percent of the tin, and 62 percent of the mercury we use comes from abroad.

At the same time, global interdependence means other countries of the world depend on the United

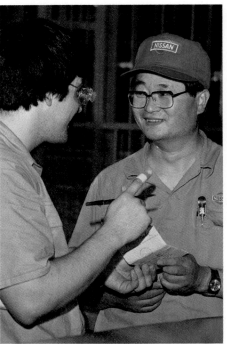

Examples of our shrinking world can be seen in all corners of the world. (above) Smyrna, Tennessee, auto workers recently visited Japan to learn Japanese manufacturing and management techniques. The employees work at a new Japanese-owned truck manufacturing plant in Smyrna. (Right) A McDonald's restaurant in Tokyo, Japan. In December, 1989, a McDonald's opened in Moscow, the capital of the Soviet Union.

States. The United States sells computers, telecommunications equipment, aircraft, medical machines, farm equipment, and countless other products around the world. In addition, many smaller, poorer countries look to the United States for food, medicine, or weapons.

The Effects of Interdependence

You can see the effects of interdependence in your own life. Think about your daily routine. You might be awakened by a Japanese clock radio. At breakfast, you might drink hot chocolate from central Africa. You might ride to school in a German-made car on tires made of Malayan rubber. On the way, you might stop to buy Saudi Arabian gas. During your ride, you might listen to a British rock group or hear a news report about a group of Chinese scientists visiting the city. Your clothes for the day might include a jacket made in Hong Kong, a sweater with Argentine wool, and shoes with leather from Brazil.

Growing global interdependence is affecting the way people live in many other ways. One example is that new and interesting jobs have opened up. Job advertisements such as these show the effects of global interdependence:

"International executive wanted. Must have solid educational background and experience in international business. Must be able to speak and read Spanish. Duties involve travel."

"Metcalf and Eddy, an international leader in water management, wants candidates to work in the Middle East."

"The Solar Energy Research Institute needs men and women with expertise in these areas: thermal conversion; solar data bank; international cooperation."

Today people all over the world communicate with each other, trade with each other, and learn from each other in greater numbers than ever before in history.

Interdependence has brought the world directly into our communities. Today we can find many examples of links with other parts of the world in our own towns and cities. We will look more closely at these global links at the end of this chapter.

Finally, interdependence has created many new foreign-policy decisions for the United States. We will look at these decisions in the next section.

Section Review

Vocabulary:
global interdependence.

Reviewing the Main Ideas:
1. What is meant by the phrase "our shrinking world"?
2. Define "global interdependence" and give two examples.
3. Describe two effects of increasing global interdependence.

Skill Building
Summarize the main ideas of this section in a paragraph.

Section 2
Dealing with Global Issues

As a result of global interdependence, the United States faces many new foreign-policy decisions. Some of the toughest decisions involve how to deal with **global issues**. These are problems which affect a large part of the world's population and which cannot be solved by the actions of any single nation. At the same time, every nation must decide how it will respond to such issues.

Five examples of global issues facing American foreign-policy makers are (1) growing economic inequality among nations, (2) world hunger, (3) use of the oceans, (4) the spread of weapons, and (5) global pollution.

Growing Economic Inequality

There is a growing split between the rich and poor nations of the world. This is one of the most basic and serious global issues today. An old saying describes what is happening: "The rich get richer and the poor get poorer." As this occurs, conflict between rich and poor grows, and the United States faces new decisions.

On one side are the twenty or so rich, industrial countries including the United States, Japan, West Germany, Canada, Britain, France, and the Soviet Union. These nations are called **developed countries** because they have used natural resources to develop a way of life based on business and industry.

The developed countries have natural resources such as coal and iron. They have many large industries such as steel, electronics, and automotives. Citizens of these nations consume most of the world's resources. They also make most of the goods sold around the world. They enjoy a high standard of living.

On the other side are about 140 poor nations. Many of their citizens live in the shadow of death by starvation or disease. **Life expectancy** in the poorest of these is only thirty-seven years. Because most of the poor countries are trying to develop industrial economies, they are called **developing countries.**

Some of these developing countries, such as Ethiopia, Afghanistan, Chad, and Uganda, are very poor. They have few natural resources. They cannot farm enough food to feed their populations. They make few products to sell to others. They have high levels of unemployment, disease, and poverty.

Other developing countries have natural resources. The countries of the Middle East, such as Saudi Arabia and Iran, have oil. Colombia grows coffee. Zaire has copper. But these developing countries have little industry. They do not have the health and educational facilities to develop their human resources. It takes scientists, engineers, business leaders, and designers to develop industry. These countries are dependent on the more developed nations.

Developed nations are mostly found in the Northern Hemisphere. Developing nations are mostly in the

Southern Hemisphere. As a result, policy makers as well as the news media often talk about the "North-South conflict" when discussing this global issue.

Mutual Dependence. Obviously, the needs of people in the developing countries are very different from those in the developed ones. One leader of an oil-producing country explained his people's point of view to an American: "My people need money from oil for food, schools, and medicine. You use energy to light ballparks at night and to drive large cars to the corner store for a pack of cigarettes."

Despite such differences, both developed and developing nations need each other. Rich nations sell their products to the poorer nations. In a recent year, 37 percent of American goods shipped abroad went to developing countries. Developed nations also get much of the raw materials they need, such as tin, zinc, and oil, from developing countries. For their part, the developing nations badly need the food, technology, and money of the developed nations.

A study headed by the chancellor (leader) of West Germany put it this way: "The South cannot grow adequately without the North." Yet, the report added, "The North cannot prosper or improve its situation unless there is greater progress in the South."

Some Policy Choices. The developing nations demand creation of "a new international economic order." They want to find better ways to transfer resources from the rich, developed nations to the poor nations. They want more aid with fewer strings attached. They argue that the developed nations became rich by exploiting the poor nations.

In addition, many of the poor nations are very critical of the United States. They argue the United States uses foreign aid only to further its own national security interests. Others, however, have been very grateful for American aid.

American officials point out that the United States gives foreign aid to nations for many reasons. Over the last 30 years the United States has given more than $130 billion to developing nations. "The American people," President Reagan explained, "have proven themselves to be as compassionate and caring as any on earth. And we will remain so."

At the same time, President Reagan has said it may be wrong to simply assume that giving huge amounts of aid "somehow, miraculously, will produce new well-being." The United States faces these kinds of choices. Is it better to encourage poor nations to get help from private investors rather than governments like ours? Should we give more aid to nations that are strongly anti-communist even if other poor nations might need it more? Should we keep giving as much aid or spend more of our money on problems at home?

World Hunger

Another aspect of the tension between rich and poor nations is the question of who will feed the

(top) Resources that many people take for granted are scarce or nonexistent in some nations. (above) Bountiful harvest of corn in Nebraska. (chart) What is the relationship between calories and life expectancy?

Countries with Calorie Surpluses or Deficits

	Per capita calorie supply as % of requirements	Life expectancy at birth (years)
Calorie surplus countries: the top ten		
Belgium	149%	72
Luxembourg	149	72
Ireland	149	73
Bulgaria	145	72
Greece	145	73
Libya	144	57
Italy	144	73
East Germany	142	72
Czechoslovakia	140	70
United States	138	74
Calorie deficit countries: the bottom ten		
Ethiopia	74%	40
Afghanistan	75	40
Chad	75	40
Uganda	79	54
Zimbabwe	79	53
Mozambique	80	47
Dem. Kampuchea	80	37
Guinea	83	45
Haiti	83	52
Mali	84	43

hungry. Every week 10,000 people in Africa die of starvation. Around the world more than 500 million people are starving. And, if the world's population continues to grow rapidly, the problems will get worse. As a result, food is becoming an important political resource for America. A communist leader recently said: "America has something more powerful than atom bombs. You have protein."

The United States has given food aid to its political allies in the Cold War since 1954. But when our food supply is smaller because of bad harvests, our food prices go up. At such times the United States faces a hard decision. Should we keep giving food to our allies and selling it to other nations or should we cut back on our food aid to keep prices down at home? And what about poor nations that cannot pay

Member of Greenpeace, an international organization whose goals include the preservation of the world's oceans, patrolling an area where illegal whale hunting has been reported.

for food but need it desperately? Do we have a duty to give them food before we give it or sell it to richer nations?

Use of the Oceans

Oceans cover 71 percent of the earth. And the oceans are rich. They contain badly needed food, oil, and scarce minerals. All countries of the world need these resources. Who owns the seas?

Until recently the law of the sea has been simple. Each nation had control of its coastal waters up to three miles from shore—the distance a cannonball could be shot. Beyond three miles, the seas were free for all.

Today the rich nations like France, England, Japan, and the Soviet Union want to keep things pretty much that way. They would like each nation to control its own coastal waters. They want to let all countries mine the open sea under the supervision of the International Seabed Authority.

Over seventy of the coastal developing nations like Ecuador and Ghana think that arrangement would be unfair. To them it would let the big, industrial nations "loot" the seabed at the expense of the poor nations. They say the poor nations don't have the technology to mine the deep sea.

The United Nations has sponsored several conferences aimed at writing a new law of the sea. But the issues are complex. It may be years before the more than 138 nations involved will reach an agreement.

One basic foreign-policy decision for the United States here is: Should the United States cooperate with poorer nations to create a new law of the sea or should we start mining the sea on our own no matter what other countries do?

The Spread of Weapons

The world is arming itself as never before. Many nations of the world devote increasingly larger amounts of their incomes to military expenditures. Recently, military expenses

(above) Volunteers cleaning up the effects of an off-shore oil spill. (above, right) Defoliated trees in Vermont—the victims of acid rain. Acid rain, which is thought to be a product of the burning of coal and oil, has destroyed many forests around the world. The problem has been reported in Canada, Brazil, China, South Africa, and even in the Arctic.

were up in the United States by 62 percent, in Denmark by 116 percent, in Greece by 182 percent, in East Germany by 685 percent, and in Brazil by 338 percent.

For years America gave military aid to its allies. But until quite recently the Soviet Union, France, England, and China have been selling weapons too. The biggest buyers have been the Arab states and other developing nations such as Zaire, Guinea, and Nigeria.

The result has been insecurity in the poor countries as each races to have more weapons than its neighbors. United States foreign-policy makers face a choice. Should we continue to sell weapons or should we begin to limit our military sales in an effort to halt the growing arms race among poor countries?

Global Pollution

Another major problem today is worldwide destruction of our natural environment. Some people say the earth is in danger of becoming a global sewer.

Poisonous metals such as mercury and lead have been dumped into the seas and air by the world's industries and automobiles. Giant oil spills from tankers have spread millions of gallons of oil into the oceans and onto beaches. These spills kill fish, sea birds, and important food for marine life.

DDT, a poison, has been spread all over the world. It is found in fish, animals, and humans in the most faraway places—even in Antarctic penguins. And more than 150 species of birds and animals have become extinct because of human actions.

Rich and poor nations have disagreed on what to do about pollution problems. Rich nations want to cut down on new global pollution. Many of the changes they want are expensive. These changes would make it harder to gather natural resources.

508

Poor nations think antipollution regulations are unfair. New rules controlling pollution would make it harder for them to develop their own industries. They argue that the developed nations polluted freely while they were becoming rich, but now they do not want to let the poor countries do the same.

One decision facing the United States is: Should we push for the same pollution-control rules for everyone or should the poorer nations be given the chance to develop their economies without worrying about pollution?

Section Review

Vocabulary:

developed countries, developing countries, global issues, life expectancy.

Reviewing the Main Ideas

1. What do the developed countries have in common?
2. What do the developing countries have in common?
3. List and briefly explain four foreign-policy issues that divide the developed and developing countries.

Skill Building

1. How are the foreign-policy issues today different from the issues faced during the Cold War?
2. Which of today's foreign-policy problems, if any, do you think are more important than problems of containment and Cold War? Give reasons for your answer.

Section 3
The United Nations

Many of the new foreign-policy issues between the poor and rich nations are being argued in the **United Nations** (UN). The UN is an international organization with over 150 nations as members.

The United States and other nations started the planning for the UN during the years of World War II. In 1944, delegates from the United States, Britain, and the Soviet Union drafted a charter for the UN. In 1945, representatives from fifty countries signed it at a meeting in San Francisco. By October of that year, twenty-nine of those countries had ratified it, and the UN was born. Its headquarters are in New York City.

The basic purposes of the UN are to help maintain international peace and security, to promote friendly relations among all nations, and to work on the solution of global problems.

The United Nations General Assembly.

The United Nations

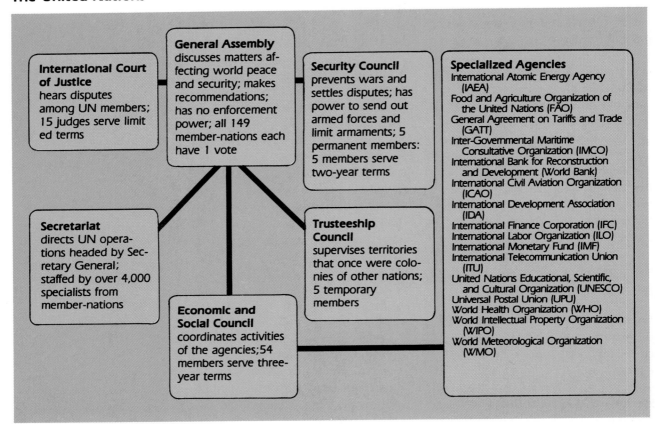

International Court of Justice
hears disputes among UN members; 15 judges serve limited terms

General Assembly
discusses matters affecting world peace and security; makes recommendations; has no enforcement power; all 149 member-nations each have 1 vote

Security Council
prevents wars and settles disputes; has power to send out armed forces and limit armaments; 5 permanent members: 5 members serve two-year terms

Specialized Agencies
International Atomic Energy Agency (IAEA)
Food and Agriculture Organization of the United Nations (FAO)
General Agreement on Tariffs and Trade (GATT)
Inter-Governmental Maritime Consultative Organization (IMCO)
International Bank for Reconstruction and Development (World Bank)
International Civil Aviation Organization (ICAO)
International Development Association (IDA)
International Finance Corporation (IFC)
International Labor Organization (ILO)
International Monetary Fund (IMF)
International Telecommunication Union (ITU)
United Nations Educational, Scientific, and Cultural Organization (UNESCO)
Universal Postal Union (UPU)
World Health Organization (WHO)
World Intellectual Property Organization (WIPO)
World Meteorological Organization (WMO)

Secretariat
directs UN operations headed by Secretary General; staffed by over 4,000 specialists from member-nations

Trusteeship Council
supervises territories that once were colonies of other nations; 5 temporary members

Economic and Social Council
coordinates activities of the agencies; 54 members serve three-year terms

Study the chart above. What is the main job of the General Assembly? What does the Security Council do?

Organization. The chart above shows the organization of the UN. The six major parts of the UN are the General Assembly, the Security Council, the Economic and Social Council, the Trusteeship Council, the International Court of Justice, and the Secretariat.

The **General Assembly** has been called the "town meeting of the world." Each member-nation is represented in the General Assembly. Each nation has one vote regardless of size or wealth.

The General Assembly may admit, suspend, or expel members. It has many powers. It can recommend actions to the Security Council, other UN agencies, and the member-nations.

The **Security Council** has the power to carry out the UN's peace-keeping purpose. The Security Council decides when to send an international armed force into a country to stop aggression and restore law and order. When North Korea invaded South Korea in 1950, the UN sent in troops.

The Security Council has fifteen members. Real power in the Council is held by the five permanent members: the United States, the Soviet Union, China, Great Britain, and France. The ten other members are chosen by the General Assembly for two-year terms. Five are elected each year.

All important decisions in the Security Council must have nine yes votes. All five permanent members must vote yes. This gives any one of them a veto power over actions they oppose.

The UN has been successful in several ways. It has served as a meeting place where decision makers of many nations can discuss mutual problems. It has been able to settle fights between several smaller nations. Some special agencies of the UN (see chart, page 510), like the World Health Organization, have done a great deal to fight sickness, poverty, and ignorance around the world.

Poor vs. Rich in the UN. Until recently the United States and other rich nations were able to control things in the UN. They were able to have things pretty much their own way. But this does not always happen today.

In the mid-1970s, the UN became a truly global organization. Since 1955, over seventy new nations have joined the UN. Most of these new UN members are poor nations.

In recent years the poor nations have pushed for many new programs. They have asked for new trade policies, foreign aid, and money from the rich nations. The poor nations have voted together against some United States foreign policies in the General Assembly. On the other hand, the United States still dominates the Security Council.

This cartoon is titled "The Small Society." The UN building is in the background. What is the cartoonist's point of view?

Some people say the United States should ignore the UN since the majority of members no longer agree with American foreign policy. These critics say that the UN is not in America's interest.

Others think the rich countries, including the United States, must learn to live with the poor nations of the world. They argue that the United States should try to strengthen the UN, not weaken it.

Section Review

Vocabulary:
General Assembly, Security Council, United Nations.

Reviewing the Main Ideas
1. Why and when was the UN created?
2. In what part of the UN are all member-nations equally represented?

Skill Building
Summarize the main jobs of the Security Council.

511

Law and Freedom

Our Constitution and the World

The Constitution of the United States, written in 1787, is the oldest of its kind in the world. More than half of the world's constitutions have been written since 1970. The constitutions of less than twelve countries of today's world were written before World War II.

The U.S. Constitution has been the world's most honored and influential written constitution. In 1887, William Gladstone, the British Prime Minister, offered a glowing tribute: ". . . the American Constitution is the most wonderful work ever struck off [written] at a given time by the brain and purpose of man."

Britain's Influence on the American Constitution

The Americans who wrote the Constitution were influenced by European ideas. The legal heritage of England, Wales, and Scotland was especially important. Most Americans of the 1780s had either come from the British Isles, or their ancestors had originated there. They brought to America the strong English belief in government according to law. In particular, they treasured their civil liberties listed in the English Declaration of Rights, which the Parliament had won from the monarchy in 1688. English, Welsh, and Scottish immigrants to America taught their children and grandchildren the values of government limited by law, of popular representation in government through a parliament or other legislative body, and of civil liberties guaranteed by statutes.

In 1775, Americans rebelled against Britain to secure traditional legal rights and liberties which, they claimed, had been withdrawn. After winning independence, the United States established government in the name of the people. Legal rights and liberties inherited from England became part of the U.S. Constitution.

The Beginning of America's Constitutional Heritage

Americans went beyond their English legal heritage to create their constitutional government. They rejected monarchy and created a republic, a government that is run by representatives of the people. Few other republics existed in the world of 1787. Among them were Holland, Switzerland, Venice, and Genoa.

The American republic was the only country with a written constitution. Britain had a constitutional government, but it was based on a large collection of laws and customs. There was no single document, such as the U.S. Constitution.

Americans were the first people in the world to hold a convention for the single purpose of creating their government. James Wilson represented the people of Pennsylvania at the Constitutional Convention. He said that "The United States exhibit to the world the first instance, as far as we can learn, of a nation . . . assembling voluntarily, deliberating fully, and deciding calmly, concerning that system of government under which they would wish that they and their posterity should live. . . ."

The American people were asked to ratify the plan for government created at the Constitutional Convention. For the first time anywhere in the world, the people were invited to approve or reject the supreme laws under which they would live. In 1788, George Washington wrote: "We exhibit at present the astonishing spectacle of a whole people deliberating calmly on what form of government will be most conducive to their happiness."

512

Law and Freedom

★ ★ ★

Worldwide Influence of the U.S. Constitution

In a rather short time, other nations were influenced by the U.S. Constitution. The French overthrew their king in 1789 and established a republic. American ideas influenced their "Declaration of the Rights of Man and the Citizen." Since 1789, the French have had several constitutions, all of them influenced, more or less, by the American model.

In 1810, Mexicans followed the American example and rebelled against their mother country, Spain. During the next fifteen years, rebellions against Spain spread throughout Latin America. Several Latin American republics were created and each one was influenced, more or less, by constitutional government in the United States. The current constitutions of Argentina, Brazil, Ecuador, Mexico, and Venezuela have been influenced by the U.S. Constitution with respect to separation of powers, the two-house legislature, the holding of regular elections, and the office of the presidency.

Of course, the manner in which these legal ideas are practiced varies from place to place under the influence of different national traditions.

In modern Europe, West Germany and France are the two republics with constitutions that have been most influenced by America. The West German constitution, for example, emphasizes civil rights and liberties and a federal system of government.

India and Japan are two Asian countries that have been influenced considerably by American constitutional government. For example, the American idea of judicial review is used in India, and opinions of the U.S. Supreme Court are used as precedents for decisions by the Supreme Court of India. American federalism was studied by Indians who established their own federal system of government.

The Constitution is one of America's grandest achievements. It has been acclaimed as the most successful constitution in world history. Senator Orrin Hatch of Utah said: "The whole world has looked to the U.S. experience as a possible precedent to be considered in each country's own constitution-making."

Washington presiding over the Constitutional Convention.

Review

1. How did British ideas influence the Americans who wrote the Constitution?
2. Give an example of how the Americans "went beyond" their English legal heritage to create their constitutional government.
3. Name three nations whose constitutions have been affected by the United States Constitution.

Case Study

Columbus and the World

Ken Shulman answered the phone. Ken worked in the international division of a bank in Des Moines, Iowa. The caller asked about investing money in a new housing project in Africa. Yes, Ken said, he could arrange an investment without any trouble.

Ken Shulman is one of many millions of people involved in international activity as a result of increasing global interdependence. These people help bring the world into their community and their community into the world.

Most of today's international activity is carried out from cities and towns around the world. Cities and towns provide the many services that people in international activity depend on. These include banks, airports, shipping, travel agencies, convention services, and many more.

Columbus, Ohio, is a good example. In many ways Columbus is a typical midwestern city. It is located near the center of Ohio. It does not have a seaport. Yet like most communities Columbus is connected to other parts of the world in many ways. Here are some of the ways Columbus is linked to the world.

Travel. At least 29,000 international trips were made out of Columbus in a recent year. Many of the people traveling from Columbus go to Western Europe, Canada, and Mexico. Over one-third go to Africa, Asia, and the Middle East. Many Columbus

Columbus's Ohio Theatre, which has recently been restored to look much like it did when it was built in the 1800s.

residents travel for pleasure. Others travel for business.

At the same time Columbus has more than five thousand visitors from other countries each year. Some of these visitors come as students, some come on business, and still others come for a vacation.

Business Connections. The Columbus business community is closely linked with the rest of the world. More than 3,000 jobs in the Columbus area result from the international activities of such businesses. Banks in Columbus deal with more than 500 foreign banks around the world. At the same time, these firms import more than $88 million worth of goods each year. Other Columbus businesses export over $140 million worth of machinery.

Recently, in a twenty-month period, Columbus companies sent:

- sixteen shipments of goods to Nigeria, including cars, hospital supplies, road-safety reflectors, and chemicals.
- forty-four shipments to Colombia, including cement, steel, paint, water fountains, locomotive parts, and air conditioners.
- eight shipments to Denmark, including bowling balls, tractor parts, and fabric softeners.

Agriculture. As in any American city today, Columbus shoppers can go into a supermarket and select from more than 70 imported items. These include bananas from Panama, wine from Italy, sausage from Germany, oranges from Japan, and cheese from Denmark.

In addition, a large part of the crops grown in the nearby countryside are exported. For example, 60 percent of the wheat crop is sold to other countries. In Columbus, large companies export $53 million worth of corn, soybeans, wheat, and oats. These companies store, sell, and ship the crops for Ohio farmers.

The Arts. As with most cities, the Columbus arts menu has a growing international flavor. Recently, for example, the city welcomed the Vienna Choir Boys from Austria, several British rock groups, a well-known opera star from Italy, an outstanding violinist from Israel, the Royal Tahitian Dance Company, Romanian dancers, Spanish guitarists, and, just in time for St. Patrick's Day, the Irish Rovers.

In addition, the Columbus Gallery of Fine Arts is one of many places people can visit to see pictures and statues from all over the world. The gallery has Chinese vases, Greek statues, and many wood carvings from Pacific islands.

Art galleries in cities around the world share art work with each other. So a citizen in Columbus may look at a French painting in August. In December, a person in Tokyo, Japan, may be looking at the same painting.

Ethnic Groups. Many members of the ethnic groups in Columbus—Italians, Germans, Serbians, Irish, Croatians, Greeks, and Hungarians—keep up ties with their countries of origin. These ties link Columbus

to the world. Activities in the black and Jewish communities also link Columbus to the world. Black churches, for example, send people abroad to teach and to learn from people in Africa, Asia, Latin America, and Europe.

Review

You have seen some ways one city is linked with the world. Now here are some ideas for how you can chart the global linkages of your own community.

1. Make a list of the items in your own household that come from another country. These could include food, television and stereo sets, furniture, and sports equipment. Some of these items will say: "Made in _____." Others will be unmarked, such as the rubber from Asia used to make balls and boots.

2. Use the yellow pages of the telephone book to find examples of global links. Look under such headings as: restaurants, automobiles, cameras, churches, travel agencies, manufacturing firms, civic and professional organizations.

3. Collect ads from your local newspapers that describe products or services from another country. Collect articles from the newspaper describing ways your community is linked to the world.

4. Keep a record of the number of stories about other countries, foreign policy, or international problems on the nightly news on television.

Basic Social Studies Skills
Using an Atlas to Find Information

An atlas is a book of maps and related information. For example, the *Times Atlas of the World* is a collection of maps and information about various nations and regions.

There are atlases on special topics. The *Times Atlas of World History*, for instance, only includes maps about different periods of events in history.

You need to know how to interpret maps in order to find information in an atlas. Knowing the main parts of a map is a key to reading it.

The map title tells what its main topic or subject is. The map legend, or key, is a guide to interpretation of symbols that appear on the map. The legend shows symbols

used for the national capitals, state capitals, and other cities. The scale provides a way to measure distances on a map. Most map scales are divided into both miles and kilometers.

Skill Practice

There are two maps in your textbook's atlas. Use these maps and the one below to answer these questions.
1. What is the subject or topic of each map?
2. What are the capital cities of Indiana, Maine, Alabama, Colorado, and Oregon?
3. How many OPEC nations are there in South America?

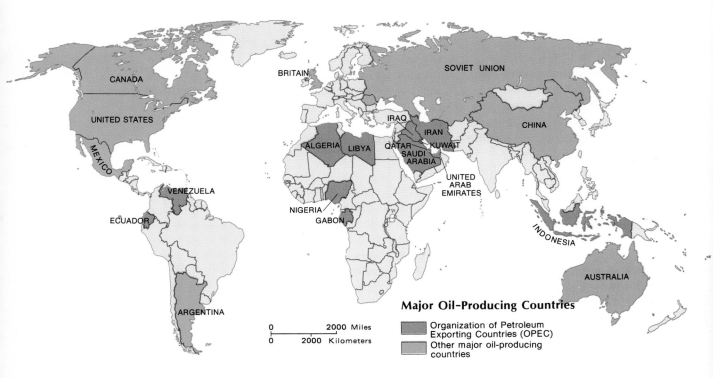

Major Oil-Producing Countries

Organization of Petroleum Exporting Countries (OPEC)

Other major oil-producing countries

Chapter 27 Review

Summary

Section 1: Our Shrinking World
Global interdependence means that nations the world over now depend upon one another for many goods and services. It also means that what happens in one part of the world can affect what happens in other areas of the world. Many nations depend upon the United States for food, technology, and weapons. At the same time, our country depends on other nations for many types of raw materials needed by our industries.

Section 2: Dealing With Global Issues
Global issues are problems which cannot be solved by any one nation. Such issues affect a large part of the world's population. They pose tough decision problems for American foreign-policy makers. Key global issues include: (1) growing economic inequality among nations, (2) world hunger, (3) global pollution, (4) use of the oceans, and (5) the spread of weapons.

Section 3: The United Nations
The United Nations (UN) is an international organization created in 1945. More than 150 nations, including the United States, are members. The UN seeks to prevent war and to work on the solution of global problems. The UN has six major parts including the General Assembly, which has been called the "town meeting of the world."

Vocabulary
Define the following terms.
1. developing countries
2. developed countries
3. global interdependence
4. United Nations
5. General Assembly
6. Security Council
7. life expectancy
8. global issues

Reviewing the Main Ideas
1. Developing countries usually have _____.
a. a shortage of food
b. great industries
c. many natural resources
d. a high standard of living
2. True or false: Developed nations make many products to sell in other parts of the world.
3. Which of the following are examples of foreign-policy concerns?
a. feeding the world
b. sale of weapons
c. use of oceans
d. all of the above

Thinking Critically
Finding Information
1. Name the five permanent members of the UN Security Council.
2. Name three things in your community that give evidence of global interdependence.
Communicating Ideas
Explain in your own words why the differences between the United States and the developing countries make for difficult foreign-policy decisions.
Evaluating Information
Suppose you could influence a government decision about giving food to a developing nation.
a. What are the alternatives involved?
b. What are the consequences of each alternative for the people of the developing nation?
c. What are the consequences of each alternative for Americans?
d. What decision would you support? Why?

Unit Nine Test

Vocabulary

Write *true* if the underlined word or phrase is used correctly. Write *false* if it is used incorrectly. Rephrase each false statement so that the underlined word or phrase is used correctly.

1. International relations are dealings with other countries.

2. Isolationism is becoming involved in foreign affairs.

3. Foreign policy is our plan for how we act toward other nations in the world.

4. The Department of State is the major agency for foreign-policy decision making.

5. The Secretary of State directs the Department of Defense.

6. The Security Council is an advisory group for the Secretary of State.

7. Foreign-policy money powers must be approved by Congress.

8. *Das Kapital* was written by Karl Marx.

9. During the Cold War the Soviet Union and the United States were competing with each other.

10. Our policy of containment meant that the U.S. would try to stop Soviet expansion.

11. Massive retaliation is a very dangerous containment tool.

12. What happens in one part of the world affects what happens in other places. This is global interdependence.

13. Developing countries are very wealthy and have clearly defined goals.

14. Global pollution can be described as worldwide destruction of our natural environment.

15. The developed countries include England, Canada, and the United States.

Recalling Information

1. Goals of our foreign policies include
a. promoting peace.
b. protecting the United States.
c. encouraging trade.
d. all of the above.

2. The chief diplomat of the United States is
a. the President.
c. the Secretary of State.
b. the Vice-President.
d. none of the above.

3. Our foreign-policy bureaucracy is made up of
a. the Department of Defense.
b. the Department of State.
c. the CIA.
d. all of the above.

4. The purpose of the CIA is
a. to distribute food and money to foreign countries.
b. to gather information about foreign countries for use in foreign-policy decision making.
c. to gather information about American citizens' activities inside the United States.
d. all of the above.

5. True or false: The President is able to reject ideas of the National Security Council.

6. True or false: The State Department sells American arms to countries around the world.

7. True or false: Only a few government agencies are involved in foreign affairs.

8. True or false: Congress has a great deal of direct control over foreign-policy decisions.

9. Which of the following can the President do without Congressional approval?
a. make treaties with other countries
b. make executive agreements with other countries
c. appoint ambassadors
d. spend money for foreign-policy activities

10. Foreign aid involves
a. making defense treaties.
b. sending troops.
c. giving economic goods.
d. carrying on secret activities.

11. Which of the following are examples of the effects of global interdependence?
a. increased numbers of jobs
b. more opportunities for trade
c. more links with other countries in your community
d. all of the above

12. True or false: Interdependence has created new foreign-policy decisions.

13. Examples of developed countries are
a. U.S. and Ethiopia.
b. Japan and Canada.
c. Mexico and Peru.
d. USSR and Zambia.

14. Most foreign-policy decisions involve
a. young people vs. old people.
b. educated people vs. people who can't read.
c. rich countries vs. poor countries.
d. bad weather.

15. True or false: Africa is the only continent faced with a starvation problem.

16. True or false: Food is an important political resource of the United States.

17. True or false: The Security Council was organized to give the developed nations the most influence.

Skill Building

1. Where would you look in this unit to find the foreign-policy roles of such government agencies as the Treasury Department, Department of Agriculture, or Department of Commerce? Give page numbers.

2. Compare communism and democracy. List three ways they are similar and three ways they are different.

3. Which Presidents were involved in decision-making roles in Vietnam and Korea?

4. You want to summarize this unit for a friend who hasn't read it. Which four pictures or charts would you use? Identify each by page and location (if there is more than one). Explain your choices.

5. Explain how coffee is an example of global interdependence.

6. Give three examples of natural resources found in the oceans.

7. Do you agree that the earth is in danger from worldwide pollution? Explain your viewpoint.

8. List three powers of the UN General Assembly.

Students' Resource Section

Table of Contents

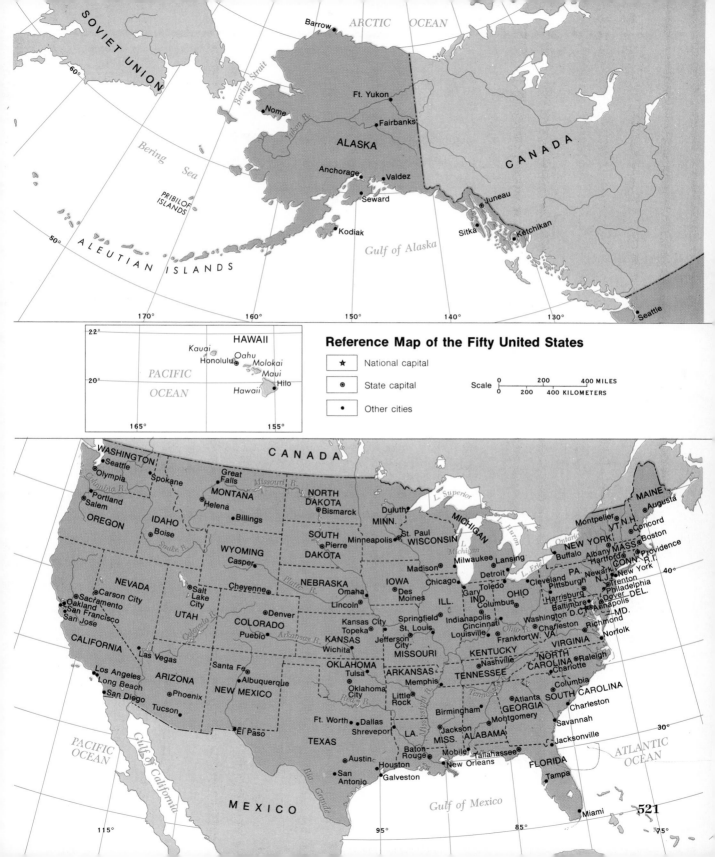

Reference Map of the Fifty United States

★ National capital

◉ State capital

• Other cities

Scale

| 0 | 200 | 400 MILES |

| 0 | 200 | 400 KILOMETERS |

521

World: Political

ARCTIC OCEAN

180°   160°W   140° West Longitude   80°W

80°N

Arctic Circle   Alaska (U.S.)   Gre (DE

60°N   CANADA

NORTH
AMERICA   ATLAN
OCEA

Aleutian Islands

40°North Latitude   UNITED STATES   Azo (PO

PACIFIC
OCEAN   Bermuda (U.K.)

Midway Islands
(U.S.)   MEXICO   BAHAMAS

Tropic of Cancer   CUBA   DOMINICAN
REPUBLIC   Puerto Rico (U.S.)

20°N   Hawaii (U.S.)   HAITI   ST. CHRISTOPHER AND NEVIS
JAMAICA   ANTIGUA-BARBUDA
GUATEMALA   BELIZE   DOMINICA
HONDURAS   ST. VINCENT AND   ST. LUCIA
EL SALVADOR   NICARAGUA   THE GRENADINES   BARBADOS
COSTA RICA   GRENADA   TRINIDAD AND TOBAGO
VENEZUELA   GUYANA
KIRIBATI   PANAMA   SURINAME
COLOMBIA   FR. GUIANA
(FRANCE)

POLYNESIA   Virgin Is. (U.S.-U.K.)   CAPE

0°   Equator   Galapagos
Islands
(ECUADOR)   ECUADOR
PERU   SOUTH
AMERICA

WESTERN
SAMOA   American
Samoa (U.S.)   BRAZIL

TONGA   French   BOLIVIA

20°S   Polynesia
(FRANCE)   PARAGUAY

Tropic of Capricorn   Easter Island
(CHILE)   CHILE   URUGUAY

PACIFIC
OCEAN   ARGENTINA

40°S

Falkland Islands
(U.K.)

South Georgia
(Falkland Is.)

60°S

Antarctic Circle

80°S   ANTARCTICA

180°   160°W   140°W   120°W   100°W   80°W   60°W

EUROPE

60°N   0°W   0°

NORWAY

SWEDEN

IRELAND   UNITED
KINGDOM   DENMARK

50°N   NETHERLANDS   EAST
GERMANY   POLAND   U.S.S.R.
BELGIUM   WEST
LUX.   GERMANY   CZECHOSLOVAKIA

ATLANTIC
OCEAN   FRANCE   AUSTRIA   HUNGARY
SWITZERLAND   ROMANIA
YUGOSLAVIA

PORTUGAL   ITALY   BULGARIA

SPAIN   ALBANIA

GREECE

20°E   0°E   CYPRUS

MALTA

0   500 Miles
0   500 Kilometers

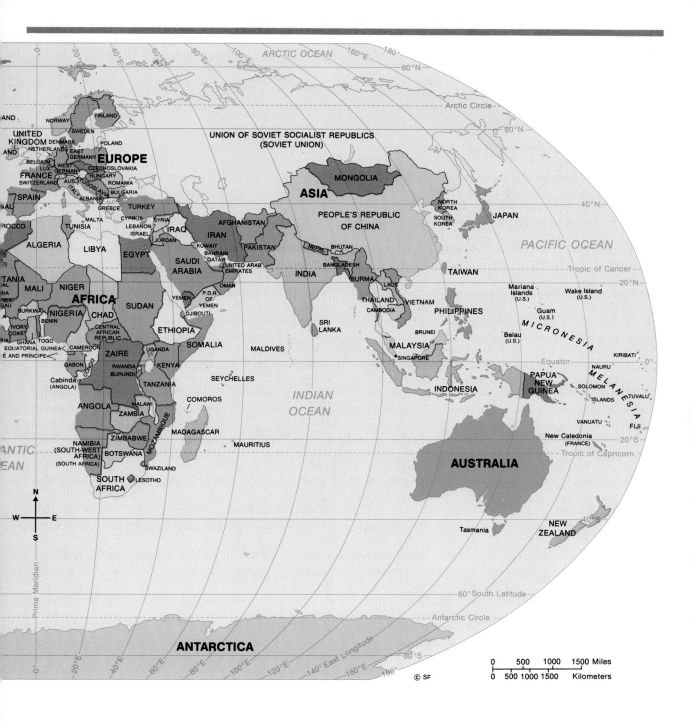

AUS.—AUSTRIA
LUX.—LUXEMBOURG
P.D.R. OF YEMEN—PEOPLE'S DEMOCRATIC REPUBLIC OF YEMEN
PORT.—PORTUGAL
U.K.—UNITED KINGDOM
U.S.—UNITED STATES
U.S.S.R.—UNION OF SOVIET SOCIALIST REPUBLICS

☆ The Declaration of Independence in Congress, July 4, 1776

The unanimous declaration of the thirteen United States of America:

When in the course of human events it becomes necessary for one people to dissolve the political bands which have connected them with another, and to assume among the powers of the earth the separate and equal station to which the laws of nature and of nature's God entitle them, a decent respect to the opinions of mankind requires that they should declare the causes which impel them to the separation.

We hold these truths to be self-evident, that all men[1] are created equal, that they are endowed by their Creator with certain unalienable rights, that among these are life, liberty, and the pursuit of happiness.

That to secure these rights, governments are instituted among men, deriving their just powers from the consent of the governed. That whenever any form of government becomes destructive to these ends, it is the right of the people to alter or to abolish it, and to institute new government, laying its foundation on such principles and organizing its powers in such form as to them shall seem most likely to effect their safety and happiness.

Prudence, indeed, will dictate that governments long established should not be changed for light and transient causes; and accordingly all experience hath shown, that mankind are more disposed to suffer, while evils are sufferable, than to right themselves by abolishing the forms to which they are accustomed. But when a long train of abuses and usurpations, pursuing invariably the same object, evinces a design to reduce them under absolute despotism, it is their right, it is their duty, to throw off such government, and to provide new guards for their future security. Such has been the patient sufferance of these colonies, and such is now the necessity which constrains them to alter their former systems of government.

The history of the present King of Great Britain is a history of repeated injuries and usurpations, all having in direct object the establishment of an absolute tyranny over these states. To prove this, let facts be submitted to a candid world:

He has refused his assent to laws, the most wholesome and necessary for the public good.

He has forbidden his governors to pass laws of immediate and pressing importance, unless suspended in their operation till his assent should be obtained; and when so suspended, he has utterly neglected to attend to them.

He has refused to pass other laws for the accommodation of large districts of people, unless those people would relinquish the right of representation in the legislature, a right inestimable to them and formidable to tyrants only.

He has called together legislative bodies at places unusual, uncomfortable, and distant from the depository of their public records, for the sole purpose of fatiguing them into compliance with his measures.

He has dissolved representative houses repeatedly, for opposing with manly firmness his invasions on the rights of the people.

He has refused for a long time, after such dissolutions, to cause others to be elected; whereby the legislative powers, incapable of annihilation, have returned to the people at large for their exercise; the state remaining in the meantime exposed to all the dangers of invasion from without and convulsions within.

He has endeavored to prevent the population of these states; for that purpose obstructing the laws for naturalization of foreigners; refusing to pass others to encourage their migration hither, and raising the conditions of new appropriations of lands.

He has obstructed the administration of justice, by refusing his assent to laws for establishing judiciary powers.

He has made judges dependent on his will alone, for the tenure of their offices, and the amount and payment of their salaries.

He has erected a multitude of new offices, and sent hither swarms of officers to harass our people and eat out their substance.

He has kept among us, in times of peace, standing armies without the consent of our legislatures.

He has affected to render the military independent of and superior to the civil power.

---

[1]"Men" refers to women as well as men.

He has combined with others to subject us to a jurisdiction foreign to our constitution, and unacknowledged by our laws; giving his assent to their acts of pretended legislation:

For quartering large bodies of armed troops among us.

For protecting them, by a mock trial, from punishment for any murders which they should commit on the inhabitants of these states.

For cutting off our trade with all parts of the world.

For imposing taxes on us without our consent.

For depriving us in many cases, of the benefits of trial by jury.

For transporting us beyond seas to be tried for pretended offenses.

For abolishing the free system of English laws in a neighboring province, establishing therein an arbitrary government, and enlarging its boundaries so as to render it at once an example and fit instrument for introducing the same absolute rule into these colonies.

For taking away our charters, abolishing our most valuable laws, and altering fundamentally the forms of our governments.

For suspending our own legislatures, and declaring themselves invested with power to legislate for us in all cases whatsoever.

He has abdicated government here, by declaring us out of his protection and waging war against us.

He has plundered our seas, ravaged our coasts, burnt our towns, and destroyed the lives of our people.

He is at this time transporting large armies of foreign mercenaries to complete the works of death, desolation and tyranny, already begun with circumstances of cruelty and perfidy scarcely paralleled in the most barbarous ages, and totally unworthy the head of a civilized nation.

He has constrained our fellow citizens taken captive on the high seas to bear arms against their country, to become the executioners of their friends and brethren, or to fall themselves by their hands.

He has excited domestic insurrections amongst us, and has endeavored to bring on the inhabitants of our frontiers, the merciless Indian savages, whose known rule of warfare is an undistinguished destruction of all sexes and conditions.

In every stage of these oppressions we have petitioned for redress in the most humble terms. Our repeated petitions have been answered only by repeated injury. A prince, whose character is thus marked by every act which may define a tyrant, is unfit to be the ruler of a free people.

Nor have we been wanting in attentions to our British brethren. We have warned them from time to time of attempts by their legislature to extend an unwarrantable jurisdiction over us. We have reminded them of the circumstances of our emigration and settlement here. We have appealed to their native justice and magnanimity, and we have conjured them by the ties of our common kindred to disavow these usurpations, which would inevitably interrupt our connections and correspondence. They too have been deaf to the voice of justice and of consanguinity. We must, therefore, acquiesce in the necessity, which denounces our separation, and hold them, as we hold the rest of mankind, enemies in war, in peace friends. We, Therefore, the representatives of the United States of America, in general congress, assembled, appealing to the Supreme Judge of the world for the rectitude of our intentions, do, in the name, and by authority of the good people of these colonies, solemnly publish and declare, that these united colonies are, and of right ought to be free and independent states; that they are absolved from all allegiance to the British crown, and that all political connection between them and the state of Great Britain, is and ought to be totally dissolved; and that as free and independent states, they have full power to levy war, conclude peace, contract alliances, establish commerce, and to do all other acts and things which independent states may of right do. And for the support of this Declaration, with a firm reliance on the protection of divine providence, we mutually pledge to each other our lives, our fortunes and our sacred honor.

John Hancock	William Paca	Benjamin Rush	Philip Livingston	Robert Treat Paine
Button Gwinnett	Thomas Stone	Benjamin Franklin	Francis Lewis	Elbridge Gerry
Lyman Hall	Charles Carroll	John Morton	Lewis Morris	Step Hopkins
George Walton	of Carrollton	George Clymer	Richard Stockton	William Ellery
William Hooper	George Wythe	James Smith	John Witherspoon	Roger Sherman
Joseph Hewes	Richard Henry Lee	George Taylor	Francis Hopkinson	Samuel Huntington
John Penn	Thomas Jefferson	James Wilson	John Hart	William Williams
Edward Rutledge	Benjamin Harrison	George Ross	Abra Clark	Oliver Wolcott
Thomas Heyward, Jr.	Thomas Nelson, Jr.	Caesar Rodney	Josiah Bartlett	Matthew Thornton
Thomas Lynch, Jr.	Francis Lightfoot Lee	George Read	William Whipple	
Arthur Middleton	Carter Braxton	Thomas M. Kean	Samuel Adams	
Samuel Chase	Robert Morris	William Floyd	John Adams	

The Declaration has been modernized in spelling, capitalization, and punctuation.

The above names have been spelled out for clarity.

★ The Mayflower Compact   November 11, 1620

In the name of God, Amen. We, whose names are underwritten, the Loyal Subjects of our dread Sovereign Lord, King *James*, by the Grace of God, of *Great Britain*, *France* and *Ireland*, King, *Defender of the Faith*, &,

Having undertaken for the Glory of God, and Advancement of the Christian Faith, and the Honour of our King and Country, a voyage to plant the first colony in the northern Parts of Virginia; do by these Presents, solemnly and mutually in the Presence of God and one of another, covenant and combine ourselves together into a civil Body Politick, for our better Ordering and Preservation, and Furtherance of the Ends aforesaid; And by Virtue hereof to enact, constitute, and frame, such just and equal Laws, Ordinances, Acts, Constitutions and Offices, from time to time, as shall be thought most meet and convenient for the General good of the Colony; unto which we promise all due Submission and Obedience.

In Witness whereof we have hereunto subscribed our names at *Cape Cod* the eleventh of *November,* in the Reign of our Sovereign Lord, King *James* of *England*, *France* and *Ireland*, the eighteenth, and of *Scotland* the fifty-fourth. *Anno Domini*, 1620.

John Carver	John Ridgate	Miles Standish	John Allerton	Edward Tilly
Digery Priest	Christopher Martin	Richard Bitteridge	Richard Warren	John Craxton
William Brewster	William Mullins	Francis Eaton	Edward Liester	Thomas Rogers
Edmund Margesson	Thomas English	John Tilly	William Bradford	John Goodman
John Alden	John Howland	John Billington	Thomas Williams	Edward Fuller
George Soule	Stephen Hopkins	Thomas Tinker	Isaac Allerton	Richard Gardiner
James Chilton	Edward Winslow	Samuel Fuller	Peter Brown	William White
Francis Cooke	Gilbert Winslow	Richard Clark	John Turner	Edward Doten
Moses Fletcher				

⭐ The Emancipation Proclamation January 1, 1863

By the President of the United States of America:
A Proclamation.

Whereas on the 22d day of September, A.D. 1862, a proclamation was issued by the President of the United States, containing, among other things, the following, to wit:

"That on the 1st day of January, A.D. 1863, all persons held as slaves within any State or designated part of a State the people whereof shall then be in rebellion against the United States shall be then, thenceforward, and forever free; and the executive government of the United States, including the military and naval authority thereof, will recognize and maintain the freedom of such persons and will do no act or acts to repress such persons, or any of them, in any efforts they may make for their actual freedom.

"That the executive will on the 1st day of January aforesaid, by proclamation, designate the States and parts of States, if any, in which the people thereof, respectively, shall then be in rebellion against the United States; and the fact that any State or the people thereof shall on that day be in good faith represented in the Congress of the United States by members chosen thereto at elections wherein a majority of the qualified voters of such States shall have participated shall, in the absence of strong countervailing testimony, be deemed conclusive evidence that such State and the people thereof are not then in rebellion against the United States."

Now, therefore, I, Abraham Lincoln, President of the United States, by virtue of the power in me vested as Commander-in-Chief of the Army and Navy of the United States in time of actual armed rebellion against the authority and government of the United States, and as a fit and necessary war measure for suppressing said rebellion, do, on this 1st day of January, A.D. 1863, and in accordance with my purpose so to do, publicly proclaimed for the full period of one hundred days from the first day above mentioned, order and designate as the States and parts of States wherein the people thereof, respectively, are this day in rebellion against the United States the following, to wit:

Arkansas, Texas, Louisiana (except the parishes of St. Bernard, Plaquemines, Jefferson, St. John, St. Charles, St. James, Ascension, Assumption, Terrebonne, Lafourche, St. Mary, St. Martin, and Orleans, including the city of New Orleans), Mississippi, Alabama, Florida, Georgia, South Carolina, North Carolina, and Virginia (except the forty-eight counties designated as West Virginia, and also the counties of Berkeley, Accomac, Northhampton, Elizabeth City, York, Princess Anne, and Norfolk, including the cities of Norfolk and Portsmouth), and which excepted parts are for the present left precisely as if this proclamation were not issued.

And by virtue of the power and for the purpose aforesaid, I do order and declare that all persons held as slaves within said designated States and parts of States are, and henceforward shall be, free; and that the Executive Government of the United States, including the military and naval authorities thereof, will recognize and maintain the freedom of said persons.

And I hereby enjoin upon the people so declared to be free to abstain from all violence, unless in necessary self-defense; and I recommend to them that, in all cases when allowed, they labor faithfully for reasonable wages.

And I further declare and make known that such persons of suitable condition will be received into the armed service of the United States to garrison forts, positions, stations, and other places, and to man vessels of all sorts in said service.

And upon this act, sincerely believed to be an act of justice, warranted by the Constitution upon military necessity, I invoke the considerate judgment of mankind and the gracious favor of Almighty God.

⭐ The Star-Spangled Banner Francis Scott Key, 1814

O say, can you see, by the dawn's early light,
What so proudly we hail'd at the twilight's last
  gleaming?
Whose broad stripes and bright stars, thro' the perilous
  fight,
O'er the ramparts we watch'd, were so gallantly
  streaming?
And the rockets' red glare, the bombs bursting in air,
Gave proof thro' the night that our flag was still there.
O say, does that star-spangled banner yet wave
O'er the land of the free and the home of the brave?

On the shore dimly seen thro' the mists of the deep,
Where the foe's haughty host in dread silence reposes,
What is that which the breeze, o'er the towering steep,
As it fitfully blows, half conceals, half discloses?
Now it catches the gleam of the morning's first beam,
In full glory reflected, now shines on the stream:
'T is the star-spangled banner: O, long may it wave
O'er the land of the free and the home of the brave!

And where is that band who so vauntingly swore
That the havoc of war and the battle's confusion,
A home and a country should leave us no more?
Their blood has wash'd out their foul footsteps'
  pollution.
No refuge could save the hireling and slave
From the terror of flight or the gloom of the grave:
And the star-spangled banner in triumph doth wave
O'er the land of the free and the home of the brave.

O thus be it ever when free-men shall stand
Between their lov'd home and the war's desolation;
Blest with vict'ry and peace, may the heav'n-rescued
  land
Praise the Pow'r that hath made and preserv'd us a
  nation!
Then conquer we must, when our cause it is just,
And this be our motto: "In God is our trust!"
And the star-spangled banner in triumph shall wave
O'er the land of the free and the home of the brave!

⭐ Lincoln's Gettysburg Address November 19, 1863

Fourscore and seven years ago our fathers brought forth on this continent a new nation conceived in liberty and dedicated to the proposition that all men are created equal. Now we are engaged in a great civil war testing whether that nation, or any nation so conceived and so dedicated, can long endure. We are met on a great battlefield of that war. We have come to dedicate a portion of that field as a final resting-place for those who here gave their lives that that nation might live. It is altogether fitting and proper that we should do this. But, in a larger sense, we cannot dedicate, we cannot consecrate, we cannot hallow this ground. The brave men, living and dead, who struggled here have consecrated it far above our poor power to add or detract. The world will little note nor long remember what we say here, but it can never forget what they did here. It is for us the living rather to be dedicated here to the unfinished work which they who fought here have thus far so nobly advanced. It is rather for us to be here dedicated to the great task remaining before us—that from these honored dead we take increased devotion to that cause for which they gave the last full measure of devotion—that we here highly resolve that these dead shall not have died in vain, that this nation under God shall have a new birth of freedom, and that government of the people, by the people, for the people shall not perish from the earth.

Parliamentary Procedure

What do your student council, your local school board, and the U.S. Congress have in common?

Like all organizations, whenever these groups hold a meeting they need rules to help them get their business done. **Parliamentary procedure** provides rules for holding a meeting. These rules are called "parliamentary" because they are based on rules and customs developed in the British Parliament (legislature).

A meeting can easily become confused unless group members understand and follow a set of rules. Of course, all groups do not use exactly the same rules of order. The U.S. Congress uses a very complicated form of parliamentary procedure. The rules for operating Congress take up more than 400 pages of fine print. Smaller groups, such as student councils, social clubs, and church groups, can follow simpler rules of order.

Any system of rules, or parliamentary procedure, should have two features. First, it should be democratic. This means the rules should: (1) give all members of the group a chance to contribute their ideas and (2) let the majority make the final decisions. Second, the rules should be efficient. They should help the group get its work done with little delay or confusion.

Robert's Rules of Order

You can find the rules of parliamentary procedure in *Robert's Rules of Order*. This book is the basic guide to accepted procedure. It is very widely used.

The book was written in 1876 by Major Henry Robert, a U.S. Army engineer. Major Robert decided to write the book after leading business meetings of his local church. He studied the rules used by lawmaking bodies like the British Parliament. He then adapted the rules so they would be useful for private groups like PTAs, churches, and clubs.

Major Robert's book has been revised several times. The book is not easy to read. However, the League of Women Voters, the Future Farmers of America, and several other organizations publish simplified guides to the main ideas in *Robert's Rules of Order*. Studying such guides can help you quickly learn the basic ideas of parliamentary procedure.

Another widely used book is *Sturgis Standard Code of Parliamentary Procedure*. Alice Sturgis, a university teacher, wrote this book. She spells out parliamentary procedure in easy-to-understand terms.

Conducting a Meeting

How do you conduct a meeting using parliamentary procedure? To get started, you need a **quorum.** This is the minimum number of members needed to do the group's business. Every group can set its own number.

Usually it is a majority of the total membership. Requiring a quorum prevents a few group members from making decisions for the entire group when others cannot be present.

Steps in a Meeting. A meeting begins when the presiding officer, usually the president, calls the group to order. Most groups then follow steps such as these:

1. *Minutes* from the last meeting are read by the secretary.
2. *Treasurer's Report* is given and questions about the group's budget may be asked.
3. *Standing Committees* report on their activities.
4. *Special Committees* report on their work.
5. *Unfinished Business.* Items left over from previous meetings are discussed.
6. *New Business.* Members deal with any new matters.
7. *Announcements* about matters of interest to members are made.
8. *Adjournment.* The meeting is officially ended, usually by majority vote.

Voting on Motions

Key decisions are made in the meeting by voting on motions. This is how a group conducts its business.

Motions. A **motion** is a brief statement of a proposed action. A student council member could make a motion to hold the Valentine's Day dance on a certain date. "I move we hold next year's Valentine dance on the Saturday closest to February 14."

A member can only make a motion when he or she "has the floor" (has been given permission to speak by the presiding officer). Another member must **second** the motion before the group can discuss it. "I second the motion on the date of the Valentine dance."

Members can now discuss the motion. Routine motions may cause little discussion. Other motions may cause lengthy debate and arguments. Parliamentary procedure can keep things in order. Members can offer to amend a motion. "I move we have the Valentine dance on Friday instead of Saturday." If the group accepts the amendment, then the discussion continues on the amended motion.

Motions must be dealt with one at a time. If the group cannot agree or wants to get more information, they may vote to "table the motion." This means they will postpone discussion of the motion for a later meeting.

Voting. When each member who wants to speak on a motion has done so, the group votes yes or no. The president usually restates the motion or has the secretary read it. Then the president may call for a **voice vote.** "All those in favor say 'aye;' all opposed 'nay.'" On a close vote the president may ask members to vote by raising their hands. The president usually does not vote except to break a tie.

Presidents of the United States

President	Party	State[2]	Term of Office
George Washington (1732-1799)	None	Virginia	1789-1797
John Adams (1735-1826)	Federalist	Massachusetts	1797-1801
Thomas Jefferson (1743-1826)	Republican[1]	Virginia	1801-1809
James Madison (1751-1836)	Republican[1]	Virginia	1809-1817
James Monroe (1758-1831)	Republican[1]	Virginia	1817-1825
John Quincy Adams (1767-1848)	Republican[1]	Massachusetts	1825-1829
Andrew Jackson (1767-1845)	Democratic	Tennessee (S.C.)	1829-1837
Martin Van Buren (1782-1862)	Democratic	New York	1837-1841
William Henry Harrison (1773-1841)	Whig	Ohio (Va.)	1841
John Tyler (1790-1862)	Whig	Virginia	1841-1845
James K. Polk (1795-1849)	Democratic	Tennessee (N.C.)	1845-1849
Zachary Taylor (1784-1850)	Whig	Louisiana (Va.)	1849-1850
Millard Fillmore (1800-1874)	Whig	New York	1850-1853
Franklin Pierce (1804-1869)	Democratic	New Hampshire	1853-1857
James Buchanan (1791-1868)	Democratic	Pennsylvania	1857-1861
Abraham Lincoln (1809-1865)	Republican	Illinois (Ky.)	1861-1865
Andrew Johnson (1808-1875)	Republican	Tennessee (N.C.)	1865-1869
Ulysses S. Grant (1822-1885)	Republican	Illinois (Ohio)	1869-1877
Rutherford B. Hayes (1822-1893)	Republican	Ohio	1877-1881
James A. Garfield (1831-1881)	Republican	Ohio	1881
Chester A. Arthur (1829-1886)	Republican	New York (Vt.)	1881-1885
Grover Cleveland (1837-1908)	Democratic	New York (N.J.)	1885-1889
Benjamin Harrison (1833-1901)	Republican	Indiana (Ohio)	1889-1893
Grover Cleveland (1837-1908)	Democratic	New York (N.J.)	1893-1897
William McKinley (1843-1901)	Republican	Ohio	1897-1901
Theodore Roosevelt (1858-1919)	Republican	New York	1901-1909
William H. Taft (1857-1930)	Republican	Ohio	1909-1913
Woodrow Wilson (1856-1924)	Democratic	New Jersey (Va.)	1913-1921
Warren G. Harding (1865-1923)	Republican	Ohio	1921-1923
Calvin Coolidge (1872-1933)	Republican	Massachusetts (Vt.)	1923-1929
Herbert C. Hoover (1874-1964)	Republican	California (Iowa)	1929-1933
Franklin D. Roosevelt (1882-1945)	Democratic	New York	1933-1945
Harry S. Truman (1884-1972)	Democratic	Missouri	1945-1953
Dwight D. Eisenhower (1890-1969)	Republican	New York (Tex.) Pennsylvania	1953-1961
John F. Kennedy (1917-1963)	Democratic	Massachusetts	1961-1963
Lyndon B. Johnson (1908-1973)	Democratic	Texas	1963-1969
Richard M. Nixon (1913-	Republican	New York (Calif.)	1969-1974
Gerald R. Ford (1913-	Republican	Michigan (Neb.)	1974-1977
James Earl Carter (1924-	Democratic	Georgia	1977-1981
Ronald W. Reagan (1911-	Republican	California (Ill.)	1981-

[1]The party is often called the Democratic-Republican party because in the 1820s it became the Democratic party.
[2]State of reference at time of election. If state of birth is different, it is shown in parentheses.

Facts About the States

Order of Admission to the Union[1]	State Name	Year admitted to the Union[1]	Area in square miles	Population[2]	Number of Representatives in Congress
22	Alabama	1819	51,609	3,893,888	7
49	Alaska	1959	586,412	401,851	1
48	Arizona	1912	113,909	2,718,215	5
25	Arkansas	1836	53,104	2,286,435	4
31	California	1850	158,693	23,667,902	45
38	Colorado	1876	104,247	2,889,964	6
5	Connecticut	1788	5,009	3,107,576	6
1	Delaware	1787	2,057	594,338	1
27	Florida	1845	58,560	9,746,324	19
4	Georgia	1788	58,876	5,463,105	10
50	Hawaii	1959	6,450	964,691	2
43	Idaho	1890	83,557	943,935	2
21	Illinois	1818	56,400	11,426,518	22
19	Indiana	1816	36,291	5,490,224	10
29	Iowa	1846	56,290	2,913,808	6
34	Kansas	1861	82,264	2,363,679	5
15	Kentucky	1792	40,395	3,660,777	7
18	Louisiana	1812	48,523	4,205,900	8
23	Maine	1820	33,215	1,124,660	2
7	Maryland	1788	10,577	4,216,975	8
6	Massachusetts	1788	8,257	5,737,037	11
26	Michigan	1837	58,216	9,262,078	18
32	Minnesota	1858	84,068	4,075,970	8
20	Mississippi	1817	47,716	2,520,638	5
24	Missouri	1821	69,686	4,916,686	9
41	Montana	1889	147,138	786,690	2
37	Nebraska	1867	77,227	1,569,625	3
36	Nevada	1864	110,540	800,493	2
9	New Hampshire	1788	9,304	920,610	2
3	New Jersey	1787	7,836	7,364,823	14
47	New Mexico	1912	121,666	1,302,894	3
11	New York	1788	49,576	17,558,072	34
12	North Carolina	1789	52,586	5,881,766	11
39	North Dakota	1889	70,665	652,717	1
17	Ohio	1803	41,222	10,797,630	21
46	Oklahoma	1907	69,919	3,025,290	6
33	Oregon	1859	96,981	2,633,105	5
2	Pennsylvania	1787	45,333	11,863,895	23
13	Rhode Island	1790	1,214	947,154	2
8	South Carolina	1788	31,055	3,121,820	6
40	South Dakota	1889	77,047	690,768	1
16	Tennessee	1796	42,244	4,591,120	9
28	Texas	1845	267,339	14,229,191	27
45	Utah	1896	84,916	1,461,037	3
14	Vermont	1791	9,609	511,456	1
10	Virginia	1788	40,817	5,346,818	10
42	Washington	1889	68,192	4,132,156	8
35	West Virginia	1863	24,181	1,949,644	4
30	Wisconsin	1848	56,154	4,705,769	9
44	Wyoming	1890	97,914	469,557	1
	District of Columbia	1791	67	638,333	0

Total number of representatives[3]   435

[1]For the thirteen original states, the order of admission and year of admission represent their ratification of the Constitution.
[2]United States Bureau of the Census figures for 1980.
[3]The total number of representatives in Congress does not include the representative from the District of Columbia, who does not vote.

Writing and Research Skills

Preparing a Report

Choosing a Suitable Topic

The first step in writing a report is choosing a suitable topic. Before you decide on a topic, find out how long your report should be. Its length will determine how broad your topic can be. In a short report, for instance, you could not possibly cover a topic as broad as *Presidents of the United States.* This covers far too many different people. However, you might be able to cover one President.

When the choice of a topic is up to you, pick one that you are interested in and want to learn more about. If you are enthusiastic about a topic, your enthusiasm will probably show in the writing of the report and make it more interesting to the reader. Be sure your topic is not too narrow or too dull to interest many possible readers. For example, you may be curious about the history of can openers and want to write about it. You should ask yourself, "Who else would be interested in the topic?" If you are not sure your topic will be of interest to others, choose another one with a wider appeal.

When choosing your topic, follow a process similar to the one below. Notice, too, how asking questions can help you narrow your topic.

- Could you cover the topic *United States Government* in a short report? Why or why not?
- Why is the topic *The Supreme Court* still too large?
- What specific aspect of the Supreme Court is suggested for a report?
- Can you think of any other topics for a report on the Supreme Court?
- What in particular would you like to know about the Court?

One more consideration in choosing a topic is to pick one that you can find plenty of information on quickly and easily. You will need to base your report on some facts, which you will have to find in books and other references. You should also support each of your main points with informative details to make your report effective.

Using the Library

After you choose a topic, you need to research it. A library is the best place to begin. Libraries contain a treasure of information. To use that information, you need to learn how to use the **card catalog**.

The card catalog is an alphabetical file that contains cards on all the books in the library. For most books the card catalog has at least three cards: an **author card, title card,** and one or more **subject cards.** All of these cards are similar, but they are organized differently. Notice the first line of each card on the opposite page.

Each of the cards gives the author, book title, publisher, and place and date of publication. These cards also tell you that the book is 64 pages long and is illustrated.

Suppose you wanted to find this book in a library, but you only remembered the author's name. Then you would look up the author's name in the card catalog. If you knew only the title of the book, *Be a Smart Shopper*, you would look up the title in the card catalog. Maybe you knew nothing of Kathlyn Gay and her book, but you wanted to find some books on the subject of consumer education. Then you would look up *consumer education*, and under that subject you would find a subject card for Kathlyn Gay's book.

All of the cards in a card catalog are filed alphabetically according to the first word on the first line of each card, unless the word is *a*, *an*, or *the*. In the upper left-hand corner of every card is a **call number.** The call number will help you locate the book on the library shelf. When you copy the call number of a book, be sure to copy it exactly.

The call number is the library's system of classifying books. One of the most common is the **Dewey Decimal System.** In this system books are assigned a number based on their subject. Books on the same subject have similar call numbers and are grouped together in the library. At right are the major headings in the Dewey Decimal System.

Writing and Research Skills

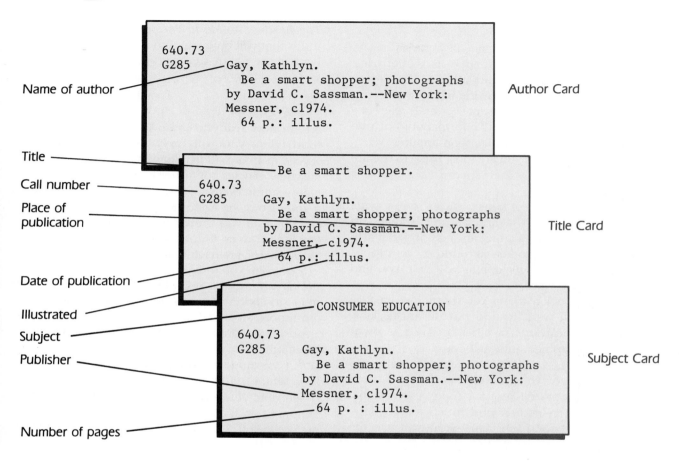

Name of author

```
640.73
G285    Gay, Kathlyn.
           Be a smart shopper; photographs
        by David C. Sassman.--New York:
        Messner, c1974.
           64 p.: illus.
```

Author Card

Title

Call number

Place of publication

```
                        Be a smart shopper.
640.73
G285    Gay, Kathlyn.
           Be a smart shopper; photographs
        by David C. Sassman.--New York:
        Messner, c1974.
           64 p.: illus.
```

Title Card

Date of publication

Illustrated

Subject

Publisher

```
                    CONSUMER EDUCATION
640.73
G285    Gay, Kathlyn.
           Be a smart shopper; photographs
        by David C. Sassman.--New York:
        Messner, c1974.
           64 p. : illus.
```

Subject Card

Number of pages

Dewey Decimal System

000—099   General works (reference materials)
100—199   Philosophy (includes psychology)
200—299   Religion (includes mythology)
300—399   Social Sciences (includes government, economics, law, education, transportation, and communication)
400—499   Language (includes foreign languages)
500—599   Science (includes physics, biology, astronomy)

600—699   Technology (includes inventions, aviation, engineering)
700—799   The Arts (includes sports, architecture, and all fine arts, such as music and dance)
800—899   Literature (includes poems, plays, essays)
900—999   History (includes geography, biography, travel)

Writing and Research Skills

Using Reference Books

In addition to the card catalog, all libraries have a section for reference books, such as dictionaries, encyclopedias, almanacs, and atlases. The key to using reference books is knowing which one to use for the information you want. Several reference books may have the needed information, but one book is usually a better choice than another.

The reference books you are most likely to use are described below. Study their special uses and how each might help you.

- An **encyclopedia** contains articles on a wide range of subjects. The articles are arranged in alphabetical order. Reading an encyclopedia article will give you a good background for your topic. The index of the encyclopedia will help you find the article you want.
- An **atlas** is a book of maps. You should use an atlas whenever you want to find out distances, locations, or populations of cities, as well as other similar geographical information.
- An **almanac** is a collection of facts on many and diverse subjects. An almanac gives the names and achievements of well-known people, sports statistics, population figures, and much more. Almanacs are updated each year, so always use the most current one.
- The **dictionaries** and **thesauri** are also located in the reference section. Use a dictionary whenever you are unsure about the spelling, pronunciation, meaning, or use of a word. Use a thesaurus to find synonyms and antonyms for a word.
- **Specialized dictionaries** may also be helpful in your research. This kind of dictionary defines terms in a particular area, such as science, dance, music, or medicine. Such dictionaries are useful for the definition of a special term or information about a person in a particular field.
- The **biographical reference books** are works such as *Who's Who in America* and *Current Biography*. They give short biographies of well-known people in politics, literature, and the arts.

- *The Readers' Guide to Periodical Literature* is an index that will help you find magazine articles. To learn more about this guide see page 36 in this text.

Taking Notes

You are now ready to begin the research for your report. First, you will need to find several good sources of information. They may be entire books, magazine articles, or articles in reference books. Begin reading quickly at first. Then, when you find an interesting or important piece of information, slow down. If you think you may want to use it in your report, write it down.

Index cards are useful for taking notes. Be sure to write notes in your own words, except when you are quoting an expert on your topic. An occasional direct quotation can add interest or authority to your report. Most of your notes, however, should be in your own words. This will make it easier for you to write the report in your own words.

Read the sample note cards for a report on *A Visit to the White House* on the opposite page.

Each note you read gave the source of the note, the note itself, and the page number from which the note was taken. The number on the top line of each note keys the note to the **bibliography**, or list of books, magazines, and reference works you used in preparing the report. The bibliography appears at the end of your report. The bibliography shows your readers where you gathered your information. It allows readers to judge how good your sources are and to locate the material you used.

Look closely at the bibliography on page 535. It shows the sources of the information given in the notes. The first entry shows a magazine article source, the second a book source, and the third an encyclopedia source. Notice that the entries are in alphabetical order, beginning with the author's last name (or, in reference works, the name of the article). Study the use of capital letters, commas, periods, parentheses, and underlining.

Writing and Research Skills

---

1. "Inside the White House"
Cornerstone was laid in 1792.
First official building. Designed
by Irish architect James Hoban.
p. 20

---

2. The White House
"In place of formal receptions, Jefferson
gave small dinner parties, ... Dinner at
the President's House was usually served at
four in the afternoon, in a small room
now known as the Green Room." pp. 22, 23

---

3. "White House"
132 rooms in middle of 18-acre plot
at 1600 Pennsylvania Ave. Main
building 175 feet long, 85 feet
wide. p. 240

Sample Bibliography

Aikman, Lonnell, "Inside the White House" National Geographic, Volume 119, No. 1 (January, 1961), p. 20.

Leish, Kenneth W., The White House, Newsweek Book Division, 1972; 1977 edition.

"White House," World Book Encyclopedia, 1985. Volume 21, pp. 240–242.

Writing and Research Skills

Organizing Your Information

Organizing the information you have on your note cards is the next step in planning a good report. First, identify the main ideas you want to cover in the report. Then make sure you can support each of them with relevant facts, examples, or details. Keep in mind that one paragraph is usually required for each well-developed main idea.

As you sort your note cards, discard any information that does not keep to your topic. By eliminating irrelevant notes—those that don't support any of your main ideas—you will see more clearly what information you need to cover. You can then decide on the most logical order and number your cards accordingly.

Here are some notes for *A Visit to the White House.* Decide which one expresses a main idea, which two notes support that idea, and which one should be discarded.

> The White House is a storehouse of American history.

> George Washington helped to choose its site.

> Every President since John Adams has lived in the White House.

> President John Adams was a native of Massachusetts.

Making an Outline

Making an outline for all the reports you do will help you focus, refine, and finish organizing your information. Here is a sample outline.

A Visit to the White House

  I. Introductory description of State Dining Room
 II. Storehouse of American history
    A. Attracts 1.5 million per year
    B. Historical background
      1. Washington helped to choose site
      2. Home of all other Presidents
      3. Important historical decisions
 III. Design information
    A. James Hoban architect
    B. Dimensions
 IV. Other rooms shown to visitors
    A. East Room
      1. Abigail Adams' laundry room
      2. Dead Presidents lie in state
    B. Green Room
    C. Blue Room
      1. Formal reception room
      2. Furnishings
    D. Red Room
 V. Impressive place to visit
    A. Only part is open to public
    B. Vivid impression of history

In making your outline, plan at least three main topics and two subtopics for each main topic. You may use two or more details for any subtopic to develop and illustrate your point. If you have only one subtopic or one detail under a subtopic, include the ideas in a larger category. Use an abbreviated version of your notes when writing items in an outline.

Writing Your Report

In the report below you will find three distinct sections. The **introduction** is a paragraph designed to get the reader's attention. The **body** of the report gives the information collected in research. It follows the outline as a general guide. Finally, the **conclusion** sums up the report.

A Visit to the White House

You go through a doorway into a large room. A few days ago on television you saw the President of the United States in this room entertaining a foreign head of state at a large dinner. Now the room is empty. The tables are set with china, and a portrait of Abraham Lincoln gazes pensively down from its place over the mantel. You are a visitor to the White House, official home of the President. You are in the State Dining Room, where formal dinners are held.

Each year more than one and a half million people come to this house at 1600 Pennsylvania Avenue in Washington, D.C. It is a storehouse of American history. George Washington helped to choose its site, but the mansion was not ready for occupancy until 1800 when his successor, John Adams, was President. Since then, all the Presidents have lived here. Many decisions important in United States and world history have been made within its walls.

James Hoban, an Irish-born architect, designed the White House. He also supervised its construction. The cornerstone was laid in 1792. The original mansion, built of white sandstone, is 175 feet long, 85 feet wide, and three stories high. The east and west wings were added much later.

As a visitor to the White House, you see five rooms. The East Room, largest in the mansion, is used for formal entertaining. Abigail Adams, who hung laundry in it, would never recognize it today. Every president who died in office has laid in state in this room. The Green Room is furnished in a style popular around 1800. Thomas Jefferson used it for dining. The Blue Room, a formal reception room, has a lovely view of the gardens. Much of its furniture dates from the presidency of James Monroe. A wonderful portrait of Jefferson is in this room. The Red Room is a parlor furnished in a style popular from 1810 to 1830. A couch in this room belonged to Dolley Madison.

The White House rooms shown to the public, of course, represent only a small part of its 132 rooms. However, a visit to the White House is an experience you will never forget. Every visitor brings away a vivid and impressive picture of the continuity of American history and the power of the presidency.

You should also attach a bibliography, or list of sources, to your report. See the sample on page 535.

Writing and Research Skills

Writing Letters to Government Leaders

Citizens write to government leaders to influence their decisions about making and enforcing laws. They also write for information about laws and activities of the government.

Just as you can do a good or bad job of painting a fence or baking a cake, you can write a good or bad letter. A carefully written letter is more likely to influence a government leader than a poorly written letter. Read the tips for effective letter writing below.

Tips for Effective Letter Writing

1. Address the official properly. For example, when writing to a member of the Senate or House, write "The Honorable (name), Senate (or House) Office Building, Washington, D.C., 20510." When addressing the official in the letter itself, say "Dear Senator (or Representative) (name)."

2. Make sure that your handwriting or typewriting is neat.

3. Include your name and address. This will enable your representative to write back to you.

4. Be as brief as possible.

5. Try to explain why you feel as you do about an issue. A flat statement of support or opposition to a bill is OK as far as it goes, but it means more if there is some reasoning behind it.

6. Talk about only one issue in a letter. If you can, give the name or number of the bill you are interested in.

7. Be courteous and reasonable. Even if you are angry, do not be rude.

8. Use your own words and stationery. This shows you are interested enough in a problem to make an effort to write a personal letter.

9. Don't apologize for writing or taking the official's time. Your government official will be glad to hear from you.

10. Write often. Let communication between you and your representatives become a good habit. Stay informed.

Read the tips for effective letter writing again. Then utilize these tips to write a letter to one of the following officials. Explain to the official your views about a particular issue.

a. one of your United States senators

b. your United States congressman

c. your mayor

d. your governor

Flag Etiquette

The proper way to honor and display the flag has been set forth in Public Law 829. This is a summary of the main ideas of that law.

1. On buildings and stationary flagstaffs in the open, the flag should be displayed only from sunrise to sunset. However, when a special patriotic effect is desired, the flag may be displayed for twenty-four hours a day if it is properly lighted. It should not be displayed on days when the weather is bad unless an all-weather flag is used.

2. The flag should be displayed on or near the main building of all public institutions. It should be displayed in or near every polling place on election days. It should be displayed during school days in or near every school.

3. There are certain correct ways to display the flag. The blue field, called the union, must always be at the top. The union hangs from the peak of a flagstaff. It is on the observer's left, the flag's right, if the flag is hung on a wall. In a group of state and local flags, the United States flag is in the center and at the highest point. When they are flown from the same halyard, the United States flag is at the peak. The United States flag is hoisted first and lowered last. No other flag should fly higher or be placed to the United States flag's right. When flags of two or more nations are displayed, they are to be flown from separate staffs of the same height.

4. When the flag is displayed over the middle of the street, it should be suspended vertically with the union to the north in an east and west street or to the east in a north and south street.

5. The flag, when flown at half-staff, should first be hoisted to the peak for an instant and then lowered to the half-staff position. It should again be raised to the peak before it is lowered for the day.

6. When the flag is used to cover a casket, it should be placed so the union is at the head and over the left shoulder. The flag should not be lowered into the grave or allowed to touch the ground.

7. When the flag hangs across a corridor or lobby in a building it should hang vertically with the union to the observer's left upon entering. If the building has more than one entrance, the flag should hang near the center of the corridor with the union to the north when entrances are to the east and west or to the east when entrances are to the north and south. If there are entrances in more than two directions, the union should be to the east.

In a group of state and local flags.

With other flags on a halyard.

With another flag with crossed staffs.

Permission is given to reproduce pages 539–540.

539

Horizontally on a wall.

Vertically on a wall.

From a staff projecting from a window or wall.

In an auditorium or meeting place.

8. No disrespect should be shown to the flag. It should not be dipped to honor any person or thing. It should never be displayed union down, except as a signal of dire distress. It should never touch anything beneath it. It should never be carried flat or horizontally, but always aloft and free. It should never be used as wearing apparel, drapery, bedding, nor to cover a ceiling. Nothing should be placed on it, drawn on it, or attached to it. It should not be used for advertising purposes, and should not be printed, sewn, or embroidered on anything disposable, like paper napkins. A flag patch may be put on uniforms, and should be worn on the left lapel, near the heart.

9. When the flag is raised or lowered and during the national anthem, all present should face the flag and stand at attention with the right hand over the heart. People in military uniform should give a military salute. Men wearing a hat should remove it with the right hand and hold the hat at the left shoulder, the hand being over the heart. The same rules apply while saying the Pledge of Allegiance:

"I pledge allegiance to the Flag of the United States of America, and to the Republic for which it stands, one Nation under God, indivisible, with liberty and justice for all."

10. When the flag is in such condition that it is no longer a fitting emblem for display, it should be destroyed in a dignified way, preferably by burning.

Glossary

Pronunciation Key

hat, āge, fär; let, ēqual, tèrm; it, īce; hot, ōpen, ôrder; oil, out; cup, pùt, rüle; ə represents *a* in about, *e* in taken, *i* in pencil, *o* in lemon, *u* in circus.

The references in parentheses following each definition refer to the places in the text where each of the boldface terms is defined. Refer to these sections whenever a more in-depth explanation of the glossary terms is needed.

abstain (ab stān′), *v.* to choose *not* to vote. (Ch. 2, Sec. 1)

adjudicatory hearing a hearing that determines the facts in a juvenile case. (Ch. 21, Sec. 2)

administrative law law made by a government agency. (Ch. 10, Sec. 1)

agenda (ə jen′də), *n.* list of items of business brought before a meeting to be dealt with. (Ch. 6, Sec. 1)

alien (ā′lyən, ā′lē ən), *n.* person living in a country but remaining a citizen of another country. (Ch. 1, Sec. 2)

almanac (ôl′mə nak), *n.* an annual reference book containing summaries of information on particular subjects. (Ch. 7, *Basic Social Studies Skills*)

alternative (ôl tèr′ə tiv), *n.* one of two or more choices faced when making a decision. (Ch. 1, Sec. 1)

amendment (ə mend′mənt), *n.* change offered or made in a law. (Ch. 3, Sec. 3)

Anti-Federalist (an′tī fed′ər ə list), *n.* opponent of the new Constitution and supporter of individual liberties and rights under state governments. (Ch. 3, Sec. 3)

appellate court court that hears appeals from trial courts. (Ch. 16, Sec. 1)

apprentice (ə pren′tis), *n.* a person learning a trade or art. (Ch. 25, Sec. 1)

appropriations (ə prō′prē ā′shənz), *n.pl.* money that is set aside by law for a stated purpose. (Ch. 14, Sec. 1)

aptitude (ap′tə tüd), *n.* natural capacity or talent for a particular trade or profession. (Ch. 25, Sec. 2)

arraignment (ə rān′mənt), *n.* the stage in a criminal proceeding in which the accused person comes before a judge, hears the charges, and pleads guilty or not guilty. (Ch. 16, Sec. 2)

articles (är′tə kəlz), *n.pl.* the seven parts of the main body of the United States Constitution; each contains rules and procedures for organizing and carrying out its business. (Ch. 4, Sec. 2)

attorney general chief law officer of a state or country. In the President's cabinet, the Attorney General is head of the Department of Justice. Forty-two states elect an attorney general to fight crime. (Ch. 15, Sec. 1)

bail (bāl), *n.* money or property an accused person gives the court to hold as a guarantee of returning for trial, so he or she may stay out of jail in the meantime. (Ch. 5, Sec. 1)

bait and switch to advertise an item at a low price to attract customers with the intention of selling them, instead, a higher priced item. (Ch. 24, Sec. 1)

balanced budget a budget in which income is equal to expenses. (Ch. 7, Sec. 3)

ballot (bal′ət), *n.* piece of paper, ticket, or other object used in secret voting. (Ch. 13, Sec. 1)

bandwagon (band′wag′ən), *n.* propaganda technique of persuading others to join what appears to be the winning candidate or group. (Ch. 13, Sec. 2)

bank (bangk), *n.* an institution in the business of lending, protecting, and handling money. (Ch. 24, Sec. 2)

bar graph type of graph that utilizes rectangles of different lengths to show quantities. (Ch. 5, *Basic Social Studies Skills*)

barter (bär′tər), *v.* to trade one good directly for another without using money. (Ch. 22, Sec. 3)

benefit (ben′ə fit), *n.* anything that is for a person's good; advantage. (Ch. 1, Sec. 3)

biased (bī′əsd), *adj.* favoring one side too much. (Ch. 12, *Basic Social Studies Skills*)

bicameral legislature a legislature divided into two houses. (Ch. 6, Sec. 1 and Ch. 14, Sec. 1)

bill of attainder law that deprives a person of property or rights without benefit of a trial. (Ch. 5, Sec. 1)

Bill of Rights the first ten amendments to the United States Constitution. (Ch. 5, Sec. 1)

block grant an award of money from the federal government given to cities for specific projects. (Ch. 19, Sec. 3)

board of directors people elected by stockholders to run a corporation. (Ch. 23, Sec. 1)

bond (bond), *n.* a certificate stating that the government has borrowed a certain amount of money from the owner of the bond. (Ch. 17, Sec. 3)

borough (bèr′ō), *n.* in Alaska, a district similar to a county. In some states a borough is an unincorporated town, and in New York City there are five divisions called boroughs. (Ch. 17, Sec. 1)

boycott (boi′kot), *n.* the act of collectively refusing to buy or use the services or goods of a government or company. (Ch. 5, Sec. 2)

breach of contract the breaking of a contractual promise. (Ch. 24, *Law and Freedom*)

brief (brēf), *n.* written document that explains one side's position in a legal case. (Ch. 5, *Case Study*)

budget (buj′it), *n.*, *v.*—*n.* plan for gathering, spending, and saving money. —*v.* to make a plan for gathering, spending, and saving money; allot. (Ch. 7, Sec. 3 and Ch. 24, Sec. 1)

burden (bèrd′n), *n.* a duty or responsibility that a person or group takes on for the benefit of another person or group. (Ch. 1, Sec. 3)

bureaucracy (byù rok′rə sē), *n.*, *pl.* **-cies.** the departments, divisions, and commissions in the executive branch of government. (Ch. 9, *Introduction* and Ch. 15, Sec. 3)

bureaucrat (byùr′ə krat), *n.* government official in the executive branch who administers a government program or supervises the carrying out of regulations. (Ch. 15, Sec. 3)

business cycle the ups and downs in the production phase of a market system. (Ch. 22, Sec. 3)

bylaws (bī′lôz′), *n.pl.* the written constitution for a company, club, city, or other group. (Ch. 20, Sec. 2)

Cabinet (kab′ə nit), *n.* group of advisers to the President. Most members head departments in the national government. (Ch. 8, Sec. 3)

Cabinet department an executive agency of the national government, headed by a member of the President's Cabinet and responsible for a special area of activity. (Ch. 9, Sec. 1)

Cabinet secretaries top leaders in federal agencies who are named by the President. (Ch. 9, Sec. 2)

calendar (kal′ən dər), *n.* schedule of the order in which bills are considered by a legislature and court cases are considered by a court. (Ch. 16, Sec. 3)

canvass (kan′vəs), *v.*, *n.* —*v.* to contact the people of a district systematically in support of a candidate, asking for votes and counting supporters and opponents. —*n.* a systematic coverage of a district to measure support. A person conducting a canvass may be supporting a candidate or may be attempting to predict results of a coming election. (Ch. 12, Sec. 3)

capital goods products that can be used to make other goods. (Ch. 22, Sec. 1)

capitalism (kap′ə tə liz′əm), *n.* an economic system in which property and the means of production are privately owned and in which the market system is the means of economic decision making. (Ch. 22, Sec. 2)

card-stacking (kärd′stak′ing), *n.* propaganda technique of presenting only one-sided facts favorable to a candidate or issue. (Ch. 13, Sec. 2)

career worker permanent employee. (Ch. 8, Sec. 1)

caucus (kô′kəs), *n.* a meeting of members or leaders of a political party to make plans, choose candidates, or decide how to vote. (Ch. 8, Sec. 1)

Central Intelligence Agency (CIA) federal agency that gathers and evaluates information important to the President and other foreign-policy decision makers. (Ch. 26, Sec. 3)

chamber of commerce group of business people organized to protect and promote the business interests of a city, state, or country. (Ch. 18, Sec. 3)

chambers (chām′bərz), *n.pl.* office of a lawyer or a judge. (Ch. 16, Sec. 3)

charge account system of buying on credit. (Ch. 24, Sec. 2)

charter (chär′tər), *n.* a plan for government granted by a state legislature to cities, towns, and other local governments. (Ch. 14, Sec. 1)

chief executive person in charge of seeing that the laws passed by the legislature are carried out. (Ch. 4, Sec. 2 and Ch. 8, Sec. 2)

chief legislator the person with the largest role in proposing new laws. In the role of chief legislator, the President suggests most of the new laws that Congress considers. (Ch. 8, Sec. 2)

chief school officer superintendent or commissioner who directs the state department of education in carrying out state laws and providing service related to schools. (Ch. 15, Sec. 1)

chronology (krə nol′ə jē), *n.* arrangement of dates of events in the order in which they happened. (Ch. 11, *Basic Social Studies Skills*)

circle graph type of graph that shows percentages or fractions of a whole within a circle. (Ch. 5, *Basic Social Studies Skills*)

circuit (sėr′kit), *n.* area served by one of the eleven federal appellate courts. (Ch. 10, Sec. 2)

civics (siv′iks), *n.* the study of the duties, rights, privileges, and responsibilities of citizenship. (Ch. 1, Sec. 1)

civil case court case involving a dispute between people over property, money, or damages of some kind. (Ch. 16, Sec. 1)

civil service workers workers who are appointed to their jobs in the federal government. (Ch. 9, Sec. 2)

classify (klas′ə fī), *v.* to arrange or organize in classes or groups. (Ch. 4, *Basic Social Studies Skills*)

client group the group of citizens an agency serves. Farmers are a client group of the Department of Agriculture. (Ch. 9, Sec. 3)

closed primary an election in which only declared party members are allowed to choose the party's nominees. (Ch. 12, Sec. 3)

closed shop union-employer contract providing that only union members may be hired. (Ch. 23, Sec. 2)

coalition (kō′ə lish′ən), *n.* combined pool of two or more interest groups working together to reach a goal. (Ch. 11, Sec. 3)

Cold War the contest for power after World War II between communist nations, headed by the Soviet Union, and western nations, headed by the United States. (Ch. 26, Sec. 2)

collective bargaining negotiation between an employer and a union representing the employees. (Ch. 23, Sec. 2)

column (kol′əm), *n.* part of a newspaper or magazine used for a special subject or written by a special writer. (Ch. 18, Sec. 3)

commander in chief person in charge of all the armed forces. In national government, the President is commander in chief of the armed forces. In state government, the governor is commander in chief of the National Guard. (Ch. 8, Sec. 2)

command system, pure an economy in which the government makes all major economic decisions. (Ch. 22, Sec. 2)

commission plan a plan of city government in which a small group of elected commissioners, each heading a city department, makes and carries out the laws. (Ch. 18, Sec. 1)

committee hearings congressional hearings that investigate special problems in an agency. (Ch. 6, Sec. 2)

committee staff people who work directly for House and Senate committees. (Ch. 6, Sec. 2)

common law law that has developed

from custom, common practice, or previous decisions judges have made in similar cases. (Ch. 10, Sec. 1)

communism (kom′yə niz′əm), *n.* a type of command economic system practiced in the Soviet Union and other nations. Under communism, the government owns all the land, factories, and stores and strictly controls the production of goods and services. (Ch. 22, Sec. 2)

competition (kom′pə tish′ən), *n.* rivalry; effort to obtain something wanted by others. (Ch. 22, Sec. 2)

complaint (kəm plānt′), *n.* a formal accusation, or charge. (Ch. 16, Sec. 2)

compromise (kom′prə mīz), *n., v.* —*n.* settlement of a dispute in which each side gives up something so agreement can be reached. —*v.* to settle a difference by having each side give up part of what is wanted. (Ch. 3, Sec. 2)

concurring opinion an opinion of one or more judges who agree with the decision of the court but for reasons that are different from those given in the majority opinion. (Ch. 10, Sec. 3)

confederation (kən fed′ə rā′shən), *n.* a group of independent states joined together for a special purpose. A confederation may not make laws that apply directly to individuals without agreement of the member states. Some people say the United Nations is a confederation. (Ch. 3, Sec. 1)

conference committee group of legislators from both houses who work out a compromise version of a bill when both houses have passed different versions of the bill. (Ch. 6, Sec. 3 and Ch. 14, Sec. 2)

conflict (kon′flikt), *n.* disagreement between people; a fight, struggle, or clash. (Ch. 1, Sec. 4)

congressional district area in a state from which a representative is elected to Congress as a member of the House of Representatives. (Ch. 6, Sec. 1)

consequences (kon′sə kwen′siz), *n.pl.* outcomes or results of a decision; effects. (Ch. 2, Sec. 1)

consolidation (kən sol′ə dā′shən), *n.* a joining to form one unit. In several urban areas, people have combined the government departments of city and county to make a city-county consolidation. (Ch. 17, Sec. 2)

constituent (kən stich′ü ənt), *n.* a voter in a legislator's district. (Ch. 14, Sec. 3)

constitution (kon′stə tü′shən, kon′stə-tyü′shən), *n.* the basic plan of government that sets up the government's framework, lists the powers and duties of its sections or parts, and describes the connection between the people and their government. (Ch. 1, *Law and Freedom*)

constitutional law law based on the Constitution or an interpretation of the Constitution described in a Supreme Court decision. (Ch. 10, Sec. 1)

consumer advocate person who works on getting consumer problems corrected. (Ch. 24, Sec. 3)

consumer goods items produced to be used up, such as food or clothing. (Ch. 22, Sec. 1)

containment (kən tān′mənt), *n.* the confinement of a possibly hostile political force in existing geographical boundaries; American policy, 1947 to the present, of limiting the expansion and influence of the Soviet Union. (Ch. 26, Sec. 2)

contingency fee lawyer's fee, usually one-fifth to one-half of the total money won in a lawsuit. (Ch. 16, Sec. 2)

continuance (kən tin′yü əns), *n.* postponement of a court date to allow lawyers time to gather evidence and prepare their case. (Ch. 16, Sec. 1)

contract (kon′trakt), *n.* a formal agreement between two parties that can be enforced by law. (Ch. 24, *Law and Freedom*)

contraction phase the phase of the business cycle in which production is cut back. (Ch. 22, Sec. 3)

convention (kən ven′shən), *n.* a meeting or gathering of people representing the sections of an organization; an assembly of delegates. (Ch. 3, Sec. 1)

cooperative (kō op′ər ə tiv), *n.* a business association that is set up to provide services for its own members. (Ch. 23, Sec. 1)

corporate income tax a tax on a corporation's profits. (Ch. 7, Sec. 1)

corporation (kôr′pə rā′shən), *n.* a business owned by its stockholders. Those who own stock in a corporation elect a board of directors who pick top management people to run the business. (Ch. 23, Sec. 1)

council (koun′səl), *n.* the legislative branch of most city governments. (Ch. 18, Sec. 1)

council-manager plan a plan of city government in which voters elect a council which hires, and can fire, a manager to carry out the laws. (Ch. 18, Sec. 1)

Council of Economic Advisers (CEA) unit of the Executive Office of the President that helps the President carry

out the role of economic leader. (Ch. 8, Sec. 3)

county (koun′tā) *n., pl.* **-ties.** a division of a state set up to help carry out state law. (Ch. 17, Sec. 1)

credit (kred′it), *n.* payment later for what you buy now. (Ch. 24, Sec. 2)

credit card a card that identifies its holder as entitled to charge goods and services. (Ch. 24, Sec. 2)

credit union a consumer cooperative that provides banking services. (Ch. 23, Sec. 1)

criminal case court case in which the government charges someone with a crime. (Ch. 16, Sec. 1)

custody (kus′tə dē), *n.* **in custody,** under someone's care; detained by the police. (Ch. 21, Sec. 2)

customs duty tax on a product brought into the United States. (Ch. 7, Sec. 1)

decision (di sizh′ən), *n.* choice among alternatives; a making up of one's mind. (Ch. 1, Sec. 1)

deduction (di duk′shən), *n.* **1.** an amount subtracted from the income tax a person has to pay, based on an allowable expense of some kind. **2.** conclusion that is the result of deductive thinking. (Ch. 7, Sec. 1 and Ch. 10, *Basic Social Studies Skills*)

deductive thinking type of thinking that requires the use of premises, or assumed truths. (Ch. 10, *Basic Social Studies Skills*)

defendant (di fen′dənt), *n.* a person accused of a crime or sued in a court of law. (Ch. 16, Sec. 1)

deficit (def′ə sit), *n.* shortage; the difference between income and greater expenses. (Ch. 7, Sec. 3)

deflation (di flā′shən), *n.* a decline in prices during the contraction phase of the business cycle. (Ch. 22, Sec. 3)

delegate (del′ə gāt, del′ə git), *n.* person sent to a convention to represent the people from one place; a person with power to act for others. (Ch. 3, Sec. 1)

denaturalization (dē nach′ər ə lə-zā′shən), *n.* loss of naturalized citizenship through proof that the citizenship was falsely obtained. (Ch. 1, Sec. 2)

Department of Defense the largest department in the executive branch of government in money spent and in civilian employment. The department helps form military policies and maintains the armed forces. (Ch. 26, Sec. 3)

Department of State department in the

executive branch of government headed by the Secretary of State and responsible for advising the President on foreign policy. (Ch. 26, Sec. 3)

depression (di presh′ən), *n.* a time when business activity slows down and many people are out of work. (Ch. 22, Sec. 3)

deregulate (dē reg′yə lāt), *v.* to remove regulations or restrictions placed on a business or industry. (Ch. 9, Sec. 1 and Ch. 23, Sec. 1)

developed country one of the twenty or so built-up nations of the world having a comparatively high standard of living based on business and industry. (Ch. 27, Sec. 2)

developing country one of the 100 or so poor nations that are trying to increase industry and business to raise the standard of living of their people. (Ch. 27, Sec. 2)

diplomat (dip′lə mat), *n.* person skilled in managing relations between nations. A nation's diplomats include its ambassadors, envoys, and chargés d'affaires. (Ch. 26, Sec. 3)

direct democracy democracy in which political decisions are made *directly* by the people rather than their elected representatives. (Ch. 1, Sec. 1 and Ch. 14, Sec. 4)

direct primary a preliminary election in which voters choose candidates to represent a political party in the general election. (Ch. 12, Sec. 3)

dispositional hearing a juvenile hearing at which a judge determines what shall be done with an offender. (Ch. 21, Sec. 2)

dissenting opinion an opinion of one or more judges who disagree with the court's decision. (Ch. 10, Sec. 3)

district court federal court where most federal cases are tried. Every state has at least one United States district court. (Ch. 10, Sec. 2)

domestic tranquility peace in all the states, with people's health, safety, and property free from threat. (Ch. 4, Sec. 1)

due process lawful treatment. A person is entitled to the protection of due process of law, with all the standard legal steps and no shortcuts, anytime government threatens his or her life, freedom, or property. (Ch. 5, Sec. 1)

duress (dù res′), *n.* use of force. The law does not require a person to fulfill a contract made under duress. (Ch. 24, *Law and Freedom*)

duties (dü′tēz), *n.pl.* taxes, including imposts, on imported goods.

economic leader person who guards the welfare of the people as a whole in their requirements for working, earning, and surviving. (Ch. 8, Sec. 2)

economic system a nation's way of producing and distributing goods and services. (Ch. 22, Sec. 2)

editorial (ed'ə tôr'ē əl, ed'ə tōr'ē əl), *n.* article in a newspaper or magazine giving the editor's or publisher's opinion on some subject; radio or television broadcast expressing the opinion of the program, station, or network. (Ch. 18, Sec. 3)

electoral college group of people chosen by the voters to elect the President and Vice-President of the United States. (Ch. 8, Sec. 1)

emolument (i mol'yə mənt), *n.* salary paid to someone for performing a job. (Ch. 8, Sec. 2)

entrepreneur (än'trə prə nėr'), *n.* person who organizes and manages a business, attempting to make a profit but taking the risk of a loss. (Ch. 23, Sec. 1)

entrepreneurship (än'trə prə nėr'ship), *n.* a type of business in which a person starts and accepts the risks of operating a business in a market economy. (Ch. 23, Sec. 1)

equal justice an ideal on which the legal system of the United States is based, that every person is treated the same under the law. (Ch. 10, Sec. 1)

equal-protection clause clause in the Fourteenth Amendment that declares that no state shall deny to any person the "equal protection of the law." (Ch. 14, *Law and Freedom*)

equity suit a civil case in which a person or group seeks to prevent some kind of damaging action by another person or group. (Ch. 16, Sec. 2)

estate tax a tax on money, property, and other valuables left by a person who has died. (Ch. 7, Sec. 1)

excise tax a tax on the manufacture, sale, or use of goods. (Ch. 7, Sec. 1)

exclusionary rule Supreme Court ruling that says that evidence obtained in violation of a person's Fourth Amendment rights may not be used in court as evidence against the person. (Ch. 19, *Law and Freedom*)

executive branch the branch of government that enforces laws. The executive branch of the national government is headed by the President. (Ch. 4, Sec. 2)

Executive Office of the President (EOP) large general staff that helps the President carry out the duties of being President. Many agencies are part of the EOP. (Ch. 8, Sec. 3)

executive order rule issued by the President, a governor, or an administrative authority, that has the effect of law. (Ch. 15, Sec. 2)

expansion phase the part of the business cycle in which business activity is increasing. (Ch. 22, Sec. 3)

expatriate (*n.*, ek spā'trē it, ek spā'trē āt; *v.*, ek spā'trē āt), *n., v.* —*n.* person who loses citizenship by becoming a citizen of another country; exile. —*v.* to withdraw from citizenship by becoming a citizen of another nation. (Ch. 1, Sec. 1)

expatriation (ek spā'trē ā'shən), *n.* the loss of citizenship by means of becoming a citizen of another nation. (Ch. 1, Sec. 2)

exports (ek'spôrts), *n.pl.* articles or goods that are sold to other nations. (Ch. 3, Sec. 2)

ex post facto law law that applies to actions committed before the law was passed. (Ch. 5, Sec. 1)

extradition (ek'strə dish'ən), *n.* return by one state to another of a person accused of a crime; surrender of a fugitive or prisoner to another state or nation for trial or punishment. (Ch. 4, Sec. 3)

factors of production the resources required to produce goods or services: natural resources, capital goods, labor, and entrepreneurship. (Ch. 23, Sec. 1)

federal agency a unit set up in the executive branch of government to carry out laws by running a government program, making rules, and settling disputes. (Ch. 9, Sec. 1)

federalism (fed'ər ə liz'əm), *n.* plan of government in which powers are divided between national and state governments. (Ch. 4, Sec. 3)

Federalist (fed'ər ə list), *n.* supporter of the new Constitution and a strong central or national government. (Ch. 3, Sec. 3)

federal judge a chief decision maker in the judicial branch of government. (Ch. 10, Sec. 2)

felony (fel'ə nē), *n., pl.* **-nies.** crime more serious than a misdemeanor. Armed robbery is a felony. (Ch. 16, Sec. 1)

fiscal year year-long period set up for budget purposes. (Ch. 7, Sec. 1)

fixed expense a necessary cost that stays the same from month to month. (Ch. 24, Sec. 1)

flexible expense a cost that changes from month to month. (Ch. 24, Sec. 1)

floor leader member of the House of Representatives (national or state), elected by members of his or her political party, who times the introduction of bills and organizes the voting of party members. (Ch. 6, Sec. 1 and Ch. 14, Sec. 2)

foreign policy the plans a national government makes about how to act toward other nations and groups. (Ch. 26, Sec. 1)

foreign-policy leader person who directs a country's relations with other nations. The President is foreign-policy leader in the United States. (Ch. 8, Sec. 2)

foster family court-appointed family that assumes temporary responsibility for a neglected or troubled child or juvenile. (Ch. 21, Sec. 2)

free enterprise the right of private business to select and run a business for profit with little government regulation. (Ch. 22, Sec. 2)

fringe benefits benefits received by an employee in addition to pay, such as insurance plans, retirement plans, and paid vacations. (Ch. 23, Sec. 2)

General Assembly central body of the United Nations, in which every member-nation has one vote. The General Assembly is sometimes described as the "town meeting of the world." (Ch. 27, Sec. 3)

general trial court a court of law that handles all major criminal and civil cases. (Ch. 16, Sec. 1)

general welfare good living conditions for all; people's health, happiness, and prosperity. (Ch. 4, Sec. 1)

gift tax a tax on any gift, including cash, that is worth more than a certain amount set by law. (Ch. 7, Sec. 1)

glittering generality propaganda technique of using broad, vague statements in support of one's views, avoiding specific ideas that can be debated or corrected. (Ch. 13, Sec. 2)

global interdependence the need of people around the earth for each other. Foreign interchanges of products, services, and information are indications of global interdependence. (Ch. 27, Sec. 1)

global issues problems that concern or affect a large segment of the world's population. (Ch. 27, Sec. 2)

goal (gōl), *n.* something a person or group tries to reach; something desired. (Ch. 1, Sec. 3)

goods (gủdz), *n.pl.* things for sale; products. (Ch. 22, Sec. 1)

government (guv'ərn mənt), *n.* group

that has power to make and enforce laws. In the United States, governments (local, state, and national) have the power and duty to furnish public services, settle conflicts, keep order, and provide security against outside threats. (Ch. 1, Sec. 3)

government corporation a business run by the government, such as the Federal Deposit Insurance Corporation which insures bank deposits. (Ch. 9, Sec. 1)

governor (guv′ər nər, guv′nər), *n.* chief executive officer in state government. (Ch. 15, *Introduction*)

grand jury panel of people chosen to investigate accusations of crime and decide whether there is enough evidence for a trial in court. (Ch. 5, Sec. 1)

grants-in-aid (grants′in ād′), *n.pl.* contributions from the national government to a state or local government for specific programs. States also issue grants-in-aid to local governments. (Ch. 7, Sec. 2 and Ch. 17, Sec. 3)

grass roots neighborhood level; the ordinary citizens. (Ch. 12, Sec. 1)

gross national product (GNP) the total value of goods and services produced for money in a country during a year. (Ch. 22, Sec. 3)

guarantee (gar′ən tē′), *n., v.* —*n.* a pledge to replace or repair a purchased product or return the money if the product is not as represented. —*v.* to stand behind one's merchandise. (Ch. 24, Sec. 1)

head of state person who represents all the people of a nation in greeting people, awarding honors, and filling other ceremonial requirements. (Ch. 8, Sec. 2)

hearing (hir′ing), *n.* a public information-gathering session of a legislative committee; a formal listening to evidence. (Ch. 21, Sec. 2)

human resources the skills, knowledge, energy, and physical capabilities of people. (Ch. 21, Sec. 1)

hung jury a jury that is unable to reach a unanimous verdict. (Ch. 16, Sec. 2 and Ch. 21, *Law and Freedom*)

hypothesis (hī poth′ə sis), *n.* something assumed because it seems likely to be a true explanation. (Ch. 13, *Basic Social Studies Skills*)

ideal (ī dē′əl), *n.* **1.** belief about the way something should be; goal. **2.** a perfect type; model to be imitated. (Ch. 5, *Introduction*)

immigrant (im′ə grənt), *n.* person from a foreign country who comes into a country to stay. (Ch. 1, Sec. 2)

imports (im′pôrtz), *n.pl.* goods or services purchased by one nation from another nation. (Ch. 3, Sec. 2)

independent executive agency unit of the executive branch of government set up to do a special job not covered by any Cabinet department (Ch. 9, Sec. 1)

independent voter person who votes for a person or an issue, regardless of political party. (Ch. 12, Sec. 2)

indictment (in dīt′mənt), *n.* formal charge against an accused person, made by the prosecutor or by the grand jury. (Ch. 16, Sec. 2)

inductive thinking thinking that involves using information about parts of the whole to draw general conclusions about the whole. (Ch. 9, *Basic Social Studies Skills*)

inflation (in fla′shən), *n.* a general increase in prices of goods and services during the later stages of the expansion phase of the business cycle. (Ch. 22, Sec. 3)

initiative (i nish′ē ə tiv), *n.* procedure by which citizens introduce new laws. (Ch. 11, Sec. 2)

injunction (in jungk′shən), *n.* a judge's order to a person or group to stop doing something that might do harm to others. (Ch. 16, Sec. 2)

Inner Cabinet Cabinet members who have an important influence upon the decisions made by the President. (Ch. 8, Sec. 3)

interest (in′tər ist), *n.* money paid for the use of money. (Ch. 7, Sec. 1)

interest group organization of people who share common beliefs and interests, and who try to influence government decisions. (Ch. 11, Sec. 1)

irrelevant (i rel′ə vənt), *adj.* not to the point; off the subject. (Ch. 12, *Basic Social Studies Skills*)

isolationism (ī′sə lā′shə niz′əm, is′ə-lā′shə niz′əm), *n.* principle or policy of avoiding political and economic relations with other nations. (Ch. 26, Sec. 1)

issue (ish′ü), *n.* matter of dispute or discussion representing an occasion for decision. (Ch. 2, Sec. 1)

joint committee a committee with members from both houses of the legislature, selected to consider problems and bills in a particular field. (Ch. 6, Sec. 1)

judgment (juj′mənt), *n.* opinion about the worth of an action, object, idea, or person. (Ch. 2, Sec. 2)

judicial branch the branch of government that judges laws and decides legal cases. The courts are in the judicial branch of government. (Ch. 4, Sec. 2)

judicial review the power of the courts to declare acts of the legislative or executive branches unconstitutional. (Ch. 10, Sec. 3)

jurisdiction (jùr′is dik′shən), *n.* authority to judge and administer the law. (Ch. 10, Sec. 1)

jury (jùr′ē), *n.* group of persons selected to hear evidence in a court of law and give a decision in accordance with the evidence presented to them. (Ch. 21, *Law and Freedom*)

juvenile court a special court that deals with juvenile delinquency. (Ch. 21, Sec. 2)

juvenile delinquency violation of the law by a person considered to be legally a minor. In most states, a juvenile is anyone under eighteen. (Ch. 21, Sec. 2)

label (lā′bəl), *n.* a tag attached to anything and marked with information about the item. (Ch. 24, Sec. 1)

labor union an organization of workers that seeks to improve working conditions and pay through collective bargaining. (Ch. 23, Sec. 2)

laws (lôz), *n.pl.* rules made by government. (Ch. 1, Sec. 3)

lawsuit (lô′süt′), *n.* case in a court of law started by one person to claim something from another. (Ch. 16, Sec. 2)

legislative branch the branch of government that makes laws. Congress is the legislative branch of the national government. (Ch. 4, Sec. 2)

legislative districts areas in each state that are represented by lawmakers in Congress and state legislatures. (Ch. 13, *Law and Freedom*)

legislative program the group of bills a President, governor, or legislator will introduce and work to get passed. (Ch. 8, Sec. 2)

legislature (lej′ə slā′chər), *n.* group of persons that has the duty and power of making laws for a state or nation. (Ch. 1, *Law and Freedom*)

letters-to-the-editor a section of a newspaper containing letters of opinion by people not connected with the paper. (Ch. 18, Sec. 3)

libel (lī′bəl), *n., v.* —*n.* a written or published statement, picture, etc., tending to damage a person's reputation. —*v.* to write or publish a libel. (Ch. 5, Sec. 1)

lieutenant governor public official next in rank to the governor of a state. (Ch. 15, Sec. 1)

life expectancy average number of years a person or a group of persons live. (Ch. 27, Sec. 2)

limited liability having only certain obligations and no others. Limited liability is one of the advantages of organizing a business as a corporation. (Ch. 23, Sec. 1)

limited war a war fought without the use of nuclear weapons and for objectives other than complete defeat of the enemy. (Ch. 26, Sec. 2)

line graph graph in which points representing quantities are plotted and then connected by a series of short straight lines. (Ch. 5, *Basic Social Studies Skills*)

lobbyist (lob′ē ist), *n.* person hired by a special interest group to influence government decision makers. (Ch. 6, Sec. 2)

lower courts courts that hear only special cases, usually only minor violations of state law or lawsuits involving small amounts of money. (Ch. 16, Sec. 1)

loyalty (loi′əl tē), *n.* a feeling of faithfulness to a friend, group, or nation. Loyalty to a friend can make a person defend that friend, even against heavy odds. (Ch. 1, Sec. 1)

magistrate (maj′ə strāt, maj′ə strit), *n.* a minor judicial officer with power to try cases for lesser offenses. A federal magistrate holds preliminary hearings in federal criminal cases and helps with the work of the federal district court. (Ch. 10, Sec. 2)

majority party in either legislative chamber, the political party having the most members. (Ch. 6, Sec. 1)

majority rule political doctrine that choices are made by more than half of the members of a group. (Ch. 1, Sec. 1)

major party one of the two main political parties; Republican Party or Democratic Party. (Ch. 12, Sec. 1)

manager (man′ə jər), *n.* director; person who runs a business, a department, a city, etc. (Ch. 18, Sec. 1)

mandatory referendum type of referendum that requires that certain bills be referred to the voters before they become law. (Ch. 14, Sec. 4)

market system, pure an economy in which consumers and producers make all economic decisions. (Ch. 22, Sec. 2)

marshal (mär′shəl), *n.* the official who performs police duties in connection with a federal district court. The United States marshal is in the Department of Justice. (Ch. 10, Sec. 2)

massive retaliation the use of all one's weapons, especially nuclear weapons, upon provocation. (Ch. 26, Sec. 2)

mass media the forms of communication, such as the press, TV, and radio, which reach large numbers of people. (Ch. 9, Sec. 3)

maturity (mə chur′ə tē), *n.* time a note or debt is payable. (Ch. 7, Sec. 1)

Mayflower Compact the agreement to form a government, signed by men on the Pilgrim ship *Mayflower* before landing at Plymouth. (Ch. 1, Sec. 1)

mayor (mā′ər), *n.* the main executive official in most American cities. (Ch. 18, Sec. 1)

mayor-council plan a plan of city government with an elected mayor for executive officer and elected council members for a law-making body. (Ch. 18, Sec. 1)

megalopolis (meg′ə lop′ə lis), *n.* an area where large metropolitan areas have started to overlap; a large metropolitan area, often including several cities. (Ch. 19, Sec. 1)

merit system system under which federal employees are hired because of their particular abilities and skills. (Ch. 9, Sec. 2)

metropolitan area a large city with its nearby suburbs and small towns. (Ch. 19, Sec. 1)

minority party in either legislative chamber, the major political party having fewer members than the other party. (Ch. 6, Sec. 1)

minor party a political party with few supporters compared to the major parties. (Ch. 12, Sec. 1)

minutes (min′its), *n.pl.* the formal notes of what happens at a meeting of a club, board, committee, or other group. (Ch. 20, Sec. 2)

misdemeanor (mis′di mē′nər), *n.* least serious crime or breaking of a law, such as a minor traffic offense. (Ch. 16, Sec. 1)

Missouri Plan plan that combines election and appointment to choose judges. (Ch. 16, Sec. 1)

monopoly (mə nop′ə lē), *n., pl.* **-lies.** a business with no competition; exclusive control of a product or service people want to buy. (Ch. 23, Sec. 1)

Monroe Doctrine doctrine that European nations—including Russia—should not interfere with American nations or try to acquire more territory in the Western Hemisphere. (Ch. 26, Sec. 1)

municipal charter a local constitution granted by the state to a heavily populated community. (Ch. 17, Sec. 1)

municipality (myü nis′ə pal′ə tē), *n., pl.* **-ties.** city, town or other district having local self-government under a charter granted by the state. (Ch. 17, Sec. 1)

name-calling (nām′kô′ling), *n.* propaganda technique of labeling an opponent in a bad way. (Ch. 13, Sec. 2)

national debt a nation's total indebtedness to lenders. (Ch. 7, Sec. 1)

National Emergencies Act law that requires Presidents to inform Congress in advance of the need to declare a national emergency. (Ch. 8, Sec. 1)

National Security Council President's advisory group on foreign policy. (Ch. 8, Sec. 3 and Ch. 26, Sec. 3)

national supremacy the constitutional principle that national government is the highest law in the land, and that no state can pass a law that goes against the Constitution. (Ch. 4, Sec. 3)

naturalized citizen person who becomes a citizen of a nation through a legal process designed by the nation. (Ch. 1, Sec. 2)

natural resources the supplies that come from nature, or from the earth, such as soil, water, and minerals. (Ch. 22, Sec. 1)

news story factual article in a newspaper. (Ch. 18, Sec. 3)

nominate (nom′ə nāt), *v.* to name as candidate for an office. (Ch. 8, Sec. 1)

nominating committee group of people that selects candidates for office. (Ch. 20, Sec. 2)

nomination (nom′ə nā′shən), *n.* selection of candidates for the ballots in an election. (Ch. 12, Sec. 3)

nonpartisan (non pär′tə zən), *adj.* not identified with either major political party. (Ch. 18, Sec. 2)

Office of Management and Budget (OMB) agency in the executive branch of the national government that prepares the federal budget. (Ch. 8, Sec. 3)

Office of Personnel Management the central personnel agency of the national government, charged with impartially selecting among job applicants and with carrying out laws about fairness in government employment. (Ch. 9, Sec. 2)

ombudsman (om budz′mən), *n.* a government official with the power to investigate a citizen's complaint against a public official. (Ch. 15, Sec. 3)

open primary a nominating election in which qualified voters may take part without telling their party preference. (Ch. 12, Sec. 3)

open shop contract allowing each worker to join the union or not. (Ch. 23, Sec. 2)

opinion (ə pin′yən), *n.* statement by a judge of the reasons for a court decision. (Ch. 5, *Case Study*)

optional referendum referendum that requires that certain bills, often those dealing with taxes, must be referred to the voters before they become law. (Ch. 14, Sec. 4)

ordinance (ord′n əns), *n.* a local law. (Ch. 17, Sec. 2)

parish (par′ish), *n.* in Louisiana, a district similar to a county. (Ch. 17, Sec. 1)

parliamentary procedure structured rules and procedures for conducting a formal meeting. (Ch. 20, Sec. 2)

partnership (pärt′nər ship), *n.* a business owned by two or more people who share the costs, profits, and responsibilities of the business. (Ch. 23, Sec. 1)

party chief leader of his or her political party. (Ch. 8, Sec. 2)

party convention method of nomination in which party members pick delegates in all parts of the state, then the delegates meet and select candidates; meeting at which candidates are chosen. (Ch. 12, Sec. 3)

party platform written series of statements on election issues that a particular party stands for. (Ch. 12, Sec. 2)

party whip member of Senate or House of Representatives whose job it is to keep after members of the same political party to get their votes registered when a bill is on the floor. (Ch. 6, Sec. 1)

patriotism (pā′trē ə tiz′əm), *n.* loyalty to a country or nation; love and support of one's country. (Ch. 1, Sec. 1)

patronage (pā′trə nij, pat′rə nij), *n.* power to give jobs or favors. (Ch. 14, Sec. 3)

peak phase the part of the business cycle in which production is at full capacity. (Ch. 22, Sec. 3)

Pendleton Act act that limited the spoils system and created the civil service system (Ch. 9, Sec. 2)

peremptory challenge lawyer's privilege of being able to dismiss a certain number of jurors without giving a reason for their dismissal. (Ch. 21, *Law and Freedom*)

personal income the total money earned by all individuals, measured before taxes; the PI. (Ch. 22, Sec. 3)

personal income tax tax charged on the income each person earns in a year. (Ch. 7, Sec. 1)

personal staff people who work directly for a senator or representative. (Ch. 6, Sec. 2)

petition (pə tish′ən), *n., v.* —*n.* a request signed by qualified voters asking that a wrong be corrected or that a particular candidate or issue be on the ballot. —*v.* to ask the government for a corrective action, a right guaranteed by the First and Fourteenth Amendments. (Ch. 12, Sec. 3)

petition referendum the most common type of referendum. This referendum allows voters to change or reject a bill after it has been passed by the legislature and signed into law by a governor. (Ch. 14, Sec. 4)

plain folks propaganda technique of influencing people to think one is just like them—a worker among workers, a farmer among farmers, etc. (Ch. 13, Sec. 2)

plaintiff (plān′tif), *n.* person who begins a lawsuit. (Ch. 16, Sec. 2)

plank (plangk), *n.* a position statement from a party platform giving the party view on an election issue. Support for federal aid to education is often a plank in both parties' platforms. (Ch. 12, Sec. 2)

plea bargaining arrangement between a prosecutor and an accused person (or the defense lawyer) to exchange a guilty plea from the accused for a reduced charge or promise of leniency. (Ch. 16, Sec. 2)

pocket veto a special way the President can veto a bill. The pocket veto is only possible with bills the President receives in the last ten days of a legislative session. If the President does not sign the bill (carries it around in a pocket is the implication), it is the same as a veto. (Ch. 6, Sec. 3)

police state state in which the government exercises great power. Police states have little or no regard for personal freedoms or liberties. (Ch. 1, Sec. 4)

political action committee (PAC) members of a special interest group who collect contributions from the group and then use the money to back political candidates. (Ch. 11, Sec. 2)

political party an association of voters who organize to elect members to public office, operate government, and determine public policy. (Ch. 12, Sec. 1)

political resource time, money, skill, or information available to influence government decisions. (Ch. 11, Sec. 2)

polling place a location where voting takes place. (Ch. 12, Sec. 3)

poll tax a tax one must pay in order to vote. The Twenty-Fourth Amendment prohibits poll taxes in federal elections. (Ch. 5, Sec. 1)

popular vote the votes cast by the voters as a whole. (Ch. 8, Sec. 1)

practical (prak′tə kəl), *adj.* useful; having strong possibility that results wanted will be achieved. (Ch. 2, Sec. 2)

Preamble (prē′am′bəl), *n.* preface or introduction to the Constitution, naming goals for the United States. (Ch. 1, *Law and Freedom*)

precedent (pres′ə dənt), *n.* legal decision in a preceding case; action or case that serves as a pattern in future cases that are similar. (Ch. 10, Sec. 3 and Ch. 16, Sec. 3)

precinct (prē′singkt), *n.* **1** neighborhood election district. **2** district within certain boundaries, such as a police precinct. (Ch. 12, Sec. 1)

preliminary hearing a procedure in a criminal case to protect an accused person from being held if there is not sufficient cause. The judge examines the accused and decides whether or not the person should be held for trial. (Ch. 16, Sec. 2)

premise (prem′is), *n.* a statement assumed to be true and used to draw a conclusion. (Ch. 10, *Basic Social Studies Skills*)

preside (pri zīd′), *v.* to have charge of a meeting, seeing that speakers have a chance to be heard, keeping order, and urging the group to finish its business. (Ch. 3, Sec. 2)

president of the senate leader and presiding officer of the state senate, often the lieutenant governor. (Ch. 14, Sec. 2)

president pro tempore officer elected by the Senate to be chairperson in the absence of the Vice-President of the United States. (Ch. 6, Sec. 1)

presiding officer person in charge of a meeting. (Ch. 14, Sec. 2)

prestige (pre stēzh′, pre stēj′), *n.* reputation, influence, or distinction. (Ch. 14, Sec. 3)

primary election election at which voters decide who their party's candidate will be in the general election. (Ch. 8, Sec. 1)

priority (prī ôr′ə tē, prī or′ə tē), *n., pl.* **-ties.** what comes first; preference in order of importance. (Ch. 7, Sec. 3)

private property property that is owned by individual citizens. (Ch. 22, Sec. 2)

probation (prō bā′shən), *n.* system of letting juvenile offenders go free under supervision. Commonly used for first-time offenders. (Ch. 21, Sec. 2)

probation officer person appointed by a court to supervise offenders who have been placed on probation. (Ch. 21, Sec. 2)

profit (prof′it), *n.* the money left over after the cost of doing business has been subtracted from a company's income. (Ch. 7, Sec. 1 and Ch. 23, Sec. 1)

proletariat (prō′lə ter′ē ət), *n.* in socialist and communist writing, a word that means "working-class people." (Ch. 26, Sec. 2)

propaganda technique a means used to carry out a plan for spreading opinions or beliefs. (Ch. 13, Sec. 2)

property tax local tax on the value of property a person or business owns. (Ch. 17, Sec. 3)

proposition (prop′ə zish′ən), *n.* a procedure that allows citizens to propose laws for the approval of voters during an election. Propositions are also called initiatives. (Ch. 14, Sec. 4)

prosecutor (pros′ə kyü′tər), *n.* lawyer in charge of the government's side of a case against an accused person. (Ch. 16, Sec. 2)

protective tariff a customs tax that protects an American product from competition with foreign-made goods. The tariff raises the price of the foreign-made goods. (Ch. 7, Sec. 1)

public defender lawyer designated by a court, and paid from public funds, to defend accused persons who cannot afford to hire their own lawyer. (Ch. 10, *Law and Freedom*)

public employee person employed by a government. (Ch. 18, Sec. 3)

public housing project apartment buildings built with public money. (Ch. 19, Sec. 2)

public interest group an interest group that works to influence government on issues it believes are good for most citizens. (Ch. 11, Sec. 1)

public opinion what people think; citizens' views, attitudes, or beliefs. (Ch. 8, Sec. 4)

public property property that is owned by a government. (Ch. 22, Sec. 2)

public services actions of government carried on for people's health, safety, employment, or other common benefit. (Ch. 1, Sec. 4)

pure command economy (*See* command economy)

pure market economy (*See* market economy)

rapid transit system trains used to move people around a city. (Ch. 19, Sec. 2)

ratify (rat′ə fī), *v.* to approve; confirm in a formal way, as by a vote. (Ch. 3, Sec. 3)

real case rule a requirement of the Supreme Court in deciding whether a law agrees with the Constitution. The Supreme Court will not consider a case unless a law has been broken or a person has claimed injury from the carrying out of a law. (Ch. 10, Sec. 3)

recall procedure by which a public official can be removed from office before his or her term has expired by vote of the people. (Ch. 14, Sec. 4)

recession (ri sesh′ən), *n.* a period of slow business activity that is less serious than a depression. (Ch. 22, Sec. 3)

referee (ref′ə rē′), *n.* person who makes recommendations to a judge concerning the best way to deal with particular juvenile offenders. (Ch. 21, Sec. 2)

referendum (ref′ə ren′dəm), *n.* process of referring certain types of bills to the voters for approval or rejection. (Ch. 11, Sec. 2)

reformatory (ri fôr′mə tôr′ē), *n., pl.* **-ries.** an institution for reforming juvenile offenders. (Ch. 21, Sec. 2)

regulate (reg′yə lāt), *v.* to control by rule, principle, or system. (Ch. 9, Sec. 1)

regulatory commission a board, usually of three or more people, chosen to direct a particular government function. The Federal Communications Commission, for example, regulates interstate and foreign radio, television, telephone, telegraph, and cable communications. (Ch. 9, Sec. 1)

relevant (rel′ə vənt), *adj.* bearing upon or connected with the matter at hand. (Ch. 12, *Basic Social Studies Skills*)

representative democracy type of democratic government in which people elect representatives to act for them in making laws and decisions. The United States is a representative democracy. (Ch. 1, Sec. 1 and Ch. 14, Sec. 4)

respect (ri spekt′), *n., v.* —*n.* high regard, honor, or esteem for someone or something of recognized worth. —*v.* to feel or show honor or esteem for. (Ch. 5, Sec. 3)

responsibility (ri spon′sə bil′ə tē), *n., pl.* **-ties.** duty or obligation. (Ch. 5, Sec. 3)

revenue sharing a turning over of tax money by the national government to state and local governments, with little restriction on its use. States also issue revenue sharing money to local governments. (Ch. 7, Sec. 2 and Ch. 17, Sec. 3)

rider (rī′dər), *n.* anything added to a record, document, bill, or statement after it was supposed to be completed. (Ch. 8, Law and Freedom)

right-to-work laws laws that prohibit both closed shops and union shops. (Ch. 23, Sec. 2)

Rules Committee powerful committee in the House of Representatives that decides on the rules for debate on bills. (Ch. 6, Sec. 3)

sales receipt a written record, showing the amount of a sale. (Ch. 24, Sec. 1)

savings and loan association a banklike institution that specializes in large loans such as the kind given when people buy houses. (Ch. 24, Sec. 2)

scarcity (sker′sə tē, skar′sə tē), *n., pl.* **-ties.** the basic economic problem of limited resources and unlimited wants; too small a supply to meet the demand or satisfy the need. (Ch. 22, Sec. 1)

search warrant court order or legal paper allowing police to search a place where there is good reason to believe evidence of a crime will be found. (Ch. 5, Sec. 1)

secretary of state an executive officer in the national government or in one of thirty-nine state governments. The President's Secretary of State advises on foreign affairs. In most states, the secretary of state manages elections, official records, licenses, and permits. (Ch. 15, Sec. 1)

secret operations government actions in another country that are kept under cover. (Ch. 26, Sec. 2)

security (si kyùr′ə tē), *n., pl.* **-ties. 1** freedom from danger; feeling of being safe. (Ch. 1, Sec. 4) **2** Usually, **securities,** *pl.* bond or stock certificates. (Ch. 7, Sec. 1)

Security Council a major body within the United Nations, having five permanent member-nations and ten members elected for two-year terms. The Security Council has the power to send out troops. (Ch. 27, Sec. 3)

segregation (seg′rə gā′shən), *n.* separation of one race, people, etc., from another or from the rest of society. (Ch. 5, Sec. 2)

self-nomination (self′nom′ə nā′shən), *n.* announcement by a person not on the ballot that he or she is a candidate requesting a write-in vote. (Ch. 12, Sec. 3)

senatorial courtesy a tradition that allows any senator of the President's political party to "veto" a person nominated for judge in his or her state. (Ch. 10, Sec. 2)

seniority rule custom of making the majority party member with the most years on a committee the chairperson. (Ch. 6, Sec. 1)

seniority system job security based on length of service. In case of a layoff, those on the job the most years would be the last to be laid off. (Ch. 23, Sec. 2)

service charge a bill from a government agency for a certain kind of service, such as water supply or garbage collection. (Ch. 17, Sec. 3)

services (sèr′vi siz), *n.pl.* what people do in exchange for something of value; work done in the service of others rather than in the production of goods. (Ch. 22, Sec. 1)

shared tax a tax created and collected by a state, with part of the money going to local governments and part to the state government. (Ch. 17, Sec. 3)

shares of stock certificates of ownership of a corporation. (Ch. 23, Sec. 1)

single proprietorship a business owned by one person. (Ch. 23, Sec. 1)

slate (slāt), *n., v.* —*n.* list of candidates to be considered for appointment, nomination, or election. —*v.* to list for an office, a promotion, or other event. (Ch. 20, Sec. 2)

slum (slum), *n.* an old, dirty, run-down part of a city. (Ch. 19, Sec. 2)

small claims court a court that handles cases involving small amounts of money, usually a maximum of $200. (Ch. 16, Sec. 1)

socialism (sō′shə liz′əm), *n.* an economic system in which major industries are owned by government but smaller industries are owned by individual citizens. (Ch. 22, Sec. 2)

social security tax money people pay as tax, most of which is used to provide income for retired persons, their dependents, and survivors. (Ch. 7, Sec. 1)

speaker of the House the presiding officer and most powerful leader in the national or a state house of representatives, a member of the majority party. (Ch. 6, Sec. 1 and Ch. 14, Sec. 2)

special committee a committee set up to do a special job, disbanding when the job is done. (Ch. 6, Sec. 1)

special district a local government set up to supply one or a few special services. A school district is a kind of special district. (Ch. 17, Sec. 1)

special interest group organization of people who have some common interest and who try to influence the decisions of government officials. (Ch. 6, Sec. 3)

special session an extra series of meetings of the legislature called at a time when it usually does not assemble. (Ch. 14, Sec. 3)

split ticket a vote for some candidates from one party and some candidates from another. (Ch. 13, Sec. 1)

staff agencies agencies created by Congress to investigate and support matters dealing with proposed legislation and to monitor the work of certain federal agencies. (Ch. 6, Sec. 2)

Standard Metropolitan Statistical Area (SMSA) any area including city and suburbs that has a population of 50,000 or more. (Ch. 19, Sec. 1)

standard of living the level of comfort a person or community enjoys through available goods and services. (Ch. 22, Sec. 3) ˙

standing committee a permanent legislative committee that continues its work from session to session. (Ch. 6, Sec. 1 and Ch. 14, Sec. 2)

state agency a department, board, or commission in a state government. (Ch. 15, Sec. 3)

state auditor person elected to watch over state funds and make sure all money is accounted for. Thirty-one states have a person in this job. (Ch. 15, Sec. 1)

state supreme court the highest court in each state. It reviews cases appealed from general trial courts and the appellate courts. (Ch. 16, Sec. 1)

state treasurer person elected to be in charge of collecting state funds and paying the state's bills. Forty-nine states elect treasurers. (Ch. 15, Sec. 1)

station adjustment the release of a juvenile offender by the police to his or her parents. (Ch. 21, Sec. 2)

statutes (stach′üts), *n.pl.* laws enacted by a legislative body. (Ch. 1, *Law and Freedom*)

statutory law law made by a law-making body such as Congress, a state legislature, or a city council. (Ch. 10, Sec. 1)

stockholder (stok′hōl′dər), *n.* person owning shares of stock in a company. (Ch. 23, Sec. 1)

straight ticket a vote for all the candidates in one party. (Ch. 13, Sec. 1)

strike (strīk), *n., v.* —*n.* a stopping of work by employees to force agreement of the employer to improved pay or conditions of employment. —*v.* to stop work to get better pay or working conditions. (Ch. 23, Sec. 1)

strong mayor a mayor who has broad powers to appoint, to shape the budget, to suggest laws, and to veto bills from the council. (Ch. 18, Sec. 2)

subcommittee (sub′kə mit′ē), *n.* a small committee chosen from and acting under a larger general committee for some special duty. (Ch. 6, Sec. 1)

subway (sub′wā′), *n.* part of a rapid transit system that runs underground; an electric railroad running beneath the surface of streets in a city. (Ch. 19, Sec. 2)

tax (taks), *n., v.* —*n.* fee that people must pay to support the government. —*v.* to put a fee or charge on, for government support. (Ch. 7, Sec. 1)

taxable income amount of a person's income that is taxed. (Ch. 7, Sec. 1)

technology (tek nol′ə jē), *n.* the science of the mechanical and industrial arts; the capital goods that workers use. (Ch. 22, Sec. 3)

testify (tes′tə fī), *v.* to give opinions and facts about a bill being considered; give evidence. (Ch. 6, Sec. 2)

testimonial (tes′tə mō′nē əl), *n.* form of propaganda utilizing the statements of trustworthy, sometimes popular, people to sell a product, service, or idea. (Ch. 13, Sec. 2)

third party an independent political party, often organized as a protest movement, that succeeds in becoming a temporary challenger to the two major parties. (Ch. 12, Sec. 1)

time line a chart that shows the order in which events happened. (Ch. 11, *Basic Social Studies Skills*)

title of nobility name showing high rank or position of honor, such as countess, prince, or duke. The United States government may not grant titles of nobility. (Ch. 4, Sec. 2)

totalitarian society people governed by one political group which controls many aspects of citizens' lives and suppresses opposition. (Ch. 20, Sec. 3)

township (toun′ship), *n.* part of a

county, having certain powers of government. (Ch. 17, Sec. 1)

transfer (*n.* tran′sfèr′; *v.* tran sfèr′, tran′sfèr′), *n., v.—n.* propaganda technique of associating something everyone thinks is good with a candidate, idea, or product. —*v.* to give approval to someone because of his or her association with something one thinks is good. (Ch. 13, Sec. 2)

treason (trē′zn), *n.* most serious crime against a government; in the United States, carrying on war against the United States or helping its enemies. (Ch. 1, Sec. 2)

treaty (trē′tē), *n., pl.* **-ties.** agreement between governments of two or more countries, signed and approved by each nation. (Ch. 4, Sec. 3)

trough phase the part of the business cycle in which economic activity hits its lowest point. (Ch. 22, Sec. 3)

two-party system political order in which two major parties generally compete at election time, with one of the two winning. (Ch. 12, Sec. 1)

unanimous (yü nan′ə məs), *adj.* agreed on by all. (Ch. 3, Sec. 2 and Ch. 21, *Law and Freedom*)

unbiased (un bī′əst), *adj.* not prejudiced; impartial; fair. (Ch. 12, *Basic Social Studies Skills*)

unconstitutional (un′kon stə tü′shə nəl, un′kon stə tyü′shə nəl), *adj.* contrary to the Constitution. (Ch. 10, Sec. 3)

unicameral legislature a legislature with one house. (Ch. 14, Sec. 1)

union shop union-employer contract that says workers who are hired must join the union within a certain period of time. (Ch. 23, Sec. 2)

unitary government plan of government in which the central government has all the power. (Ch. 4, Sec. 3)

United Nations an international organization of about 150 nations working to promote peace, friendly relations between nations, and the solving of global problems. (Ch. 27, Sec. 3)

United States attorney the lawyer for the Department of Justice who prosecutes violations of federal law in each federal district court. (Ch. 10, Sec. 2)

unit price the cost of one part—one ounce, one quart, one inch, one meter, etc. (Ch. 24, Sec. 1)

urban area a center of population and business activity having 2,500 people or more. (Ch. 17, Sec. 2)

urban renewal the tearing down of slums to replace them with new buildings. (Ch. 19, Sec. 2)

utilities (yü til′ə tēz), *n.pl.* legal monopolies that provide services such as gas, water, sewage disposal, and electricity. (Ch. 23, Sec. 1)

values (val′yüz), *n.pl.* things people think are important or good. (Ch. 2, Sec. 1)

veto (vē′tō), *v., n., pl.* **-toes.** —*v.* to reject; refuse to consent to. —*n.* rejection; right or power of a President, governor, or such officer, to reject bills passed by a lawmaking body. (Ch. 4, Sec. 2)

vocational school school that teaches specific trades and crafts. (Ch. 25, Sec. 2)

voluntary exchange the buying and selling process that takes place in a pure market economy. (Ch. 22, Sec. 2)

voluntary group a group of people who work together for no pay to help others. (Ch. 20, Sec. 1)

volunteer (vol′ən tir′), *n., v.* —*n.* a person who gives time and effort, without pay, for the benefit of others. —*v.* to offer one's services. (Ch. 5, Sec. 3 and Ch. 20, Sec. 1)

voter registration period during which a state allows its voters to register to vote for an upcoming election. (Ch. 13, Sec. 1)

ward system a way of choosing members of a city council by electing one representative from each ward or section of the city. (Ch. 18, Sec. 2)

War Powers Act law passed in 1973 that limits the President's power to send troops into combat without a declaration of war by Congress. (Ch. 8, Sec. 4)

warranty (wôr′ən tē, wor′ən tē), *n., pl.* **-ties.** a pledge that something is what it is claimed to be. (Ch. 24, Sec. 1)

watchdog agency a government regulatory commission, responsible for protecting the public by setting up and enforcing rules within an industry that carry out the law. (Ch. 9, Sec. 1)

weak mayor a mayor who has limited power, power being with the council and other officials. (Ch. 18, Sec. 2)

White House Office group of people close to the daily work of the President, who help him or her to use time only on important matters others cannot handle. The White House Office is part of the Executive Office of the President. (Ch. 8, Sec. 3)

White House Staff a President's top advisers, including the press secretary, counsel to the President, and assistant for national security affairs. (Ch. 8, Sec. 3)

winner-take-all unit system by which the party winning the most popular votes in a state receives all of the state's electoral votes. (Ch. 8, Sec. 1)

writ (rit), *n.* a formal written order issued by a court. (Ch. 5, Sec. 1)

write-in candidate a candidate not on the ballot. (Ch. 13, Sec. 1)

writ of *habeas corpus* order requiring that a prisoner be brought before a judge or court to decide whether he or she is being held lawfully. This writ is a protection against unjust imprisonment. (Ch. 5, Sec. 1)

writ of mandamus a judge's order to a person or group to do what someone has a legal right to expect will be done. (Ch. 16, Sec. 2)

zoning ordinance a law about how land may be used in a particular area. (Ch. 19, Sec. 2)

Index

Acknowledgments

Quoted Material
112 © 1963 by Martin Luther King, Jr. Reprinted by permission of Joan Daves. 412 ©, 1981, *Los Angeles Times*. Reprinted by permission.

Illustrations
Positions of photographs are shown in abbreviated form as follows: top (t), bottom (b), center (c), left (l), right (r). All photographs not credited are the property of Scott, Foresman and Company.

Cover photo: © **1983 Peter B. Kaplan**
II Howard Millard 2 George Schaub 5, 6, 7 (l), 8 (t) Michael Goss/Scott, Foresman 7 (r) Steven E. Sutton/Duomo 8 (b) Paul Conklin 11 (t) International Museum of Photography at George Eastman House (b) Tom McCarthy/Hillstrom Stock Photo 14 (l) Bill Grimes/Black Star (r) Suzanne J. Engelmann 15 Randy Taylor/Sygma 16 P. Ledru/Sygma 17 © Kerby Smith 1985 18 Burt Glinn/Magnum 19 Michael Goss/Scott, Foresman 20 Information and Tourism Department, State of Wisconsin 22 C.S. Powell/U.S. Coast Guard 23 James Pozarik/Picture Group 27 Jim Anderson/Woodfin Camp 28 (t) Kim Komenich/San Francisco Examiner (b) Tim Davis/Focus West 29 Alan Tannenbaum/Sygma 30 (t) Daily Herald staff photo (b) Dave Tonge 32 Gregory Heisler, LIFE Magazine © 1979 Time Inc. 34 (all) John Running 40 Cary Wolinsky/Stock, Boston 43 (t) Independence National Historical Park Collection, Eastern Parks and Monuments Association (b) Rare Book Division, New York Public Library, Astor, Lenox and Tilden Foundations 44 The Metropolitan Museum of Art, Rogers Fund, 1907 45 (l) New York Public Library, Astor, Lenox and Tilden Foundations (r) Historical Society of Pennsylvania 46 (t) Independence National Historical Park Collection, Eastern Parks and Monuments Association (c) Bowdoin Museum of Fine Arts, Bowdoin College, Brunswick, Me. (b) The Metropolitan Museum of Art, Rogers Fund, 1942 47 Historical Society of Pennsylvania 50 (t) Courtesy of the Essex Institute, Salem, MA (c) Library of Congress 51 Yale University Art Gallery, Gift of Roger Sherman White, B. A. 1859 51 Historical Society of Pennsylvania 54 (t) Courtesy, The Henry Francis du Pont Winterthur Museum (b) From R. M. Devins, *Our First Century* 55 The Metropolitan Museum of Art, Edgar Williams and Bernice Chrysler Garbish, 1963 59 Everett C. Johnson 60 Spider Martin/Photo Options 61 Paul Conklin 62 Andrew Popper/Picture Group 66 (t) Werner Stoy/Camera Hawaii (b) Leif Skoogfers/Woodfin Camp 67 James Steinberg/Photo Researchers 69 UPI/Bettmann Newsphotos 70 Mark Godfrey/Archive Pictures 71 (t) Reprinted by permission of the Chicago Tribune-New York News Syndicate, Inc. (b) UPI/Bettmann Newsphotos 72 Wide World 101 Tom Myers 103 Kastytis Izokaitis 104 *Harper's Weekly*, November 16, 1867 105 (t) UPI/Bettmann Newsphotos (b) Michael Sullivan 107 Reprinted by permission of United Feature Syndicate, Inc. 108 Ed Clark, LIFE Magazine © Time Inc. 109 (both) UPI/Bettmann Newsphotos 110 A.F.P. from Pictorial Parade 111 Rick Friedman/Black Star 112 Photo by Shannon Matheny. Permis-

sion to reprint by the Close Up Foundation. All other rights reserved by the Close Up Foundation. 115 Michal Heron 116 (l) Carl Iwasaki, LIFE Magazine © Time Inc. (r) Wide World 122, 125, 126, 127 National Geographic Society Photographer, Courtesy U.S. Historical Society 128 Bruce Hoertel 129 Sloan/Gamma-Liaison 130-131 Paul Hosefros/NYT Pictures 131 Rick Friedman/Black Star 132 (t) Paul Conklin (b) Chris Cross/Uniphoto 133 Courtesy of Congressman Julian C. Dixon 135 Mary Ellen Mark/Archive Pictures 137 (l) Paul Conklin (r) Rodney E. Mims/Uniphoto 141 (l) Mickey Pfleger/Picture Group (r) Dan McCoy/Black Star 145 Mark Godfrey/Archive Pictures 146 Stayskal/84 Tampa Tribune 147 © Sidney Harris 148 Stephen Shames/Visions 150 Bryce Flynn/Picture Group 152 (t) Paul Conklin (lc) Ted Wathen/MDS (rc) R.J. North/Picture Group (b) Kevin Horan/Picture Group 155 Reprinted by permission of United Feature Syndicate, Inc. 156-157 Darryl Heikes/U.S. News & World Report 163 Wally McNamee/Newsweek 165 Robert R. McElroy/Newsweek 166 (t) Alan Tannenbaum/Sygma (b) Mickey Pfleger/Picture Group 167, 168 Bill Fitz-Patrick/The White House 169, 170 David Hume Kennerly/Gamma-Liaison 172-173 Michal Evans/The White House 176 Dennis Brack/Black Star 177 (l) Harry S. Truman Library (r) Paul Conklin 178-179 Brown Brothers 183 Rockwell International Corp. 187 Dan McCoy/Rainbow 190 Bryce Flynn/Picture Group 195 Dennis Brack/Black Star 196 Courtesy CBS 198 Courtesy British Airways 202 Fred Ward/Black Star 203 (both) Michal Heron 204 Shirl Elliott/Hillstrom Stock Photo 206 The Supreme Court Historical Society 211 (t) Robert S. Oakes/The Supreme Court Historical Society (b) Yoichi Okomoto/Photo Researchers 212 The Supreme Court Historical Society 213 Des Moines Register & Tribune 217 (both) The Supreme Court Historical Society 222 Tom Myers 225 Mark J. Palmer 226 (both) Paul Conklin 227 Pete Souza/The White House 228 David Burnett/Contact Stock Images 229 (l) National Rifle Association (r) Shepard Sherbell/Picture Group 231 Dirck Halstead/Gamma-Liaison 232 Thomas England 234 Darryl Heikes/U.S. News & World Report 236 Engelhardt/St. Louis Post-Dispatch 241 Max Winter/Picture Group 242 Brown Brothers 243 Paul Hosefros/NYT Pictures 245 Owen Franken 247 Thomas England 249 Bryce Flynn/Picture Group 250 (t) Bryce Flynn/Picture Group (b) Owen Franken 253 Brad Bower/Picture Group 257 David Burnett/Contact Press Images 258 Collection of the Boatmen's National Bank of St. Louis 259 Michael Sullivan 262 (l) Ira Wyman/Sygma (r) Michael Sullivan 264 Dennis Brack/Black Star 269 Daniel Brody/Stock, Boston 274 Susan Griffith 277 Peter Vandermark/Stock, Boston 280 Ron Lindsey/TIME Magazine 282, 285 Susan Griffith 286 Wide World 287 Paul Conklin 291 Glenn Short 295 Tom McHugh/Photo Researchers 296 Don Hesse, © 1985, St. Louis Globe Democrat. Reprinted with permission, Los Angeles Times Syndicate 299 Wally McNamee/Woodfin Camp 300 Courtesy of Kentucky Department of the Arts 303 (t) Michael Goss/Scott, Foresman (bl) Ray F. Hillstrom Jr./Hillstrom Stock Photo (br) Tony O'Brien/Picture Group 304 Charles Harbutt/Archive 306 J. Berndt/Stock, Boston 307 Dennis Brack/Black Star 308 (l) Stacy Pick/Uniphoto

310 Chris Brown/Stock, Boston 315 David Woo/Stock, Boston 316 Bill Bachman/Photo Researchers 319 (t) © John Jonik. From PSYCHOLOGY TODAY 321 Charles Cherney/Paddock Publications, Inc. 323 John Lopinot/Black Star 324 Bruno Torres/UPI/Bettman Newsphotos 325 John Running/Stock, Boston 327 John Coletti/Stock, Boston 332 Michael Goss/Scott, Foresman 335 Courtesy of Metropolitan Sanitary District of Greater Chicago 336 David R. Frazier/Hillstrom Stock Photo 339 Stephen Green 340 (l) Bill Luster/SPORTS ILLUSTRATED (r) Rick Smolan/Woodfin Camp 347 Christopher Springman 351 Bart Bartholomew/Black Star 352 Ray R. Hillstrom Jr./Hillstrom Stock Photo 353 Jim Markham 355 Dennis Brack/Black Star 357 Michal Heron 362 Donald Dietz/Stock, Boston 367 Photography by Milt and Joan Mann 369 Courtesy of Museum of the City of New York 372 A. Tannenbaum/Sygma 373 John Lopincot/Black Star 375 (t) © News Group Chicago, Inc., 1984. Photo by Jack Lenahan. Reprinted with permission of the Chicago Sun-Times. (b) A. Epstein and Sons International, Inc. 376 Rick Browne/Picture Group 377 David Strickler/Picture Cube 380 Harborplace in Baltimore, Maryland. Photo courtesy of The Rouse Company 382 Library of Congress 386 Annie Griffiths 389 Mario Ruiz/Picture Group 390 Ken Kobre/Black Star 391 Courtesy of St. Jude Children's Research Hospital, Memphis, TN 393 Tom Myers 394 Robert George Gaylord 395 R. P. Kingston/Stock, Boston 397 John Stearns/The News-Sentinel, Fort Wayne, IN 401 Marc Pokempner/Black Star 404 (t) Bart Bartholomew/Black Star (b) Richard Casler 405 Richard Casler 407 Christopher Morris/Black Star 409 Stephen Shames/Visions 412 © 1981 Los Angeles Times 418 Photography by Milt and Joan Mann 421 Michael Goss/Scott, Foresman 422 Liane Enkels/Stock, Boston 424 Chris Niedenthal/Black Star 425 Arnold Zann/Black Star 426 Gunvor Jorgsholm/Pressehuset 428 Lynn Johnson/Black Star 429 James Balog/Black Star 433 Braniff International 441 Sara Krulwich/NYT Pictures 443 Free Library of Philadelphia 445 Group III Kerr/Uniphoto 447 Paolo Koch/Photo Researchers 454 Jim Harrison/Stock, Boston 456 Don and Pat Valenti, Hillstrom Stock Photo 458 Susan McElhinney/Woodfin Camp 467 Michael L. Abrahamson 469 (r) Earl Kubis/R/C Photo Agency 471 (b) NASA 480 Neil Leifer/TIME Magazine 483 Dennis Brack/Black Star 484 Sygma 485 Courtesy of Chicago Historical Society 486 Bill Nation/Sygma 487 Courtesy of The Imperial War Museum 488 Wide World 489 Dennis Brack/Black Star 490 (t,b) James Nachtwey/Black Star 494 Frank Fournier/Contact Press Images 496 Library of Congress 497 Owen D.B./Black Star 501 R. Bruce Thompson 502 (t) Steve Harbison/Black Star (b) Fred Ward/Black Star 506 (t) David Burnett/Contact Press Images 507 Sygma 508 (l) Chris Springman/Black Star (r) Michael Melford/Wheeler Pictures 509 Courtesy of United Nations 511 Permission granted by King Features Syndicate, Inc. 513 Signing of the Constitution by Howard Chandler Christy. National Geographic photographer George F. Mobley. Courtesy U.S. Capital Historical Society 514 D. R. Goff, Quicksilver Photography. Courtesy Columbus Association of the Performing Arts 538 Paul Conklin